S0-CFZ-537

CIVIL PROCEDURE

By

Steven L. Emanuel

Harvard Law School, J.D. 1976

with the assistance of

**Peter Banos,
Kevin O'Connor**
and
Stephen Gang

all Harvard Law School, J.D. 1976

16th Edition prepared with
the assistance of

Erika Gorrin
Columbia Law School,
Class of 1996

emanuel law outlines, inc.

Civil Procedure, 16th Edition, © 1974, 1994 by Steven L. Emanuel
Emanuel Law Outlines, Inc. • 1865 Palmer Avenue • Larchmont, NY 10538

To my beloved wife Marilyn,
mother of my five (5!) children

Preface

I intend for you to use this book both throughout the semester and for exam preparation.

Here are some suggestions about how to use it:[1]

1. During the semester, use the book in preparing each night for the next day's class. To do this, first read your casebook. Then, use the *Casebook Correlation Chart* at the front of the outline to get an idea of what part of the outline to read. Reading the outline will give you a sense of how the particular cases you've just read in your casebook fit into the overall structure of the subject. You may want to use a yellow highlighter to mark key portions of the *Emanuel*.

2. If you make your own outline for the course, use the *Emanuel* to give you a structure, and to supply black letter principles. You may want to rely especially on the *Capsule Summary* for this purpose. You are hereby authorized to copy small portions of the *Emanuel* into your own outline, provided that your outline will be used only by you or your study group, and provided that you are the owner of the *Emanuel*.

3. When you first start studying for exams, read the *Capsule Summary* to get an overview. This will probably take you all or part of two days.

4. Either during exam study or earlier in the semester, do some or all of the *Quiz Yourself* short-answer questions, supplied at the end of most sub-chapters. You can find these quickly by looking for *Quiz Yourself* entries in the Table of Contents. When you do these questions: (1) record your short "answer" on the small blank line provided after the question, but also: (2) try to write out a "mini essay" on a separate piece of paper. Remember that the only way to get good at writing essays is to write essays.

5. A couple of days before the exam, review the *Exam Tips* that appear at the end of each chapter. You may want to combine this step with step (4), so that you use the *Tips* to help you spot the issues in the short-answer questions. You'll also probably want to follow up from many of the *Tips* to the main outline's discussion of the topic; the number references after some of the *Tips* (e.g., "[145]") point you to the main outline's discussion.

6. Some time during the week or so before the exam, do some or all of the full-scale essay exams at the back of the book. Write out a full essay answer under exam-like conditions (e.g., closed-book if your exam will be closed book.) If you can, exchange papers with a classmate and critique each other's answer.

7. The night before the exam: (1) do some *Quiz Yourself* questions, just to get your writing juices flowing; and (2) re-read the various *Exam Tips* sections (you should be able to do this in 1-2 hours).

Good luck. Write to me with any comments or suggestions. Or, you can reach me via E-mail at: 74224.3600@compuserve.com.

Steve Emanuel

---

1. The suggestions below relate only to this book. I don't talk here about taking or reviewing class notes, using hornbooks or other study aids, joining a study group, or anything else. This doesn't mean I don't think these other steps are important — it's just that on this one page I've chosen to focus on how I think you can use this outline.

Abbreviations Used in Text

CASEBOOKS

C,F,M&S — Cound, Friedenthal, Miller and Sexton, *Civil Procedure* (6th Ed. 1993; with 1994 Supplement)

F,K&C — Field, Kaplan and Clermont, *Materials for a Basic Course in Civil Procedure* (6th Ed. 1990; with 1994 Supplement)

L,H&T — Louisell, Hazard and Tait, *Pleading and Procedure* (6th Ed. 1989; with 1994 Supplement)

R,S&D — Rosenberg, Smit and Dreyfuss, *Elements of Civil Procedure* (5th Ed. 1990; with 1994 Supplement)

Y,L&M — Yaezell, Landers & Martin, *Civil Procedure* (3rd Ed. 1992; with 1994 Supplement)

HORNBOOKS & NUTSHELLS

F,K&M — Friedenthal, Kane and Miller, *Civil Procedure* (2nd Ed. 1993)

James & Hazard — James, Hazard & Leubsdorf, *Civil Procedure* (4th Ed. 1992)

James (1st Ed.) — Fleming James, Jr., *Civil Procedure* (1965)

J & H (3d Ed.) — James and Hazard, *Civil Procedure* (3rd Ed. 1985)

Jurisdiction Nutshell — Ehrenzweig, Louisell, and Hazard, *Jurisdiction in a Nutshell* (4th Ed. 1980)

Moore's Manual — Moore, Vestal and Kurland, *Moore's Manual —Federal Practice and Procedure* (2 Vols. 1980)

Res Judicata Nutshell — Robert C. Casad, *Res Judicata in a Nutshell* (1976)

Study... — American Law Institute, *Study of the Division of Jurisdiction between State and Federal Courts*

W&M — Wright and Miller, *Federal Practice and Procedure* (multi- volume treatise, with annual supplementation)

Wr. — Charles A. Wright, *Law of Federal Courts* (4th Ed. 1983)

CASEBOOK CORRELATION CHART

Emanuel's Civil Procedure Outline *(by chapter heading)*	Cound, Friedenthal, Miller, & Sexton **Civil Procedure** (6th Ed. 1993; w/ 1994 Supp.)	Yaezell, Landers & Martin **Civil Procedure** (3rd Ed. 1992; w/ 1994 Supp.)	Field, Kaplan, & Clermont **Materials for a Basic Course in Civil Procedure** (6th Ed. 1990; w/ 1994 Supp.)	Rosenberg, Smit, & Dreyfuss **Elements of Civil Procedure** (5th Ed. 1990; w/ 1994 Supp.)	Louisell, Hazard, & Tait **Pleading and Procedure** (6th Ed. 1989; w/ 1994 Supp.)
JURISDICTION OVER THE PARTIES					
I. Jurisdiction over Individuals	65-77, 85-96, 166-182	9-10, 69, 61-85, 94-95, 99-100, 153-159, 172-180	49-50, 203-204, 216, 909-956, 977, 980-981, 1067	186-187, 222-258, 261-288, 481-482, 1136	4, 281-303, 306-307, 312-314, 320-383, 386-415, 481-487
II. Jurisdiction over Corporations	77-85, 96-149, 747-756	72-73, 76-82, 84, 99-131	918, 924-945, 956-1003	241-250, 255-257, 259-289, 513-521	294-314, 337-345, 354-370, 476-498
III. Federal Jurisdiction over the Parties	182-191, 208-226	169-180	1005-1016	226, 232-235, 325-330	3-4, 280, 415, 458-464
IV. Jurisdiction over Things	149-166	70-71, 75-76, 85-101, 160-169	202, 893-906, 956-982, 1031, 1063	289-325	284-293, 306-307, 312-337, 411-418, 422-427
V. Notice and Opportunity to be Heard	196-207, 232-260	69, 71, 72, 159-172	1046-1067	312-320, 330-335	3-4, 284-287, 303-312, 440-464
VI. Defenses to Claims of Jurisdiction	191-195, 226-232	68, 73-74, 153, 204, 967-977	905-910, 913, 915, 920-924, 970, 983, 1012	227-228, 230-232	418-422, 437-439, 1198-1199, 1201-1202
VII. Venue	339-371	10-12, 172, 180-193	199-201, 1016-1045	335-350, 360, 1068	3, 427-437, 514-522, 615-627
SUBJECT MATTER JURISDICTION					
I. Diversity Jurisdiction	265-276	5-9, 204-212	13, 188-196, 205-206, 210, 216, 824-827, 843-851, 853-858, 1347-1348	181-189, 210-216, 218-222, 412, 431, 450	16, 64-65, 524-525, 731-737, 739, 747-750, 819
II. Federal Question Jurisdiction	282-304	196-204, 220-228	13, 185-188, 827-834	189-200, 210-219	16, 65, 526-527
III. Amount in Controversy	276-282	210-212	215-216, 859-867	183, 185-186, 200-205, 511-512	16, 503-504, 527
IV. Supplemental (Pendent and Ancillary) Jurisdiction	304-323	212-219, 475-484	834-853	206-219, 220, 436-437, 456-457	64-66, 528-547, 710-713, 731-737, 739, 747-750, 752
V. Removal of Cases to the Federal Courts	323-333	220-228	197-198, 205-206, 855-858, 867-872	219-221	526-527, 538-544
VI. Court's Power to Punish Disobedience	333-338	213-217, 146-159	872-884	145-152	545-546
PLEADING					
I. Pleading at Common Law	458-464	349-350, 354-359	409-415	547-548	91-94
II. Code Pleading	505-511	366-375	454-455, 484, 495, 502-520	548-549, 551-555, 579-581	108-110
III. Modern Federal Pleading Generally	7-9, 581-598	12-14, 387-405	35-66, 42-45, 87, 100, 473-476, 484-548, 825-826	543-557, 563-574	90, 94, 96-97, 102-105, 134-143, 897-900
IV. The Complaint	505-541	14-16, 375-385, 405-409, 411-423	15, 35-45, 502-531	575-587, 589-603	3-5, 52-111
V. Motions Against the Complaint	541-551	17, 375-386, 422-427	46-53, 56, 99, 107, 516-517, 530-532, 534-537	32-33, 557-559, 560-562	5, 6, 86, 106, 111-116
VI. The Answer	552-564	17-21, 423-438	47-50, 537-540	32-33, 32, 555, 609	119-124
VII. Amendment of the Pleadings	566-581	21-22, 439-452	50, 62-66, 490-495	614-629	125-131
VIII. Variance of Proof from Pleadings			486-495		

CASEBOOK CORRELATION CHART (Cont.)

Emanuel's Civil Procedure Outline *(by chapter heading)*	Cound, Friedenthal, Miller, & Sexton **Civil Procedure** (6th Ed. 1993; w/ 1994 Supp.)	Yaezell, Landers & Martin **Civil Procedure** (3rd Ed. 1992; w/ 1994 Supp.)	Field, Kaplan, & Clermont **Materials for a Basic Course in Civil Procedure** (6th Ed. 1990; w/ 1994 Supp.)	Rosenberg, Smit, & Dreyfuss **Elements of Civil Procedure** (5th Ed. 1990; w/ 1994 Supp.)	Louisell, Hazard, & Tait **Pleading and Procedure** (6th Ed. 1989; w/ 1994 Supp.)
DISCOVERY AND PRETRIAL CONFERENCE					
I. Scope of Discovery	764-784, 820-844	574-576, 582-610	68-69, 140-142, 549-576	658-671, 679-710, 713-719	902-903, 912-929, 929-943, 961-962
II. Methods of Discovery					
Oral Depositions	785-791	29, 577-578	69-74, 585-586	731-734	7, 904, 907-908
Written Depositions	791	577-578	74-75, 585-586	731-734	904-905
Interrogatories to Parties	791-796	29, 576-578, 601-602	75-79, 84-87, 567	671-679	7, 903-904, 908-909
Requests for Admission	812-815	580-582	79, 83, 89, 567	727-729	906, 909
Requests to Produce Documents	797-803	29, 576, 578-580	70, 79-80		905
Physical and Mental Exams	804-812	29-30, 579-580, 605-607, 610-619	5-31, 80-82	719-727	909, 943-952
III. Orders and Sanctions	844-854	582, 609, 621, 623-637	71, 74, 79, 82-83, 576-587	736-748	904, 906, 963-967
IV. Use of Discovery Results at Trial	816-819		87-89, 150		
V. Appellate Review of Discovery Orders			17, 590-592	1068-1070	911, 1305-1310, 1319
VI. Pretrial Conference	11, 855-880	38, 685-698	91-97, 593-620	34-35, 813-827	8, 969-981
ASCERTAINING APPLICABLE LAW					
I. *Erie* and Other Fundamentals	372-383	229-240	218-228	351-359	558-569
II. *Erie* Problems	383-429	241-282	5-10, 228-266	359-389	569-615
III. Federal Common Law	429-447	240-241	266-279	389-395	561-569, 612
TRIAL PROCEDURE					
I. Burden of Proof	1001-1004	765-772	36-37, 130, 540-548, 642-643	842-851	66-75
II. Presumptions		772-774	643-654	844	75-83
III. Preponderance of the Evidence	1065		130, 654-667	844	1113-1135
IV. Adjudication Without Trial					
Voluntary Dismissal	911-912	649-653	673-674, 1100	650-654, 918-921	982-983
Involuntary Dismissal	912-914	642-659	131-132, 586-587, 675-677,1099-1100	654-657	9, 983, 1134
Summary Judgment	10-11, 881-910	33-38, 653-667	99-107, 516-517, 621-638	631-650	8, 134, 143-174
V. Trials Without a Jury	1049-1053	826-831	143, 159, 757-760, 1353-1355	772-773, 779-780, 922-929	1178-1197
VI. The Jury	11-15, 921-926, 966-999	732-752	124-130, 156-159, 700-705, 708-712	35-37, 41-42, 758-760, 829-836, 838-842, 871-872	9-10, 1099-1100, 1144-1157, 1160-1168, 1070
VII. Directed Verdict/ Judgment as a Matter of Law	1008-1033	41, 765-786	131-133, 155-156, 673-697	39, 895-910	9-10, 1128-1131, 1134-1135
VIII. Special Verdict and Interrogatories	1042-1049	803-807	157-158, 714-723	851-852, 856-858	10, 1158-1159
IX. New Trial	1053-1092	803-812, 813-816	159-161, 678-679, 726-774	872-895	11, 1159-1169, 1173-1178
X. Review of Grant or Denial of New Trial	1183-84	825-826	746-757, 767-774, 1391	868-878, 911-915, 1047-1049	1286, 1296
XI. Judgment Notwithstanding the Verdict	1020-1033	816-826	159-161, 760-774	911-918	11, 1118-1125, 1168-1173
XII. Review of Combined New Trial and JML Motions		817-825	161, 760-774	911-916	1169, 1170-1173
XIII. Consitutional Right to Jury Trial	927-966	700-734	775-823	753-754, 771-778	1001-1083

CASEBOOK CORRELATION CHART (Cont.)

Emanuel's Civil Procedure Outline (by chapter heading)	Cound, Friedenthal, Miller, & Sexton **Civil Procedure** (6th Ed. 1993; w/ 1994 Supp.)	Yaezell, Landers & Martin **Civil Procedure** (3rd Ed. 1992; w/ 1994 Supp.)	Field, Kaplan, & Clermont **Materials for a Basic Course in Civil Procedure** (6th Ed. 1990; w/ 1994 Supp.)	Rosenberg, Smit, & Dreyfuss **Elements of Civil Procedure** (5th Ed. 1990; w/ 1994 Supp.)	Louisell, Hazard, & Tait **Pleading and Procedure** (6th Ed. 1989; w/ 1994 Supp.)
MULTI-CLAIM AND MULTI-PARTY LITIGATION					
I. Counterclaims	602-617	455-464	56-61, 540-546	417-426	708-715
II. Joinder of Claims	599-625	453-454	41, 58, 60, 204, 218	412-417	705-719
III. Joinder of Parties	629-654	22, 464-504	46-50, 206-209, 1200-1218, 1332-1333	426-434, 437-453, 969-974	719-896
IV. Class Actions	703-760	533-571	213-216, 1221-1306, 1333-1335	483-542	823-896
V. Intervention	684-702	26-27, 505-522	217, 1307-1317, 1335-1336	459-469	751-770
VI. Interpleader	662-684	522-533	210, 1318, 1330, 1336-1337	469-483	770-779
VII. Real Party in Interest	625-629	501-503	1218-1220	400-405	797-800, 802-803
VIII. Third Party Practice (Impleader)	655-661	469-474	211-212, 490-492, 1136-1137, 1172-1174	453-458	748-749
IX. Cross-Claims	617-625	18, 475, 490-491	212-213	435-437	740-750
FORMER ADJUDICATION					
I. Claim Preclusion (Merger and Bar)	1210-1223	887-920, 950-958	1068-1069, 1073-1108	417-426, 955-977	630-679
II. Collateral Estoppel	1228-1289	920-949, 958-967	1069, 1109-1134, 1140-1172	978-1002	630-679
III. Full Faith and Credit	1289-1304	967-987	910-911, 1175-1199	1004-1030	679-700

TABLE OF CONTENTS

Chapter 1

INTRODUCTION

Chapter 2

JURISDICTION OVER
THE PARTIES

Chapter 3

SUBJECT-MATTER JURISDICTION

Chapter 4

PLEADING

Chapter 5

DISCOVERY AND PRETRIAL CONFERENCE

Chapter 6

ASCERTAINING
APPLICABLE LAW

Chapter 7

TRIAL PROCEDURE

Chapter 8

MULTI-PARTY AND
MULTI-CLAIM LITIGATION

Chapter 9

FORMER
ADJUDICATION

CAPSULE SUMMARY

This Capsule Summary is intended for review at the end of the semester. Reading it is not a substitute for mastering the material in the main outline. Numbers in brackets refer to the pages in the main outline where the topic is discussed.

INTRODUCTION

I. CIVIL PROCEDURE GENERALLY

A. A road map: Here is a *"road map"* for analyzing a Civil Procedure problem:

1. Personal jurisdiction: First, make sure that the court has *"personal jurisdiction"* or *"jurisdiction over the parties."* You must check to make sure that: (1) D had **minimum contacts** with the forum state (whether the court is a state or federal court); and (2) D received such **notice and opportunity to be heard** as to satisfy the constitutional requirement of due process. [7-92]

2. Venue: Then, check whether **venue** was correct. In federal court suits, the venue requirement describes what judicial **district** the case may be heard in. Essentially, the case must be heard either: (1) in any district where the **defendant resides** (with special rules for multi-defendant cases; or (2) in any district in which a **substantial part of the events** giving rise to the claim occurred. See 28 U.S.C. §1391. [79-91]

3. Subject matter jurisdiction: If the case is a federal case, you must then ask whether the court has **subject matter** jurisdiction. Essentially, this means that one of the following two things must be true: [93-135]

    a. Diversity: Either the case is between **citizens of different states** (with "complete diversity" required, so that no plaintiff is a citizen of the same state as any defendant) and at least $50,000 is at stake; or

    b. Federal question: The case raises a *"federal question."* Essentially, this means that plaintiff's right to recover stems from the U.S. Constitution, a federal treaty, or an act of Congress. (There is no minimum amount required to be at stake in federal question cases.)

4. Pleading: Next, you must examine whether the **pleadings** are proper. [137-167]

5. Discovery: Next, you may have a complex of issues relating to pre-trial **discovery**. [168-216]

6. Ascertaining applicable law: Now, figure out **what jurisdiction's law** should be used in the case. The most important problem of this type is: In a diversity case, may the federal court apply its own concepts of "federal common law", or must the court apply the law of the state where the federal court sits? If the state has a **substantive law** (whether a statute or a judge-made principle) that is on point, **the federal court sitting in diversity must apply that law**. This is the "rule" of **Erie v. Tompkins**. (*Example:* In a diversity case concerning negligence, the federal court must normally apply the negligence law of the state where the court sits.) [217-244]

7. **Trial procedure:** Next, you may face a series of issues relating to *trial procedure*. [245-285]

8. **Multi-party and multi-claim litigation:** If there is more than one claim in the case, or more than the basic two parties (a single plaintiff and a single defendant), you will face a whole host of issues related to the *multi-party* or *multi-claim* nature of the litigation. You must be prepared to deal with the various methods of bringing multiple parties and multiple claims into a case. In federal courts: [287-356]

   a. **Counterclaim:** D may make a claim against P, by use of the *counterclaim*. See FRCP 13. Check whether the counterclaim is *"permissive"* or *"compulsory."* (Also, remember that third parties, who are neither the original plaintiff nor the original defendant, may make a counterclaim.) [289]

   b. **Joinder of claims:** Once a party has made a claim against some other party, she may then make *any other claim* she wishes against that party. This is *"joinder of claims."* See Rule 18(a). [296]

   c. **Joinder of parties:** Multiple parties may *join* their actions together. Check to see whether either *"permissive* joinder" or *"compulsory* joinder" is applicable. Also, remember that each of these two types of joinder can apply to *either multiple plaintiffs* or *multiple defendants*. See FRCP 19 and 20. [297]

   d. **Class actions:** Check whether a *class action* is available as a device to handle the claims of many similarly-situated plaintiffs, or claims against many similarly-situated defendants. See FRCP 23. Look for the possibility of a class action wherever there are 25 or more similarly-situated plaintiffs or similarly-situated defendants. [309]

   e. **Intervention:** A person who is not initially part of a lawsuit may be able to enter the suit on his own initiative, under the doctrine of *intervention*. See FRCP 24. Check whether the intervention is "of right" or "permissive." [332]

   f. **Interpleader:** Where a party owes something to two or more other persons, but isn't sure which, that party may want to use the device of *interpleader* to prevent being made to pay the same claim twice. After checking whether interpleader might be desirable, decide whether the stakeholder should use *"statutory* interpleader" or "Rule interpleader." See 28 U.S.C. §1335 (statutory interpleader) and FRCP 22 (Rule interpleader). [336]

   g. **Third-party practice (impleader):** Anytime D has a potential claim against some *third person* who is not already in the lawsuit, by which that third person will be liable to D for some or all of P's recovery against D, D should be able to *"implead"* the third person. (*Example:* Employee, while working for Employer, hits Victim with a company car. Victim sues Employer in diversity, under the doctrine of *respondeat superior*. Under traditional concepts of indemnity, Employer will be able to recover from Employee for any amount that Employer is forced to pay Victim. Therefore, Employer should "implead" Employee as a "third party defendant" to the Victim-Employer action.) See FRCP 14(a). Once a third-party defendant is brought into the case, consider what other claims might now be available (e.g., a counterclaim by the third-party defendant against the third-party plaintiff, a cross-claim against some other third-party defendant, a counterclaim against the original plaintiff, etc.). [343]

h. **Cross-claims:** Check to see whether any party has made, or should make, a claim against a *co-party*. This is a *cross-claim*. See FRCP 13(g). [350]

i. **Jurisdiction:** For any of these multi-party or multi-claim devices, check to see whether the requirements of *personal jurisdiction* and *subject matter jurisdiction* have been satisfied. To do this, you will need to know whether the doctrine of *"supplemental"* jurisdiction applies to the particular device in question. If it does not, the new claim, or the new party, will typically have to *independently* meet the requirements of federal subject matter jurisdiction. (*Example:* P, from Massachusetts, sues D, from Connecticut, in diversity. X, from Massachusetts, wants to intervene in the case on the side of D. Because supplemental jurisdiction does not apply to intervention, X must independently satisfy the requirement of diversity, which he cannot do because he is a citizen of the same state as P. Therefore, X cannot intervene.)

9. **Former adjudication:** Lastly, check whether the results in some *prior litigation* are *binding* in the current suit. Distinguish between situations in which the *judgment* in the prior suit is binding on an entire cause of action in the present suit (under the doctrines of *merger* and *bar*), and the situation where a *finding of fact* is binding on the current suit, even though the judgment itself is not binding (the *"collateral estoppel"* situation).

a. **Non-mutual collateral estoppel:** Where a *"stranger"* to the first action (one not a party to that first action) now seeks to take advantage of a finding of fact in that first suit, consider whether this *"non-mutual"* collateral estoppel should be allowed. [358]

b. **Full Faith and Credit:** Lastly, if the two suits have taken place in *different jurisdictions*, consider to what extent the principles of *Full Faith and Credit* limit the second court's freedom to ignore what happened in the first suit. [388]

CHAPTER 2

JURISDICTION OVER THE PARTIES

I. GENERAL PRINCIPLES

A. **Two kinds of jurisdiction:** Before a court can decide a case, it must have jurisdiction over the *parties* as well as over the *subject matter*. [7]

1. **Subject matter jurisdiction:** *Subject matter* jurisdiction refers to the court's power to decide the *kind* of case before it. (*Examples of subject matter jurisdiction issues:* (1) Does the federal court for the District of New Jersey have the power to decide cases in which the two parties are citizens of different states? (2) Does the Binghamton Municipal Court have the power to decide cases involving more than $1,000?)

2. **Jurisdiction over the parties:** Jurisdiction over the *parties* refers to whether the court has jurisdiction to decide a case *between the particular parties*, or *concerning the property*, before it. (*Examples of issues concerning jurisdiction over the parties:* (1) Does Court X have jurisdiction over D, who is a citizen of State X, but who is temporarily out of the state? (2) Does Court Y have jurisdiction over property in State Y where the action is one by P to register title to the land in his name?)

B. Jurisdiction over the parties: There are two distinct requirements which must be met before a court has jurisdiction over the *parties*: [8]

    1. Substantive due process: The court must have *power* to act, either upon given property, or on a given person so as to subject her to personal liability. The Constitution's Fourteenth Amendment Due Process Clause imposes this requirement of power to act, as a matter of *"substantive due process."*

    2. Procedural due process: Also, the court must have given the defendant *adequate notice* of the action against him, and an *opportunity to be heard*. These, taken together, are requirements of *procedural due process*, also imposed by the Fourteenth Amendment's Due Process Clause.

C. Three kinds of jurisdiction over the parties: There are *three different kinds* of jurisdiction which a court may exercise over the parties — one of these three *must be present* for the case to go forward. [8]

    1. In personam: *In personam* jurisdiction, or jurisdiction over the defendant's "person," gives the court power to issue a judgment against her *personally*. Thus *all* of the person's *assets* may be seized to satisfy the judgment, and the judgment can be sued upon in other states as well. [8]

    2. In rem: *In rem* jurisdiction, or jurisdiction over a *thing*, gives the court power to adjudicate a claim made about a *piece of property* or about a *status*. (*Examples:* An action to quiet title to real estate, or an action to pronounce a marriage dissolved.) [8]

    3. Quasi in rem jurisdiction: In *quasi in rem* jurisdiction, the action is begun by seizing property owned by (*attachment*), or a debt owed to (*garnishment*) the defendant, within the forum state. The thing seized is a pretext for the court to decide the case without having jurisdiction over the defendant's person. Any judgment affects only the property seized, and the judgment cannot be sued upon in any other court. [8]

    4. Minimum contacts requirement: If jurisdiction in the case is *in personam* or *quasi in rem*, the court may not exercise that jurisdiction unless D has *"minimum contacts"* with the state in which the court sits. In brief, the requirement of minimum contacts means that D has to have taken *actions* that were *purposefully directed* towards the forum state. (*Examples of the required action:* D sold goods in the state, or incorporated in the state, or visited the state, or bought property in the state, etc.) Without such minimum contacts, exercise of jurisdiction would violate D's Fourteenth Amendment federal constitutional right to due process. [8]

        a. Unreasonable exercise: Even if D has the requisite "minimum contacts" with the forum state, the court will not exercise jurisdiction if considerations of *"fair play* and substantial justice" would require making D defend in the forum state so *unreasonable* as to constitute a due process violation. But in most cases, if D has the required minimum contacts with the forum state, it will not be unreasonable for the case to be tried there.

D. Long-arm statute: Most states have *"long-arm statutes."* A long-arm statute is a statute which permits the court of a state to obtain jurisdiction over *persons not physically present within the state at the time of service*. (*Example:* A long-arm might allow jurisdiction over an out-of-stater who has committed a tort in the state.) [9]

    1. Substitute service: Long-arms typically provide for "substitute" means of *service*, since in-state personal service is not possible. (*Example:* A long-arm statute might allow the plaintiff to cause the defendant to be served out of state by registered mail.)

II. JURISDICTION OVER INDIVIDUALS

A. Different categories: In most states, there are a number of different criteria which will enable the court to take personal jurisdiction over an individual. Some of the most common (each of which will be considered in detail below) are: [10]

1. *Presence* within the forum state;

2. *Domicile* or *residence* within the forum state;

3. *Consent* to be sued within the forum state;

4. *Driving a car* within the forum state;

5. Committing a *tortious act* within the state (or, perhaps, committing an out-of-state act with in-state tortious consequences);

6. Ownership of *property* in the forum state;

7. Conducting *business* in the forum state;

8. Being *married in*, or living while married in, the forum state.

> **Note:** Regardless of the criteria used by the state and its long-arm for establishing personal jurisdiction over the individual, due process requires that the individual have *minimum contacts* with the forum state before personal jurisdiction may be exercised over her. The meaning of "minimum contacts" is discussed further below in the treatment of jurisdiction over corporations.

B. Presence: Jurisdiction may be exercised over an individual by virtue of his *presence within the forum state*. That is, even if the individual is an out-of-state resident who comes into the forum state only briefly, personal jurisdiction over him may be gotten as long as *service was made* on him while he was in the forum state. [10]

> **Example:** D and his wife, P, separate while residing in New Jersey. P moves to California with their children. D visits California on business, and stops briefly to visit the children. While D is visiting, P serves him with process in a California suit for divorce. D never visits the state again.
>
> *Held*, California can constitutionally assert personal jurisdiction over D based on his presence in the state at the time of service, even though that presence was brief, and even though D had virtually no other contacts with the state. [*Burnham v. Superior Court*].

C. Domicile: Jurisdiction may be exercised over a person who is *domiciled* within the forum state, even if the person is temporarily absent from the state. A person is considered to be domiciled in the place where he has his *current dwelling place*, if he also has the *intention to remain* in that place for an *indefinite period*. [11-13]

D. Residence: Some states allow jurisdiction to be exercised on the basis of D's *residence in the forum state*, even though he is absent from the state. A person may have several residences simultaneously. (The Supreme Court has not yet passed on the due process validity of jurisdiction based solely on residence, so this remains presumptively a valid method of gaining jurisdiction.) [13]

E. Consent: Jurisdiction over a party can be exercised by virtue of her *consent*, even if she has no contacts whatsoever with the forum state. [14]

C
A
P
S
U
L
E

S
U
M
M
A
R
Y

C
A
P
S
U
L
E

S
U
M
M
A
R
Y

Example: P, who does not reside in Ohio or have any other contacts with Ohio, brings suit against D in Ohio. By filing the suit in Ohio, P will be deemed to have consented to Ohio's jurisdiction. D may then counterclaim against P. Even if P dismisses his own suit, his consent to the action will be binding, and the Ohio courts will have personal jurisdiction over him on the counterclaim.

F. **Non-resident motorist:** Most states have statutes allowing the courts to exercise jurisdiction over *non-resident motorists* who have been involved in *accidents in the state*. [14]

> **Example:** P is a resident of the forum state. D, not a resident of the forum state, is driving his car in the forum state, and has a collision with P's car. Even if D has no other contacts with the state, a non-resident motorist statute will probably be in force in the state, and will probably give the forum state's courts jurisdiction over a tort suit by P against D.

1. **Service on state official:** Most of the non-resident motorist statutes provide for in-state service of process on a *designated state official* (e.g., the Director of Motor Vehicles) and for *registered mail service* on the out-of-state defendant himself. [15]

G. **In-state tortiousness:** Many states have statutes allowing their courts jurisdiction over persons committing *tortious acts within the state*. [15]

> **Example:** D, an out-of-stater, gets into a fight with P at a bar in P's home state. P wants to bring a civil battery claim against D in the state. If, as is likely, the state has a long-arm provision governing tortious acts within the state, P will be able to get personal jurisdiction over D in the battery action.

1. **Out-of-state acts with in-state consequences:** Some "in-state tortious acts" long-arm clauses have been interpreted to include acts done *outside the state* which produce *tortious consequences within the state*. In a *products liability* situation, a vendor who sells products that he knows will be used in the state probably may constitutionally be required to defend in the state, if the product causes injury in the state. [*Gray v. American Radiator Corp.*] [15]

H. **Owners of in-state property:** Many states exercise jurisdiction over *owners of in-state property* in causes of action arising from that property. [16]

I. **Conducting business:** States often exercise jurisdiction over non-residents who conduct *businesses* within the state. Since states may regulate an individual's business conduct in the state, they may constitutionally exercise jurisdiction relating to that doing of business. [16]

J. **Domestic relations cases:** Courts sometimes try to take personal jurisdiction over a non-resident party to a *domestic relations* case. However, the requirement of "minimum contacts" applies here (as in every personal jurisdiction situation), and that requirement may bar the state from taking jurisdiction. [24]

> **Example:** A father resides in New York, and permits his minor daughter to go to California to live there with her mother. *Held*, the father does not have sufficient minimum contacts with California to allow the mother to bring an *in personam* suit in California against him for increased child support. [*Kulko v. Superior Court*]

III. JURISDICTION OVER CORPORATIONS

A. **Domestic corporations:** *Any* action may be brought against a *domestic corporation*, i.e., one which is incorporated in the forum state. [18]

B. Foreign corporations generally: A state is much more limited in its ability to exercise jurisdiction over a *foreign* corporation (i.e., a corporation not incorporated in the forum state). [20-24]

    1. Minimum contacts: The forum state may exercise personal jurisdiction over the corporation only if the corporation has *"minimum contacts"* with the forum state "such that the maintenance of the suit does not offend 'traditional notions of fair play and substantial justice.' " [*International Shoe Co. v. Washington*] [20-21]

    2. Dealings with residents of forum state: Usually, a corporation will be found to have the requisite "minimum contacts" with the forum state only if the corporation has somehow *voluntarily sought* to *do business* in, or with the residents of, the forum state. [21-24]

        Example 1 (minimum contacts found): D has no activities in Washington except for the activities of its salesmen, who live in the state and work from their homes. All orders are sent by the salesmen to the home office, and approved at the home office. The salesmen earn a total of $31,000 per year in commissions.

        Held, the company has minimum contacts with Washington. [*International Shoe Co.*]

        Example 2 (minimum contacts found): D is a Texas insurance company. It does not solicit business in California. However, it takes over, from a previous insurance company, a policy written on the life of X, a California resident. D sends X a new policy; X sends premiums from his California home to D's out-of-state office. X dies; P (the beneficiary under the policy) is a California resident. P sues D in California for payment under the policy.

        Held, D has minimum contacts with California, and can thus be sued *in personam* there in a suit by P for payment on the policy. [*McGee v. International Life Insur. Co.*]

        Example 3 (minimum contacts not found): D is a Delaware bank, which acts as trustee of a certain trust. S, the settlor of the trust, is a Pennsylvania resident at the time she sets up the trust. Years later, she moves to Florida. Later, her two children, also Florida residents, want to sue D in Florida for a judgment that they are entitled to the remaining trust assets. D has no other contacts with Florida.

        Held, D does not have minimum contacts with Florida, and therefore, cannot be sued *in personam* there. [*Hanson v. Denckla*]

        Note: The key idea is that D will be found to have minimum contacts with the state only if D has *purposely availed* itself of the chance to do business in the forum state. Thus in *McGee* (Example 2 above), the insurance company offered a policy to someone who it knew was a resident of the forum state. In *Hanson* (Example 3 above), by contrast, the trustee never voluntarily initiated business transactions with a resident of the forum state or otherwise voluntarily did business in the state — it was only S's unilateral decision to move to the forum state that established any kind of connection with that state, so minimum contacts did not exist.

C. Use of agents: Sometimes an out-of-state company does not itself conduct activities within the forum state, but uses another company as its *agent* in the state. Even though all business within the state is done by the agent, the principal (the foreign corporation) can be sued there, if the agent does a significant amount of business on the foreign company's behalf. [24]

D. Claims unrelated to in-state activities: All of the above law assumes that the claim relates to D's *in-state activities*. Where the cause of action does *not* arise from the company's in-state activities, ***greater contacts*** between D and the forum state are required. The in-state activities in this situation must be ***"systematic and continuous."*** [25-27]

> **Example:** D is a South American corporation that supplies helicopter transportation in South America for oil companies. D has no contacts with Texas except: (1) one negotiation there with a client, (2) the purchase by D of 80% of its helicopter fleet from a Texas supplier, (3) the sending of pilots and maintenance people to Texas for training, and (4) the receipt out-of-state of two checks written in Texas by the client. D is sued in Texas by the Ps (Texas residents) when they are killed in South America while being transported by D.
>
> *Held*, the Ps cannot sue D in Texas. Because the Ps' claims did not arise out of D's in-Texas activities, those Texas contacts had to be "systematic and continuous" in order to be sufficient for jurisdiction. The contacts here were too sparse for that. [*Helicopteros Nacionales de Colombia v. Hall*]

E. Products liability: The requirement of "minimum contacts" with the forum state has special bite in ***products liability*** cases. [28-32]

1. Effort to market in forum state: The mere fact that a product manufactured or sold by D outside of the forum state finds its way into the forum state and causes injury there is ***not enough*** to subject D to personal jurisdiction there. Instead, D can be sued in the forum state only if it made some ***effort to market in the forum state***, either directly or indirectly. [28]

> **Example:** The Ps are injured in Oklahoma in an accident involving an allegedly defective car. They had purchased the car in New York while they were New York residents. The Ps sue in Oklahoma. D1 is the distributor of the car, who distributed only on the East Coast. D2 is the dealer, whose showroom was in New York. Neither D1 nor D2 sold cars in Oklahoma or did any business there.
>
> *Held*, neither D may be sued in Oklahoma. Neither D had made efforts to "serve directly or indirectly" the Oklahoma market. Any connection between the Ds' product and Oklahoma was merely an isolated occurrence, completely due to the unilateral activity of the Ps. [*World-Wide Volkswagen v. Woodson*]

2. Knowledge of in-state sales enough: But if the out-of-state manufacturer makes or sells a product that it ***knows*** will be eventually sold in the forum state, this fact by itself is probably enough to establish minimum contacts. However, if this is the only contact that exists, it may nonetheless be ***"unreasonable"*** to make D defend there, and thus violate due process. [29-32]

> **Example:** P is injured while riding a motorcycle in California. He brings a products liability suit in California against, *inter alia*, D, the Taiwanese manufacturer who made the cycle's rear innertube. D "impleads" X, the Japanese manufacturer of the tube's valve assembly, claiming that X must pay D any amount that D has to pay to P. X has no contacts with California, except that X knew that: (1) tires made by D from X's components were sold in the U.S., and (2) 20% of the U.S. sales were in California. The P-D suit has been settled but the D-X case is to be tried.
>
> *Held*, X had minimum contacts with California, because it put its goods into a stream of commerce that it knew would lead many of them to California. But despite these minimum contacts, it would be "unreasonable and unfair" — and thus a violation of due process — for California to hear the case, because of the burden to X of having to defend in California, the slenderness of California's interest in having the case heard there, and the

foreign relations problems that would be created by hearing an indemnity suit between two foreign corporations. [*Asahi Metal Industry Co. v. Superior Court*]

F. Unreasonableness: As the case in the above example shows, even where minimum contacts exist, it will be a violation of due process for the court to hear a case against a non-resident defendant where it would be *"unreasonable"* for the suit to be heard. The more burdensome it is to the defendant to have to litigate the case in the forum state, and the slimmer the contacts (though "minimum") with the forum state, the more likely this result is to occur. [30]

G. Suits based on contractual relationship: The requisite "minimum contacts" are more likely to be found where one party to a *contract* is a resident of the forum state. But the fact that one party to a contract is a resident does not by itself automatically mean that the other party has "minimum contacts" — the existence of a contract is just one factor to look at. [32-34]

    1. Contractual relationship involving the state: Where the contract itself somehow ties the parties' business activities into the forum state, this will be an important factor tending to show the existence of minimum contacts. For instance, if one party is to make payments to the other, and the latter will be receiving the payments in the forum state, this stream of payments coming into the state is likely to establish minimum contacts and thus to permit suit against the payor.

        Example: D runs a fast food restaurant in Michigan under franchise from P, which has its headquarters in Florida. The contract requires D to make royalty payments to P in Florida.
        Held, P may sue D in Florida. The fact that the payment stream comes into Florida is an important factor, though not by itself dispositive, in the court's conclusion that there were minimum contacts with Florida. [*Burger King Corp. v. Rudzewicz*]

    2. Choice-of-law clause: Where there is a contract between the parties to the suit, the fact that the contract contains a *choice of law clause* requiring use of the forum state's law will also be a factor (though not a dispositive one) tending towards a finding of minimum contacts. (*Example:* On the facts of the above example, the franchise contract stated that Florida law would be used. This was a factor helping lead the court to conclude that D had minimum contacts with Florida.) [34]

    3. "Reasonable anticipation" of defendant: In suits relating to a contract, as with any other kind of suit, the minimum contacts issue always boils down to this: *Could the defendant have reasonably anticipated being required to litigate in the forum state?* The fact that the other party was a resident of the forum state, the fact that a stream of payments went into the forum state, and the fact that the forum state's law was to be used in the contract, are all non-dispositive, but important, factors tending towards the conclusion that the out-of-stater had minimum contacts with the forum state. [35]

H. Class action plaintiffs: An "absent" plaintiff in a class action that takes place in the forum state may be *bound* by the decision in the case, even if that plaintiff did not have minimum contacts with the forum state. [*Phillips Petroleum Co. v. Shutts*] [35-36]

I. Libel and slander cases: The First Amendment imposes certain limits on the substantive *libel* and *slander* laws of the states (e.g., that no "public figure" may recover without a showing of "actual malice"). But this special first amendment protection does *not* affect the personal jurisdiction requirements for libel and slander suits — no more extensive contacts between D and the forum state must be shown in defamation suits than in any other type of case. [*Calder v. Jones*] [37]

IV. FEDERAL JURISDICTION OVER THE PARTIES

A. **General principles:** To determine whether a *federal* court has personal jurisdiction over the defendant, you must check *three things*: [39]

    1. **Territory for service:** Whether service took place within the appropriate *territory*;

    2. **Manner of service:** Whether the service was carried out in the correct *manner*; and

    3. **Amenability:** Whether the defendant was *"amenable"* to the federal suit.

B. **Territory for service:** [39-44]

    1. **General rule:** As a general rule, in both diversity actions and federal question cases, *service of process* may be made only: (1) *within the territorial limits of the state in which the District Court sits*; or (2) anywhere else permitted by the state law of the state where the District Court sits. FRCP 4(k)(1)(A). [39]

        Example (within the territorial limits of state): P sues D in a federal action in the Northern District of Ohio. Whether the suit is based on diversity or federal question, service will be territorially valid if P is served with process anywhere within the state of Ohio, since this is the state where the district court sits. This is true even if service is physically made in the Southern District of Ohio.

        Example (out-of-state service based on state law): Under the New Jersey long-arm statute, if a non-resident is involved in a motor vehicle accident inside New Jersey with a New Jersey resident, the New Jersey resident may serve the non-resident outside New Jersey, and the New Jersey courts may then exercise personal jurisdiction. P, a New Jersey resident, and D, a California resident, have an accident in New Jersey. P may sue D in diversity in federal District Court for New Jersey; P may serve D with process in California, because the long-arm of the state where the district court sits (Montana) would allow such service. FRCP 4(k)(1)(A).

    2. **100-mile bulge:** A special *100-mile bulge* provision (FRCP 4(k)(1)(B)) allows for out-of-state service sometimes, even if local law does not permit it. When the provision applies, it allows service anywhere (even across a state boundary) within a 100-mile radius of the federal courthouse where suit is pending. The bulge provision applies only where out-of-staters will be brought in as *additional parties* to an *already pending* action. There are two types of parties against whom it can be used: [41-42]

        a. **Third-party defendants:** *Third-party defendants* (FRCP 14) may be served within the bulge.

        Example: P sues D in a New Jersey federal district court diversity action. D claims that if D is liable to P, X is liable to D as an indemnitor. The suit is pending in Newark, less than 100 miles from New York City. D may serve X in New York City, even if no New Jersey long-arm statute would allow the suit.

        b. **Indispensable parties:** So-called *"indispensable parties"* — that is, persons who are needed in the action for just adjudication, and whose joinder will not involve subject matter jurisdiction problems — may also be served if they are within the bulge.

C
A
P
S
U
L
E

S
U
M
M
A
R
Y

Example: P sues D for copyright infringement in federal district court for the Eastern District of Kentucky, located in Lexington. D files a counterclaim against P. D wants to join X as a co-defendant to this counterclaim, arguing that P and X conspired to violate D's copyrights. X resides in Cincinnati, Ohio, located 78 miles from Lexington. If the court agrees that X is required for just adjudication of D's counterclaim, service on X in Cincinnati is valid, even if the Kentucky long-arm would not allow service there.

3. **Nationwide service of process:** In several kinds of cases, Congress has provided for *nationwide* service of process. Suits against *federal officials and agencies*, and suits based on *statutory interpleader*, are examples of nationwide service. [40]

4. **Foreign defendant not servable in any state:** Rule 4(k)(2) allows a *federal question* suit to be brought against any person or organization who cannot be sued in *any state* court (almost always because they are a *foreigner*).

    Example: D, a French company, without setting foot in the U.S., solicits business by phone and mail from residents of a large number of states. D does not solicit enough from the residents of any one state to satisfy that state's long-arm. Therefore, D could not be sued in any state court for a claim concerning its activities. P, a New York investor, brings a suit based upon the federal securities laws against D in the federal district court for the Southern District of New York. Assuming that D can be said to have had minimum contacts with the United States as a whole, the New York federal court will have personal jurisdiction over D for this federal-question claim, because D is not subject to the jurisdiction of the courts of any state. FRCP 4(k)(2) .

5. **Gaps possible:** A defendant who is not located in the state where the district court sits may *not* be served if he does not fall within one of the four special cases described above (servable pursuant to state long-arm, 100-mile bulge, nationwide service or foreign defendant not servable in any state), *even if he has the constitutionally-required minimum contacts* with the forum. This is true whether the case is based on diversity or federal question. [44]

    Example: P, a Connecticut resident, wants to bring a federal diversity suit in Connecticut against D, a New Yorker. The suit involves an accident that occurred in New York. D owns a second home in Connecticut, as well as lots of other real estate there. Assume that this ownership gives him not only minimum contacts but "systematic and continuous" contacts with Connecticut. However, Connecticut has a very narrow long-arm, which would not allow service on D in New York for a Connecticut state action.

    P will not be able to serve D in New York in his federal action, because none of the special cases is satisfied. This is true even though it would not be a violation of due process for either the Connecticut courts or the federal court in Connecticut to exercise personal jurisdiction over D.

C. **Manner of service:** Once you determine that the party to be served lies within the territory described above, you must determine if the service was carried out in the correct *manner*.

1. **Individual:** Service on an *individual* (Rule 4(e)) may be made in any of several ways:

   a. **Personal:** By serving him *personally*;

   b. **Substitute:** By handing the summons and complaint to a person *"suitable age and discretion"* residing at D's residence;

C
A
P
S
U
L
E

S
U
M
M
A
R
Y

    c. **Agent:** By serving an *agent* appointed or designated by law to receive process. (*Example:* Many states designate the Director of Motor Vehicles as the agent to receive process in suits involving car accidents);

    d. **Local state law:** By serving D in the manner provided by either: (1) the *law of the state where the district court sits*, if that state has such a provision, or (2) the *law of the state where the person is being served*. (*Example*: P brings an action against D, a resident of California, in New Jersey federal court, and wishes to serve him by certified mail. Service will be possible if *either* the courts of New Jersey *or* California allow certified-mail service.)

2. **Corporation:** Service on a *corporation* may be made by leaving the papers with an *officer*, a managing or general *agent*, or any other agent authorized by appointment or by law to receive process for the corporation. FRCP 4(h)(1).

    a. **Local state law:** As with individuals, service on a corporation may also be made in the manner provided by the local law of (i) the state where the *action is pending* or (ii) the state where the *service is made*. FRCP 4(h)(1), first sentence.

3. **Waiver of service:** Rule 4(d) allows plaintiff to in effect serve the summons and complaint by *mail*, provided that the *defendant cooperates*. P mails to D a *"request for waiver of service";* if D agrees, no actual in-person service is needed.

    a. **Incentives:** D is free to refuse to grant the waiver, in which case P must serve the summons by the in-person methods described above. But, if D refuses the waiver, the court will impose the *costs* subsequently incurred by P in effecting service on D unless "good cause" is shown for D's refusal. (FRCP 4(d)(2), last sentence.)

D. **Amenability to suit:** If D was served in an appropriate territory, and in an appropriate manner, you still have to determine whether D is closely-enough linked to the state where the federal district court sits to make him *"amenable to suit"* in that court. [46-49]

1. **Federal question:** In *federal question* cases, most courts hold that D is amenable to suit in their court if jurisdiction could *constitutionally be exercised* over him in the *state courts* of the state where the federal court is sitting, even if the state court itself would not (because of a limited long-arm) have jurisdiction. [46]

    Example: P sues D for copyright infringement. The suit is brought in the Northern District of Ohio. D's only contact with Ohio is that he sold 100 copies of the allegedly infringing book in Ohio. The state courts of Ohio, although they could constitutionally take personal jurisdiction over D in a similar state-created claim — libel, for instance — would not do so because the Ohio long-arm is very limited and would not cover any action growing out of these facts. However, the federal district court will hear the federal question copyright claim against D, because P has minimum contacts with the state where the federal court sits.

    a. **Foreign defendants:** In general, if the defendant is a *foreign* corporation or resident, most federal courts will exercise jurisdiction over the defendant only if that defendant has minimum contacts with the state where the federal court sits, not merely minimum contacts with the United States as a whole. (Again, as with an out-of-state but not foreign defendant, the federal court will hear the federal question claim even though the state courts might not exercise jurisdiction over the defendant due to a limited state long-arm.)

C
A
P
S
U
L
E

S
U
M
M
A
R
Y

      i. **Narrow exception:** If a foreign defendant could not be sued in *any state*, he may be sued on a federal-question claim in any federal judicial district, assuming that he has minimum contacts with the U.S. as a whole. (FRCP 4(k)(2).) But assuming that the foreign defendant could be sued in at least some state court, the general rule described in the prior paragraph (D must have minimum contacts with the state where the federal court sits, not just with the U.S. as a whole) continues to apply.

    2. **Diversity:** In *diversity* cases, the federal courts exercise only the jurisdiction that is allowed *by the statutory law of the state in which they sit*. So if the state statutory law does not go to the limits of due process, the federal court will follow suit. [48-49]

V. JURISDICTION OVER THINGS

A. **Two types of actions:** There are two types of actions that relate primarily to *"things"* rather than to people: (1) *in rem* actions; and (2) *quasi in rem* actions. [51-53]

    1. *In rem* **actions:** *In rem* actions are ones which do not seek to impose personal liability on anyone, but instead seek to affect the interests of persons in a specific thing (or *res*). (*Examples:* Probate court actions; admiralty actions concerning title to a ship; actions to quiet title to real estate or to foreclose a lien upon it; actions for divorce.)

       a. **No personal liability:** In all of these types of *in rem* actions, no judgment imposing personal liability on anyone results — all that happens is that the status of a thing is adjudicated. (*Example:* In a quiet title action, a determination is reached that A, rather than B, is the owner of Blackacre).

    2. *Quasi in rem* **actions:** *Quasi in rem* actions are actions that would have been *in personam* if jurisdiction over D's person had been attainable. Instead, property or intangibles are seized not as the object of the litigation, but merely as a *means of satisfying a possible judgment* against D.

B. *In rem jurisdiction:* [51-52]

    1. **Specific performance of land sale contract:** One important type of *in rem* action is an action for *specific performance* of a contract to *convey land*. Even if the defendant is out of state and has no connection with the forum state other than having entered into a contract to convey in-state land, the forum state may hear the action. D does not have to have minimum contacts with the forum state for the action to proceed — it is enough that the contract involved in-state land, and that D has received reasonable notice. [52]

    2. **Effect of *Shaffer*:** The landmark case of *Shaffer v. Heitner*, discussed below, has almost no effect on *in rem* suits. *Shaffer* holds that there must be minimum contacts before a *quasi in rem* action may proceed; but no minimum contacts are needed for the court to adjudicate the status of property or some other thing located in the state, even though it affects the rights of an out-of-state defendant. [52]

C. *Quasi in rem jurisdiction:* [52-62]

    1. **Definition:** As noted, a *quasi in rem* action is one that would have been *in personam* if jurisdiction over D's person had been attainable. Instead, property or intangibles are seized not as the **object** of the litigation, but merely as a means of satisfying a possible judgment against D. [52]

C
A
P
S
U
L
E

S
U
M
M
A
R
Y

Example: P wants to sue D on a contract claim in California state court. The contract has no connection with California, nor does D himself have sufficient contacts with California to allow that state to exericise personal jurisdiction over him. D does, however, own a bank account in California. Putting aside constitutional due process problems, P could attach that bank account as a basis of jurisdiction, and bring a *quasi in rem* action on the contract claim. If P wins, he will be able to collect only the value of the bank account, and D will not be personally liable for the remainder if the damages exceed the value of the account.

2. **No res judicata value:** *Quasi in rem* judgments have **no res judicata value**. (*Example:* If P wins against D in a *quasi in rem* action in Connecticut, he cannot in a later suit against D in California claim that the matter has been decided for all time. Instead, he must go through another trial on the merits if he wishes to subject D to further liability.) [53]

   a. **Possible exception:** Some courts hold that if D makes a *limited appearance* (an appearance that does not confer personal jurisdiction over him) and fully litigates certain issues, he will not be allowed to re-litigate those issues in a subsequent trial. But other courts hold that even here, the first suit will not prevent D from re-litigating the same issues later on.

3. **Requirement of minimum contacts (*Shaffer*):** *Quasi in rem* jurisdiction over D cannot be exercised unless D had such *"minimum contacts"* with the forum state that *in personam jurisdiction could be exercised over him*. This is the holding of the landmark case of *Shaffer v. Heitner*. [56-60]

   Example: P brings a shareholder's derivative suit in Delaware on behalf of XYZ Corp. against 28 of XYZ's non-resident directors and officers. None of the activities complained of took place in Delaware, nor did any D have any other contact with Delaware. P takes advantage of a Delaware statute providing that any stock in a Delaware corporation is deemed to be present in Delaware, allowing that stock to be attached to provide *quasi in rem* jurisdiction against its owner. Thus P is able to tie up each D's XYZ stockholdings even though there is no other connection with Delaware.

   Held, this use of *quasi in rem* jurisdiction violates constitutional due process. No D may be subjected to *quasi in rem* jurisdiction unless he has minimum contacts with the forum state. Here, neither the Ds' actions nor the fact that those actions related to a Delaware corporation were sufficient to create minimum contacts, so the exercise of jurisdiction was improper. [*Shaffer v. Heitner*]

4. **Jurisdiction based on debt, insurance or other obligation:** *Shaffer* basically abolishes the utility of *quasi in rem* jurisdiction — since *quasi in rem* is only used where there is no personal jurisdiction, and since the same minimum contacts needed for *quasi in rem* will suffice for personal jurisdiction, *quasi in rem* will rarely be advantageous. (The one exception is where minimum contacts are present, but the state long-arm for personal jurisdiction is too narrow to reach the defendant, yet a state attachment statute applies.) One big practical effect is that attachment of a third party's *debt* to the defendant, or attachment of an insurance company's *obligation to defend and pay a claim*, are largely wiped out as bases for jurisdiction. [55-56]

   Example 1: Harris, of North Carolina, owes $180 to Balk, of North Carolina. Epstein, of Maryland, has a claim against Balk for $300. While Harris is visiting in Maryland, Epstein attaches Harris' debt to Balk by serving Harris with process in a Maryland suit.

Under pre-*Shaffer* law, this established *quasi in rem* jurisdiction over the $180 debt, on the theory that the debt goes wherever the debtor goes. If Epstein won, he could require Harris to pay the $180 to him rather than to Balk. [*Harris v. Balk*] [54]

But after *Shaffer*, the fact that Balk's debtor happened to be in North Carolina and available for personal service was irrelevant. Since Balk himself did not minimum contacts with Maryland, and thus could not be sued there personally, *Shaffer* means that a *quasi in rem* suit based on Harris' debt to him may also not be heard in Maryland.

Example 2: Same facts as above, except assume that instead of Harris' being sued, Insurance Co., which had an obligation to defend Balk and pay judgments issued against Balk, was served in Maryland. Pre-*Shaffer*, this would have been enough for *quasi in rem* jurisdiction over Balk. [55]

But because of *Shaffer*, the fact that Insurer had minimum contacts with Maryland would be irrelevant — an insurance company's obligation to defend the debtor in the forum state and to pay claims arising out of suits in the forum state is not enough to subject the insured to a *quasi in rem* suit in the forum state.

D. **Limited appearance:** [60]

1. **Definition:** Some states allow a *"limited appearance."* Under a limited appearance, D appears in an *in rem* or *quasi in rem* suit, contests the case on its merits, but is subjected to liability only to the extent of the property or debt attached or garnished by the court.

   a. **Distinguished from special appearance:** Distinguish limited appearances from special appearances — in the latter, a defendant against whom personal jurisdiction is asserted is allowed to argue the invalidity of that jurisdiction without having this argument, or his presence in the court, itself constitute a submission to the court's jurisdiction.

2. **Federal limited appearances:** Federal courts usually follow the rule of the *state in which they are sitting* in determining whether to allow a limited appearance.

E. **Federal *quasi in rem* jurisdiction:** [60-62]

1. **General rule:** *Quasi in rem* jurisdiction is allowed in a federal court if: (1) *the law of the state in which the federal court sits permits* such *quasi in rem* jurisdiction, and (2) P cannot obtain *personal* jurisdiction over D in the state through reasonable efforts. Rule 4(n). (*Examples of conditions satisfying (2)*: D is a fugitive, or the local long-arm is too weak to reach D even though he has minimum contacts with the state where the district court sits.)

2. **Amount in controversy:** In a federal *quasi in rem* case, courts are split as to whether it is the value of the attached property, or the amount claimed, which should control for the $50,000 amount in controversy requirement.

VI. NOTICE AND OPPORTUNITY TO BE HEARD

A. **Notice generally:** Even if the court has authority to judge the dispute between the parties or over the property before it (covered in the above sections), the court may not proceed unless D received *adequate notice* of the case against him. [63-72]

1. **Reasonableness test:** In order for D to have received adequate notice, it is not necessary that he *actually* have learned of the suit. Rather, the procedures used to alert him must have been *reasonably likely to inform him*, even if they actually failed to do so. [65]

Example: P's process server leaves the summons and complaint at D's house, with D's wife. D's wife throws it in the garbage, and D never learns of it. D has received adequate notice, so the court can exercise jurisdiction over him. Conversely, if P's process server had left the papers on the sidewalk outside the house, and D had happened to pick them up, this would ***not*** be adequate notice to D — the procedures used were not reasonably likely to give D notice, and they are not saved by the fact that D in fact learned of the suit.

2. **Substitute service:** Personal service — handing the papers to D himself — will always suffice as adequate notice. But all states, and the federal system, also allow *"substitute service"* in most instances. Substitute service means "some form of service other than directly handing the papers to the defendant." [64]

   a. **Leave at dwelling:** The most common substitute service provision allows the process papers to be left at D's ***dwelling*** within the state, if D is not at home. These provisions usually require the papers to be left with an adult who is reasonably likely to give them to D. (*Example:* FRCP 4(e)(2) allows the papers to be left with a person of "suitable age and discretion residing in the dwelling place in question.")

   b. **Mail:** Some states, and the federal system, allow service to be made by ordinary ***first class mail***. However, usually this method is allowable only if D returns an acknowledgement or waiver form to P's lawyer. If D does not return the form, some other method of service must then be used. See FRCP 4(e)(1).

3. **Service on out-of-staters:** Where D is not present in the forum state, he must somehow be served ***out of state***. Remember that in a state court suit, this can only be done if the state has a long-arm statute covering the type of case and defendant in question. Once the long-arm covers the situation, the out-of-state defendant must still be given some sort of notice. [65]

   a. **Mail notice:** Many states provide for notice by ***registered or certified mail*** on the out-of-state defendant.

   b. **Public official:** Sometimes, service may be made by serving a ***state official***, plus giving notice by mail to D. (*Example:* Many non-resident motorist statutes allow P to serve the state Director of Motor Vehicles with a matching mailing to the out-of-state defendant.)

   c. **Newspaper publication:** If D's identity or residence are unknown, some states allow service by ***newspaper publication***. But this may only be used where D truly cannot be found by reasonable effort.

4. **Corporations:** Several means are commonly allowed for giving notice of suit to ***corporations***. [66]

   a. **Corporate officer:** Many states require that a corporation, if it wishes to be incorporated in the state or to do business in the state, must ***designate a corporate official*** to receive process for suits against the company. Service on this designated official is, of course, deemed to be adequate notice.

   b. **Federal Rule:** The Federal Rules, and the rules of many states, are more liberal, in that they allow service on any person associated with the corporation who is of sufficiently high placement. Thus FRCP 4(h)(1) provides that service on a corporation may be made by giving the papers to "an officer, a managing or general agent, or to any other agent authorized by appointment or by law to receive service of process."

B. Constitutional due process: Just as the Fourteenth Amendment's Due Process Clause prohibits jurisdiction over a defendant who lacks minimum contacts with the forum state (*International Shoe*), so that clause prohibits the exercise of jurisdiction over a defendant who has not been given *"reasonable notice"* of the suit. [*Mullane v. Central Hanover Bank*] [66-68]

1. **Mail notice to all the identifiable parties:** For instance, if a party's name and address are "reasonably ascertainable," publication notice will not be sufficient, and instead notice by *mail* (or other means equally likely to ensure actual notice) must be used. [*Mennonite Board of Missions v. Adams*] [67]

2. **Actual receipt doesn't count:** Remember that what matters is the *appropriateness* of the notice prescribed by statute and employed, *not* whether D actually *got* the notice. [68]

C. Opportunity to be heard: D must not only be notified of the suit against him, but must also be given an *opportunity to be heard*. That is, before his property may be taken, he must be given a chance to defend against the claim. This "opportunity to be heard" must be given to D not only when his property will be taken forever, but even before there is any *significant interference* with his property rights.

1. **Pre-judgment remedy:** Opportunity-to-be-heard questions arise most frequently in the context of *pre-judgment remedies*, which protect plaintiff against the defendant's hiding or squandering his assets during litigation. Two common forms of pre-judgment remedies are the *attachment* of D's *bank account* and the placing of a *lis pendens* against her *real estate*.

2. **Three-part test:** The court will weigh *three factors* against each other to determine whether due process was violated when D's property was interfered with through a pre-judgment remedy: [70-72]

   a. First, the degree of *harm* to *D's interest* from the pre-judgment remedy;

   b. Second, the risk that the deprivation of D's property right will be *erroneous* (especially if the state could have used additional procedural safeguards against this but did not); and

   c. Third, the strength of the interest of the party (typically P) *seeking* the prejudgment remedy.

   [*Connecticut v. Doehr*] [70]

   Example: A state statute allows P to get a prejudgment attachment of D's real estate without D's having a hearing first, so long as P "verifies by oath" that there is probable cause to sustain his claim. Factor 1 above (the strength of D's interest) works against allowing attachment, since an attachment clouds D's title and affects his credit rating. Factor 2 (risk of erroneous deprivation) also supports not allowing the attachment, since the judge can't accurately determine the likely outcome of the litigation based solely on P's one-sided conclusory statements in the oath. Factor 3 (strength of P's interest) also works against the attachment, since P is not required to show D is dissipating his assets. Consequently, the grant of a prejudgment attachment of D's property violates his due process rights. [*Connecticut v. Doehr*]

VII. DEFENSES TO CLAIMS OF JURISDICTION

A. Special appearance: In a *"special appearance,"* D appears in the action with the express purpose of making a jurisdictional objection. By making a special appearance, D has *not consented* to the exercise of jurisdiction. [73]

C
A
P
S
U
L
E

S
U
M
M
A
R
Y

1. **Appeal:** Most courts allow a defendant who has unsuccessfully made a special appearance to then defend on the merits, without losing his right to appeal the jurisdictional issue. [73]

2. **Federal substitute for special appearance:** The federal courts (and the many state courts with rules patterned after the Federal Rules) have *abolished* the special appearance. Instead, D makes a *motion* to dismiss for lack of jurisdiction over the parties; making this motion does not subject D to the jurisdiction that he is protesting. FRCP 12(b)(2). [74]

   a. **Waiver:** The right to make a motion to dismiss for lack of personal jurisdiction is *waived* in the federal system if: (1) D makes a motion raising any of the defenses listed in Rule 12, and the personal jurisdiction defense is not included; or (2) D neither makes a Rule 12 motion nor raises the defense in his answer.

B. **Collateral attack:** [75-76]

   1. **General enforcement of judgments:** A judgment entered in one jurisdiction may generally be *enforced* in another. That is, if State 1 enters a judgment against D, D's property in State 2 (or wages owed him in State 2) may be seized to satisfy the earlier State 1 judgment. [74]

   2. **Collateral attack on default judgment:** If D *defaults* in an action in State 1, she may *collaterally attack* the default judgment when it is sued upon in State 2. Most commonly, D collaterally attacks the earlier judgment on the grounds that State 1 did not have personal jurisdiction over her, or did not have valid subject matter jurisdiction. [75-76]

      Example: D has no contacts with Iowa. P, an Iowa resident, sues D in Iowa court. D never appears in the action, and a default judgment is entered against him for $100,000. P then brings a suit in D's home state of New Jersey to enforce the earlier Iowa judgment. D will be permitted to collaterally attack the Iowa judgment, by arguing that Iowa lacked personal jurisdiction over him. The New Jersey court will undoubtedly agree with D that, because D did not have minimum contacts with Iowa, Iowa could not constitutionally take jurisdiction over him. Therefore, the New Jersey court will decline to enforce the Iowa judgment.

   3. **Waiver by D:** A defendant who *appeared in the original action* without objecting to jurisdiction, or one who unsuccessfully litigated the jurisdictional issue in the first action, may *not* collaterally attack the judgment. (Instead, a defendant who unsuccessfully litigates jurisdiction in the first action must appeal to the first state's system, rather than later making a collateral attack.) [76]

C. **Defense of fraud or duress:** A court may constitutionally exercise jurisdiction over a defendant found within the forum state, even if D's presence was the result of *fraud* or *duress* on the part of the plaintiff. But the court may exercise its *discretion* not to exercise jurisdiction. (*Example:* P entices D into the jurisdiction with a false love letter and a false statement that she is leaving the country forever and wants to see D once more. When D arrives at the airport in the forum state, P serves him with papers. *Held*, the forum state will decline to exercise its jurisdiction because of P's fraud. [*Wyman v. Newhouse*]) [76-77]

D. **Immunity:** Most jurisdictions give to non-residents of the forum state an *immunity* from service of process while they are in state to *attend a trial*. This is true whether the person is a *witness*, a *party*, or an *attorney*. Most states also grant the immunity for related proceedings such as depositions. [77-78]

   1. **Federal suits:** Out-of-state parties, witnesses, and attorneys also generally receive immunity from *federal* court suits (whether diversity or federal question). [78]

VIII. VENUE

A. Definition: *"Venue"* refers to the ***place within a sovereign jurisdiction*** in which a given action is to be brought. It matters only if jurisdiction over the parties has been established. (*Example:* State X is found to have jurisdiction over the person of B, in a suit against him by A. Venue determines in which ***county*** or ***district*** of State X the case should be tried.) [79]

B. State action: In state trials, venue is determined by statute. The states are free to set up virtually any venue rules they wish, without worrying about the federal constitution. [80]

   1. Basis for: Most commonly, venue is authorized based on the county or city where the ***defendant resides***. Many states also allow venue based on where the cause of action arose, where the defendant does business, etc. [80]

   2. Forum non conveniens: Under the doctrine of ***forum non conveniens***, the state may use its discretion not to hear the case in a county where there is statutory venue. Sometimes, this involves shifting the case to a different place within the state. At other times, it involves the state not having the case take place in-state at all. Usually, it is the defendant who moves to have the case dismissed or transferred for *forum non conveniens*. [81-83]

      a. Factors: Three factors that state courts often consider in deciding whether to dismiss for *forum non conveniens* are: (1) whether the plaintiff is a state ***resident*** (if so, he has a stronger claim to be able to have his case heard in his home state); (2) whether the witnesses and sources of proof are more available in a different state or county; and (3) whether the forum's own state laws will govern the action (transfer is more likely if a different state's law controls).

C. Venue in federal actions: In ***federal*** actions, the venue question is, ***"Which federal district court shall try the action?"*** Venue is controlled by 28 U.S.C. §1391. [83-90]

   1. Still need personal jurisdiction: When you consider a venue problem, remember that venue is ***not a substitute*** for personal jurisdiction: the fact that venue lies in a particular judicial district does not automatically mean that suit can be brought there. Suit can be brought only in a district that satisfies ***both*** the venue requirements and the personal jurisdiction requirements as to all defendants. [84]

   2. Three methods: There are three basic ways by which there might be venue in a particular judicial district: (1) if ***any*** defendant ***resides*** in that district, and ***all defendants reside in the state*** containing that district; (2) if a ***"substantial part of the events***…giving rise to the claim ***occurred***, or a substantial part of property that is the subject of the action is situated," in the district; and (3) if all defendants are ***"reachable"*** in the district. Each of these is considered below, as sections 3, 4 and 5. [84]

   3. "Defendant's residence" venue: For both diversity and federal question cases, venue lies in any district where ***any defendant resides***, so long as, if there is more than one defendant, ***all the defendants*** reside in the ***state*** containing that district. [85]

      Example: P, from Massachusetts, brings a diversity suit against D1, from the Southern District of New York, and D2, from the Eastern District of New York. Venue will lie in either the Southern District of New York or the Eastern District of New York — each of these is home to at least one defendant, and each of these two districts is in a state that is home to all the defendants. But if D2 had been a resident of the District of Connecticut instead of any New York district, there would not be any "defendant's residence" venue anywhere.

4. **"Place of events or property" venue:** For both diversity and federal question cases, venue lies in any district "in which a *substantial part* of the *events* or omissions giving rise to the claim *occurred*, or a substantial part of *property* that is the subject of the action is *situated*...." This is "place of events" venue. [85]

   a. **Multiple districts:** There can be *multiple* districts qualifying for "place of events" venue, as long as each district was the locus for a "substantial part" of the events relating to the claim. (*Example:* P, from Massachusetts, sues D, a car dealer from Connecticut. P alleges that D sold P a car in Connecticut, that P drove the car to Massachusetts, and that a defect in the car caused P to be injured in Massachusetts. Probably venue in *either* the District of Massachusetts or the District of Connecticut would be allowed under the "place of events" provision, since probably both the selling of the defective car and the incurring of the accident were a "substantial part" of the events.)

5. **"Catch all" provision:** Finally, for both diversity and federal question cases, there is a *"catch all,"* by which venue may be founded in a district with which some or all defendants have close ties. [86-88]

   a. **Diversity:** In a case founded solely on diversity, the catch-all gives venue in any judicial district "in which the defendants are *subject to personal jurisdiction* at the time the action is commenced." §1391(a)(3). This means that *all* defendants must be subject to personal jurisdiction in that district.

   Example: P, from Massachusetts, brings a diversity suit against D1, who resides in the Southern District of New York, and D2, who lives in the District of Connecticut. P's suit is brought in the Southern District of New York. P serves D2 while D2 happens to be in New York City (S.D.N.Y.) on business one day.

   The catch-all applies — even though there is no "defendant's residence" venue or "place of events" venue in S.D.N.Y., the catch-all works because D1 is subject to personal jurisdiction in S.D.N.Y. by virtue of his residence there, and D2 is subject to personal jurisdiction there by virtue of his "transitory presence" at the moment of service. Probably, this would be true even if D2 was not served while in S.D.N.Y. on business, if he otherwise had substantial contacts with New York City and the New York State long-arm would cover him.

   b. **Federal question cases:** In federal question cases, the catch-all provision gives venue in any judicial district "in which *any defendant* may be *found*, if there is *no district in which the action may otherwise be brought*." §1391(b)(3). (Note the difference from the diversity catch-all: here, only one defendant must be "found" in the district, not "all defendants" — all the Ds must still be made subject to personal jurisdiction, but this might happen even though not all can be "found" in the district because not all have ever had any contacts with the district, merely with some other part of the state where the district court sits.)

6. **No "plaintiff's residence" venue:** There is *no* venue (as there used to be) based on *plaintiff's residence*. [88]

7. **Corporation:** The residence of a *corporation* for venue purposes matters only if the corporation is a defendant. A corporation is deemed to be a resident of *any district as to which the*

corporation would have the "minimum contacts" necessary to support personal jurisdiction if that district were a separate state. Thus a corporation is a resident of at least the district where it has its **principal place of business**, any district where it has **substantial operations**, and probably any district in its **state of incorporation**. But merely because a corporation does business somewhere in the state, this does not make it a resident of all districts of that state. [88-89]

> **Example:** XYZ Corp. is incorporated in Delaware, and has its only office in San Francisco. XYZ has no contacts with any part of California other than San Francisco. If XYZ is a defendant, it will reside, for venue purposes, in the district of Delaware and in the Northern District of California. XYZ is not a resident of any other districts in California — thus "defendant's residence" venue would not lie against XYZ, for instance, in a suit brought in the Central District of California, located in Los Angeles.

8. **Removal:** A case **removed** from state to federal court passes to "the district court of the U.S. for the district and division embracing the place **where such action is pending**." 28 U.S.C. §1441(a). [89]

9. **Federal forum non conveniens:** In the federal system, when a defendant successfully moves for *forum non conveniens*, the original court **transfers** the case to another district, rather than dismissing it. Under 28 U.S.C. §1404(a), "for the convenience of parties and witnesses ... a district court may transfer any civil action to any other district or division where it might have been brought." [89-90]

   a. **Defendant's motion:** Usually, it is the defendant who moves for *forum non conveniens*. When this happens, the case may be transferred only to a district where P would have had the right, **independent of the wishes of D**, to bring the action. (*Example:* If suit on a particular district would not have been possible, as an initial matter, because one or more of the Ds could not be personally served there, or because venue would not have been proper there, even the consent by all Ds would not authorize the action to be transferred to that district.)

   b. **Choice of law:** When federal *forum non conveniens* is granted, the state law of the **transferor** court is to be applied by the transferee court. (*Example:* P brings a diversity action against D in Mississippi federal court. That court grants D's motion to have the case moved to Pennsylvania District Court. If, as is likely, Mississippi federal court would have applied Mississippi state law rather than Pennsylvania state law under *Erie* principles, the Pennsylvania federal court must also apply Mississippi state law.) This is true whether the *forum non conveniens* was sought by P or by D. [*Ferens v. John Deere Co.*] [90]

CHAPTER 3
SUBJECT MATTER JURISDICTION

I. GENERAL PRINCIPLES

A. **Diversity vs. federal question:** In the federal courts, there are two basic kinds of controversies over which the federal judiciary has subject matter jurisdiction: (1) suits between **citizens of different states** (so-called **diversity** jurisdiction); and (2) suits involving a **"federal question."** [94]

1. **Other cases:** Certain other kinds of cases specified in the constitution also fall under the federal judicial power. These are cases involving *ambassadors*, cases involving *admiralty*, and cases in which the *United States* is a party. But except in these very unusual cases, when you are considering a case that is brought in the federal courts, you must ask: Does it fall within the diversity jurisdiction or federal question jurisdiction? If it does not fall within either of these, probably it cannot be heard by the federal courts.

B. **Amount in controversy:** In federal suits based on diversity, an amount in excess of *$50,000* must be in dispute. This is the *"amount in controversy"* requirement. In federal question cases, there is no amount in controversy requirement. [94]

C. **Burden:** The party seeking to *invoke the jurisdiction* of a federal court must make an *affirmative showing* that the case is within the court's subject matter jurisdiction. (*Example:* If P wants to invoke diversity jurisdiction, in her pleading she must allege the relevant facts about the citizenship of the parties.) [94]

D. **Dismissal at any time:** *No matter when* a deficiency in the subject matter jurisdiction of a federal court is noticed, the suit must be stopped, and *dismissed* for lack of jurisdiction. See FRCP 12(h)(3), requiring the court to dismiss the action at any time if it appears that the court lacks subject matter jurisdiction. [94]

> **Example:** A case brought under federal question jurisdiction goes through trial and through one level of appeals, and is then heard by the Supreme Court. The Supreme Court decides that there was no federal question in the first place. *Held*, the entire case must be dismissed for lack of federal subject matter jurisdiction. [*Louisville & National Railroad v. Mottley*]

II. DIVERSITY JURISDICTION

A. **Definition:** The Constitution gives the federal courts jurisdiction over *"controversies … between the citizens of different states…."* This is the grant of "diversity jurisdiction." [96-104]

> **Example:** P, a citizen of California, wants to sue D, a citizen of Oregon, for hitting P with D's car. Assuming that P's damages exceed $50,000, P can bring her negligence suit against D in federal court, because it is between citizens of different states.

1. **Date for determining:** The existence of diversity is determined *as of the commencement of the action*. If diversity existed between the parties on that date, it is not defeated because one of the parties later moved to a state that is the home state of the opponent. [98]

2. **Domicile:** What controls for citizenship is *domicile*, not residence. A person's domicile is where she has her true, fixed and permanent home. (*Example:* P has his main home in New York, but has an expensive second home in Florida. D has her only home in Florida. P can bring a diversity action against D, because P is deemed a citizen only of New York, not Florida, even though P has a "residence" in Florida.) [98]

a. **Resident alien:** A *resident alien* (an alien who lives in the United States permanently) is deemed a citizen of the state in which he is domiciled.

b. **Presence of foreigner:** In a suit between citizens of different states, the fact that a *foreign* citizen (or foreign country) is a party does *not destroy* diversity. (Example: P, a citizen of Ohio, sues D1, a citizen of Michigan, and D2, a citizen of Canada. Diversity jurisdiction exists.) (In situations where one side consists *solely* of foreign citizens or foreign countries, "alienage" jurisdiction applies. See below.)

3. **Complete diversity:** The single most important principle to remember in connection with diversity jurisdiction is that ***"complete diversity" is required***. That is, it must be the case that *no plaintiff is a citizen of the same state as any defendant*. [96-97]

    Example: P, a citizen of New York, brings a suit against D1, a citizen of New York, and D2, a citizen of New Jersey. We ask, "Is there any plaintiff who is a citizen of the same state as any defendant?" Since the answer is "yes," the requirement of complete diversity is not satisfied, and there is no diversity jurisdiction.

4. **Pleading not dispositive:** In order to determine whether diversity exists, the pleadings do not settle the question of who are adverse parties. Instead, the court looks beyond the pleadings, and arranges the parties according to their real interests in the litigation. [97]

    a. **Nominal parties ignored:** In determining the existence of diversity, *nominal* or purely *formal* parties are ignored. (*Example:* Where a guardian of an infant sues, the guardian is deemed to be a citizen only of the same state as the infant. See 28 U.S.C. §1332(c)(2).) [97-98]

B. **Alienage jurisdiction:** Related to diversity jurisdiction, but analytically distinct, is ***"alienage"*** jurisdiction. Alienage jurisdiction exists where there is a suit between citizens of a state, on one side, and foreign states or citizens thereof, on the other. (*Example:* P, a citizen of Mexico, sues D, a citizen of Illinois. Even if there is no federal question issue, there will be federal subject matter jurisdiction of the "alienage" variety, assuming that the amount in controversy requirement is satisfied.) [99-100]

1. **Suit between two foreign citizens:** But a suit solely between citizens of *two foreign countries* does *not* fall within the alienage jurisdiction. (*Example:* If P, a citizen of Canada, sues D, a citizen of Mexico, there is no alienage jurisdiction.)

C. **Diversity involving corporations:** For diversity purposes, a *corporation* is deemed a citizen of *any state where it is incorporated* and of the state where it has its *principal place of business*. In other words, for diversity to exist, no adversary of the corporation may be a citizen of the state in which the corporation is incorporated, or of the state in which it has its principal place of business. (*Example:* XYZ Corp., a corporation which is incorporated in Delaware, has its principal place of business in New York. In order for there to be diversity, no adverse party may be a citizen of *either* Delaware or New York.) [100-01]

1. **Principal place of business:** Courts have taken two different views about where a corporation's "principal place of business" is.

    a. **Home office:** Some courts hold that the corporation's principal place of business is ordinarily the state in which its *corporate headquarters*, or "home office," is located. This is sometimes called the ***"nerve center"*** test.

    b. **Bulk of activity:** Other courts hold that the principal place of business is the place in which the corporation carries on its main *production or service activities*. This is sometimes called the ***"muscle"*** test. This is the more commonly-used standard.

D. **Devices to create or destroy diversity:** The federal courts will not take jurisdiction of a suit in which any party has been ***"improperly or collusively joined"*** to obtain jurisdiction. 28 U.S.C. §1359. [101-02]

1. **Assignment:**   This means that a claimant may *not assign her claim* in order to create diversity. (*Example:* Alex and Dennis are both citizens of Florida. Alex wants to bring a diversity action against Dennis. Alex assigns his claim to Barbara, a Massachusetts citizen, with the understanding that Barbara will remit to Alex 80% of any recovery. The court will not take diversity jurisdiction over the Barbara-vs.-Dennis action, because Barbara's presence in the suit was an improper or collusive joinder. [*Kramer v. Caribbean Mills*]) [101]

2. **Devices to defeat removal:**   A plaintiff suing in state court may sometimes seek to defeat her adversary's potential right to *remove to federal court*. There is no federal statute prohibiting "improper or collusive" joinder for the purpose of defeating jurisdiction. However, as a matter of judge-made law, courts will often *disregard* obvious removal-defeating tactics (e.g., joinder of a defendant who has nothing to do with the underlying dispute, but who is a citizen of the same state as a plaintiff.) [101-02]

   a. **Low dollar claim:**   But the state-court plaintiff is always free to make a claim for *less than the amount in controversy* ($50,000), in order to defeat removal, even if P has really suffered a loss greater than this amount. (But the less-than-$50,000 amount must be named *before* D removes.)

III. FEDERAL QUESTION JURISDICTION

A. **Generally:**   The Constitution gives the federal courts authority to hear *"federal question"* cases. More precisely, under 28 U.S.C. §1331, the federal courts have jurisdiction over "all civil actions *arising under the Constitution, laws, or treaties of the United States.*" [104-06]

   1. **Federal claim:**   There is no precise definition of a case "arising under" the Constitution or laws of the United States. But in the vast majority of cases, the reason there is a federal question is that federal law is the *source of the plaintiff's claim*. (*Examples:* A claim of copyright infringement, trademark infringement or patent infringement raises a federal question, because in each of these situations, a federal statute — the federal copyright statute, trademark statute or patent statute — is the source of the right the plaintiff is asserting.) [104]

      a. **Interpretation of federal law:**   It is *not* enough that P is asserting a *state-created* claim which requires *interpretation* of federal law. (*Example:* P brings a state-court product liability suit against D for injuries sustained by taking a drug made by D. P claims that D violated the federal FDA statute by mislabeling the drug, and that this mislabeling automatically constitutes common-law negligence. D wants to remove to federal court, so it claims that the case is within federal question jurisdiction, because its disposition requires interpretation of a federal statute. *Held*, no federal question is raised, because P's claim did not "arise under" federal law. [*Merrell Dow Pharmaceuticals, Inc. v. Thompson*]) [104]

      b. **Claim based on the merits:**   If P's claim clearly "arises" under federal law, it qualifies for federal question jurisdiction *even if the claim is invalid on the merits*. Here, the federal court must dismiss for failure to state a claim upon which relief may be granted (FRCP 12(b)(6)), not for lack of subject matter jurisdiction. [105-06]

      c. **Anticipation of defense:**   The federal question must be *integral* to P's cause of action, as revealed by P's complaint. It does *not* suffice for federal question jurisdiction that P *anticipates a defense* based on a federal statute, or even that *D's answer* does in fact raise

C
A
P
S
U
L
E

S
U
M
M
A
R
Y

a federal question. Thus the federal question must be part of a "well pleaded complaint." [105]

Example: P claims that D Railroad has breached its agreement to give P free railroad passes. A recently-passed federal statute prohibits the giving of such passes. In P's complaint, he anticipates the railroad's federal statutory defense, claiming that the statute violates the Fifth Amendment.

Held, since P's claim was merely a breach of contract claim, and the federal statute was not essential to that claim, there was no federal question — the fact that federal law was an integral part of D's anticipated defense is irrelevant. [*Louisville & Nashville RR v. Mottley*]

IV. AMOUNT IN CONTROVERSY

A. **Diversity only:** In *diversity* cases, but *not* in federal question cases, plaintiff must satisfy an *"amount in controversy"* requirement. In all diversity cases, the amount in controversy must exceed *$50,000*. [106]

   1. **Interest not included:** The $50,000 figure does not include interest or court costs.

B. **Standard of proof:** The party seeking to invoke federal diversity jurisdiction does not have to *prove* that the amount in controversy exceeds $50,000. All she has to show is that there is *some possibility* that that much is in question. [106]

   1. **"Legal certainty" test:** To put it another way, the claim cannot be dismissed for failing to meet the $50,000 requirement unless it appears to a *legal certainty* that the claim is really for less than the jurisdictional amount. [*St. Paul Mercury Indemnity Co. v. Red Cab*]

   2. **Eventual recovery irrelevant:** The fact that P *eventually recovers* far *less* than the jurisdictional amount does *not* by itself render the verdict subject to reversal and dismissal on appeal for lack of jurisdiction.

      a. **Discretion to deny costs:** But the federal court has discretion to *deny costs* to P, and even to impose costs on him, if he recovers less than $50,000. 28 U.S.C. §1332(b).

C. **Whose point of view followed:** The courts are split as to *which party's* point of view is to be considered in calculating the amount at stake. Most courts hold that the controversy must be worth $50,000 to the *plaintiff* in order to satisfy the jurisdictional amount. [107]

D. **Aggregation of claims:** In multi-plaintiff or multi-claim litigation, you must understand the rules governing when *aggregation* of claims is permissible for meeting the jurisdictional amount: [108-110]

   1. **Aggregation by single plaintiff:** If a single plaintiff has a claim in excess of $50,000, he may add to it *any other claim of his against the same defendant*, even though these other claims are for less than the jurisdictional amount. This is done by the doctrine of supplemental jurisdiction. [108]

      a. **No claim exceeds $50,000:** Even if a plaintiff does *not* have any single claim worth more than $50,000, he may add together all of his claims against a single defendant. So long as these claims against a single defendant *total* more than $50,000, the amount in controversy requirement is satisfied.

   b. Additional defendants: But a plaintiff who has aggregated his claim against a particular defendant, usually may *not* join claims against *other* defendants for less than the jurisdictional amount.

       Example: P has two claims, each for $30,000, against D1. P will be deemed to meet the amount in controversy requirement as to these claims, because they aggregate more than $50,000. But if P tries to bring D2 into the lawsuit, and has a single claim worth $20,000 against D2, most courts will not allow this claim, because P's total claims against D2 do not exceed $50,000, and the doctrine of supplemental jurisdiction does not apply.

  2. Aggregation by multiple plaintiffs: [108-10]

    a. At least one plaintiff meets amount: If one plaintiff meets the jurisdictional amount, courts are *split* about whether the other plaintiffs may join their related claims against that same defendant. The plaintiffs may be able to use the doctrine of "supplemental jurisdiction" so as to enable the low-amount plaintiffs to join their claims together with the high-amount plaintiff.

    b. No single claim meets the amount: If no single plaintiff has a claim or claims meeting the jurisdictional amount, aggregation by multiple plaintiffs is *not allowed*. (*Exception:* Where two or more plaintiff unite to enforce a single title or right in which they have a common and undivided interest, aggregation is allowed.)

    c. Special restrictions for class actions: In *class actions*, there is an especially stringent, and clear, rule: *every member of the class must satisfy the jurisdictional amount*. This means that class actions in diversity cases will rarely be possible. [*Zahn v. International Paper Co.*] [109-10]

E. Counterclaims: [110]

  1. Suit initially brought in federal court: If P sues in federal court for less than the jurisdictional amount, and D *counterclaims* for an amount which (either by itself or added to P's claim) exceeds the jurisdictional amount, probably the amount in controversy requirement is *not* met.

  2. Removal by defendant: If P originally sues in state court for less than $50,000, and D tries to *remove* to federal court, amount in controversy problems work out as follows:

    a. Plaintiff removal: The *plaintiff* may never remove, even if D counterclaims against him for more than $50,000. (The removal statute simply does not apply to plaintiffs, apart from amount-in-controversy problems.)

    b. Defendant removal: If the *defendant* counterclaims for more than $50,000, but plaintiff's original claim was for less than $50,000, the result depends on the type of counterclaim. If D's counterclaim was permissive (under state law), all courts agree that D may *not* remove. If D's claim was compulsory under state law, courts are split about whether D may remove.

V. SUPPLEMENTAL JURISDICTION

A. "Supplemental" jurisdiction: Suppose new parties or new claims are sought to be added to a basic controversy that by itself satisfies federal subject-matter jurisdictional requirements. Under the doctrine of *"supplemental"* jurisdiction, the new parties and new claims may not have to independently satisfy subject-matter jurisdiction — they can in effect be "tacked on" to the "core" controversy. See 28 U.S.C. §1367. [112-25]

1. **Pendant and ancillary doctrines replaced:** Supplemental jurisdiction replaces two older judge-made doctrines, "pendent" jurisdiction and "ancillary" jurisdiction.

2. **Provision generally:** Section 1367(a) says that "in any civil action of which the district courts have original jurisdiction, the district courts *shall have supplemental jurisdiction* over all other claims that are *so related* to claims in the action within such original jurisdiction that they form part of the *same case or controversy* under Article III of the United States Constitution. Such supplemental jurisdiction shall include claims that involve the joinder or intervention of additional parties." [112]

3. **Federal question cases:** Where the original claim comes within the court's *federal question* jurisdiction, §1367 basically allows the court to hear any *closely related state-law claims*. [112]

   a. **Pendent state claims with no new parties:** Supplemental jurisdiction clearly applies when a related state claim involves the *same parties* as the federal question claim.

      Example: P and D are both citizens of New York. Both sell orange juice nationally. P sues D in federal court for violation of the federal trademark statute, arguing that D's brand name infringes a mark registered to P. P also asserts that D's conduct violates a New York State "unfair competition" statute. There is clearly no independent federal subject matter jurisdiction for P's state law unfair competition claim against D — there is no diversity, and there is no federal question. But by the doctrine of supplemental jurisdiction, since the federal claim satisfies subject-matter jurisdictional requirements, P can add the state law claim that is closely related to it.

   b. **Additional parties to state-law claim:** Section 1367 also allows *additional parties* to the state-law claim to be brought into the case. [113]

      Example: P's husband and children are killed when their small plane hits power lines near an airfield. P sues D1 (the U.S.) in federal court, under the Federal Tort Claims Act, for failing to provide adequate runway lights. Then, P amends her complaint to include state-law tort claims against D2 and D3 (a city and a private company) who maintain the power lines. There is no diversity of citizenship between P and D2 and D3, and no federal-question claim against them. But because P's state-law claim against D2 and D3 arises from the same chain of events as P's federal claim against D1, P may bring D2 and D3 into the suit under the supplemental jurisdiction concept, and the last sentence of §1367(a). [This overrules *Finley v. U.S.*] [113-14]

4. **Diversity cases:** There is also supplemental jurisdiction in many cases where the "core" claim — the claim as to which there is independent federal subject matter jurisdiction — is based solely on *diversity*. But there are some important *exclusions* to the parties' right to add additional claims and parties to a diversity claim.

   a. **Claims covered:** Here are the principal diversity-only situations in which supplemental jurisdiction *applies*: [120-21]

      i. Rule 13(a) *compulsory counterclaims*.

      ii. Rule 13(h) joinder of *additional parties to compulsory counterclaims*. (*Example:* P, from New York, brings a diversity suit against D, from New Jersey. The claim is for

C
A
P
S
U
L
E

S
U
M
M
A
R
Y

$60,000. D counterclaims that in the same episode, D was injured not only by P but also by Y; D's injuries total $1,000. Y is from New Jersey. D may bring Y in as a Rule 13(h) additional defendant to D's compulsory counterclaim against P, even though D and Y are both from New Jersey, and even though D's claim does not total $50,000 — supplemental jurisdiction applies, and obviates the need for D-Y diversity or for D to meet the amount in controversy requirement.)

iii. Rule 13(g) *cross-claims*, i.e., claims by one defendant against another. (*Example:* P, from Ohio, brings a diversity suit against D1 and D2, both from Kentucky. D1 brings a Rule 13(g) cross-claim against D2 — since it is a cross-claim, it necessarily relates to the same subject matter as P's claim. Even though there is no diversity as between D1 and D2, the cross-claim may be heard by the federal court.)

iv. Rule 14 *impleader* of third-party defendants, for claims *by and against third-party plaintiffs*, and claims *by third-party defendants*, but *not* claims by the *original plaintiff* against third-party defendants. (*Example:* P, from California, sues D, a retailer from Arizona, claiming that a product D sold P was defective and injured P. The suit is solely on diversity. D brings a Rule 14 impleader claim against X, the manufacturer of the item, claiming that if D owes P, X must indemnify D. X is a citizen of Arizona. Because D's suit against X falls within the court's supplemental jurisdiction, the lack of diversity as between D and X makes no difference. Supplemental jurisdiction would also cover any claim by X against P. But any claim by P against X would *not* be within the court's supplemental jurisdiction, so P and X must be diverse and the claim must meet the amount in controversy requirement.)

b. Claims not covered: Where the core claim is based on diversity, some important types of claims do *not* get the benefit of supplemental jurisdiction: [117-120]

i. Claims against third-party defendants: Claims made by a plaintiff against a *third-party defendant*, pursuant to Rule 14(a), are *excluded*. (*Example:* P sues D, and D brings a third-party claim against X, asserting that if D is liable to P, X is liable to D. P and X are citizens of the same state. P does not get supplemental jurisdiction for her claim against X, so the P-vs.-X claim must be dismissed. [*Owen Equipment v. Kroger*, codified in §1367(b).])

ii. Compulsory joinder: When a person is joined under Rule 19(a) as a person to be "joined if feasible" (*"compulsory joinder"*), neither a claim *against* such a person, nor a claim *by* that person, comes within the supplemental jurisdiction in a diversity-only case.

iii. Rule 20 joinder: When a plaintiff sues multiple defendants in the same action on common law and facts (Rule 20 *"permissive joinder"*), supplemental jurisdiction does not apply. (*Example:* P is hit by D1's car, then negligently ministered to by D2. P is from New York, D1 is from Connecticut, and D2 is from New Jersey. P's claim against D2 is for $20,000. The federal court cannot hear the P-D2 claim, because it does not meet the amount in controversy and does not fall within supplemental jurisdiction.)

iv. Intervention: Claims by prospective plaintiffs who try to *intervene* under Rule 24 do not get the benefit of supplemental jurisdiction. This is true whether the intervention is permissive or of right. (*Example:* P1 sues D in diversity. P2, on her own motion, moves for permission to intervene under Rule 24(b), because her claim against D has a question of law or fact in common with P1's claim. P1 is a citizen of Indiana, P2 of Illinois, and D of Illinois. Because there is no supplemental jurisdiction over intervention, the fact that P2 and D are citizens of the same state means that the court may not hear P2's claim. The same result would occur even if P2's claim was so closely related to the main action that P2 would otherwise be entitled to "intervention of right" under Rule 24(a).)

    c. **Defensive posture required:** If you look at the situations where supplemental jurisdiction is allowed in diversity-only cases, and those where it is not allowed, you will see that basically, additional claims asserted by *defendants* fall within the court's supplemental jurisdiction, but additional claims (or the addition of new parties) by *plaintiffs* are generally not included. So expect supplemental jurisdiction only in cases where the claimant who is trying to benefit from it is in a *"defensive posture."* [117]

5. **Discretion to reject exercise:** Merely because a claim is within the court's supplemental jurisdiction, this does not mean that the court *must* hear that claim. Section 1367(c) gives four reasons for which a court may *decline to exercise* supplemental jurisdiction that exists. Most importantly, the court may abstain if it has already *dismissed all claims* over which it has original jurisdiction. This discretion is especially likely to be used where the case is in its early stages. (*Example:* P sues D1 (the U.S.) under a federal statute, then adds state-law claims against D2 and D3, as to which there is neither diversity nor federal question jurisdiction. Soon after the pleadings are filed, the court dismisses P's claim against D1 under FRCP 12(b)(6). Probably the court will then exercise its discretion to decline to hear the supplemental claims against D2 and D3.) [121]

6. **No effect on personal jurisdiction:** The application of the supplemental jurisdiction doctrine does *not* eliminate the requirement of *jurisdiction over the parties*, nor does it eliminate the requirement of *service of process*. It speaks solely to the question of subject matter jurisdiction. (But often in the supplemental jurisdiction situation, service in the *100-mile bulge* area will be available.) [121-22]

    a. **Venue:** Where supplemental jurisdiction applies, probably *venue* requirements do not have to be satisfied with respect to the new party. But usually, venue will not be a problem anyway in these kinds of situations.

VI. REMOVAL TO THE FEDERAL COURTS

A. **Removal generally:** Generally, any action brought in *state court* that the plaintiff could have brought in federal court may be *removed* by the defendant to federal district court. [126]

    Example: P, from New Jersey, sues D, from New York, in New Jersey state court. The suit is a garden-variety automobile negligence case. The amount at issue is $100,000. D may remove the case to federal district court for the District of New Jersey.

1. **Diversity limitation:** The most important single thing to remember about removal jurisdiction is this: In *diversity* cases, the action may be removed only if *no defendant is a citizen of the state in which the action is pending*.

Example: P, from New Jersey, brings a negligence action against D, from New York, in the New York state court system. D may not remove the case to federal court for New York, because he is a citizen of the state (New York) in which the action is pending. (But if P's suit was for trademark infringement — a kind of suit that raises a federal question but may be brought in either state or federal court — D would be able to remove, because the "not a citizen of the state where the action is pending" requirement does not apply in suits raising a federal question.)

2. **Where suit goes:** When a case is removed, it passes to the federal district court for the district and division embracing the place where the state cause of action is pending. (*Example:* If a suit is brought in the branch of the California state court system located in Sacramento, removal would be to the federal district court in the Eastern District of California encompassing Sacramento.) [126]

B. **Diversity and amount in controversy rules applicable:** In removal cases, the usual rules governing existence of a federal question or of diversity, and those governing the jurisdictional amount, apply. (*Example:* If there is no federal question, diversity must be "complete.") [126]

C. **No plaintiff removal:** Only a *defendant* may remove. A plaintiff defending a counterclaim may not remove. (*Example:* P brings a suit for product liability against D. D counterclaims for libel in an amount of $100,000. P is from Ohio; D is from Indiana. The suit is pending in Michigan state court. Even though P is not a resident of the state where the action is pending, P may not remove, because the right of removal is limited to defendants.) [127]

D. **Look only at plaintiff's complaint:** The right of removal is generally decided from the face of the pleadings. The jurisdictional allegations of plaintiff's complaint control. [127]

    Example: P is badly injured in an automobile accident caused by D's negligence. P's medical bills total $60,000, but P sues only for $40,000, for the express purpose of thwarting D's right to remove. The jurisdictional allegations of P's complaint control, so that D may not remove even though more than $50,000 is "really" at stake.

E. **Removal of multiple claims:** Where P asserts against D in state court two claims, one of which could be removed if sued upon alone, and the other of which could not, complications arise. [128-30]

1. **Diversity:** If the claim for which there is federal jurisdiction is a *diversity* claim, the presence of the second claim (for which there is no original federal jurisdiction) *defeats* the defendant's right of removal entirely — the whole case must stay in state court. [128-29]

2. **Federal question case:** Where the claim for which there is original federal jurisdiction is a *federal question* claim, and there is another, "separate and independent," claim for which there is no original federal jurisdiction, D may remove the whole case. 28 U.S.C. §1441(c). [129]

    Example: P and D1 are both citizens of Kentucky. P brings an action in Kentucky state court alleging federal antitrust violations by D1. P adds to that claim a claim against D1 and D2, also from Kentucky, asserting that the two Ds have violated Kentucky state unfair competition laws. Section 1441(c) will allow D1 and D2 to remove to federal court, if the antitrust claim is "separate and independent" from the state unfair competition claim.

C
A
P
S
U
L
E

S
U
M
M
A
R
Y

a. Remand: If §1441(c) applies, and the entire case is removed to federal court, the federal judge need not hear the entire matter. The court may instead remand all matters in which state law predominates.

i. Remand even the federal claim: In fact, the federal court, after determining that removal is proper, may remand *all claims* — even the properly-removed federal claim — if state law predominates in the whole controversy.

F. Compulsory remand: If the federal judge concludes that the removal did not satisfy the statutory requirements, she *must remand* the case to the state court from which it came. (*Example:* If in a diversity case it turns out that one or more of the Ds was a citizen of the state in which the state suit was commenced, the federal judge must send the case back to the state court where it began.) [130]

G. Mechanics of removal: [131]

1. Time: D must usually file for removal within *30 days* of the time he receives service of the state-court complaint.

2. All defendants joined: *All defendants* (except purely nominal ones) must *join* in the notice of removal. (However, if removal occurs under §1441(c)'s "separate and independent federal claim" provision, then only the defendant(s) to the separate and independent federal claim needs to sign the notice of removal.)

CHAPTER 4
PLEADINGS

I. FEDERAL PLEADING GENERALLY

A. Approach generally: [136-45]

1. Two types: In most instances, there are only two types of pleadings in a federal action. These are the *complaint* and the *answer*. The complaint is the document by which the plaintiff begins the case. The answer is the defendant's response to the complaint. [139]

a. Reply: In two circumstances, there will be a third document, called the *reply*. The reply is, in effect, an "answer to the answer." A reply is allowable: (1) if the answer contains a *counterclaim* (in which case a reply is *required*); and (2) at plaintiff's option, if plaintiff obtains a court order allowing the reply.

2. No verification generally: Pleadings in a federal action normally need not be *"verified,"* i.e., sworn to by the litigant. However, there are a couple of exceptions, two of which are: (1) the complaint in a stockholders' derivative action (see FRCP 23.1); and (2) the complaint is seeking a *temporary restraining order* (FRCP 65(b)). [140]

3. Attorney must sign: The pleader's *lawyer* must *sign* the pleadings. This is true for both the complaint and the answer. By signing, the lawyer indicates that to the best of her belief, formed after reasonable inquiry, the pleading is not interposed for any *improper purpose* (e.g., harassing or causing unnecessary delays), the claims and defenses are warranted by existing law or a nonfrivolous argument for changing existing law, and (in general) the allegations or denials have evidentiary support. FRCP 11. [141]

  a. Sanctions: If Rule 11 is violated (e.g., the complaint, as the lawyer knows, is not well grounded in fact, or supported by any plausible legal argument), the court must impose an ***appropriate sanction*** on either the signing lawyer, the client, or both. The most common sanction is the award of ***attorneys' fees*** to the other side.

  b. Safe harbor: A party against whom a Rule 11 motion is made has a 21-day *"safe harbor"'* period in which she can withdraw or modify the challenged pleading and thereby avoid any sanction.

4. Pleading in the alternative: The pleader, whether plaintiff or defendant, may plead *"in the alternative."* "A party may set forth two or more statements of a claim or defense alternately or hypothetically." FRCP 8(e). (*Example:* In count 1, P claims that work done for D was done under a valid written contract. In count 2, P claims that if the contract was not valid, P rendered value to D and can recover in *quantum meruit* for the value. Such alternative pleading is allowed by Rule 8(e).) [145]

II. THE COMPLAINT

A. Complaint generally: The complaint is the initial pleading in a lawsuit, and is filed by the plaintiff. [145]

1. Commences action: The filing of the complaint is deemed to "commence" the action. The date of filing of the complaint is what counts for statute of limitation purposes in federal question suits (though in diversity suits, "commencement" for statute-of-limitations purposes depends on how state law defines commencement.)

2. Elements of complaint: There are three essential elements that a complaint must have (FRCP 8(a)): [146]

  a. Jurisdiction: A short and plain statement of the grounds upon which the court's ***jurisdiction*** depends;

  b. Statement of the claim: A short and plain ***statement of the claim*** showing that the pleader is entitled to relief; and

  c. Relief: A demand for judgment for the ***relief*** (e.g., money damages, injunction, etc.) which the pleader seeks.

B. Specificity: Plaintiff must make a ***"short and plain statement"*** of the claim showing that she is entitled to relief. The level of factual detail required is not high — gaps in the facts are usually remedied through discovery. Plaintiff needs to state only the facts, not the legal theory she is relying upon. [146]

C. Special matters: Certain *"special matters"* must be pleaded with ***particularity*** if they are to be raised at trial. [148-49]

1. Catalog: The special matters (listed in FRCP 9) include: (1) denial of a party's legal ***capacity to sue*** or be sued; (2) the circumstances giving rise to any allegation of ***fraud*** or ***mistake***; (3) any denial of performance or occurrence of a ***condition precedent***; (4) the existence of ***judgments*** or ***official documents*** on which the pleader plans to rely; (5) material facts of ***time and place***; (6) ***special damages***; and (7) certain aspects of admiralty and maritime jurisdiction. [148]

    a. Note: The above matters requiring special pleading apply to the ***answer*** as well as to the complaint.

  2. Effect of failure to plead: The pleader takes the full risk of failure to plead any special matter. (*Example:* P brings a diversity claim for breach of contract against D. P has suffered certain unusual consequential damages, but fails to plead these special damages as required by FRCP 9(g). Even if P proves these items at trial, P may not recover these damages, unless the court agrees to specially permit this "variance" between proof and pleadings.) [148]

III. MOTIONS AGAINST THE COMPLAINT

A. Defenses against validity of complaint: Either in the ***answer***, or by separate ***motion***, defendant may attack the validity of the complaint in a number of respects. Rule 12(b) lists the following such defenses: [149]

  1. Lack of ***jurisdiction over the subject matter;***

  2. Lack of ***jurisdiction over the person***;

  3. Improper ***venue***;

  4. Insufficiency of ***process***;

  5. Insufficiency of ***service of process***;

  6. Failure to ***state a claim upon which relief may be granted***; and

  7. Failure to ***join a necessary party*** under Rule 19.

B. 12(b)(6) motion to dismiss for failure to state a claim: Defense (6) above is especially important: if D believes that P's complaint does not state a legally sufficient claim, he can make a Rule 12(b)(6) motion for to dismiss for ***"failure to state a claim upon which relief can be granted."*** The motion asserts that on the facts as pleaded by P, no recovery is possible under ***any legal theory***. (*Example:* If P's complaint is barred by the statute of limitations, D should move under 12(b)(6) for failure to state a valid claim.) [150-52]

  1. Different motion once D files answer: A Rule 12(b)(6) motion to dismiss is generally made ***before*** D files his answer. After D has filed an answer, and the pleadings are complete, D can accomplish the same result by making a Rule 12(c) motion for "judgment on the pleadings." [152]

C. Amendment: If the complaint is dismissed in response to D's dismissal motion, P will almost always have the opportunity to ***amend*** the complaint. [151]

  1. Amendment as of right: If D makes a motion against the complaint before filing his answer, and the court grants the dismissal, P may ***automatically*** amend — Rule 15(a) allows amendment without leave of court any time before a responsive pleading is served, and motions made under 12(b) are not deemed to be responsive pleadings.

  2. Amendment by leave of court: If D serves his answer before making the Rule 12(b) motion, and is then successful with the motion, P may amend only by getting ***leave of court*** (i.e., permission). But the court will almost always grant this permission following a 12(b) dismissal.

D. Motion for more definite statement: If the complaint is so "vague or ambiguous that [the defendant] cannot reasonably be required to frame a responsive pleading," D may move for a *more definite statement* under Rule 12(e). [152]

E. Motion to strike: If P has included "redundant, immaterial, impertinent or scandalous" material in the complaint, D may move to have this material *stricken* from the pleading. Rule 12(f). [153]

IV. THE ANSWER

A. The answer generally: The defendant's response to the plaintiff's complaint is called an *"answer."* In the answer, D states in short and plain terms his *defenses* to each claim asserted, and admits or denies each count of plaintiff's complaint. Rule 8(b). [156]

   1. Alternative pleading: Defenses, like claims, may be pleaded in the *alternative*. (*Example:* In a breach of contract suit brought by P, D can in count 1 of his answer state that no contract ever existed, and in count 2 state that if such a contract did exist, it was breached by P, not D.)

B. Signed by defendant's attorney: The answer must be *signed* by the defendant's lawyer. As with the complaint, the attorney's signature constitutes a certificate that the signer has read the pleading, believes it is well founded, and that it is not interposed for delay. Rule 11. [157]

C. Denials: The defendant may make various kinds of *denials* of the truth of plaintiff's allegations. [156-57]

   1. Where not denied: Averments in a complaint, other than those concerning the amount of damages, are "admitted when not denied…in [an answer]." Rule 8(d).

   2. Kinds of denials: There are five kinds of denials in federal practice:

      a. General denial: D may make a *"general"* denial, by which he denies each and every allegation in P's complaint. (But D must then contest all of P's allegations, or face sanctions.)

      b. Specific denial: D may make a *"specific"* denial, which denies all of the allegations of a particular paragraph or count of the complaint.

      c. Qualified denial: D may make a *"qualified"* denial, i.e., a denial of a particular *portion* of a particular allegation.

      d. Denial of knowledge or information (DKI): D may make a denial of *knowledge or information* (DKI), by which he says that he does not have enough knowledge or information sufficient to form a belief as to the truth of P's complaint (but D must do this in good faith).

      e. Denial based on information and belief: D may deny *"based on information and belief."* By this, D effectively says, "I don't know for sure, but I reasonably believe that P's allegation is false." This kind of denial is often used by large corporate defendants.

D. Affirmative defenses: There are certain defenses which must be *explicitly pleaded* in the answer, if D is to raise them at trial. These are so-called *"affirmative defenses."* [157-58]

   1. Listing: Rule 8(c) lists 19 specific affirmative defenses, of which the most important are *contributory negligence*, *fraud*, *res judicata*, *statute of limitations*, and *illegality*.

   2. General formulation: Also, Rule 8(c) contains a more general requirement, by which D must plead affirmatively "any other matter constituting an avoidance or affirmative defense."

C
A
P
S
U
L
E

S
U
M
M
A
R
Y

Any defense which relies on facts *particularly within the defendant's knowledge* is likely to be found to be an affirmative defense.

E. **Counterclaim:** In addition to defenses, if D has a claim against P, he may (in all cases) and must (in some cases) plead that claim as a *counterclaim*. If the counterclaim is one which D is *required* to plead, it is called a *compulsory* counterclaim. If it is one which D has the option of pleading or not, it is called a *permissive* counterclaim. A counterclaim is compulsory if it "arises out of the transaction or occurrence that is the subject matter of the [plaintiff's] claim...." Rule 13(a). [158]

V. TIME FOR VARIOUS PLEADINGS

A. **Time table:** Here is the time table for various pleading steps (see Rule 12(a)): [158-57]

1. **Complaint:** Filing of the complaint usually occurs before it is served. Service must then normally occur within 120 days. Rule 4(m).

2. **Answer:** The *answer* must be served within *20 days* after service of the complaint, except that

a. **Different state rule:** If P has served D *out of state*, by using the state long-arm (see Rule 4(k)(1)(A)), the time to answer allowed under that state rule (typically longer) controls.

b. **Rule 12 motion:** If D makes a Rule 12 motion against the complaint and loses, D has 10 days after the court denies the motion to answer.

c. **Waiver of formal service:** If D *waives* formal service pursuant to Rule 4(d), then he gets *60 days* to answer running from the date the request for waiver was sent by P. Rule 12(a)(1)(B).

3. **Reply to counterclaim:** If the answer contains a *counterclaim*, P must serve his *reply* within *20 days* after service of the answer.

VI. AMENDMENT OF THE PLEADINGS

A. **Liberal policy:** The Federal Rules are extremely *liberal* in allowing amendment of the pleadings. [159]

B. **Amendment as of right:** A pleading may be amended *once as a matter of right* (i.e., without leave of court) as follows: [159]

1. **Complaint:** The complaint may be amended once *at any time before the answer is served*. (A motion is not the equivalent of an answer, so the fact that D has made a motion against the complaint does not stop P from amending once as a matter of right.)

2. **Answer:** The *answer* may be amended once within *20 days* after D has served it. (If the answer contains a counterclaim, the answer may be amended up until the time P has served her reply.)

C. **Amendment by leave of court:** If the above requirements for amendment of right are not met, the pleading may be amended only by *leave of court*, or by *consent of the other side*. But leave by the court to amend "shall be freely given when justice so requires." (Rule 15(a).) Normally, the court will deny leave to amend only if amendment would cause *actual prejudice* to the other party. [159-60]

D. Relation back: When a pleading has been amended, the amendment will *relate back* to the date of the original pleading, if the claim or defenses asserted in the amended pleading "arose out of the conduct, transaction or occurrence set forth or attempted to be set forth in the original pleading." Rule 15(c). This "relation back" doctrine is mainly useful in meeting statutes of limitations that have run between filing of the original complaint and the amendment. [160-62]

> **Example:** On Jan. 1, P files a complaint against D for negligently manufacturing a product that has injured P. The case is brought in diversity in Ohio federal district court. On Feb. 1, the Ohio statute of limitations (which controls in a diversity case) on both negligence and product liability claims arising out of this episode runs. On March 1, P amends to add a count alleging strict products liability. Because the products liability claim arises out of the same conduct or transaction as set forth in the original negligence complaint, the amendment will relate back to Jan. 1, and P will be deemed to have met the statute of limitations for his products liability claim.

1. When action is deemed "commenced": According to Rule 3, an action is deemed "commenced" as of the *date on which the complaint is filed*. In federal question cases, it is to this date that the amendment relates back. In diversity cases, by contrast, it is the date that state law regards as the date of commencement which controls. [160]

> **Example:** In a diversity case, assume that state law regards the date on which the complaint is served, not the filing date, as being the commencement. In a diversity action in that state, any relation back will be to the date the complaint was served, not to the filing date.

2. Change of party: Where an amendment to a pleading *changes the party* against whom the claim is asserted, the amendment "relates back" only if three requirements are met: (1) the amendment covers the *"same transaction or occurrence"* as the original pleading (the same rules discussed above); (2) the party to be brought in by amendment received *actual notice* of the action before the end of the *120 days following original service*; and (3) before the end of that 120-day service period, the new party knew or should have known that "but for a mistake concerning the identity of the proper party, the action *would have been brought against the [new] party*." Rule 15(c)(3). [161-62]

> **Example:** P's complaint names D1, and is filed just prior to the expiration of the statute of limitations. Ten days after the running of the statute, P discovers that the complaint really should have named D2. P amends the complaint to name D2, and serves D2 60 days after the filing of the original complaint. The amendment as to D2 relates back to the original, timely filing, because within 120 days of the original filing, D2 received notice of the action and learned that but for P's mistake about the proper party, the action would have been brought against D2 rather than D1.

VII. VARIANCE OF PROOF FROM PLEADINGS

A. Federal practice: The Federal Rules allow substantial *deviation* of the proof at trial from the pleadings, so long as the variance does not seriously prejudice the other side. Rule 15(b). Unless omission of the issue from the pleading was intentional, and was designed to lead the objecting party into wasted preparation, the court will almost certainly allow amendment at trial. [162-63]

> **Example:** P brings a diversity action for breach of contract against D. P's complaint does not allege any special damages. At trial, P shows that P lost considerable business and

profits. D objects that special damages were not pleaded. Since D probably cannot show the court that D has wasted preparation, the court will almost certainly allow P to amend his pleadings to allege the special damages. If necessary, the court will give D extra time to develop evidence to rebut P's newly-claimed special damages.

CHAPTER 5

DISCOVERY AND PRETRIAL CONFERENCE

I. GENERAL PRINCIPLES

A. Forms of discovery: Discovery under the Federal Rules includes six main types: [169]

1. *Automatic disclosure;*

2. *Depositions*, taken from both written and oral questions;

3. *Interrogatories* addressed to a party;

4. Requests to *inspect documents* or property;

5. Requests for *admission* of facts;

6. Requests for physical or mental *examination*.

II. SCOPE OF DISCOVERY

A. Scope generally: Rule 26(b), which applies to all forms of discovery, provides that the parties "may obtain discovery regarding *any matter, not privileged, which is relevant to the subject matter involved in the pending action*." So the two principal requirements for discoverability of material are that it is: (1) *not privileged*; and (2) *relevant* to the subject matter of the suit. [170]

B. Relevant but inadmissible: To be discoverable, it is *not required* that the information necessarily be *admissible*. For example, inadmissible material may be relevant, and thus discoverable, if it: (1) is likely to serve as a *lead* to admissible evidence; or (2) relates to the identity and whereabouts of any *witness* who is thought to have discoverable information. [171]

C. Privilege: Only material which is *not privileged* may be discovered. [172]

1. **Who may assert:** Only the *person who could assert the privilege at trial* may resist discovery on the grounds of privilege. (*Example:* P sues D1 and D2 for conversion. At P's deposition of D1, P asks D1 questions relating to the facts. D1 knows the answer and is willing to respond, but D2's lawyer objects on the grounds that the questions may violate D1's privilege against self-incrimination. D2's objection is without substance, because only D1 — the person who could assert the privilege at trial — may assert the privilege during discovery proceedings.)

2. **Determining existence of privilege:** Generally, in *diversity cases, state law of privilege applies*. See Federal Rule of Evidence 501. (*Example:* P brings a diversity action against D, asserting that D intentionally inflicted emotional distress on him. D seeks to depose P's psychotherapist, to determine the extent of P's anguish. The suit is brought in Ohio Federal District Court. The privilege laws of the state of Ohio, not general federal principles, are looked to to determine whether patient-psychotherapist confidences are privileged.)

C
A
P
S
U
L
E

S
U
M
M
A
R
Y

D. Trial preparation immunity: Certain immunity from discovery is given to the *materials prepared by counsel for trial purposes*, and to the *opinions of experts* that counsel has consulted in trial preparation. This immunity is often referred to as *"work-product"* immunity. [172-78]

    1. Qualified immunity: *"Qualified"* immunity is given to documents prepared *"in anticipation of litigation"* or for trial, by a party or that party's *representative*. [174-75]

        a. "Representative" defined: A party's "representatives" include his *attorney*, consultant, insurance company, and anybody working for any of these people (e.g., a private investigator hired by the attorney).

        b. Hardship: The privilege is "qualified" rather than "absolute." This means that the other side might be able to get discovery of the materials, but only by showing *"substantial need of the materials in preparation of [the] case"* and an inability to obtain the equivalent materials "without *undue hardship*." Rule 26(b)(3).

        Example: A car driven by D runs over P. D's insurance company interviews X, a non-party witness to the accident. The insurer then prepares a transcript of the statement. This transcript was prepared "in anticipation of litigation," so it is protected by the qualified work-product immunity. Therefore, P will be able to obtain discovery of it only if he can show substantial need, and the inability without undue hardship to obtain the substantial equivalent by other means. Since P could conduct his own interview of the witness, the court will probably find that the qualified immunity is not overcome.

    2. Absolute immunity: In addition to the qualified work-product immunity discussed above, there is also *"absolute"* immunity. Rule 26(b)(3) provides that even where a party has substantial need for materials (in other words, the showing for qualified immunity has been made), the court "shall protect against disclosure of the *mental impressions*, *conclusions*, *opinions*, or *legal theories* of an attorney or other representative of a party concerning the litigation." [175-77]

        Example: Same facts as above example. Now, D's lawyer reads X's statement, and writes a memo to the file stating "X appears to be lying for the following three reasons...." This lawyer memo, since it reflects the mental impressions and conclusions of an attorney or other representative of a party, will receive absolute immunity, and no showing by P will entitle him to get the memo.

E. Statements by witnesses: A person who makes a *statement* to a party or the party's lawyer may obtain a *copy* of that statement without any special showing. Rule 26(b)(3). This is true whether the person making the statement is a party or a non-party. [178]

    Example: In an accident suit, D's insurance company takes P's statement about the accident, and transcribes it. D must give P a copy of P's statement, without any special showing of need by P.

F. Names of witnesses: The *"identity and location of persons having knowledge of any discoverable matter"* (so-called "occurrence witnesses") are discoverable. Rule 26(b)(1). This means, for instance, that each party must disclose to the other the identity and whereabouts of any *eyewitness* to the events of the lawsuit. (*Example:* In an accident case, D's lawyer and investigator locate all eight people who saw the accident. D must furnish this list to P.) [178]

1. **Disclosure is automatic:** The 1993 amendments to Rule 26 make disclosure of the name and address of any occurrence witness *automatically* disclosable (even without a specific request from the adversary), early on in the litigation. See Rule 26(a)(1)(A).

G. **Discovery concerning experts:** [179-81]

1. **Experts to be called at trial:** Where one side expects to call an expert *at trial*, the other side gets extensive discovery:

   a. **Identity:** First, a party must automatically (without a request) give the other side a list *identifying* each expert who will be called at trial.

   b. **Report:** Second, the party who intends to call an expert at trial must have the expert prepare and sign a *report* containing, among other things: (i) the expert's *opinions*, and the basis for them; (ii) the *data* considered by the expert; (iii) any *exhibits* to be used by the expert at trial; (iv) the expert's *qualifications*; (v) her *compensation*, and (vi) the names of all *other cases* in which she testified as an expert in the preceding 4 years.

   c. **Deposition:** The expert who will be called at trial must also be made available for *deposition* by the other side.

   See Rule 26(a)(2)(A); 26(a)(2)(B); 26(b)(4)(C).

2. **Experts retained by counsel, but not to be called at trial:** Where an expert has been retained by a party, but will *not* be called at trial, discovery concerning that expert (her identity, knowledge and opinions) may be discovered only upon a showing of *exceptional circumstances* making it impractical for the party seeking discovery to obtain the information by other means. Rule 26(b)(4)(B). [180]

3. **Unretained experts not to be called at trial:** Where an expert is *consulted* by a party, but *not retained*, and not to be called at trial, there is virtually no way the other side can discover the identity or opinions of that expert. [180]

4. **Participant experts:** A *participant* expert — one who actually took part in the transactions or occurrences that are part of the subject matter of the lawsuit — is treated like an *ordinary witness*. (*Example:* P's estate sues to compel D, an insurance company, to pay off on a policy covering P's life. D claims that it was a suicide, based on the results of an autopsy conducted by X, a pathologist. P may depose X, even though X is an expert — because X participated in the events, he is treated like an ordinary witness for purposes of discovery.) [181]

   a. **Expert is a party:** Similarly, a *party* who is herself an expert (e.g., a doctor who is a defendant in a malpractice suit) is treated like an ordinary witness for discovery purposes, not like an expert.

H. **Insurance:** A party may obtain discovery of the existence and contents of any *insurance agreement* under which any insurer will be liable to satisfy any judgment that may result. (*Example:* P brings an automobile negligence suit against D in diversity. P may ask D, in an interrogatory, whether D has insurance, and in what amount by what insurer. P may do this without any special showing of need.) [182]

I. **Mandatory disclosure:** Certain types of disclosure are now (since 1993) *automatic* and *mandatory*. [182-87]

1. **Automatic pre-discovery disclosure:** Under Rule 26(a)(1), a party must, even without a request from the other side, automatically disclose, early in the litigation, certain things. The most important are:

    a. All witnesses with discoverable information: First, each party must disclose the name, address and phone number of *each individual* likely to have *discoverable information* relevant to any *disputed fact* alleged with *particularity* in the pleadings. So any occurrence witness, and any other type of witness who may know something relevant to a disputed factual issue, must be identified.

    b. Documents: Second, a party must furnish a *copy*, or else a *description* by category and location, of all *documents* and *tangible* things in that party's possession, relevant to any disputed fact alleged with particularity.

    Note: A judicial district or an individual judge may *"opt out"* of these mandatory-disclosure rules. Many judicial districts have done so.

  2. Other: Later in the litigation, each party must automatically disclose to the other the details of expert testimony (as discussed above) and witnesses and exhibits to be used at trial.

J. Privilege log: If a party is declining to furnish documents or information because of a claim of *privilege* or *work product* immunity, the party must make the claim *expressly*, and must describe the nature of the documents or communications. (Thus the party can't keep silent about the fact that such a claim is being made or about the nature of the documents/communications as to which it is being made). Rule 26(b)(5). [188]

K. Duty to supplement: A party who makes a disclosure during discovery now normally has a duty to *supplement* that response if the party then learns that the disclosed information is incomplete or incorrect. [187]

  1. How it applies: This "duty to supplement" applies to any *automatic pre-discovery disclosure* (mainly witness names and documents); to any disclosure regarding *experts* to be called at trial; and to any responses to an *interrogatory*, a request for production, or request for admission. Rule 26(e)(1); 26(e)(2).

    Example: P is suing D regarding a car accident in which P was injured. Early in the litigation, P gives D a list of all witnesses to the accident that P knows of, as required by Rule 26(a)(1)(A). If P later learns of another person who saw the accident, P must "supplement" her earlier disclosure by telling D about the new witness.

III. METHODS OF DISCOVERY

A. Characteristics: The various forms of discovery (depositions, interrogatories, requests to produce, requests for admission and requests for examination) have several common characteristics: [191]

  1. Extrajudicial: Each of these methods (except requests for physical examination) operates *without intervention of the court*. Only where one party refuses to comply with the other's discovery request will the court intervene.

  2. Scope: The scope of discovery is the same for all of these forms: the material sought must be relevant to the subject matter for the suit, and unprivileged.

  3. Signature required: Every request for discovery of each of these types, and any response or objection to discovery, must be *signed* by the lawyer preparing it. Rule 26(g).

4. **Only parties:** Each of these types — except for depositions — may only be addressed to a *party*. Depositions (whether upon oral or written questions) may be addressed to either a party or to a non-party who possesses relevant information.

B. **Oral depositions:** After the beginning of an action, any party may take the *oral testimony* of any person thought to have information within the scope of discovery. This is known as an *oral deposition*. Rule 30. [192-94]

1. **Usable against non-party:** Not only parties, but any non-party with relevant information, may be deposed.

2. **Subpoena:** If a non-party is to be deposed, then the discovering party can only force the deponent to attend by issuing a *subpoena*. This subpoena must require the deposition to be held no more than *100 miles* from the place where the deponent resides, is employed, or regularly transacts business in person. Rule 45(c)(3)(A)(ii).

   a. **No subpoena for party:** If a *party* is to be deposed, a subpoena is not used. Instead, non-compliance with the notice can be followed up by a motion to compel discovery or to impose sanctions under Rule 37.

3. **Request to produce:** The person seeking discovery will often also want documents held by the deponent. If the deponent is a party, the discovering party may attach a Rule 34 *request to produce* to the notice to the party. But if the deponent is a non-party, the discovering party must use a subpoena *duces tecum*. [193]

4. **Limits to ten:** Each side is limited to a total of *ten depositions*, unless the adversary agrees to more or the court issues an order allowing more. Rule 30(a)(2)(A).

5. **Method of recording:** The party ordering the deposition can arrange to have it recorded by stenography (court reporter), by *audio tape recorder*, or by *video recorder*. Rule 30(b)(2).

C. **Depositions upon written questions:** Any party may take the oral responses to *written questions*, from *any person* (party or non-party) thought to have discoverable information. Rule 31. This is called a "deposition on written questions." [194-95]

1. **Distant non-party witnesses:** Depositions on written questions are mainly used for deposing *distant non-party witnesses*. Such witnesses cannot be served with interrogatories (since these are limited to parties), and cannot be compelled to travel more than 100 miles from their home or business.

D. **Interrogatories to the parties:** An *interrogatory* is a set of *written questions* to be *answered in writing* by the person to whom they are addressed. Interrogatories may be addressed *only to a party*. Rule 33(a). [195]

1. **Limit of 25 questions:** Each party is limited to *25 interrogatory questions* directed to any other party, unless the parties stipulate otherwise or the court orders otherwise. Rule 33(a).

E. **Requests for admission:** One party may serve upon another party a written request for the *admission, for the purposes of the pending action only, of the truth of any discoverable matters*. Rule 36. This is a *"request for admission."* [196-97]

1. **Coverage:** The statements whose genuineness may be requested include statements or opinions of fact, the application of law to fact, and the genuineness of any documents. (*Example:* P, in a breach of contract action, may request that D admit that the attached document is a contract signed by both P and D.) [196]

2. **Expenses for failure to admit:** If a party fails to admit the truth of any matter requested for admission under Rule 36(a), and the party making the request *proves* the truth of the matter at trial, the court may then require the party who refused to admit to pay *reasonable expenses* sustained by the movant in proving the matter. Rule 37(c). (But no expenses may be charged in several situations, including where the party who failed to admit had reasonable grounds to think he might prevail on the issue at trial.) [197]

3. **Effect at trial:** If a party makes an admission under Rule 36, the matter is normally *conclusively established at trial*. (However, the court may grant a motion to withdraw or amend the admission, if this would help the action to be presented on its merits, and would not prejudice the other side.) [197]

F. **Request to produce documents or to inspect land:** A party may require any other party to *produce documents and things*. Rule 34. Thus any papers, photos or objects relevant to the subject matter of the case may be obtained from any other party, but not from a non-party. (*Example:* P sues D1 and D2 for antitrust and price fixing. P believes that the records of both Ds will show that they set prices in concert. P may require D1 and D2 to produce any documents in their control relating to the setting of prices.) [197-98]

1. **Only to parties:** A request to produce can only be addressed to *parties*. If documents in the possession of a non-party are desired, a subpoena *duces tecum* must be used.

2. **Party's control:** A party may be required to produce only those documents or other objects which are in her *"possession, custody or control."* Rule 34(a). [197]

3. **Land:** Rule 34 also allows a party to demand the right to inspect, photograph and survey any *land* within the control of another party. (*Example:* P sues D, a merchant, for negligence, because P fell on D's slippery floor. P may require D to open the premises so that P may inspect and photograph them.)

G. **Physical and mental examination:** When the mental or physical condition of a *party* is *in controversy*, the court may order the party to submit to a *physical or mental examination* by a suitably licensed or certified examiner. Rule 35. [198]

1. **Motion and good cause:** Unlike all other forms of discovery, Rule 35 operates only by *court order*. The discovering party must make a *motion* upon notice to the party to be examined, and must show *good cause* why the examination is needed. [198]

2. **Controversy:** The physical or mental condition of the party must be *in controversy*. In other words, it is not enough (as it is for other forms of discovery) that the condition would be somehow relevant. (*Example:* If P is suing D for medical malpractice arising out of an operation, P's condition would obviously be in controversy, and D would be entitled to have a physician conduct a physical examination of P. But if P were suing D for breach of contract, and D had some suspicion that P was fabricating the whole incident, a mental examination of P to find evidence of delusional behavior would probably not be found to be supported by good cause, so the court order granting the exam would probably not be made.) [198]

3. **Reports from examiner:** The *actual medical report* produced through a Rule 35 examination is discoverable (in contrast to the usual non-discoverability of experts' reports).

   a. **Who may receive:** A *person examined* (typically the opposing party) may request, from the party causing the exam to be made, a copy of the examiner's written report.

b. Other examinations: Once the examined party asks for and receives this report, then the other party is entitled to reports of any ***other*** examinations made at the request of the examinee for the same condition. (*Example:* P sues D for automobile negligence. D causes P to be examined by a doctor retained by D, to measure the extent of P's injuries. P asks for a copy of the report, and D complies. Now, D is entitled to receive from P copies of any other reports of examinations made of P at P's request. In other words, by asking D for the report, P is deemed to have waived the physician-patient privilege as to exams conducted at P's request.) [199]

IV. ORDERS AND SANCTIONS

A. Two types: Discovery normally proceeds without court intervention. But the court where the action is pending may intercede in two main ways, by issuing orders and by awarding sanctions. The court may order abuse of discovery stopped (a protective order) or may order a recalcitrant party to furnish discovery (order compelling discovery). Sanctions can be awarded for failing to handle discovery properly.

B. Abuse of discovery: One party sometimes tries to use discovery to harass her adversary. (*Example:* P requests that D reveal trade secrets, or schedules 10 repetitive depositions of D.) The discoveree may fight back in two ways: (1) by simply ***objecting*** to a particular request; or (2) by seeking a Rule 26 ***protective order***. [201-03]

1. Objection: A party may ***object*** to a discovery request the same way a question at trial may be objected to. Typical grounds are that the matter sought is not within the scope of discovery (i.e., not ***relevant*** to the subject matter) or that it is privileged. [201]

a. Form of objection: The form depends on the type of discovery. An objection to an ***interrogatory*** question is written down as part of the set of answers. Similarly, an objection to a request to admit is made in writing. An objection to a ***deposition*** question, by contrast, is raised as an oral objection by the lawyer representing the deponent or the party opposing the deposition. The deposition then continues, and the objections are later dealt with en masse by the judge.

2. Protective order: Where more than a few questions are at stake, the party opposing discovery may seek a *"**protective order**."* Rule 26(c) allows the judge to make "any order which justice requires to protect a party or person from ***annoyance***, ***embarrassment***, ***oppression***, or undue ***burden*** or expense...." [201-03]

Example 1: In a simple automobile negligence case brought under diversity, D schedules P for ten different depositions, and asks substantially the same questions each time. P may seek a protective order in which the judge orders that no further depositions of P may take place at all. The court will probably grant this request.

Example 2: P sues D for patent infringement, alleging that D's manufacturing methods violate P's patents. In a deposition of D's vice president, P asks the details of D's secret manufacturing processes. D may seek a protective order preventing P from learning these trade secrets, perhaps on the grounds that P does not need to know these secrets in order to pursue his patent case.

a. Prohibition of public disclosure: One common type of protective order allows trade secrets or other information to be discovered, but then ***bars the public disclosure*** of the information by the discovering litigant. (*Example:* On the facts of the above example, the

C
A
P
S
U
L
E

S
U
M
M
A
R
Y

judge might allow P to get discovery of D's trade secrets, but prevent P from disclosing that information to any third party.) [202]

C. Compelling discovery: Conversely, if one party refuses to cooperate in the other's discovery attempts, the aggrieved party may seek an ***order compelling discovery*** under Rule 37(a). [203-04]

    1. When available: An order to compel discovery may be granted if the discoveree fails to: (1) answer a written or oral deposition question; (2) answer an interrogatory; (3) produce documents, or allow an inspection; (4) designate an officer to answer deposition questions, if the discoveree is a corporation.

D. Sanctions for failing to furnish discovery: The court may order a number of ***sanctions*** against parties who behave unreasonably during discovery. Principally, these sanctions are used against a party who fails to cooperate in the other party's discovery efforts. [204-07]

    1. Financial sanctions: If a discovering party seeks an order compelling discovery, and the court grants the order, the court may require the discoveree to pay the ***reasonable expenses*** the other party incurred in obtaining the order. These may include attorney's fees for procuring the order. Rule 37(b). [204]

    2. Other sanctions: Once one party obtains an order compelling the other to submit to discovery, and the latter ***persists in her refusal*** to grant discovery, then the court may (in addition to the financial sanctions mentioned above) impose additional sanctions: [205]

        a. Facts established: The court may order that the matters involved in the discovery be taken to be ***established***. (*Example:* In a product liability suit, P wants discovery of D's records, to show that D made the product that injured P. If D refuses to cooperate even after the court issues an order compelling discovery, then the court may treat as established D's having manufactured the item.)

        b. Claims or defenses barred: The court may prevent the disobedient party from making certain claims or defenses, or introducing certain matters in evidence.

        c. Entry of judgment: The court may also ***dismiss*** the action, or enter a default judgment.

        d. Contempt: Finally, the court may hold the disobedient party in ***contempt*** of court.

V. USE OF DISCOVERY RESULTS AT TRIAL

A. Use at same trial: The rules for determining whether the fruits of discovery can be ***introduced at trial*** vary depending on the type of discovery. [207]

B. Request to produce: The admissibility of ***documents*** and ***reports*** that were obtained through a Rule 34 ***request to produce*** is determined ***without regard*** to the fact that these items were obtained through discovery. These documents will thus be admissible unless their contents constitute prejudicial, hearsay, or other inadmissible material. [207]

C. Depositions: The admissibility of ***depositions*** is determined through a two-part test. Both parts must be satisfied: [207-09]

    1. Test 1: First, determine whether the deposition statement sought to be introduced would be admissible ***if the deponent were giving live testimony***. If not, the statement is automatically inadmissible. (*Example:* Deponent says, "X told me that he committed the murder." If the hearsay rule would prevent deponent from making this statement live at trial, it will also prevent the deposition statement from coming in.)

2. **Test 2:** Second, apply the *"four categories"* test. Since the use of a deposition statement rather than live testimony is itself a form of hearsay, the deposition statement must fall within one of the four following categories, which are in effect exceptions to the hearsay rule:

    a. **Adverse party:** The deposition of an *adverse party*, or of a *director or officer* of an adverse *corporate* party, may be admitted for *any purpose at all*. See Rule 32(a)(2). [208-09]

    b. **Impeachment:** The deposition of any witness, *party or non-party*, may be used to *impeach the witness' credibility*. See Rule 32(a)(1).

    c. **Adverse witness' deposition for substantive purposes:** A party may use a deposition of an *adverse witness* for *substantive* purposes, if it conflicts with that witness' trial testimony. (*Example:* In a suit by P versus D, W, a witness favorable to D and called by D, states at trial, "The light was red when P drove through it." P may introduce W's statement in a deposition, "The light was green when P drove through," not just for impeachment but to prove the substantive fact that the light was green.)

    d. **Other circumstances:** The deposition of any person (party or non-party) can be used for any purpose if one of the following conditions, all relating to the witness' *unavailability*, exists: (1) the deponent is *dead*; (2) the deponent is located *100 or more miles* from the trial; (3) the deponent is *too ill* to testify; (4) the deponent is *not obtainable by subpoena*; or (5) there are *exceptional circumstances* that make it desirable to dispense with the deponent's live testimony. See Rule 32(a)(3).

3. **Partial offering:** If only *part* of a deposition is offered into evidence by one party, an *adverse* party may introduce *any other parts* of the deposition which in *fairness* ought to be considered with the part introduced. Rule 32(a)(4). (*Example:* If one side reads part of an answer, the other side may almost always read the rest of the answer.)

D. **Interrogatories:** The *interrogatory answer* of a party can be used by an *adverse party* for *any purpose*. [209-10]

    1. **Not binding:** Statements made in interrogatories, like statements made in depositions, are *not binding* upon the maker — he may contradict them in court. (Obviously the witness' credibility will suffer, but the witness is not legally bound to the prior statement.)

E. **Admissions:** *Admissions* obtained under Rule 36 *conclusively establish* the matter admitted. [210]

F. **Physical and mental examinations:** The results of *physical and mental examinations* made under Rule 35 are almost always *admissible at trial*. (Also, remember that if the examined party requests and obtains a report of the examiner, the examinee is held to waive any privilege associated with the report, such as the doctor/patient privilege.) [210]

> **Note:** All of the above discussion of use at trial assumes that the use takes place during the very proceeding that gave rise to the discovery itself. Where the fruits of discovery in Action 1 are sought to be used in Action 2, different, more complicated, rules apply.

CAPSULE SUMMARY

VI. PRETRIAL CONFERENCE

A. Generally: Many states, and the federal system, give the judge the authority to conduct a *pretrial conference*. The judge may use such a conference to simplify or formulate the issues for trial, and to facilitate a settlement. See Rule 16(a) and 16(c). [214-15]

1. **Scheduling:** The federal judge must issue a *"scheduling order"* within 120 days after filing of the complaint. This order sets a time limit for filing of motions, completion of discovery, etc. Rule 16(b). The trial judge may, but need not, conduct a pretrial conference.

2. **Pretrial order:** If the judge does hold a pretrial conference, she then must enter a *pretrial order* reciting the actions taken in the conference (e.g., narrowing the issues to be litigated, and summarizing the admissions of fact made by the lawyers).

CHAPTER 6

ASCERTAINING APPLICABLE LAW

I. NATURE OF PROBLEM

A. Generally: A particular controversy that is litigable in federal court may also, in most situations, be brought in state court. This chapter is about which law — federal law or state law — should be applied in cases brought in federal court. [218-222]

1. **Forum shopping:** A key concept to keep in sight is the federal courts' desire to *discourage "forum shopping."* If a particular case could be brought in either state or federal court, and the state courts would apply rules of law different from those that would be applied by the federal court, the plaintiff (and in situations where removal is possible, the defendant) will have an incentive to *choose the court more favorable to her case.* To prevent forum shopping of this sort, the courts *generally apply state law* in diversity cases. [218-21]

2. **Rules of Decision Act:** The Rules of Decision Act (RDA), 28 U.S.C. §1652, based upon the Supremacy Clause of the Constitution, is the main statute stating when the federal court should apply federal law, and when it should apply state law. [218-21]

   a. **Federal law applied:** According to the clear language of the RDA, the federal Constitution, treaties, and constitutional *statutes* enacted by Congress, always take precedence, where relevant, over all *state* provisions. (In fact, this rule applies not only to federal proceedings but also to state court proceedings.)

   b. **State statutes:** The RDA also clearly provides that in the absence of a federal constitutional or statutory provision on point, the federal courts must follow *state constitutions and statutes.* [218]

   c. **Dispute about common law:** The interesting question, and one on which the RDA is silent, is what the federal court should do where there is *no controlling constitutional or statutory provision*, federal *or* state. In other words, the key question is, what law should the federal court follow where what is at issue is *"common,"* or *judge-made*, law. [218]

   Example: P sues D in a diversity action arising out of an automobile accident that took place in Kansas. The Kansas courts apply common-law contributory negligence. Must the federal judge hearing the case apply Kansas' common-law contributory negligence, or is the court free to make its own determination that comparative negligence is a sounder principle? The answer, as set forth in *Erie v. Tompkins* (discussed below), is that Kansas common law must be followed.

B. Erie v. Tompkins: The most important Supreme Court case in all of Civil Procedure is **Erie Railroad v. Tompkins**. That case holds that when the Rules of Decision Act says that the federal courts must apply the "law of the several states, except where the Constitution or … acts of Congress otherwise require…," this language applies to state *common law* as well as state statutory law. The net result is that *in diversity cases, the federal courts must apply state judge-made law on any substantive issue*. [220-21]

   1. Discrimination against citizens: The contrary rule that had been followed before *Erie* — *Swift v. Tyson*'s holding that federal judges could ignore state common law in diversity cases — allowed non-citizens to *discriminate against citizens of the state where the federal court sat*. (*Example:* P, an Ohio resident, sues D, a Kansas resident, in federal district court for the District of Kansas. Kansas law would be favorable to D. *Swift v. Tyson*, which would allow P to choose federal or state court in Kansas, whichever was more favorable to him, would thus allow P to profit at D's expense. *Erie v. Tompkins*, by forcing the federal court to apply Kansas law, guarantees D, the Kansas citizen, the benefits of his own state's law.)

   2. Facts of Erie: The facts of *Erie* remain a good illustration of the case's principle, that state rather than federal common law is to be followed on substantive matters in diversity cases. P, a Pennsylvania citizen, was injured while walking on the right of way maintained by D, a New York railroad. Under Pennsylvania judge-made law, P would probably have lost his negligence suit, because P was a trespasser, to whom D would be liable only for gross, not ordinary, negligence. P instead sued in New York federal district court, expecting the federal court to follow *Swift v. Tyson* and make its own "federal common law" which P hoped would make the railroad liable to him for ordinary negligence.

      a. Holding: But the Supreme Court held that the federal court must follow state law on substantive issues, and that "state law" included judge-made (common) law as well as state statutes. So Pennsylvania law on the railroad's duty of care was to be followed (though the Court did not specify why Pennsylvania rather than New York law was what should be followed).

II. *ERIE* PROBLEMS

A. Ascertaining state law: Several problems arise when the federal court tries to determine what *is* the "state law," when there is no state statute on point. Obviously if the highest court of the state where the federal court sits has recently spoken on the issue, the problem is easy. But where this is not the case, life gets trickier. The general principle is that the federal court must try to determine *how the state's highest court would determine the issue if the case arose before it today*. [222-23]

   1. Intermediate-court decisions: If there is no holding by the highest state court, the federal court looking for state law to apply *considers intermediate-court* decisions. These intermediate-court decisions will normally be followed, unless there are other reasons to believe that the state's highest court would not follow them. [222]

   2. Where no state court has spoken: If no court in the state has ever considered the issue in question, then the court can look to other sources. One important source is decisions in *prior federal diversity cases* which have attempted to predict and apply the law of the same state.

C
A
P
S
U
L
E

S
U
M
M
A
R
Y

Similarly, the federal court may look at the practice of other states, other authorities (e.g., Restatements), etc. But the issue is always: What would the highest state court decide today? [222]

3. **State decision obsolete:** Where there is an *old* determination of state law by the highest state court, the federal court hearing the present case is always free to conclude that the state court would decide the issue differently if confronted with the present case. In that situation, the old ruling is not binding. [223]

4. **Change to conform with new state decision:** The federal court (even an appellate court) must give effect to a *new* decision of a state's highest court, even if the state court decision was handed down *after* the federal district court action was completed. [223]

B. **Conflict of laws:** The federal court must also apply state law governing *conflict of laws*. In other words, the conflict of laws rules of the state *where the federal court sits* must be followed. [*Klaxon Co. v. Stentor Electric Mfg. Co.*] [224]

> **Example:** The Ps, soldiers, are injured in Cambodia by an explosion of a shell manufactured by D. The Ps sue D in Texas federal court. Texas tort law allows strict liability. The law of Cambodia does not allow strict liability.
>
> *Held*, Texas conflict-of-laws principles must apply. Since the Texas courts would apply the tort law of the place where the accident occurred — Cambodia — so must the federal court. Therefore, strict liability will not be applied, and the Ps lose. [*Day & Zimmermann, Inc. v. Challoner*]

C. **Burden of proof:** The federal court must also follow the rules governing the *allocation of the burden of proof* in force in the state where the federal court is sitting. [225]

D. **Procedure/substance distinction:** *Erie v. Tompkins* says that state common law controls in "substantive" matters. But federal rules and policies control on matters that are essentially "procedural." Here are some guidelines for handling the *procedure/substance distinction*: [225-36]

1. **Federal Rules take precedence:** *Erie* is only applicable where there is no controlling federal statute. Since the Federal Rules of Civil Procedure are adopted pursuant to a congressional statute (the Rules Enabling Act), *the FRCP, when applicable, take precedence over state policy*. So if a Federal Rule arguably applies to the situation at hand, ask two questions: (1) Does the Rule in fact apply to the issue at hand? and (2) Is the Rule valid under the Rules Enabling Act? If the answer to both questions is "yes," then the Federal Rule takes precedence. [225]

   a. **Does Rule apply:** The mere fact that a Federal Rule seems to have something to do with the issue at hand does not mean that the Rule applies — the Rules are *construed narrowly*, to cover just those situations that Congress intended them to cover. [227-29]

   > **Example:** FRCP 3 provides that a civil action "is commenced by filing a complaint with the court." P files a complaint against D with the court on Feb. 1. The statute of limitations on P's right of action expires on Feb. 15. On March 1, P causes D to be served with process. The suit takes place in Kentucky federal district court. Kentucky state law provides that the statute of limitations is satisfied only by service upon the defendant, not by mere filing with the court.
   >
   > The federal court for Kentucky must ask, "Does Rule 3 really apply to this situation?" The Supreme Court has held on these facts that Rule 3 does *not* speak to the issue of when a state statute of limitations is tolled, but is merely designed to give a starting point for the

measurement of various time periods in the federal suit. Since neither Rule 3 nor any other Federal Rule is on point, state common law — in this case, Kentucky's principle that the date of service is what counts — must be applied in the federal action. [*Ragan v. Merchants Transfer; Walker v. Armco Steel Corp.*]

b. **Is Rule valid:** If you conclude that the Rule applies to the issue at hand, the next question is, "Is the Rule valid?" The Rules Enabling Act provides that to be valid, a Rule must not "abridge, enlarge, [or] modify the substantive rights of any litigant." But as long as the Rule is arguably "procedural," it will be found to satisfy this test. No Federal Rule has ever been found to violate the "no abridgement, enlargement or modification of substantive rights" test of the Rules Enabling Act. [225-26]

c. **Illustration:** To see how the two part test works, consider this famous example: [232-34]

Example: P sues D in diversity in Massachusetts federal court. D is the executor of an estate. P causes process to be served on D's wife, by leaving copies of the summons and complaint with her at D's dwelling place. Federal Rule 4(d)(1) (now Rule 4(e)(2)) allows service on a defendant by leaving copies of the summons and complaint at the defendant's dwelling place with a person of suitable age and discretion, a standard met here. But a Massachusetts statute sets special standards for service on an executor of an estate, which were not complied with here.

   Held, first, Rule 4(d)(1) is in harmony with the Enabling Act, since it is basically procedural. Second, the Rule clearly applies to the issue here, since it specifies the allowable method of service in a federal action. Therefore, the Rule takes priority over any contrary state policy or statute, even if applying the Rule might help produce a different outcome than had the state rule been applied. [*Hanna v. Plumer*]

2. **Case not covered by a Federal Rule:** If the issue at hand is *not* covered by anything in the FRCP, but is nonetheless arguably "procedural," the situation is more complicated: [230-32]

   a. **Rejection of "outcome determination":** At one time, the test was whether the choice between state and federal policy was *"outcome determinative"* — if the choice was at all likely to influence who won the lawsuit, then the litigants' substantive rights would be affected by the choice, and the state policy must be followed. But the Supreme Court has *rejected outcome-determinativeness as the standard.* [*Byrd v. Blue Ridge*] [230]

   b. **Balance state and federal policies:** Today, the federal court *balances* the state and federal policies against each other. *Where the state interest in having its policy followed is fairly weak, and the federal interest strong, the court is likely to hold that the federal procedural policy should be followed.* Here are some illustrations of how this balancing works out: [230-32]

      i. **Judge/Jury allocation:** Where the question is, "Who decides a certain factual issue, judge or jury?" *federal* policies are to be followed. (*Example:* Whether P was an employee rather than an independent contractor is to be determined by following the federal policy of having factual matters determined by a jury, not the state policy of having such an issue decided by the judge, because the federal policy on judge-jury allocation is strong, the state policy is not tightly bound up with the rights of the parties, and the choice is not very outcome determinative. [*Byrd v. Blue Ridge*]) [230]

ii. **Door-closing statute:** Similarly, state procedural rules limiting in-state suits by non-residents against foreign corporations — *"door-closing"* rules — need not be followed by the federal court; the state interest here is weak, and the federal interest in furnishing a convenient forum for litigants is a strong one. [*Szantay v. Beech Aircraft*] [230-31]

iii. **Unanimity for jury trials:** Federal policy requiring a **unanimous jury verdict** will be applied in diversity suits, at the expense of the state policy allowing a verdict based on a less-than-unanimous majority. The state's policy (reducing hung juries) has little weight here, since the case is not taking place in the state system; the federal policy is strong, supported by tradition; the choice is not heavily outcome-determinative. [*Masino v. Outboard Marine Corp.*] [231-32]

iv. **Statute of limitations:** But a state *statute of limitations* must be followed in a diversity case. Here, the state's interest is heavily outcome-determinative, and deeply bound up with the rights of the parties. The federal interest is relatively weak, and there is little to be gained from district-to-district uniformity. [*Guaranty Trust Co. v. York*, an older case that is still valid.] [228]

3. **Federal statute (not Rule) on point:** Where there is a federal procedural *statute* (as distinct from a Federal Rule) that is directly on point, it will control over any state law or policy, even though this may promote forum shopping. [232]

III. FEDERAL COMMON LAW

A. **Federal common law still exists:** Even though *Erie* makes it clear that there is no *general* federal common law, there are still *particular instances* in which federal common law is applied. That is, the federal court is occasionally free to disregard state law in deciding the case. [238]

B. **Federal question cases:** Most importantly, in *federal question* cases, *federal common law, not state common law, usually applies*. (*Example:* P sues D, the United States, in federal district court for the Northern District of Texas. This suit raises a federal question, since it involves the U.S. as a party. Even if there is no federal statute on point, and even if it is clear that under Texas law the U.S. would not be negligent, the federal court may and should apply general federal common law principles in deciding whether the U.S. was negligent and is thus liable.) [239]

C. **Diversity cases:** Occasionally, federal common law may even be applied where the basis for federal jurisdiction is diversity. For instance, if P's claim does not raise issues of federal law, but a defense asserted by D does raise federal law, the validity of that defense will be determined under federal common law principles. [240]

D. **Federal common law in state courts:** Conversely, the *states* are occasionally required to apply *federal* common law. If concurrent jurisdiction (state and federal) exists concerning a particular claim, and the suit is brought in state court, federal common law applies there if it would apply in federal court. [240-41]

> **Example:** P brings a state-court action against D, a city, under a federal statute giving a cause of action for deprivation of civil rights. State law requires that P give notice to D within 120 days of injury before suing D if D is a city. *Held*, the state court may not impose this state-created procedural rule, since it would abridge federally-granted rights. [*Felder v. Casey*]

CHAPTER 7
TRIAL PROCEDURE

I. BURDEN OF PROOF

A. Two meanings of "burden of proof": There are two kinds of "burden of proof" which a party may have to bear. Assuming that the issue is called *A*: [246]

1. **Burden of production:** The party bears the "burden of *production*" if the following is true: unless the party produces *some* evidence that *A* exists, the judge must direct the jury to find that *A* does not exist. [246]

2. **Burden of persuasion:** The party bears the "burden of *persuasion*" if the following is true: at the close of the evidence, if the jury cannot decide whether *A* exists or not, the jury must find that *A* does not exist. [246]

> **Example of two burdens:** P sues D, arguing that D failed to use reasonable care in driving his car, and therefore hit P, a pedestrian. P bears both the burden of production and the burden of persuasion as to D's negligence. To meet the burden of production, P will have to come up with at least some evidence that D was careless; if P does not do so, the judge will not let the jury decide the issue of negligence, and will instead direct the jury to find that there was no negligence. If P comes up with some evidence of negligence, and the case goes to the jury, the fact that P also bears the burden of persuasion means that the judge will tell the jury, "In order to find that D was negligent, you must find it more likely than not that D was negligent. If you find exactly a 50-50 chance that D was negligent, you must find non-negligence."

II. PRESUMPTIONS

A. Definition: A *presumption* is a convention that when a designated *basic fact* exists (call the designated basic fact *B*), another fact, called the *presumed fact* (call it *P*) *must* be taken to exist unless there is rebuttal evidence to show that *P* does not exist. [247]

B. Effect of presumption: The existence of a presumption always has an effect on the burden of production, and sometimes has an effect on the burden of persuasion. (In the following discussion, assume that there is a legal presumption that if *B*, then *P*. Assume also that plaintiff is trying to prove *P*. Also assume that if there were no presumption, plaintiff would bear the burden of persuasion as to *P*.) [247-49]

1. **Effect on burden of production:** The party against whom the presumption is directed bears the initial burden of *producing* evidence of non-*P*. If he produces no evidence, he *suffers a directed verdict*. [247]

> **Example:** A statute establishes a presumption that when a railroad locomotive causes damage, the railroad was negligent. P proves that D's locomotive caused damage to him. Neither party puts on any evidence about D's actual negligence. Assume that if there were no presumption, P would have the burden of production on negligence. By showing damage, P has carried his burden of production; if D does not come up with any rebutting evidence of non-negligence, the judge will direct the jury to find for P on the negligence issue.

C
A
P
S
U
L
E

S
U
M
M
A
R
Y

2. **Burden of persuasion:** If the defendant offers enough evidence of non-*P* that a reasonable jury might find non-*P*, it is clear that defendant has met his production burden, and that the case will go to the jury. But courts are *split* as to who bears the burden of *persuasion*. [247]

    a. **Federal Rules of Evidence:** Most states, and federal courts in federal-question cases, follow the approach set out in the Federal Rules of Evidence. Under this approach, the presumption has *no* effect on the burden of persuasion, merely on the burden of production. This approach is sometimes called the *"bursting bubble"* approach — *once evidence tending to show the non-existence of the presumed fact is introduced, the presumption bursts like a bubble*. See FRE 301 ("A presumption imposes on the party against whom it is directed the burden of going forward with evidence to rebut or meet the presumption, but does not shift to such party the burden of proof in the sense of the risk of non-persuasion...").

        Example: Same facts as above example. After P shows evidence of damage by the locomotive, D comes forward with evidence that it was not negligent. This is enough to send the case to the jury. Now, under the FRE "bursting bubble" approach, P will still bear the burden of persuasion — unless P convinces the jury that it is more likely than not that D was negligent, D will win on the issue of negligence. This is because the presumption — that where there is locomotive damage, there is railroad negligence — has no effect on the burden of persuasion.

    b. **State law in diversity cases:** But in *diversity* cases, the federal courts must defer to any contrary state rule concerning the effect of a presumption on the burden of persuasion. See FRE 302. In other words, FRE 301, applying the bursting bubble approach, applies only where a federal claim or defense is at issue, or state law is silent.

III. PREPONDERANCE OF THE EVIDENCE

A. **"Preponderance" standard generally:** The usual standard of proof in civil actions is the *"preponderance of the evidence"* standard. A proposition is proved by a preponderance of the evidence if the jury is convinced that it is *"more likely than not"* that the proposition is true. [249]

B. **Adversary's denials:** A party who has the burden of proving a fact by a preponderance of the evidence may *not rely solely on the jury's disbelief of his adversary's denials of that fact*. [250]

    Example: P asserts that D behaved negligently by driving through a red light. P produces no affirmative evidence of this allegation. D takes the stand, and says, "The light was green when I drove through." P does not cross-examine D on this point. There is no other relevant evidence. The court must hold that P could not possibly have satisfied the "preponderance of the evidence" standard as to D's negligence — the fact that the jury might possibly disbelieve D's denials of negligence is not enough, and the court must enter a directed verdict for D on this point.

IV. ADJUDICATION WITHOUT TRIAL

A. **Voluntary dismissal by plaintiff:** A plaintiff in federal court may *voluntarily dismiss* her complaint *without prejudice* anytime before the defendant serves an answer or moves for summary judgment. The fact that the dismissal is "without prejudice" means that she may *bring the suit again*. See Rule 41(a)(1). [251]

1. **Only one dismissal:** Only the *first* dismissal of the claim is without prejudice.

2. **After answer or motion:** After D has answered or moved for summary judgment, P may no longer automatically make a voluntary dismissal. Instead, P must get the court's approval. FRCP 41(a)(2).

B. **Involuntary dismissal:** P's claim may also be *involuntarily* dismissed by court order. [251]

    1. **Examples:** Some of the grounds for which, under FRCP 41(b), the court may grant an involuntary dismissal, are: (1) P's failure to *prosecute*; (2) P's failure to *obey court orders*; (3) lack of *jurisdiction* or *venue*; or (4) P's failure to join an *indispensable party*.

    2. **Prejudice:** Normally an involuntary dismissal is *with prejudice*. But some kinds of dismissals are *not* with prejudice (and thus the action may be brought anew): (1) dismissal for *lack of jurisdiction*, of both parties and subject matter, or for insufficient service; (2) improper *venue*; and (3) failure to *join* an indispensable party under Rule 19.

C. **Summary judgment:** If one party can show that there is *no "genuine issue of material fact"* in the lawsuit, and that she is "entitled to judgment as a matter of law," she can win the case without going to trial. Such a victory without trial is called a *"summary judgment."* See FRCP 56. [252-55]

    1. **Court goes behind pleadings:** The court will go *"behind the pleadings"* in deciding a summary judgment motion — even if it appears from the pleadings that the parties are in dispute, the motion may be granted if the movant can show that the disputed factual issues presented by the pleadings are *illusory*. [252]

    2. **How shown:** The movant can show the lack of a genuine issue by a number of means. For example, the movant may produce *affidavits*, or use the fruits of *discovery* (e.g., depositions and interrogatory answers) to show that there is no genuine issue of material fact. [253]

        a. **Burden of production:** The person moving for summary judgment bears the initial burden of production in the summary judgment motion — that is, the movant must come up with at least some affirmative evidence that there is no genuine issue of material fact. [253]

    3. **Opposition:** The party *opposing* the summary judgment usually also submits affidavits, depositions and other materials. [254]

        a. **Opponent can't rest on pleadings:** If materials submitted by the movant show that there is no genuine material issue of fact for trial, the non-movant cannot avoid summary judgment merely by repeating his pleadings' denial of the allegations made by the movant. In other words, the party opposing the motion may not rest on restatements of her own pleadings, and must instead present by affidavits or the fruits of discovery *specific facts* showing that there is a genuine issue for trial. Rule 56(e). [254]

        b. **Construction most favorable to non-movant:** On the other hand, once the opponent of the motion does submit opposing papers, he receives the *benefit of the doubt*. All matters in the motion are construed *most favorably to the party opposing the motion*. The fact that the movant is extremely likely to win at trial is not enough; only if there is *no way*, legally speaking, that the movant can lose at trial, should the court grant summary judgment. [254]

    4. **Partial summary judgment:** Summary judgment may be granted with respect to *certain claims* in a lawsuit even when it is not granted with respect to all claims. This is called *partial*

summary judgment. See Rule 54(b). (*Example:* Where P sues D for breach of contract, the court might grant P partial summary judgment on the issue of liability, because there is no genuine doubt about whether a breach occurred; the court might then conduct a trial on the remaining issue of damages.) [254]

V. TRIALS WITHOUT A JURY

A. When tried to court: A case will be tried without a jury if *either* of the two following conditions exists: [256]

1. No right to a jury trial exists; or

2. All parties have **waived** the right to a jury trial.

    a. When waived: A party who wants a jury trial on a particular issue must file a *demand* for jury trial to the other parties within *10 days* after the service of the *last pleading* directed to that issue. FRCP 38(b). Otherwise, the party is deemed to have waived her right to jury trial.

B. Effect: If there is no jury, the trial judge serves as both the *finder of fact* and the decider of law. [256]

C. Evidence rules: The rules of evidence followed by the judge (in federal trials, these are the Federal Rules of Evidence) are officially the *same* in non-jury trials as in jury trials. However, in practice, judges tend to *relax the rules* where there is no jury present. [256]

D. Findings of fact: If an action is tried without a jury, FRCP 52 requires the trial court to "*find the facts* specially and [to] state separately its conclusions of law thereon...." So the trial judge must set forth the facts with *particularity*, and must in a separate section of her opinion state the law which she believes applies to those facts. [256-57]

1. Where separate findings required: The federal judge must make separate findings of fact and conclusions of law not only in cases that are fully tried, but also: [256]

    a. Where requests for interlocutory *injunctions* are made (whether granted or denied); and

    b. Where *"judgment on partial findings"* is given pursuant to Rule 52(c).

2. Separate findings not required: The trial judge is *not* obligated to make separate findings of fact and conclusions of law when disposing of a *motion*, except a Rule 52(c) motion for judgment on partial findings. (*Examples:* If the judge denies a motion for summary judgment, or grants a 12(b)(6) motion to dismiss for failure to state a claim, the judge need not make detailed findings of fact.) [256]

3. Judgment on partial findings: The judge can conduct a *"mini trial"* of just one issue, if the judge thinks that this will dispose of the case. If the judge then finds against the party bearing the burden of proof on that issue, the judge issues a "judgment on partial findings." See FRCP 52(c). (*Example:* In an auto accident case, D pleads the three-year statute of limitations. The judge can conduct a mini trial concerning only the date of the accident; if the date is more than three years before P started the action, the judge can issue a judgment in D's favor based on the partial finding that the action is time-barred.) [256-57]

E. Appellate review of findings of fact: Although the appellate court has the full record of the case before it, it does *not* review the evidence for the purpose of making its own determination of what really happened. Appellate review as to factual matters is much more *limited*: [257]

1. **General "clearly erroneous" standard:** The general standard is that the trial judge's findings of fact *will be set aside only if they are "clearly erroneous."* FRCP 52(a). (*Example:* If the trial judge finds that D behaved negligently in an auto accident case, the appellate court will not set aside the verdict merely because it believes that there was only a 40% chance that D was negligent. Only if the trial judge's findings seem to the appellate court to be "clearly erroneous," a test not satisfied here, will the court reverse.) [257]

2. **Witnesses' credibility:** Where the findings of fact relate to trial *testimony* given by live witnesses, the appellate court must give "due regard…to the opportunity of the trial court to judge of the *credibility of the witnesses*." FRCP 52(a). In other words, the appellate court should be *particularly loathe* to overturn the trial judge's findings of fact regarding such testimony. [257]

   a. **Standard:** Where the trial judge believes one of two witnesses who are telling *conflicting stories*, as long as the favored witness' story is *internally consistent*, "facially plausible," and not contradicted by extrinsic evidence, the appellate court will not overturn the findings of fact. [*Anderson v. Bessemer City*]

VI. THE JURY

A. **Seventh Amendment generally:** The Seventh Amendment to the U.S. Constitution says that "in suits at *common law … the right of trial by jury shall be preserved….*" This Amendment applies to *federal trials*, but does *not* apply to *state* trials. [260]

B. **Number of jurors:** Traditionally, juries have been composed of 12 members. But this is breaking down today. [260-61]

   1. **Federal:** Even in federal civil cases, the Seventh Amendment does *not* require a 12-member jury. FRCP 48 provides that a jury of at least *six* members will be seated.

      a. **Too few remaining:** Normally the federal court seats more than six jurors, so that if some have to leave the panel, there will be at least six at the time of verdict. If there are fewer than six at the time of verdict, the court must declare a mistrial unless both parties agree to continue.

   2. **State trials:** The number of jurors in *state trials* varies from state to state.

C. **Unanimity:** [261]

   1. **Federal:** The verdict of a *federal* civil jury must be *unanimous*, unless the parties stipulate otherwise. FRCP 48.

   2. **States:** Most states allow a *less-than-unanimous* civil verdict.

D. **Jury selection:** The process by which the jury is selected is called the *"voir dire."* In most states, the *voir dire* consists of oral questions by both sides' counsel to the prospective jurors. These questions are designed to discover whether a juror would be biased, or has connections with a party or prospective witness. [261]

   1. **Dismissal for cause:** Any juror who is shown through the *voir dire* to be biased or connected to the case must be dismissed upon motion by a party (dismissal *"for cause"*). There is no limit to the number of for-cause challenges by either party.

C
A
P
S
U
L
E

S
U
M
M
A
R
Y

2. Challenges without cause: In addition to the jurors dismissed for cause, each party may dismiss a certain number of other prospective jurors *without showing cause* for their dismissal (*"peremptory challenges"*).

    a. Federal practice: In federal civil trials, each party receives *three* peremptory challenges.

3. Balanced pool: The Seventh Amendment requires that the jury, and the pool from which it is drawn, be roughly *representative of the overall community*.

4. Alternates: In most states, the court orders the selection of up to six *alternates* after the "regular" members of the jury have been selected. But under federal practice, alternates are no longer used (FRCP 48).

E. Instructions: The judge must *instruct* the jury as to the *relevant law*. (*Example:* If P sues D for negligence, the judge must instruct the jury about the "reasonable person" standard, and the requirement of proximate cause.) [262]

    1. Objections: A party who wants to raise the inadequacy of the instructions on appeal must *object* to those instructions *before the jury retires*. (Sometimes courts make an exception to this rule for "plain error.")

F. Juror misconduct: A jury verdict may be set aside, and a *new trial* ordered, for certain types of *jury misconduct*. (*Examples:* Talking to a party, receiving a bribe, concealing a bias on voir dire.) [262-63]

    1. Traditional impeachment rule: The traditional rule, still followed in most states, is that the jury may *not impeach its own verdict*. That is, the verdict will not be set aside because of a juror's testimony of his own or another juror's misconduct — only evidence from a *third party* will suffice. [262]

        a. Federal Rule: But the Federal Rules of Evidence have modified this principle slightly for federal trials. The general "jury can't impeach its own verdict" rule still applies, except that a juror may testify about whether extraneous prejudicial information was improperly brought to the jury's attention, or whether any *outside influence* was improperly brought to bear upon a juror. FRE 606(b). (*Examples:* One juror can testify that another read a newspaper article about the case, or was bribed by one of the parties. But a juror cannot testify that the jury disregarded the judge's instructions.)

    2. Post-trial discovery of bias: If, after the trial, it turns out that a juror *failed to disclose* information during voir dire that would have indicated bias, the party may move for a new trial. In federal trials, the movant must show: (1) that the juror failed to answer honestly a material question during the voir dire; and (2) that a correct response would have led to a valid challenge for cause. [*McDonough Power Equipment Inc. v. Greenwood*] (*Example:* A party can get a new trial if he proves that a juror lied about knowing one of the parties, but not if the juror honestly gave a mistaken answer in voir dire because of confusion about the question.) [263]

VII. DIRECTED VERDICT

A. Defined: In both state and federal trials, either party may move for a *directed verdict*. Such a verdict *takes the case away from the jury, and determines the outcome as a matter of law*. [264]

1. **Federal trials:** In federal trials, the phrase "directed verdict" is no longer used — instead, a party moves for "judgment as a matter of law."

2. **When made:** Motions for directed verdict or judgment as a matter of law are made when the opposing party has been *fully heard* on the relevant issues. Thus D can move for directed verdict at the close of P's case, and either party may move for directed verdict after both sides have rested.

B. **Standard for granting:** Generally, the court will direct a verdict if the evidence is such that *reasonable people could not differ* as to the result. [264]

1. **Federal standard:** In federal trials, the standard is that the judge may enter judgment as a matter of law "if during a trial by jury, a party has been fully heard with respect to an issue and there is *no legally sufficient evidentiary basis* for a *reasonable jury* to have found for that party with respect to that issue...." FRCP 50(a)(1).

VIII. SPECIAL VERDICT AND INTERROGATORIES

A. **Special verdict defined:** A "special verdict" is a *specific finding of fact*, as opposed to a general verdict (which merely grants victory to one side or the other). (*Example:* In a contract case, the jury might be asked to render a special verdict as to whether a valid contract existed between the parties.) [266]

B. **General verdict with interrogatories:** The judge may, instead of requiring a special verdict, require a general verdict, supported by *interrogatories* as to specific findings of fact. See FRCP 49(b). This "general verdict with interrogatories" approach is more common than the specific verdict approach. [267]

IX. NEW TRIAL

A. **Generally:** The trial court, in both state and federal courts, usually has wider discretion to grant a *new trial* motion than to direct a verdict or disregard the jury's verdict (JNOV). The reason is that the grant of a new trial interferes less with the verdict winner's right to jury trial. [267]

B. **Federal rules for granting:** Here is a summary of the rules on grants of new trials in federal civil cases: [267-68]

1. **Harmless error:** A new trial may not be granted except for errors in the trial which are serious enough that they affect the substantial rights of the parties. FRCP 61. This is the so-called *"harmless error"* doctrine. Basically, unless the trial judge believes that the error *might have made the case come out differently*, she cannot grant a new trial motion. [267]

2. **Evidence error:** One common ground for granting a new trial is that the trial judge *erroneously admitted or excluded evidence*. [267]

3. **Objection:** For most types of error at the trial court level, the party injured by the error must make a *timely objection*, in order to preserve the right to cite that error on appeal as a ground for a new trial. (*Example:* If evidence is erroneously admitted or excluded, this cannot serve as grounds for a new trial unless the injured party immediately objects at the time the evidence is admitted or excluded.) [267]

4. **Improper conduct:** A new trial may be granted because of *improper conduct* by a *party*, *witness* or *lawyer*, posing a substantial risk that an unfair verdict will result. Similarly, a new

trial may be granted where there is evidence that the *jury* behaved improperly (e.g., a juror was bribed or was contacted by a party). [268]

5. **Verdict against weight of evidence:** The trial judge (or the appeals court) may set aside a verdict as *"against the weight of the evidence."* Courts vary as to the standard for doing this. [268-69]

    a. **Federal standard:** In federal courts, a verdict must be against the *clear weight* of the evidence, be based upon evidence which is *false*, or result in a miscarriage of justice. It is not enough that there is substantial evidence against the verdict, or that the trial judge disagrees with the verdict and would vote otherwise if he were a juror. (But it is still easier to get a federal judge to grant a new trial as against the weight of the evidence than to get the trial judge to direct judgment as a matter of law.)

6. **Verdict excessive or inadequate:** A new trial may be granted where a verdict is *excessive* or *inadequate*. [269-70]

    a. *Remittitur* **and** *additur:* Where the verdict is excessive or inadequate, the judge may grant a *conditional* new trial order — the new trial will occur unless the plaintiff agrees to a reduction of the damages to a specified amount (called *"remittitur"*) or the new trial to occur unless the defendant consents to a *raising* of the damages (called *"additur"*). Most state courts allow both *additur* and *remittitur*. In federal practice, only *remittitur* is allowed. If a party accepts the *remittitur/additur*, he may not thereafter *appeal*.

7. **Partial new trial:** The trial judge may grant a *partial* new trial, i.e., a retrial limited to a particular issue. Most typically, this occurs when the trial judge feels that the jury's conclusion that D is liable is reasonable, but feels that the damages awarded are inadequate or excessive — the judge can grant a new trial limited to the issue of damages. [270-71]

8. **Newly-discovered evidence:** The trial judge may grant a new trial because of *newly-discovered evidence*. The person seeking the new trial must show that: (1) the evidence was discovered since the end of the trial; (2) the movant was *"reasonably diligent"* in his search for the evidence before and during the trial, and could not reasonably have found the evidence before the end of the trial; (3) the evidence was *material*, and in fact likely to produce a different result; and (4) injustice would otherwise result. [271]

C. **Review of orders granting or denying new trial:** Both the grant of a new trial by the trial judge, and his denial of a new trial, may be reviewed upon appeal. Where the judge orders a new trial, the party who won the verdict may not appeal the new trial order, and must instead wait until the end of the new trial. [271]

X. JUDGMENT NOT WITHSTANDING VERDICT / JUDGMENT AS A MATTER OF LAW

A. **Definition:** Most states allow the judge to set aside the jury's verdict, and enter judgment for the verdict-loser. This is called a Judgment Notwithstanding Verdict, or *JNOV*. In federal practice, the device is called *"judgment as a matter of law"* (JML). [273-74]

1. **Usefulness:** Judges like the JNOV procedure better than directed verdicts, because it allows the jury to reach a verdict — then, if the judge is reversed on appeal, a new trial is not necessary (as would be the case if the trial judge erroneously directed a verdict).

B. Federal practice: Federal practice for "judgment as a matter of law" is spelled out in FRCP 50: [273-74]

1. **Motion before jury retires:** The most important thing to remember about JML in federal practice is that the party seeking the JML must make a *motion* for that judgment *before the case is submitted to the jury.* The movant also specifies why (in terms of law and facts) she thinks she is entitled to the JML. The judge reserves decision on the motion, then submits the case to the jury. If the verdict goes against the movant, and the judge agrees that no reasonable jury could have found against the movant, then the judge may effectively overturn the verdict by granting JML. [273]

2. **Appeal:** Appellate courts frequently reverse both grants and denials of JML. Since a JML is granted based on the legal sufficiency of the parties' cases, not a detailed consideration of the evidence, the appellate court is quicker to second-guess the trial judge than in the case of a motion for a new trial. [275]

XI. CONSTITUTIONAL RIGHT TO JURY TRIAL

A. Seventh Amendment: The Seventh Amendment provides that "in suits at *common law*...the right of trial by jury shall be preserved...." [275]

1. **No state application:** The Seventh Amendment has never been applicable to *state* trials, only federal ones.

2. **Federal Rule:** The Seventh Amendment does apply to all federal civil jury trials, and is incorporated in Rule 38(a).

   a. **Party must demand:** The right to a jury trial in federal practice is *not* self-executing. A party who wishes a jury trial on a particular issue must file a *demand* for that jury trial to the other parties within *10 days* after the service of the last pleading directed to that issue. (Rule 38(b).)

   b. **Equitable claim:** There is no jury trial right as to *"equitable"* claims (e.g., a claim for injunction). The distinction between legal and equitable claims is very important, and is discussed further below.

B. Law in diversity cases: In a *diversity* case, the issue of whether a party has a right of jury trial on a particular claim is to be determined by *federal*, not state, law. (*Example:* Federal principles, not local state law, are used to determined whether a particular claim is "legal" rather than "equitable," even in diversity cases.) [276]

C. Suits with both legal and equitable claims: If a case presents both *legal* and *equitable* claims, and one party wants a jury trial on the legal claims, the court must normally *try the legal claims first.* [*Beacon Theatres v. Westover*] If the court allowed the equitable claims to be tried first, without a jury, this might effectively dispose of some of the legal issues as well, thus thwarting the party's right of jury trial on the legal claims. [276-78]

> **Example:** P sues D for an injunction against certain contract violations. D counterclaims for damages for breach of contract. D demands a jury trial on its counterclaim. Assuming, as seems likely, the injunction claim is equitable and the damages counterclaim is legal, the judge must try the counterclaim to a jury *before* it conducts a bench trial of the injunction claim, as long as there may be some issues common to both claims.

D. Distinguishing "legal" vs. "equitable" claims: In deciding whether a claim is "legal" rather than "equitable," the issue is whether the claim is a claim "at common law." The main test is whether the claim is one in which the courts of law (as opposed to equity) would have recognized prior to the 1789 adoption of the Seventh Amendment. Here are the general rules for deciding this: [277]

1. **Damages:** Claims that basically involve *money damages* are almost always *legal*.

2. **Injunctions are equitable:** An action where the principal relief sought is an *injunction* will almost always be *equitable*. [278]

3. **Shareholder derivative suit:** A *shareholder's derivative* suit is either legal or equitable, depending on the status of the corporation's own suit — if the corporation's own suit would be legal, the derivative action is legal. (*Example:* P, a stockholder in X Corp., brings a derivative suit attempting to enforce X's rights against D, a former officer of X Corp., for an alleged embezzlement by D from X Corp. The suit seeks money damages. Since a suit on the same cause of action by X Corp. directly against D would be legal, P's shareholder's derivative suit is also legal. [*Ross v. Bernhard*]) [279-80]

4. **Declaratory judgment:** A *declaratory judgment* suit can be either legal or equitable, depending on the underlying issues in the suit. [278]

5. **Bankruptcy is equitable:** A claim asserted as part of *bankruptcy* proceedings will generally be treated as equitable, and will thus not involve a right to jury trial. [*Katchen v. Landy*] [281]

CHAPTER 8

MULTI-PARTY AND MULTI-CLAIM LITIGATION

I. COUNTERCLAIMS

A. Federal Rules generally: A "counterclaim" is a claim *by a defendant against a plaintiff*. The Federal Rules provide for both *"permissive"* and *"compulsory"* counterclaims. FRCP 13. [289]

1. **Permissive counterclaim:** Any defendant may bring against any plaintiff "any claim...not arising out of the transaction or occurrence that is the subject matter of the opposing party's claim." Rule 13(b). This is a *"permissive"* counterclaim. This means that no claim is too far removed from the subject of P's claim to be allowed as a counterclaim. [289]

> **Example:** P sues D in diversity for a 1989 car accident. D counterclaims for breach of a 1990 contract having nothing to do with the auto accident. D's counterclaim is allowed, and is a "permissive" one because it has nothing to do with the subject matter of P's claim against D.

2. **Compulsory counterclaim:** If a claim *does* arise "out of the *transaction or occurrence that is the subject matter of the opposing party's claim....*," it is a *"compulsory"* counterclaim. See Rule 13(a). [290]

   a. **Failure to state compulsory counterclaim:** If D does not assert her compulsory counterclaim, she will *lose* that claim in any future litigation. [290]

Example: Cars driven by P and D collide. P sues D in diversity, alleging personal injury. D makes no counterclaim. Later, D wants to bring either a federal or state suit against P for property damage sustained by D as part of the same car accident. Neither federal nor state courts will permit D to bring this action, because it arises out of the same transaction or occurrence as P's original claim — the car accident — and is thus barred since D did not assert it as a compulsory counterclaim in the initial action.

   i. **Exceptions:** There are a couple of main *exceptions* to the rule that any claim involving the same "transaction or occurrence" as P's claim is compulsory: (1) claims by D which for *"just adjudication"* require the presence of *additional parties* of whom the court *cannot get personal jurisdiction*; and (2) claims by D in which the suit against D is *in rem* or *quasi in rem* (assuming D is not making any other counterclaim in the action). See Rule 13(a), including 13(a)(2).

   b. **Default by plaintiff:** If D asserts a counterclaim (whether compulsory or permissive), and P neglects to either serve a reply or make a motion against the counterclaim, a *default judgment* may be entered against P on the counterclaim. Rule 55(d). [290]

B. **Claims by third parties:** A counterclaim may be made by *any party* against *"any opposing party."* Rule 13(a), Rule 13(b). [291]

   1. **By third-party defendant:** Thus a *third-party defendant* may counterclaim against either the original defendant, or against the original plaintiff. (In the latter case, a claim by the plaintiff against the third-party defendant must first have been made.) [291]

   2. **By plaintiff:** If D has counterclaimed against P, P may then assert a "counterclaim" against D, even though P has already asserted "regular" claims against D. In fact, P's "counter-counterclaim" will be compulsory if it relates to the same subject matter as D's counterclaim. (*Example:* P sues D about a car accident. D sues P for breach of an unrelated contract. Any claims P might have against D relating to that same contract are now compulsory counterclaims.) [291]

   3. **New parties:** *New parties* to a counterclaim can be brought into a suit. Rule 13(h). (*Example:* P sues D for an auto accident. D believes that P and X conspired to ruin D's business, in an unrelated action. D may not only counterclaim against P for this conspiracy — a permissive counterclaim — but D may bring in X as a new party to D's counterclaim.) [291]

C. **Subject-matter jurisdiction:** The *subject-matter jurisdiction* treatment of counterclaims depends on whether the counterclaim is compulsory or permissive: [292]

   1. **Compulsory counterclaim:** A *compulsory* counterclaim in a federal action is within the federal courts' *supplemental jurisdiction*. Therefore, it requires *no independent subject-matter jurisdictional grounds*.

      Example: A, a New Yorker, sues B, from Massachusetts. The suit relates to an accident involving cars driven by A and B. B, in a counterclaim, asserts that A was at fault, and that the accident caused B $30,000 of damages. A's car was owned by C, a Massachusetts resident not yet in the action whom B would also like to sue. B may bring C in as an additional party to his counterclaim. Because supplemental jurisdiction applies to B's compulsory counterclaim, and even to the entrance of the new party defending that counterclaim, the fact that B and C are not diverse, and the fact that B's counterclaim does not meet the jurisdictional amount, are irrelevant.

2. **Permissive counterclaims:** A *permissive* counterclaim is probably *not* within the court's supplemental jurisdiction, and must therefore independently satisfy the requirements of federal subject matter jurisdiction. (*Example:* Same facts as above example, except that now, B's claim against A and C does not relate to the same transaction as A's claim against B. The absence of diversity as between B and C, and the fact that B's claim does not meet the jurisdictional amount, are both fatal, so B's permissive counterclaim may not go forward against either A or C.)

D. **Statute of limitations for counterclaims:** [293-94]

1. **Time-barred when P sues:** If D's counterclaim was already *time-barred* at the time P sued, few if any federal courts will allow D to make an affirmative recovery. Some courts will allow the counterclaim to be used as a defense; the court is more likely to do this if the counterclaim is compulsory than if it is permissive.

2. **Time-barred after P sued:** Where the statute of limitations on the counterclaim runs *after* P commenced the suit, but before D asserted his counterclaim, a federal court will probably allow the counterclaim. [*Azada v. Carson*]

II. JOINDER OF CLAIMS

A. **Joinder of claims generally:** *Once a party has made a claim against some other party*, he may then make *any other claim he wishes against that party*. Rule 18(a). (*Example:* P sues D, claiming that D intentionally assaulted and battered him. P may join to this claim a claim that D owes P money on a contract entirely unrelated to the tort.) [296]

1. **Never required:** Joinder of claims is *never required* by Rule 18(a), but is left at the claimant's option. (However, the rules on former adjudication, especially the rule against splitting a cause of action, may cause a claimant to lose the ability to bring the unasserted claim in a later suit.)

2. **Subject-matter jurisdiction not affected:** *Supplemental* jurisdiction probably does *not* apply to a claim joined with another under Rule 18(a). Thus the requirements of subject-matter jurisdiction must be *independently satisfied* by the joined claim. However, usually there will not be a subject-matter jurisdiction problem for joinder of claims (since diversity will not be affected, and since P may add all claims together for purposes of meeting the $50,000 requirement, under the aggregation doctrine).

III. JOINDER OF PARTIES

A. **Permissive joinder:** Joinder under Rule 20, done at the discretion of the plaintiffs, is called *"permissive"* joinder. ("Compulsory" joinder under Rule 19 is described below.) FRCP 20 allows two types of permissive joinder of parties: (1) the right of *multiple plaintiffs* to join together; and (2) a plaintiff's right to make several parties *co-defendants* to her claim. [298-300]

1. **Joinder of plaintiffs:** Multiple *plaintiffs* may join together in an action if they satisfy two tests: [298]

   a. **Single transaction or occurrence:** Their claims for relief must arise from a *single "transaction, occurrence, or series of transactions or occurrences,"* and

   b. **Common questions:** There must be a *question of law or fact common to all plaintiffs* which will arise in the action.

Note: Normally, permissive joinder is "voluntary." That is, if P1 wants P2 to join in the action, but P2 does not want to join, P1 cannot compel P2 to come in as a co-plaintiff. There is a limited exception for "involuntary plaintiffs." [298]

2. **Joinder of defendants:** If one or more plaintiffs have a claim against *multiple defendants*, these defendants may be joined based on the same two tests as plaintiff-joinder. That is, claims against the co-defendants must: (a) arise from a *single "transaction*, occurrence, or series of transactions or occurrences"; and (b) contain a *common question* of law or fact. [298]

   a. **At plaintiff's option:** Joinder of multiple defendants is at the *option of the plaintiff* or plaintiffs.

B. **Jurisdiction in permissive joinder cases:** [299-300]

1. **Personal jurisdiction:** Where joinder of multiple *defendants* is involved, the requirements of personal jurisdiction must be met with regard to *each defendant individually*. That is: [299]

   a. **Service:** Each D must be *personally served*;

   b. **Contacts:** Each D must individually fall within the *in personam jurisdiction* of the court (by having "minimum contacts"); and

   c. **Long-arm limits:** Each D must be *"amenable"* to suit. Since federal courts in diversity suits follow the long-arm of the state where they sit, if a potential co-defendant cannot be reached by the state long-arm, he cannot be part of the federal diversity action even if he has the requisite minimum contacts. (But in federal question suits, it doesn't matter that the state long-arm can't reach D.)

2. **Subject-matter jurisdiction:** There is *no supplemental jurisdiction* for Rule 20 joinder. Thus all parties (whether plaintiffs or defendants) joined under Rule 20 must meet federal *subject-matter jurisdiction* requirements. [299-300]

   a. **Complete diversity:** Thus if diversity is the basis, there must be *complete* diversity, with no state represented on both sides of the action. (*Example:* P, from Massachusetts, may not join as co-defendants D1, from New York, and D2, from Massachusetts, in a diversity action.)

   b. **Aggregation:** It is not clear whether *multiple plaintiffs* may *aggregate* their claims to meet the jurisdictional amount in a diversity case. If no plaintiff meets this amount, aggregation is not allowed. If one or more does, but others do not, it is not clear whether either the aggregation doctrine or supplemental jurisdiction will allow the less-than-$50,000 plaintiffs to be part of the action.

      i. **Each defendant must meet:** If the Rule 20 joinder involves *multiple defendants*, supplemental jurisdiction definitely does *not* apply, so *each D* in a diversity case must have claims against him equal to $50,000.

C. **Compulsory joinder:** There are certain situations in which additional parties *must* be joined, assuming the requirements of jurisdiction can be met. Such joinder, specified by Rule 19, is called *"compulsory"* joinder. The basic idea is that a party must be joined if it would be uneconomical or unfair to litigate a claim without her. [300-305]

1. **Two categories:** There are two categories of parties who must be joined where possible: [300]

a. **"Necessary" parties:** The "less vital" group consists of parties: (1) who must be joined if this can be done; but (2) in whose absence because of jurisdictional problems the action will nonetheless be permitted to go forward. These parties are called *"necessary"* parties. See Rule 19(a).

b. **"Indispensable" parties:** The second, "more vital" group consists of parties who are so vital that if their joinder is impossible for jurisdictional reasons, the whole action must be *dropped*. These are called *"indispensable"* parties. See Rule 19(b).

2. **"Necessary" defined:** A party is "necessary" — and must be joined if jurisdictionally possible — if the party is not "indispensable" (defined below) *and either* of the two following tests is met: [300]

   a. **Incomplete relief:** In the person's absence, *complete relief* cannot be accorded among those already parties; or

   b. **Impaired interest:** The absentee has an interest relating to the action, and trying the case without the absentee will either *impair the absentee's interest* or leave one of the people already parties subject to *multiple or inconsistent obligations*.

   Example: P, a Californian, sues D, a bank, which is holding stock P says P owns. D is incorporated and based in Oregon. D knows that X, a citizen of Nevada, asserts a conflicting claim to own the stock. X will almost certainly be found to be at least a "necessary" party — if the P-D suit is decided without X, P could obtain title, yet a later X-D suit might find that X should have title, leaving D with multiple inconsistent obligations and perhaps leaving X without a real remedy. Therefore, X must be joined, probably as a co-defendant.

3. **"Indispensable" defined:** If a party meets the test for "necessary" given in paragraph (2) above, but the party's joinder is *impossible* because of jurisdictional problems, the court has to decide whether the party is *"indispensable."* [301]

   a. **Consequence of indispensability:** If the party is "indispensable," then the action must be *dismissed* in that party's absence.

   b. **Factors:** When the court decides whether a party is "indispensable," the factors are: (1) the extent of *prejudice* to the absentee, or to those already parties; (2) the possibility of framing the judgment so as to *mitigate* such prejudice; (3) the *adequacy* of a *remedy* that can be granted in the party's absence; and (4) whether the plaintiff will have an adequate remedy if the action is dismissed. Rule 19(b).

   Example: P sues D, a bank holding some stock. P alleges that although the stock is registered solely in the name of X, P and X in fact co-own the stock. P and D are citizens of different states, but X is a citizen of the same state as P. X thus cannot be joined as a co-defendant, because his presence would destroy diversity. The issue is whether X is "necessary" or "indispensable."

   Held: (1) X is definitely a person who must be joined if feasible under Rule 19(a), because his absence will expose D to the risk of double obligation — a judgment that P owns the stock will not bind X, who can later sue D for the whole value of the stock; (2) X is in fact "indispensable" — his presence is so important that the suit must be dismissed rather than proceed in X's absence. Continuing the suit might prejudice D's interests; there is no way to adjust the decree to protect either D or X since the issue is title; and P will have an adequate remedy (a new state court action) if the action is dismissed. [*Haas v. Jefferson Bank*] [303]

4. **Jurisdiction:** Where a non-party is one who must be "joined if feasible," the doctrine of *supplemental jurisdiction* does *not* apply to overcome any jurisdictional problems. So if the person who is sought to be joined as a defendant is not diverse with all plaintiffs, or if the claim against that would-be defendant does not meet the amount-in-controversy requirement in a diversity case, the joinder may not take place. [301]

IV. CLASS ACTIONS

A. **Definition:** The class action is a procedure whereby a single person or small group of co-parties may *represent* a larger group, or *"class,"* of persons sharing a *common interest*. [309]

1. **Jurisdiction:** In the class action, *only the representatives* must satisfy the requirements of personal jurisdiction, subject-matter jurisdiction, and venue. (*Example:* P1 and P2 are the named co-plaintiffs who bring a diversity class action against D. There are 2,000 non-named class members. Only P1 and P2 must meet the requirements of diversity vis-a-vis D, so the fact that many non-named plaintiffs are citizens of the same state as D is irrelevant.)

2. **Binding on absentees:** The results of a class action are generally *binding on the absent members*. Therefore, all kinds of procedural rules (discussed below) exist to make sure that these absentees receive *due process* (e.g., they must receive notice of the action, and notice of any proposed settlement).

3. **Defendant class:** In federal practice, as well as in states permitting class actions, the class may be composed *either* of plaintiffs or defendants. The vast majority of the time, the class will be composed of plaintiffs. [309]

B. **Rule 23 generally:** The federal procedures for *class actions* are spelled out in FRCP 23. [310]

1. **Four prerequisites:** *Four prerequisites* (discussed below) must be met before there is any possibility of a class action.

2. **Three categories:** Once these prerequisites are met, a class action will still not be allowed unless the action fits into one of *three categories*, represented by Rule 23(b)(1), 23(b)(2), and 23(b)(3).

C. **Prerequisites:** Here are the four prerequisites which must be met before any federal class action is allowed: [310-11]

1. **Size:** The class must *so large* that joinder of all members is impractical. Nearly all class actions involve a class of at least 25 members, and most involve substantially more (potentially tens of thousands). The more *geographically dispersed* the claimants are, the fewer are needed to satisfy the size requirement. [310]

2. **Common questions:** There must be *"questions of law or fact common to the class."* This is seldom a problem. [310]

3. **Typical claims:** The claims or defenses of the representatives must be *"typical"* of those of the class. This requirement of "typicality" is also rarely a problem. [310-11]

4. **Fair representation:** Finally, the representatives must show that they can *"fairly and adequately protect the interests of the class."* Thus the representatives must not have any *conflict of interest* with the absent class members, and they must furnish *competent legal*

counsel to fight the suit. Even after the suit, the adequacy of representation can be attacked by an absent class member who now wants to be exempted from an adverse judgment in the class action. [311]

D. Three categories: As noted, there are three categories of class actions, all of which must meet the four prerequisites listed above. They are covered in Rules 23(b)(1), 23(b)(2) and 23(b)(3). [313-16]

   1. 23(b)(1) actions: The first of the three categories, **23(b)(1)**, applies to situations similar to the circumstances requiring the *joinder of necessary parties* under Rule 19. [313-14]

      a. Test: A class action is allowed under 23(b)(1) if individual actions by or against members of the class would create a *risk* of either: (a) *inconsistent decisions* forcing an opponent of the class to observe *incompatible standards of conduct* (Rule 23(b)(1)(A)); or (b) the *impairment of the interests* of the members of the class who are not actually parties to the individual actions (23(b)(1)(B)).

      Example: Taxpayers residing in City XYZ are unhappy with a municiple bond issue by XYZ. Some taxpayers want the issue declared invalid; others want merely to have the terms of the issue changed. If each taxpayer brought his own action, as the result of one suit XYZ might have to refrain from floating the issue altogether, but as the result of the other suit might just be forced to limit the size of the issue. XYZ thus faces a risk of incompatible standards of conduct. Therefore, a Rule 23(b)(1) action would be suitable on these facts.

      b. No opting out: Members of the 23(b)(1) class *may not "opt out" of the class*. Any absentee will therefore *necessarily be bound* by the decision in the suit.

      c. Mass tort claims: Courts are increasingly allowing use of the 23(b)(1) class action in *mass tort cases*, where there are so many claims that D may be *insolvent* before later claimants can collect. See the further discussion of this topic *infra*, p. C-70.

      Example: Tens of thousands of women may have been injured by breast implants manufactured by D. If each brings an individual suit, D's financial resources may be exhausted, leaving nothing for those who bring suit later. A federal court might therefore hold that a 23(b)(1) action is suitable for determining, once and for all, whether D sold a defective device and whether it typically caused a certain type of medical injury. Each P would then have a separate claim on causation and damages only. [314]

   2. 23(b)(2) actions: The second category, 23(b)(2), allows use of a class action if "the party opposing the class has acted or refused to act on *grounds generally applicable to the class*, thereby making appropriate final injunctive relief or … declaratory relief with respect to the class as a whole." In other words, if the suit is for an *injunction* or declaration that would affect all class members, (b)(2) is probably the right category. [314-15]

      a. Civil rights case: The main use of 23(b)(2) is for *civil rights cases*, where the class says that it has been discriminated against, and seeks an *injunction* prohibiting further discrimination. (*Example:* A class action is brought on behalf of all black employees of XYZ Corp., alleging that executives of XYZ have paid them less money and given them fewer promotions than white employees. The suit seeks an injunction against further discrimination, as well as money damages. This would be an appropriate suit for a 23(b)(2) class action.)

C A P S U L E   S U M M A R Y

b. No opt-out: Members of a 23(b)(2) class may not *"opt out"* of the class. See Rule 23(c)(3).

3. 23(b)(3) actions: The final type of class action is given in Rule *23(b)(3)*. This is the *most common* type. [315-16]

    a. Two requirements: The court must make *two findings* for a (b)(3) class action:

        i. Common questions: The court must find that the "questions of law or fact *common* to members of the class *predominate* over any questions affecting only individual members…"; and

        ii. Superior method: The court must also find that "a class action is *superior to other available methods*" for deciding the controversy. In deciding "superiority," the court will consider four factors listed in 23(b)(3), including: (1) the interest of class members in *individually controlling* their separate actions; (2) the presence of any suits that have *already been commenced* involving class members; (3) the desirability of *concentrating the litigation* of the claims in a *particular forum*; and (4) any difficulties likely to be encountered in the *management* of a class action.

    b. Securities cases: (b)(3) class actions are especially common in *securities fraud* cases, and in *antitrust* cases.

    c. Mass torts: (b)(3) actions are sometimes brought in *mass tort* cases (e.g., airline crashes) and mass *product liability* cases (e.g., mass pharmaceutical cases). But many courts still frown on (b)(3) class action status for such suits, because individual elements typically predominate. See *infra*, C-70.

E. Requirement of notice: Absent class members (i.e., those other than the representatives) must almost always be given *notice* of the fact that the suit is pending. [316-17]

1. When required: The Federal Rules explicitly require notice only in *(b)(3)* actions. But courts generally hold that notice is required in (b)(1) and (b)(2) actions as well.

    a. Individual notice: *Individual* notice, almost always *by mail*, must be given to all those class members whose names and addresses can be obtained with *reasonable effort*. This is true even if there are millions of class members, each with only small amounts at stake. [*Eisen v. Carlisle & Jacquelin*] [316]

    b. Publication notice: For those class members whose names and addresses cannot be obtained with reasonable effort, *publication* notice will usually be sufficient.

2. Contents: The most important things notice does is to tell the claimant that he may *opt out* of the class if he wishes (in a (b)(3), but not (b)(1) or (b)(2), action); and that the judgment will affect him, favorably or unfavorably, unless he opts out.

3. Cost: The cost of both *identifying* and *notifying* each class member must normally be borne by the *representative plaintiffs*. If the plaintiff side is unwilling to bear this cost, the case must be *dismissed*. [*Eisen v. Carlisle*; *Oppenheimer Fund v. Sanders*] [317]

F. Binding effect: Judgment in a class action is *binding*, whether it is *for or against the class*, on all those whom the court finds to be members of the class. [317]

1. Exclusion: In the case of a (b)(3) action, a person may *opt out*, i.e., exclude himself, from the action, by notifying the court to that effect prior to a date specified in the notice of the action sent to him. A person who opts out of the action will not be bound by an adverse judgment, but conversely may not assert collateral estoppel to take advantage of a judgment favorable to the class. (Absent class members in (b)(1) and (b)(2) actions do *not* have the right to opt out and thereafter bring their own suit.)

G. Amount in controversy: Only the named representatives of a class have to meet the requirements of *diversity* and *venue*. However, *every member of the class* must satisfy the applicable *amount in controversy* requirement. [318]

   1. Diversity: Thus in *diversity* cases, each member of the class must have more than $50,000 at stake. [*Zahn v. International Paper Co.*] This obviously makes diversity class actions difficult to bring (but has not stood in the way of such actions in mass-tort cases).

   2. Federal question suits: In federal question cases, there is no general amount in controversy requirement, so the problem does not arise.

H. Certification and denial of class status: Soon after an action purporting to be a class action is brought, the court must decide whether to *"certify"* the action. By certifying, the court agrees that the class action requirements have been met, and allows the suit to go forward as a class action. If the court refuses to certify the action: [319-20]

   1. Continued by representative: The suit may still be continued by the "representatives," but with no *res judicata* effect for or against the absent would-be class members. Usually, the representatives will not want to proceed on this non-class-action basis. [319]

   2. Sub-class: Alternatively, the suit may be continued by a *sub-class* of the original class. If so, *res judicata* extends to the members of the sub-class, but not to the other members of the original class. [319]

   3. No appeal: The denial of class action status may *not* be immediately appealed, because it is not deemed to be a *"final order."* [*Coopers & Lybrand v. Livesay*] [319]

I. Settlements: Any proposed *settlement* of the class action must be *approved by the court*. FRCP 23(e). The court will approve the settlement only if it is convinced that the interests of the absent class members have been adequately protected (e.g., that settlement is not being urged by greedy contingent-fee lawyers who will pocket most of the settlement money). [320]

   1. Notice requirement: If the class has already been certified, *notice* of any proposed settlement must be given to *each class member*.

J. Attorneys' fees: The court may award *reasonable attorneys fees* to the lawyers for the class. These fees are generally in rough proportion to the size of the recovery on behalf of the class. [320]

   1. Federal statute requires: In the usual case of a class action brought under a *federal statute*, attorneys fees may be awarded *only if a federal statute so provides*. [*Alyeska Pipeline Service Co. v. Wilderness Society.*] Congress has authorized attorneys fees for many important federal statutes that are frequently the subject of class action suits (e.g., civil rights and securities law).

K. Mass tort cases: Class actions have begun to be used increasingly in *"mass tort"* cases. [321-27]

   1. Definition of "mass tort":   Mass torts fall into two categories. In a *"mass accident,"* a large number of persons are injured as a result of a single accident. (*Examples:* an airplane crash, the collapse of a building, or the explosion of a factory accompanied by the release of toxic substances.) In a *"mass product liability"* case, a *defective product* is sold to thousands of buyers, who are thereby injured. [321]

2. **Modern trend towards accepting class status:** Courts have grown increasingly willing to grant class certification in mass accident and mass product liability situations. [324]

   a. **b(1) mandatory class actions:** Courts often certify actions as *b(1) "mandatory"* class actions rather than b(3) "common question" optional class actions. Courts are especially likely to certify a class action where there are so many thousands of claimants that there is reason to believe that D (or even all D's taken collectively) will be *insolvent* before the last claimants have recovered, and that what is at issue is thus a *"limited fund"*. [324]

      i. **Punitive damages:** Where early claimants seek *punitive damages*, the case for (b)(1) "limited fund" certification is especially strong. The size of the punitive damage award bears no foreseeable relation to the size of a compensatory damage award, so just a few very successful early punitive-damage claimants can wipe out a small or midsized defendant. [324]

   b. **Common questions don't predominate:** If the court believes that individual questions of law or fact predominate, rather than common questions, the court won't grant class certification. (*Example:* If the suit involves a defective prescription drug, a court might deny certification on the grounds that each plaintiff would present a separate case as to proximate cause of injury, damages, affirmative defenses like assumption of risk, etc.)

   c. **Amount in controversy:** Nearly all mass tort actions are brought as diversity, rather than federal question, cases (since they are based on state tort law). Recall that under the *Zahn* decision, each claimant in a federal diversity class action must have a claim of at least $50,000. Most courts have held that this requirement is *satisfied* by each class member who has a personal injury claim, even if that person's likely recovery is less than $50,000.

V. INTERVENTION

A. **Intervention generally:** By the doctrine of *"intervention,"* certain persons who are not initially part of a lawsuit may enter the suit *on their own initiative*. The person who intervenes is called an "intervenor." [332]

   1. **Two forms:** In federal suits, FRCP 24 creates two forms of intervention:

      a. *"Intervention of right"* (Rule 24(a)); and

      b. *"Permissive intervention"* (Rule 24(b)).

   2. **Distinction:** Where the intervention is "of right," *no leave of court* is required for the party's entry into the case. Where the facts are such that only "permissive" intervention is possible, it is up to the court's *discretion* whether to allow intervention.

B. **Intervention of right:** [332-34]

   1. **Three tests:** A stranger to an existing action may intervene *"of right,"* under Rule 24(a), if she meets *all* of the three following criteria: [332]

      a. **Interest in subject-matter:** She must "claim an interest relating to the *property or transaction* which is the *subject* of the action";

C
A
P
S
U
L
E

S
U
M
M
A
R
Y

b. Impaired interest: She must be "so situated that the disposition of the action may as a *practical matter impair or impede [her] ability to protect that interest*"; and

c. Inadequate representation: She must show that this interest is *not "adequately represented by existing parties."*

Note: Even if the outsider cannot meet one or more of these criteria, she may nonetheless automatically intervene under Rule 24(a) if a federal *statute* gives her such a right. (*Example:* The U.S. may intervene in any action involving the constitutionality of an act of Congress.) [333]

Example: P (the U.S. government) sues D, a local Board of Education, charging that D has drawn school boundaries on racially-discriminatory lines. X, the parent of a black public school student attending D's schools, wants to intervene. Probably X's intervention will be of right, since X has an interest in the subject-matter, and his ability to bring his own action in the future will be compromised if the U.S. loses the case. X will have to show that the U.S. may not adequately represent X's interest, which he can do by showing that the U.S. may be pursuing other objectives, such as settling a lot of suits quickly.

2. Jurisdiction: *Independent subject-matter* jurisdictional grounds are *required* for intervention of right in a diversity case. In other words, such intervention does not fall within the court's *supplemental* jurisdiction. [334]

Example: P, from California, sues D, from New York, in a diversity suit. X, from New York, would like to intervene. Even if the court concludes that the requirements of intervention of right are met by X, X cannot intervene because there is no supplemental jurisdiction for intervention of right; after X's intervention there would have to be complete diversity, and this would not be the case since X and D are both citizens of New York.

C. Permissive intervention: For a person to seek *"permissive intervention,"* she merely has to have a "claim or defense" that involves a *"question of law or fact in common" with the pending action.* [334]

1. Discretion: Where the outsider seeks permissive intervention, it is up to the trial court's *discretion* whether to allow the intervention. The trial court's decision — whichever way it goes — is rarely reversed on appeal.

2. Jurisdiction: Like any intervenor of right, a permissive intervenor in a diversity case must independently meet federal subject-matter jurisdictional requirements. (*Example:* There must be diversity between the intervenor and all defendants.) [334]

VI. INTERPLEADER

A. Definition: Interpleader allows a party who owes something to one of two or more other persons, but is not sure whom, to force the other parties to argue out their claims among themselves. The technique is designed to allow the "stakeholder" to avoid being made to pay the same claim twice. [336]

Example: X and Y both claim a bank account at Bank. Y demands the money from Bank. If Bank had to litigate against Y, and then possibly defend a second suit brought by X, Bank might have to pay the amount of the account twice. By using the interpleader doctrine, Bank can force X and Y to litigate between themselves as to the ownership of the account, with Bank paying only the winner.

C
A
P
S
U
L
E

S
U
M
M
A
R
Y

1. **Federal practice:** In federal practice, *two* kinds of interpleader are allowed:

   a. *"Statutory interpleader"* under 28 U.S.C. §1335; and

   b. *"Rule interpleader"* under FRCP 22.

B. **Federal statutory interpleader:** 28 U.S.C. §1335 allows a person holding property which *is* or *may be* claimed by two or more "adverse claimants" to interplead those claimants. [338-40]

   1. **Jurisdictional benefits:** The main benefits to the stakeholder from using statutory interpleader instead of Rule interpleader relate to *jurisdiction* and *service*: [338]

      a. **Nationwide service:** *Nationwide service of process* is allowed in statutory interpleader actions. See 28 U.S.C. §2361. Thus the court where the stakeholder files a statutory interpleader suit may serve its process on any claimant, *no matter where in the U.S. that claimant resides or is found*.

      b. **Diversity:** Diversity is satisfied as long as *some two claimants are citizens of different states*. (*Example:* Two New York residents and a Californian all claim the proceeds of a particular insurance policy. Since either New Yorker and the Californian form a diverse pair, the diversity requirement for statutory interpleader is satisfied. The citizenship of the insurance company is irrelevant.)

      c. **Amount in controversy:** The property which is the subject of the suit must merely exceed *$500* in value, in contrast to the usual $50,000.

   2. **How commenced:** A statutory interpleader suit is commenced by the *stakeholder*. The stakeholder must, to begin the suit, *deposit into court* the amount of the property in question, or post a *bond* for that amount. [339]

      a. **Right to deny debt:** Even though the stakeholder must deposit the amount of the property with the court, he is not estopped from claiming at trial that he does *not owe the money to any claimant at all*. [339]

   3. **Restraint on other suits:** Once the statutory interpleader suit is begun, the court may *restrain all claimants* from starting or continuing any other action, in any state or federal suit, which would affect the property. (*Example:* On the facts of the above example, the court could prevent the two New Yorkers and the Californian from starting any state action to collect on the policy.) [339]

C. **Rule interpleader:** FRCP 22 provides an interpleader remedy for any person who "is or may be exposed to double or multiple liability." This is so-called *"Rule interpleader."* The stakeholder may invoke interpleader by coming into court on his own initiative (i.e., as plaintiff), or by counterclaiming or cross-claiming as *defendant* in an action already commenced against him by one claimant. [340]

   1. **Jurisdiction:** The main difference between statutory interpleader and Rule interpleader is that *Rule 22 interpleader has no effect on ordinary jurisdictional and venue requirements*.

      a. **Complete diversity:** Thus *diversity* must be *complete* between the stakeholder on one hand and all claimants on the other (assuming there is no federal question). (*Example:* Two New Yorkers and a Californian all claim a particular insurance policy, which is issued by a California-based insurer. Rule 22 interpleader cannot be used, because it is not the case that all claimants are of different citizenship than the insurer.)

    b. Service: Service of process must be carried out as in any other diversity action — that is, within the state where the district court sits, or pursuant to the long-arm of the state. There is *no "nationwide service of process"* as in statutory interpleader.

    c. Amount in controversy: The *$50,000* amount in controversy requirement must be met.

  2. No deposit: The stakeholder is *not required* to *deposit* the property or money into the court (as she is in statutory interpleader).

  3. Denial of liability: The stakeholder may "aver that the plaintiff is not liable in whole or in part to any or all of the claimants." FRCP 22(1). In other words, the stakeholder may *deny liability*.

VII. REAL PARTY IN INTEREST

A. Generally: FRCP 17, and most states, require that a complaint be in the name of the *"real party in interest."* This means, for instance, that an *assignee* — a person to whom the original holder of a claim assigned that claim — must sue in the assignee's own name. [343]

  1. Subrogation: This "real party in interest" rule covers *subrogation*. An insurer who has compensated its policy holder may sue the tortfeasor in lieu of suit by the policy holder — but the insurance company must sue in its own name, not in the name of the policy holder.

  2. Representatives: Executors, administrators, bailees and other *representatives* are considered to be themselves "real parties in interest." Therefore, they may bring suit in their own names, not in the names of persons they represent (e.g., the estate). But the *citizenship* of the *represented party* (e.g., the estate) generally controls for diversity purposes.

VIII. THIRD-PARTY PRACTICE (IMPLEADER)

A. Impleader right generally: A defendant who believes that a third person is *liable to him* "for all or part of the plaintiff's claim against [the defendant]" may "*implead* such a person as a *'third party defendant.'* " FRCP 14(a). [343]

> **Example:** Victim is injured when a van driven by Employee and owned by Employer runs her over. Victim brings a diversity action against Employer, on a *respondeat superior* theory. Employer believes that if Employer is required to pay a judgment to Victim, Employee, under common law indemnity rules, will be required to reimburse Employer. Instead of waiting until the end of the Victim-Employer suit, Employer may instead "implead" Employee. That is, Employer (the third-party plaintiff or TPP) brings Employee into the action as a "third party defendant" (TPD), so that in a single action, the court may conclude that Employer owes Victim, and that Employee owes indemnity to Employer.

B. Claim must be derivative: For a third-party claim to be valid, the TPP may not claim that the TPD is the *only* one liable to the plaintiff, and that he himself is not liable at all. (*Examples:* Impleader works for claims for *indemnity*, *subrogation*, *contribution* and *breach of warranty*, since as to each of these, the TPD is liable only if the TPP is liable.) [344]

  1. Alternative pleading: However, the TPP is not precluded from claiming in an *alternative* pleading that neither she nor the TPD is liable.

2. **Partial claim:** Also, the TPP may allege that only a *portion* of the recovery is due from the TPD. (*Example:* If TPP claims that TPD is liable for "contribution" rather than "indemnity," TPP will recover from TPD at most only part of any judgment that TPP owes to P.)

C. **Leave of court:** Leave of court is *not* necessary for impleader, as long as the TPP serves a summons and complaint on a TPD within *10 days* after the time the TPP served his answer to P's claim. FRCP 14(a), second sentence. After this 10-day period, however, the court's permission to implead is necessary. [344]

D. **Impleader by plaintiff:** Just as the defendant may implead a TPD, so a *plaintiff* against whom a *counterclaim* is filed may implead a third person who is liable to him for any judgment on the counterclaim. FRCP 14(b). [344]

E. **Jurisdictional requirements relaxed:** Both personal and subject-matter *jurisdictional* requirements are *relaxed* with respect to the third-party claim: [344]

1. **100-mile bulge:** Service of the third-party complaint may be made anywhere within the *100-mile bulge* surrounding the courthouse, even if the place of service is outside the state and is beyond the scope of the local long-arm. FRCP 4(k)(1)(B). [344]

   Example: In the above Victim/Employer/Employee example, if the suit is pending in the Southern District of New York (Manhattan), Employee could be served in Newark, New Jersey, even if the New York State long-arm would not reach him.

2. **Supplemental jurisdiction:** A third-party claim falls within the court's *supplemental jurisdiction*. Thus the TPD's citizenship is unimportant, and no amount-in-controversy requirement must be satisfied. [345]

3. **Venue:** Similarly, if *venue* is proper between the original parties, it remains valid regardless of the residence of the TPD. [345]

F. **Additional claims involving the TPD:** [345-47]

1. **Claim by TPD:** Once a TPD has been impleaded, she may make *claims of her own*, including: (1) counterclaims against the TPP (either permissive or compulsory); (2) cross-claims against any other TPDs; (3) any claim against the original plaintiff, but only if it arises out of the same transaction or occurrence that is the subject of the plaintiff's claim against the TPP; (4) any counterclaim against the original plaintiff, if the original plaintiff has made a claim against the TPD; and (5) impleader claims against persons not previously part of the suit, if these persons may be liable to the TPD for all or part of the TPP's claim against the TPD. [345]

   a. **Supplemental jurisdiction:** All of the above kinds of claims, except permissive counterclaims, fall within the court's *supplemental jurisdiction*, and thus need no independent federal subject-matter jurisdictional grounds.

   b. **Defenses:** A TPD may also raise against the original plaintiff the same *defenses* that the original defendant could have raised.

2. **Claims by original plaintiff:** The original plaintiff may assert any claims against the TPD arising out of the transaction or occurrence that is the subject-matter of that plaintiff's claim against the TPP. [346]

   a. **Jurisdiction:** A claim by a plaintiff against the TPD must *independently satisfy jurisdictional requirements* — supplemental jurisdiction does not apply in this situation.

C
A
P
S
U
L
E

S
U
M
M
A
R
Y

(*Example:* In a diversity case, the original plaintiff's claim against the TPD must be supported by diversity between the plaintiff and the TPD, and that claim must satisfy the $50,000 amount in controversy.)

G. Dismissal of main claim: If the main claim is *dismissed* before or during trial, the court has *discretion* whether to hear the third-party claims relating to it (assuming that these are within the court's supplemental jurisdiction, as they will be in the case of an ordinary impleader claim). [347]

IX. CROSS-CLAIMS

A. Definition: A claim by a party against a *co-party* is called a *"cross-claim."* A cross-claim is made only against a party who is on the *same side* of an already-existing claim (e.g., a claim by one co-defendant against another, or by one co-plaintiff against another). [350]

B. Requirements: A cross-claim must meet two main requirements: [350]

1. **Transaction requirements:** It must have arisen out of the *"transaction or occurrence"* that is the subject of the original action or the subject of a counterclaim. FRCP 13(g). (A cross-claim is thus comparable to a compulsory counterclaim, in terms of how closely related it must be to the original claim.)

2. **Actual relief:** The cross-claim must ask for *actual relief* from the co-party against whom it is directed. (*Example:* D1 claims that he is blameless, and that D2 is the one who should be liable for all of P's claims. This is not a cross-claim, since D1 is not asking for actual relief from D2 — instead, D1 is merely asserting a defense.)

C. Not compulsory: A cross-claim, no matter how closely related it is to the subject of the existing action, is *never compulsory*. [350]

D. Jurisdiction: Cross-claims are within the *supplemental jurisdiction* of the court, and thus need no independent jurisdictional grounds. [350]

CHAPTER 9

FORMER ADJUDICATION

I. GENERAL PRINCIPLES

A. Former adjudication generally: There is a set of rules that prevents re-litigation of claims and issues; the set is sometimes collectively called the doctrine of *"res judicata"* (Latin for "things which have been decided"). [358]

1. **Two categories:** There are two main categories of rules governing re-litigation:

   a. **Merger and bar:** One set of rules prevents a *claim* (or "cause of action") from being re-litigated. These rules are collectively called the rules of *claim preclusion*. They break down into two sub-rules:

   i. **Merger:** Under the rule of *"merger,"* if P *wins* the first action, his claim is "merged" into his judgment. He cannot later sue the same D on the same cause of action for higher damages.

ii. **Bar:** Under the doctrine of *"bar,"* if P *loses* his first action, his claim is extinguished, and he is barred from suing again on that cause of action.

b. **Collateral estoppel:** The second main set of rules prevents re-litigation of a particular *issue of fact or law.* When a particular issue of fact or law has been determined in one proceeding, then in a subsequent proceeding between the same parties, *even on a different cause of action*, each party is *"collaterally estopped"* from claiming that that issue should have been decided differently than it was in the first action. This is known as the doctrine of "collateral estoppel" or *"issue preclusion"*.

i. **Use by stranger:** Today, even one who is not a party to the first action (a *"stranger* to the first action") may in some circumstances assert in the second suit that her adversary, who was a party to the first action, is collaterally estopped from re-litigating an issue of fact or law decided in that first action.

B. **Applicable only to new actions:** The rules discussed in this "Former Adjudication" chapter apply only to *new actions* subsequent to the action in which the original judgment was rendered — they do not apply to *further proceedings* in the same action in which the original judgment was rendered. (*Examples:* These rules do not apply to a party seeking a *new trial*, or to one seeking to have a judgment reversed on *appeal.*) [359]

C. **Privies:** The rules of claim preclusion and collateral estoppel apply not only to the parties to the first action, but also to other persons who are said to be in *"privity"* with the litigants in the other action. [359]

> **Example:** Victim is injured when hit by a van driven by Employee and owned by Employer. Victim sues Employer under *respondeat superior.* Employer notifies Employee of the latter's right to control the defense, but Employee does nothing. Victim gets a judgment against Employer, but Employer goes bankrupt before Victim can collect. Victim then sues Employee. Employee, as an indemnitor of Employer, will be covered by the same rules of claim preclusion and collateral estoppel in the Victim-Employee suit as Employer would be in a new suit by Victim. Therefore, Employee will be collaterally estopped from denying that he was at fault.

II. CLAIM PRECLUSION (MERGER AND BAR)

A. **Definition:** If a judgment is rendered for the plaintiff, his claim is "merged" into the judgment — the claim is extinguished and a new claim to enforce the judgment is created. If a judgment is for the defendant on the merits, the claim is extinguished and nothing new is created; plaintiff is "barred" from raising the claim again. [359]

> **Example 1:** P sues D for $1,000 damages resulting from an automobile accident. The verdict and judgment grant P only $500. His claim, or cause of action, is "merged," meaning that P cannot start a new suit for the other $500.

> **Example 2:** Same as Example 1, but D is found not to be liable at all. P is now "barred" from making the same claim in a second suit against D.

B. **No claim-splitting:** The basic concept of claim preclusion is that a judgment is conclusive with respect to the *entire "claim"* which it adjudicates. Consequently, P *may not split her claim* — if she sues upon *any portion* of the claim, the other aspects of that claim are merged in her judgment if she wins, and barred if she loses. [360-61]

Example: P believes that D has breached a contract with him, and that P has lost $100,000 as a result. If P sues for $25,000 and loses, P may not bring a second suit for the other $75,000. The same is true if P wins the $25,000 — the rule is "one suit per claim."

1. **Installment contracts:** Where the claim relates to payments due under a *lease* or *installment contract*, generally P must sue at the same time for *all payments* due at the time the suit is filed. (*Example:* If Tenant is six months behind in the rent at the time Landlord brings suit, Landlord must sue for the entire six months at once — any months missed that are not sued for when the suit is brought are waived.) [360]

2. **Personal and property damage from accident:** Today, most states hold that claims for *personal injuries* arising from an auto accident are part of the *same cause of action* as a claim for *property damage* sustained in the same accident. Thus generally, P must bring a single suit for property damage and personal injuries from a given accident. [363]

3. **Multi-theory actions:** The rule against splitting a claim also applies where P has several claims, all arising from the same set of facts, but involving *different theories* or remedies. The modern rule is that there will be merger or bar of all of P's rights against D with respect to all or any part of the *transaction*, or series of connected transactions, out of which the action arose. [361-62]

   Example: P works for D, and is then fired. P sues D for breach of an alleged oral contract promising two years of employment. P loses. P then sues D, alleging the same facts, and asserting the right to recover in *quantum meruit* for the reasonable value of services he performed for D. A modern court would probably hold that the two suits related to a single transaction or series of transactions, and that the first judgment against P therefore barred him from bringing the second suit.

   a. **Equitable/legal distinction:** A demand for *legal* relief (generally, money damages) and a demand for *equitable* relief (e.g., an injunction) will both be deemed to be part of the same claim if they relate to the same facts — therefore, demands for both types of relief will have to be made in the same action. (*Example:* If P believes that D is violating P's copyrights, P cannot bring a suit for an injunction, followed by a separate suit for money damages.) [363-64]

4. **Exceptions based on jurisdictional requirements:** There is one important *exception* to the rule against splitting a cause of action — if the court trying the first action would not have had *subject matter jurisdiction* for a claim now asserted in the second action, there will be no bar or merger. (*Example:* P sues D in state court under state antitrust law, and loses on the merits. P then sues D in federal court alleging the same facts, and charging a violation of federal antitrust laws. Because the federal courts have exclusive jurisdiction of antitrust claims, the state court could not have heard the federal claim. Therefore, the second — federal court — action will not be barred.) [364]

5. **State law followed in diversity cases:** In diversity cases, the federal courts follow *state law* with respect to the application of the rules of claim preclusion (as well as collateral estoppel). In other words, if (and only if) the law of the state where the district court sits would have granted claim preclusion or collateral estoppel effect to an earlier state court judgment, the federal court will do the same. [364]

C. Adjudication on merits: Not every loss by the plaintiff in the first action will act as a "bar" to subsequent suits on the same claim. Plaintiff will be barred only if the original adjudication in favor of the defendant was *"on the merits."* [365-66]

   1. **Non-prejudicial grounds:** In other words, some of the ways that a plaintiff may "lose" the first suit are deemed to be "without prejudice" to future suits. For instance, if the first suit is brought in federal court, plaintiff will *not* be barred from bringing a new action if the first action is dismissed because of: (1) lack of jurisdiction; (2) improper venue; or (3) failure to join an indispensable party. See FRCP 41(b). Any other type of dismissal (e.g., dismissal for failure to state a claim under 12(b)(6)) *does* bar a future claim by P, unless the court granting the dismissal specifies otherwise in its order. FRCP 41(b), last sentence. [365]

D. Counterclaims: A defendant who pleads a *counterclaim* is, in effect, a plaintiff with respect to that claim. He is bound by the outcome, just as a plaintiff is bound by the outcome of his original claim. [366-67]

   1. **No splitting:** Thus D may not split his counterclaim into two parts. (*Example:* P sues D for damages from an auto accident. D counterclaims for his property damage from that same accident, but not for personal injuries. Whether D wins or loses with the counterclaim, he may not bring a second suit against P for personal injury arising from that same accident.) [366]

   2. **Compulsory counterclaim:** Observe that state and federal rules making certain counter-claims "compulsory" serve a similar function to the merger or bar doctrine. (*Example:* P sues D for damages arising out of an auto accident. The rules of merger and bar do not by them-selves force D to assert either his claim for property damage, or for personal injury, arising out of that same accident. But in the federal court and in most state courts, any counterclaim by D for either of these things would be "compulsory," so that D would not be able to use that claim in a subsequent suit against P.) [366-67]

E. Change of law: Once a final judgment has been rendered (and any appeals resolved), *not even a change in the applicable law* will prevent claim preclusion from operating. The fact that the losing party would, because of such an overruling of legal precedent, win the lawsuit if she were allowed to start it again, is irrelevant. [367]

F. Privies not party to the first action: Remember that sometimes, a non-party may be *so closely related* to a party to the first judgment, that she will be both burdened and benefited by that judg-ment as if she had been a party to it. The non-party is said to be a *"privy"* to the first judgment. A trustee and his beneficiary, and an indemnitor and her indemnitee, are examples of privity rela-tionships. [367-68]

III. COLLATERAL ESTOPPEL

A. Definition: Regardless of which of the parties to an action wins, the judgment decides for all time any *issue actually litigated* in the suit. A party who seeks to re-litigate one of the issues dis-posed of in the first trial is said to be *"collaterally estopped"* from doing so. [369]

> **Example:** Cars driven by A and B collide. A sues B for property damage. Assume that the jurisdiction has no rules making any counterclaim a compulsory counterclaim. B declines to assert any counterclaim in the suit brought by A. A recovers $1,000 of dam-ages. The jurisdiction follows common-law contributory negligence, by which even a

small amount of contributory negligence by A would have barred him from recovery. In a subsequent suit, B sues A for personal injuries arising out of the same accident.

The court will hold that B is "collaterally estopped" from re-litigating the issue of whether A was negligent — the first judgment in A's favor amounted to a specific finding that A was not negligent, because contributory negligence would have barred recovery if he had been. Therefore, B cannot recover from A on a negligence theory. [*Little v. Blue Goose*]

1. **Distinguished from merger and bar:** There are two major differences between collateral estoppel and claim preclusion (merger and bar): [369]

    a. **Issue vs. claim:** Whereas claim preclusion applies only where the "cause of action" or "claim" in the second action is the *same* as the one in the first action, collateral estoppel applies as long as any *issue* is the same, even though the causes of action are different.

    b. **Suit not prevented:** Whereas claim preclusion prevents the second suit altogether, collateral estoppel does not prevent suit, but merely compels the court to make the *same finding of fact* that the first court made on the identical issue.

2. **To whom applied:** Collateral estoppel always applies where *both* the parties in the second action were present in the first action. Collateral estoppel sometimes, but not always, applies where only the person against whom estoppel is sought to be used was present in the first action. [375]

B. **Issues covered:** For an issue to be subject to collateral estoppel, three requirements concerning that issue must be satisfied: (1) the issue must be the *same* as one that was *fully and fairly litigated* in the first action; (2) it must have been actually *decided* by the first court; and (3) the first court's decision on this issue must have been *necessary* to the outcome in the first suit. [370-75]

1. **Same issue:** For the re-litigation of an issue to be collaterally estopped, that issue must be *identical* to an issue litigated in the earlier trial. [370]

2. **Actually litigated and decided:** The issue must have been actually *litigated* and *decided* at the first trial. [370-71]

    a. **Need not raise all defenses:** This means that D in the first trial is *not obligated to raise all of his defenses*. D does not forfeit these defenses by not raising them as he would forfeit a compulsory counterclaim. (*Example:* P sues D for an installment of rent under a lease, and wins. In a later suit for subsequent installments due on the same lease, D will not be collaterally estopped from denying that the lease was ever executed — since the issue of execution was not actually litigated and decided in the first action, collateral estoppel does not apply even though D *could* have raised this as a defense the first time. [*Jacobson v. Miller*])

    b. **"Full and fair" litigation:** Also, the party against whom collateral estoppel is sought to be used must have had a *"full and fair opportunity"* to litigate the claim. (*Example:* In a negligence case by P against D, D asserts his own due care, but the trial court unjustly excludes relevant evidence tending to prove that D was careful. In a subsequent suit by D against P for his own injuries, D will not be estopped from contending that he behaved with due care, since he lacked a full and fair opportunity to litigate the due care issue in the first suit.)

3. **Issue essential to verdict:** Not only must the issue have been litigated and decided in the first action, but the finding on that issue must have been *necessary to the judgment*. [371]

Example: A sues B for common-law negligence, and loses. The court's findings state that both parties were negligent, and recovery is denied on the grounds that A was contributorily negligent. B then sues A. A claims that the earlier finding of B's negligence, together with the doctrine of contributory negligence, mean that B cannot now recover as plaintiff.

Held, collateral estoppel should not be applied against B. The first case's finding that B was negligent was not necessary to the first verdict, since A's contributory negligence would have been enough to dispose of the case. Collateral estoppel applies only to issues whose adjudication was necessary to the verdict in the first action. [*Cambria v. Jeffery*]

   a. Alternate findings: Where a judgment rests upon *alternate* findings, either of which would be sufficient to sustain it, courts are split about whether either finding should be given collateral estoppel effect. The modern (and Restatement) view is that *neither* should be given collateral estoppel effect, since the case could have turned out the same way without that finding. [371]

4. Reasonably foreseeable future litigation: Many courts today apply collateral estoppel in a subsequent action only where that action was *reasonably foreseeable* at the time of the initial suit. Otherwise, "defeat in one suit might entail results beyond all calculation…; a trivial controversy might bring utter disaster in its train." [*The Evergreens v. Nunan*] [372]

5. Court of limited jurisdiction: A finding made by a court of *limited jurisdiction* may be denied collateral estoppel effect in a subsequent suit that would have been beyond the first court's jurisdiction. This is especially true where the first court has jurisdiction limited to a dollar amount, and also has *informal procedures*. (*Example:* If the first suit is in a small claims court, most of which have no pleadings, no rules of evidence, and usually no lawyers, a finding will generally not be held to have collateral estoppel effect in a later suit that could not have been brought in the small claims court.) [372-73]

6. Differences in burden of proof: If in the first action the allocation of the *burden of proof* was more favorable to the party now seeking to apply collateral estoppel than it was in the second action, collateral estoppel will not be allowed. [373]

7. Settlement: In most jurisdictions, the *settlement* of an action by consent of the parties has *no* collateral estoppel effect. (The settlement document may, of course, provide otherwise.) [373-74]

8. Findings of law: A court's conclusion of *law*, like a conclusion of fact, is generally given collateral estoppel effect. [374-75]

   a. Exceptions: But there are two situations in which a conclusion of law generally will *not* be given collateral estoppel effect: (1) where the two actions involve claims that are *substantially unrelated* to each other; and (2) where there has been a significant *change in legal principles* between the two suits, especially where use of collateral estoppel would impose on one of the parties a significant disadvantage, or confer on him a significant benefit, with respect to his *competitors*.

   Example: D is a liquor wholesaler. P, a state liquor licensing agency, sues to have D's license revoked on the grounds that D is really functioning as a retailer. The trial court finds in D's favor. P then sues X, whose conduct is the same as D's; a higher court finds in favor of P, and orders X's license revoked. Now, P brings a second suit against D for revocation.

Collateral estoppel effect will probably not be given to the first P-D suit, since there has been an intervening change in legal principles, and since use of collateral estoppel would give D a perpetual, and unfair, advantage over X and other similar competitors.

C. Persons who can be estopped: Generally, only the ***actual parties*** to the first action can be ***bound*** by the finding on an issue. [375-78]

   1. Privies: But someone who is very closely ***related*** to a party in the first action can also be bound. Such ***"privies"*** include successors in interest to real property, beneficiaries of trusts, and indemnitors. [375-77]

   2. Strangers to first action: The most important thing to remember is that a true ***stranger*** to the first action cannot be ***collaterally estopped*** by the former judgment. [377-78]

   Example: A bus owned by Bus Co. collides with a car driven by Driver. In a suit between these two, Bus Co. is held to have full responsibility. Passenger, who was riding in Driver's car, now sues Driver. Even though the court in the first action decided that Driver was not at all at fault, Passenger is not bound by this finding. This is because Passenger was a complete stranger to the first action (the rules about who was a privy do not apply to the passenger-driver situation where the two are not related), and a stranger can never be bound by any finding of fact in the first action.

D. Persons who can benefit from estoppel: [378-83]

   1. Mutuality: Originally, it was held that a party ***not bound*** by an earlier judgment (because not a party to it) could not use that judgment to bind his adversary who ***was*** a party to the first action. This rule prohibiting a stranger's use of collateral estoppel was known as the doctrine of ***"mutuality."*** [378]

   a. Abandoned: Nearly all courts have ***abandoned*** the general principle of mutuality. While many courts refuse in ***particular circumstances*** to allow the use of estoppel by one not a party to the first action, it is no longer a general rule that a stranger to the first action cannot benefit from findings of fact made against her adversary.

   Example: A bus owned by Bus Co. and a car driven by Driver collide. Also involved in the collision is Pedestrian, who is badly injured. Bus Co. sues Driver for negligence, and the court decides that Driver was totally at fault. In a separate suit, Pedestrian now sues Driver. Application of the doctrine of mutuality would prevent Pedestrian from collaterally estopping Driver on the issue of negligence. But most courts today would give Pedestrian the benefit of collateral estoppel in this situation, even though Pedestrian was a stranger to the first action.

   2. Offensive/defensive distinction: Courts are ***more willing*** to allow the ***"defensive"*** use of collateral estoppel by a stranger than they are to allow the ***"offensive"*** use. "Offensive" use refers to use by a stranger to the first action who is a ***plaintiff*** in the second action; "defensive" use refers to use by a stranger who is a ***defendant*** in the second action. [379-80]

   a. Offensive use sometimes OK: But even offensive use is sometimes approved by the courts, just not as often as defensive use. (The above example is an illustration of offensive use that would probably be accepted by a court.) [380-81]

   Example: The SEC sues D, a corporation, based on a false proxy statement D has issued. The trial court decides in the SEC's favor, concluding that the proxy statement contained certain falsehoods. P then brings a stockholder's derivative action against D, based on the same proxy statement. P wants to collaterally estop D from relitigating the falsity of the proxy statement.

    Held, P may use collateral estoppel. This is true even though P was a stranger to the first action, and even though P's use is offensive, in the sense that the person seeking collateral estoppel is the plaintiff in the second action. [*Park Lane Hosiery Co. v. Shore*]

b. Factors: Here are some of the factors courts consider in deciding whether to allow offensive non-mutual estoppel in a particular case: [381-83]

    i. Alignment: Whether the party sought to be bound (the defendant in the second suit) was a *plaintiff* or *defendant* in the *first* suit. (If she was a defendant, this will militate against use of estoppel.)

    ii. Incentive to litigate: Whether the person to be estopped had a reasonable *incentive* to litigate the issue fully in the first suit, which will depend in part on whether the second suit was *foreseeable* at the time of the first suit. (The more incentive the party had to litigate the first time, the fairer it is to bind him now.)

    iii. Discouraging break-away suits: Whether the plaintiff in the second action *could have joined* in the first action, but instead sat out that first action in order to derive a tactical advantage.

    iv. Multiple plaintiff anomaly: Whether permitting offensive estoppel would present a danger of the *"multiple plaintiff anomaly."* (*Example:* All 200 passengers are killed when a plane owned by D crashes. If each P sues *seriatim*, and offensive estoppel is allowed, D might win the first 20 suits, lose the 21st, and then be estopped from denying liability in the next 179. This would be unfair to D.)

    v. Procedural opportunities: Whether there are *procedural opportunities* not available to the party in the first action but available now in the second action — if there are, allowing offensive estoppel is less likely. (*Examples:* There was less extensive discovery available in the first action, or no jury trial right.)

    vi. Issue of law: Whether the issue is one of *law* or merely of "fact." (Where the issue is one of law, the court is likely to use the more flexible doctrine of *stare decisis*, rather than collateral estoppel.)

    vii. Government as party: Whether the defendant in the second action is the *government* — non-mutual offensive use of collateral estoppel will virtually *never* be allowed against the government. [*U.S. v. Mendoza*]

3. Criminal conviction: Courts are split as to whether a party's previous *criminal conviction* may serve to collaterally estop him in the subsequent civil action. (*Example:* D is convicted of drunk driving after getting into an accident in which V is injured. In a subsequent civil suit by V, some but not all courts will allow V to collaterally estop D from denying that he was drunk.) [383]

a. Guilty plea: Courts are also split about whether offensive collateral estoppel effect should be given to a *guilty plea* in the first proceeding.

b. Acquittal: *Acquittal* in a criminal case is *never binding* in a subsequent civil action. The main reason is that to grant estoppel effect to an acquittal would be to allow the criminal defendant to bind a non-party. (*Example:* D is prosecuted by the state for drunk driving in an accident in which V was injured. D is acquitted. V now brings a civil action for negligence against D, and seeks to show that D was drunk. V will not be collaterally estopped by the acquittal, because V was not a party to the earlier action. A second reason for rejecting estoppel is that the "beyond a reasonable doubt" standard of proof necessary in a criminal case was tougher for the prosecution to meet than the "preponderance of the evidence" standard used in the later civil suit, so estopping V would be extra unfair to him.) [383]

IV. FULL FAITH AND CREDIT

A. Full Faith and Credit generally: Special problems arise when two related suits occur in *different jurisdictions*. There may be two different states involved, or a state court and a federal court. In either situation, the second court's handling of the first court's judgment is governed by a general principle called "full faith and credit." [388]

1. Two states: When the courts of *two different states* are involved, the result is dictated by the *Full Faith and Credit* Clause of the U.S. Constitution (Article IV, Section 1). This clause requires each state to give to the judgment of any other state *the same effect that that judgment would have in the state which rendered it*. [388-89]

Example: P wins a judgment against D in Connecticut, but cannot find any property in Connecticut on which to levy. P then locates property held by D in Illinois. P may collect in Illinois by bringing a suit based on the Connecticut judgment. Because of the Full Faith and Credit Clause, the courts of Illinois must accept this judgment at face value, and may not reconsider any issues which it concluded. The Illinois courts must therefore give P all the rights that a judgment creditor would have if he got an Illinois judgment, including the right to have the sheriff sell D's Illinois assets.

a. Misinterpretation: The rule of full faith and credit applies even where the second court is convinced that the first court made a *mistake* on law or facts. Indeed, State A must give full faith and credit to an adjudication of State B even if that judgment was based on a *misinterpretation of the laws of State A*. [*Fauntleroy v. Lum*] [388]

b. Collateral attack on jurisdiction: There is *one exception* to the rule that the second court may not reconsider any aspect of the original judgment: the second court may reconsider whether the first court had *jurisdiction* (either personal or subject-matter), provided that the jurisdictional question was *not litigated or waived* in the first action. This is the doctrine of *"collateral attack."*

Example: P sues D in Connecticut. D defaults, by never appearing in the suit at all. The Connecticut court enters a judgment in favor of P. P then sues in Illinois, having found property of D there. At D's request, the Illinois court may consider whether the Connecticut court ever had valid personal jurisdiction over D. If it concludes that Connecticut did not, the Illinois court need not enforce the judgment. (But if D had litigated the jurisdictional issue in Connecticut, Illinois could not reconsider the jurisdiction question, even if it was convinced that Connecticut wrongly determined that it had jurisdiction.)

2. State followed by federal court: If the first court is a state court, and the second court is a *federal* court, a similar full faith and credit principle applies, but this is not dictated by the Constitution. Instead a federal statute, 28 U.S.C. §1738, requires every federal court to give to the judgment of any state court the same effect that that judgment would have in the courts of the state which rendered it. [389]

3. **Federal followed by state court:** Conversely, if the first judgment is in a federal court and the second suit is in a state court, full faith and credit again applies, though the mechanism by which this happens is not so clear. (Probably the Constitution's Supremacy Clause dictates that the state court honor a federal court judgment). [392]

B. **Duty to follow the *res judicata* effect of first judgment:** The full faith and credit principle — that one jurisdiction's courts must honor the judgments of another jurisdiction — applies not only generally, but specifically to the issue of *res judicata effect*. In other words, the earlier judgment must be given *exactly the same effect*, in terms of claim preclusion and collateral estoppel, as the judgment would have in the court that rendered it. [389]

1. **Two states:** Thus a state must give to the judgment of any other state at least the *res judicata* effect that that judgment would have in the state of its rendition. (*Example:* P litigates an issue with D in State 1. The issue is decided in favor of P. X now sues D in State 2 in a suit raising the same issue. The State 2 court determines that the courts of State 1 would allow X to use offensive collateral estoppel in this situation. The courts of State 2 must follow suit, even if the State 2 courts do not themselves generally allow offensive collateral estoppel in this situation.) [389]

   a. **Greater effect:** Courts are split about whether they may or should give **greater effect** to another state's judgment than it would have in that other state. Probably no constitutional principle prevents the second state from giving greater effect to the first state's judgment, so it is within the second court's discretion whether to do so. (*Example:* On the facts of the above example, assume that State 2 would allow offensive collateral estoppel, but State 1 would not. Probably State 2 is free to give the State 1 judgment collateral estoppel effect, but State 2 might choose not to do so.)

2. **State followed by federal:** Similarly, if the first judgment is in a state court and the second suit is in a federal court, the federal court must grant the state court judgment the same *res judicata* effect that it would have in that state. [389-92]

   a. **Right of Congress to specify otherwise:** There is an exception to this rule: Congress is always free to provide *otherwise*, in a specific context. If Congress does provide otherwise, then the federal court may be free to deny the earlier state court judgment the *res judicata* effect it would have in the rendering state. (*Example:* 42 U.S.C. §1983 gives a person the right to bring a federal suit against anyone who violates his constitutional rights "under color of" state law. Suppose Congress added a clause to §1983 saying that any state court criminal proceeding absolving an official of unconstitutional conduct should be ignored by the federal court hearing the §1983 action. If Congress did this, a federal court hearing a §1983 suit would be free to deny any state judgment the collateral estoppel effect it would have in the courts of the state that rendered it. But Congress has not in fact done this in §1983, so the federal courts must honor the collateral estoppel effect of state court judgments in §1983 suits.)

   b. **Can't give greater effect:** The federal court may *not* give *greater* preclusive effect to the prior state court judgment than that state would give it. [*Migra v. Warren City Board of Ed.*] (*Example:* If the initial state judgment comes from a state that does not allow non-mutual offensive use of collateral estoppel, the federal court hearing the second suit may not apply such collateral estoppel, even if the situation is one in which the Supreme Court allows the use of collateral estoppel.) [391-92]

3. **Federal suit followed by state suit:** If the federal suit comes first and the state suit second, the state court must give to the federal judgment the same *res judicata* effect that that federal court would give to its own judgment. [392]

INTRODUCTION

I. CIVIL PROCEDURE GENERALLY

A. "Civil" procedure vs. "criminal" procedure: "Civil" procedure refers to the rules of litigation for *"civil" actions*. Civil actions are best defined by contrasting them to "criminal" proceedings. In a criminal proceeding, the state is a party, and is asserting that an individual has committed a crime requiring punishment. In a civil action, by contrast, there is no assertion that the defendant has committed a crime. Instead, one private party (the plaintiff) has brought the suit, and is asserting that the other private party (the defendant) has wronged the plaintiff. Typically, the plaintiff in a private civil action is seeking money damages; however, the plaintiff may also be seeking "equitable" relief, such as an injunction to prevent the defendant from doing something.

> **Example 1 (money damages):** P and D are in an automobile accident. P sues D for $30,000 for personal injury. This is a civil action of the "money damages" type. If P wins, he will get a judgment from the court. This judgment will entitle P to collect (assuming the judgment is for the full amount sought) $30,000 from D. If D does not pay promptly, P will be able to use the state's judgement-collection mechanisms, such as a sheriff's auction, to forcibly collect the money from D.

> **Example 2 (equitable relief):** As part of P's purchase of D's business, D agrees not to start up a competing business within a five-mile radius for five years. D violates the agreement, and opens up a competing business. P sues D to enforce the non-compete. Here, P's action is an "equitable" action, for an injunction. That is, P is not asking principally for money damages (though he may ask for these as well). Instead, he is asking the court to order D not to do something, namely, carry on the new, competing, business. An action for an injunction is known as an *"equitable"* rather than *"legal"* action, because, historically, injunctions were the sort of relief granted by courts of "equity" as opposed to courts of "law."

B. Two court systems: There are *two entirely distinct court systems* in the U.S.

1. State courts: First is the system of *state courts*. Each state has its own system of courts. In a typical state, courts which can entertain civil proceedings are likely to include: (1) *small claims* courts, which are typically limited to suits seeking no more than a certain dollar amount, say $5,000; (2) courts of *general jurisdiction*, in which civil trials are held without any limit on the amount being sought; (3) an *intermediate appeals* court, to which anyone who loses a verdict in the general trial court has a right of appeal; and (4) a highest state court (typically called a "Supreme" court, but bearing a different name in certain states, such as the "Court of Appeals" in New York). In many states, there is no automatic right of appeal to the highest state court, since the litigant has already had an appeal "of right" to the intermediate appeals court; instead, it is up to the state's highest court to decide which requests for appeal it will accept.

    a. Appeal to U.S. Supreme Court: The losing litigant in a state court proceeding does *not* have an automatic right to appeal to the *U.S. Supreme Court*. In brief, the Supreme Court may only hear appeals from state court judgments where the state court has decided a *federal question*. And, in fact, the Supreme Court may only hear those state cases in which the federal-question decision was *necessary* to the outcome (so that it will not hear cases whose outcome rests on an "independent and adequate state ground"). For a more full discussion of when the Supreme Court can hear an appeal from a state court proceeding, see Emanuel on *Constitutional Law*.

  2. The federal courts: There is a second, entirely distinct, set of courts in the U.S.: the *federal* judicial system. This set of courts has three levels: (1) district courts; (2) circuit courts of appeal; and (3) the U.S. Supreme Court.

    a. District courts: Each state is divided into one or more "federal judicial *districts*." Each district has at least one *federal district court*, and some states have multiple courts. (For example, New York has four judicial districts, some of which have district courts in multiple places, each representing a "division" of a district.) The federal district courts are the *trial* courts of the federal system.

    b. Circuit courts of appeal: The federal judicial districts described in the prior paragraph are grouped into 13 *"judicial circuits."* In each of these circuits, there is a *"Court of Appeals."* The circuits are numbered First through Eleventh, plus the District of Columbia Circuit and the Federal Circuit. The First through Eleventh each cover the district courts in three or more states. (For example, the Ninth Circuit covers all districts located in Alaska, Arizona, California, Idaho, Montana, Nevada, Oregon, Washington, Guam and Hawaii, and thus hears all appeals from federal district courts in any of these states.)

      i. Appeal: Any litigant who loses in federal district court has a right to appeal to the Court of Appeals. Typically, an appeal is heard not by the entire Court of Appeals (which contains from 4-23 judges, depending on the circuit), but rather by a 3-judge *panel* of that circuit. (Occasionally, the entire set of judges in the circuit will re-consider a decision by a panel; in that case, the resulting decision is said to be "en banc.")

    c. Supreme Court: When a federal civil litigant loses in the Court of Appeals, she may petition the Supreme Court to hear the case. It is up to the Supreme Court to decide whether to "grant certiorari," i.e., to hear the appeal. The Supreme Court is never *required* to hear an appeal; the Court exercises its discretion to hear the case only if four Justices vote to grant certiorari.

    d. Federal Rules of Civil Procedure: Procedure in the federal courts is mainly governed by the *Federal Rules of Civil Procedure*. Changes in these Rules are proposed from time to time by the U.S. Supreme Court, and go into effect unless Congress specifically objects (which it rarely does).

C. Grounds for federal court jurisdiction: The *jurisdiction* of the federal court system is *limited* by the U.S. Constitution. In other words, it is not the case that the federal courts can hear any controversy they wish to hear. It is not even the case that Congress could, by passing a broad jurisdictional statute, empower the federal courts to hear any case they wish. Instead, the Constitution lists certain types of cases as to which the federal judicial power is deemed to exist, and only cases falling within that power may be heard by the federal system. (Furthermore, Congress can, and frequently has, cut back the federal judicial power to exclude cases that would be within the Constitution's grant.) At present, there are two main kinds of civil cases that the federal district courts may hear:

1. **Diversity cases:** First, the federal district courts may hear cases arising between *"citizens of different states,"* in which at least $50,000 is involved. See 28 U.S.C. §1332. (Also, the courts may hear a case between a citizen of an American state and any foreign subject.) The right to hear cases between citizens of different states is known as the grant of *"diversity"* jurisdiction, and the cases are called "diversity cases."

2. **Federal question cases:** Second, the federal district courts may hear any civil action "arising under the Constitution, laws, and treaties of the United States." 28 U.S.C. §1331. Cases falling under this provision are typically called *"federal question"* cases.

D. **Both systems studied:** In a typical first-year Civil Procedure course, both judicial systems are studied. However, certain "chapters" of the course typically focus on just state-court concerns or just federal concerns. Other chapters relate heavily to both systems. Thus "jurisdiction over the parties" relates to both federal and state systems; "subject matter jurisdiction," on the other hand, is limited to the federal-court context.

E. **A road map:** Here is a sort of *"road map"* for analyzing a Civil Procedure problem. If you are currently at the beginning of your Civil Procedure course, just look at this road map quickly, to get some sense of the lay of the land. If you are towards the end, and studying for exams, try to memorize this map so that you can use it as a checklist for spotting issues:

1. **Personal jurisdiction:** First, make sure that the court has *"personal jurisdiction"* or *"jurisdiction over the parties."* In brief, this means that you must check to make sure that the court can hear the case against the particular defendant. You must check to make sure that: (1) D had *minimum contacts* with the forum state (whether the court is a state or federal court); and (2) D received such *notice and opportunity to be heard* as to satisfy the constitutional requirement of due process.

2. **Venue:** Then, check whether *venue* was correct. In federal court suits (which are the only types of suits as to which venue problems are usually covered in a Civil Procedure course), the venue requirement describes what judicial *district* the case may be heard in. Essentially, the case must be heard either: (1) in any district where the *defendant resides* (with special rules for multi-defendant cases); or (2) in any district in which a *substantial part of the events* giving rise to the claim occurred. See 28 U.S.C. §1391. (There are special provisions giving venue for other districts in special cases, but most of the time you should be concerned with just "defendant's residence" or "place of events" venue.)

3. **Subject matter jurisdiction:** If the case is a federal case, you must then ask whether the court has *subject matter* jurisdiction. Essentially, this means that one of the following two things must be the case:

   a. **Diversity:** Either the case is between *citizens of different states* (with "complete diversity" required, so that no plaintiff is a citizen of the same state as any defendant) and at least $50,000 is at stake; or

b. **Federal question:**   The case raises a *"federal question."* Essentially, this means that plaintiff's right to recover stems from the U.S. Constitution, a federal treaty, or an act of Congress. (There is no minimum amount required to be at stake in federal question cases.)

4. **Pleading:**   Next, you must examine whether the *pleadings* are proper. This can involve a whole range of questions, most of which will be fairly easy to spot. Typical questions might include: Did D answer in time? Can D make a motion to get the complaint dismissed for failure to state a claim? May P now amend her pleadings?

5. **Discovery:**   Next, you may have a complex of issues relating to pretrial *discovery*, the process by which each side finds out details about the other side's case. Again, you should be able to spot discovery questions fairly readily from the fact pattern. Typical issues might include: May P take the oral deposition of W, an expert witness whom D is planning to call at trial? May D obtain court-ordered sanctions against P for failing to cooperate with discovery? May P use at trial the results of a deposition taken of W in a different case?

6. **Ascertaining applicable law:**   Now, figure out *what jurisdiction's law* should be used in the case. The most important problem of this type is: In a diversity case, may the federal court apply its own concepts of "federal common law" (i.e., federal judge-made law), or must the court apply the law of the state where the federal court sits? In brief, the answer is that if the state has a *substantive law* (whether a statute or a judge-made principle) that is on point, *the federal court sitting in diversity must apply that law*. (*Example:* In a diversity case concerning negligence, the federal court must normally apply the negligence law of the state where the court sits.) This whole set of problems relating to ascertaining applicable law is commonly referred to as *"Erie"* problems, after *Erie v. Tompkins*, probably the most important case in federal Civil Procedure.

7. **Trial procedure:**   Next, you may face a series of issues relating to *trial procedure*. Typical questions here are: What burden of proof does P bear, both to avoid having the case dismissed before it is fully tried, and to prevail in front of the judge or jury? May the case be dismissed before trial pursuant to the doctrine of summary judgment? Is there a right to jury trial here? May the judge order a directed verdict, effectively taking the case away from the jury? Should the judge grant a new trial or a judgment notwithstanding the verdict?

8. **Multi-party and multi-claim litigation:**   If there is more than one claim in the case, or more than the basic two parties (a single plaintiff and a single defendant), you will face a whole host of issues related to the *multi-party* or *multi-claim* nature of the litigation. You must be prepared to deal with the various methods of bringing multiple parties and multiple claims into a case.

a. **Various devices:**   Following is a brief checklist of devices by which multiple parties, or multiple claims, may be brought into the case. (In most Civil Procedure courses, and for our discussion here, the multi-claim and multi-party discussion focuses on the Federal Rules of Civil Procedure. Most states have roughly similar rules.)

b. **Counterclaim:**   D may make a claim against P, by use of the *counterclaim*. See FRCP 13. Check whether the counterclaim is *"permissive"* or *"compulsory."* (Also, remember that third parties, who are neither the original plaintiff nor the original defendant, may make a counterclaim.)

c. Joinder of claims: Once a party has made a claim against some other party, she may then make *any other claim* she wishes against that party. This is *"joinder of claims."* See Rule 18(a).

d. Joinder of parties: Multiple parties may *join* their actions together. Check to see whether either *"permissive* joinder" or *"compulsory* joinder" is applicable. Also, remember that each of these two types of joinder can apply to *either multiple plaintiffs* or *multiple defendants*. See FRCP 19 and 20.

e. Class actions: Check whether a *class action* is available as a device to handle the claims of many similarly-situated plaintiffs, or claims against many similarly-situated defendants. See FRCP 23. Look for the possibility of a class action wherever there are 25 or more similarly-situated plaintiffs or similarly-situated defendants.

f. Intervention: A person who is not initially part of a lawsuit may be able to enter the suit on his own initiative, under the doctrine of *intervention*. See FRCP 24. Check whether the intervention is "of right" or "permissive."

g. Interpleader: Where a party owes something to two or more other persons, but isn't sure which, that party may want to use the device of *interpleader* to prevent being made to pay the same claim twice. After checking whether interpleader might be desirable, decide whether the stakeholder should use *"statutory* interpleader" or "Rule interpleader." See 28 U.S.C. §1335 (statutory interpleader) and FRCP 22 (Rule interpleader).

h. Third-party practice (impleader): Anytime D has a potential claim against some *third person* who is not already in the lawsuit, by which that third person will be liable to D for some or all of P's recovery against D, D should be able to *"implead"* the third person. (*Example:* Employee, while working for Employer, hits Victim with a company car. Victim sues Employer in diversity, under the doctrine of *respondeat superior*. Under traditional concepts of indemnity, Employer will be able to recover from Employee for any amount that Employer is forced to pay Victim. Therefore, Employer should "implead" Employee as a "third-party defendant" to the Victim-Employer action.) See FRCP 14(a). Once a third-party defendant is brought into the case, consider what other claims might now be available (e.g., a counterclaim by the third-party defendant against the third-party plaintiff, a cross-claim against some other third-party defendant, a counterclaim against the original plaintiff, etc.).

i. Cross-claims: Check to see whether any party has made, or should make, a claim against a *co-party*. This is a *cross-claim*. See FRCP 13(g).

j. Jurisdiction: For any of these multi-party or multi-claim devices, check to see whether the requirements of *personal jurisdiction* and *subject matter jurisdiction* have been satisfied. To do this, you will need to know whether the doctrine of *"supplemental"* jurisdiction applies to the particular device in question. If it does not, the new claim, or the new party, will typically have to *independently* meet the requirements of federal subject matter jurisdiction. (*Example:* P, from Massachusetts, sues D, from

Connecticut, in diversity. X, from Massachusetts, wants to intervene in the case on the side of D. Because supplemental jurisdiction does not apply to intervention, X must independently satisfy the requirement of diversity, which he cannot do because he is a citizen of the same state as P. Therefore, X cannot intervene.)

9. **Former adjudication:**   Lastly, check whether the results in some *prior litigation* are *binding* in the current suit. Distinguish between situations in which the *judgment* in the prior suit is binding on an entire cause of action in the present suit (under the doctrines of *merger* and *bar*), and the situation where a *finding of fact* is binding on the current suit, even though the judgment itself is not binding (the *"collateral estoppel"* situation).

   a. **Non-mutual collateral estoppel:**   Where a *"stranger"* to the first action (one not a party to that first action) now seeks to take advantage of a finding of fact in that first suit, consider whether this *"non-mutual"* collateral estoppel should be allowed.

   b. **Full Faith and Credit:**   Lastly, if the two suits have taken place in *different jurisdictions*, consider to what extent the principles of *Full Faith and Credit* limit the second court's freedom to ignore what happened in the first suit.

CHAPTER 2

JURISDICTION OVER THE PARTIES

ChapterScope

This Chapter examines "jurisdiction over the parties," that is, a court's power to decide a case between the *particular parties* before it. The most important concepts in this Chapter are:

■ **Minimum contacts:** Whether the defendant is an individual or a corporation, the court may proceed only if D has *"minimum contacts"* with the state in which the court sits. This is true for all state-court actions and most federal-court actions.

■ **Voluntariness:** Usually a corporation will be found to have the requisite minimum contacts with the forum state only if the corporation has somehow *voluntarily sought to do business in*, or *with the residents of*, the forum state.

■ **Limits on service of process:** As a general rule, in federal cases (both diversity actions and federal question cases), *service of process* may be made only: (1) *within the territorial limits of the state in which the District Court sits*; or (2) anywhere else permitted by the state law of the state where the District Court sits.

■ **Notice:** Even if the court has authority to judge the dispute between the parties or over the property before it, the court may not proceed unless D received *adequate notice* of the case against him.

  ❑ **Reasonableness test:** In order for D to have received adequate notice, it is not necessary that he *actually* have learned of the suit. Rather, the procedures used to alert him must have been *reasonably likely to inform him*, even if they actually failed to do so.

■ **Venue:** In addition to requirements of jurisdiction, requirements of *venue* must also be satisfied. Venue refers to the place within a jurisdiction in which a particular action may be brought. In a state-court action, venue determines in what county or district of the state the action may be brought. In federal actions, venue determines which federal district court may try the action.

I. GENERAL PRINCIPLES

A. Two kinds of jurisdiction: Before a court can decide a case, it must have jurisdiction over the *parties* as well as over the *subject matter*. That is, it must have jurisdiction not only to decide the *kind* of case before it (subject matter jurisdiction) but also jurisdiction to decide a case *between the particular parties*, or *concerning the property*, before it.

  1. Examples of *subject matter* jurisdictional problems:

    a. *Does Court X have the power to decide cases in which the two* parties are citizens of different states? (The answer would be "yes" if Court X were a federal court; the subject matter jurisdiction would be "diversity jurisdiction." Of course, the amount in controversy requirement, *infra*, p. 106, would also have to be met.)

    b. *Does Court X have the power to decide cases involving more than* **i.*$1,000?***   (The answer might be "no" if Court X were a municipal court.)

Note: Questions of subject matter jurisdiction are discussed in the chapter on Subject Matter Jurisdiction, *infra*, p. 93.

  2. Examples of problems of jurisdiction *over the parties:*

    a. *Does Court X have jurisdiction* over a defendant who is a citizen of State X, but who is temporarily out of the state? (The answer would be "yes" in almost every state, as long as the defendant were given reasonable notice that the Court in X was going to exercise its jurisdiction over him.)

    b. *Does Court Y have jurisdiction over* property in State Y where the action is one by the plaintiff to register title to the land in his name? (The answer is "yes," even though no defendant is personally known to the plaintiff or to the court. Even though the jurisdiction here is over land rather than people, it is still referred to as a kind of jurisdiction *over the parties* as distinguished from *subject matter* jurisdiction.)

B. Requirements for jurisdiction over the parties: There are two distinct requirements which must be met before a court can be said to have jurisdiction over the parties:

  1. The court must have *power* to act, either upon given property, or on a given person so as to subject him to personal liability. This is a requirement of *substantive due process*.

  2. The court must have given the defendant *adequate notice* of the action against him, and an *opportunity to be heard*. This is a requirement of *procedural due process*.

C. Three kinds of jurisdiction over the parties: There are three kinds of jurisdiction which a court may exercise over the parties. These will be distinguished more fully in the treatment of *in rem* and *quasi in rem* jurisdiction, *infra*, p. 51.

  1. *In personam:* *In personam* jurisdiction, or jurisdiction over the defendant's person, gives the court power to issue a judgment against him personally. This judgment can then be sued upon in other states, and *all of his assets* may be seized to satisfy the judgment.

  2. *In rem:* *In rem* jurisdiction, or jurisdiction over a *thing*, gives the court power to adjudicate a claim made about a *piece of property* or about a *status*. An action to quiet title to real estate, and an action to pronounce a marriage dissolved, are example.

  3. *Quasi in rem jurisdiction:* In *quasi in rem* jurisdiction, the action is begun by seizing property owned by (*attachment*), or a debt owed to (*garnishment*) the defendant, within the forum state. This is different from *in rem* jurisdiction because here the action is not really *about* the "thing" seized; instead the thing seized is a pretext for the court to decide the case without having jurisdiction over the defendant's person. Any judgment affects only the property seized, and the judgment cannot be sued upon in any other court.

D. Minimum contacts requirement: Regardless of which type of jurisdiction over the parties is involved, a court may not exercise it unless the defendant has *"minimum contacts"* with the state in which the court sits. What constitutes "minimum contacts" is a complex issue that is discussed extensively beginning *infra*, p. 20. In brief, the notion is that the defendant must have taken **actions** that were **purposefully directed** toward the forum state. (These might include selling goods in the state, incorporating in the state, visiting the state, etc.) Without such minimum contacts, exercise of jurisdiction would violate the defendant's federal constitutional right to due process.

1. **Balancing test:** Furthermore, even if the defendant has the requisite "minimum contacts" with the forum state, the court may not exercise jurisdiction if considerations of "**fair play** and **substantial justice**" would make requiring the defendant to defend the action in the forum state so **unreasonable** as to constitute a due process violation. This might be the case, for instance, if the burden to the defendant of defending in the forum state was unusually great, and the interests of the plaintiff in having the controversy heard in the forum state were very slight. See, e.g., *Asahi Metal Industry Co. v. Superior Court*, *infra*, p. 29. Generally, however, if the defendant has the requisite minimum contacts with the forum state, it will not be unreasonable for the case to be tried there, and there will thus be constitutionally-exercisable jurisdiction over him.

E. **Long-arm statutes:** Even where the above due process requirements (minimum contacts, etc.) are satisfied, the defendant may not be served **outside** of the forum state unless the forum state has enacted a **statute** authorizing out-of-state service under certain circumstances. Such a statute allowing the courts of a state to obtain jurisdiction over persons **not physically present** within the state at the time of the service are called "**long-arm** statutes." Long-arm statutes allow jurisdiction on the basis of certain links between the defendant and the forum state, such as domicile there, ownership of property in the state, commission of a tortious act inside the state, etc.

F. **Continuing jurisdiction:** Once jurisdiction over the parties is gained, it continues during the entire litigation. But at each significant new step in the litigation process, notice and opportunity to appear must be given.

G. **Due process:** The exercise of jurisdiction by a state or federal court must meet the requirements of the **due process** clause of the 14th Amendment, as that clause is interpreted by the U.S. Supreme Court. Virtually all of the Supreme Court cases outlined below concern this due process requirement.

H. **State and federal:** Most of the material which follows relates to the exercise of jurisdiction by **state** courts. Federal jurisdiction follows roughly similar principles, and will be outlined in detail in the section on Federal Jurisdiction over the Parties, *infra*, p. 39.

II. JURISDICTION OVER INDIVIDUALS

Note: This section will consider various bases which have been employed for the exercise of jurisdiction over natural persons. These bases include **presence within the forum state, domicile within the state, consent to being sued within the state, tortious acts committed within the state, business done within the state**, etc. **Jurisdiction over corporations** will be considered separately in the section following the present one.

A. Individual's presence: Jurisdiction may be exercised over an individual by virtue of his *presence within the forum state*.

    1. Originally chief basis: *Originally, presence within the state was the chief, if not sole, basis for personal jurisdiction*. This is illustrated by the leading case of *Pennoyer v. Neff*, 95 U.S. 714 (1877). *Pennoyer* stated that "the authority of every tribunal is necessarily restricted by the territorial limits of the State in which it is established."

        a. Power as basis for: Since the state's *power* only extends to the edge of its borders, *Pennoyer* held, "Process from the tribunals of one State cannot run into another State, and summon parties there domiciled to leave its territory and respond to proceedings against them."

    2. Presence still enough: Today, presence within the forum state is only one of numerous ways to get jurisdiction over a person. But it continues to be a *constitutionally valid method* of getting jurisdiction, even where the individual is an *out-of-state resident* who comes into the forum state only briefly — so long as *service is made* on the person while he is in the forum state, the entire case probably may be tried in the forum state, even though the defendant then leaves the forum state and has no other contacts with it. This is the result of a very important Supreme Court decision, *Burnham v. Superior Court*, 495 U.S. 604 (1990).

        a. Facts: In *Burnham*, Dennis and Francie Burnham, a married couple with children, separated. Mrs. Burnham and the children moved to California, and Mr. Burnham remained in New Jersey. The next year, Mr. Burnham visited California on business. That same trip, he went to visit his children, and was served with process in a California suit by Mrs. Burnham for divorce. Mr. Burnham then returned to New Jersey. Mr. Burnham argued that California could not constitutionally exercise personal jurisdiction over him, because his only contacts with the state were a few short visits there for business, and a few visits with his children.

        b. Court upholds jurisdiction: But the Supreme Court held that on these facts, California *could* constitutionally assert jurisdiction. There was no majority opinion. But all members of the court agreed that on these facts, personal jurisdiction was not a violation of Mr. Burnham's due process rights.

            i. Plurality: Four justices seemed to feel that as long as the defendant was personally served while present in the forum state, no matter how briefly, this would always suffice for personal jurisdiction. The plurality reasoned that all American jurisdictions apparently continue to allow in-state service as a basis for jurisdiction, so that this means of jurisdiction cannot be said to violate "traditional notions of fairness," the standard for determining whether a practice violates due process.

            ii. Other justices: The other justices in *Burnham* believed that presence would almost always suffice, but appeared to think that there might be occasional instances where this would lead to great unfairness and might thus be unconstitutional.

        c. Summary: So as the result of *Burnham*, so long as the defendant voluntarily travels to the forum state, and is *served while present there*, that state will have personal jurisdiction over him in virtually all instances, even though the defendant may have no other contacts with the state at all apart from the visit on which he was served. (If the defendant was *involuntarily* in the forum state at the time of service, e.g., because he was forcibly abducted and brought there, this rationale would presumably not apply, so jurisdiction would probably be a violation of due process. But this rarely happens.)

    d. **Service on airplane:** Even *service on an airplane* flying *over* the forum state has been held valid, on the theory that the persons in the plane were "present in" that state. *Grace v. MacArthur*, 170 F.Supp. 442 (E.D. Ark. 1959).

B. **Domicile:** Jurisdiction may be exercised over an individual who is *domiciled* within the forum state, even if he is temporarily absent from the state.

    1. *Milliken:* The leading case allowing jurisdiction based on domicile is *Milliken v. Meyer*, 311 U.S. 457 (1940). Meyer was domiciled in Wyoming, and was served in Colorado, pursuant to a Wyoming statute allowing out-of-state service on a resident defendant who has attempted either to escape his creditors or to avoid being served with process. The U.S. Supreme Court held that such service was valid: "Domicile in the state is alone sufficient to bring an absent defendant within the reach of the state's jurisdiction for purposes of a personal judgment. ..." The Court noted that the defendant still had to be served out of state in a way "reasonably calculated to give him actual notice of the proceedings and an opportunity to be heard." (See the section on Notice and Opportunity to be Heard, *infra*, p. 63.)

    2. **Rationale for jurisdiction based on domicile:** The rationale for allowing jurisdiction based on domicile was explained in *Milliken* as follows: *"A state which accords privileges and affords protection to [a person] and his property by virtue of his domicile may also exact reciprocal duties."*

    3. **Necessity for statutory authorization:** Most courts have held that they have jurisdiction based on domicile only if they have been given this by statute. (See F,K&C, p. 915.) Such a statute may be enacted retroactively, so as to apply to a cause of action arising before the statute's enactment. *McGee v. Int'l Life Insurance Co.*, 355 U.S. 220 (1957), upheld a California statute granting jurisdiction over companies writing insurance policies on California residents, even though the statute was enacted after the policy in question was written.

    4. **Domicile and citizenship:** Domicile is usually held to be synonymous with citizenship for personal jurisdiction purposes. A person can have only one domicile at a time for this purpose.

    5. **Domicile and residence:** Domicile is more limited than residence, since people can have several residences at one time.

    6. **Formula for domicile:** A person is considered to be domiciled in the place where he has his *current dwelling-place*, if he also has an *intention to remain* in that place for an *indefinite period*. The formula is sometimes expressed:

        domicile = current dwelling place + intent to remain indefinitely

        a. **Indefinite plan to return:** A "floating intention to return [to a previous domicile] at some future period" does not prevent a person's present residence from being his domicile; *Baker v. Keck*, 13 F.Supp. 486 (E. D. Ill. 1936). The key is that the intention to return must be indefinite in time.

b. **The 2nd Restatement of Conflicts (§18)** says "To acquire a domicile of choice in a place, a person must intend to make that place his home *for the time at least.*"

Example: A moves to state B to be near his mother, who has cancer, and who will probably die within the next year. A rents an apartment, and plans to stay in State B until his mother dies, at which time he plans to return to his old state of residence. A court would probably hold that he was domiciled in State B, since the date of his mother's death is not known with certainty, and his intention to stay in the state is therefore indefinite.

c. **Criteria for determining intention:** In determining a person's intention to remain indefinitely or permanently, the court will look at whether he has *registered to vote*, whether he has *left property behind* in his former state of residence, *where he works*, whether his *family has moved* with him, etc.

Example: A moves to State B, taking with him his family and all of his household goods, except two beds and other small items. He rents the farm he left behind in State A for five years, leaving his livestock on that farm. He registers to vote in State B as soon as he is eligible to do so (after 1 year of residence). He has never voted there, but the only day he could have voted was a day in which he had to be in court. He has returned to State A for short visits three or four times.

Held, A has changed his state of domicile from State A to State B, even though he admits that he plans to go back to State A to live after the litigation is completed. *Baker v. Keck*, 13 F. Supp. 486 (E.D. Ill. 1936).

d. **Prior residence as domicile:** Observe that the equation given above means that a person is domiciled in the place where he has his current dwelling-place only if he has the intention to remain there indefinitely. What happens if a person has a residence in a particular state, but does *not* intend to remain there indefinitely? Generally, his *prior* residence will be looked at; if there was a time when he intended to remain in that prior state indefinitely (so that it became his domicile), the court will treat it as *continuing* to be his domicile until he both resides in, and intends to remain indefinitely in, some new place. This can produce the anomaly that a person is treated as a domiciliary of a place that he no longer resides in and intends never to return to.

Example: P1 and P2, a husband and wife, sue D in federal court under diversity of citizenship. (See *infra*, p. 96.) It becomes relevant to determine the domicile of P1, the wife. P1 formerly lived in Mississippi. She then moved to Louisiana to attend graduate school; subsequently, she moved to Illinois, where she lives at the time the trial begins. She intends to move back to Louisiana so her husband can complete his schooling there, and does not know where she will reside thereafter.

Held, P1 is domiciled in Mississippi. Her move to Louisiana did not change her domicile since she never intended to remain there indefinitely. Nor did her temporary move to Illinois change her domicile. Therefore, her domicile remains Mississippi, and this will continue to be the case until she moves to a place in which she intends to reside indefinitely. This is true even though she has *no* intent ever to return to Mississippi to live. *Mas v. Perry*, 489 F.2d 1396 (5th Cir. 1974).

e. **Avoidance of jurisdiction:** As long as the intention to remain indefinitely in the new domicile exists, it is *irrelevant* that a defendant has *moved in order to avoid the jurisdiction* of his former state. (But he must make the move *before* the action against him is begun — see, e.g., *Owens v. Superior Court*, 345 P.2d 921 (Cal. 1959).)

f. **Diversity of citizenship:** The same definition of "domicile" described above is used to determine whether diversity of citizenship exists in federal cases. (The *Mas* case, *supra*, illustrates this.) See the discussion of diversity in the Subject Matter Jurisdiction chapter, *infra*, p. 93. See also Wr., pp. 146-48.

g. **"Dwelling place" not required:** An actual "dwelling-place" within the state is not necessary for domicile to be in the state; a hotel room can suffice, as long as the requisite intention to remain is present. The physical presence of the domiciliary must coincide with the requisite intention, if only for a brief period. 2 Rest. Confl., §16.

h. **Service on absent domiciliaries:** If the requirements for jurisdiction on the basis of domicile are met, service may be made on the absent defendant by personal service, or by any other method that is reasonably calculated to give him actual notice. (See Section on Notice and Opportunity to be Heard, *infra*, p. 63.)

7. **Effect of *Shaffer*:** *Milliken v. Meyer*, *supra*, p. 11, has never been explicitly overruled. Therefore, it apparently remains the case that jurisdiction may be exercised over a person who is domiciled within the forum state, even if he is absent from that state. However, *Shaffer v. Heitner*, discussed *infra*, pp. 56-60, may imply that the defendant's mere domicile in the forum state is *not always enough* to constitutionally confer jurisdiction over him. The Supreme Court held in *Shaffer* that it is unfair to subject a defendant to jurisdiction over his property located in the forum state if he does not have "minimum contacts" with that state. It would be equally unfair to make the defendant personally liable in the forum state merely because he was domiciled there, if he has subsequently moved his residence somewhere else but has not established a new domicile.

Example: In *Mas v. Perry*, above, plaintiff was treated by the court as still being domiciled in Mississippi, even though she had subsequently moved to Louisiana and then Illinois, and did not intend ever to return to Mississippi. It is questionable whether the Mississippi courts could constitutionally exercise jurisdiction over her based on domicile. See F,K&M, p. 160.

C. **Residence:** Some states allow jurisdiction to be exercised on the basis of defendant's *residence in the forum state*, even though he is absent from the state. Since a person may have several residences, but only one domicile, this is a looser ground for jurisdiction than domicile.

1. **Rationale:** The argument that the forum state grants certain privileges and protection to the property owner (police, fire, streets, etc.) and is thus entitled to exert jurisdiction in return, would apply almost as strongly to the resident as to the domiciliary.

2. **No Supreme Court decision:** The U.S. Supreme Court has not yet passed on the due process validity of jurisdiction based solely on residence.

D. Consent: Jurisdiction over a party can be exercised by virtue of his *consent*, even if he has no contacts whatsoever with the forum state.

1. Consent by filing action: A plaintiff is considered to have submitted to the court's jurisdiction by filing an action. A counterclaim may therefore be filed against him, by service on his attorney. He cannot escape jurisdiction by dismissing the action, or by failing to prosecute it. *Adam v. Saenger*, 303 U.S. 59 (1938).

2. Consent before claim arises: A party may agree to submit to the jurisdiction of a certain court even before any cause of action has arisen.

> **Example:** Defendants were Michigan farmers who signed a rental equipment leasing contract with a farm equipment company. The contract stated that the defendants agreed to designate a third person to receive process for them for a suit in New York, should one arise. The court found that the defendants had consented to the jurisdiction of the New York federal district court. *National Equipment Rental v. Szukhent*, 375 U.S. 311 (1964).

3. Cognovit: A party may not only agree to submit to the jurisdiction of a certain court in advance of a cause of action, he may even agree to *waive his right of notice and appearance*, and to allow a judgment to be entered against him by consent. The instrument indicating such consent is known as a *cognovit* note.

4. Implied consent: Certain state statutes recognize the doctrine of *implied consent*, by which a defendant is said to have impliedly consented to the jurisdiction of a state over him by virtue of acts which he had committed within the state. This doctrine will be discussed more fully in the sections on Non-resident Motorist Statutes, *infra*, and Jurisdiction over Corporations, *infra*, p. 18.

5. General appearance: If a suit is brought seeking personal liability over a defendant, his appearance in the court to contest the case *on the merits* constitutes consent to the court's jurisdiction, even if jurisdiction would not otherwise have been valid. Such an appearance on the merits is called a *general appearance*. If defendant first makes an objection to lack of jurisdiction, and then contests the case on the merits, the matter is more complicated — see the Section on Special Appearances, *infra*, p. 73.

E. Non-resident motorist statutes: Many states have statutes allowing their courts to exercise jurisdiction over *non-resident motorists* who have been involved in *accidents in the state.*

1. Implied consent: Formerly this jurisdiction over non-resident motorists was based on the fiction of *implied consent.*

> **Example:** A former Massachusetts statute held that Massachusetts had jurisdiction over anyone who operated a motor vehicle within the state, on the grounds that such a person could be said to have *impliedly consented* to jurisdiction by the act of operating the vehicle. *Hess v. Pawloski*, 274 U.S. 352 (1927).

a. Rationale: Statutes like the one in *Hess* justified the implying of consent by the following syllogism:

i. The state has a right to require entering non-resident motorists to appoint an in-state agent to receive process served against them.

ii. **The state has a right to exclude** those who refuse to make this appointment.

iii. **Therefore the state may infer that those** who drive into the state without being forced to appoint agents would have done so if they had been forced to, and they may be said to have impliedly consented to substitute service.

2. **Rejection of "implied consent" theory:** The modern trend in non-resident motorist statutes is to **reject the theory of implied consent**, in favor of a theory that the states have the right to use their **police power** and their court system to protect their own citizens who are injured by the automobile, a dangerous object.

3. **Cases where non-resident statutes used:** Non-resident motorist statutes have been applied in the following situations:

a. P is a resident of the forum state, and D was driving the car in the forum state, when the accident injuring P occurred. This is the most common situation in which non-resident motorist statutes are applied.

b. Neither P nor D is a resident of the forum state, but the accident occurred there. W&M, v. 4, p. 242.

c. D was never in the state at all, but merely lent his car to a friend, who had the accident in the state. *Id.*

d. D is the representative of the dead motorist. *Id.*

4. **Service on state official:** Most of the non-resident motorist statutes provide for in-state service of process on a **designated state official**, such as the Director of Motor Vehicles, and for **registered mail service** on the defendant himself.

F. **In-state tortious acts:** Many states have statutes allowing their courts jurisdiction over persons committing **tortious acts within the state**. The Illinois long-arm statute, for instance (the first really far-reaching long-arm, enacted in 1956) permits Illinois courts to exercise jurisdiction over any person in a cause of action arising from "the commission of a tortious act within this state" by that person or his agent.

Note: Remember that the term **"long-arm statute"** refers to a statute which permits the courts of a state to obtain jurisdiction over **persons not physically present within the state at the time of service**. Such statutes may allow jurisdiction on the basis of factors such as citizenship in the forum state, in-state property ownership, in-state tortious acts, etc.

1. **Measure of proof for jurisdiction:** Long-arm statutes based on in-state tortious acts allow jurisdiction if the plaintiff shows at the outset merely that it is **reasonably likely** that the defendant has committed a tortious act within the state. Proof of the kind that would suffice at trial is not required.

2. **Out-of-state acts with in-state consequences:** The clauses in long-arm statutes referring to "a tortious act within the state" or "tortious conduct within the state" have sometimes been interpreted to include acts done **outside the state** which produce **tortious consequences within the state**. This has happened most often in products liability cases, when the issue is whether there is a sufficient connection between the manufacturer or

vendor, and the state where the injury occurred, to permit personal jurisdiction over the former.

> **Example:** Titan (an Ohio company) makes valves which it sells to another company, which incorporates them into a boiler which it sells to Plaintiff. The boiler explodes in Illinois, injuring Plaintiff, who sues Titan in Illinois. The Illinois long-arm allows suit in Illinois based upon a "tortious act within the state." *Held*, a tortious act is committed where the resultant damage occurs. Therefore, the Illinois courts have jurisdiction in the present case. "In law the place of the wrong is where the last event takes place which is necessary to render the actor liable." *Gray v. American Radiator Corp.*, 176 N.E.2d 761 (Ill. 1961)

    a. *Gray* **case may be invalid:** But the assertion of jurisdiction in *Gray v. American Radiator Corp., supra,* may be invalid as the result of the Supreme Court's decision in *World-Wide Volkswagen Corp. v. Woodson*, discussed *infra*, p. 28. Certainly the mere fact that a product made out of state has found its way into the forum state, and has caused injury there, is not sufficient for the assertion of jurisdiction under *Volkswagen*. However, the majority opinion in *Volkswagen* noted that jurisdiction is permissible over a corporation that "delivers its products into the stream of commerce with the ***expectation that they will be purchased by consumers in the forum State.***" If the defendant in *Gray* had reason to expect that Illinois customers would buy a product containing its valves, *Gray* may survive the *Volkswagen* decision.

3. Libel: Statutes based on tortious acts committed in-state or with in-state consequences have been applied to *libel* cases. The special issues involved in jurisdiction over libel cases are discussed in detail *infra*, p. 37.

G. Owners of in-state property: Some statutes allow states to exercise jurisdiction over *owners of in-state property* in causes of action arising from that property.

1. Constitutional: These statutes are probably constitutional, since a person who chooses to own property in a state may reasonably anticipate that he will be required to defend a lawsuit in the state, at least where the suit relates to the property.

> **Example:** D lives in New York, but owns a vacation home in Florida. P, a Florida resident, slips on the sidewalk in front of D's Florida property, and sues D in Florida for negligently maintaining the sidewalk. Even if D has no other contacts with the state of Florida, it is almost certainly not a violation of due process for Florida to exercise jurisdiction over this case, since D voluntarily chose to own property in Florida, and should reasonably have anticipated that Florida might require him to defend lawsuits there that related to the property.

H. Conducting business: Some states have statutes allowing jurisdiction over non-residents who conduct *unincorporated businesses* within the state.

1. Constitutionality: It seems clear that such statutes are *constitutional*, i.e., that a state does not violate due process when it exercises jurisdiction over out-of-state individuals who do business within the state. Virtually all modern Supreme Court cases that have involved jurisdiction over out-of-staters transacting business in the state have concerned foreign *corporations*. These cases indicate that jurisdiction is valid whenever a defendant's contacts within the state are such as to make it "reasonable and just" and "not offensive to traditional notions of fair play" that the defendant be forced to defend within the state (the so-called *"minimum contacts"* standard). See, e.g., *International Shoe*, *infra*, p. 20. Almost certainly, the same "minimum contacts" standard applies to out-of-staters who transact business in-state as *individuals* rather than in corporate form.

I. **Recent statutory treatment:** Two long-arms, the Illinois statute and the Uniform Interstate and International Procedure Act, illustrate the significant reach which most states attempt to exercise today over out-of-state defendants.

    1. **Illinois long-arm:** Any person, whether a resident or not, submits himself to the jurisdiction of the Illinois courts for any cause of action arising from any of the following acts, among others:

        a. "The *transaction of any business* within this State."

        b. "The *commission of a tortious act* within this State."

        c. "The *ownership, use, or possession* of any real estate situated in this State."

        d. "The *making or performance of any contract or promise* substantially connected with this State."

    2. **Means of service under Illinois statute:** When jurisdiction is valid according to the Illinois long-arm, service may be made outside the state in person, and has the same effect as if it had been personally made within the state. Only *personal* (this presumably excludes mail) service seems to be contemplated by the statute.

    3. **UIIP:** The *Uniform Interstate and International Procedure Act* is similar to the Illinois long-arm with the following major differences:

        a. **Out-of-state torts with in-state consequences:** The UIIP statute asserts jurisdiction where out-of-state tortious conduct has in-state injurious consequences; but this provision applies only where the defendant *"regularly does or solicits business or engages in any other persistent course of conduct in this state or derives substantial revenue from goods or services used or consumed in this state."* By contrast, the Illinois long-arm does not seem, on its face, to allow jurisdiction for out-of-state torts having in-state consequences (though in *Gray v. American Radiator*, *supra*, p.16 , the tortious act was held to have taken place where the injury occurred, even though all physical motions by the defendant took place out of state.)

            i. **UIIP interpreted by Supreme Court:** The UIIP provision was given a strict reading by the Supreme Court in *World-Wide Volkswagen Corp. v. Woodson*, discussed *infra*, p. 28. The fact that the defendant derived revenue from goods used in the forum state is not sufficient for jurisdiction under *Volkswagen*; direct efforts to derive *substantial* revenue from the foreign state, rather than merely an occasional isolated sale for use in that state, must occur for there to be jurisdiction.

        b. **Contracts:** The UIIP Act includes jurisdiction over persons *"contracting to supply services or things in the state"* even though the contract is signed outside the state, and is breached before performance is begun.

c. Service: The UIIP Act does not require *personal* out-of-state service; presumably notice may be made by registered or certified mail, as long as this method meets Constitutional due process requirements.

4. Claim must relate to state: The UIIP applies *only to causes of action arising from the acts enumerated by the statute.* That is, transacting business within the forum state is not sufficient to confer jurisdiction for a cause of action not arising out of in-state business.

    a. Jurisdiction where cause of action is unrelated to in-state activities: The Supreme Court has never explicitly laid down the rules governing jurisdiction over individuals based on their in-state activities, where the cause of action sued on is not related to those activities. In the case of foreign corporations, the Court has required that in-state contacts must be *"systematic and continuous"* if the cause of action is unrelated to those contacts. In other words, the in-state activities must be *greater* to confer jurisdiction for a cause of action based on out-of-state acts, than to support jurisdiction for a claim arising from the in-state activities. (See *infra*, p. 25.) This distinction will almost certainly also be applied to unincorporated individuals.

J. Foreign nationals: Some long-arm statutes exercise jurisdiction over non-resident individuals located in *foreign countries*.

K. Statutes going to limits of due process: Some states have enacted long-arm statutes that purport to extend jurisdiction *as far as the due process clause* of the 14th Amendment will allow.

    Example: The California long-arm provides that "A court of this state may exercise jurisdiction *on any basis not inconsistent with the Constitution of this state or of the United States."*

1. Limits undefined: It is difficult to define what the limits of due process are with respect to jurisdiction over individuals. Probably the *"minimum contacts"* test applied to corporations, described *infra*, p. 20, would be applied by the Supreme Court if the issue were before it.

III. JURISDICTION OVER CORPORATIONS

A. General Principles:

1. Domestic corporations: *Any* action may be brought against a *domestic* corporation, i.e. one which is incorporated in the forum state.

    Note: The test of whether a corporation is a "resident" of the forum state is different for the purposes of state *in personam* jurisdiction (i.e. jurisdiction over the parties) than it is for the purposes of determining the existence of *federal diversity* jurisdiction. For state *in personam* purposes, a corporation is "domestic" or "resident" only if it is incorporated within the state; if it is not, the corporation must meet one of the other criteria described below for the state to have jurisdiction over it. For *federal diversity* purposes, a corporation is a "citizen" of not only the state in which it is incorporated, but also of the state where it has its *principal place of business*.

2. **Presence of corporate agent:** Whereas an individual can perhaps be "tagged" with process in a state where his presence is transient, the same *cannot be done* with a corporation whose presence is occasional and casual. Thus a corporate agent who comes into the state only occasionally to conduct a small piece of business does not render the corporation liable to service through him. The corporation must meet minimum standards of contact with a state beyond mere presence by an agent, before that state may exercise jurisdiction over it. These minimum contacts are described below.

3. **Cessation of in-state contacts:** Once an act or the systematic doing of in-state business has rendered a corporation subject to the state's jurisdiction, as outlined below, the fact that the corporation has ceased to do business within the state will not undo this "amenability to process." W&M, V.4, p. 262.

B. **Older tests for jurisdiction over foreign corporations:** Before the landmark 1945 case of *International Shoe*, courts had a number of theories justifying the exercise of jurisdiction over "foreign" corporations, i.e., ones not incorporated in the forum state. These ideas are mostly of historical interest today. Here is a brief overview of this pre-*International Shoe* law:

1. **Existence only where incorporated:** A corporation was originally held not to legally exist outside of the state which incorporated it, since the only reason a corporation could "exist" at all was because its home state had incorporated it.

   a. **Where corporation suable:** This meant that although the corporation was capable of bringing suit in states where it was not incorporated, it could not itself be sued anywhere but in its state of incorporation.

2. **Corporate agent to receive process:** Many states have always required foreign corporations to be *licensed* within the state before they are allowed to transact in-state business. These states have often made the express *appointment by the corporation of an agent to receive in-state process* a part of the licensing procedure. James & Hazard, p. 61.

   a. **Consent:** This express appointment of an agent has been held to confer jurisdiction by "consent."

3. **Implied consent:** On the theory that a state could exclude a foreign corporation from doing business in the state at all, the notion was developed that a corporation which *was* allowed to do business had *"impliedly consented"* to the state's jurisdiction over it. *St. Clair v. Cox*, 106 U.S. 350 (1882).

   a. **Interstate Commerce clause:** But the notion of implied consent, since it was based on the idea that the state could, if it wished, exclude the foreign corporation altogether, ran afoul of the Constitutional prohibition against excessive restraints on interstate commerce. James & Hazard, p. 61.

4. **Corporate presence:** The "implied consent" doctrine gave way to the idea of *"corporate presence."*

   a. **Brandeis' view:** This view was expressed by Justice Brandeis: "A foreign corporation is amenable to process to enforce a personal liability, in the absence of consent, *only if it is doing business within the State in such manner and to such extent as to warrant the inference that it is present there."* *Philadelphia & Reading Railway v.*

McKibbin, 243 U.S. 264 (1917). More than a single act or limited activity was generally required for "presence."

b. Residence of corporate agent: The "presence" test was *not* satisfied by the mere presence or even in-state residence of a *stockholder, officer*, or *agent*, who did not carry out the corporation's business inside the state.

 i. Modern rule: It has remained true today, under *all* theories, that the *mere presence within the state of a corporate employee or officer, is not by itself enough to confer jurisdiction over the corporation*. The employee or officer must at least do some corporate business within the state. (See discussion of *Perkins v. Benguet Mining Co., infra*, p. 25.)

C. Modern ideas on jurisdiction over foreign corporations: The modern view of jurisdiction over foreign corporations derives mainly from *International Shoe Co. v. Washington*, 326 U.S. 310 (1945).

 1. The "minimum contacts" test of *International Shoe:* In *International Shoe*, the state of Washington sought to collect unemployment taxes based on commissions paid by the firm to its Washington-based salesmen. The company's status with respect to Washington was as follows:

  a. Incorporation: The company was incorporated in Delaware, and its principal place of business was in Missouri.

  b. Washington activities: The firm conducted no business in Washington except for the activities of its Washington-based salesmen, who solicited orders for the firm.

  c. Office: The firm had no Washington office, but the salesmen sometimes rented display rooms in the state.

  d. Salesmen's authority: The salesmen had no authority to enter into contracts; all orders had to be approved by the home office.

  e. Shipping: All orders were shipped to Washington from the home office in Missouri.

  f. Commissions: Total commissions paid annually to the Washington salesmen were about $31,000.

 2. Holding: On the basis of the above facts, the Supreme Court concluded that the state of Washington could *constitutionally exercise jurisdiction* over the Shoe Company.

  a. Test: The Court established a new test based on *minimum contacts* with the forum state: "Due process requires only that in order to subject a defendant to a judgment *in personam*, if he be not present within the territory of the forum, he have *certain minimum contacts with it such that the maintenance of the suit does not offend 'traditional notions of fair play and substantial justice'.*"

  b. Applicability to individuals: The *Shoe* case involved a *corporate defendant*, but the language used above, with its implicit rejection of the requirement that jurisdiction be limited by territoriality (the theory of *Pennoyer*) seems applicable to *individuals* as well.

    c. Inconvenience: The test of "fair play" may include "an *'estimate of the inconveniences'* which would result to the corporation from a trial away from its 'home' or principal place of business."

    d. Claims not arising from in-state contacts: While *Shoe* involved a cause of action arising from activities within the state of Washington (the unemployment taxes sought were based on the payments of commissions by the firm to its salesmen for work done in Washington) the court left open the possibility that a firm might have sufficient contacts with the forum state to subject it to jurisdiction even on a cause of action independent of any instate activities.

3. Black's concurrence: A concurrence in *International Shoe* by Justice Black argued that a state has an ***absolute Constitutional right to protect its own citizens*** by allowing them to sue a corporation on ***any claim arising from their in-state dealings with the firm***.

    a. "Inconvenience" criterion rejected: The concurrence strongly rejected the idea that the "inconvenience" to the corporation of being forced to defend away from home should be considered.

    b. Black's rejection of "fair play" idea: The concurrence also rejected basing the jurisdictional test on notions of "fair play" and "substantial justice"; "For application of this natural law concept … makes judges the supreme arbiters of the country's laws and practices … and means that tomorrow's judgment may strike down a State or Federal enactment on the ground that it does not conform to this Court's idea of natural justice."

D. The limits of the "minimum contacts" test: Several post-*International Shoe* cases have spelled out the limits of "minimum contacts."

1. *McGee:* *McGee v. International Life Insurance Co.*, 335 U.S. 220 (1957), was a California case involving an insurance policy written by a Texas company on a California resident.

    a. Contacts with forum state: The *contacts* between the insurance company and the forum state were as follows:

        i. Assumption of obligation: The company assumed the insurance obligations of the deceased's previous insurer, and sent the deceased a reinsurance offer which he accepted.

        ii. Mailing of premiums: The deceased mailed all premiums to the defendant from California until his death.

        iii. California residents: Both the deceased and the plaintiff (the beneficiary under the policy) were California residents.

        iv. Witnesses: The insurance company refused to pay the benefits, claiming that the deceased's death was a suicide; the witnesses to this death were all residents of California.

        v. Offices and solicitation: The defendant insurance company had no offices in California, and had apparently never solicited or done any business in the state, apart from the policy in this case.

b. **Basis for jurisdiction:** California's jurisdiction over the insurance company in *McGee* was based on a statute allowing jurisdiction in suits on insurance contracts with California residents, even if the insurer could not otherwise be sued in the state.

c. **Holding:**   The U.S. Supreme Court held that these contacts were **sufficient** to allow jurisdiction in California over the Texas insurance company. The key point in *McGee* was that California had a strong interest in **protecting its citizens**, by giving them a local forum to sue the out-of-state company with which they had dealings. As Justice Black wrote, "It is sufficient for purposes of due process that the suit was based on a contract which had **substantial connection** with [the forum state]. ... It cannot be denied that California has a manifest interest in providing effective means of redress for its citizens when their insurers refuse to pay claims. These residents would be at a severe disadvantage if they were forced to follow the insurance company to a distant state in order to hold it legally accountable."

    i. **Broad application of *McGee*:** It is not clear whether the holding in *McGee* applies to all contracts which have substantial connection with the forum state, or only to industries, like the insurance industry, that are susceptible to regulation. The language of *McGee* seems to be broadly applicable to all businesses, and the holding has been so interpreted.

    ii. **Importance of *McGee*:**   *McGee* represents the **least contact with the forum state** that has been approved by the Supreme Court as the basis for personal jurisdiction. Note that the cause of action here involved the defendant's **in-state** activities. In cases where the claim does not involve in-state activities, **significantly greater contacts with the forum state** have always been required. (See *Perkins v. Benguet*, *infra*, p. 25.)

2. ***Hanson v. Denckla:* *Hanson v. Denckla*, 357 U.S. 235 (1958), involved the decisions of two states about the disposition of the funds from a trust.

a. **Facts:** The general (and unfortunately complicated) facts of *Hanson* are as follows:

    i. A Mrs. Donner, while she was domiciled in Pennsylvania, created a trust, the trustee of which was a Delaware bank. The terms of the trust gave her a life estate in the trust, and gave her the power to dispose of the remainder of the trust either by will or by an instrument taking effect during her lifetime.

    ii. Ten years after making the trust, she moved to Florida, and several years after that, assigned the remainder of the trust to her grandchildren in trust.

    iii. In her will, the remaining assets of the trust (assuming that her assignment of the trust assets to her grandchildren was invalid) passed to her two daughters, residents of Florida.

    iv. The daughters, claiming that the appointment of the remainder of the trust to the grandchildren was invalid, argued that the trust funds should pass to them through the will. They sued in Florida for a declaratory judgment to that effect; the Delaware trustee was notified by mail and in-state publication, as provided by Florida law.

v. The Florida court, in a trial at which the Delaware trustee did not appear, found that the funds passed through the will to the daughters.

vi. Meanwhile, the Delaware trust beneficiaries (the grandchildren) sued in Delaware for a declaratory judgment that the funds passed to them through the assignment Mrs. Donner had made, and not through the will. The daughters, although notified by mail, did not appear. The Delaware court found that the property passed to the grandchildren.

vii. The two decisions, inconsistent with each other, were appealed to the Supreme Court. The two issues decided by the Court were: (1) Did Florida have jurisdiction over the Delaware trustee? and (2) If so, did Delaware err in refusing to give the Florida judgment full faith and credit?

b. Holding: The Supreme Court in *Hanson* found that the Florida court could ***not*** constitutionally exercise jurisdiction over the Delaware trustee, since the trustee's contacts with Florida were insufficient. The Court emphasized the following:

i. The trustee bank had never done any other business in Florida.

ii. The cause of action sued on could not be said to have arisen out of business done in Florida, since the trustee's obligation was created in Pennsylvania, and merely continued when the settlor of the trust, Mrs. Donner, moved to Florida.

c. Importance of *Hanson*:   *Hanson* was the first major post-*International Shoe* case in which the Supreme Court ***invalidated*** asserted jurisdiction over a foreign corporation.

i. Limits on state court personal jurisdiction: The Court noted that it would be a mistake to assume that the liberalized jurisdiction requirements of *International Shoe* heralded the demise of all restraints on the personal jurisdiction of state courts.

ii. Nature of restraints on jurisdiction: Restrictions on jurisdiction "are more than a guaranty of immunity from inconvenient or distant litigation. They are a consequence of ***territorial limitations on the power of the respective states***. However minimal the burden of defending in a foreign tribunal, a defendant may not be called upon to do so unless he had had the 'minimum contacts' with that state that are a prerequisite to its exercise of power over him."

d. *Hanson* distinguished from *McGee*: The Court distinguished *Hanson* from *McGee* partly on the grounds that in *Hanson*, the contacts with the forum state were initiated by the settlor, not the defendant. "The unilateral activities of those who claim some relationship with a non-resident defendant cannot satisfy requirements of contact with the forum state. ... It is essential that in each case there be ***some act by which the defendant purposely avails itself of the privilege of conducting activities within the forum State***, thus involving the benefit and protections of its laws."

i. "Center of gravity" ignored: The Court noted that a state court "does ***not*** acquire ... jurisdiction by being '*the center of gravity*' of the controversy, or the ***most convenient location*** for litigation." 357 U.S. at 254.

e.   Full Faith and Credit issue: Since the Florida judgment was void for want of jurisdiction, the Delaware court was not bound to give it full faith and credit.

f.   Black's dissent in *Hanson*: A dissent in *Hanson*, by Justice Black, stressed that Florida:

   i.   was the home of all the principal contenders for the money;

   ii.   was a reasonably convenient forum for all litigants; even the Delaware trustee had maintained correspondence voluntarily with Mrs. Donner for eight years after her move to Florida, and could therefore be subjected to suit there without fundamental unfairness;

   iii.   had an interest in the trust funds, since Mrs. Donner's will was probated in that state.

g.   Minimum contacts still required: "The principal significance of *Hanson* is probably that the Court still insists on minimum contacts ***between the state and the non-resident***. It is not enough that the subject matter of the action has ample connection with the forum state; nor that the balance of convenience favors it." James (1st Ed.), 643.

   Note: See also *Rush v. Savchuk*, *infra*, p. 55, similarly holding that minimum contacts between defendant and forum state are always necessary.

3.   Minimum contacts in domestic relations cases: The minimum contacts rule has been applied in the ***domestic relations*** context. In ***Kulko v. Superior Court***, 436 U.S. 84 (1978), the Supreme Court held that a father residing in New York does not acquire "minimum contacts" with California merely by permitting his minor daughter to go there to live with her mother. The Court therefore refused to allow the mother to bring an *in personam* suit in California against the father for increased child support.

a.   State interest: The Court conceded that California had a strong interest in assuring the financial support of children residing in it. But this interest was adequately protected by the Uniform Reciprocal Enforcement of Support Act, in force in both California and New York, which would have allowed the wife to obtain a New York adjudication on the support issue, without requiring her to leave California.

   i.   Distinguished from *McGee*: The Court therefore distinguished this case from *McGee*, *supra*, p. 21, where citizens of the forum state would have been severely disadvantaged by an inability to bring suit there against out-of-state insurers who refused to pay claims.

b.   Divorce allowed: But California's right to grant effect to a Haitian divorce was not questioned — this was adjudication of a status, which is considered to be *in rem*, and permissible where *either* spouse is domiciled — see *infra*, p. 51.

E.   Use of agents: Suppose a foreign company does not itself conduct activities within the forum state, but uses another company as its ***agent*** within the state. If all business within the state is done by the agent, can the principal (the foreign corporation) be sued there? The answer is ***"yes,"*** if the agent does a significant amount of business on the foreign company's behalf.

1.   Test: One court has phrased the test as follows: "A foreign corporation is doing business in [the forum state] 'in the traditional sense' when its [forum state] representative provides services beyond 'mere solicitation' and these services are sufficiently important to the foreign corporation that *if it did not have a representative to perform them, the corporation's own officials would undertake to perform substantially similar services.*" *Gelfand v. Tanner Motor Tours*, 385 F.2d 116 (2d Cir. 1967).

   a. **Application:** In *Gelfand*, this test was held to be satisfied, since the agent (a non-profit organization which booked travel tours for the foreign corporation and other companies) accounted for 40% of the foreign corporation's total business, maintained an office in the forum state, and actually advertised and promoted the foreign corporation's tours in the state.

2. **Jurisdiction not automatic:** But the mere fact that a foreign corporation has an agent representing it in the forum state does not by itself suffice to bring the foreign corporation within the forum state's jurisdiction. The agent must do a significant volume of business in the state on the defendant's behalf, and the defendant must have at least some control over how the agent does that business. For instance, in *Cook Associates v. Lexington United Corp.*, 429 N.E. 2d 847 (Ill. 1981), D was a non-Illinois corporation which manufactured dinnerware. The fact that D had an Illinois-based manufacturer's representative (who represented other companies' products as well as D's), was held insufficient to constitute the "doing of business" in Illinois by D.

   a. **Factors:** The court in *Cook* indicated that the relevant factors would include the *dollar volume* of sales of D's products by the representative in Illinois, the extent to which D had *"control"* over the representative's actions, and whether the representative was *authorized to contract* for D (as opposed to being required to send orders to D's out-of-state office for acceptance). (The decision in *Cook* revolved around whether D was "doing business" in the state, a concept which the court defined in terms of common-law, not constitutional, notions. Therefore, the court never reached the issue of whether D had the constitutionally-required "minimum contacts" with Illinois. However, it seems unlikely that even this minimal standard was satisfied by the representative's actions.)

3. **Combination of agent's and principal's actions:** Where the foreign corporation has an agent acting for it in the state, the court will often *aggregate* the actions taken for the corporation by the agent together with the corporation's *own* actions in the state.

F. **Claims unrelated to in-state activity:** All of the cases discussed so far involved claims related to the defendant's activities within the forum state. Where the cause of action *does not arise from the company's in-state activities, greater contacts* between the defendant and the forum state have been required. The standard seems to be that the in-state activities must be *"systematic and continuous."*

1. **"General" jurisdiction:** Where the claim does not arise from the in-state contacts, the *in personam* jurisdiction asserted is sometimes called *"general"* jurisdiction. This term contrasts with *"specific"* jurisdiction, the situation in which the claim does arise from the in-state contacts.

2. *Perkins:* The leading case on claims not arising out of in-state activities is *Perkins v. Benguet Consolidated Mining Co.*, 342, U.S. 437 (1952), in which the defendant was an out-of-state mining company.

a. **Facts:** The general facts of *Perkins* were as follows:

    i. **The company's mining operations,** all of which were in the Philippines, were suspended during the Second World War by the Japanese invasion of the Islands.

    ii. **During that time, the president** (who was also the principal stockholder) returned home to Ohio, where he maintained an office, did business on behalf of the company, and kept the company files.

    iii. **The plaintiff was suing for dividends** she claimed the company owed her based on its profits from its Philippine operations. The cause of action thus did not involve the company's Ohio activities.

b. **Test of *Perkins*:** The Court held that where the cause of action does not arise from business done within the forum state, Constitutional due process requires that the in-state business actually conducted be so ***systematic and continuous*** as to make it not unjust that the corporation be forced to defend a suit there. "The essence of the issue here, at the constitutional level, is … one of general fairness to the corporation."

c. **Holding in *Perkins*:** The mining company president's in-state activities were held to be extensive enough so that Constitutional due process neither prohibited nor compelled Ohio's jurisdiction over the mining company; the matter was to be left to the discretion of the Ohio courts. But the Court emphasized that notice requirements must also be met (as they were here by personal service on the president).

3. **In-state purchases:** The more rigorous "systematic and continuous activities" standard for claims not arising out of the defendant's in-state activities is ***still in force***. The Supreme Court applied the test, and cited *Perkins*, in ***Helicopteros Nacionales de Colombia, S.A. v. Hall***, 466 U.S. 408 (1984). *Helicopteros* also establishes that, where the claim does not arise out of the defendant's in-state activities, the mere fact that ***purchases*** have been made by the defendant in the forum state, even if they have occurred regularly, will not be sufficient to establish the requisite minimum contacts.

a. **Facts:** The defendant in *Helicopteros* was a Colombian corporation in the business of providing helicopter transportation in South America for oil construction companies. It signed a contract to provide such services to Consorcio, in connection with a pipeline in Peru. Plaintiffs were the estates of employees of Consorcio who were killed when a helicopter supplied by and piloted by D crashed in Peru.

b. **Defendant's contacts with forum:** D's contacts with Texas (the forum state) consisted of the following: (1) one negotiating session between the president of D and officials of Consorcio; (2) the purchase by D of 80% of its helicopter fleet from Bell Helicopter Co. of Texas, at a cost of more than $4 million; (3) the sending of pilots and maintenance personnel to Bell Helicopter for training; and (4) the receipt in two non-Texas American banks of payments by Consorcio drawn upon a Texas bank.

c. **Holding:** The Supreme Court held that these contacts did ***not***, in the aggregate, constitute the requisite "minimum contacts." The wrongful death claims did not "arise out of" the defendant's in-Texas activities; therefore, the issue was whether those activities "constitute the kind of ***continuous*** and ***systematic*** general business contacts the Court found to exist in *Perkins*." The Court concluded that they did not.

    i. Rationale: The Court quickly dismissed the significance of the negotiating session and the checks; the single trip to negotiate was not a contact of a "continuous and systematic" nature; the receipt of checks drawn on a Texas bank was a "unilateral activity of another party" and was therefore not to be taken into account (the Court cited *Hanson* and *Kulko* on this point.) The sending of personnel to be trained did not have any independent significance; it was "part of the package of goods and services purchased by [D]." Therefore, the question boiled down to whether those purchases within the forum state sufficed to establish the requisite minimum contacts.

    ii. Mere purchases not sufficient: In the most significant part of its decision, the Court held that "***Mere purchases, even if occurring at regular intervals***, are ***not enough*** to warrant a State's assertion of *in personam* jurisdiction over a non-resident corporation in a cause of action not related to those purchase transactions." The Court gave little reasoning in support of this conclusion; instead, it cited a 1923 Supreme Court decision involving the owner of a small clothing store in Tulsa who made occasional trips to New York to buy from wholesalers there.

  d. Dissent: Justice Brennan, the sole dissenter in *Helicopteros*, argued that the cause of action was ***"related to"*** (even though not "arising out of") the defendant's in-Texas contacts. Therefore, he argued, the stricter standard of *Perkins* should not be applied. Since the negotiations that led to the providing of the transportation services involved in the crash were conducted in Texas, and since the helicopter that crashed was purchased (and its pilot trained) in Texas, Defendant "should have expected to be amenable to suit in the Texas courts for claims directly related to these contacts." Therefore, in Brennan's view, it was "fair and reasonable" to allow the suit to go forward in Texas.

  e. Scope: The majority in *Helicopteros* did not definitively reject the assertion that claims that "relate to" (but do not "arise out of") the defendant's in-state contacts should not be subjected to the stringent approach of *Perkins*; the majority declined to address this contention, on the theory that it had not been briefed by the parties. Therefore, ***the possibility remains that a claim "related to" the in-state activities will be enough*** to trigger the ***less demanding standard*** applied for "specific" jurisdiction.

4. Newspaper publication: Still another illustration of the principle that greater contacts are required where the cause of action does not arise from contacts with the forum state, came in a Supreme Court *libel* decision, *Keeton v. Hustler Magazine, Inc.*, 465 U.S. 770 (1984) (discussed more extensively *infra*, p. 37).

  a. Facts: D's contacts with the forum state (New Hampshire) consisted solely of the circulation there of from 10-15,000 copies per month of its magazine, *Hustler*; P (who was not a resident of New Hampshire and had no other contacts with it) claimed that articles in *Hustler* injured her reputation in New Hampshire and elsewhere.

  b. Holding: The Court found that there was jurisdiction, because the cause of action arose "out of the very activity being conducted, in part, in New Hampshire." But it noted that D's activities in the forum "may not be so substantial as to support jurisdiction over a cause of action unrelated to those activities." (The Court also observed that

D's contacts with the forum state were less extensive than those of the defendant in *Perkins.*)

G. **Jurisdiction involving products liability:** Much litigation against out-of-state corporations has been in *products liability* cases, where the foreign corporation is charged with making or selling (out-of-state) a product which is shipped into the forum state and which causes personal injury there. Not surprisingly, injured plaintiffs have sought to bring suit in the state where the injury occurred (usually the plaintiff's home state).

1. **Statutes:** Such attempts are supported, at least partially, by the language of many long-arm statutes. For instance, most long-arm statutes (e.g. the Ill. long-arm; *supra*, p. 17) allow jurisdiction over corporations in cases where an in-state tortious act is sued on. Such statutes have sometimes been interpreted to include tortious conduct outside the state producing in-state injury. (See *Gray, supra*, p. 16.)

   a. **Explicit provision:** Some long-arm statutes even explicitly provide for jurisdiction in cases of out-of-state tortious conduct having in-state consequences (e.g., the UIIP long-arm, *supra*, p. 17).

2. *Volkswagen* **case:** But the Supreme Court has placed significant limits on the use of long-arm statutes in products liability suits against out-of-state manufacturers and vendors. The mere fact that a product finds its way into a state and causes injury there is *not enough* to subject the out-of-state manufacturer or vendor to personal jurisdiction there. Instead, some *effort to market in the forum state*, either directly or indirectly, is required, as the result of *World-Wide Volkswagen Corp. v. Woodson*, 444 U.S. 286 (1980).

   a. **Facts of *Volkswagen:*** In *Volkswagen*, the Ps sued in Oklahoma for injuries suffered there in an accident involving an allegedly defective car; they had purchased the car in New York while they were New York residents. The Ds were, *inter alia*, the distributor of the car (a non-Oklahoma resident who distributed only in New York, New Jersey and Connecticut) and the dealer (a non-Oklahoma resident whose showroom was in New York). Neither the distributor nor the dealer sold cars in Oklahoma or did any other business there.

   b. **Holding:** The Supreme Court held that even though it may have been foreseeable that the defendants might derive revenue from a car ultimately used in Oklahoma, this was *not sufficient to confer jurisdiction* on the Oklahoma courts. The Court stated that "the foreseeability that is critical to due process analysis is not the mere likelihood that a product will find its way into the forum State. Rather, it is that the defendant's conduct and connection with the forum state are such that he should reasonably *anticipate being haled into court there.*"

      i. **Application of test:** Thus if either of the defendants had made efforts "to serve directly or indirectly, the market for its products" in Oklahoma, it would not be unreasonable to subject it to that state's jurisdiction. But here, the use of the defendants' products in Oklahoma was merely an "isolated occurrence," and was completely due to the *unilateral activity of the Ps.*

      ii. **Ordered from forum state:** Under this analysis, one critical fact seems to be that the Ps bought the car in New York, and were New York residents at the time they did so. If they had placed the order from Oklahoma, and had had the car shipped by the dealer to them directly there, this would seem to be enough to subject the dealer (and perhaps the distributor as well) to Oklahoma's jurisdiction, even if that were the only car shipped directly to the state. (Alternatively, if the Ds advertised in Oklahoma, or shipped more than an occasional car there, there would probably be jurisdiction even for a suit involving a car bought from the Ds in New York, at least if the accident took place in Oklahoma.)

c. **Dissent:** Three Justices dissented in *Volkswagen*. One of them, Justice Brennan, noted that the car accident occurred in Oklahoma, that the Ps were hospitalized there when they brought the suit, and that essential witnesses and evidence were there. Also, he argued, Oklahoma has a legitimate interest in enforcing its laws designed to keep its highway system safe.

d. **Single out-of-state tort:** The rule of *Volkswagen* is also supported by the potential paralyzing effect on commerce which might result if jurisdiction were based on a single out-of-state tortious act with in-state consequences (even where the in-state consequences were foreseeable).

   Example: Suppose a California retailer is asked to sell a tire to a customer whose car has Pennsylvania license plates. If he can be forced to defend in Pennsylvania if the tire blows out there, he may refuse to make such sales altogether. The judge who posed the above example said that "it is difficult to conceive of a more serious threat and deterrent to the free flow of commerce between states." *Erlanger Mills v. Cohoes Fibre Mills*, 239 F.2d 502 (4th Cir. 1956).

3. **Awareness of sales in foreign state (*Asahi*):** *Volkswagen* establishes that the mere fact that a user of a product takes it into the forum state is not sufficient to confer jurisdiction over the manufacturer, even if the latter should have foreseen that the user might do so. Suppose, however, that Manufacturer, a foreign company, repeatedly sells to Merchant, a non-forum-state business, who repeatedly resells some of the goods in the forum state, that Manufacturer *knows* that this is happening, but that Manufacturer makes no other efforts directed at the forum state (e.g., advertising, sales office, exclusive distributor for that state, etc.). Arguably, there could be jurisdiction over Manufacturer notwithstanding *Volkswagen*, since he has benefited continually, albeit indirectly, from what he knows to be sales of his product by Merchant in the forum state. In *Asahi Metal Industry Co. v. Superior Court*, 480 U.S. 102 (1987), the Supreme Court considered this issue. The Court was badly split on the proper analysis: five members believed that the foreign manufacturer had the requisite minimum contacts with the forum state (California), but eight members believed that because of the unusual posture of the parties, it would be so unreasonable as to be violative of due process to exercise that power.

   a. **Facts of *Asahi*:** Gary Zurcher lost control of his motorcycle while riding in California, and was seriously injured. He brought a products liability suit in California state court, claiming that the cycle's rear tire and tube were defective. One of the co-defendants was Cheng Shin, the Taiwanese manufacturer of the tube. Cheng Shin in turn impleaded (see p. 343, *infra*) Asahi, the Japanese manufacturer of the tube's valve assembly — in the impleader suit, Chen Shin sought indemnity from Asahi for the full amount of Cheng Shin's payment to Zurcher. Zurcher eventually settled all of his claims against the various defendants, leaving only Cheng Shin's impleader suit against Asahi.

b.   Contacts: Asahi ships valve assemblies from Japan to Taiwan. Over a five-year period, Asahi shipped over a million valve assemblies to Cheng Shin; Cheng Shin sold tires containing the valve assemblies throughout the world, including an unspecified number in the U.S. Cheng Shin claimed that 20% of its U.S. sales were in California, and presented evidence that nearly 20% of the tire tubes found in a typical motorcycle store had been produced by Asahi. There was evidence that Asahi was aware that the valves it sold to Cheng Shin and others would end up in the U.S. and in California. However, Asahi made no direct sales in California, had no offices or agents there, and did not control the system of distribution that carried its products into the state. (Apparently, Cheng Shin was free to sell the tubes incorporating the valves anywhere in the world.)

c.   Line-up of opinions: All nine members of the Court believed that California could not, consonant with due process, adjudicate Cheng Shin's indemnity claim against Asahi. But the Court was badly split as to the rationale. Five Justices (Brennan, joined by White, Marshall, and Blackmun, and Stevens in a separate concurrence) believed that Asahi *had minimum contacts* with California, because it put its goods into a stream of commerce that it knew would lead many of them to the state. But all Justices except Scalia believed that despite these minimum contacts, it would be "unreasonable and unfair" for California to hear the case, because of: (1) the burden to Asahi of defending in a foreign legal system; (2) the slenderness of California's and Cheng Shin's interests in having the indemnity claim heard in California; and (3) the strong federal and state interest in not creating foreign relations problems by deciding an indemnity claim between two foreign defendants.

d.   O'Connor's opinion: Justice O'Connor's opinion was the main one in *Asahi.*

i.   No minimum contacts: On the issue of whether Asahi had minimum contacts with California, she concluded that it did not. Such contacts could only come about "by an action of the defendant *purposefully directed toward the forum State*." And "[t]he placement of a product into the stream of commerce, without more, is not an act of the defendant purposefully directed toward the forum State." Had Asahi designed the valves for the California market, advertised in that state, established "channels for providing regular advice to customers" in the state, or marketed the product through a distributor who agreed to serve as sales agent there, any of these acts would have been sufficient "purposeful direction." "But a defendant's awareness that the stream of commerce may or will *sweep the product* into the forum State does not convert the mere act of placing the product into the stream into an act purposefully directed toward the forum State." On this "minimum contacts" issue, Justice O'Connor was joined *only* by Rehnquist, Powell, and Scalia; as noted, the other five Justices believed that Asahi did have minimum contacts with California.

ii.   Reasonableness: O'Connor then concluded that even if Asahi had minimum contacts with California, it would be so unreasonable as to constitute a violation of due process for California to *exercise* the jurisdiction. "[R]easonableness" should be determined by a consideration of "the burden on the defendant, the interests of the forum state, ... the plaintiff's interest in obtaining relief, ... 'the interstate judicial system's interest in obtaining the most efficient resolution of controversies; and the shared interest of the several States in furthering fundamental substantive social policies.' " Here, the burden on Asahi of having to defend in California would be great, not only because of distance but because it would have to submit to a foreign nation's judicial system. California's interests in hearing the controversy were very weak, since the third-party plaintiff (Cheng Shin) was not a California resident, and the transaction which gave rise to the indemnification claim took place in Taiwan. The third-party plaintiff's own interest in having a California forum was also weak, for the same reasons. And the need for the whole system to resolve controversies most efficiently meant that in a multi-national situation like this, U.S. courts should be especially leery of extending their notions of jurisdiction into the international field. On this "reasonableness" or balancing step, Justice O'Connor spoke for all members of the Court except Justice Scalia (who agreed that there were no minimum contacts and who remained silent on the issue of reasonableness).

e. **Brennan's concurrence:** Four Justices (Brennan, joined by White, Marshall, and Blackmun), in a concurrence, disagreed with O'Connor on the minimum contacts issue. The Brennan group believed that "[a]s long as a participant in [the manufacturing-to-distribution-to-retail-sale] process is aware that the final product is being marketed in the forum State, the possibility of a lawsuit there cannot come as a surprise," and the participant should thus be regarded as having the requisite minimum contacts. Asahi *benefited economically* from the regular retail sale of the final product in California, so it was fair for it to be treated as having the requisite contacts with the state. There is a big difference, the Brennan group believed, between a situation where a single consumer fortuitously transports the defendant's goods into the forum state (insufficient contacts, as in *Volkswagen, supra*, p. 28) and the situation where the defendant's products are *regularly sold* there (sufficient contacts, as here).

   i. **Unreasonable:** But Brennan implicitly agreed with O'Connor's view that it would be *unreasonable* to require Asahi to defend the third-party indemnity claim, given the settlement of the primary Zurcher-Cheng Shin claim.

f. **Stevens' concurrence:** Justice Stevens, in a separate concurrence, similarly agreed that it would be unreasonable to exercise jurisdiction here. Stevens saw no need to decide the minimum contacts issue, although he noted in dictum that "[i]n most circumstances I would be inclined to conclude that a regular course of dealing that results in deliveries of over 100,000 units annually over a period of several years would constitute 'purposeful availment' even though the item delivered to the forum State was a standard product marketed throughout the world."

g. **Significance:** *Asahi* is significant for two main reasons:

   i. **Reasonableness:** First, it marks the first time in recent years that the Court has found it to be unreasonable and thus *violative of due process* for a state to exercise jurisdiction over a defendant that, a majority of the Court believed, *had minimum* *contacts* with the forum state. As Justice Brennan put it, "[t]his is one of those rare cases in which 'minimum requirements inherent in the concept of fair play and substantial justice' ... defeat the reasonableness of jurisdiction even [though] the defendant has purposefully engaged in forum activities." The burden on the defendant was so great, and the interests of the forum state and the plaintiff were so weak, that these difficulties were enough to overcome what a majority thought were weak minimum contacts and a minority thought were no minimum contacts at all.

    ii. Minimum contacts issue: Second, the case is notable for being probably the *slenderest contact* with the forum state that a majority has believed constitutes "minimum contacts." In the view of five members of the Court, a foreign manufacturer who makes a product that he knows will be incorporated in another product, and eventually sold in the forum state, has by these facts developed minimum contacts with that state. (But where this is the only contact that exists, a substantial burden to the defendant in being required to defend in the forum state, or relatively weak interests on the part of the forum state or the plaintiff, will be sufficient to make it unreasonable for the forum court to exercise jurisdiction despite the minimum contacts.)

   h. Original case preserved: Suppose that Gary Zurcher had not settled his claims, and had wanted to litigate a claim against Asahi as co-defendant. (In the actual case, there was apparently no claim by Zurcher against Asahi.) The minimum contacts analysis would not have changed at all; O'Connor and three other Justices would have continued to hold that there were no minimum contacts, and the other five members of the Court would have continued to find minimum contacts to exist. However, on the "reasonableness" issue, a sharply different result might well have ensued: a majority of the Court might well have held that the interests of both California and Zurcher in having California hear the case were sufficiently strong as to outweigh the burden to Asahi in having to defend in a foreign nation. Zurcher's interest in having his home state hear his claim, especially when it was already hearing his claims against other defendants arising from the same transaction, would have been an extremely strong one. California's interest in offering a forum for protection of its residents, similarly, would have been very strong. Furthermore, the only alternative forum for Zurcher would have been a non-U.S. one; thus the burden to him of losing his California forum would have been far greater than had he merely been required to bring the suit in another American jurisdiction. While it is impossible to say what a majority would have decided on these facts, probably most members of the Court would have found the exercise of jurisdiction to be reasonable.

H. Suits based on contractual relationship: What effect on jurisdictional analysis should result from the fact that the in-state plaintiff and the out-of-state defendant have a *contractual* relationship? The Supreme Court has held that although the mere fact that one party to the contract is a resident of the forum state does not by itself mean that the other party has "minimum contacts" with that state, the whole contractual relationship may well, in a particular case, be sufficient to confer jurisdiction. In *Burger King Corp. v. Rudzewicz*, 471 U.S. 462 (1985), the Supreme Court held that the courts of Florida (and therefore, a federal district court sitting in Florida — see *infra*, p. 46) could constitutionally exercise jurisdiction over a Michigan resident who had signed a franchise contract with a Florida franchisor, even though the franchise was operated in Michigan.

1. **Facts:** The contract allowed D, an individual residing in Michigan, to run a fast- food restaurant in Michigan under franchise from P (Burger King Corp.), which had its headquarters in Florida. The lawsuit was brought by Burger King in order to terminate the franchise agreement and to collect payments alleged to be due under it. The franchise agreement provided that *Florida law* would control, but expressly stated that this choice of Florida law "does not require that all suits concerning this Agreement be filed in Florida."

   a. **Contacts with state:** D never travelled to Florida in connection with the contract or the restaurant (though his partner in the franchise went there once for a training session). D's face-to-face meetings with Burger King officials all involved people from the local Michigan office of Burger King, not the Florida headquarters. However, there were some phone and mail negotiations between D and the Florida headquarters. The contract required that all payments and notices be sent by D to the Florida office.

   b. **Long-arm:** Service was made under a provision of the Florida long-arm statute allowing jurisdiction over one who "[b]reach[es] a contract in this state by failing to perform acts required by the contract to be performed in this state," so long as the cause of action arose from the alleged breach of contract.

2. **Designation of law:** In concluding that Florida could constitutionally entertain personal jurisdiction over D (at least in a suit arising out of the contract), the Court attached special importance to the contract's *designation of Florida law* as the controlling law. While it is true that, under *Hanson v. Denckla* (*supra*, p. 22), the state that is the "center of gravity" of the controversy (i.e., the state whose law will normally control for conflict of laws purposes) is not automatically entitled to jurisdiction, the rule is somewhat different where the out-of- stater has signed a contract expressly designating the forum state's law as the controlling law. By signing a contract with such a provision, the out-of-stater has "purposely availed himself of the benefits and protections of [the forum state's] laws." (The Court observed that this provision *by itself* would not be sufficient to confer jurisdiction; however, the provision was clearly a major factor in the Court's analysis.)

3. **Other factors:** In addition to the mere existence of the contract, the Court said, other significant factors were "prior negotiations and contemplated future consequences, along with the terms of the contract and the parties' actual course of dealing" — all of these must be evaluated to determine "whether the defendant purposefully established minimum contacts within the forum."

4. **No surprise:** The Court also asserted that D was *not unfairly surprised* by being required to defend in Florida against a suit having to do with the franchise relationship. Both the contractual provisions and the course of dealing should have put D on notice that the franchise relationship would be supervised from Florida, not from the local Michigan office — the Court implied that P's suit was merely an aspect of its supervision of the franchise relationship.

5. **Fraud or bargaining advantage:** The Court took pains to point out that had D been able to show that the contract or particular terms in it were obtained through *"fraud, undue*

influence, or *overweening bargaining power*," the contractual provisions would *not* have supplied the basis for jurisdiction. Here, however, D was an experienced accountant who spent five months negotiating the contract, and who was represented by counsel. Although Burger King may have had a bargaining advantage, its advantage was not so great as to constitute fraud or economic duress.

6. **Inconvenience:** The Court rejected D's plea that it would be materially *inconvenient* for him to have to defend the suit in Florida (e.g., that he would not be able to obtain witnesses as easily). D did not demonstrate which witnesses he was forced to do without, and in any event any inconvenience could have been relieved by a *change of venue* (see *infra*, p. 89.) Nor was it relevant that Burger King, with its great wealth and national operations, would have found it easier to litigate in Michigan than D found it to litigate in Florida — "absent compelling considerations ... a defendant who has purposefully derived commercial benefit from his affiliations in a forum may not defeat jurisdiction simply because of his adversary's greater net wealth."

7. **Dissent:** Justice Stevens (joined by Justice White) dissented. Stevens stressed these points: (1) D's entire conduct of the business took place in Michigan, not Florida; (2) D's face-to-face dealings with Burger King's representatives, and even all or most of his telephone contacts with them, were with people who worked in D's Michigan, not Florida, office; (3) D had reason to believe that since the Michigan office was the office that negotiated and supervised the contract, any suit would be brought in Michigan, not Florida; and (4) there was a substantial inequality in bargaining power, which deprived D of the practical ability to get concessions in return for bearing the risk of having to defend a possible suit in Florida. All in all, the contract and the negotiations leading to it "left [D] bereft of reasonable notice and financially unprepared for the prospect of franchise litigation in Florida."

8. **Significance of case:** *Burger King* appears to establish several useful principles:

   a. **Significance of contract:** The existence of a contractual relationship, one party to which resides or has its headquarters in the forum state, will go a significant distance towards establishing the out-of-state party's minimum contacts with the forum state (even though the existence of the contract will not be dispositive on the jurisdiction issue);

   b. **Choice of law:** The presence in a contract of a "choice of law" provision making the forum state's law the law to be used in any lawsuit will carry significant weight in the analysis, since such a provision indicates that the out-of-stater has chosen to receive the benefit of the forum state's legal system;

   c. **Payment stream:** The fact that the out-of-stater is required by contract to send payments and reports into the forum state will also be a significant factor.

   d. **Limitations:** However, *Burger King* does *not* mean that any franchisor will be able to sue its franchisee in the franchisor's home state. If the size of the contract claim is small (in contrast to the $228,000 judgment in *Burger King*), if the contract terms are obtained through "fraud, undue influence, or overweening bargaining power," if the franchise is "primarily intrastate in character" or if the franchisor's decision-making structures are different (e.g., more authority is vested in the local office and less in the forum-state-based home office), there may not be jurisdiction. The underlying question is whether the franchisee should *"reasonably anticipate out-of-state litigation."*

I. **Class action plaintiffs:** The vast majority of the time, personal jurisdiction challenges involve defendants. There is, however, at least one context in which the issue of the jurisdiction over a *plaintiff* can arise: the *"class action."* The class action (discussed extensively beginning *infra*, p. 309) is a device by which the claims of many similarly-situated parties (usually plaintiffs) can be adjudicated in one proceeding. Not all of these plaintiffs will participate actively in the lawsuit: indeed, some will not even know that it is going on. Yet under federal class action rules, as well as the rules of most states, such an "absent" plaintiff may nonetheless be *bound* by the decision in the case — if the class loses the case, he loses his claim, and if the class wins, the case will determine the size of his award. What contacts, if any, must the "absent plaintiff" have with the state hearing the class action suit in order for the result to be binding upon him? In brief, the Supreme Court has decided that "minimum contacts" of the sort needed for personal jurisdiction over a defendant *need not exist* between the absent plaintiff and the forum state.

1. **Setting of the case:** The case raising this issue was *Phillips Petroleum Co. v. Shutts*, 472 U.S. 797 (1985). The plaintiff class was composed of all persons owning a royalty interest in certain oil and gas leases being exploited by the defendant, Phillips Petroleum. The claim was for interest alleged to be owed by Phillips to the class members on account of late royalty payments. Of the 28,000 members of the class, fewer than 1,000 lived in Kansas, in whose state courts the suit was brought. Only about 1/4 of 1% of the oil and gas leases involved in the suit were on Kansas land.

    a. **Defense contention:** The defendant asserted that those members of the class who did not live in Kansas were not properly class members, since they did not have "minimum contacts" with Kansas, and thus could not constitutionally be bound by the decision. Phillips claimed to be worried that if it won, the absent plaintiffs would subsequently make an objection to jurisdiction and would end up not being bound by the result, whereas if Phillips lost, it would be bound, a "heads you win, tails I lose" result.

    b. **Opt-out provision:** The Kansas class action rules, like those of most states and the federal system, required that all prospective members of the class be *notified* of the suit, and that they be given the opportunity to *"opt out"* of the class. Those who took advantage of this "opt-out" provision (over 10% of the potential members of the plaintiff class) were not bound by the results in the case, but could not take advantage of the favorable result either. Those to whom notice of the suit could not be delivered were also excluded from the class. But those who received notice and who *remained silent* were made members of the class. It was as to these silent, absent plaintiffs (or at least those who were not Kansas residents and who did not have minimum contacts of the sort that would be sufficient to make them defendants) that Phillips made its jurisdictional challenge.

2. **Result:** The Supreme Court *rejected* Phillips' jurisdictional argument. The Court conceded that these absent class members might, as a result of the suit, lose a constitutionally protected property interest (namely, their claim, or "chose in action"). But this limited loss was far less than the damage that virtually any defendant can suffer as a result of a judg-

ment against him — there could be no monetary recovery against the absent class members, nor were such absent members required to do anything (in contrast to a defendant, who must ordinarily retain counsel and appear). Furthermore, the "opt-out" procedure gave each absentee the ability to escape even this limited impact.

3. **Standard:** However, the Court held, there are some safeguards which must be observed before absent members who remain silent can be deemed part of the class and thus bound: the forum state must provide *"minimal procedural due process protection."* The protection must consist of the following elements:

   a. **Notice and opportunity to be heard:** The plaintiff must receive *notice* plus have an opportunity to be heard to and participate in the litigation.

      i. **Type of notice:** The notice must be "the best practicable, 'reasonably calculated, under all the circumstances, to apprise interested parties of the pendency of the action …' " (quoting *Mullane v. Central Hanover Bank & Trust, infra,* p. 66).

   b. **Opt-out provision:** The absent plaintiff must be given the opportunity to *"opt out"* of the class by returning a form to the court.

      i. **No "opt-in" requirement:** It is *not* required that the class members affirmatively *"opt in."* Such a requirement would "probably impede the prosecution of those class actions involving an aggregation of small individual claims, where a large number of claims are required to make it economical to bring suit."

   c. **Adequate representation:** The named plaintiff(s) must *adequately represent* the interests of the absent class members. (See *Hansberry v. Lee, infra,* p. 311.)

4. **Open questions:** The decision in *Phillips Petroleum* leaves some unanswered questions:

   a. **Actual notice:** The trial court in *Phillips Petroleum* excluded from the class any person as to whom attempts to give notice by first class mail failed. But is such an exclusion of those who do not receive *actual* notice constitutionally required? The answer is probably *"no."* In a non-class action context, the Supreme Court has held that actual notice is not required: all that is required is "notice reasonably calculated, under all the circumstances, to apprise interested parties of the pendency of the action. … " *Mullane v. Central Hanover Bank,* 339 U.S. 306 (1950) (discussed *infra,* p. 66). *Mullane* indicates that *publication* can be a reasonable method of notice where the actual address of the party to be notified is not ascertainable with reasonable economy. This rationale seems at least as strongly applicable to the context of an absent plaintiff in a class action, who normally has less at stake than a defendant would, and whose interests are being protected by the named members of the class.

   b. **Defendant class:** There are a few class actions in which the class consists of *defendants* rather than plaintiffs. The *Phillips Petroleum* Court noted that its analysis did not deal with defendant class actions. Since even where the class that is sought to be established consists of defendants, no class will be certified unless the court is convinced that the named defendants will adequately represent the interests of the absent ones, it is possible that absent defendants might be bound even though they did not have minimum contacts with the forum state. However, in those cases where the absent defendants face significant liability, the Supreme Court is unlikely to hold that they may be bound if they do not have minimum contacts with the forum.

J. Libel and slander suits: Suits for *libel* and *slander* have been recognized as posing significant dangers to the First Amendment freedoms of defendants, especially publishers. The Supreme Court has held in a series of decisions dating back to *New York Times v. Sullivan*, 376 U.S. 254 (1964), that the First Amendment imposes certain limits on the substantive libel and slander laws of the states (e.g., that no "public figure" may recover without a showing of "actual malice." See Emanuel on *Constitutional Law.*) Do these First Amendment concerns also dictate that more extensive contacts between the defendant and the forum state must be shown in defamation suits than in other types of cases? A pair of Supreme Court decisions on the jurisdictional aspects of libel cases makes it clear that the answer is *"no"* — essentially the *same standard* applies in libel and slander cases as in other types of suits. These two decisions also establish some other points of significance for jurisdiction cases outside of the defamation area. *Calder v. Jones*, 465 U.S. 783 (1984); *Keeton v. Hustler Magazine, Inc.*, 465 U.S. 770 (1984).

K. Plaintiff's lack of contacts: The fact that the *plaintiff has no contacts* with the forum state will *not block* jurisdiction. For instance, in *Keeton v. Hustler Magazine, supra,* the plaintiff was a New York resident who sued Hustler in New Hampshire only because that was the sole state where the suit would not have been barred by the statute of limitations. Plaintiff had no contacts with New Hampshire at all, except for the fact that her reputation in that state (as in every other state) was allegedly libeled. Nonetheless, the Supreme Court held that "Plaintiff's residence in the forum state is not a separate requirement, and lack of residence will not defeat jurisdiction established on the basis of Defendant's contacts."

L. Limits on choice-of-law: Once it is established that a state court defendant has the minimum contacts with the forum state needed to support jurisdiction, does it follow that the forum state is constitutionally entitled to *apply its own laws* to the controversy? The entire subject of "conflict of laws" is an illustration of the fact that a court, merely because it has jurisdiction, will not necessarily choose to apply its own laws, and may instead apply the laws of some other jurisdiction having closer ties to the controversy. But only recently has it been established that the Due Process Clause (which is of course the source of the "minimum contacts" requirement) also places limits on the forum state's right to apply its own law to a particular controversy. It is therefore possible that a state may have jurisdiction over the parties to a controversy, yet have such tenuous ties with that controversy that that state is constitutionally required to apply the law of *some other state.*

1. *Phillips Petroleum case:* The case establishing this possibility is *Phillips Petroleum Co. v. Shutts*, 472 U.S. 797 (1985). That case, which is discussed more extensively *supra*, p. 35, was a class action in which the plaintiff class consisted of the owners of royalty interests in oil and gas leases being exploited by the defendant. The case was brought in Kansas state court, but 97% of the plaintiffs resided outside of Kansas, and 99 3/4% of the leases at issue were on non-Kansas land. Although the Supreme Court held that absent members of the plaintiff class could be bound by the Kansas court's decision in the case, the Court also held that as to those claims which involved neither a Kansas plaintiff nor Kansas land, it was a *violation of due process* for the trial court to apply Kansas law. For Kansas law to be applied to a particular claim, Kansas must have a "significant contact or aggregation of contacts" to that claim; the contacts must be sufficient to " 'create ... state interests' in order to ensure that the choice of Kansas law is not arbitrary or unfair."

2. **State may usually apply its law:** But outcomes like that in *Phillips Petroleum* — that is, situations where the court of State X has jurisdiction, but is constitutionally required to apply the laws of some other state because State X's contacts with the controversy are too slim — will be *rare*. Only when there is *virtually no connection* between the underlying facts of the suit and the forum state will the forum state's decision to apply its own law be a violation of due process.

Quiz Yourself on
JURISDICTION OVER INDIVIDUALS AND CORPORATIONS

1. D lived in Connecticut until 1988. His company then transferred him to California to take over a troubled operation. Even though D expected to return to Connecticut eventually, he sold his Connecticut house, figuring that when he returned there he would buy a different house. D did not know for sure how long he would be residing in California, but he did not expect to remain there for more than two or three years. After D took up residence in California, he was sued in the Connecticut state courts concerning a transaction which he had carried out in New York some years before. Can the Connecticut state courts constitutionally take jurisdiction over this suit? _____

2. D owns and runs a small bakery in Portland, Maine. P is a truck driver who lives in South Carolina. One day, P visited D's bakery just before embarking on the long truck ride from Maine to South Carolina. He bought a dozen cream filled doughnuts from D, and remarked, "I'm going to eat one of these every two hours, so I'll still have a couple left by the time I get home to South Carolina." P followed this plan, and ate the last two doughnuts while inside the South Carolina state limits. P then fell violently ill of food poisoning, causing him to lose control of his truck, so that it went off the road and flipped over, seriously injuring P. Later, medical evidence showed that it was one of the last two doughnuts, eaten in South Carolina, that caused the food poisoning. P sued D in the South Carolina courts. Not only was P a resident of South Carolina, but at the time of the suit he was hospitalized there, and all witnesses to the accident, as well as all witnesses to the medical findings concerning the food poisoning, resided in South Carolina. Assuming that the South Carolina long-arm statute can fairly be interpreted to give jurisdiction over D on these facts, may the courts of South Carolina constitutionally hear the suit? _____

3. Corporation is a manufacturer of ladies' dresses. In the state of Arkansas, Corporation does not maintain any official office. Corporation conducts no advertising directed at Arkansas residents, and derives only a small portion of its total revenues from that state. Corporation's sole activities in the state consist of the activities of Jones, a commission salesman for Corporation, who works out of his house soliciting orders from Arkansas-based department stores. When an Arkansas department store places an order, the order is not accepted by Jones, but is instead sent to the home office in New York for approval. All orders are shipped from New York directly to the department store which placed the order. P, an Arkansas department store that placed one order with Corporation via Jones, received what it believed to be defective merchandise, and sued Corporation in the Arkansas courts. May the Arkansas courts constitutionally take jurisdiction over Corporation? _____

Answers

1. **Yes.** It is quite clear that a court may constitutionally exercise jurisdiction over anyone who is *domiciled*

in that state. Even though D has temporarily changed his residence to California, his domicile remains Connecticut. This is because one's domicile is the last place of which it was true both that one resided there and that one had the indefinite intent to remain there. Since D does not intend to remain in California, California cannot be his domicile, so we look at the next prior place he resided, Connecticut. (In fact, Connecticut would still be D's domicile even if he intended to move to New York after he finished his California job.)

2. **No, probably.** According to *Worldwide Volkswagen v. Woodson*, 444 U.S. 286 (1980), the mere fact that a product finds its way into a state and causes injury there is not enough to subject the out-of-state manufacturer or vendor to personal jurisdiction there. Instead, the defendant must have made some effort to *market* in the forum state. Here, D was not attempting to market in South Carolina, even though he knew that the doughnuts in question would find their way to South Carolina. Therefore, even though P resides in and is presently located in South Carolina, and all the witnesses are there, it would probably be a violation of due process for the South Carolina courts to subject D to personal jurisdiction there.

3. **Yes.** These facts are quite similar to those of *International Shoe v. Washington*, 326 U.S. 310 (1945), in which the Supreme Court held that the out-of-state company had the requisite *"minimum contacts"* with the forum state. Since Corporation sought business from within Arkansas, and had a salesman based there, the fact that it had no office, conducted no advertising directed at the state, and derived only a small portion of its total revenues from the state, are all irrelevant. The basic idea is that Corporation purposefully availed itself of the opportunity to sell goods within Arkansas, so it is therefore not unfair for Corporation to be required to defend suits there relating to those sales.

IV. FEDERAL JURISDICTION OVER THE PARTIES

Introductory Note: Many of the technical aspects of federal court jurisdiction over the parties are governed by Rule 4 of the FRCP. A 1993 amendment to Rule 4 completely reorganized that rule, and added an important new section, Rule 4(n). All references to Rule 4 in this outline have been changed to match the 1993 amendments.

A. **General principles:** To determine whether a *federal* court has personal jurisdiction over the defendant, you must check *three things*:

1. **Territory for service:** Whether service took place within the appropriate *territory*;

2. **Manner of service:** Whether the service was carried out in the correct *manner*; and

3. **Amenability:** Whether the defendant is *"amenable"* to the federal suit.

B. **Territory for service:** As a general rule, in *both diversity actions and federal question cases, service of process* may be made *only* (1) *within the territorial limits of the state in which the District Court sits*; or (2) *anywhere else that the state law of the state where the District Court sits permits*. FRCP 4(k)(1)(A). (There are some additional possibilities for special situations, such as the "100-mile bulge" provision discussed *infra*, p. 41, and the "foreign defendant not servable in any state" provision discussed *infra*, p. 42.)

Example 1 (service within the territorial limits of state): P sues D in a federal action in the Northern District of Ohio. Whether the suit is based on diversity or federal question, service will be territorially valid if P is served with process anywhere within the state of Ohio, since this is the state where the district court sits. This is true even if service is physically made in the Southern District of Ohio.

Example 2 (out-of-state service based on state law): Assume that under the Montana long-arm statute, if a non-resident is involved in a motor vehicle accident inside Montana with a Montana resident, the Montana resident may serve the non-resident outside Montana, and the Montana courts may then exercise personal jurisdiction. P, a Montana resident, and D, a Texas resident, have an accident in Montana. P may sue D in diversity in federal District Court for Montana; P may serve D with process in Texas, because the long-arm of the state where the district court sits (Montana) would allow such service. FRCP 4(k)(1)(A).

Example 3 (no territory available for service): P and D are involved in an auto accident in Nevada. P is a Nevada resident. D is a Vermont resident. Because P is an invalid, he cannot leave Nevada to litigate. Assume that the Nevada long-arm statute is extremely limited, and would not allow service to be made on D anywhere outside of Nevada for the Nevada negligence action. Assume further that D has never set foot in Nevada again after the accident, and is unlikely to do so in the future. There is no way that P can bring a federal court *diversity* action in Nevada against D. He cannot serve D within Nevada, because D will not be physically there to receive service. He cannot serve D in Vermont (or anywhere else), because the Nevada long-arm would not allow out-of-state service on these facts. Therefore, even though there is diversity of citizenship between P and D, there is no way for P to make service for his Nevada federal court action, and he is stuck.

The same result would follow if P's suit against D was based on a federal question (say a violation of the federal securities laws) rather than on diversity — since P cannot make service on D within Nevada, and the local long-arm does not allow out-of-state service, P cannot bring his federal suit in Nevada. FRCP 4(k)(2) (see *infra*, p. 42), added in 1993, looks as though it might help P, but it doesn't — the section only applies to allow jurisdiction over a defendant for a federal-question claim where the defendant "is not subject to the jurisdiction of the courts of general jurisdiction of *any* state." Since D is subject to jurisdiction in the courts of his home state, Vermont (any resident of a state can always be sued in that state), Rule 4(k)(2) does not apply.

1. **Not imposed by Constitution:** These limits — requiring service to be made either within the state when the District Court sits or where permitted by the local law of that state — are *not* imposed by the U.S. *Constitution*. "The sovereignty of the U.S. is, of course, nationwide and Congress could constitutionally provide for the service of process, issuing out of any federal court, throughout the length and breadth of the land, just as New York may provide that process of a state court in Manhattan may be served in Buffalo." James (1st Ed.), 616. Rather, these limits come principally from the Federal Rules of Civil Procedure and the way the federal courts have interpreted those Rules.

   a. **Nationwide service of process:** In fact, in several kinds of cases, Congress has provided for *nationwide service of process*. An example of such a statute is 28 U.S.C.

§1391(e), permitting service by registered mail anywhere in the country in a suit against *federal officials and agencies*. See also the Federal Interpleader Act, 28 U.S.C. §2361, discussed *infra*, p. 338. See FRCP 4(k)(1)(C) and (D), referring to interpleader and other special federal statutes allowing for nationwide service.

2. **Service out of state:** As noted, service outside the state where the District Court sits may be made *if the law of that state so permits*. Federal Rule 4(k)(1)(A).

> **Example:** New Jersey enacts a long-arm statute which provides that if a non-resident is involved in a motor vehicle accident inside New Jersey with a New Jersey resident, the New Jersey resident may serve the non-resident outside New Jersey, and the New Jersey courts may then exercise personal jurisdiction over the non-resident in a suit relating to the accident. P, a New Jersey resident, and D, a California resident, are involved in an automobile accident in New Jersey.
>
> P may bring a diversity suit against D in federal district court for New Jersey. Since the New Jersey long-arm would allow service to be made on D (in California) if P sued on the accident in the New Jersey courts, Federal Rule 4(k)(1)(A) allows service in the federal action to be made on D in California under similar circumstances. (The "manner" of service — for instance, service by certified mail, or service by a process server licensed to make service in California — may be made either as expressly permitted in the federal rules, as provided in the New Jersey long-arm, or as allowed under the law of the state where service is made (California). See *infra*, pp. 44-46.)

3. **100-mile bulge:** A special *100-mile bulge* provision (FRCP 4(k)(1)(B)) allows for out-of-state service sometimes, even if local law does not permit it. When the provision applies, it allows service anywhere (even across a state boundary) within a *100-mile radius of the federal courthouse where suit is pending*. The bulge provision applies only where out-of-staters will be brought in as *additional parties* to an *already pending* action.

   a. **Two types of parties:** There are two types of parties against whom the 100-mile bulge can be used:

      i. **Third-party defendants:** First, third-party defendants (FRCP 14) may be served within the bulge.

      > **Example:** P sues D in a New Jersey federal district court diversity action. D claims that if D is liable to P, X is liable to D as an indemnitor. The suit is pending in Newark, less than 100 miles from New York City. D may serve X in New York City, even if no New Jersey long-arm statute would allow the suit.

      ii. **Indispensable parties:** Second, so-called *"indispensable parties"* (FRCP 19(a)) — that is, persons who are needed in the action for just adjudication, and whose joinder will not involve subject matter jurisdictional problems — may also be served if they are within the bulge.

      > **Example:** P sues D for copyright infringement in federal district court for the Eastern District of Kentucky, located in Lexington. D files a counterclaim against P. D wants to join X as a co-defendant to this counterclaim, arguing that P and X conspired to violate D's copyrights. X resides in Cincinnati, Ohio, located 78 miles from Lexington. If the court agrees that X is required for just adjudication of

D's counterclaim, service on X in Cincinnati is valid, even if the Kentucky long-arm would not allow service there.

b. **Minimum contacts with the bulge:** As noted above, an out-of-state defendant in a diversity suit may only be required to defend if she would be reachable by the long-arm of the state where the District Court sits for purposes of a state suit. Does this limitation apply to out-of-state defendants served in the "bulge"? The case law on this question is quite confused; most states seem to hold that the defendant may be required to defend so long as he is reachable by the long-arm of the state *where service is made* (i.e., the "bulge state'"), even if he could not be reached according to the law of the state where the federal suit is pending.

Example: P sues D in a federal court diversity action pending in the Southern District of New York. D claims that if he is liable to P, X is liable to D as an indemnitor. X, a California corporation, has a small sales office in Trenton, New Jersey (less than 100 miles from the New York City courthouse where the suit is pending), but has no contacts whatsoever with New York. Assume that the New Jersey long-arm would permit suit in a New Jersey state court suit against X. Most federal courts would probably hold that since X can be reached under the New Jersey long-arm for a suit in the courts of New Jersey (the "bulge state"), and X has minimum contacts with New Jersey, X can be required to defend the third-party New York federal court complaint even though X does not have minimum contacts with New York and could not be reached by the New York state long-arm for purposes of a New York state suit. See, e.g., *Coleman v. American Export Isbrandtsen Lines, Inc.*, 405 F.2d 250 (2d Cir. 1968). Some courts would make it even easier to get X into the action, by holding that as long as X had the constitutionally-required "minimum contacts" with New Jersey (the bulge state), even the fact that the New Jersey long-arm might not allow service on X would be irrelevant. See W&M, p. 4A, pp. 336-37. A few courts might hold that X can be reached only if X has mimimum contacts with the bulge itself, not just with New Jersey as a whole.

4. **Foreign defendant not servable in any state:** Another special provision in Rule 4, added in 1993, allows a *federal-question* suit to be brought against a person or organization who cannot be sued in *any state* court (almost always because they are a *foreigner*). FRCP 4(k)(2) provides that "if the exercise of jurisdiction is consistent with the Constitution and laws of the United States, serving a summons … is also effective, with respect to claims arising under *federal law*, to establish personal jurisdiction over the person of any defendant who is *not subject* to the jurisdiction of the courts of general jurisdiction of *any state*."

a. **Old law:** To see the significance of this new 4(k)(2), consider the leading case demonstrating how, under the old law, a foreign defendant having extensive contacts with the U.S. as a whole could escape service by the fortuity that it did not have minimum contacts with the state where the federal action was pending:

Example: The Ps bring a civil suit against D for violation of the federal Commodity Exchange Act (CEA). D attempts to implead X and Y, citizens of England who participated in the transactions in question and who D claims should be liable to D if D is liable to the Ps. (See *infra*, p. 343, for a discussion of impleader.) The suit is filed in Louisiana, where the Ps reside. X and Y have minimum contacts with the U.S. as a whole, but not with Louisiana. No federal statute authorizes nationwide service in private CEA actions. The Louisiana long-arm does not allow service on X and Y, because they lack the statutorily-required connections with Louisiana. D argues that since X and Y's connections with the U.S. are sufficient for the court to exercise personal jurisdiction over them without violating the due process clause (which X and Y concede), the district court should exercise that jurisdiction despite the lack of an applicable Congressional or Louisiana long-arm.

Held (by the U.S. Supreme Court), the impleader claim against X and Y must be dismissed for lack of personal jurisdiction. Whether or not jurisdiction could constitutionally be exercised over X and Y, a federal court may only exercise jurisdiction where either a federal statute or a statute of the state where the federal court sits explicitly authorizes service of process. Since the CEA does not contain any provision authorizing nationwide service of process in private actions brought under it, and since the Louisiana long-arm clearly does not apply, no service is possible. It is for legislatures, not courts, to decide the circumstances under which service of process is to be allowed. *Omni Capital Int'l v. Rudolf Wolff & Co.*, 484 U.S. 97 (1987).

b. **Significance of amendment:** New FRCP 4(k)(2) is designed to deal precisely with the problem posed by *Omni Capital*. But this provision is in fact extremely narrow, and will apply only if three conditions (one of them rarely met) are satisfied:

i. The claim against D is based on a *federal question*, rather than on diversity;

ii. D has such contacts with the United States as a *whole* that it is not a violation of D's Fifth Amendment *due process* rights for D to be required to defend the action in the United States; and

iii. D "is not subject to the jurisdiction of the courts of general jurisdiction of *any state*." It will be a very rare case in which D has enough contacts with the United States as a whole to satisfy (ii) above, but not enough contacts to subject it to jurisdiction in any individual state. Certainly D will have to be a *foreigner* for this requirement to be met.

c. **Application to facts of *Omni Capital*:** The Advisory Committee's Note to Rule 4(k)(2) expressly states that that provision "responds to the suggestion of the Supreme Court made in *Omni Capital*. ..." Yet it is not clear that even on the very facts of *Omni Capital* itself, the defendants there (called X and Y in our treatment) would be subject to jurisdiction under the new rule. Observe that the rule kicks in only if the defendants are not subject to personal jurisdiction in *any state*. In *Omni Capital*, the essence of the claim against X and Y was that they participated in soliciting business from D, a New York corporation. If X and Y had conducted enough activities in or relating to New York to subject them to jurisdiction in a New York state court action (determined by looking at New York's long-arm), then new 4(k)(2) would not apply. Furthermore, if X and Y did not have enough contacts with the U.S. as a whole to make it "fair" as a matter of due process law for them to be required to defend an American action, the new rule would also not apply. Only if X and Y's activities fell within a very peculiar and narrow range — collectively, enough contacts with the U.S. as a whole to satisfy due process, but not enough contacts with any state to satisfy that state's long-arm — would 4(k)(2) spring into action. The situations where it does so should be very rare. (One possible illustration might be where a foreigner, without setting foot in the U.S., solicited business by phone or mail from people in a large number of states, but did not solicit from the residents of any one state enough to satisfy that state's long-arm so as to subject the defendant to process in that state.)

    d. Not applicable to diversity claim standing alone: Also, observe that new 4(k)(2) applies only to a *federal question* claim. If the only claim against D is based on diversity, then even though D has minimum contacts with the United States as a whole, and does not have minimum contacts with any particular state, P is out of luck. (But if P does have a federal claim against D, then a related diversity claim could be added to the suit, under the doctrine of "supplemental jurisdiction," discussed *infra*, p. 112.)

 5. Gaps possible: Even after new 4(k)(2), there can be *"gaps of service,"* whereby a person will not be servable in a federal action even though the person has minimum contacts with the state where the federal court sits. A defendant who is not located in the state where the District Court sits may *not* be served if she does not fall within one of the four special cases described above (servable pursuant to state long-arm, 100-mile bulge, special nationwide-service provision, or the new "foreign defendant not servable in any state" provision), *even if she has the constitutionally-required minimum contacts* with the forum. Example 3, *supra*, p. 40, shows how this can be true, both as to a case based on diversity and one based on federal question.

C. Manner of service: Once you determine that the party to be served lies within the territory described above, you must determine whether the service was carried out in the correct *manner*. The allowable manner of service is somewhat different, depending on whether the defendant is an individual or a corporation.

 1. Individual: The manner for serving an *individual* is set out in new 4(e). Service on the individual may be made in any of several ways:

    a. Personal: By serving him *personally* (4(e)(2));

    b. Substitute: By leaving the summons and complaint at D's *residence* with a person of *"suitable age and discretion"* residing there (4(e)(2));

    c. Agent: By serving an *agent* appointed or designated by law to receive process. (4(e)(2)). (For instance, many states designate the Director of Motor Vehicles as the agent to receive process in suits involving car accidents);

    d. Local state law: By serving D in the manner provided by either: (1) the *law of the state where the District Court sits*, if that state has such a provision; or (2) in the manner provided by the *law of the state where the person is being served*. (4(e)(1).)

    Example: P sues D in an action brought in federal court for the District of New Jersey. D resides in California. P wishes to serve D by certified mail. If *either* the New Jersey courts or the California courts allow service by certified mail, P may use this method for serving D. (Prior to the 1993 amendments to Rule 4, only the law of the state where the action was pending, not the state where the service was to be effected, could be relied on by the plaintiff.)

e. **Foreign defendants:** A special rule governs service *outside the United States* on an individual. Essentially, any method allowed by a particular international treaty (the Hague Convention) or any method allowed by the country where service occurs, can be used. See FRCP 4(f).

2. **Corporation:** Service on a *corporation* may be made by leaving the papers with an *officer*, a managing or general *agent*, or any other agent authorized by appointment or by law to receive process for the corporation. FRCP 4(h)(1).

    a. **Test for suitability:** Whether a given corporate employee is an "officer or managing or general agent" and is thus qualified to receive process is established by examining her position within the corporation; if that position makes her likely to pass the papers on to the lawyers or directors who would be expected to prepare the defense, she is qualified. Wr., 416.

    b. **Local state law:** As with individuals, service on a corporation may also be made in the manner provided by the law of the *state* where the action is *pending* or the law of the *state* where the *service is made*. FRCP 4(h)(1), first clause.

    c. **Foreign defendants:** As with individuals, special rules for serving corporations that are *not present in the U.S.* are provided, in Rule 4(h)(2). These rules are essentially the same as for individuals.

3. **Waiver of service:** Nearly all the methods of service discussed above require a person acting as the plaintiff's agent to personally deliver the summons and complaint to the defendant or to someone acting on behalf of the defendant. But Rule 4(d) (added in 1993) allows the plaintiff to in effect serve the summons and complaint by *mail*, provided that the *defendant cooperates*. Actually, what the plaintiff does is to mail to the defendant a *"request for waiver of service;"* if the defendant agrees, no actual in-person service is needed. The rule gives the defendant financial and other incentives to grant the waiver request.

    a. **Procedure:** The plaintiff begins the waiver-of-service procedure by sending the defendant a notice that the action is being commenced, a request that the defendant waive service of the summons, and a copy of the complaint. The notice may be sent "through *first-class mail* or *other reliable means*" (4(d)(2)(B)). Thus *facsimile transmission* is valid — see Advisory Committee's Notes to 4(d).

    b. **Time to respond:** The defendant has 30 days to respond to the request for waiver (60 days for a foreign defendant).

    c. **Incentives:** The defendant is free to refuse to grant the waiver, in which case the plaintiff must serve the summons by the in-person methods described above (personal service, substitute service, service on agent, or service pursuant to local state law; see *supra*, p. 44). But Rule 4(d) gives the defendant two significant incentives, one a "carrot" and the other a "stick," to grant the waiver:

       i. **Additional time to answer:** The "carrot" is that if the defendant grants the waiver, she gets *60 days* following the date on which the request for waiver was sent, in which to *answer* the complaint (compared with 20 days from service of process, provided by Rule 12(a)). (Foreign defendants get 90 days.)

ii. D must pay costs of service: Probably more significantly, the "stick" is that if the defendant refuses the waiver, and requires plaintiff to bear the expense of serving the summons. "The court *shall impose* the *costs subsequently incurred in effecting service* on the defendant unless good cause for the failure be shown." (4(d)(2), last sentence.) So the costs of hiring a process server (even the attorneys fees involved in moving to collect the cost of the process server) will normally be assessed against the defendant. (But these rules only apply to a defendant "located within the United States"; foreign defendants suffer no monetary sanction if they refuse to grant the waiver.)

d. No waiver of personal jurisdiction or venue: A defendant who grants the waiver of personal service will not be deemed to have waived any objection to venue or personal jurisdiction over him. Rule 4(d)(1). So D can still make a motion for dismissal on either of these counts, under FRCP 12(b)(2). See *infra*, p. 74.

D. Amenability to suit: If D was served in an appropriate territory, and in an appropriate manner, you still have to determine whether D is *closely-enough linked* to the state where the federal district court sits to make him *"amenable to suit"* in that court. The test for determining "amenability" varies depending on whether the suit is brought based on existence of a federal question or on diversity.

1. Federal question: In federal question cases, amenability to suit depends solely on federal law and concepts of due process. Wr. 419-20.

a. Same as state court limits: Most federal courts in federal question cases have held a defendant to be amenable to suit in their court if jurisdiction *could constitutionally be exercised* over him in the *state courts* of the state where the federal court is sitting. The result of this rule is that it will often be possible to bring a federal question suit against the defendant in federal court even if suit *could not be brought against him in the courts of that state* (because of a weak state long-arm); the reason for this is that the federal courts will allow suit whenever the state court *could* constitutionally hear the suit, not merely in those cases where, under the state's statutes, the state courts *will* hear the suit.

Example: P sues D for copyright infringement. The suit is brought in the Northern District of Ohio. D's only contact with Ohio is that he sold 100 copies of the allegedly infringing book in Ohio. Assume that the state courts of Ohio, although they could constitutionally take personal jurisdiction over D in a similar state-created claim — libel, for instance — would not do so because the Ohio long-arm is very limited and would not cover any action growing out of these facts. The federal district court will nonetheless hear the federal question copyright claim against D, because P has minimum contacts with the state where the federal court sits.

i. Less far than it could go: But even the rule just stated — that the federal court may hear the suit if D has minimum contacts with the state where the federal court sits — may extend federal court jurisdiction in federal question cases *less far* than it constitutionally could. The Fifth Amendment, which sets the federal government's due process standard, might plausibly be interpreted to allow jurisdiction in federal question suits to be exercised by *any federal court* over any U.S. citizen, in whatever state he resided. In fact, in those situations in which Congress has authorized *nationwide service of process* (*supra*, p. 40), it is quite clear that there need be no "minimum contacts" between the defendant and the state in which the federal court sits, merely minimum contacts with *some* state.

b. Foreign defendants: A comparable issue arises when the defendant is a *foreign* corporation or resident. If the claim is based upon a federal question, need the defendant have minimum contacts with the state where the federal district court sits, or merely with the United States as a whole? At least in those situations where the service of process that is used relies upon state law rules for service, most federal courts have concluded that *there must be minimum contacts with the state where the federal court sits.*

Example: P, who has suffered personal injuries while working aboard a ship moored in New Jersey, sues D (a Japanese corporation), which did work on the vessel in Japan. The suit is brought in New Jersey federal district court. D does not have minimum contacts with New Jersey, but probably does have minimum contacts with the United States as a whole, if D's contacts with all states are added together. No federal statute explicitly allows service of process on D in this situation.

Held, D is not amenable to service in this action, because it lacks minimum contacts with New Jersey. It probably would not violate the Fifth Amendment's Due Process Clause (the applicable clause here) for D to be subjected to suit based on its aggregate contacts with the United States as a whole. However, service on D here was made based upon the New Jersey long-arm (on which federal litigants may rely; see Federal Rule 4(e)(1), discussed *supra*, p. 44). But Federal Rule 4(e)(2) (in force at the time of decision but since amended) requires that if the state's long-arm is to be relied on, service must be made "under the circumstances and in the manner prescribed by statute." Therefore, this rule only allows service upon those defendants over whom New Jersey could constitutionally exercise jurisdiction (namely, those who have minimum contacts with New Jersey).

However, if the case were one in which service were made under a federal statute allowing for nationwide service of process, or one where service were made pursuant to former Federal Rule 4(d)(3)'s (now 4(h)(1), second clause) purely federal method of service, these contacts within the United States as a whole could probably be aggregated. *DeJames v. Magnificence Carriers*, 491 F.Supp. 1276 (D.N.J. 1980).

Note: The Third Circuit affirmed *DeJames;* 654 F.2d 280 (3d Cir. 1981). However, that court noted that even if service could be made by wholly federal means (e.g., a nationwide service of process statute), "We are not sure that some geographic limit short of the entire United States might not be incorporated into the 'fairness' component of the Fifth Amendment." For instance, the court observed, if D's only contacts were in Hawaii, Alaska or a few states on the West Coast, it is not clear that it would be "fair" to subject D to suit in New Jersey federal court. (But the court implicitly indicated that suit in, say, California federal court would be valid based on D's contacts not only with California but with other states in that same geographic portion of the country.)

i. Small exception: There is a recent, narrow exception to the principle that in a federal-question suit, the defendant must have minimum contacts with the state where the federal District Court sits: under new Rule 4(k)(2), if the defendant to a federal-question claim is not "subject to the jurisdiction of the courts of general jurisdiction of *any state*," he may be sued in any federal judicial district, provided that this exercise of jurisdiction is "consistent with the Constitution and laws of the United States. ..." This seems to mean that if there is no state with which D has minimum contacts (or no state whose long-arm would reach D, regardless of whether there is a state with which he has minimum contacts), a federal court can hear a federal claim against D provided that D has minimum contacts with the United States as a whole, and the particular choice of federal forum is not grossly unfair to D. But situations satisfying Rule 4(k)(2)'s conditions will be rare; see *supra*, p. 42. In the usual case of a foreign defendant who has minimum contacts with some state, a federal-question action against that defendant in some other state with whom the defendant does not have minimum contacts will still not be allowed.

2. Diversity: In *diversity* cases, the Federal courts exercise only the jurisdiction that is allowed *by the statutory law of the state in which they sit*, even if this state statutory law does not go to the limits of what the state could do commensurate with due process.

a. Supreme Court silent: The Supreme Court has not yet passed on whether this restraint is either constitutionally required (which it probably is not) or even desirable as a matter of policy.

b. *Arrowsmith:* The leading case establishing the policy of following local law in determining amenability to suit in diversity cases is *Arrowsmith v. United Press International*, 320 F.2d 219 (2d Cir. 1963). The majority opinion was written by Judge Friendly.

i. No strong federal policy: The court said: "We finally concede that the constitutional doctrine announced in *Erie v. Tompkins*, (*infra*, p. 220) would not prevent Congress or its rule-making delegate from authorizing a district court to assume jurisdiction over a foreign corporation in any ordinary diversity suit although the state court would not. ... But we find no federal policy that should lead federal courts in diversity cases to override valid state laws as to the subjection of foreign corporations to suit, in the absence of direction by federal statute or rule."

ii. State interests: State jurisdiction rules embody a valid state policy, the court held, and should not lightly be overruled by federal courts sitting in diversity cases. State interests represented in jurisdiction statutes include "affording a forum for wrongs connected with the state and conveniencing resident plaintiffs, while avoiding the discouragement of activity within the state by foreign corporations." Federal interest in uniform jurisdiction rules is not sufficiently strong to outweigh these valid state interests, in the absence of legislation.

iii. Holding: The result of *Arrowsmith* is that "the amenability of a foreign corporation to suit in a federal court in a diversity action is determined in accordance with the law of the state where the court sits, with 'federal law' entering the picture only for the purpose of deciding whether a state's assertion of jurisdiction contravenes a constitutional guarantee."

 c. Followed everywhere: The rule of *Arrowsmith* has been followed by all courts of appeals. See F,K&C, p. 1012.

 d. Applied to individuals: *Arrowsmith* has been applied not only to corporations, but also to individuals not reached by the local state long-arm, but over whom *in personam* jurisdiction in the local court would be constitutional. The state limited-jurisdiction rule has thus been followed both for corporations and individuals.

Quiz Yourself on
FEDERAL JURISDICTION OVER THE PARTIES

 4. D is a toy manufacturer whose sole office is located in New York. P is a young Florida citizen who claims to have been seriously injured in Florida by a toy made by D in New York and shipped to a store in Florida, from which P's mother bought it. P has brought a diversity action against D, based on strict product liability, in the U.S. District Court, Southern District of Florida. Assume that if the action had been brought in the Florida state courts, no Florida statute would have permitted P to serve process on D outside the boundaries of Florida. In the federal action, P caused a licensed process server to travel to New York, where the process server visited D's headquarters, and personally handed the summons and complaint to D's president. Does the federal court for the Southern District of Florida now have personal jurisdiction over D? _____

 5. Same facts as prior question. Now, however, assume that Florida has a long-arm statute that provides that service may be made on a corporation located outside of the state, by first-class mail sent to any officer of that corporation, in any suit in which the claim arises out of a tort allegedly committed by the defendant outside of the state but causing injury in the state. P caused a summons in his Florida federal court action to be sent by first-class mail to the president of D in New York. May the U.S. District Court for the Southern District of Florida take jurisdiction over D? _____

 6. Software Co. is a Washington-based publisher of computer software, particularly a program called "3-2-1." Clone Co., which is also a software publisher, has come out with a competing program called "4-3-2." Clone Co. has sold over 1,000 copies of 4-3-2 in the state of Washington. Software Co. has sued Clone Co. for federal copyright infringement in U.S. District Court for the Western District of Washington. The complaint alleges that 4-3-2 is so similar to 3-2-1 that it has the same "look and feel," and is therefore a violation of Software Co.'s copyrights. Assume that Clone Co., by selling over 1,000 copies in Washington, has the constitutionally-required minimum contacts with Washington to make it not violative of due process for Clone Co. to have to defend a suit there. Assume further, however, that due to the Washington state legislature's desire to cut down on the "litigation explosion," Washington's long arm is quite restrictive, and would not permit the Washington courts to take jurisdiction of any suit against a company which, like Clone Co., has no contacts with the state except for selling 1,000 copies of a product in the state. May the federal court for the Western District of Washington take personal jurisdiction over Clone Co. for purposes of the Software Co. copyright suit? (Assume that the method by which service is made on Clone Co. is satisfactory.) _____

 7. Driver borrowed a car owned by Owner (a New Mexico resident), with Owner's permission. While Driver was driving the car in Arizona, he hit and injured Pedestrian, an Arizona resident. Pedestrian, realizing that Driver is so poor as to be judgment-proof, has brought a diversity action against Owner in Arizona Federal District Court. Applicable Supreme Court decisions indicate that Owner, by permitting his car to be driven into Arizona, has such minimum contacts with Arizona that it is not a violation of due process for him to be required to defend a suit brought in the Arizona state courts arising out of the accident. However, Arizona's non-resident motorist statute is relatively restrictive; it allows suit against one who is the driver in an Arizona-based accident, but not against one who owns a car (which he is not driving) that is involved in an Arizona accident. Therefore, Pedestrian would not have been permitted to sue Owner in the Arizona courts unless Owner was served while in Arizona. Pedestrian instituted his federal court suit by making personal service on Owner in New Mexico. May the Arizona district court hear the suit against Owner? _____

Answers

4. No. Normally, service in a federal court action (whether based on diversity or federal question) must either take place within the confines of the state where the federal court sits, or must be made out of state in a way that is expressly permitted by that state's own long-arm statute. (There is an exception for situations where Congress has allowed for nationwide service of process, and for the 100-mile bulge provision of Federal Rule 4(f), neither of which is applicable here.) Since the facts tell us that Florida would not allow service on the New York corporation to be made in New York on these facts, and since D is not found within Florida (as it would be if, say, it had its principal place of business there), the federal court may not take jurisdiction either.

5. Yes. According to Federal Rule 4(e), if the long-arm statute of the state in which the District Court is located would permit a particular type of out-of-state service on a particular defendant, that same form of out-of-state service will suffice to confer jurisdiction on the federal district court (whether the case is based on diversity or federal question).

6. Yes. Software Co.'s suit is a "federal question" suit. That is, Software Co.'s claim "arises under the constitution, laws, or treaties of the United States," since the source of the claim is the federal copyright statute. In federal question suits, the federal court will hear the case if the defendant has minimum contacts with the forum state, even though the courts of the state might not (due to restrictive long arms) have heard a suit against that defendant. So the fact that the Washington long arm would not permit the courts of Washington to hear any suit against Clone Co. is irrelevant — since Clone Co. has the constitutionally-required minimum contacts with Washington, the federal court will hear the suit. (But this is not the rule for suits based on diversity.)

7. No. In diversity cases, the federal courts only exercise the personal jurisdiction that is allowed by the statutory law of the state in which they sit, even if the state statutory law does not go to the limits of what the state could do commensurate with due process. See, e.g., *Arrowsmith v. United Press International*, 320 F.2d 219 (2d Cir. 1963). So the rule for diversity actions is quite different from that for federal question actions — this fact pattern is virtually identical to the fact pattern of the prior question, except for the fact that we are dealing with diversity rather than federal question, yet the result is that here there is no federal-court jurisdiction and in the prior question there is.

V. JURISDICTION OVER THINGS

A. General Principles

1. ***In rem* actions:** *In rem* actions are ones which do not seek to impose personal liability on anyone, but seek rather to affect the interests of persons in a specific thing (or *res*).

   a. **Interest of all persons in *res*:** A few *in rem* actions purport to affect the interest of *all* persons in the *res*. Examples are *admiralty actions* where the ship itself is in a sense the defendant; actions under *land registration statutes; probate court* decisions. The Restatement of Conflicts, V. 1, p. 190, takes a narrow view of *in rem*, limiting it to those actions, just described, which affect the rights of the whole world in the thing.

   b. **Interest of only some persons in *res*:** Most *in rem* actions, however, according to the general usage of the term, affect the interests of only certain specified persons in the thing. Typical examples are actions to *quiet title* to, or to *foreclose a lien* on, real estate.

   c. **Status as *res*:** The concept of *in rem* has been extended to cover actions which seek to affect *status*, for instance, *divorce* actions. In such an action, the marital status is considered to be the "thing" on which jurisdiction is exercised; it is often considered to be located wherever one of the two spouses is domiciled.

2. ***Quasi in rem actions:*** *Quasi in rem* actions are those which would have been *in personam* if jurisdiction over the defendant's person had been attainable. Instead, property or intangibles are seized not as the *object* of the litigation, but merely as a *means of satisfying a possible judgment* against the defendant.

3. **Method of attachment:** In an *in rem* action, *description* of the property in the papers filed with the court is sufficient to bring the property within the control of the court for the purposes of the suit. But in a *quasi in rem* action, the property must be actually *attached*, or seized (generally by having the sheriff post official notice on the land). This is the actual holding of *Pennoyer*. (The statements about the lack of personal jurisdiction in that case are essentially dicta).

B. *In rem* jurisdiction

1. **Constitutionality of *in rem judgments*:** The constitutionality of *in rem* judgments has never been seriously in question.

   a. **Lack of personal notice:** In the early case of *Tyler v. Judges of the Court of Registration*, 55 N.E. 812 (Mass. 1900), the plaintiff argued that a land registration proceeding which registered land in the name of a third person violated plaintiff's due process rights, since he was *not personally notified*. The *in rem* proceedings in question provided for notification by mail to all persons known to claim an interest in the land, and for newspaper publication announcing the proceedings in the hopes of reaching unknown claimants.

      i. **Constitutionality upheld:** Justice Holmes *rejected* plaintiff's argument that the lack of personal notice violated the due process rights of the unknown claimants: "If it does not satisfy the Constitution, a judicial proceeding to clear titles against all the world hardly is possible, for the very meaning of such a proceeding is to get rid of unknown as well as known claims — indeed certainty against the unknown may be said to be its chief end — and unknown claims cannot be dealt with by personal service upon the claimant. ... But we cannot bring ourselves to doubt that the Constitutions of the U.S. and of Massachusetts at least permit it as fully as did the common law."

2. **Specific performance of land sale contracts:** In actions for *specific performance of contracts to convey land, in rem* jurisdiction in the state where the land is located has been constitutionally upheld.

   a. **Conveyance by sheriff:** If the plaintiff wins, the court may order the sheriff to make the conveyance of land to the plaintiff, as long as the out-of-state defendant was given reasonable notice.

3. **Effect of *Shaffer*:** *Shaffer v. Heitner*, discussed *infra*, p. 56, probably has little effect on *in rem* as opposed to *quasi in rem* jurisdiction. The *Shaffer* opinion states that "... when claims to the property itself are the source of the underlying controversy between the plaintiff and the defendant, it would be unusual for the state where the property is located not to have jurisdiction. In such cases the defendant's claim to property located in the state would normally indicate that he expected to benefit from the state's protection of his interest." Moreover, the state has an interest in making its real estate marketable.

   a. **Specific performance:** Thus a court can almost certainly continue to order specific performance of contracts to convey land within its borders (even if the defendant resides out-of-state). By owning in-state real estate, the defendant has evidenced his expectation of receiving the benefit of the state's laws, and it is reasonable to require him to litigate claims regarding that land in-state. This is different from the usual *quasi in rem* case, where the property has nothing to do with the litigation.

4. **Federal *in rem* jurisdiction:** If federal subject matter jurisdiction exists (either diversity or federal question), a *federal in rem* case may be brought concerning land (e.g., to clear title, or to foreclose a lien).

   a. **Nationwide service:** 28 U.S.C. §1655 allows *nationwide service* on defendants in District Court actions "to enforce any lien upon or claim to, or to remove any incumbrance or lien or cloud upon the title to, real or personal property within the district. ..."

   b. **Only lien property affected by default:** If the defendant in a §1655 suit defaults, the judgment affects *only the property involved in the lien*, and not the defendant's other assets.

C. *Quasi in rem* jurisdiction

1. **Nature of *quasi in rem*:** A *quasi in rem* action is one which would have been *in personam* if jurisdiction over the defendant's person had been attainable. Instead property or intangibles are seized not as the *object* of the litigation, but merely as a *means of satisfying a possible judgment* against the defendant.

   Example: P wishes to sue D on a contract claim in California state court. The contract has no connection with California, nor does D himself have sufficient contacts with

California to allow it to exercise *in personam* jurisdiction over him. D does, however, own some property in California. Putting aside constitutional due process problems, P could attach that property as a basis of jurisdiction, and bring a *quasi in rem* action on the contract claim. If P wins, he will be able to collect only the value of the attached property, and D will not be personally liable for the remainder if the damages exceed the value of the property.

2. **"Half-way house":** *Quasi in rem* jurisdiction has been referred to as a ***"half-way house"*** between *in rem* and *in personam* jurisdiction; it is *in rem* in the sense that the court is able to adjudicate the case only because the defendant has property within the state that has been attached by the court; it is *in personam* in the sense that the subject matter of the suit is unrelated to the property seized.

3. **Two definitions:** Definitions of *"in rem"* and *"quasi in rem"* are not all consistent. Some authorities include within the definition of *quasi in rem* not only the kinds of actions described above, but also those which are "about" a particular piece of property, but which affect ***only*** the interest of ***certain specified people*** in the property, not the interest of the whole world. These commentators would, for instance, include within the definition of *quasi in rem* proceedings to foreclose a mortgage on real property, since only the interest of the mortgagor and mortgagee, and not that of a person with superior title to either, will be affected. See Res Judicata in a Nutshell, p. 233. The Supreme Court's opinion in *Shaffer v. Heitner, infra*, p. 56, refers to this additional kind of suit as *"quasi in rem* of the first type"; see footnotes 17 and 24.

   a. **Our definition:** Here, the term *"quasi in rem"* is not used to include these cases, and includes ***only*** those cases which are "aimed primarily at the satisfaction of a personal claim, but which proceed under the guise of actions to apply property or other assets to the satisfaction of the claim." Res Judicata in a Nutshell, p. 232. (In *Shaffer*, this is *quasi in rem* "of the second type." See footnote 29.)

4. **Means of satisfying judgment:** *Quasi in rem* actions are generally for money damages, which are awarded by ***selling the property***, or ***garnishing the debt***, owned by or owed to the defendant within the forum state.

   a. **Limited to attached property:** A *quasi in rem* judgment may be satisfied ***only out of the attached property***. Even if there is other property belonging to the defendant within the forum state, unless this property has been attached prior to the suit, it may not be seized and sold to satisfy the judgment subsequently. A new action must be brought, and litigated on the merits, in order to reach this new property.

   b. **No *res judicata*:** *Quasi in rem* judgments have ***no res judicata value;*** if P wins against D in a *quasi in rem* action in State X, he cannot in a later suit against D in State Y claim that the matter has been decided for all time. Instead, he must go through another trial on the merits if he wishes to subject D to further liability.

      i. **Exception:** Some courts recognize one exception to the general rule that *quasi in rem* judgments to do not have res judicata value. These courts hold that if the defendant makes a ***limited appearance*** (*infra*, p. 60) and fully litigates certain issues, he will not be allowed to relitigate those issues in a subsequent trial. Nor will the plaintiff be allowed to relitigate those issues. The Restatement, Second, Judgments §75(c), takes this view.

    ii. Contrary view: Other courts, however, hold that even if the defendant makes a limited appearance and litigates all the issues, the judgment has no *res judicata* effect. These courts point out that to allow res judicata in this situation would destroy the utility of the limited appearance (a device which allows the defendant to contest on the merits without subjecting himself to personal liability) since the defendant will be bound as to all his other property by the results of the first *quasi in rem* suit. See Res Judicata in a Nutshell, p. 236.

5. Jurisdiction based on debt: *Quasi in rem* jurisdiction has frequently been exercised not only over tangible property (e.g., real estate) located in the forum state, but also over *intangible property*, such as a *debt.*

    a. Harris v. Balk: In the leading case of ***Harris v. Balk***, 198 U.S. 215 (1905), it was held that jurisdiction could be exercised *quasi in rem* over a ***debt owed to a defendant***, if personal jurisdiction could be obtained over the ***defendant's debtor.*** Personal jurisdiction over the defendant himself was therefore unnecessary; the debtor could be ordered to pay the debt to the plaintiff, rather than to his own creditor (the defendant) in order to satisfy the judgment if the plaintiff won.

    b. Facts of Harris v. Balk: The facts of *Harris v. Balk* were as follows:

        i. Harris, a North Carolina resident, owed $180 to Balk, also a North Carolina resident. Epstein, a Maryland resident, claimed Balk owed him $300.

        ii. Harris spent a few days in Maryland, during which Epstein garnished Harris' debt to Balk by serving Harris with process. This furnished the Maryland court with *quasi in rem* jurisdiction to consider Balk's debt to Epstein, and to satisfy a possible judgment in Epstein's favor.

        iii. Harris did not contest the attachment process; the Maryland court found that Balk owed Epstein the money, and ordered Harris to pay the $180 to Epstein instead of to Balk. Harris did this.

        iv. Balk then sued Harris in North Carolina for the $180 originally owed him by Harris. Harris claimed the payment to Epstein under the Maryland judgment as a defense.

    c. Jurisdiction validated: The Supreme Court found that the exercise of *quasi in rem* jurisdiction by the Maryland court was valid.

        i. Rationale: The court stated, "The obligation of the debtor to pay his debt clings to and *accompanies him wherever he goes*. ... If there be a law of the State providing for the attachment of the debt, then if the garnishee be found in that State, and process be personally served upon him therein, we think the court thereby acquires jurisdiction over him, and can garnish the debt due from him to the debtor of the plaintiff and condemn it. ..."

        ii. Right to sue garnishee: The ability of the Maryland court to exercise *quasi in rem* jurisdiction over the debt was contingent on the creditor's (Balk) being able to sue the garnishee (Harris) in that court. Since Balk could have sued Harris for the debt in Maryland, there is no reason why Epstein should not be able to sue for the same debt.

d. Garnishee's defense against second suit: Since the Maryland court's jurisdiction was valid, the payment of the judgment by Harris was a defense against the action against him by Balk.

   i. Notice to creditor required: The availability of the first judgment as a defense by the garnishee in an action against him by his original creditor was contingent on the *garnishee's giving notice of the suit to his creditor.* By receiving such notice, the creditor (Balk) got a chance to prove that the plaintiff's (Epstein's) claim was invalid. Had Harris not given notice of the suit to Balk, Harris would not have been allowed to use his payment to Epstein as a defense to Balk's suit against him (Harris).

   ii. Creditor's right of appeal: In *Harris*, Maryland law allowed Balk one year to appeal the decision condemning Harris' debt. Since Balk had notice of the condemnation right after it was issued, he had a year to protect his rights, and could not therefore claim that Harris had been negligent in not informing him. The payment of the debt by Harris to Epstein therefore protected him against having to pay it again to Balk.

e. Criticism of *Harris v. Balk:* *Harris v. Balk* has often been criticized because it results in a defendant (Balk) being forced to defend, if he wishes to protect the debt owed him, in a place which has *no connection with his own activities*. W&M, V.4, 275. Observe that this happens only where *intangible* property (like the debt in *Harris*), not tangible property, is the subject of the attachment; using the defendant-in-interest's real property within the forum state as the basis for suit there is less patently unfair, since the mere ownership of property within the forum state constitutes a connection with that state.

   i. Effect of *Shaffer:* Unfairness in the attachment-of-debt situation was one of the considerations which led the Supreme Court to sound the virtual death-knell for *quasi in rem* jurisdiction in *Shaffer v. Heitner*, discussed *infra*, p. 56. As a result of *Shaffer*, it is probably safe to say that Balk would today be able to argue successfully that the attachment of Harris' debt to him to confer jurisdiction violated his constitutional right to due process.

6. Jurisdiction based on insurance obligations: Until the 1980's, some courts allowed *quasi in rem* jurisdiction over a *liability insurer's obligation to defend a policyholder* in an action against the latter. See, e.g., *Seider v. Roth*, 17 N.Y. 2d 111 (1966).

a. Insurer-based jurisdiction rejected by Supreme Court: However, the U.S. Supreme Court explicitly *rejected* jurisdiction based upon the attachment of an insurance company's duty to defend, in *Rush v. Savchuk*, 444 U.S. 320 (1980).

   i. Facts of *Rush:* P and D in *Rush* were both Indiana residents at the time of their involvement in an automobile accident, which occurred in Indiana. P then moved to Minnesota, and sued D in Minnesota state court. Jurisdiction was based upon the obligation of D's insurance company to defend him in Minnesota. (The insurer, State Farm, did business in Minnesota, as in all other states.)

    ii. Due process violated: The Court held that the exercise of jurisdiction over D based on the insurer's obligation to defend *violated the due process requirements* of *International Shoe* and *Shaffer v. Heitner, infra,* p. 58. The Court stressed that D himself had never had any contact with Minnesota, and that the underlying controversy had no connection with that state either. The Court rejected the contention that the insurance policy itself was so important to the litigation that it furnished the requisite contacts with Minnesota; the policy pertained "only to the conduct, not the substance, of the litigation" and therefore did not amount to a contact between Minnesota and D.

7. *Shaffer v. Heitner:* The utility of *quasi in rem* jurisdiction was radically curtailed in the landmark Supreme Court case, ***Shaffer v. Heitner***, 433 U.S. 186 (1977). That case held that *quasi in rem* jurisdiction over a defendant could not be exercised unless the defendant had such *"minimum contacts"* with the forum state that *in personam jurisdiction could be exercised over him* under *International Shoe.*

    a. Facts of *Shaffer:* Plaintiff Heitner brought a shareholder's derivative suit in Delaware on behalf of Greyhound Corporation against 28 of the corporation's non-resident directors and officers. The suit alleged that wrongdoing by the defendants had caused the corporation to be liable for large antitrust damages and fines.

        i. Place of activities complained of: None of the activities complained of took place in Delaware, nor had any of the defendants had any other contacts with Delaware. The corporation's business activities were conducted mostly at its home headquarters in Phoenix, Arizona.

        ii. Sequestration of stock: In order to gain jurisdiction, the plaintiff took advantage of a Delaware statute providing that any stock in a Delaware corporation could be *"sequestered,"* i.e. attached, to provide *quasi in rem* jurisdiction against its owner. The shares themselves were not physically present in Delaware, but the statute provided that the situs of stock in a Delaware corporation should be "deemed" to be Delaware, regardless of its actual physical location. 21 of the 28 defendants owned Greyhound stock, so jurisdiction was obtained only as to their property.

        iii. Consequence: The consequence of all this was that the plaintiff was able to attach over $1 million worth of stock as a basis for *quasi in rem* jurisdiction against most of the defendants. Furthermore, since Delaware *does not allow a limited appearance*, these defendants had to choose between not defending the action, and forfeiting the $1 million in stock, or defending it, and subjecting themselves to possibly unlimited personal liability. Instead, they maintained that *quasi in rem* jurisdiction violated their due process rights, because of their lack of contacts with Delaware.

    b. Holding: The Court, in an opinion by Justice Marshall, agreed that Delaware's statute *violated the defendants' due process rights.* The Court noted that all actions, even true *in rem* ones, adjudicate the interests of *people* in things, and are therefore really "against" people. Where, as here, the suit is not even "about" the in-state property, and the property is merely a means of giving the court jurisdiction, the suit is even more clearly against the owner than in the true *in rem* case. And this is still more obviously the case insofar as Delaware allows no limited appearance, and the express purpose of its sequestration statute is to force the defendant to enter a general appearance.

c. **Conclusion:** Therefore, the Court concluded, "If a direct assertion of personal jurisdiction over the defendant would violate the Constitution, it would seem that an indirect assertion of that jurisdiction should be equally impermissible." ***The same test, the "minimum contacts" test of International Shoe, should therefore apply to determine whether the exercise of quasi in rem in a particular case is constitutional.***

   i. **Arguments for *quasi in rem rejected*:** The Court rejected several traditional arguments in favor of *quasi in rem*. The most important of these was the argument that a defendant "should not be able to avoid payment of his obligations by the expedient of removing his assets to a place where he is not subject to an *in personam* suit." Even if the defendant attempts to do this, the Court said, the plaintiff is always free to bring an *in personam* suit where the defendant resides, regardless of the presence of assets, and then after recovering a judgment, sue to enforce that judgment in the state where the assets are. He has a right to bring the second suit under the Full Faith and Credit Clause (see *infra*, p. 75.)

d. **Lack of minimum contacts:** The Court also found that Delaware did not have an interest in adjudicating the controversy sufficient to make such an adjudication fair to the defendant.

   i. **Lack of connection between state and cause of action:** First, no acts alleged in the complaint had any contact with Delaware.

   ii. **Regulatory interest:** Secondly, Delaware's interest in "supervising the management of a Delaware corporation" is insufficient. This interest couldn't really be that strong, the Court said, or the sequestration statute wouldn't have been designed as it was. That statute would not allow the court to exercise *quasi in rem* jurisdiction over a director or officer who owned no stock in the Delaware corporation, or other Delaware property (as was indeed the case with 7 of the 28 defendants). Furthermore, the statute was overinclusive, since it would grant jurisdiction over any stockholder of a Delaware corporation, even on a claim having nothing to do with the corporation, or Delaware, at all (e.g., a claim for a personal breach of contract occurring in California).

   iii. **Delaware law applies:** Delaware's interest in supervising corporations is given adequate protection, the Court said, by the fact that Delaware *law* would apply to this suit no matter where it was brought, because of conflict of laws principles. But, the Court stated, the fact that a state's laws apply does not mean that that state has the right to adjudicate the controversy; the Court quoted *Hanson v. Denckla*: "[The State] does not acquire … jurisdiction by being the 'center of gravity' of the controversy, or the most convenient location for the litigation. The issue is personal jurisdiction, not choice of law."

   iv. **Implied consent:** The Court also rejected the plaintiff's *"implied consent"* argument, i.e., that by accepting positions as officers or directors of a Delaware corporation, the defendants had impliedly consented to be subject to Delaware law. Again, the Court stated, the fact that they may have consented to be bound by Delaware law did not mean that they had agreed to be sued in Delaware courts. Furthermore, "It strains reason … to suggest that anyone buying securities in a corporation formed in Delaware 'impliedly consents' to subject himself to Delaware's … jurisdiction on any cause of action."

e. **Concurrences:** Justice Powell concurred, but indicated that there might be some kinds of property "whose situs is indisputably and permanently located within a State" and which might therefore, and without anything else, provide the necessary contacts to make *quasi in rem* jurisdiction constitutional. He thought that this was particularly likely to be true of real estate, and that such jurisdiction "would avoid the uncertainty of the general *International Shoe* standard. …" Justice Stevens concurred in the result only, stating that the test should be whether the defendant had a *"fair warning"* of the chance of litigation within a particular forum; one who owns real estate or keeps a bank account within the state probably has received such warning, he indicated, but someone who buys a share of stock in a Delaware corporation on a national stock exchange certainly has not.

i. **Brennan's concurrence and dissent:** Justice Brennan concurred in part and dissented in part. He agreed that "minimum contacts" should be required to sustain *quasi in rem* jurisdiction. However, he felt that such contacts should be found to exist whenever a shareholders' derivative suit is brought in the state where the corporation is chartered, in view of the chartering state's "unusually powerful interest in insuring the availability of a convenient forum for litigating claims involving a possible multiplicity of defendant fiduciaries and for vindicating the State's substantive policies regarding the management of its domestic corporations." He argued that the defendants, by associating themselves with a Delaware corporation, had invoked the "benefits and protections" of Delaware law, and should have been apprised that "the State may seek to offer a convenient forum for redressing claims of fiduciary breach of trust."

8. **Significance of *Shaffer*:** Generally speaking, the utility of *quasi in rem* jurisdiction is at an end. Prior to *Shaffer*, its utility lay precisely in the fact that where personal jurisdiction was not available, it provided a "second best" form of jurisdiction, in which the plaintiff could get satisfaction at least to the extent of the in-state property (and perhaps induce the defendant into a general appearance). If, as the majority suggests, *quasi in rem* jurisdiction may only be exercised where the *International Shoe* minimum contacts test is satisfied, *quasi in rem* will never do anything that *in personam* jurisdiction couldn't do better.

a. **Insurer's duty to defend:** One example of *Shaffer's* effect is the demise of *quasi in rem* jurisdiction over an **insurance company's duty to defend its policyholder** in the forum state. As noted *supra*, p. 55, the Supreme Court in *Rush v. Savchuk* rejected this type of jurisdiction.

9. **Open questions:** The decision in *Shaffer* left a number of open questions, some of which are as follows:

a. **Transient presence:** Will mere *presence in the forum state* at the time of service continue to be enough for *in personam* jurisdiction, if the defendant has no other contacts? The answer to this has turned out to be *"yes"* — the Supreme Court held in 1990 that because virtually all states continue to allow presence in the forum state at the time of service as a basis for jurisdiction, use of presence does not violate "traditional notions of fairness," and thus does not violate due process. See *Burnham v. Superior Court, supra,* p. 10.

b. **Claims not connected with the forum:** In *in personam* cases, will greater contacts with the forum state be required where the claim does not arise in the forum state (perpetuating the "systematic and continuous" contacts requirement of *Perkins v. Benguet, supra,* p. 25)? In view of the stress the *Shaffer* opinion placed on the fact that the claim there had no connection with Delaware, the answer is probably *"yes."*

c. **Vitality of *Harris v. Balk*:** Is *Harris v. Balk* overruled? The answer is almost certainly *"yes."* The mere fact that the defendant's debtor happens to be physically present in the forum state does not by itself mean that the defendant has the necessary "minimum contacts" with that state. The *quasi in rem* jurisdiction exercised in *Harris* is objectionable under *Shaffer* in at least two respects: (1) it subjects the defendant to litigation in unforeseeable forums, with no advance warning; and (2) It makes him litigate in a forum that has no necessary connection with the claim against him.

d. ***In rem* jurisdiction:** What will become of the familiar kinds of *in rem* jurisdiction, such as mortgage foreclosures, specific performance actions involving land sale contracts, etc.? Since these actions are "about" the property in the state, they are probably not affected by *Shaffer.* See the discussion of this question *supra,* p. 52.

e. **Effect of limited appearance:** Will the fact that the forum state permits a *limited appearance* save an exercise of *quasi in rem* jurisdiction from what would otherwise be unconstitutionality? It is true that the Court attached some significance to the fact that Delaware did not allow such a limited appearance, and forced defendants to choose between forfeiting their property or submitting themselves to unlimited personal liability. But in a footnote, the Court observed that "It is true that the potential liability of a defendant in a [*quasi in rem*] action is limited by the value of the property. ... [But] the fairness of subjecting a defendant to state court jurisdiction does not depend on the size of the claim being litigated. ..." This indicates that the availability of a limited appearance is probably completely *irrelevant* to the constitutionality of *quasi in rem* jurisdiction in any particular case.

f. **Suit to enforce judgments:** If the plaintiff obtains a personal judgment against the defendant in one state, may he sue to *enforce it* against the defendant's assets in another state with which the defendant does not have minimum contacts? The answer certainly seems to be "yes," that judgments may be sued on for enforcement under the Full Faith and Credit Clause, just as before. See footnote 36 of the Court's opinion.

g. **Significance of plaintiff's connection with forum:** Does the extent of the *plaintiff's* contacts with the forum state have any significance? The Court focused almost exclusively on the connections between the defendant and the forum, and cited *Hanson v. Denckla's* statement that a state does not get jurisdiction by being the "center of gravity" of the controversy. (This theme was repeated in *Rush v. Savchuk, supra*, p. 55, where the court emphasized that only the contacts between defendant and forum state mattered.) But there are two situations in which the plaintiff's close ties with the forum state might be a factor (although not the only one) tending to make jurisdiction (whether *in personam* or *quasi in rem*) constitutional.

    i. **Plaintiff's activities local and defendant's activities interstate:** If the defendant is a large corporation with far-reaching interstate activities (although not doing business in the forum state itself), and the plaintiff's activities are strictly local, a court might decide that the hardship to the defendant in being required to come to the plaintiff's "home court" was not so substantial as to violate due process. See Note, 91 Harv. L. Rev. 152, 161.

    ii. **No other forum:** The court explicitly declined to consider "the question whether the presence of a defendant's property in a State is a sufficient basis for jurisdiction when *no other forum is available* to the plaintiff." (Footnote 37). This might be the case if there were multiple defendants, and no state with which all had minimum contacts, or if there were a foreign defendant. In this situation, the Court might well find the balance to be tipped in favor of *quasi in rem* jurisdiction, particularly if the plaintiff had close ties with the forum.

D. Limited appearances

    1. **Nature of limited appearance:** Some states allow what is called a ***limited appearance***. In a limited appearance, the defendant appears in an *in rem* or *quasi in rem* suit, contests the case on its merits, but is subjected to liability ***only to the extent of the property or debt attached or garnished by the court.***

        Example: In order to sue D in State X (where personal jurisdiction over D cannot be obtained), P has the court garnish wages owed to D by T, a State X corporation. P claims $10,000 damages for the wrong done by D, but the garnished wages only amount to $2,000. If D is allowed to make a limited appearance, he may contest the case on the merits (that is, argue that he does not in fact owe P the money) without subjecting himself to unlimited personal liability. If he loses, he loses only the $2,000 in wages. If P sues him again in another state where jurisdiction is obtained, P must retry the case on the merits — there is no *res judicata* effect of the judgment, even though D contested on the merits in the original action.

    2. **Distinguished from special appearance:** The doctrine of *limited appearance* should be distinguished from that of *special appearance*. The former allows the defendant to contest on the merits while limiting his liability to the property previously attached or garnished by the court. The latter allows a defendant against whom personal jurisdiction is asserted to argue the invalidity of that jurisdiction, without having his argument, or presence in the court, itself constitute a submission to the court's jurisdiction. See the discussion of Special Appearances, *infra*, p. 73.

    3. **Federal limited appearances:** A limited appearance is sometimes allowed in *federal* actions. See *infra*, p. 61.

E. Federal *quasi in rem* jurisdiction

1. **Not allowed before 1963:** Prior to 1963, original federal *quasi in rem* jurisdiction did not exist. Once a valid *quasi in rem* action had been commenced in *state* court, it could be *removed* by the defendant to federal court. But the action could not be commenced as an original federal action based on attachment or garnishment.

2. **Rule 4(n):** The Federal Rules were first amended to allow original quasi-in-rem jurisdiction in the federal courts in 1963. Today, Rule 4(n) (added in 1993) allows a court to exercise *quasi-in-rem* jurisdiction over a person by seizure of his assets within the jurisdiction, "under the circumstances and in the manner provided by the law of the state in which the District Court is located." 4(n)(2). Thus *quasi-in-rem* may be used only *if the law of the state in which the federal court sits permits* such *quasi-in-rem* jurisdiction. Furthermore, *quasi-in-rem* jurisdiction may be used only "upon a showing that *personal* jurisdiction over a defendant *cannot*, in the district where the action is brought, *be obtained with reasonable efforts* by service of summons in any manner authorized by this rule. ..." *Id.* So the main utility of federal *quasi-in-rem* jurisdiction will be where either D is a *fugitive* who cannot be located (though he has minimum contacts with the state where the District Court sits), the assets themselves are in imminent danger of *disappearing*, or the local state long-arm is too narrow to reach D even though he has minimum contacts with the forum state. See Advisory Committee Notes to new Rule 4(n).

3. **Limited appearance:** The federal courts are split on whether a *limited appearance* may be made, i.e., whether the defendant may defend on the merits in a federal *quasi in rem* suit without thereby subjecting himself to unlimited personal liability.

   a. **Federal Rules silent:** The Federal Rules of Civil Procedure neither allow nor prohibit limited appearances — these are simply not mentioned at all.

   b. **Follow state law:** Most federal courts that have considered the issue have followed the rule of the *state in which they are sitting* in determining whether to allow a limited appearance. That is, if the state would allow a limited appearance in a state-court *quasi in rem* suit, the federal court similarly allows it; if not, not.

   c. **Follow federal law:** But a few federal courts have made their own decision about whether to allow a limited appearance, without regard to state law. See, e.g., *Campbell v. Murdock*, 90 F.Supp. 297 (N.D. Ohio 1950), following general federal-law policies (rather than state law) in deciding not to allow a limited appearance.

4. **Practical effect:** Since general *venue* statutes must still be met in federal *quasi in rem* actions, the practical effect is to give rise to such suits only in the *state where a substantial part of the relevant events occurred*. 28 U.S.C. §1391. See discussion of Venue in Federal Actions, *infra*, p. 83.

   a. **Use where state's long arm is narrow:** Recall that the federal courts in diversity cases follow the long arm of the state in which the federal court sits. See *supra*, p. 41. Therefore, the principal use of federal *quasi in rem* jurisdiction is likely to be in those diversity cases where the local state long arm is narrow, so that personal jurisdiction over the defendant would not be exercised by the state, even though it could be exercised constitutionally. Thus if D has contacts with the forum state that would suffice for personal jurisdiction over him, but the long arm of the state would not reach him, the federal court may use *quasi in rem* jurisdiction if the state court would permit such jurisdiction.

5. **Amount in controversy:** In federal *quasi in rem* cases, the courts have not been able to agree on whether it is the value of the attached or garnished property, or the amount claimed, which should control for the $50,000 amount in controversy requirement. F,K&C, p. 906.

> **Example:** The plaintiff claims $51,000 of damages against the defendant. The court has attached property belonging to the defendant within the state as the basis for *quasi in rem* jurisdiction; this property is worth only $3,000. (If the plaintiff wins, he will only win the $3,000. He will have to sue for the other $48,000, if he can get personal jurisdiction or attach other property, by ***relitigating on the merits***, since there is no res judicata effect to the *quasi in rem* judgment. Also, if defendant wins, he can still be sued again either *in personam* or on the basis of other attached property; here, too, he must relitigate the merits to defend.) If it is the amount claimed that determines whether the Federal Amount in Controversy requirement is met (*infra*, p.106) then the plaintiff has met the requirement and may bring suit. But if the value of the property attached controls, he has not fulfilled the requirement. Courts and commentators are in disagreement about whether the plaintiff may bring suit on these facts, with perhaps a majority of opinion on the side of allowing the suit to go forward. F,K&C, *id*.

Quiz Yourself on
JURISDICTION OVER THINGS

8. D is a resident of Pennsylvania. While driving one day in Pennsylvania, D collided with P, a pedestrian, who is an Ohio resident who happened to be visiting his sister in Pennsylvania. D has no contacts with Ohio except for the fact that D works in Pennsylvania for a corporation whose state of incorporation and principal place of business are Ohio. P commenced an action for negligence against D in the Ohio state courts. P obtained from the Ohio state courts an order of pre-judgment garnishment (authorized by Ohio statutes) whereby D's employer was required to deposit with the court each week 20 of D's take-home pay until the action is resolved. Under the terms of the garnishment order, if P prevails, P will be given the garnished amount (up to the amount of his judgment), but D will have no other liability, assuming that he does not make a general appearance. May the Ohio courts constitutionally proceed with P's action on this basis? _____

Answer

8. **No.** The landmark case of *Shaffer v. Heitner* states that *quasi in rem* jurisdiction over a defendant may not be exercised unless the defendant has such minimum contacts with the forum state that *in personam* jurisdiction could be exercised over him. Since D has no contacts at all with Ohio (except for the very fortuitous fact that D's Pennsylvania-based job is with an Ohio-headquartered company), the Ohio courts could not exercise personal jurisdiction over D. Consequently, under *Shaffer v. Heitner*, Ohio may not achieve the same result by seizing part of D's wages to serve as the means for satisfying a possible judgment. The fact that P happens to be an Ohio resident is irrelevant — what counts is D's contacts with the forum state. The type of garnishment-based action described in this fact pattern is similar to that of *Harris v. Balk*, a pre-*Shaffer* case in which *quasi in rem* jurisdiction over a debt located in the forum state was

permitted — but *Harris v. Balk* is almost certainly now invalid in light of *Shaffer* (though the Supreme Court has not expressly so held).

VI. NOTICE AND OPPORTUNITY TO BE HEARD

A. General Principles:

1. **Notice:** Once it has been established that the court has the ***authority*** to adjudicate a dispute between the parties or over the property before it, it must still be established that the defendant received ***adequate notice*** of the case against him.

   a. **Reasonableness test:** In order for the defendant to have received adequate notice, it is not necessary that he ***actually*** have learned of the suit. Rather, the procedures used to alert him must have been ***reasonably likely to inform him***, even if they actually failed to do so.

   b. ***In rem and quasi in rem:*** Less strict notice requirements are generally applied in *in rem* and *quasi in rem* cases than in *in personam* cases.

   c. **Mail notice:** Many statutes today allow service by registered mail or certified mail, in addition to the traditional personal "in-hand" service required in the 19th century (as in *Pennoyer*). The applicability of these "constructive" service statutes will be considered more fully below.

2. **Opportunity to defend:** The defendant must be given ***adequate time*** to prepare a defense, and an ***opportunity*** to present that defense. This requirement is in addition to the requirement that he be given reasonable notice of the case against him.

3. **Constitutional standard:** The adequacy of notice and hearing are measured by a Constitutional due process standard.

B. Traditional Notice Requirements:

1. **In-hand service:** In *in personam* cases, until this century, ***personal*** "in-hand" service within the forum state was generally required. Personal service is still the best and surest means of satisfying the notice requirement.

2. **Attachment:** In *in rem* and *quasi in rem* cases, if the suit is begun by the attachment of ***tangible property***, the traditional view has been that this attachment suffices to give the defendant property owner notice.

   a. **Rationale:** This rule was based on the idea that the act of attaching tangible property (by sending the sheriff to post notices on the land) would be almost certain to effectively inform the absent owner of the land of the suit against him.

   b. **Modern requirement:** Since, however, the owner of the land was usually an out-of-state resident (hence an *in rem* or *quasi in rem* suit, rather than one *in personam*) attachment might well not give him actual notice. Most modern statutes therefore require some ***additional*** means of informing the defendant, such as publication of the fact of the impending suit, or mailing of notice to the defendant.

3. Garnishment: In a *quasi in rem* suit involving **garnishment of a debt** (as opposed to attachment of tangible property), some statutes rely on the **garnishee** (i.e., the defendant's debtor) to inform the defendant of the suit.

    a. Rationale: The rationale for relying on the garnishee to give notice is two-part:

        i. Garnishee gets notice: First, the garnishee is certain to get notice, since the means of garnishing the debt is by making personal service of garnishment papers on the garnishee. (It is the garnishee's amenability to personal service that makes it constitutionally possible to garnish the debt he owes the defendant.)

        ii. Garnishee's obligation to notify: Second, the rule in *Harris v. Balk* established that if the garnishee does not inform the defendant of the action, the garnishee cannot later plead the garnishment and subsequent payment by him of the debt as a defense in an action by the original defendant against him for the debt. Thus if the garnishee does not want to run the risk of having to pay twice, once to the garnishor (the plaintiff in the first suit) and secondly to the original creditor, he must give notice to the creditor (defendant in the first action).

    b. Modern statutory rule: Most modern statutes, however, nonetheless require that the original plaintiff give **notice to the defendant**, rather than relying solely on the garnishee.

C. Modern Notice Requirements:

    1. "Substitute" service: When personal "in-hand" service was required, an unscrupulous defendant could thwart a plaintiff either by staying out of the forum state (since only in-state personal service was allowed) or by remaining **hidden within the state**. To deal with such evasion of process-servers, the concept of **"substitute service"** was established.

        a. Papers left at dwelling: The most common substitute service provision allows the process papers to be left at the defendant's dwelling house or usual place of abode within the state.

        b. Court order: Some statutes make substitute service available only after a court order is obtained showing personal service was unsuccessfully attempted.

        c. "Suitable age and discretion" standard: Some statutes require that the papers be left "at the individual's dwelling house ... with some person of suitable age and discretion then residing within" (as the formula is phrased in Federal Rule 4(e)(2)) or some similar formula.

        d. Left at unattended dwelling: Some states permit papers in certain types of actions to be left even at an **unattended dwelling**; usually such statutes require that the papers be **affixed to the door**. However, in some fact situations, use of provisions like these may violate the constitutional due process right to adequate notice.

            i. *Greene case:* For instance, in *Greene v. Lindsey*, 456 U.S. 444 (1982), notice of eviction proceedings was given by posting copies of summonses on the door of several tenants' apartments. The tenants claimed that they never saw the posted summonses, and that they did not learn of the eviction proceedings until default judgments had been taken. The Court held that, at least on these facts, service had *not* met the requirements of due process — there was substantial risk that the summonses would be torn down by children in the building (a factor which presumably would not be present if the defendant lived in a house). Even more importantly, *use of the mails* was a better way to ensure that the tenants actually received service; this more effective means should have been used.

e. **Service by mail:** Some states (e.g., California) and the federal court system allow service to be made by ordinary *first-class mail*, if the defendant returns an acknowledgment or waiver form to the plaintiff's lawyer. For a more complete description of the federal mail service provision, see *supra*, p. 45.

f. **Domicile requirement:** Some states have statutes requiring that the defendant must have his *domicile* in the forum state in order for substitute service to be performed. Other statutes, however, have been construed to allow substitute service on the *temporary residence* of a transient, such as a hotel room, as long as the service is made during the period when the dwelling is still the defendant's local residence.

2. **"Constructive" notice to out-of-staters:** The notion of *"constructive service"* was developed to notify defendants who could not be located within the state. (The growth of long-arm statutes has made the need for a means of notifying out-of-state defendants increasingly pressing.)

a. **Mail notice:** These statutes generally provide for notice by *registered or certified mail*, or sometimes by publication, upon defendants over whom jurisdiction has been asserted. Such defendants include in-state domiciliaries or residents who are temporarily absent, non-resident tortfeasors, etc., as described in the discussion of Jurisdiction over Individuals, *supra*, pp. 9-18.

b. **Reasonableness test:** The standard that has generally been used for determining whether such constructive service is constitutionally adequate has been whether the procedure used was *reasonably likely* to give the defendant actual notice.

   i. **Rationale:** Thus in *McDonald v. Mabee*, 243 U.S. 90 (1917), Justice Holmes stated, "To dispense with personal service the substitute that is most likely to reach the defendant is the least that ought to be required if substantial justice is to be done."

c. **Service on state official:** Many of the non-resident motorist statutes described *supra*, p. 14, provide for constructive service on a *state official* (e.g. the State Director of Motor Vehicles) plus notice by mail to the defendant. *Hess v. Pawloski*, 274 U.S. 352 (1927).

d. **Estoppel of defendant:** A manner of notice otherwise insufficient may be sufficient by virtue of the fact that it is the *defendant's own acts* which make traditional service impossible. F,K&C, p. 1054.

   Example: An automobile owner who has moved from the address at which his car is registered without informing any authority of his move might be constructively served by service on his insurance company, if the insurer's identity is known.

e. Publication: Service by *newspaper publication* announcing the suit has been upheld in certain cases, e.g. where the defendant's identity is unknown. (This is discussed more fully in the analysis of *Mullane v. Central Hanover Bank, infra.*)

   i. Service on domiciliary in hiding: Service by publication has been upheld against a domiciliary of the forum state who *hides himself* within the state.

   ii. Publication insufficient: But service by publication will virtually never be constitutionally sufficient if the defendant's *name and address* are *known*. See, e.g., *Walker v. City of Hutchinson*, 352 U.S. 112 (1956).

3. Service on corporations: There are several means which are commonly allowed for giving notice of suit to *corporations*.

   a. Official to receive process: The licensing procedures of many states require that a corporation, if it wishes to do business within the state, must *designate a corporate official* to receive process for suits against the company.

   b. Notice to official: Many other statutes merely provide for notice to be given to any corporation official or manager.

   i. Constitutional test: Under such general statutes, the constitutional test seems to be whether the official occupies a position within the firm such that it is likely that he will pass on the process papers to the corporate lawyers or directors who will prepare the defense. Wr., 416.

   c. Federal Rule: Federal Rule 4(h)(1) states that service on a corporation may be made by giving the papers to "an officer, a managing or general agent, or to any other agent authorized by appointment or by law to receive service of process." (See *supra*, p. 45.)

4. The *Mullane* balancing test: In *Mullane v. Central Hanover Bank,* 339 U.S. 306 (1950), a *balancing test* to determine the sufficiency of notice was announced by the Supreme Court.

   a. Facts: The facts of *Mullane* were as follows:

   i. The Hanover Bank administered numerous small trust funds. The bank wished to settle the year's accounts for the funds, which it had pooled together for investment purposes.

   ii. The Bank brought proceedings to certify the settlement of the accounts, pursuant to state law. The court appointed Mullane to represent all those who had an interest in the trust funds.

   iii. The only notice given to the beneficiaries of the trust funds was through a newspaper announcement. The Bank had available to it the names and addresses of the beneficiaries, but claimed that it would be too costly for it to notify them all of the proceedings to settle the accounts, in view of the small sums involved in most of the accounts.

   iv. Mullane, the court-appointed beneficiaries' representative, objected to the court's jurisdiction, claiming that the requirement of reasonable notice to the beneficiaries was not met, and that therefore the court's certification of the accounts could not be binding.

b. Holding: The Court held that the *expense* of notification by mail, and the *availability of names and addresses* of beneficiaries, were factors that could be taken into account in determining whether publication was sufficient notice.

    i. Reasonableness standard: "The means [of notice] employed must be such as one desirous of actually informing the absentee might reasonably adopt to accomplish it." But this may be *limited by reasonable considerations of economy.*

    ii. Names and addresses known: Publication was *insufficient* notice to those beneficiaries whose names and addresses were *known* to the Bank.

    iii. Names and addresses unknown: But for those beneficiaries who were unknown or unlocatable, *publication was a reasonable method of notice.* Cf. the dictum in *Walker v. City of Hutchinson, supra,* p. 66.

c. Basis for jurisdiction not stated: *Mullane,* in determining what constituted reasonable notice, declined to determine whether the case was *in rem* or *in personam.* Instead, the Court simply relied on a state's interest in "providing means to close trusts that exist by the grace of its laws ..." This indicates that old distinctions between the notice required in *in personam* actions and that required in *in rem* actions are dying out. Instead, the standard is becoming one of *general reasonableness in view of all the circumstances* (e.g. cost, importance of proceedings, availability of other, better, notification methods, etc.).

5. *Mullane* **reasonableness test curtailed:** The *Mullane* test of "reasonableness in view of all the circumstances" seems to have been *undercut* by the Supreme Court's 1974 decision in *Eisen v. Carlisle & Jacquelin,* 417 U.S. 156. That case, discussed more fully *infra,* p. 327, held that the plaintiff in a federal class action must pay the costs of notifying by mail all members of the class whose names and addresses could be ascertained by "reasonable effort." Since the class in *Eisen* numbered 2,250,000, and the individual plaintiff's stake in the litigation was only $70, the reasonableness test of *Mullane* does not seem to have been followed. (The Court in *Eisen* did refer to *Mullane,* but cited it for the proposition that publication notice could never satisfy due process where the names and addresses of the beneficiaries were known.)

a. Mail notice to all identifiable parties: Similarly, the *Mullane* "reasonableness in view of all the circumstances" test seems not to have been followed in the case of *Mennonite Board of Missions v. Adams,* 462 U.S. 791 (1983). There, the Court held that publication notice will not suffice as to *any party* having any liberty or property interest in the controversy, if its name and address are "reasonably ascertainable." Instead, notice by *mail* or other means equally likely to insure actual notice, must be used.

b. Summary: So the *Mullane* "reasonableness" test probably survives today, but only as a very general principle. That general principle is *overridden* by the more specific rule that *publication* notice will *not* be enough as to any party with an interest in the controversy whose name and address are *reasonably ascertainable.* In the "reasonably ascertainable" situation, notice by mail or other personalized means must be used, even if its cost is very high relative to the interest at stake.

6. **Contents of notice:** To be constitutionally adequate, the notice must give the recipient reasonably full information about his rights. For instance, in one case, a power company sent its customer a notice saying, in effect, "Pay up or we'll cut you off." Because the notice did not advise the customer that he had a right to contest the accuracy of the bill, the notice was held insufficient to meet due process requirements. *Memphis Light, Gas & Water Div. v. Craft*, 436 U.S. 1 (1978).

D. **Statutory provisions vs. actual results:** Generally what matters is the ***appropriateness*** of the notice prescribed by statute and employed, ***not*** whether the defendant actually ***got*** the notice.

1. **Actual notice not required:** Thus if a reasonable means of notification is prescribed by statute, and followed in the individual case, it does not matter that the defendant did not ***in fact*** receive notice. F,K&C, p. 1053. (Most states allow a statutory period after the entry of default judgments for defendants to claim their failure to receive actual notice, and to prepare a defense on the merits.)

2. **Actual notice not sufficient:** Conversely, if the prescribed statutory method is either insufficient, or is not followed, the fact that the individual defendant actually received notice does ***not*** make the service valid.

> **Example:** In *Wuchter v. Pizzutti*, 276 U.S. 13 (1928), the state notice statute (of the non-resident motorist variety) did not provide for actual mail notice on the defendant, but merely for constructive service on a state official. The Supreme Court held that the statute's notice provisions were invalid, even though in this case the state official mailed a copy of the summons to the defendant on his own initiative. ***Notice in the actual case did not resuscitate a formally invalid statute***, and service under the statute was held invalid.

E. **Opportunity to be heard:** The defendant must not only be notified of the suit against him, but must also be given an ***opportunity to be heard***. That is, in order for the state to "take" defendant's property from him (even if the taking is only temporary), the defendant must be given a chance to appear in court to tell his side of the story. This hearing requirement is imposed by the Due Process Clause of the 14th Amendment. See, e.g., *Roller v. Holly*, 176 U.S. 398 (1900).

1. **Notice alone not enough:** For instance, suppose that a state were to provide that P can serve D with a summons and complaint alleging that D is liable to P for money damages, and that without any further fact-finding by the state, D must pay the amount demanded to P. (Obviously, no rational state would enact such a statute.) Clearly, it would be a violation of due process for the state to give plaintiffs this kind of power over defendants — it is not enough that the defendant be given notice that the state (acting on behalf of the plaintiff) will be taking the defendant's property; the defendant must be given a chance to show a neutral state fact-finder (e.g., a judge) that on the merits, P's claim is wrong.

F. **Prejudgment remedies, including attachment:** Actually, it has always been pretty clear that states must give the defendant notice and an opportunity to be heard before the state renders a *final* decision on the defendant's civil liability. What is not so clear is the procedures that must be observed before states give plaintiffs *temporary prejudgment relief*. Litigation can take a long time, and a plaintiff may reasonably fear that during the course of litigation, a defendant may hide his assets, fraudulently dispose of them, move from the jurisdiction, or otherwise act in such a way that the plaintiff will end up with a judgment but also an assetless defendant. Therefore, all states give plaintiffs various ways to try to prevent this kind of during-the-litigation litigation dissipation of assets. Most commonly, states let the plaintiff under certain circumstances *"attach"* (i.e., tie up) the defendant's property after the litigation begins. Once the litigation is finished, if plaintiff wins, the attached assets can be used to satisfy the judgment; if defendant wins, the attachment is released.

1. **Illustrative techniques:** Thus, states typically allow a plaintiff who meets certain requirements to (1) attach the defendant's real property by placing a "lis pendens" on it, which has the effect of preventing defendant from selling the property to anyone else; and (2) attach the defendant's bank accounts, by informing the bank that the account proceeds are to be frozen and not released to the defendant. Other devices help a plaintiff gain possession of property which, the plaintiff alleges, the plaintiff owns or has rights to even though the property is still in the defendant's possession. An example of this kind of procedural help is a statute allowing a creditor to *repossess* goods which the creditor claims to have sold to the defendant under agreements giving the creditor the right to repossess if the defendant does not pay. Finally, all states have statutes letting one who has already obtained judgment against the defendant *garnish the defendant's wages* (but since federal and state laws limit the garnishment rights even of a creditor who has obtained a final judgment against the defendant.) In all of these situations, the question becomes: *What procedures must be followed before the state* (acting on behalf of the creditor) *impairs the defendant's interest in the property in question?*

2. **Significant property interest:** Before we look at the detailed procedures that are required, we must first understand the circumstances under which the defendant has some right to procedural due process. Essentially, the rule is that the defendant has the right to notice and a hearing before there is a state-sponsored deprivation of *any significant property interest* on the part of the defendant. In other words, it is not just a final taking of the defendant's property that triggers due process, but even a *temporary* and *less-than-total* taking. For instance, if the state lets the plaintiff block the defendant from selling the defendant's real estate for even a few days, this is still a sufficiently significant property deprivation that due process must be obeyed.

   a. **Significance of prior hearing:** Furthermore, the mere fact that the state gives some sort of a *hearing* before the deprivation is not enough to automatically establish that due process has been respected. Most battles over pre-judgment attachment techniques have focused on techniques that do not give the defendant a hearing until after the deprivation has already begun. (The recent leading case of *Connecticut v. Doehr*, discussed extensively below, is one illustration of this.) But even if the state gives the defendant notice and some sort of hearing before the deprivation occurs, the deprivation may violate due process if the hearing itself is conducted in such a way that it is too easy for the plaintiff, and too hard for the defendant, to win. For instance, if a state statute required a hearing before defendant's bank account could be attached, but provided that the attachment should be granted if, as a result of the hearing, "the court finds that there is *some possibility* that the plaintiff will prevail at trial and that the defendant will not have sufficient assets to satisfy a judgment," the Supreme Court would almost certainly hold that the rules of the game had been so rigged in favor of the plaintiff that due process was not followed.

3. **Test for due process:** Here, then, are the rules for determining when a state-sponsored deprivation of any significant property interest on the part of the defendant, made before a full trial on the merits, violates the defendant's due process rights:

   a. **Three-part test:** A *three-part test* is to be used, the Supreme Court held in *Connecticut v. Doehr*, 501 U.S. 1 (1991). In judging the validity of a state statute that enables an individual to enlist the aid of the state to deprive another person of his property by means of a prejudgment attachment or similar procedure, the following three factors must be *balanced* against one another:

      i. **Strength of D's private interest:** First, the interest of the private party who is being *harmed* by the prejudgment attachment or other procedure. The more important the defendant's property right (or the greater the interference with that property right), the harder it is for due process to be satisfied.

      ii. **Risk of erroneous deprivation:** Second, the risk of an *erroneous determination*. The greater the risk that the particular *procedures* being used will result in an erroneous interference with defendant's property rights, the harder it is for the procedure to pass due process scrutiny. For instance, a procedure that makes it probable that the attachment will be granted even in circumstances where the defendant would eventually prevail on the merits is less likely to satisfy due process than a procedure that grants the prejudgment relief only to a plaintiff who shows that she is very likely to prevail ultimately on the merits. (The availability of *alternative procedural safeguards* is part of this examination of the risk of an erroneous deprivation.)

      iii. **Interest of the party seeking the remedy:** Finally, on the other side of the scale, the strength of the interest of the party *seeking the prejudgment remedy*. For instance, where plaintiff has a large sum at stake and will probably prevail at trial, and it is also likely that the defendant will dissipate or conceal his assets if the prejudgment remedy is not granted, this "plaintiff's interest" factor weighs more strongly in favor of a finding that due process has been observed than where, say, a large percentage of the defendant's property is being tied up to protect a small or weak claim on the part of the plaintiff which the defendant will probably be able to satisfy anyway even without prejudgment relief.

      Example applying the three-part test: The facts of *Connecticut v. Doehr* show how the three-part test will be applied in practice (and, in fact, represent the only Supreme Court case so far applying this test, which originated in *Doehr*.) A Connecticut statute allows prejudgment attachment of D's real estate without giving D opportunity for a prior hearing, if P "verifies by oath" that there is probable cause to sustain the validity of his claim.

As to the first factor — the strength of the private interest (D's) that will be hurt by the prejudgment measure — here, the impact on D is significant; the attachment clouds title to the property, prevents D from selling it, affects his credit rating, and prevents him from getting a home equity loan or new mortgage. As to the second factor — the risk of erroneous deprivation — this, too, is substantial here. Even if the statute is read to mean that a judge must independently find that P will probably prevail (as opposed to determining merely that plaintiff honestly believes that he will prevail), "the judge could make no realistic assessment concerning the likelihood of an action's success based upon these one-sided, self-serving, and conclusory submissions." This factor also weighs against the validity of the procedure because the state fails to use other protections that it might have used, such as requiring the plaintiff to post a bond. (The fact that the property owner can get a reasonably prompt *post-attachment* hearing helps somewhat, but even a temporary interference with one's property rights is significant.) Finally, the last factor — the strength of the interest in favor of the attachment — works against a finding of validity; for instance, P was not required to show that D was about transfer or encumber his real estate or do anything else that would impair P's ability to collect a judgment if he should obtain one.

In summary, these three factors all mean that the Connecticut practice of allowing a pre-judgment attachment of real estate without a prior hearing, without a bond and without a showing of exigent circumstances, violates the property owner's Fourteenth Amendment due process rights. *Connecticut v. Doehr, supra.*

4. **Some other examples of bad statutes:** Here are some other examples of statutes which have been found to be violations of a property owner's due process rights (these are all pre-*Doehr* decisions, but they probably remain valid).

   a. **Wage garnishment:** A defendant's *wages* may not be *garnished* unless she has first been given a chance to show that the garnishor has no right to garnish. See *Sniadach v. Family Finance Corp.*, 395 U.S. 337 (1969).

   b. **Bank account garnishment:** A defendant's *bank account* may not be attached unless he is given the right to argue against the attachment either before it occurs or immediately thereafter. See *North Georgia Finishing, Inc. v. Di-Chem*, 419 U.S. 601 (1975).

   c. **Repossession of goods:** A statute allowing a creditor to obtain *repossession of goods* before a hearing, violates due process where it (1) allows repossession merely on the creditor's conclusory statement that he owns the property; (2) provides for a writ of possession issued by a clerk rather than a judge; and (3) does not provide for an immediate post-repossession hearing. See *Fuentes v. Shevin*, 407 U.S. 67 (1972). (But a statute allowing repossession by a creditor will be valid if it requires presentation of specific facts about the claim, requires that the facts be presented to a judge rather than to a clerk, and provides for an immediate post-repossession hearing at which the defendant can present his case. See *Mitchell v. W.T. Grant Co.*, 416 U.S. 600 (1974).)

5. **Clues to a bad statute:** Here are some statutory provisions that make it more likely that a due process violation will be found:

a. **No bond by P:** Due process is likely to be violated if the provision for pre-judgment attachment does ***not*** require the plaintiff to ***post a bond***, from which damages to the defendant can be paid if the attachment turns out to have been wrongful. See *Connecticut v. Doehr, supra* (four Justices conclude that due process virtually always requires the plaintiff to post a bond or other security even if a hearing and some showing of exigency are also required).

b. **Deprivation before hearing:** If the defendant does not get notice or opportunity for a hearing until sometime ***after*** the attachment, a due process violation is much more likely to be found than where the notice and hearing come before the deprivation. (But even a pre-attachment hearing does not insulate the procedure from due process attack, if the risk of an erroneous deprivation is too high or the plaintiff's interest in having the attachment is too weak.)

c. **Clerk rather than judge:** If the decision whether to allow the attachment is made by a ***clerk*** rather than by a judge, a due process violation is more likely to be found.

d. **Conclusory statements:** If the plaintiff is able to obtain the attachment by making ***conclusory statements*** rather than by making detailed disclosure of the underlying facts of the dispute, due process is more likely to be found to be violated.

6. **State action:** A due process violation can occur only where the state ***actively participates*** in the interference with the defendant's property rights. Usually, some action by a state official in connection with the particular case is necessary before state action will be found. Thus where the only state involvement is, say, passing a statute (like U.C.C. §7-210) that allows a warehouse operator to conduct a public sale to enforce his lien for storage charges (with no state officials conducting the sale), no state action is present, and thus due process requirements do not need to be met. *Flagg Bros., Inc. v. Brooks*, 436 U.S. 149 (1978). Similarly, the procedure under U.C.C. Article 9, whereby a creditor holding a security interest can repossess property that has not been paid for, does not involve state action and does not, therefore, need to meet due process requirements.

Quiz Yourself on
NOTICE AND OPPORTUNITY TO BE HEARD

10. A statute of the state of Ames provides that in any action for personal injuries arising out of an automobile accident, the plaintiff may obtain a pre-judgment attachment of the defendant's bank account simultaneously with the filing of the plaintiff's suit. However, the plaintiff may obtain the attachment only by filing an affidavit stating that, to the best of P's knowledge, D was involved in, and was the cause of, the accident; the judge must then find that P appears to be acting in good faith. The statute also provides that the court must grant D a hearing, within one month after issuance of the attachment, at which D may show that he will probably not be found liable in the suit; if D makes such a showing, the attachment must be rescinded. D now attacks the statute as a violation of his right to due process. Should D prevail? _____

Answer

10. Yes. Under *Connecticut v. Doehr*, 501 U.S. 1 (1991), the court is to apply a three-part balancing test in determining whether a statute allowing for prejudgment attachment satisfies the due process rights of the person whose property is being attached (here, D): the court weighs the harm to D's property right, the risk of an erroneous deprivation, and the strength of the other party's (here, P) interest in obtaining the prejudgment attachment. Here, the impact on D is significant, since D can't spend the money in the account (and even a temporary, up-to-one-month deprivation would probably be found to be material). The risk of erroneous deprivation is substantial, because P's one-sided conclusory allegations (with no rebuttal by D or opportunity to cross-examine P or to present witnesses) leave the judge no real ability to assess the likelihood that P will prevail on the merits. The strength of P's interest in the attachment is weak, because the statute does not require P to show that D is about to transfer funds or do anything else that would make it hard for P to collect any judgment he might obtain. All in all, the statute here is marginally better than the one struck down in Doehr, but similar enough to it that it, too, would almost certainly be found to violate due process.

VII. DEFENSES TO CLAIMS OF JURISDICTION

A. **General principles:** We examine in this section several defenses to claims of jurisdiction, including (1) the *special appearance* (by which the defendant may litigate the jurisdiction issue without automatically subjecting himself to personal jurisdiction by his mere appearance); (2) the *collateral attack* on another court's default judgment (and the companion issue of enforcement of sister state judgments); (3) the defense that jurisdiction was obtained by *fraud or duress*; and (4) the defense that the defendant is *immune* from service of the process of the court where the suit is in progress.

B. **Special appearance:** A *special appearance* is distinguished from a *general appearance*; in the latter, the defendant appears before the court to defend *on the merits*, and is thereby concluded to have *consented* or submitted to the court's personal jurisdiction over him. In the special appearance, the defendant appears with the *express purpose of making a jurisdictional objection*; his doing so is *not a consent* to the exercise of jurisdiction.

1. **Appeal:** Most courts allow a defendant who has unsuccessfully made a special appearance to then defend on the merits, *without losing his right to appeal* the jurisdictional issue.

   a. **Minority rule:** Some courts do not follow this majority rule, and thereby force a defendant to make the following unpleasant choice:

      i. **Appeal:** He can stick to his unsuccessful jurisdictional objection, refuse to defend on the merits, allow a default judgment to be entered against him, and then appeal. He thereby puts all his hopes on winning the jurisdictional question on appeal; he has lost his right to defend on the merits.

      ii. **Defend:** Alternatively, he can forget his unsuccessful jurisdictional objection, and defend on the merits. But by so doing, he loses the right to appeal the jurisdictional question.

      iii. **Interlocutory appeal:** Some of the majority-rule jurisdictions have alleviated the above dilemma by allowing an *interlocutory* appeal when a jurisdictional objection is made unsuccessfully. This lets the defendant make the appeal as soon as the trial court rules against him on jurisdiction — if he wins on appeal, the suit is dismissed; if he loses, he can then defend on the merits.

2. **Federal and state substitutes for special appearance:** The federal courts, and many state courts whose rules are patterned after the Federal Rules, have *abolished the special appearance*. Instead, a *motion* to dismiss for lack of jurisdiction over the parties may be made, without subjecting the mover to the jurisdiction he is protesting. Fed. Rule 12(b)(2).

   a. **Waiver:** The right to make a motion to dismiss for lack of jurisdiction of the parties is *waived* in the federal system if:

      i. **Omitted from 12(b) motion:** a motion is made raising any of the defenses listed in Rule 12 (e.g., failure to state a claim on which relief may be granted — Rule 12(b)(6)), and the personal jurisdiction defense is not included; or

      ii. **Not made by motion or answer:** the personal jurisdiction defense is not made either by a Rule 12 motion or in the answer. See Rule 12(h)(1).

   b. **Distinguished from lack of subject matter jurisdiction:** For waiver purposes, an objection to lack of jurisdiction over the *person* must be distinguished from one to lack of *subject matter* jurisdiction. The latter (e.g. "lack of diversity"; "jurisdictional amount not satisfied") may be made *at any time*, even after trial, and even at the court's own initiative. Rule 12(h)(3).

3. **Special appearance in *quasi in rem* and *in rem* actions:** In state courts, when suit is begun by attachment or garnishment (i.e., the plaintiff proceeds on the basis of asserted *quasi in rem* or *in rem* jurisdiction), the general rule is that D may appear specially to contest the validity of the attachment, without giving the court jurisdiction over his person. But not all courts allow this.

   a. **Federal practice:** In the *federal courts, both quasi in rem* (Rule 4(n)) and *in rem* (28 U.S.C. §1655) jurisdiction may be protested through a Rule 12(b) jurisdictional objection, just as for lack of *in personam* jurisdiction. This objection, by motion or answer, has the effect of a special appearance.

C. **Enforcement of judgments:** A judgment entered in one jurisdiction may be *enforced* in another. That is, the defendant's property in one state, or wages owed him in that state, may be seized to satisfy the judgment entered in another state.

1. **Procedure:** In order to sue on a foreign judgment, the victorious plaintiff must institute a new suit in the second state, and then prove that he has received the original judgment. The second court must then enter an identical judgment, which serves as the basis for levy and/or garnishment in the second state.

   a. **Merits not reviewable:** The second court may not reconsider the merits of the original controversy, even if the first court's conclusion was patently incorrect. The only exception to this rule is if the first court is shown to have lacked personal or subject matter jurisdiction, and the jurisdictional issue was *not* litigated in that first court, i.e., a "collateral attack," discussed *infra*, p. 75.

2. **Rules:** The following rules govern the effect given to one jurisdiction's judgment in another jurisdiction:

a. **Two state courts (Full Faith and Credit):** If both judgments are in *state* courts, the second court is compelled to give the first judgment the same effect it would have had in the first state. This is required by the Full Faith and Credit Clause of the Constitution (Art. IV, § 1).

b. **State judgment followed by federal suit:** If the first judgment is in state court, then a federal court is obligated to give the first judgment full faith and credit by a statutory provision, 28 U.S.C. §1738.

c. **Federal judgment followed by state suit:** If the first judgment is in federal court, the *Supremacy Clause* of the U.S. Constitution (Art. 6) requires a subsequent state court to give the federal judgment the same effect it would have if sued on in federal court.

d. **Both courts federal:** If both judgments are in federal courts, the second court respects the first because they are both arms of the same sovereignty, just as two trial courts in the same state respect each other's judgments.

    i. **Registration of judgments:** A judgment entered in any federal court may be *registered* in any other federal court, thus abolishing the need for a separate suit for enforcement. 28 U.S.C. §1963.

    ii. **State registration:** A similar registration procedure has been proposed for the states, and a number of states have adopted it. F,K&C, p. 911.

D. Collateral attack: A defendant who *defaults* in an action in one jurisdiction may *collaterally attack* the default judgment when it is sued upon in a second jurisdiction.

1. **Basis of attack:** The defendant may make such a collateral attack either upon the first court's jurisdiction over the parties, or upon its subject matter jurisdiction.

a. **Personal jurisdiction:** The defendant may argue that the first court lacked *in personam* jurisdiction over him.

b. *In rem:* He may argue that the *quasi in rem* or *in rem* jurisdiction purportedly exercised over his property by the first court was invalid.

c. **Extrinsic fraud:** He may argue that his failure to appear in the first action was the result of *fraud* by the plaintiff. Fraud inducing a party not to appear is often classified as "extrinsic fraud" (as distinguished from "intrinsic fraud," which relates to the litigation itself, and which is not grounds for collateral attack). See, e.g., *Britton v. Gannon*, 285 P.2d 407 (Ok. 1955), in which D successfully avoided an Oklahoma suit to enforce a prior Illinois judgment, on the grounds that he had been fraudulently induced to default by P's statement that he (D) was a necessary defendant, but that P only wanted to recover property and would not pursue a money judgment against him.

d. **Subject matter jurisdiction:** He may also argue that the first court had no statutory authority to try the kind of case or grant the kind of relief in question (i.e., that it lacks subject matter jurisdiction). For instance, if the first court, a municipal court not empowered to try matrimonial actions, had granted a divorce, the defendant could attack this.

2. **Waiver:** A defendant who *appeared in the original action* without objecting to jurisdiction, or one who *unsuccessfully litigated the jurisdictional issue* in the first action, may *not* collaterally attack the judgment. The unsuccessful objection to jurisdiction may, of course, be repeated on appeal to a court superior to the first trial court; but this is a *direct*, rather than *collateral*, attack.

    > **Example:** Defendant makes a special appearance in a Missouri District Court, loses on his jurisdictional objection, then declines to answer. A default judgment is entered against him. Plaintiff then sues in Iowa District Court to enforce the judgment. Defendant raises the jurisdictional objection again. *Held* (by the U.S. Supreme Court), Defendant had no right to raise the jurisdictional objection a second time. *Baldwin v. Iowa State Traveling Men's Ass'n.*, 283 U.S. 522 (1931).

E. **Defense of fraud or duress:** Presence, however transient, has been held a basis for personal jurisdiction. *Darrah v. Watson*, 36 Iowa 116 (1873). But if this presence is the result of *fraud* or *duress* on the part of the plaintiff, the court may decide not to exercise jurisdiction.

1. **Discretionary:** If the defendant has been *induced into the jurisdiction* by fraud or duress, it is probably not a violation of Constitutional due process for the court to exercise jurisdiction over him, but most courts will, as a matter of *discretion, refuse to exercise* this jurisdiction. Rest. Conflicts 2nd, §82.

    a. **No collateral attack:** If the court does decide to exercise jurisdiction where fraud or duress was involved, this jurisdiction may not be collaterally attacked, if this issue or any other was litigated in the first court. (This is by the general principle of Full Faith and Credit — *even if the first court's exercise of jurisdiction was clearly unconstitutional*, the second state court must respect it, if the defendant appeared in the first court. Only the U.S. Supreme Court can overrule a final, non-default, state court judgment.)

    b. **Where first court's judgment is by default:** But if the first court enters a default judgment, the defendant may raise the fraud or duress defense as part of a collateral attack when enforcement is sought in a second state. Thus in *Wyman v. Newhouse*, 93 F.2d 313 (2d Cir. 1937), the defendant defaulted in the first action, and raised fraud as a collateral attack in the suit to enforce the judgment in a different state court. Since the first court's judgment was by default, the second court had the right to find the first court without jurisdiction. It is not clear whether the second court should have decided the first court's jurisdiction according to the latter court's general principles, or according to its own. Probably the first court's principles should control.

    > **Example:** In *Wyman*, defendant's claim was that plaintiff had enticed him into the jurisdiction with a false love letter and a false statement that she was leaving the country forever, and wished to see him once more. When he arrived at the airport, he was served with papers. The court in which the original judgment was sought to be enforced found this defense of fraud *valid.*

2. **Person already in state:** Where a potential defendant is *already within the forum state*, most jurisdictions hold that he may be served by *resort to subterfuge*. It might seem inconsistent to allow subterfuge in this situation, but not to allow it when it is used to

induce the defendant into the forum state. One case, *Gumperz v. Hofmann*, 245 App. Div. 622 (N.Y., 1st Dept. 1935), distinguished the two situations by arguing that trickery used to serve a person already in the jurisdiction voluntarily does not confer a right which the court would not otherwise have had; the court has the ***power*** to exercise jurisdiction over a person just by virtue of his presence in the state. When deception is used to induce a person into the jurisdiction, by contrast, the trickery puts a person into the court's power who would not otherwise be within that power.

    a. Criticism: However, the conclusion of the *Gumperz* court is open to question — should the court be a party to "dirty tricks" at all? The problem is somewhat less severe today than formerly, since many states have statutes providing for substitute service (e.g., at the last known dwelling place) for one who is known to be within the state but who is in hiding.

    3. Federal practice: The federal courts follow their own, rather than state, principles with respect to immunity. In general, service on a party induced into the jurisdiction by fraud or deceit is ***invalid.*** Wr., 415.

F. Immunity: Most jurisdictions give to nonresidents of the forum state an immunity from service of process while they are in the state to ***attend a trial*** either as witnesses, parties, or attorneys. James & Hazard, p. 79. Immunity is also granted for a reasonable time period before and after trial, for the journey into and out of the state. Most states also grant the immunity for related proceedings such as ***depositions***.

    1. Witnesses: Of the persons listed in the preceding paragraph, the case for immunity is strongest for ***witnesses.*** *Id.*

        a. Rationale: Witnesses cannot be forced to testify in a state of which they are not residents. Therefore, the forum state has an interest in having them come in voluntarily, and to the extent to which immunity from service induces them to do so, it is justifiable.

    2. Defendants: Immunity for ***defendants*** is also probably a good idea on balance. If immunity is not granted, some defendants will not attend trial, resulting in a default judgment being entered against them. Since such a judgment can be collaterally attacked when it is sued on for enforcement in another jurisdiction, plaintiff is forced not only to sue a second time, but also to run the risk that the second court will find that the first lacked jurisdiction.

        a. Actions concerning related facts: The case for defendant immunity is especially strong where the two suits involve ***related facts***, and the defendant is making a special or limited appearance in the first suit. If the plaintiff in the case for which a special or limited appearance was being made by the defendant were allowed to serve him on a cause of action closely related to the original cause of action, the doctrines of special and limited appearance would be vitiated; defendants would always be afraid of being subjected to personal jurisdiction if they set foot in the forum state at all.

        b. Immunity for criminal defendants: The courts are split on whether to grant immunity from civil suit to defendants in ***criminal actions***. If the defendant comes in voluntarily, there is good reason to grant him this immunity, and thus spare the expense and bother of extradition proceedings. But if the defendant is in the forum state only because extradition proceedings have brought him there, the weight of authority denies him immunity from process, since his presence in the state would not have been facilitated by immunity. James & Hazard, 643-44.

3. **Plaintiffs:** Immunity for ***non-resident plaintiffs*** is harder to justify than for witnesses and defendants, since the plaintiff is pursuing his own self-interest in the forum state. But there is nonetheless good reason for a state to encourage in-state suits against at least those of its citizens who could be reached by the long-arms of other states, since it is more convenient for those citizens to be sued at home than elsewhere.

4. **Federal immunity:** In *federal* suits, both diversity and federal question, the fact that a person would be immune from service in the courts of the state where the federal court sits is irrelevant; the federal courts treat immunity as a matter of *federal*, not state, law. Wr., 415.

   a. **Federal rule:** In general, the federal courts grant immunity from a federal suit to *parties*, *witnesses* and *attorneys* coming into the state in connection with a different (state or federal) suit. Wr., p. 415.

Quiz Yourself on
DEFENSES TO CLAIMS OF JURISDICTION

10. P is a resident of New Mexico. D is a resident of Arizona. P sued D in diversity in federal court for New Mexico, and made service on D in Arizona in a manner that he believed to be authorized by the New Mexico long-arm statute. D filed a motion under Federal Rule 12(b)(6) for failure to state a claim upon which relief can be granted; this motion asserted that P's claim was barred by the applicable statute of limitations. The court considered and rejected D's motion. D then made a motion pursuant to Rule 12(b)(2), claiming that the federal court lacked personal jurisdiction over D. D does not in fact have minimum contacts with New Mexico. Should the court grant D's second motion? _____

11. Same facts as prior question. Now, however, assume that D has not made a 12(b)(6) motion or a motion to dismiss for lack of jurisdiction. This is because he has placed his lawyer on a tight budget, and has told her not to make any motions at all. What should D's lawyer do to assert D's claim of lack of personal jurisdiction, without subjecting D to the court's general jurisdiction by the very act of raising the lack-of-jurisdiction objection? _____

12. P is a resident of New York. D is a resident of New Jersey. While P was driving through New Jersey, D (who operates a fast food restaurant) served P a hamburger. P ate the hamburger in New Jersey, but became violently ill upon his return to New York. P sued D in New York state court for negligence and product liability. Service on D was carried out by means authorized by the New York long-arm statute. D never appeared in the New York courts in any way, and thus did not contest New York's jurisdiction over him. The New York court issued a default judgment against him.

Since all of D's assets were in New Jersey, P brought a suit in New Jersey to enforce the New York judgment. In the New Jersey suit on the judgment, D convinced the New Jersey court that under applicable U.S. Supreme Court decisions, the New York court had erred in deciding that it could constitutionally exercise personal jurisdiction over D, because D did not knowingly and voluntarily take action that would bring his products into New York. Must the New Jersey court enforce the New York judgment against D, thus allowing P to seize D's property to satisfy that judgment? _____

Answers

10. **No.** D has *waived* his meritorious claim of lack of personal jurisdiction by failing to make it as part of the initial motion under Rule 12(b) that he made. Under Rule 12(h)(1), a defense of lack of jurisdiction over the person is waived if it is "omitted from a motion in the circumstances described in subdivision (g) …," which is a sub-section that allows a party only one 12(b) motion per case. (If D had not made his 12(b)(6) motion, he could have asserted his claim of lack of personal jurisdiction as part of his answer.)

11. **Assert the defense as part of D's answer.** Any defense, including the defense of lack of jurisdiction, may in the federal system be asserted as part of the defendant's answer. The defendant's right to do this is implied by Federal Rule 12(b) and 12(h)(1)(B).

12. **No.** The Full Faith and Credit Clause of the Constitution (Article IV, Section 1) provides that where a judgment from State 1 is sued upon in State 2, the courts of State 2 must give that judgment the same effect as it would have in State 1. Thus normally, a defendant may not "collaterially attack" the first court's jurisdiction when the judgment is sued upon in the second court. However, there is one exception to this general rule: the defendant *will* be permitted in the State 2 proceedings to collaterally attack the judgment issued against him in State 1 if: State 1 issued a *default judgment* against the defendant, *and* the defendant *did not appear* for *any reason* in the State 1 proceeding (even to unsuccessfully contest jurisdiction there). Observe, however, that D took a big chance by letting a default judgment be issued against him in the New York proceedings: if the New Jersey court had disagreed with D's jurisdictional argument, D would have lost his right to defend on the merits in the New Jersey courts, since under the Full Faith and Credit Clause the New Jersey courts would have had no choice but to enforce New York's judgment against D once the court concluded that the New York court had personal jurisdiction over D.

VIII. VENUE

A. General Principles:

1. **Definition of venue:** Venue refers to the ***place within a sovereign jurisdiction*** in which a given action is to be brought. It becomes a consideration only when jurisdiction over the parties has been established.

   Example: State X is found to have jurisdiction over the person of B, in a suit against him by A. Venue determines in which *county* or *district* of State X the case shall be tried.

2. **Venue in state courts statutory:** Venue in state trials is almost exclusively determined by statute, and has few if any Constitutional implications.

3. **Land:** Courts frequently refuse to try cases involving certain transactions relating to *land* lying in another jurisdiction. Sometimes the court bases this refusal on *venue* principles, sometimes on *subject matter jurisdictional* ones.

4. ***Forum non conveniens:*** Courts will sometimes refuse to exercise their jurisdiction over the parties, on the grounds that it would be more convenient to try the case elsewhere,

either in a court of their own jurisdiction, or in one of another jurisdiction. This refusal, based on principles of venue, is known as the doctrine of *forum non conveniens.*

5. **Venue in federal cases:** Venue in federal cases is controlled by 28 U.S.C. §1391, the general federal venue statute. It provides mainly for venue based on the *defendant's residence*, the place where a substantial part of the relevant *events occurred*, or the place where defendant can be made *subject to personal jurisdiction*. See *infra*, p. 83.

B. **Venue in state actions:** Venue in state actions is determined by many different tests. Generally, plaintiff has a choice of several different criteria in determining where he may bring his action.

1. **Places for state court venue:** Among the places (usually a county or judicial district of the state) where venue is sometimes held to lie are the following: (F,K&C, pp. 1016-17.)

   a. where the *cause of action arose;*

   b. where the *defendant resides;*

   c. where the *defendant has a place of business*, or agent;

   d. where the *plaintiff does business;*

   e. where the *seat of government is located; or*

   f. in the county *designated in plaintiff's complaint.*

2. **Most common test:** "The most common provision today, and the basic one, appears to be venue based upon the *residence of the defendant*." J & H (3d ed.), 607.

3. **Waiver:** Objections to venue are *waived* unless they are seasonably made, generally speaking. The time for making an objection to improper venue is often at an early stage in the proceedings.

4. **Effect of improper venue:** If jurisdiction is good, but venue improper, a judgment is good against a defendant who defaults, and may *not be collaterally attacked* when sued upon for enforcement in another jurisdiction. F,K&C, p. 1016.

   a. **Rationale:** The courts' refusal to allow collateral attacks on venue may be justified as follows: since the venue privilege is purely a matter of convenience for the defendant, and involves no element of the forum state's *power* to adjudicate the case before it, its absence is in a sense less severe than the absence of personal jurisdiction. Thus where a default judgment is open to collateral attack in the state where it is sought to be enforced, on the grounds that personal jurisdiction was lacking, the sovereignty of the original forum is brought into question. But an objection to originally improper venue would involve only the discretionary decision of the original forum state to use the power of adjudication which it had; the objection is thus less serious, since the venue privilege is not mandated by any Constitutional principles. (Presumably a state could, once it had jurisdiction over the parties, try an action in any county it wished.)

C. **Transitory vs. local actions:** State courts will sometimes refuse to try actions involving *land* located in other jurisdictions. These actions intimately involving land are often called *local* actions (as distinguished from *transitory* actions).

Example: A sues B for trespass to land lying in State X. State Y may decline to try the suit, even though it may have personal jurisdiction over B. See *Livingston v. Jefferson*, 15 Fed.Cas. 660, No. 8,411 (C.C.D.Va. 1811).

1. **Basis for court's refusal:** It is often unclear whether this refusal to try such a land-related case is based on lack of *in rem* jurisdiction (under the theory that the *res* of the suit is land, which is not within the state's boundaries, and thus not within the control of its courts) or on a lack of venue.

    a. **Discretionary:** Probably the refusal to exercise jurisdiction is a discretionary one, mandated not by any constitutional principles, but by considerations of comity and convenience. James & Hazard, 49.

2. **No test:** No clear rule exists for distinguishing *local* actions (trial of which a court is likely to decline because the land lies elsewhere) from *transitory* ones (which the court will try even though the suit relates in some way to out-of-state land).

    Example: When a plaintiff seeks specific performance of a contract to sell land, it is generally held that any court which has jurisdiction over the defendant's person has jurisdiction to enter a judgment commanding specific performance, although such an action concerns land intimately.

    a. *Livingston* **followed:** *Livingston v. Jefferson, supra,* has been followed in almost all states, which therefore refuse generally to try suits for damages from trespass to land lying in other states.

    b. **Conversion; specific performance:** Actions for *conversion*, and actions for *specific performance* of land-sale contracts, are generally *not considered local* for venue purposes, and may thus be brought wherever personal jurisdiction may be had. Similarly, where the action affecting land in State X took place in State Y, most courts will allow suit in either place.

D. *Forum non conveniens:* Under the doctrine of *"forum non conveniens,"* a court having jurisdiction over a particular case may use its *discretion* to *decline to exercise* that jurisdiction, if the court concludes that the action could be more appropriately tried in *some other jurisdiction*.

    Example: Suppose that P1, P2 and W, all New York residents, are travelling in a car that crashes while passing through Oklahoma. P1 and P2 are injured. The Ps bring suit in Oklahoma state court against D1 and D2, the retailer and manufacturer of the car, respectively, on a products liability theory. D1 and D2 have their principal place of business in New York, and are incorporated there. Assume that these two defendants have just enough contacts with Oklahoma for it to be constitutional for the Oklahoma courts to hear suits against them. The only witness to the accident is W, who has no other connection with Oklahoma.

    The Oklahoma court clearly has constitutionally-sufficient jurisdiction to hear the suit. But the Oklahoma court might invoke the doctrine of *forum non conveniens* to decline to hear the suit, on the grounds that the parties' and witness's links to New York are far stronger than those to Oklahoma, and that the suit is therefore better heard in New York. (Probably the dismissal on grounds of *forum non conveniens* would come in response to a motion by the defendants, but the Oklahoma court might decide on its own to dismiss.)

1. **Rationale:** Two independent policy considerations seem involved in a court's decision to invoke the doctrine of *forum non conveniens* (James & Hazard, p. 87):

   a. **Parties' convenience:** The *parties* have an interest in having the litigation conducted in the *most convenient locale*. (When the doctrine is invoked, it is generally the *defendant* whose convenience is being respected, since the plaintiff has usually indicated his own convenience in his original choice of forum.)

   b. **State's interest:** The state has an interest in *not burdening its courts* with litigation not connected with the State. (This only becomes a consideration when the more convenient forum lies outside the original forum state; a court's decision to transfer the case to another court within the same jurisdiction is also sometimes referred to as invoking the *forum non conveniens* doctrine, but does not reflect the state's interest in being free of litigation unrelated to the state.)

2. **Factors in decision:** Among the factors which have been considered by courts in determining whether to invoke the doctrine are the following (James & Hazard, pp. 87):

   a. Is the plaintiff a state *resident* and taxpayer? (If so, he should have a right to the judicial machinery of his state.)

   b. In which forum are the *witnesses* and sources of proof most available?

   c. Which forum will be *familiar with* the state law that must govern the case? Conflict-of-laws principles may require a court to apply the law of a different state; it is generally undesirable to have "a court in some other forum untangle problems in conflict of laws, and in law foreign to itself." *Gulf Oil v. Gilbert*, 330 U.S. 501 (1947).

3. **Unfavorable change in law insufficient:** The mere fact that the law of the alternative forum is *less favorable to the plaintiff* is *not* by itself grounds for denying the defendant's *forum non conveniens* motion. This is illustrated by a Supreme Court case, *Piper Aircraft Co. v. Reyno*, 454 U.S. 235 (1981).

   a. **Facts:** In *Piper*, a plane built by an American manufacturer crashed in Scotland, killing all aboard. Plaintiff, the decedents' representative, brought a wrongful death action in Pennsylvania Federal District Court. (The American manufacturer of the plane's propellers, as well as the plane's manufacturer, were joined as defendants.) The defendants, in moving for a dismissal based on *forum non conveniens*, argued that Scotland was a more appropriate forum: the decedents and their heirs were all Scottish citizens, and the necessary witnesses to the crash and to the prior maintenance of the airplane were located in Scotland and Great Britain. (Also, because of choice-of-law principles, Scottish law would have had to be applied to one, but not the other, defendant.) However, the plaintiff opposed the *non conveniens* motion because Scottish law was much less favorable to her. For instance, it did not recognize strict tort liability, and also limited the items of damages.

   b. **Grant of motion upheld:** The Supreme Court rejected plaintiff's assertion that a *forum non conveniens* motion should be denied wherever it would result in application of law less favorable to the plaintiff than the law applying in the plaintiff's originally-chosen forum. In fact, the Court stated that the likelihood of an unfavorable change in law should not even be given "substantial," let alone "conclusive," weight in the *forum non conveniens* decision.

    i.   **Rationale:** The Court stressed that the essential purpose of the *forum non conveniens* doctrine is to assure that the litigation takes place in the most **convenient** forum. Since most litigations could take place (at least from the standpoint of jurisdiction) in two or more forums, a rule that *forum non conveniens* will not be applied where the law would be less favorable to the plaintiff would strip *forum non conveniens* of most of its utility, and would lead to trials in "plainly inconvenient" forums.

    ii.   **Foreign plaintiff:** Where the plaintiff (or, as here, the real party in interest) is a *foreigner*, the considerations against stripping the plaintiff of an American forum are even weaker, the Court noted. For the usual presumption that the plaintiff has chosen a convenient forum is not applicable where a foreign plaintiff has selected a United states forum.

    iii.   **No real remedy available:** But the Court indicated that if the remedy provided by the alternative forum was "so clearly inadequate or unsatisfactory that it is no remedy at all", the unfavorable change in law could be given substantial weight in the *forum non conveniens* decision. For instance, if the alternative forum did not allow litigation of the very **subject matter** of the dispute, this might be a reason for denying the *forum non conveniens* motion. But here, all that would be lost to plaintiff was a more favorable rule on liability and a somewhat broader gamut of damages, not all possibility of a reasonably adequate remedy.

E.   **Venue in federal actions:** In *federal* actions, the venue question is: "Which federal district court shall try the action?"

    1.   **Federal statute:** 28 U.S.C. §1391, the general federal venue statute, was extensively rewritten in 1990. The main provisions of §1391 are as follows:

> **(a)** A civil action wherein jurisdiction is founded only on diversity of citizenship may, except as otherwise provided by law, be brought only in (1) a judicial district where any defendant resides, if all defendants reside in the same State, (2) a judicial district in which a substantial part of the events or omissions giving rise to the claim occurred, or a substantial part of property that is the subject of the action is situated, or (3) a judicial district in which the defendants are subject to personal jurisdiction at the time the action is commenced.

> **(b)** A civil action wherein jurisdiction is not founded solely on diversity of citizenship may, except as otherwise provided by law, be brought only [in] (1) a judicial district where any defendant resides, if all defendants reside in the same State, (2) a judicial district in which a substantial part of the events or omissions giving rise to the claim occurred, or a substantial part of property that is the subject of the action is situated, or (3) a judicial district in which any defendant may be found, if there is no district in which the action may otherwise be brought.

> **(c)** For purposes of venue under this chapter, a defendant that is a corporation shall be deemed to reside in any judicial district in which it is subject to personal jurisdiction at the

time the action is commenced. In a State which has more than one judicial district and in which a defendant that is a corporation is subject to personal jurisdiction at the time an action is commenced, such corporation shall be deemed to reside in any district in that State within which its contacts would be sufficient to subject it to personal jurisdiction if that district were a separate State, and, if there is no such district, the corporation shall be deemed to reside in the district within which it has the most significant contacts.

a. **Definition of "judicial district":**   The venue statute, as you can see, uses the term *"judicial district."* A federal judicial district can consist either of a whole state, or a portion of a state. Generally, the more populous a state, the more federal judicial districts it is likely to contain. Thus in Rhode Island, there is only one district, and one district court, the Rhode Island federal district court. In New York, on the other hand, there are four districts, the Southern (which includes Manhattan), Eastern, Northern and Western Districts.

b. **Still need personal jurisdiction:**   When you consider a venue problem, remember that venue is *not a substitute* for *personal jurisdiction*: the fact that venue lies in a particular judicial district does not automatically mean that suit can be brought there. Suit can be brought only in a district that satisfies *both* the venue requirements and the personal jurisdiction requirements as to all defendants. (Remember that in federal question cases, the defendant is generally held to be subject to personal jurisdiction as long as jurisdiction could constitutionally be exercised over him in the state courts of the state where the federal court is sitting, and service is validly made. In diversity cases, there is personal jurisdiction only if this would not only be constitutional but also would be allowed by the long-arm of the state in which the federal court sits. See *supra*, p. 45.)

Example: P is a citizen of Massachusetts. D, a car dealer, is a citizen of Connecticut. D sold a Buick to P in Connecticut. P then drove the car to Massachusetts, where he was involved in an accident. P brings suit in Massachusetts federal district court against D, in diversity, alleging that D is liable for P's injuries based on a strict product liability theory. Assume that Massachusetts has a very limited long-arm statute, which covers tortious actions occurring in Massachusetts, but which does not cover the sale of a defective product outside Massachusetts which later causes injury in Massachusetts.

The federal venue statute, 28 U.S.C. §1391, gives P venue in Massachusetts: §1391(a)(2) puts venue in a judicial district "in which a substantial part of the event or omissions giving rise to the claim occurred …," a test which is satisfied here. But the federal district court of Massachusetts will *not* exercise jurisdiction over D. Why? Because in diversity cases a federal court will exercise only that personal jurisdiction which would be exercised by the state in which the federal court sits, and here, by hypothesis, Massachusetts would not exercise personal jurisdiction over D because of the limited Massachusetts long-arm. Consequently, the fact that there is *venue* in Massachusetts is irrelevant — the case cannot be heard there because of lack of personal jurisdiction over D.

c. **Three methods:**   Section 1391 gives three basic methods for determining whether there is venue in a particular judicial district: (1) if *any* defendant *resides* in that district, and all defendants reside in the state containing that district (a test applicable in both diversity and federal question cases); (2) if "a substantial part of the *events* or omissions giving rise to the claim *occurred*, or a substantial part of property that is the subject of the action is situated ..." in the district (again, a test that is applicable whether the case is based on diversity or federal question); and (3) if all defendants are in some sense "reachable" in the district (though the test here varies slightly depending on the basis for subject matter jurisdiction: all defendants must be "subject to personal jurisdiction" in the district if the case is based solely on diversity; it must merely be the case that one defendant "may be found" in the district if there is a federal question, and if there is no district in which the action may otherwise be brought.) We consider each of these three main bases for venue separately below.

2. **"Defendant's residence" venue:** For both diversity and federal question cases, venue lies in any district where *any defendant resides*, so long as, if there is more than one defendant, *all* the defendants reside in the *state* containing that district.

> **Example 1:** P, a citizen of Massachusetts, brings a diversity suit against D1, a resident of the Southern District of New York, and D2, a resident of the Eastern District of New York. Based on §1391(a)(1), venue will lie in either the Southern District of New York or the Eastern District of New York — each of these is home to at least one defendant, and each is in a state that is home to all defendants.

> **Example 2:** P, a citizen of Massachusetts, brings a diversity suit (or, for that matter, a federal question suit) against D1, a resident of the Southern District of New York, and D2, a resident of the District of Connecticut. Now, §1391(a)(1) (applicable in diversity cases) and §1391(b)(1) (applicable where there is a federal question) do *not* furnish any "defendant's residence" venue anywhere. This is because there is no state in which all defendants reside. P will have to rely either on "place of events" venue, or on the "catch all" of §1391(a)(3)/§1391(b)(3).

3. **"Place of events or property" venue:** For both diversity and federal question cases, venue will lie in any judicial district "in which a *substantial part* of the *events* or omissions giving rise to the claim occurred, or a substantial part of *property* that is the subject of the action is situated. ..." §1391(a)(2) (for diversity cases) and §1391(b)(2) (for federal question cases).

a. **Replacement of "where claim arose" language:** This language is an important change to pre-1990 language, under which there was venue in the district "in which the claim arose." The most important effect of this change is that we no longer have to find a *single* district where "the claim arose." Instead, there can be *multiple* districts qualifying for "place of events" venue, as long as a *"substantial part"* of the events relating to the claim occurred in each of those districts.

> **Example:** P, a citizen of Massachusetts, sues D, a car dealer who is a citizen of Connecticut. The claim alleges that D sold P a car in Connecticut, that P drove the car to Massachusetts, and that a defect in the car caused P to be injured in Massachusetts. Probably venue in *either* the District of Massachusetts or the District of Connecticut would be allowed under the "place of events" provision (§1391(a)(2)), since probably

both the selling of a defective car, and the incurring of an accident, are a "substantial part" of the events giving rise to P's product liability claim.

4. The "catch all" provision: Finally, for both diversity and federal question cases, there is a kind of *"catch all,"* by which venue may be founded in a district with which some or all defendants have close ties. The test is somewhat more restrictive for diversity cases (*all* defendants must be "subject to personal jurisdiction" there) than it is for federal question cases (where only one defendant must be "found" in the district).

a. Diversity cases: In a case founded solely on diversity, the catch-all gives venue in any judicial district "in which *the defendants* are *subject to personal jurisdiction* at the time the action is commenced." §1391(a)(3). The reference to "the defendants" in the plural means that *all* defendants must be subject to personal jurisdiction in that district.

    i. Served while in district: This provision clearly applies where all non-resident defendants are *actually served* with proper process while in the district.

    Example: P, a resident of Massachusetts, brings a diversity action against D1, a resident of the Southern District of New York, and D2, a resident of Connecticut. P's suit is brought in the Southern District of New York. D2 is served while he happens to be in New York City on business one day. The suit relates solely to matters which occurred in Massachusetts. "Defendant's residence" venue, based on §1391(a)(1), does not exist, because it is not the case that *all* the defendants reside in SDNY. Similarly, "place of events" venue does not lie in the Southern District, because it is not the case that a "substantial part" of the relevant events occurred in that district. But §1391(a)(3) saves the day — D1 is obviously subject to personal jurisdiction of the district in which he resides, and D2 is subject to personal jurisdiction there by virtue of his *"transitory presence"* at the moment of service. See *Burnham v. Superior Court, supra,* p. 10.

    ii. Defendants amenable to service but not actually served in district: Now, consider a harder scenario: suppose one of the defendants is *not actually served* in the district, but is *amenable* to service there. This might be because the local long arm would have authorized out of state service on that defendant, or because of Rule 4(k)(1)(B)'s 100-mile bulge (see *supra,* p. 41.) Since §1391(a)(3) merely requires that the defendants all be "subject to personal jurisdiction" in the district, rather than that they be "actually served" in the district, presumably venue lies there in this situation as well.

    Example: Same facts as prior example. Now, however, assume that D2 never comes into the Southern District of New York, or indeed, into New York State at all. However, D2, from Connecticut, sells goods into New York State, sends letters and faxes to the state, and otherwise has "systematic and continuous" contacts with New York, such that New York could constitutionally take personal jurisdiction over D2 (see *supra,* p. 83.) Assume further that the New York long-arm would apply to give the New York courts personal jurisdiction over D2 in this suit had it been pending in state court, despite the fact that D2's contacts with the state don't relate to the existing suit. It seems highly probable that venue lies in SDNY on these facts, because D2, like D1, is "subject to personal jurisdiction" in SDNY at the time P has brought suit.

b. Federal question cases: In federal question cases, the catch all provision gives venue in any judicial district "in which *any defendant* may be *found*, if there is *no district in which the action may otherwise be brought*." §1391(b)(3).

   i. Only one defendant needed: First, observe that one big difference between this provision and the catch all applicable for diversity cases is that here, it is only required that *one* defendant be "found" in the district, not "all defendants." Of course, all the defendants must still be made subject to personal jurisdiction, but this might happen even though not all can be "found" in the district.

   Example: P is a resident of Massachusetts. D1 resides in Massachusetts. D2 resides in the Northern District of California. P brings an antitrust claim based on the federal Clayton Act. Service is made on D1 and D2 in their home states pursuant to the "nationwide service of process" provision of the Clayton Act, 15 U.S.C. §22. Nearly all of the monopolistic acts asserted by P took place in Canada. P's suit is brought in the District of Massachusetts.

   There is no "defendants' residence" venue anywhere, since D1 and D2 reside in different states. There is no "place of events" venue anywhere, since there is no American state in which even a "substantial part" of the events leading to the claim took place (all of that occurred in Canada). But §1391(b)(3)'s catch-all provision gives venue in Massachusetts since: (1) without the catch-all, there is no district where the action may be brought; and (2) D1, by virtue of his residence in Massachusetts, may be "found" in the state.

   ii. Meaning of "found": What does it mean to say that a defendant is "found" in the district? A defendant is clearly "found" if she can be physically served with process in the district. But it is possible that a defendant is *also* "found" in the district merely if process from that district will suffice to give personal jurisdiction over the defendant, despite the defendant's physical absence from that district. If so, §1391(b)(3) may even apply to allow venue in a district where *no* defendant resides, as long as all are amenable to service under the local long arm.

   Example: Suppose that on the facts of the above example, D1 is a citizen of Connecticut, but one who had frequent contacts with Massachusetts unrelated to the events at issue in P's suit. If the Massachusetts long arm would have given personal jurisdiction over D1, then P might plausibly argue that D1 was "found" in Massachusetts (in the sense of being amenable to suit there in a state-court action), and that the requirements for §1391(b)(3) are therefore met as to the District of Massachusetts. However, it is not clear whether a court would agree. See 133 F.R.D. 61, 74.

   iii. Foreign events: Always remember that § 1391(b)(3)'s catch all applies only "if there is no district in which the action may otherwise be brought." Therefore, you must analyze, especially, the places where the *events occurred* to make sure that there is no "place of events" venue in a district from which personal jurisdiction over all defendants could be gotten. The main utility of §1391(b)(3) is probably for federal question cases where nearly all of the events occurred *abroad* (since this would knock out "place of events" venue anywhere). The section might also help in the rare situation in which events are so spread out that no district accounts for a "substantial part" of the events.

5. **No "plaintiff's residence" venue:** Under the pre-1990 version of §1391, venue based on *plaintiff's residence* was allowed, though paradoxically it was allowed only in diversity cases, not federal question cases. The 1990 rewrite *removes plaintiff's residence completely*.

   a. **Back door:** However, sometimes the plaintiff may get a *back door* route to suit in his own district of residence, even if no defendant resides there and no relevant events took place there.

      Example: P is a resident of the District of Colorado. D is a resident of the Southern District of Illinois. P would like to bring a diversity suit against D, and would like to do so in P's home district. No events associated with the suit took place in Colorado. D happens to visit Colorado, and P is lucky enough to serve him there. P will end up getting, in effect, "plaintiff's residence" venue — there is venue in Colorado under § 1391(a)(3), since the District of Colorado is "a judicial district in which the defendants are subject to personal jurisdiction at the time the action is commenced." This is true even though no defendant resides in Colorado, and no substantial part of the events occurred there.

6. **Corporation:** The residence of a *corporation* for venue purposes matters only if the corporation is a defendant. A special section, §1391(c), deals with the residence of corporate defendants. (See *supra*, p. 83, for the text of §1391(c).) Under that section, a corporation will be deemed to be a resident of *any* district as to which it would have the "minimum contacts" necessary to support personal jurisdiction if that district were a separate state. This means in practice that the corporation will be deemed a "resident" of at least the district where it has its principal place of business, any district where it has substantial operations, and probably any district in its state of incorporation. But it is no longer the case (as it was before 1988) that if a corporation does business anywhere in a state, it is deemed to reside in *all districts* of that state.

   Example: Corporation is incorporated in Delaware, has its principal place of business in Manhattan, and has a branch office in San Francisco. It does not do business in, or have significant contacts with, any part of New York except Manhattan, or in/with any part of California except San Francisco. If Corporation is a defendant, it will reside (for venue purposes) in: (1) the District of Delaware (its state of incorporation); (2) the Southern District of New York (its principal place of business) and (3) the Northern District of California (since the branch office in San Francisco means that there would be personal jurisdiction over Corporation in the Northern District if that District were a separate state).

   What is significant is that Corporation will *not* be deemed a resident of any other districts in New York and California. Thus P could not get "defendant's residence" venue in, for instance, the Central District of California (Los Angeles). This is so because Corporation is not deemed a resident of the Central District under §1391(c) (due to its lack of minimum contacts with that district), even though Corporation is a resident of a different district (the Northern District) in the same state.

7. **Unincorporated associations:** Unincorporated associations (e.g. partnerships, labor unions, etc.) are treated like corporations for venue purposes. Wr., 248.

   a. **Distinction:** Such associations are not treated like corporations for *citizenship* purposes, however. Thus, a union with members in every state is never able to take advantage of diversity jurisdiction, despite proper venue. Since it is a citizen of all states of which ius members are citizens, there could never be a complete diversity between it and an adversary (except a foreign one).

8. **Waiver of venue claims:** The Federal Rules provide that the objection to improper venue must be raised at the same time as one to lack of personal jurisdiction, i.e. either in the answer to the complaint or in the pre-answer motions. Rule 12(h)(1). If not made then, it is waived.

9. **Venue in federal removal cases:** A case *removed* from state to federal court passes to "the district court of the U.S. for the district and division embracing the place *where such action is pending.*" 28 U.S.C. §1441(a). (Some districts are subdivided into divisions.)

   a. **Unusual result:** Observe that there may be situations where a case properly removed from state court to federal district court may *not* end up in a federal district court in which it could have been brought as an original federal action. For instance, suppose that a federal question suit is brought in New York state court by a New York resident against a New Jersey defendant, on a cause of action arising in New Jersey. In an original action, venue could lie only in New Jersey, since that is where "defendant's residence" venue would lie, as well as where "place of events" venue would lie; the catch-all of §1391(b)(3) would not give venue in New York because there is a district (New Jersey) where the action might "otherwise be brought." Notwithstanding the unavailability of original venue in New York, the case would nonetheless be removed to New York district court, in accordance with §1441(a).

10. **Federal *forum non conveniens:***

    a. **Transfer:** In a state court, application of the *forum non conveniens* doctrine typically means that the state court *dismisses* the law suit, and the plaintiff must start a new law suit from scratch in a more appropriate state. But in *federal* courts, the court does not dismiss on grounds of *forum non conveniens*; instead, it *transfers* the action to *another district*. 28 U.S.C. §1404(a).

       i. **Burden on defendant:** The burden is on the defendant to make a convincing showing that the action would be better litigated in a different district. "Unless the balance is strongly in favor of the defendant, the plaintiff's choice of forum should rarely be disturbed." *Gulf Oil v. Gilbert*, 330 U.S. 501 (1947).

    b. **Statutory standard:** §1404(a) provides that *"for the convenience of parties and witnesses, ...* a district court may transfer any civil action to any other district or division *where it might have been brought."* A motion to invoke §1404(a) may be made by either party.

   c. Interpretation: The statutory phrase *"where it might have been brought"* has been interpreted so as to sharply limit the districts to which an action may be transferred:

     i. Plaintiff's motion: Transfer on the motion of plaintiff may be made only to a district where the defendant could *initially have been served* with process (pursuant to the long-arm of the state encompassing that district). Also, the district to which the action is transferred must be one in which *venue* would originally have been proper (as specified by 28 U.S.C. §1391).

     ii. Defendant's motion: Transfer on the motion of defendant may be made only to those districts "where plaintiff would have had the right, *independent of the wishes of the defendant*, to bring the action. This clearly establishes that *consent* by the defendant will not permit transfer to a forum where the action could not originally have been commenced." Wr., 263. *Hoffman v. Blaski*, 363 U.S. 335 (1960). So if suit in a particular district would not have been possible, as an initial matter, because one or more defendants could not be personally served there, or because venue would not have been proper there, even the consent by all defendants would not authorize the action to be transferred to that district.

     iii. Commentators' view of *Hoffman*: The *Hoffman v. Blaski* decision has been both praised as prohibiting forum-shopping by defendants, and criticized as drastically reducing the utility of 1404(a). Wr., 263-64.

   d. Choice of law: When §1404(a) is invoked, the state law of the *transferor* court is to be applied by the transferee court. "A change of venue under §1404(a) generally should be, with respect to state law, but a change of courtrooms." *Van Dusen v. Barrack*, 376 U.S. 612 (1964).

     i. Plaintiff moves for transfer: The law of the transferor forum will apply even if it is the *plaintiff*, not the defendant, who moves for the transfer. *Ferens v. John Deere Co.*, 494 U.S. 516 (1990).

   e. Transfer where original venue improper: Transfer may also be made under a different statutory section, 28 U.S.C. §1406(a), which provides that when a suit is brought in a district where venue is *improper*, the action may be transferred to a district where it could have been brought.

     i. Where jurisdiction also lacking: If the court applying §1406(a) decides that it lacks not only venue but also personal jurisdiction, the court may probably nonetheless order the transfer.

Quiz Yourself on
VENUE

13. P, a resident of Las Vegas (in the District of Nevada) wishes to bring a federal-court suit against D1, a resident of Los Angeles (in the Central District of California) and D2 a resident of San Francisco (in the Northern District of California). The suit would be based on diversity, and concerns an auto accident which occurred in San Diego (in the Southern District of California. In which federal judicial district(s) may the suit be brought? _____

14. Same facts as above question. Now, however, assume that D2 is a resident of Albuquerque, in the District of New Mexico. What district(s) have venue? _____

Answers

13. Central, Northern and Southern Districts of California. In both diversity and federal question cases, venue lies in any district where any defendant resides, so long as, if there is more than one defendant, all the defendants reside in the state containing that district. 28 U.S.C. §1391(a)(1). This yields the Central and Northern Districts of California. Additionally, for both diversity and federal question cases, venue lies in any judicial district "in which a substantial part of the events or omissions giving rise to the claim occurred, or a substantial part of property that is the subject of the action is situated. ..." 28 U.S.C. §1391(a)(2). This yields the Southern District of California, where the accident took place. There is no provision allowing venue based on the residence of the plaintiff.

14. Southern District of California. As noted in the prior answer, venue based on defendants' residence exists only if all defendants are at least residents of the same state. Since this is not true here, the fact that the Central District of California and the District of New Mexico are each home to one defendant is irrelevant. Only the "place of events" section, §1391(a)(2), gives venue, which as in the prior question is the Southern District of California.

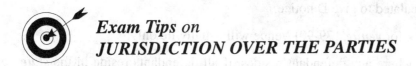

Exam Tips on
JURISDICTION OVER THE PARTIES

In any fact pattern involving the starting of a lawsuit or the service of process, you must of course be alert to issues of jurisdiction over the parties. Here are some particular things to check for:

☛ In a state-court suit, if D is served *outside* the forum state, check whether the applicable *long-arm* statute was complied with. (If not, service is invalid even if there are minimum contacts.)[9, 15-18]

   ☞ If D was served *inside* the forum state (even during a brief visit), the long-arm is irrelevant, and service is valid (though you still have to check for minimum contacts).

☛ Make sure each D has *minimum contacts* with the forum state. [8, 20-35]

   ☞ See whether D *voluntarily did business in*, or with residents of, the forum state. If yes, minimum contacts probably exists. If not, D probably doesn't have minimum contacts.

   ☞ If the suit concerns D's *in-state* activities, remember that sparser contacts will suffice than where the suit is unrelated to the in-state activities.

☛ For *federal* suits:

   ☞ Check that service took place in the correct *place.* This is either: (1) within the *territorial limits* of the state where the District Court sits; or (2) somewhere else *permitted by the state law* (i.e., the long-arm) of the state where the District Court sits. [39-44]

☞ But if D is a ***third-party defendant*** or ***indispensable party,*** think ***"100-mile bulge."*** Rule 4(k)(1)(B) allows service within a 100-mile bulge around the federal courthouse. [41-42]

☞ Check that service took place in the correct ***manner.*** This is either a method specified in the Federal Rules (e.g., delivery of summons and complaint to a person of "suitable age and discretion" at D's residence), or else a method allowed by the local law of the state where service is made or where the District Court sits. [44-46]

☞ Check that D is ***"amenable"*** to service. This means that:

☞ if the case involves a ***federal question***, it's enough that D has minimum contacts with the forum state (even if the long-arm of the state where the federal court sits wouldn't allow the state courts to exercise jurisdiction);

☞ if the case is a ***diversity*** case, the long-arm of the ***state*** where the federal court sits ***must*** allow jurisdiction, or the federal court can't exercise jurisdiction. [46-49]

☛ If P is trying to get jurisdiction based on D's ***assets*** in the forum state (***quasi in rem*** jurisdiction), remember that P can't go forward unless D has ***minimum contacts*** with the forum state, just as if this were an *in personam* suit. [52-60]

☛ Check that D was given ***notice***, and a reasonable opportunity to be ***heard.*** [63-72] (Remember that it doesn't matter whether D got actual notice, merely that the procedures used were ones reasonably calculated to give D notice.)

☛ In federal suits, check for ***venue.*** [79-90] Venue will usually lie only:

☞ in any district where any defendant resides, if all defendants reside in the ***state*** containing that district; or

☞ in any district where a "substantial part of the events" giving rise to the claim occurred.

☞ A corporation "resides" (for venue purposes) in the district where it has its principal place of business, and also in any district where it has substantial operations.

CHAPTER 3

SUBJECT MATTER JURISDICTION

ChapterScope

This Chapter examines "subject matter jurisdiction," that is, the court's power to adjudicate the kind of controversy before it. The most important concepts in this Chapter are:

■ **Two basic types:** In the federal courts, there are two basic kinds of controversies over which the federal judiciary has subject matter jurisdiction: (1) suits between *citizens of different states* (so-called *diversity* jurisdiction); and (2) suits involving a *"federal question."*

■ **Diversity suits:** In *diversity* suits:

❑ An amount in excess of *$50,000* must be in dispute. This is the *"amount in controversy"* requirement. (In federal question cases, there is no amount in controversy requirement.)

❑ *"Complete diversity" is required.* That is, it must be the case that *no plaintiff is a citizen of the same state as any defendant.*

❑ A *corporation* is deemed a citizen of *any state where it is incorporated* and of the state where it has its *principal place of business.* In other words, for diversity to exist, no adversary of the corporation may be a citizen of the state in which the corporation is incorporated, or of the state in which it has its principal place of business.

■ **Federal question suits:** A *"federal question"* suit is one *"arising under the Constitution, laws, or treaties of the United States."* Usually, the reason there is a federal question is that federal law is the *source of the plaintiff's claim.*

■ **Supplemental jurisdiction:** Under the doctrine of *"supplemental"* jurisdiction, if a basic controversy satisfies federal subject matter jurisdictional requirements, *additional claims* and *additional parties* may be brought into the litigation. This is true whether the basic claim is based on federal-question or (with important limits) diversity.

■ **Removal:** Under the doctrine of *"removal"*, any action brought in state court which the plaintiff could have brought in federal court may be transferred ("removed") by the defendant to federal district court. (But in diversity cases, the action may be removed only if no defendant is a citizen of the state in which the action is pending.)

I. GENERAL PRINCIPLES

    A. Definition of subject matter jurisdiction: Even though a state or federal court has jurisdiction over the *parties* in an action, it cannot try the case unless it has the power to adjudicate that *kind* of controversy. The power to adjudicate a certain kind of controversy is known as *subject matter jurisdiction* or *competency over the litigation.*

Example: A state court has personal jurisdiction over both parties in a divorce action. But unless the court has been granted (usually by the legislature) the power to decide divorce cases, any divorce decree granted by the court is void for lack of subject matter jurisdiction or competency. Restatement of Judgments, §7, comment 6.

B. Consent insufficient: Most courts hold that subject matter jurisdiction, unlike jurisdiction over the parties, may *not* be conferred by consent of the litigants.

C. Kinds of federal subject matter jurisdiction: In the federal courts, there are two basic kinds of controversies over which the federal judiciary has subject matter jurisdiction:

1. Suits between *citizens of different states* (so-called *diversity jurisdiction*);

2. Suits involving a *"federal question"* — this will be defined more fully in the discussion of Federal Question Jurisdiction, *infra*, p. 104.

3. Other cases: Certain other kinds of cases specified in the Constitution, Art. III, §2, also fall under the federal judicial power. These are:

a. Cases involving *ambassadors*, other public ministers and consuls;

b. Cases of *admiralty* and maritime jurisdiction;

c. Cases in which the *United States is a party.*

D. Amount in controversy: In a federal suit based on diversity (category 1 above), an amount in excess of $50,000 must be in dispute in the suit. This requirement is known as the *jurisdictional amount* or the *amount in controversy.*

Note: This chapter will be concerned with the subject matter jurisdiction of the *federal courts*. The subject matter jurisdiction of the state courts is generally controlled by state statute; each state is free to allocate the judicial power reserved to it by the 10th Amendment as it wishes among its own state courts. Most states have two or three different kinds of trial courts: a small claims or justice of the peace court, a court of general jurisdiction, a probate court, etc. Often, minimum and maximum limits are placed on the amounts in controversy in these courts. A state's court of general jurisdiction may even hear claims based on *federal* law, unless Congress has specified otherwise as to a particular type of claim. The statutes of the particular state must be consulted to determine the allocation of subject matter among its courts; this allocation will not be discussed further here.

II. FEDERAL SUBJECT MATTER JURISDICTION GENERALLY

A. Burden: The party seeking to invoke the jurisdiction of a federal court must affirmatively show that the case is within the competency of the court. Wr., 22.

Example: A plaintiff seeking to invoke diversity jurisdiction (i.e. jurisdiction based on the fact that the parties are citizens of different states) must in the pleading allege the relevant facts about the citizenship of the parties.

B. Dismissal: *No matter when* a deficiency in the subject matter jurisdiction of a federal court is noticed, the suit must be stopped, and dismissed for lack of jurisdiction.

1. **Objection:** Rule 12(h)(3) of the Federal Rules provides that the parties or the court on its own initiative can *always* object to the court's lack of subject matter jurisdiction: "Whenever it appears by suggestion of the parties or otherwise that the court lacks jurisdiction of the subject matter, the court shall dismiss the action."

2. **Appeals:** Even at the appellate level, the suit already tried may be dismissed for lack of subject matter jurisdiction. Cf. *American Fire & Casualty Co. v. Finn*, 341 U.S. 6 (1951).

   > **Example:** In *Louisville & Nashville Railroad v. Mottley*, 211 U.S. 149 (1908), the controversy reached the Supreme Court before it was dismissed for lack of subject matter jurisdiction. Neither party had raised the jurisdictional issue, but the Court found that the federal question jurisdiction alleged by the plaintiff did not exist.

   a. **Relief from judgment:** Similarly, after a judgment has been entered and any appellate proceedings concluded, a party may be entitled to have the judgment *voided* on the grounds that it was issued in a proceeding as to which the court had no subject matter jurisdiction. F.R.C.P. 60(b) allows a court to grant relief from a final judgment for a variety of reasons. Among these are that the judgment is "void" (60(b)(4)) or for "any other reason justifying relief from the operation of the judgment." (60(b)(6)). See e.g., *Bank of Montreal v. Olafsson*, 648 F.2d 1078 (6th Cir. 1981) (action based on diversity of citizenship, but both parties were foreigners, so that there was no subject matter jurisdiction; judgment set aside even though it was entered more than a year previously, on the grounds that the underlying suit could more sensibly be heard in Canada, which had a closer connection to the transaction at issue).

3. **Distinction:** Federal subject matter jurisdiction must be distinguished from jurisdiction over the parties; the latter is a *waivable* defect, which must be asserted by the party who would take advantage of it. (See Rule 12(h)(1)). Subject matter jurisdiction, on the other hand, is never waived, and may be made by the court on its own motion, as in *Louisville & Nashville, supra.*

4. **Collateral attack on subject matter jurisdiction:** The rules allowing collateral attack on the decision of the court of another jurisdiction are generally the same for both subject matter and personal jurisdiction. That is, it is only where a party to the first action had a *default judgment* entered against him that he may claim, when he is sued on the judgment in a second court, that the first court lacked subject matter jurisdiction. See *Chicot County Drainage District v. Baxter State Bank*, 308 U.S. 371 (1940), discussed *infra*, p. 388.

   > **Example:** A party who appeared in a state action against him, and who did not raise any objection to lack of subject matter jurisdiction, may not generally collaterally attack the state court's judgment when it is sued upon for enforcement in federal court. Nor would he be able usually to collaterally attack if he had made the jurisdictional objection in the state court, and lost.

   a. **Exception:** This policy limiting collateral attack is not followed when there are very strong policy considerations weighing in the opposite direction.

   > **Example:** When a federal statute has given exclusive jurisdiction over a particular type of action to the federal courts, for instance bankruptcy, patent, and copyright actions, the finding by a state court, even in a non-default situation, that it has jurisdic-

tion over such a case will not bar collateral attack on the state court's judgment, when it is sued on for enforcement in either a federal or state court. Wr., 85.

III. DIVERSITY JURISDICTION

A. Constitutional provision: The constitutional grant of jurisdiction based on diversity of citizenship extends to "Controversies ... between *Citizens of different states* ... and between a State, or the Citizens thereof, and foreign States, Citizens or Subjects." (Art. III, §2.) This grant is repeated in a statute, 28 U.S.C. §1332.

> **Example:** P, a citizen of New York, sues D, a citizen of California, in a cause of action arising out of an automobile accident. P claims damages of $100,000. Even though this suit does not involve any federal question, and P's right to recover will be determined exclusively by reference to state law, the case may be heard in federal court. This is because P and D are citizens of different states.

1. Rationale for diversity: The rationale for the existence of diversity jurisdiction has traditionally been that it offers a federal forum for an out-of-state litigant who would be exposed to *local prejudice* if suit was held in state court.

    a. Criticism: But if local prejudice is really the reason for the existence of diversity jurisdiction, it is hard to see why a *plaintiff* who is a citizen of the forum state is able to choose to sue in federal court, even if the out-of-state defendant does not wish a federal forum.

2. Possible abolition of diversity: The constitutional grant of diversity jurisdiction is permissive, rather than mandatory, in nature. Therefore, Congress is free to redraft the federal jurisdiction statutes to *curtail or abolish diversity*. Several recent sessions of Congress have seen attempts to do this. There appears to be substantial Congressional support for either a complete abolition of diversity jurisdiction or a substantial curtailment of it (e.g., a limitation to *cases where the plaintiff is a non-resident* of the state where the district court sits).

3. Amount in controversy: In all cases in which diversity is the sole basis for jurisdiction, the amount in controversy must exceed $50,000. See the section on Jurisdictional Amount, *infra*, p. 106.

B. Complete diversity required: In order to invoke diversity, it must be the case that *no plaintiff is a citizen of the same state as any defendant*. (This does not prevent a pair of plaintiffs, or a pair of defendants, from being co-citizens.) This is the rule of *"complete diversity,"* and is probably the single most important thing to remember about diversity jurisdiction.

> **Example:** P1, P2 and P3 are all citizens of Michigan. P4 is a citizen of Ohio. D1, D2 and D3 are all citizens of California. D4 is a citizen of Ohio. These plaintiffs cannot bring a joint diversity suit against these defendants, because P4 and D4 are citizens of the same state. Because it is not the case that no plaintiff is a citizen of the same state as any defendant, the required "complete diversity" is absent.

1. Basis: The requirement of complete diversity is *not* a Constitutional requirement. It is instead merely a *judge-made* interpretation of 28 U.S.C. §1332, first set forth by Justice

Marshall in *Strawbridge v. Curtiss*, 3 Cranch 267 (1806). Thus Congress is free at any time to specify that "partial" diversity (e.g., one plaintiff is from a different state than some one defendant) will suffice.

2. **Congressional modification:** In fact, Congress has *removed* the requirement of complete diversity in certain types of cases. The most common such case is that of *interpleader*, in which diversity exists as long as there are "two or more adverse claimants, of diverse citizenship." 28 U.S.C. §1335(a)(1).

> **Example:** Three competing beneficiaries, two from N.Y. and one from N.J., claim money owed to them under an insurance policy. The insurance company, by invoking the Interpleader Act, effectively tells them, "fight it out in court and we'll pay the winner." Since there are two adverse parties from different states, the fact that there are also two adverse parties from the same state does not destroy diversity, as it would in a non-interpleader action.

> **Note:** Of course, diversity is only a requirement when there is no other basis for federal jurisdiction, such as the existence of a federal question, or the presence of the U.S. as a party, etc.

3. **Presence of foreigner:** In a suit between citizens of different states, the fact that a *foreign* citizen (or foreign country) is a party does *not destroy* diversity. 28 U.S.C. §1332(a)(3).

> **Example:** P, a citizen of Ohio, sues D1, a citizen of Michigan, and D2, a citizen of Canada. Diversity jurisdiction exists. (In situations where one side consists *solely* of foreign citizens or foreign countries, "alienage" jurisdiction applies. See *infra*, p. 99.)

4. **Pleadings not dispositive:** In order to determine whether complete diversity exists, the pleadings do not settle the question of who are adverse parties. Instead, the court will *"look beyond the pleadings*, and arrange the parties according to their *sides in the dispute."* *Dawson v. Columbia Ave. Trust Co.*, 197 U.S. 178 (1905)

> **Example:** An insured tortfeasor, A, brings an action against his insurer for a declaratory judgment holding the insurer liable for certain coverage under the policy. He names B, the person suing him in tort, as a defendant along with the insurer. For the purposes of determining whether complete diversity exists, the court will probably classify B as a plaintiff, since he and A have an identical interest in having it held that the insurance covers the accident in question. Thus, as long as neither A nor B is a citizen of the same state as the insurance company (for the citizenship of a corporation, see *infra*, p. 100), diversity will not be destroyed by the fact that A and B are citizens of the same state. See *Bonell v. Gen'l Acc. & Life Assur.*, 167 F. Supp. 384 (D.C. Cal. 1958).

C. **Nominal parties ignored:** In determining the existence of diversity, *nominal* or *purely formal* parties may be *ignored*.

1. **Citizenship of trust:** A *trustee's* citizenship may or may not count for diversity purposes. If the trustee has real powers, her citizenship will count. But if the trustee is just a formal holder of title (e.g., a "straw man" in a real estate transaction), with no real deci-

sion-making authority, the trustee's citizenship will be ignored and the beneficiaries' citizenship used instead.

2. Representatives and administrators: *Representatives* and *administrators* will generally be treated as having the citizenship of the *party they represent*. Thus according to §1332(c)(2), "The legal representative of the *estate* of a decedent shall be deemed to be a citizen only of the same State as the decedent, and the legal representative of an *infant* or incompetent shall be deemed to be a citizen only of the same State as the infant or incompetent."

    a. Can't be used to affect diversity: So a representative can't be selected based on his own citizenship, for the purpose of creating (or defeating, in the case of removal) diversity jurisdiction.

    Note: Apart from the rule, just discussed, that nominal or purely formal parties may be ignored, there is a separate doctrine that parties who are "improperly or collusively joined" shall be ignored, for citizenship purposes. See the discussion of this rule *infra*, p. 101.

D. Refusal to exercise jurisdiction: Even where diversity jurisdiction as spelled out in 28 U.S.C. §1332 exists, the federal courts may still *decline to exercise* jurisdiction under certain circumstances. Among such circumstances preventing the exercise of federal jurisdiction are:

1. where diversity is the result of *improper or collusive joinder* of parties, (*infra*, p. 101);

2. where *domestic relations* (i.e., *divorce* and *child custody*) constitute the main subject matter of the suit (but civil child abuse actions don't fall within this exception, and can be heard in diversity; see *Ankenbrandt v. Richards*, 112 S.Ct. 2206 (1992);

3. where *probate* matters are the essence of the suit;

4. where the *"abstention doctrine"* is invoked. This doctrine permits a federal court to decline jurisdiction where congestion of the federal court's docket, the difficulty of the questions of state law presented by the case, the existence of related litigation in state court, etc., make it wiser to defer to a state court. Wr., 303.

E. Date of determination: The existence of diversity is determined *as of the commencement of the action*. If diversity existed between the parties at that date, it is not defeated because one of the parties later became a citizen of the same state as his opponent. Nor will a change of parties, for example by the substitution of one defendant for another, destroy jurisdiction.

1. Limitation: The above statement applies only where the nature of the cause of action remains essentially the same after the change of parties or citizenship. If the cause of action is basically *different*, the test for diversity must be made on the new situation. Wr., 157.

F. Domicile, not residence, is what counts: Residence, by itself, is not enough to make a person a citizen of a state in the sense in which the term is used in Art. III, §2 of the Constitution. Instead, *domicile* is controlling. Wr., 146. For an extended discussion of what constitutes domicile, see *supra*, p. 11.

1. **General principle:** "A person's domicile is that place where he has his *true, fixed, and permanent home* and principal establishment, and to which he has the intention of returning whenever he is absent therefrom." Wr., 146.

2. **Motive for moving irrelevant:** If a person, by moving, meets the test of domicile in his new state of residence, it is immaterial for diversity purposes that he moved in order to create or destroy diversity. But of course, the move must be made before the commencement of the action, as stated in (6.) above. Wr., 147-48.

G. **Citizens of D.C.:** Citizens of the *District of Columbia* are regarded as citizens of a state, for purposes of diversity. 28 U.S.C. §1332(d). Wr., 140.

> **Example:** P, a citizen of D.C., may bring a diversity suit against D, a citizen of any one of the 50 states.

H. **American living abroad:** It is not sufficient that each of the parties be an American citizen; each party must also be a citizen of a *particular American state*. This means that if an American citizen lives *abroad*, there will not be diversity between him and an opposing party who is a citizen of a particular American state.

> **Example:** D, a famous singer, was born in Missouri, but has since moved to England, where she intends to reside indefinitely. She has not given up her American citizenship, or become an English citizen. While she is temporarily in Missouri, she is sued in a federal action brought by P (songwriter Oscar Hammerstein); no federal question is present.
>
> *Held*, there is no federal subject matter jurisdiction. Even though D is an American citizen, she is not a citizen of any particular American state, since there is no state in which she is domiciled (i.e., there is no U.S. state in which she claims to reside permanently.) Therefore, there is no diversity. (Nor is D a citizen or a subject of a foreign country, so there is no "alienage" jurisdiction, described *infra*, p. 96.) *Hammerstein v. Lyne*, 200 F. 165 (W.D. Mo. 1912).

I. **Jurisdiction involving aliens:** Federal jurisdiction exists where there is a suit between a citizen of a state, on one side, and foreign countries, or citizens or subjects thereof, on the other. Wr., 139. Art. III, §2, U.S. Const. This is sometimes referred to as *alienage jurisdiction*. See 28 U.S.C. §1332(a)(2).

> **Example:** P, a citizen of Mexico, sues D, a citizen of Illinois. Even if there is no federal question at issue, there will be federal subject matter jurisdiction (assuming the amount in controversy requirement is satisfied). This is because the case falls under the alienage jurisdiction, since it is between a citizen of a foreign state and a citizen of an American state.

1. **Suit between two foreign citizens:** But a suit solely between or among citizens of *foreign countries* does *not* fall within the alienage jurisdiction. Thus if P, a citizen of Canada, sues D, a citizen of Mexico, there is no alienage jurisdiction; there must be a citizen of an American state on one side of the controversy.

2. **Resident alien:** A foreigner living in the U.S. (i.e., a *resident alien*) is deemed to be a citizen of whatever state in which the alien is domiciled. 28 U.S.C. §1332(a). So a resident alien is not really treated like a foreigner at all, for diversity purposes.

Example: Suppose that P, a citizen of Illinois, sues D, a Canadian citizen who now has permanent resident status in the U.S. and who lives in Illinois. Because D will be treated as a citizen of the state in which he is now domiciled, there is no diversity, and the suit cannot proceed.

3. **Aliens and U.S. citizens on same side:** Jurisdiction is not destroyed by the fact that one or more foreigners and one or more U.S. citizens are each present on each side of the litigation. Here, the jurisdiction is deemed to be conventional diversity, rather than alienage jurisdiction.

    Example: P1, a citizen of Ohio, and P2, a citizen of Canada (living in Canada), sue D1, a citizen of New Jersey, and D2, a citizen of Canada (living in Canada). The configuration is analyzed as if the foreigners were not present; therefore, the requirements for conventional diversity jurisdiction are satisfied, and the suit may proceed. See 28 U.S.C. §1332(a)(3), which specifies that in a suit between citizens of different states, the fact that "foreign states or citizens or subjects thereof are additional parties" does not destroy diversity.

J. **Diversity involving corporations:** For diversity purposes, "a *corporation* shall be deemed a citizen of any State by which it has been *incorporated* and of the State where it has its *principal place of business.*" (28 U.S.C. §1332(c)). This means that for diversity to exist, *no adversary of the corporation may be a citizen of the state in which the corporation is incorporated, or of the state in which it has its principal place of business*. Wr., 151.

    Example: Suppose a corporation is incorporated in Delaware, and has its principal place of business in New York. In order for there to be diversity, no adverse party may be a citizen of *either* Delaware or New York.

1. **Principal place of business:** Courts have taken two different views about where a corporation's "principal place of business" is.

    a. **Home office:** Some courts hold that the corporation's principal place of business is ordinarily the state in which its *corporate headquarters*, or "home office," is located. This is sometimes called the *"nerve center"* test. F,K&M, p. 34, n. 50.

    b. **Bulk of activity:** Other courts hold that the principal place of business is the place in which the corporation carries on its main *production or service activities*. This is sometimes called the *"muscle"* test. Usually, this will be the state in which the corporation has the largest share of its assets (e.g., manufacturing plants in the case of a manufacturer, or total office space, in the case of a service business).

    Note: Probably the "muscle" test is the more commonly used standard. The "nerve center" test seems to be used "only when the corporation's operations are relatively evenly divided among several states." F,K&M, p. 34.

2. **Unincorporated associations:** *Unincorporated associations*, such as *partnerships* and *labor unions*, do *not* fall under the definition of corporate citizenship given in §1332(c). Instead, the citizenship of *each member* must be considered. For instance, in a diversity suit where one of the parties is a limited partnership, every member of the partnership (even the limited partners, who have no say in how the partnership is run) must be diverse

with the opposing party; see *Carden v. Arkoma Associates*, 494 U.S. 185 (1990), so holding.

   a. **Class action:** Often, diversity can be preserved by bringing a class action, naming only those parties for whom complete diversity exists. The result is binding, through the rules of class actions, even on those members of the class who were not specifically named in the original suit. Wr., 156.

K. Devices to create or destroy diversity: Suppose a court believes that a party has used procedural tricks — such as assignment of claims, failure to join parties who have a real interest in the litigation, etc. — in order to produce diversity jurisdiction that would otherwise not exist. Congress has passed a statute to prevent such tactics. 28 U.S.C. §1359 provides that "A district court shall not have jurisdiction of a civil action in which any party, by assignment or otherwise, has been ***improperly or collusively ... joined*** to invoke the jurisdiction of such court."

   1. **Assignment of claims:** §1359 has been applied with particular strictness to the ***assignment of claims*** for the purpose of creating diversity.

      a. ***Kramer* case:** For instance, in *Kramer v. Caribbean Mills*, 394 U.S. 823 (1969), the defendant Caribbean Mills, a Haitian corporation, bought shares of the stock of the Panama Finance Co., a Panamanian Corp. The shares were bought under an installment contract, the payments for which were never made by Caribbean. Panama couldn't sue in diversity or alienage, so it assigned its contract interest to a Texas lawyer, Kramer, for $1. (Kramer, by personally suing Caribbean, invoked the alienage jurisdiction). By separate agreement, Kramer promised to return to Panama 95% of any recovery "solely as a bonus."

      b. **Assignment held invalid:** The Supreme Court in *Kramer* found that the assignment of the claim to Kramer had been made solely for the purpose of creating jurisdiction, and that the assignment was thus improper and collusive under §1359. Therefore, the court held that jurisdiction was ***void***.

   2. **Failure to name indispensable parties:** Plaintiff may not create diversity by failing to name, either as defendants or plaintiffs, ***"indispensable parties."*** That is, where the presence of a person who has not been made a party to the action is vital to the fair carrying out of the litigation, the court may classify the missing person as an "indispensable" party in whose absence the suit may not proceed. The standards for doing this are spelled out in FRCP 19(b). See the discussion of indispensable parties (and of "necessary" parties, a related category) *infra*, p. 300.

   3. **Devices to defeat removal:** A plaintiff suing in state court may sometimes seek to defeat his adversary's potential right to ***remove*** to federal court (*infra*, p. 126). There is ***no*** federal statute prohibiting "improper or collusive" joinder to ***defeat*** jurisdiction, and the courts have given plaintiffs fairly free rein in their attempts to block removal.

      a. **Assignment of part of claim:** Some courts have even held that a plaintiff bringing a state court action may ***assign*** a portion of his claim in order to defeat an undesired removal by the defendant. But the modern trend seems to be to hold that such a removal-defeating assignment *fails*. Wr., p. 172.

Example: P, a Vermont resident, sues D, a California resident, in Vermont state court. Before the action is commenced, P assigns (for a nominal consideration) 1/50th of his claim to X, a friend of his who is a California resident. X joins as co-plaintiff. By doing this, the required complete diversity for a federal action is destroyed, in an attempt to block D from removing to federal court.

Courts are split on whether this ploy should succeed. The traditional view has been that the ploy does succeed, since there is no federal statute which exists to prevent "improper and collusive" joinder to *defeat* (rather than create) jurisdiction. See, e.g., *Ridgeland Box Mfg. Co. v. Sinclair Ref. Co.*, 82 F. Supp. 274 (E.D. S.C. 1949). However, many more recent decisions have gone the other way, especially where the portion of the claim assigned was small, and the original owner of the claim remained as a party to benefit from local state court prejudice against the out-of-state defendant. See, e.g., *Gentle v. Lamb-Weston, Inc.*, 302 F. Supp. 161 (D. Me. 1969).

b. **Joinder of non-diverse defendant:** Removal may *not* be defeated by the plaintiff's *joinder as defendant* of a party against whom *no bona fide claim exists.*

Example: P (baseball great Pete Rose) brings a state-court action in Ohio against three Ds (the Commissioner of Baseball, "Major League Baseball," and the Cincinnati Reds) to prevent the Commissioner from conducting a hearing into charges that Rose gambled on baseball. The Ds remove to federal court. P claims that removal is improper, on the grounds that Major League Baseball and the Reds are citizens of Ohio, as is Rose, so that there is not complete diversity.

Held, for the Ds. Removal is proper because neither "Major League Baseball" nor the Reds are important to the case — they are both "formal or nominal" parties, with no "actual interest or control over the subject matter of the litigation." Major League Baseball and the Reds are thus, in the formal sense, "fraudulently joined," and their joinder will not prevent removal. *Rose v. Giamatti*, 721 F.Supp. 906 (S.D. Ohio 1989).

i. **Valid claim but no assets:** But if there is a valid claim against the defendant whose presence destroys diversity, the fact that he has *no assets* out of which a judgment could be satisfied does not prevent diversity from being destroyed. Wr., 173.

c. **Low dollar claim to defeat removal:** A claim for *less than the jurisdictional amount* will destroy removal jurisdiction, but this low amount must be named *before* the defendant removes. Wr., 174-75.

Quiz Yourself on
DIVERSITY JURISDICTION

15. D's sole residence is in Connecticut. Under a contract with P, D performed some construction work on P's weekend home in Connecticut. P also has a principal residence, located in New York (where P resides during the week). When D failed to do the work in the contracted-for manner, P sued D in federal court for the District of Connecticut for $60,000 (a reasonable assessment of the damages suffered by P). No federal questions are presented by P's suit. May the federal court for Connecticut hear the case?

16. P1 is a citizen of New York. P2 is a citizen of New Jersey. D1 is a citizen of California. D2 is a citizen of

New Jersey. P1 and P2 have brought a federal court action in the Southern District of New York against D1 and D2, alleging that D1 and D2 have breached a contract. No federal question is present. The Southern District of New York is the district where the claim arose. The amount at stake is $100,000. May the Southern District of New York hear the case?

_____

17. P1 is a citizen of Delaware; P2 is a citizen of New Jersey. They have brought a federal court action against D, a corporation with its principal place of business in New York and incorporated in Delaware. No federal question is present. $80,000 is at stake. Putting aside questions of venue, does the federal court have subject matter jurisdiction over the dispute? _____

18. Peter is a citizen of South Carolina. A car he was driving was involved in an accident with a car driven by Dennis, also a citizen of South Carolina. Peter wished to sue Dennis for negligence. He was aware that procedural rules would be more favorable for him in the federal court for South Carolina than in the South Carolina state courts. However, he realized that he would not be able to obtain diversity of citizenship in an action against Dennis. Therefore, he assigned his claim to his sister Paula, a citizen of North Carolina, for $1. Such an assignment is fully enforceable under the laws of both South Carolina and North Carolina. Peter and Paula had an implicit understanding that if Paula recovered, she would return the vast bulk of the award to Peter. Paula then sued Dennis on the claim in South Carolina federal court. The amount in controversy requirement is satisfied. Does the South Carolina federal district court have subject matter jurisdiction over the case? _____

_____

Answers

15. Yes. For there to be subject matter jurisdiction, there must of course be diversity of citizenship. That is, P and D must be "citizens" of different states. "Citizenship" for this purpose is not synonymous with "residence." Instead, a person is a "citizen" only of the state where he is *domiciled*, i.e., has his principal residence. On these facts, P's principal residence is clearly New York, and Connecticut is merely his secondary residence. Therefore, P is a "citizen" of New York, and he has diversity of citizenship with D. Consequently, the court may hear the case.

16. No. Since there is no federal question present, the federal subject matter jurisdiction must be supplied by diversity if at all. But by a judge-made construction of the federal diversity statute, there must be ***"complete"*** diversity. That is, it must be the case that no plaintiff is a citizen of the same state as any defendant. Since P2 and D2 are both citizens of New Jersey, diversity is deemed not to exist even though there is also a pair of opponents (P1 and D1) who are citizens of different states from each other. See *Strawbridge v. Curtiss*, 3 Cranch 267 (1806).

17. No. A corporation (whether plaintiff or defendant) is deemed to be a citizen ***both*** of the state where it has its principal place of business ***and*** the state where it is incorporated. 28 U.S.C. §1332(c)(1). Putting this rule together with the rule requiring complete diversity, it becomes the case that D can be sued only if none of the Ps is a citizen of ***either*** Delaware or New York. Since P1 is a citizen of Delaware, complete diversity is lacking and there is no diversity jurisdiction.

18. No. 28 U.S.C. §1359 provides that "a district court shall not have jurisdiction of a civil action in which any party, by assignment or otherwise, has been improperly or collusively … joined to invoke the jurisdiction of such court." Since the sole reason for which Peter made the assignment to Paula was to create diversity, and since this assignment was collusive in the sense that it was not the product of an arm's-length economic bargain between Peter and Paula, the court will invoke §1359 and refuse to take jurisdiction. The fact that the assignment may have been valid and enforceable under South Carolina law is irrelevant for purposes of §1359.

IV. FEDERAL QUESTION JURISDICTION

A. Statutory basis: The grant of original jurisdiction over federal question cases is given in 28 U.S.C. §1331: "[Jurisdiction extends to] all civil actions *arising under the Constitution, laws, or treaties of the United States.*" This language is similar to that used by Art. III, §2 of the Constitution, which gives the federal courts authority to hear federal question cases.

1. **Interpretation constricted:** The interpretation given to the statute has been narrower than that given to the Constitutional language (which applies not only to *original*, but also to *appellate*, jurisdiction).

2. **No adequate definition:** No really satisfactory definition of a case "arising under" the Constitution, etc., exists. The one that is most generally accepted is that the suit must be on *"a substantial claim founded 'directly' upon federal law."* The Supreme Court has formulated a somewhat more specific test: In order for a federal question to exist, it must be the case "either that federal law *creates the cause of action* or that the plaintiff's right to relief necessarily *depends on resolution of a substantial question* of federal law." See *Franchise Tax Bd. v. Construction Laborers Vacation Trust*, 463 U.S. 1 (1983).

   a. **Federal claim:** In the vast majority of federal-question cases, federal law will be the *source of the cause of action*. For instance, a claim for copyright or trademark violation clearly presents a federal question, because a federal statute (the federal copyright statute or trademark statute) is the source of the right the plaintiff is asserting. Conversely, if the plaintiff's cause of action derives from federal law, the case necessarily is one falling within the federal-question jurisdiction.

   b. **State-created claim:** Suppose, however, that the claim being asserted is one created by state law, but adjudication of that claim requires *interpretation* of a federal law. The Supreme Court has held that this is *not* sufficient to bring the case within the federal-question jurisdiction. See *Merrell Dow Pharmaceuticals, Inc. v. Thompson*, 478 U.S. 804 (1986). In fact, if Congress in passing a federal statute decides that there should not be a private right of action for violation of that statute, a state-created cause of action that alleges a violation of the federal statute as an element of the state-law claim will *never* be construed to "arise under the Constitution, laws, or treaties of the United States." *Merrell Dow Pharmaceuticals, supra.*

   Example: The Ps bring a state-court product liability suit against D for injuries sustained when they took a drug produced by D. The complaint alleges that D violated the federal Food, Drug and Cosmetic Act (FDCA) by mislabeling the drug, and that this mislabeling created a rebuttable presumption of negligence. D removes to federal court (see *infra*, p. 126), asserting that since Ps' claim turns upon the meaning of the FDCA, the claim "arises under" federal law.

Held, by the Supreme Court, the Ps' claim does not "arise under" federal law, and there is, therefore, no federal removal jurisdiction. Congress, when it passed the FDCA, expressly decided that there should be no private right of action for violations of the FDCA. Given this congressional decision, it would undermine the congressional scheme for the federal courts to exercise federal-question jurisdiction, and provide remedies for a violation of that statute, solely because the violation creates a rebuttable presumption of negligence under state law. *Merrell Dow Pharmaceuticals*, *supra*.

3. **Anticipation of defense insufficient:** The federal question must be *integral* to plaintiff's cause of action, as revealed by *plaintiff's complaint*. It does *not* suffice for federal question jurisdiction that the plaintiff *anticipates a defense* based on a federal statute, or even that *defendant's answer does in fact raise a federal question*. To put it another way, the federal question must be part of a "well pleaded complaint." F,K&M, 20-23; see also Wr., 98-99.

> **Example:** The Ps claim in a federal suit that D, a railroad, has breached its agreement to give the Ps free passes in return for their release of tort claims against it. A federal statute has recently been passed which prohibits the giving of such passes. The Ps, anticipating that D will raise the federal statute as a defense, assert in their complaint that the statute does not apply to their case or, alternatively, that if it applies it would violate their Fifth Amendment right not to be deprived of property without due process. The matter goes to trial, where D does in fact claim the federal statute as a defense.
>
> *Held* (by the U.S. Supreme Court on appeal), no federal question jurisdiction existed, because the federal statute was *not essential to the plaintiffs' cause of action*. It is not sufficient that the complaint mentions some anticipated defense and asserts that the validity of the defense is governed by federal law. *Louisville & Nashville R.R. v. Mottley*, 211 U.S. 149 (1908).

4. **Claim based on the merits:** If the plaintiff's claim is clearly based upon federal law, it qualifies for federal-question jurisdiction *even if it is invalid on the merits*. In this situation, the federal court will dismiss for *failure to state a claim on which relief may be granted* (see Rule 12(b)(6)), not for lack of subject matter jurisdiction. See *Bell v. Hood*, 327 U.S. 678 (1946).

   a. **Insubstantial claim:** However, if the "federal claim" is clearly made *solely for the purpose of obtaining jurisdiction*, or is "wholly insubstantial and frivolous," the court will dismiss for lack of federal-question jurisdiction. *Id.*

   b. **Supplemental claims:** It might not be obvious why there would be any practical difference between a dismissal for failure to state a claim on which relief may be granted and a dismissal for lack of subject matter jurisdiction. However, the plaintiff may be asserting multiple claims, one of which is a federal-question claim and the other of which is a state-law claim that falls within the federal court's *"supplemental"* jurisdiction. (See *infra*, p. 112 for a discussion of supplemental jurisdiction.) As a matter of subject matter jurisdiction, the federal court can (though need not) hear the state-created supplemental claim even if it dismisses the federal-law claim for failure under

Rule 12(b)(6); but it can't hear the supplemental claim if it has no subject matter jurisdiction over what is falsely alleged to be the federal-question claim.

Quiz Yourself on
FEDERAL QUESTION JURISDICTION

19. P is a franchiser of fast food restaurants. D holds a franchise issued by P for a particular restaurant location. P is incorporated in Delaware, and has its principal place of business in New York. D is incorporated in Delaware, and has its principal place of business in Florida. P wishes to terminate D's franchise. Therefore, P has brought an action in Florida federal district court for a declaratory judgment that by the terms of the franchise contract, P is entitled to terminate D's franchise. P's complaint raises no substantive issues other than issues of state contract law. D has submitted an answer asserting that P wishes to terminate D's franchise so that P can operate D's store itself; D asserts that this cancellation would be a violation of federal antitrust laws. Both P and D wish the action to proceed in federal court, to avoid the congestion of the Florida state courts. The federal judge is convinced that D's antitrust defense is not frivolous. Any applicable amount in controversy requirement is satisfied. Does the federal court for Florida have subject matter jurisdiction over the case? _____

Answer

19. **No.** Clearly there is no diversity of jurisdiction (since both parties are incorporated in Delaware, and are thus be deemed to be citizens of Delaware as well as of the state where they have their principal place of business). Therefore, the subject matter jurisdiction must be of the federal question sort. But it is well established that the federal question must be part of a "well-pleaded complaint." In other words, the federal question must be an integral part of the plaintiff's cause of action (as revealed by the plaintiff's complaint); it is not enough that the plaintiff anticipates a defense based on federal law, or even that the defendant's answer explicitly states a federal defense. Since P's claim is founded solely upon state law (contract law), it is irrelevant that D has asserted a defense that derives entirely from a federal statute. See *Louisville & Nashville R.R. v. Mottley.*

V. AMOUNT IN CONTROVERSY

A. **General rule:** In *all diversity cases*, the amount in controversy must exceed *$50,000*. 28 U.S.C. §1332(a).

   1. **Interest not included:** The $50,000 figure does not include interest or court costs.

   2. **Federal question cases:** In all *federal question* cases, there is *no* amount in controversy requirement, as the result of a 1980 amendment to 28 U.S.C. §1331.

B. **Proof not required:** The party seeking to invoke federal diversity jurisdiction does not have to *prove* that the amount in controversy exceeds $50,000. All he has to show is that there is *some possibility* that that much is in question.

1. **Standard of proof:** The usual standard of proof is that "it must appear to a *legal certainty* that the claim is really for less than the jurisdictional amount to justify dismissal." *St. Paul Mercury Indemnity Co. v. Red Cab*, 303 U.S. 283 (1938).

   a. **State law followed:** State law is consulted in determining whether it is a "legal certainty" that plaintiff cannot recover more than $50,000.

      Example: P claims $20,000 actual damages in a negligence action, and $40,000 punitive damages. If state law does not allow punitive damages for negligence, the jurisdictional amount is not satisfied in a diversity case.

2. **Good faith:** "The sum claimed by the plaintiff controls if the claim is apparently made in *good faith*." *St. Paul Mercury, supra.*

   Example: In the *St. Paul* case, plaintiff Cab Company sued defendant Insurance Company for failure to pay workmen's compensation claims; the Cab Company alleged that these claims had cost it $4000. Defendants removed from state to federal court, after which Cab Company amended its claim, still asking for $4000, but attaching a document showing an expenditure by it of only $1300 for the claims. The Insurance Company lost on the merits, and appealed. The appeals court refused to decide the appeal on the merits, holding on its own initiative that the jurisdictional amount had not been satisfied. The Supreme Court reversed the appeals court, holding that since plaintiff's claim was apparently made in good faith, and since it was not clear to a legal certainty that the claim was not worth the jurisdictional amount (then $3000), the amount requirement was satisfied.

C. **Eventual recovery irrelevant:** The fact that plaintiff *eventually recovers far less* than the jurisdictional amount does *not* by itself render the verdict subject to reversal and dismissal on appeal for lack of jurisdiction. "The inability of the plaintiff to recover an amount adequate to give the court jurisdiction does not show his bad faith or oust the jurisdiction. … [But] if, from the proofs, the court is satisfied to a legal certainty that the plaintiff never was entitled to recover that amount, and that his claim was therefore colorable for the purpose of conferring jurisdiction, the suit will be dismissed." *St. Paul Mercury, supra.*

   1. **Discretion to deny costs:** Congress has given the federal courts the discretionary power to deny costs to plaintiff, and even to impose costs on him, if he recovers less than $50,000. 28 U.S.C. §1332(b). But this power has rarely been used by the courts. F,K&C, p. 860.

D. **Whose point of view followed:** The courts are divided on the question of which party's point of view is to be considered in calculating the amount at stake.

   1. **"Plaintiff" test:** Most courts have held that the controversy must be worth $50,000 to the *plaintiff* in order to satisfy the jurisdictional amount. F,K&M, p. 46.

   2. **"Either party" test:** Other courts, however, have rejected this "plaintiff viewpoint" approach, and have held that as long as the possible benefit or cost to *one of the two parties* is greater than the jurisdictional amount, the requirement is satisfied. This would seem to serve the Congressional policy of keeping petty cases out of the courts, since any controversy which is worth $50,000 to someone is not petty. Wr., 192-93.

3. **Removal cases:** In cases which have been **removed** to federal court, the court is likely to be much less suspicious about whether plaintiff's claim meets the jurisdictional amount, if the plaintiff has stated it as being for a sum in excess of $50,000. This is because if the action meets the criteria for removal, it could have almost always been brought as an original action in the district to which it is removed. Therefore, since the plaintiff, by bringing the suit in state court, has indicated his lack of interest in having the suit tried in federal court, the amount of his claim can usually be automatically considered to have been made in good faith, if it exceeds $50,000.

    a. **Plaintiff may defeat removal:** But the **plaintiff is master of his complaint**, in removal cases as in other ones — if a plaintiff wishes to defeat removal, he may claim **less than what his cause of action is really worth**. See *supra*, p. 101.

E. **Aggregation of claims:** In multi-plaintiff and/or multi-claim litigation, it will often be the case that not all claims of all individual plaintiffs meet the jurisdictional amount. It then becomes important to determine whether some or all claims may be added together in order to satisfy the jurisdictional amount.

1. **Aggregation by single plaintiff:** If a plaintiff has a claim in excess of $50,000, he may add to it **any other claim of his against the same defendant**, even though these other claims are for less than the jurisdictional amount. These lesser claims may be "tacked on" to the big claim under the doctrine of **"supplemental jurisdiction,"** discussed *infra*, p. 112.

    a. **No claim exceeds $50,000:** Even if a plaintiff does **not** have any single claim worth more than $50,000, he may add together all of his claims against a single defendant. If these claims against a single defendant total more than $50,000, the amount in controversy requirement is satisfied. The plaintiff is thus permitted to **aggregate** his claims against a particular defendant.

        i. **Additional defendants:** Once a plaintiff has aggregated his claims against a particular defendant, and so met the jurisdictional amount, he is **not** usually permitted to join claims against other defendants for less than the jurisdictional amount. Such joinder does not fall under the supplemental jurisdiction doctrine. Wr., 31.

2. **Aggregation by multiple plaintiffs:** In suits involving multiple plaintiffs, where not all plaintiffs meet the jurisdictional amount, two analytically different cases must be considered: (1) **at least one** of the plaintiffs meets the amount, but others do not; (2) **none** of the plaintiffs singly meets the amount, but their claims when **aggregated** exceed the amount. These two cases are considered separately:

    a. **At least one plaintiff meets amount:** Courts are *split* about whether, if one plaintiff meets the amount, other plaintiffs may join their related claims against the same defendant. The Supreme Court's holding in *Zahn v. International Paper Co.* (discussed *infra*) suggests, but does not state, that in the ordinary, non-class action situation, each plaintiff must independently satisfy the jurisdictional amount. (*Zahn* dealt directly with class actions, and held that in that situation, each plaintiff must meet the amount. But the logic of *Zahn* seems to apply as well to non-class actions involving multiple named plaintiffs. See Wr., pp. 200-01; F,K&M, pp. 76.)

i. **Supplemental jurisdiction:** But the doctrine of *"supplemental jurisdiction"* may enable the low-amount plaintiffs to join their claims together with the plaintiff who independently satisfies the jurisdictional amount. This doctrine, discussed extensively beginning *infra*, p. 112, provides generally that if one claim meets federal subject matter jurisdictional requirements, certain closely-related claims, including claims involving different parties, may be joined with the "core" claim without independently meeting the subject matter jurisdictional requirements. In the case of Rule 20 joinder of co-plaintiffs, it is possible, but by no means certain, that the low-dollar-amount plaintiffs may join together with the high-dollar plaintiff. See *infra*, p. 118.

b. **No single claim meets the amount:** If no single plaintiff has a claim or claims meeting the jurisdictional amount, aggregation is normally ***not allowed***. However, an exception is made where two or more plaintiffs unite to enforce a ***single title or right*** in which they have a ***common and undivided interest.***

Example: P brings a class action suit on behalf of herself and all other stockholders in an insurance company, against the directors of the company. She alleges that the directors have sold their shares in the company at a price in excess of the market value (the buyer sought to gain control of the company) and that under local state law, the excess should be distributed among all shareholders. No individual P has a claim satisfying the jurisdictional amount, but all the Ps' claims added together do satisfy the amount.

Held (by the Supreme Court), the amount in controversy requirement is not satisfied here. No "common and undivided interest" exists among the stockholders. Therefore, aggregation is not permitted. To allow aggregation would be to expand federal jurisdiction, something which it is up to Congress, not the Supreme Court, to do. *Snyder v. Harris*, 394 U.S. 332 (1969).

c. **Special restrictions for class actions:** In *class actions*, the Supreme Court has taken an especially restrictive view of the aggregation issue. In ***Zahn v. International Paper Co.***, 414 U.S. 291 (1973), the Court held that *every* member of the class must satisfy the jurisdictional amount. The Court based its decision on *Snyder*, and held that *"one plaintiff may not ride in on another's coattails."* Any recovery by the named plaintiffs, each of whom met the amount, would have no *res judicata* effect on the plaintiffs not meeting the amount, who would all have to relitigate on the merits. The utility of Rule 23 class actions in diversity cases is thus ***virtually crippled***, since it is only a rare class action in which all members have $50,000 at stake. Wr., 485.

i. **Dissent in *Zahn*:** A dissent in *Zahn* argued that the case was totally different from *Snyder*, since in *Snyder*, *no* plaintiff satisfied the jurisdictional amount. The dissent argued that here, the doctrine of ***ancillary jurisdiction*** (since replaced by "supplemental jurisdiction"), not aggregation, was involved. (In other words, the dissent distinguished between categories (1.) and (2.) in the above analysis.) The majority rejected the dissent's argument without explanation.

ii. **Scope of ruling unclear:** It is not clear what effect, if any, *Zahn* has on non-class actions where one plaintiff satisfies the jurisdictional amount, and others seek to join claims arising out of the same transaction or occurrence. Perhaps the doctrine of supplemental jurisdiction, codified in 28 U.S.C. §1367, will permit the other low-dollar plaintiffs to join with the plaintiff who satisfies the jurisdictional amount. See *infra*, pp. 117, 298.

      iii. Federal question in class actions: Of course, class actions are still available without regard to jurisdictional amount in *federal question* cases, since there is no amount in controversy requirement in such cases.

F. Effect of counterclaim: The presence of *counterclaims* by the defendant against the plaintiff can raise questions as to jurisdictional amount.

    1. Suit brought in federal court: If the plaintiff sues in federal court for less than the jurisdictional amount, and the defendant counterclaims for an amount which, either by itself or added to the plaintiff's claim, exceeds the jurisdictional amount, it is not clear whether "aggregation" occurs, or whether the court must instead dismiss. Wright suggests (pp. 202-03) that the amount in controversy requirement is not met, by reference to the rule that the existence of federal subject jurisdiction must appear from the *plaintiff's claim*, without reference to that of the defendant (see *supra*, p. 108).

    2. Removal where counterclaim present: If the plaintiff originally sued in state court, and the defendant *removed* to federal court, amount in controversy questions also arise if a counterclaim is present. The following general rules seem to be applied:

        a. Plaintiff removal: A *plaintiff may never remove*, even if the defendant counterclaims against him for more than $50,000. The removal statute, 28 U.S.C. §1441, has been held not to apply to plaintiffs, even those who are really defendants against counterclaims. Wr., 203. See *Shamrock Oil v. Sheets, infra*, p. 127.

        b. Defendant removal: If *defendant* makes a *permissive* (by state law) counterclaim for more than $50,000, but plaintiff's original claim is for less than $50,000, defendant may *not* remove. Wr., 203.

        c. Compulsory counterclaim: Under the same facts as (b.), but where the counterclaim is *compulsory* under the state law, some courts allow defendant to remove, and some do not. Wr., 203.

Quiz Yourself on
AMOUNT IN CONTROVERSY

20. P is an individual who is a citizen of Missouri. D, also an individual, is a citizen of Indiana. P asserts that he sold goods to D under a contract whereby D was to pay him $40,000, and that D has not paid for the goods. If suit is brought in federal court for the Southern District of Indiana (the district in which D resides), may that court hear the suit? _____

21. P, an individual, is a citizen of Vermont. D, a corporation, is incorporated in and has its principal place of business in Washington. In 1988, P signed a contract with D giving D marketing rights to a software program developed by P, 4-3-2. In 1989, D issued a press release (unrelated to the P-D contract), stating that P "is a good programmer, but he's not a very good or honest guy, as evidenced by his 1986 conviction for armed robbery." P has brought suit against D in federal district court for Vermont alleging: (1) in count 1, breach of the contractual royalty provisions, for which P claims damages of $30,000; and (2) in count 2, libel, for which P claims damages of $40,000. Assume the court has personal jurisdiction over D. May the court hear the case? _____

22. P1 and P2 are individuals who are citizens of Kentucky. D is a corporation that is a citizen of North Carolina. The Ps both signed identically worded contracts with D, whereby the Ps were each to raise broiler chickens, which they would sell to D for a stated price per pound. D unilaterally cancelled both contracts at the same time. The Ps wish to sue jointly in North Carolina federal court for breach of contract, and plan to join together as plaintiffs against D under Federal Rule 20. The damages asserted by P1 are $60,000, and the damages asserted by P2 equal $20,000. May the claims by P1 and P2 be heard together in a single federal action? _____

23. Same facts as prior question. Now, however, assume that P1 and P2 each have a claim for $30,000. May they join their claims against D together pursuant to Rule 20, so that they can be adjudicated in a single federal court suit? _____

Answers

20. **No.** For diversity actions, the ***amount in controversy*** must be at least $50,000. See 28 U.S.C. §1332(a). Since P is claiming only the amount of money due under the contract, and that amount comes to less than $40,000, this requirement is not satisfied. (Nor can costs, interest or attorney's fees generally be included to meet the amount.)

21. **Yes.** A plaintiff may ***"aggregate,"*** i.e., add together, all of his claims against a single defendant, for purposes of meeting the $50,000 diversity amount in controversy requirement. This is true even if no single claim meets the jurisdictional amount by itself.

22. **No, probably.** The Supreme Court has never expressly spoken on the issue of whether, in a non-class action suit, the claim of a plaintiff who meets the jurisdictional amount may be joined together with the claim of a different plaintiff who does not meet that amount. However, the Supreme Court has explicitly refused to allow this kind of aggregation in class-action suits, where the court has held that ***each*** plaintiff must satisfy the jurisdictional amount. See *Zahn v. International Paper Co.*, 414 U.S. 291 (1973). Most courts and commentators have interpreted the rationale of *Zahn* to apply to the non-class action context as well. Thus the probability is that a court would hold that since P2 does not meet the jurisdictional amount, his claim may not be aggregated with that of P1 (whose claim does meet the amount in controversy requirement), even though both claims are very similar and arise out of the same contractual language and same conduct by D.

P1 and P2 could try to invoke subject matter jurisdiction under the new supplemental jurisdiction statute, 28 U.S.C. §1367. Section 1367(b), which applies to diversity cases, does not specifically exclude claims by persons joined as plaintiffs under Rule 20. However, because of §1367's general bias *against* allowing supplemental jurisdiction to diversity plaintiffs who join claims or parties, a judge might not allow the joinder and might instead use her discretion to "decline to exercise jurisdiction" under §1367(c).

23. **No.** Unlike the fact pattern where one claimant does meet the jurisdictional amount and others do not (dealt with in the prior question), here the Supreme Court *has* spoken and the result is quite clear: aggregation is not permitted so long as the claims are "separate and distinct." See *Snyder v. Harris*, 394 U.S. 332 (1969). Here, even though the Ps both signed similarly-worded contracts, and even though the alleged breach was carried out by D in a similar manner and at a similar time towards both Ps, a court would almost certainly regard the claims as "separate and distinct." Consequently, aggregation will not be allowed. [add Supplement answer]

Since the court does not have jurisdiction over either of the claims independently, P1 and P2 will not be able to consider the doctrine of supplemental jurisdiction as they could in the prior question. Supplemental jurisdiction requires an initial claim satisfying subject matter jurisdiction before additional claims or parties can be added.

VI. SUPPLEMENTAL (FORMERLY "ANCILLARY" AND "PENDENT") JURISDICTION

A. **Background:** Modern federal litigation typically involves more than just the basic two parties, and more than one claim. These additional claims and parties frequently present subject matter jurisdictional problems. For instance, if P brings a diversity suit against D, and D wants to "implead" X (i.e., D wants to hold X liable for any damages that D may have to pay to P; see *infra*, p. 343), what happens if D and X are citizens of the same state — is diversity ruined? Or, suppose that P sues D on an antitrust theory (clearly a federal question claim), and wants to add to the case a claim founded solely on state law (e.g., a claim for unfair competition) — may this state claim be added on to the federal case, even though there would be no federal subject matter jurisdiction if P brought just the state-law claim against D? We examine now the doctrine called *"supplemental jurisdiction,"* by which **additional claims and parties** may be brought in to a federal case without independently satisfying subject matter jurisdictional requirements, once there is a basic controversy as to which there *is* subject matter jurisdiction.

   1. **1990 amendments:** Congress completely codified this area of jurisdiction in 1990, as part of the Judicial Improvements Act of 1990. That Act added 28 U.S.C. §1367. Basically, §1367 establishes the doctrine of "supplemental jurisdiction," which is a reworking and combination of two older judge-made doctrines, "ancillary" jurisdiction and "pendent" jurisdiction.

B. **The traditional "pendent" and "ancillary" ideas:** Before we can understand the 1990 statute creating supplemental jurisdiction, we first need some sense of how courts before 1990 handled subject matter jurisdiction where new parties or new claims were sought to be added to a basic controversy that by itself satisfied federal subject matter jurisdictional requirements.

   1. **Pendent jurisdiction:** By the doctrine of *"pendent"* jurisdiction, if a federal court had jurisdiction over a *federal question claim* between two parties, it could sometimes adjudicate a *state-created claim* between those same parties, even though it would not have jurisdiction if the claim were brought separately.

      a. **Utility:** The pendent doctrine was useful in those situations where the parties were citizens of the same state, so that diversity did not exist. In such a situation, the plaintiff could gain a federal forum for her state-created claim by linking it to a federal question claim, provided that the two claims were sufficiently closely related to justify use of the pendent doctrine.

      Example: P and D are both citizens of New York. Both sell orange juice nationally. P sues D in federal court for violation of the federal trademark infringement statute, arguing that D's brand name infringes a trademark registered to P. P also believes that D's conduct violates a New York state "unfair competition" statute, in that the name of D's brand unfairly confuses New York consumers by making them think that it is P's product they are buying. There is clearly no independent federal subject matter jurisdiction for P's state-law unfair competition claim against D — there is no diversity, and there is no federal question. But by the doctrine of pendent jurisdiction, P can add the state-law claim to the federal claim, since both are closely related and stem from a "common nucleus of operative fact."

b. Must be similar: For the pendent doctrine to be applied, the Supreme Court has required fairly close *similarity* between the facts underlying the federal claim and those underlying the state-law claim. As the test was articulated in the leading case on the subject, the state and federal claims must *"derive from a common nucleus of operative fact,"* and must be so closely related that usually a plaintiff "would be expected to try them all in one judicial proceeding." *United Mine Workers v. Gibbs*, 383 U.S. 715 (1966). Initially, this meant that both must arise out of the *same event* or *transaction*. Thus in the above example, the reason pendent jurisdiction could be used is that a single act or series of acts by D — selling orange juice bearing a certain name and label — formed the basis for both the state-law claim and the federal-law one.

c. "Pendent party" jurisdiction: Suppose there was an *additional party* against whom the state-law claim was brought, but who was not a defendant to the federal-law claim. Under the doctrine of *"pendent party"* jurisdiction, this third party could be made to defend the state-law claim in federal court, even though she was not a defendant to any federal-law claim, and thus was not a defendant to any claim for which there was independent federal subject matter jurisdiction.

Example: Suppose that on the facts of the above example, P claimed that X, a retailer, orally told customers that the product that was in fact made by D was really made by P (a more prestigious and better-known producer). X is a New York citizen. P would like to be able to join X as a co-defendant to P's state-law unfair competition claim. But P has no federal trademark law claim against X. If the "pendent party" doctrine were applied, P could add X as a co-defendant to the state-law claim — X would be a "pendent party."

i. Restricted by case law: But the Supreme Court, in a series of decisions ending in 1989, made it very tough to use the pendent party doctrine. The Court held that only where Congress had *affirmatively* indicated that it wanted to allow new parties to be brought into pendent state claims may such additional parties be added without separate jurisdictional grounds. Even if the federal claim was of a type that could *only* be brought in federal court, this fact would not itself be enough to allow pendent parties to be brought in, with the result that two separate actions might be required. See *Finley v. U.S.*, 490 U.S. 545 (1989).

Example: P's husband and children are killed when their small plane hits power lines while approaching the San Diego airfield. P sues D1 (the U.S.) in federal court, under the Federal Tort Claims Act, for failing to provide adequate runway lights. (Claims against the U.S. under the FTCA can *only* be brought in federal court.) Then, P amends her complaint to include state-created tort claims against D2 and D3 (a city and a private company) who maintained the power lines. There is no diversity of citizenship between P and D2 and D3, and no federal-question claim against them. Therefore, the only way P can litigate her federal claim against the U.S. and her state-created claims against D2 and D3 in a single proceeding is if the court will allow D2 and D3 to be "pendent parties."

Held, D2 and D3 cannot be brought in as pendent parties. Unless Congress affirmatively states, for the particular federal statute in question (here, the FTCA) that new parties may be brought in to related pendent state claims, such pendent party jurisdiction will not be allowed. Since Congress has remained silent about whether additional parties to pendent state claims can be brought where jurisdiction is based on the FTCA, this silence means that P cannot bring in the additional defendants. *Finley v. U.S.*, *supra*.

ii. **Reversed by new statute:** One of the most important results of the new "supplemental jurisdiction" statute added in 1990 is that the result and logic of *Finley* are *reversed* — under the new statute, P would be permitted to bring D2 and D3 into the action. See *infra*, p. 116.

2. **Ancillary jurisdiction:** The second judge-made jurisdictional doctrine was *"ancillary"* jurisdiction. The line between "pendent" and "ancillary" jurisdictions was always somewhat blurry. But the basic use of ancillary jurisdiction was in cases where there was *diversity jurisdiction* for at least one claim between one plaintiff and one defendant, and *additional parties*, or additional *claims*, were sought to be joined to that "core" claim. Mostly, ancillary jurisdiction has been used to give the federal courts jurisdiction over certain types of claims made by *parties other than the plaintiff*, claims as to which there would not be independent federal subject matter jurisdiction because of either lack of diversity or failure to meet the amount in controversy.

Example 1: P, a citizen of Connecticut, brings suit against D1 and D2, both citizens of New York. The suit is based solely on diversity, and alleges that D1 and D2 simultaneously hit P, a pedestrian, while driving their cars. Since D1 sustained injuries of her own in the suit, D1 would like to make a claim against D2 as part of the basic federal court action brought by P. Federal Rule 13(g) allows one defendant to make a *"cross-claim"* against another defendant, if that cross-claim arises out of the "transaction or occurrence that is the subject matter ... of the original action. ..." So 13(g) authorizes D1's proposed claim against D2. But there is no diversity as between D1 and D2, so there would not be independent federal subject matter jurisdiction of D1's claim against D2. However, by the ancillary jurisdiction doctrine, D1's cross-claim against D2 is allowed to be added to the action already commenced by P, and the lack of diversity is disregarded.

Example 2: A car driven by Worker and owned by Employer hits Pedestrian. Pedestrian is a citizen of Pennsylvania; Worker and Employer are citizens of Ohio. Pedestrian starts a federal court diversity action in tort against Employer, under the doctrine of respondeat superior. Employer would like to be able to bring Worker into the action as a third-party defendant, arguing that if Employer is liable to Pedestrian, Worker must indemnify Employer for any damages which Employer is required to pay. (FRCP

14(a) allows a defendant to "implead" any non-party "who is or may be liable to the third-party plaintiff for all or part of the plaintiff's claim against the third-party plaintiff.") Since Worker and Employer are both citizens of Ohio, there is no diversity between them. Thus Employer could not bring suit against Worker as a stand-alone federal diversity action. But by the doctrine of ancillary jurisdiction — which has always been recognized for claims by a defendant against a third-party defendant — Employer may implead Worker despite the lack of diversity between them.

Note: Ancillary jurisdiction also eliminates the need to satisfy the *amount in controversy* requirement. For instance, suppose that on the facts of Example 1 above, D1's injuries amounted to only $12,000. D1 would not be able to sue D2 in a stand-alone federal action (even putting aside the lack-of-diversity problem), because D1's claim is for less than $50,000. But since ancillary jurisdiction applies to D1's cross claim against D2, her claim need not meet the amount in controversy requirement.

a. **Generally not allowed for plaintiffs:** The Supreme Court generally restricted the ancillary doctrine to claims asserted by litigants in a *defensive posture*, who would otherwise either lose forever their right to assert the claim (as in the case of a compulsory counterclaim) or be burdened by being required to start a whole new state court proceeding to litigate the right. Thus in the above two examples, it is in each instance a defendant who gets the benefit of ancillary jurisdiction. Conversely, the original plaintiff's right to use ancillary jurisdiction was cut back to almost nothing by the Supreme Court. For instance, a plaintiff has not been allowed to use ancillary jurisdiction to assert a claim against the *third-party defendant*, even if that third-party defendant has already been brought into the action by the ancillary doctrine. *Owen Equipment & Erection Co. v. Kroger*, 437 U.S. 365 (1978).

Example: P brings a wrongful death diversity action against D, a utility, for negligently maintaining a power line that electrocutes P's husband. P is a resident of Iowa, and D is a Nebraska corporation. D then makes a third-party claim against X, a contractor, alleging that X caused the accident by its negligence in operating a crane, and that X must therefore indemnify D against any judgment that P may obtain against D. X is an Iowa corporation. P now tries to make a claim against X, arguing that X is liable directly to P for X's negligence. Since P and X are citizens of the same state, P's claim may be heard by the court only if ancillary jurisdiction recognizes it.

Held (by the Supreme Court), ancillary jurisdiction may *not* be used to cover P's claim against X. If the ancillary jurisdiction doctrine were allowed in cases of a plaintiff's claim against a third-party defendant, "a plaintiff could defeat the statutory requirement of complete diversity by the simple expedient of suing only those defendants who were of diverse citizenship and waiting for them to implead non-diverse defendants." This is quite different from the situation where "a defending party [is] haled into court against his will," the kind of situation where the ancillary doctrine is allowed. *Owen Equipment & Erection Co. v. Kroger, supra*.

i. **Distinction maintained:** The 1990 codification of the pendent and ancillary doctrines *maintains* the plaintiff/defendant distinction drawn by *Owen Equipment*. It remains the case, for instance, that a diversity plaintiff may not use the ancillary doctrine against a third-party defendant, so that the result in *Owen* would be the same under the new statute. See *infra*, p. 117.

C. The new "supplemental" provision: 28 U.S.C. §1367, added in 1990, codifies the "ancillary" and "pendent" concepts, and combines them into a single notion of *"supplemental"* jurisdiction.

1. Provision generally: The core of §1367 comes in subsection (a), which says generally that "in any civil action of which the district courts have original jurisdiction, the district courts *shall have supplemental jurisdiction* over all other claims that are *so related* to claims in the action within such original jurisdiction that they form part of the same *case or controversy* under Article III of the United States Constitution. Such supplemental jurisdiction shall include claims that involve the joinder or intervention of additional parties."

a. Exceptions: This broad grant of jurisdiction is made subject to certain specific exceptions given in subsection (b) (which apply where the original action is based solely on diversity) and subject to the trial court's right, given in subsection (c), to decline to *exercise* the supplemental jurisdiction. But with these two exceptions, the grant of supplemental jurisdiction is a broad one — the federal district courts are given jurisdiction to add any claim (and any party to an additional claim) as long as that claim is so close to the original one as to be part of the same "case or controversy" as that term is used in Article III of the Constitution. The legislative history indicates that Congress was trying to codify the concept of *U.M.W. v. Gibbs*, *supra*, p. 113, whereby the two claims would be part of the same case or controversy if they "derive from a common nucleus of operative fact," i.e., derive from the same *transaction* or *occurrence*.

2. Federal question cases: Where the original claim comes within the court's *federal question* jurisdiction, §1367 basically codifies the prior judge-made *"pendent"* jurisdiction concept. Assuming that the state-law claim involves only the same parties as the federal-law claim, §1367 should produce exactly the same result as the pre-1990 pendent jurisdiction doctrine would have produced.

Example: Suppose P brings a federal-law trademark infringement claim against D, and seeks to add to its suit a state-law unfair competition claim against D. Since the state-law claim is closely related to the federal-law claim, the state-law claim would fall within the supplemental jurisdiction given by 28 U.S.C. §1367(a). Therefore, the fact that there would not be federal subject matter jurisdiction if P's only claim against D was the state-law claim becomes irrelevant.

a. "Pendent party" jurisdiction: In one very important respect, the jurisdiction given by §1367 is much *broader* than that developed by case law prior to §1367's enactment. Remember that in the *Finley* case, *supra*, p. 113, the Supreme Court held that the *"pendent party"* doctrine would be severely restricted — additional parties to the state-law claim could only be brought in if Congress affirmatively indicated that it wanted those parties brought in. But §1367 contains no such limit — the last sentence of §1367(a) states that "such supplemental jurisdiction shall include claims that involve the *joinder* or intervention of **additional parties**." The legislative history indicates that this sentence was expressly designed to overturn the result of *Finley*.

Example: Consider the facts of *Finley* itself, *supra*, p. 113. P first sues D1 (the U.S.), under the Federal Torts Claims Act. Then, P adds a state-law claim against D2 and D3 (a city and a private company) arising out of the same transaction (inadequately maintained runway lights that led to a plane crash). There is no federal claim against D2 and D3, and there is no diversity of citizenship between P and D2/D3. But because P's state-law claim against D2 and D3 arises from the same chain of events as P's federal claim against D1 — all relate to the plane crash and the reasons for it — P is now permitted to bring in D2 and D3 under the supplemental jurisdiction concept and the last sentence of §1367(a). Under the *Finley* decision, by contrast, D2 and D3, as "pendent parties," were not permitted to be brought in, because Congress, in enacting the FTCA, had not expressly provided that additional parties could be brought in on related state-law claims.

3. **Diversity exclusions:** Where the "core" claim — the claim as to which there is independent federal subject matter jurisdiction — is based solely on *diversity*, §1367's grant of supplemental jurisdiction is a bit less generous. This situation corresponds to the pre-§1367 concept of "ancillary" jurisdiction. §1367 generally allows claims that would have been ancillary to fall within the Court's supplemental jurisdiction in diversity-only cases, and thus eliminates the requirement of diversity and amount-in-controversy as to the supplemental claim. But §1367(b) sets forth some explicit and important **limits** on supplemental jurisdiction:

> (b) in any civil action of which the district courts have original jurisdiction founded solely on section 1332 of this Title [the diversity grant], the district courts shall not have supplemental jurisdiction ... over claims **by plaintiffs** against persons made parties under Rule 14, 19, 20, or 24 of the Federal Rules of Civil Procedure, or over claims by persons proposed to be joined as plaintiffs under Rule 19 of such Rules or seeking to intervene as plaintiffs under Rule 24 of such Rules, when exercising supplemental jurisdiction over such claims would be inconsistent with the jurisdictional requirements of section 1332.

a. **Theory of exclusions:** This section basically applies the same limits as pre-§1367 Supreme Court cases did, especially *Owen Equipment v. Kroger, supra*, p. 115. That is, where the core claim is founded solely on diversity, additional claims asserted by *defendants* are within the Court's supplemental jurisdiction, but additional claims (or the addition of new parties) by *plaintiffs* are severely **restricted**. The legislative history explains the reason for this limit as follows: "In diversity-only actions the district courts may not hear plaintiffs' supplemental claims when exercising supplemental jurisdiction would encourage plaintiffs to evade the jurisdictional requirement of 28 U.S.C. §1332 by the simple expedient of naming initially only those defendants whose joinder satisfies section 1332's requirements and later adding claims not within original federal jurisdiction against other defendants who have intervened or been joined on a supplemental basis." House Report to Judicial Improvements Act of 1990, p. 29.

b. **Excluded claims and parties:** Here are the claims that, according to §1367(b), should *not* get the benefit of supplemental jurisdiction in cases where the core claim is founded solely on diversity:

i. **Claims against third-party defendants:** Claims made by a plaintiff against a *third-party defendant*, pursuant to Rule 14(a), are excluded from supplemental jurisdiction.

Example: Review the facts of *Owens Equipment v. Kroger, supra.* Recall that P sued D, and D brought a third-party claim against X, asserting that if D was liable to P, X was liable to D. P and X were citizens of the same state. Section 1367(b) follows the approach of *Owens Equipment*: P does not get supplemental jurisdiction for her claim against X. Since that claim is not supported by diversity, P cannot sue X in federal court at all, and must bring a separate state-court action against X. (But D's claim against X, and any claim X might have against P arising out of the same transaction or occurrence, *do* get the benefits of supplemental jurisdiction.)

ii. **Compulsory joinder:** Rule 19(a) allows the joinder of "persons to be *joined if feasible*." Neither a claim *against* such a person, nor a claim *by* that person, comes within the supplemental jurisdiction in a diversity-only case.

Example 1: Certain stock in D Corp. is shown, on the records of D, as belonging jointly to P and to X. P and X are both Arizona residents. D is a citizen of California. P brings an action against D to compel D to issue stock certificates showing P as the sole owner. P's action is founded solely on diversity of citizenship (i.e., it involves no federal question). D asserts that X is a necessary party, who must be joined if feasible under Rule 19. But §1367(b) says that X's joinder under Rule 19 does not fall within the court's supplemental jurisdiction. Since the claim by P against X does not independently meet federal subject matter jurisdictional requirements (both P and X are citizens of the same state), X cannot be joined. The court must decide whether the entire action should be dismissed because of X's absence, or whether the action can be permitted to go forward without X. (The factors that the court should consider in deciding which of these two courses to follow are set out in 19(b).)

Example 2: Same facts as prior example. Now, however, assume that X is a citizen of California, not Arizona. Suppose that D wants X brought into the action as, in effect, a co-plaintiff, on the theory that otherwise D may be left with inconsistent obligations (ordered in the present action to convey the stock to P, and ordered in a subsequent suit brought by X to convey the stock to X). Rule 19(a) allows the absent person to be brought in as an "involuntary plaintiff." Apparently, there is *not* supplemental jurisdiction for X's "involuntary" claim against D, because §1367(b) denies supplemental jurisdiction for "claims by persons proposed to be joined as plaintiffs under Rule 19. ..." (But in this situation, D could probably use statutory interpleader instead, which requires only diversity between some two claimants. See *infra*, p. 338.)

iii. **Rule 20 joinder:** Supplemental jurisdiction also does not apply in diversity-only cases for claims by plaintiffs against parties *"permissively" joined* pursuant to Rule 20. (Rule 20 allows multiple people to be joined as defendants if "there is asserted against them jointly, severally, or in the alternative, any right to relief in respect of or arising out of the same transaction, occurrence, or series of transactions or occurrences and if any question of law or fact common to all defendants will arise in the action.")

Example: P, a pedestrian, is hit by a car driven by D1. As P is lying on the sidewalk, D2, a doctor, negligently gives him first aid, slightly worsening his condition. P is a citizen of New York; D1 is a citizen of Connecticut and D2 is a citizen of New Jersey. P brings a diversity action against D1, and then joins D2 as a second defendant, pursuant to Rule 20's "permissive joinder" provision. P's claim against D1 is for $200,000. P's claim against D2 is for $20,000 (reflecting the fact that D2 only slightly worsened P's condition). P's claim against D2 does *not* fall within the court's supplemental jurisdiction, because §1367(b) bars diversity-only claims "by plaintiffs against persons made parties under Rule ... 20." Therefore, P's claim against D2 must be dropped, because it does not meet the $50,000 amount in controversy requirement. (Remember that supplemental jurisdiction, where it applies, overcomes lack of amount in controversy as well as lack of diversity.)

iv. **Claims by Rule 20 plaintiffs not excluded:** But what about the situation where an outsider comes into the action as a Rule 20 permissive co-*plaintiff*, rather than co-defendant? Here, §1367(b) does *not* bar supplemental jurisdiction. This may have been the result simply of sloppy drafting of the statute.

Example: P1 and P2 are each women who have been seriously injured by an IUD manufactured by D. P1 is a citizen of Indiana, P2 of Illinois and D of Illinois. P1 brings a diversity-only suit against D. After the suit is filed, P1 seeks the court's permission to add P2 as a co-plaintiff pursuant to the permissive joinder provisions of Rule 20. (Rule 20(a) allows joinder by co-plaintiffs "if they assert any right to relief ... in respect of or arising out of the same transaction, occurrence, or series of transactions or occurrences and if any question of law or fact common to all these persons will arise in the action." This test is probably satisfied, since the sale of the same type of device to both women was probably the "same ... series of transactions," and the defectiveness of the product would be a common question of fact.)

Section 1367(b) seems not to prohibit the use of supplemental jurisdiction for P2's claim against D — claims by a plaintiff against persons joined *as defendants* under Rule 20 are excluded (see above example), and claims by persons proposed to be joined as plaintiffs under *Rule 19* are excluded, but claims by persons proposed to be joined as plaintiffs under Rule 20 are not mentioned at all. So P2 can probably sue D even though they are both citizens of Illinois. (But the court can always decline to exercise its supplemental jurisdiction for any of the reasons listed in §1367(c); here, the court might rely on §1367(c)(4), by which "in exceptional circumstances, there are other compelling reasons for declining jurisdiction.")

v. **Intervention:** Claims by prospective plaintiffs who try to *intervene* under Rule 24 do *not* get the benefit of supplemental jurisdiction.

Example: Consider the facts of the prior example. Suppose that, after P1 sued D, P2, on her own motion (and without any support from either P1 or D) moved for *permissive intervention* under Rule 24(b) (allowable "when an applicant's claim or defense and the main action have a question of law or fact in common"). Section 1367(b) says that in diversity-only situations, there is no supplemental jurisdiction over "claims by persons ... seeking to intervene as plaintiffs under Rule 24. ..." Since P2 and D are citizens of the same state, the absence of supplemental jurisdiction means that P2's claim cannot be heard. The same result would occur even if P2's claim was so closely related to the main action that P2 would otherwise be entitled to *"intervention of right"* under Rule 24(a). (Denial of supplemental jurisdiction to a Rule 24(a) intervenor of right changes prior case law.)

c. **Claims still allowed:** Despite the above examples, there remain a number of diversity-only situations in which supplemental jurisdiction *does* apply. In general, these are situations in which ancillary jurisdiction would have been allowed before 1990, and in which the beneficiary of the supplemental jurisdiction is a party in a defensive posture. These situations appear to include:

i. **Compulsory counterclaims:** Rule 13(a) *compulsory counterclaims*;

ii. **Additional parties to compulsory counterclaims:** Rule 13(h) joinder of *additional parties to compulsory counterclaims*;

iii. **Cross-claims:** Rule 13(g) *cross-claims* (i.e., claims by one defendant against another);

iv. **Impleader:** Rule 14 *impleader* of third-party defendants (for claims by and against third-party plaintiffs, and claims by third-party defendants, but not claims by the original plaintiff against third-party defendants). Here are some examples of situations where supplemental jurisdiction will apply:

Example 1: P, a citizen of New York, brings a diversity-only suit against D, a citizen of New Jersey. The claim is for $60,000. D may bring a Rule 13(a) compulsory counterclaim (i.e., a counterclaim arising out of the same transaction or occurrence) against P for $10,000 — supplemental jurisdiction applies, so D's claim does not independently have to meet the amount in controversy requirement.

Example 2: Same facts as above. Now, assume that D's counterclaim alleges that in the same episode that P is suing on, D was injured not only by P but also by Y. Y is a New Jersey citizen. D may bring Y in as a Rule 13(h) additional defendant to D's compulsory counterclaim against P, because supplemental jurisdiction applies and obviates the need for diversity as between D and Y.

Example 3: P, a citizen of California, sues D, a retailer located in Arizona, claiming that a product sold to P by D was defective and injured P. The suit is solely on diversity, and meets the amount in controversy requirement. D then brings a Rule 14 impleader claim against X, the manufacturer of the item, contending that if D owes damages to P, X must indemnify D. X is a citizen of Arizona. D's suit against X is within the court's supplemental jurisdiction, so the lack of diversity as between D and X makes no difference.

Example 4: Same facts as Example 3. Now, assume that once X is brought into the action under Rule 14, X asserts against P the claim that P slandered X by falsely and publicly stating that X's product was dangerously defective. X's claim is for $30,000. This claim is within the court's supplemental jurisdiction, so the fact that it does not satisfy the amount in controversy is irrelevant. (But any claim by P against X would *not* be within the court's supplemental jurisdiction — see *supra*, p. 118, and the discussion of *Owen Equipment Co. v. Kroger, supra*, p. 115.)

4. **Discretionary rejection of supplemental jurisdiction:** So far, we have examined when a claim is or is not covered by the court's supplemental jurisdiction. But merely because a claim is within the court's supplemental jurisdiction does not mean that the court *must* hear that claim. Section 1367(c) provides four reasons for which a court "may *decline to exercise* supplemental jurisdiction" that exists:

> (1) The claim raises a novel or complex issue of State law,

> (2) The claim substantially predominates over the claim or claims over which [the district court] has original jurisdiction, or

> (3) The district court has dismissed all claims over which it has original jurisdiction,

> (4) In exceptional circumstances, there are other compelling reasons for declining jurisdiction.

   a. **Dismissal of other claims:** The most important of these reasons for "abstention" is probably (3), "the district court has dismissed all claims over which it has original jurisdiction." One especially important factor is likely to be the *time* — in terms of the suit's progress — at which the original claim is dismissed. The later dismissal occurs, the less likely the court is to exercise its discretion to decline to hear the remaining, supplemental, claim.

   Example: Consider the facts of *Finley, supra*, p. 113 — P sues D1 (the U.S.) in federal court, under the Federal Tort Claims Act, for failing to provide adequate runway lights, and thus causing P's husband's death in a plane crash. Then, P amends her complaint to include state-law negligence claims against D2 and D3 (a city and a private company) whose negligence she alleges to have contributed to the accident. P is a citizen of the same state as D2 and D3, and there is no federal question claim against those two defendants. If, before the case has gone to trial and in fact before there has been very much discovery, the court grants a 12(b)(6) dismissal of the claim against D1, the court will probably exercise its discretion to decline to hear the claims against D2 and D3. But if the claim against D1 is only dismissed after discovery and after P has put on her case at trial (i.e., the dismissal is made pursuant to a Rule 50 motion for "judgment as a matter of law"), then the court will probably hear the remainder of the case against D2 and D3 anyway — here, considerations of judicial economy, and fairness to P, probably dictate that she be allowed to continue with her state-law claims rather than having to litigate them from scratch in state court.

5. **No effect on personal jurisdiction:** The application of the supplemental jurisdiction doctrine does *not* eliminate the requirement of *jurisdiction over the parties*, nor does it

eliminate the requirements of service of process. It speaks solely to the question of *subject matter jurisdiction*.

    a. Used with 100-mile bulge: Much of the time, the supplemental jurisdiction doctrine is applied in the kinds of multiparty cases in which, according to Rule 4(k)(1)(B), service in the *100-mile bulge* area may be used. (See *supra*, p. 41.)

6. Venue not required: At least under case law decided before the codification of §1367, courts held that where "ancillary" jurisdiction (one of the precursors to supplemental jurisdiction) applied, *venue* requirements did not have to be satisfied with respect to each party. Wr., p. 32. Presumably the same theory will apply in cases involving supplemental jurisdiction under §1367. In any event, the 1990 changes to the venue provisions (see *supra*, p. 83) mean that venue will rarely be a problem in any district that is in a state as to which personal jurisdiction over the supplementally-joined party is available.

> **Example:** P is a resident of the Northern District of Illinois. D is a resident of the Southern District of New York. X is a resident of the District of Rhode Island. P brings a federal court diversity-only action against D in the Southern District of New York. The events involved in the suit did not occur in New York. D impleads X, using the New York state long arm to do so (as allowed by Rule 4(k)(1)(A)). Since D's claim against X comes within the court's supplemental jurisdiction, probably we don't have to worry about whether X satisfies the requirements of venue. In any event, X's presence *does* satisfy the 1991 liberalized venue requirements, since, in diversity cases, venue is allowed in any judicial district "in which the defendants are subject to personal jurisdiction at the time the action is commenced," and by our facts, both D and X were subject to personal jurisdiction there, in part due to the New York long arm.

Quiz Yourself on
SUPPLEMENTAL JURISDICTION

24. P and D are competing furniture stores. Each is operated in the form of a corporation headquartered in Georgia (and incorporated in Georgia); both stores serve the same small town. P has sued D in federal district court for the Middle District of Georgia. P makes two claims: (1) that certain advertising and marketing practices engaged in by D are a violation of the federal antitrust statutes; and (2) that those same practices are a violation of a Georgia statute prohibiting "unfair competition." Each claim involves more than $100,000. D moves to dismiss claim (2) on the grounds that federal subject matter jurisdiction is lacking over it.

    (a) What doctrine determines the validity of D's motion? _____

    (b) Should D's motion be granted? _____

25. Paula, a pedestrian, was seriously injured when a mail truck owned by the U.S. and driven by Dexter (a post office employee), hit her while she was crossing the street. Paula reasonably believed that both the U.S. and Dexter may be liable to her. Applicable statutes and court decisions interpreting those statutes indicate that a suit against the U.S. under the Federal Tort Claims Act may only be brought in federal court. Therefore, Paula sued both the U.S. and Dexter in federal district court for Nevada. Both Paula and Dexter are citizens of Nevada. Paula's claim is for more than $200,000 against each of the defendants. Paula's claim against the U.S. is based on the Federal Tort Claims Act; her claim against Dexter is based on a state-law theory of negligence. Dexter has moved to have the claim against him dismissed for lack of subject matter jurisdiction. Should Dexter's motion be granted?

26. P and D were both injured (P more seriously than D) when a car driven by P collided with a car driven by D. P is a citizen of Oklahoma; D is a citizen of Kansas. P has sued D in federal district court for the District of Kansas, asserting a claim whose amount in controversy is $100,000. D, who sustained only a few scratches and some damage to his car, has counterclaimed against P for $12,000. P moves to dismiss D's claim for lack of subject matter jurisdiction.

   (a) What doctrine determines whether D's claim should be dismissed? _____

   (b) Should P's motion be granted? _____

27. Same facts as prior question. Now, however, assume that there was a third car involved in the collision, driven by Xavier, a citizen of Kansas. P has not filed suit against Xavier, only against D. But D has concluded that both P and Xavier were at fault and were responsible for his injuries. Therefore, he has joined Xavier as an additional party (defendant) to the counterclaim which he is making against P; he seeks $12,000 against each of P and Xavier. If Xavier moves to dismiss the claim against him for lack of federal subject matter jurisdiction, should the court grant his motion? _____

28. P is a citizen of Washington. D is a citizen of Oregon. P has sued D for negligence, arising out of an auto accident in which a car driven by D collided with a car driven by P. The amount at stake for P is $100,000. This suit has been brought in federal court for the District of Oregon. D has taken advantage of the pending suit to file a counterclaim against P for breach of a contract which the two had signed several years ago (before the auto accident). D has added Wanda as a defendant to this counterclaim, on the grounds that Wanda induced P to breach the contract with D. Wanda is a citizen of Oregon. D's counterclaim plausibly seeks $200,000 in damages from each of P and Wanda. Wanda moves to dismiss D's claim against her on the grounds that the court lacks subject matter jurisdiction over it. Should the court grant Wanda's motion? _____

29. Pedro, a pedestrian, was hit and injured in New Jersey by a car owned by Denise, and driven by her employee, Ted. Pedro (a citizen of New York) has sued Denise (a citizen of New Jersey) in federal district court for the Southern District of New York; his claim is for $100,000. Ted is a Pennsylvania resident, but Pedro has not bothered joining him (because he believes Ted is judgment-proof.) Pedro began the action by serving Denise pursuant to the New York long-arm. Denise (knowing, as Pedro does not, that Ted has a small nest egg) has brought a third-party claim against Ted, in which she asserts that if she is forced to pay anything to Pedro, Ted owes that amount to her. Denise has served Ted, claiming authority of the New York long-arm. Ted has no connection with New York, but Denise has substantial connections with New York. Ted now moves to dismiss, on the grounds that the New York federal court has no personal jurisdiction over him. Should Ted's motion be granted? _____

30. Patricia, a citizen of New York, ate dinner one night at a restaurant operated in New York by David, a citizen of Connecticut. For dessert, Patricia had an apple pie bought by David from Terry, a New York citizen who is in the business of baking and selling pies to restaurants. Patricia became violently ill shortly thereafter, and tests indicated that the pie contained botulism. After months of hospitalization, Patricia commenced a product liability action in New York federal district court against David. Her claim is for $100,000.

David then impleaded Terry as a third-party defendant pursuant to Federal Rule 14, asserting that if he is liable to Patricia, Terry is liable to him. (This represents a correct statement by David of the applicable substantive rule in a product liability action brought against a restauranteur who makes a claim over against his supplier.)

Patricia then made a product liability claim against Terry for $100,000, as allowed by Federal Rule 14. Terry now moves to dismiss Patricia's claim against her for lack of subject matter jurisdiction. Should Terry's motion be granted? _____

Answers

24. (a) Supplemental Jurisdiction.

(b) No, probably. This fact pattern is a classic illustration of what was formerly known as pendent jurisdiction, and is now covered under the doctrine of *supplemental* jurisdiction. Supplemental jurisdiction, codified in 28 U.S.C. §1367, provides that in cases where "the district courts have original jurisdiction [over a federal question], the district court shall have supplemental jurisdiction over all other claims that are so related to claims in the action within such original jurisdiction that they form part of the same case or controversy under Article III. ..." Supplemental jurisdiction applies to additional claims between the same two parties, as well as to "pendent parties" (third parties brought into the suit who are under the federal court's jurisdiction), provided that both claims derive from a *common nucleus of operative fact* (a requirement implied by the statute's reference to "Article III case or controversy").

Here, the federal court would not ordinarily have jurisdiction over the state unfair competition claim, because that claim apparently does not present a federal question, and there is no diversity between the parties (since both are citizens of Georgia). But since the antitrust claim presents a federal question, and since the practices that are being relied on by D to support that federal claim are the same as the practices that are alleged to violate the state statute, both claims derive from a "common nucleus of operative fact," and P would ordinarily be expected to try them all in one suit. The federal court would still be free to use its *discretion* under §1367(c) to decline to hear the state-law claim, but on these facts it probably would hear the claim (since considerations of judicial economy and convenience militate in favor of hearing both claims).

25. No. Paula's second claim falls within the supplemental jurisdiction of the court, as it involves a "common nucleus of operative fact" and Paula would normally try them both in the same proceeding. See 28 U.S.C. §1367. Before December 1990 (and the enactment of §1367), the Supreme Court's decision in Finley v. U.S., 490 U.S. 545 (1989) meant that the doctrine of pendent jurisdiction did not offer Paula the right to bring in "pendent parties" unless Congress had expressly stated in the applicable statute (here the FTCA) that it would allow pendent parties.

However, when Congress in 1990 codified the doctrines of pendent and ancillary jurisdiction, one of the most important changes made was to specifically overrule *Finley* and *allow "pendent parties"* in federal question cases, as indicated by the last sentence of §1367(a) — "Such supplemental jurisdiction shall include claims that involve the joinder or intervention of additional parties."

26. (a) Supplemental jurisdiction. Where the plaintiff has a valid diversity claim against the defendant, the doctrine of *supplemental jurisdiction* often allows additional claims or parties to be brought into the litigation, even though the additional claim or party does not satisfy the requirement of diversity or the amount in controversy requirement ($50,000) applied in diversity actions.

(b) No. Supplemental jurisdiction (formerly known as ancillary jurisdiction in this context) will always encompass a defendant's compulsory counterclaim. According to Federal Rule 13(a), a counterclaim is compulsory "if it arises out of the transaction or occurrence that is the subject matter of the opposing party's claim and does not require for its adjudication the presence of third parties of whom the court cannot acquire jurisdiction." By this test, D's counterclaim against P was a compulsory one, since both claims arose out of the same auto accident. Accordingly, the court will hear the counterclaim as part of its supplemental jurisdiction, even though that counterclaim does not independently meet the amount in controversy requirement for diversity suits.

27. **No.** Just as the federal courts virtually always allow supplemental jurisdiction over a compulsory counterclaim, so they also allow supplemental jurisdiction over an additional party to a compulsory counterclaim. Consequently, the fact that Xavier is a citizen of the same state as D (thus technically preventing complete diversity from existing) will be disregarded by the court. Although 28 U.S.C. §1367(b) does restrict certain types of joinder when the original claim is based on diversity, these restrictions do not apply to claims by defendants, nor do they apply to Rule 13 counterclaims.

28. **Yes.** D's claim against P is a *permissive* counterclaim (Rule 13(b)), since it does not arise out of the transaction or occurrence that is the subject matter of the plaintiff's claim. Because this permissive counterclaim and the original claim do not derive from a common nucleus of operative fact, the counterclaim does not satisfy the standard of 28 U.S.C. §1367, and it will ***not*** fall under a court's supplemental jurisdiction. For the same reason, D's claim against Wanda does not fall under supplemental jurisdiction. Therefore, D's claim must independently meet the federal subject matter jurisdictional requirements — that is, there must be either diversity or a federal question, and any applicable amount in controversy requirement must be satisfied. Since there is no federal question, and since D and Wanda are citizens of the same state (Oregon), the federal subject matter jurisdictional requirements are not satisfied, and Wanda is entitled to dismissal.

29. **Yes.** A Rule 14 third-party claim brought by a third-party plaintiff (the defendant in the main action) against a third-party defendant is always considered to be within the supplemental jurisdiction of the court. 28 U.S.C. §1367. However, the fact that supplemental jurisdiction will encompass the third-party claim against Ted under §1367 does not mean that the requirements of *personal* jurisdiction don't have to be satisfied as to Ted. For the third-party claim against Ted to be heard by the New York federal court, it must still be the case that Ted has minimum contacts with New York, which the facts say he does not.

30. **Yes.** Terry is a third-party defendant. A claim by the original plaintiff against the third-party defendant does not fall within the court's supplemental jurisdiction, so it must have independent jurisdictional grounds. Although there is now a federal statute, 28 U.S.C. §1367, codifying what was once called "ancillary jurisdiction," §1367(b) still excludes certain claims made ***by plaintiffs*** when the original claim is based on diversity. By specifically precluding claims by plaintiffs against persons made parties under Rule 14, §1367(b) preserves the result of *Owen Equipment & Erection Co. v. Kroger*, 437 U.S. 365 (1978), and thus excludes Patricia's claims against Terry. In the absence of a federal question and in the absence of supplemental jurisdiction, Patricia and Terry must be citizens of different states, which they are not. Consequently, the court has no jurisdiction over Patricia's claim against Terry, and it must be dismissed.

Observe that there is a good rationale for denying supplemental treatment to Patricia's claim against Terry: Patricia would not have been able to institute an initial suit against both David and Terry, because of the lack of diversity between Patricia and Terry; it seems improper to allow Patricia to do indirectly (by dropping Terry from the initial suit, waiting for David to implead Terry as he will surely do, then making a third-party claim against Terry) what she may not do directly.

VII. REMOVAL OF CASES TO THE FEDERAL COURTS

A. **General right to remove:** Generally, any action brought in *state court* of which the federal courts *would have had original jurisdiction* may be *removed* by the defendant to federal district court.

1. **Limitation:** The most important limitation on this is that in *diversity* cases, the action is removable *only if no defendant is a citizen of the state in which the action was brought.* (28 U.S.C. §1441(b))

B. **Removal statute:** The right of removal is statutory, and is not mentioned in the Constitution. Wr., 209. The basic removal statute is 28 U.S.C. §1441. That statute provides in brief:

1. **Where suit goes:** When a case is removed, it passes *"to the district court of the United States for the district and division embracing the place where [the state] action is pending."* Only cases which could *originally have been brought in the federal courts* may be removed. §1441(a).

2. **Federal question cases:** In *federal question* cases (of which by hypothesis the federal courts would have had original jurisdiction), the case may be removed by defendant(s) *regardless of citizenship or residence* of the parties. (§1441(b)).

3. **Diversity:** In *diversity* cases, the action may be removed only if no properly joined and served defendant is a *citizen of the state in which the action is pending.* (§1441(b)). Wr., 214.

4. **Illustrations:** Following are some examples of the practical operation of the removal statute.

   Example 1: P, a Massachusetts citizen, sues D, a Connecticut citizen, in Massachusetts state court. The only basis for jurisdiction is diversity. D may remove (to the Massachusetts Federal District Court), because he is not a citizen of the state where the action was brought.

   Example 2: Same facts as above, except that P's suit is brought in *Connecticut* state court. D may not remove, because he is a citizen of the state where the action is pending.

   Example 3: Same facts as Example 2, except that the suit is for federal trademark infringement. D may remove, even though he is a citizen of the state where the action is pending, because the citizenship of the defendant is irrelevant in cases where a federal question is present.

5. **Removal of multiple claims:** Whenever a *"separate and independent claim* or cause of action, within the [court's federal question] jurisdiction ..., is joined with one or more otherwise non-removable claims, the *entire case* may be removed and the district court may determine all issues therein. ..." (§1441(c)).

C. **Diversity and amount rules applicable:** Since removability is based on the existence of original federal jurisdiction, the usual principles governing the existence of a federal question or of diversity, and those governing the jurisdictional amount, apply. (E.g., diversity must be "complete" except in certain specified kinds of cases, such as interpleader.) Wr., 210.

1. **Anomaly:** Using the same test for original and removal jurisdiction produces the strange result that in a case where there is no diversity, "a defendant can remove a case where the plaintiff relies on federal law for his claim, though the plaintiff is perfectly willing to entrust his federal claim to a state court, but neither party can take the case to federal court where the defendant sets up federal law as a defense to a non-federal claim by plaintiff." Wr., 210.

> **Example:** In the *Louisville & Nashville v. Mottley* situation (*supra*, p. 95), the railroad could not have removed from state court even though its answer was based on a federal question claim.

D. **Removal not allowed by plaintiff:** Only a *defendant*, not a plaintiff defending a counter-claim, may remove.

1. *Shamrock* **case:** Thus where a plaintiff brought a state court suit (which happened to be for more than the federal jurisdictional amount, and against a defendant as to whom there would have been diversity), and then tried to remove when confronted by a counterclaim, the removal was not allowed. *Shamrock Oil & Gas Corp. v. Sheets*, 313 U.S. 100 (1941).

E. **Certain kinds of cases not removable:** Removal is not allowed in certain kinds of cases, even though original federal jurisdiction would have existed. This limitation reflects Congress' desire to give certain kinds of plaintiffs an *absolute choice of forum*, which cannot be frustrated by defendant's removal.

1. **Examples:** Two important examples of non-removable actions are suits under the *FELA Act* (personal injury suits against railroads) and suits under state workers' compensation laws. See 28 U.S.C. §1445. Wr., 214.

F. **Original state court jurisdiction required:** The federal courts may exercise removal jurisdiction *only if the state court in which the action was originally pending had jurisdiction.*

1. **Absurd results:** "The results to which [this doctrine] leads are often absurd. Thus a suit is brought in state court, and removed to federal court. If it is determined that the case was one over which the federal courts have exclusive jurisdiction, the federal court, remarkably enough, cannot hear the case. *It must dismiss a case falling within its exclusive jurisdiction because the court from which the case was removed had no jurisdiction.*" Wr., 212.

G. **Pleadings not pierced:** The right of removal is generally decided *from the face of the pleadings*. The jurisdictional allegations of *plaintiff's complaint* control.

1. **As of when evaluated:** The jurisdictional allegations are viewed *as of the time the notice of removal is filed.*

> **Example:** A sues B to recover accrued installments on an installment contract. The action may not be removed if the amount due on the date of removal did not satisfy the jurisdictional amount requirements, even though additional installments that have accrued *after* removal make the amount sufficient. Wr., 188.

   a. **Change in status:** A case not removable when commenced may sometimes later become removable. For instance, if plaintiff has *amended his complaint* to change the nature of his cause of action, so as to make it a federal question, or if he has dropped a party whose presence prevented diversity, the case may then be removed. Plaintiff cannot, however, take action to *defeat* federal jurisdiction after the case has been properly removed. Wr., 215.

    b. Exception for diversity cases: *Diversity cases present an exception to the rule that removability is determined as of the time when the notice of removal is filed.* In diversity cases, diversity must exist *at the time of filing the original action,* as well as at the time of notice of removal (unless plaintiff has dropped a party who had destroyed diversity).

        i. Rationale: The purpose of this limitation is to prevent the defendant from acquiring a new domicile after commencement of the suit, and then removing on the basis of diversity. But as noted above, if plaintiff drops a non-diverse party, and diversity exists with respect to the remaining parties, the action may be removed. Wr., 217.

  2. Plaintiff controls his claim: Plaintiff is master of his claim; if he chooses not to assert a federal claim, even though one is available to him, the defendant may not remove. Wr., 216.

H. Removal of multiple claims: Suppose P asserts against D in state court two claims, one of which could be removed if sued upon alone, and the other of which could not be removed if sued upon alone. May the entire case be removed by D?

  1. Old law: Before 1990, the answer was frequently "yes." The most interesting situation was one in which the "federal" claim was one based solely on diversity, and plaintiff added to it a "separate and independent" claim for which there was not diversity. Because old 28 U.S.C. §1441(c) allowed the entire case to be removed if a "separate and independent claim … which would be removable if sued upon alone, is joined with one or more otherwise non-removable claims or causes of action …," the entire case could be heard in federal court.

    Example: P is a citizen of Kentucky. D1 is a citizen of Ohio. P brings a contract claim against D1 in Michigan state court. P joins (under the liberal joinder rules of Michigan) an unrelated tort claim that P has against D1 and D2; D2 is a Kentucky citizen. Old 28 U.S.C. §1441(c) would probably have treated the contract claim as being "separate and independent" from the tort law claim. Therefore, §1441(c) could be used to allow D1 and D2 to remove the *entire case* to federal district court for Michigan, even though there was not complete diversity (or any other basis for federal subject matter jurisdiction) on the tort law claim.

  2. Present law: But §1441(c) was dramatically rewritten by Congress in 1990, in a way that removes most or all of its usefulness. Section 1441(c) now provides that "whenever a separate and independent claim or cause of action within the [federal question] jurisdiction … is joined with one or more otherwise non-removable claims or causes of action, the entire case may be removed and the district court may determine all issues therein, or, in its discretion, may remand all matters in which State law predominates."

    a. Not available in diversity cases: The most important aspect of the rewrite of §1441(c) is that it *no longer applies at all to diversity cases*. Therefore, on the facts of the above example, D1 and D2 would not be able to remove, and the whole case would remain in state court. This means that even if the sole reason P added the tort claim against D1 and D2 was to prevent D1 from removing the contract claim (as to which there was diversity), D1 would nonetheless be stuck in state court. (Congress seems to have acted in part out of a dislike of diversity generally, and thus out of a desire to cut it down where possible.)

i. **Tactic for plaintiff:** The unavailability of §1441(c) in diversity cases means that a plaintiff who wants to defeat diversity has a potent weapon: as long as some additional claim can be found that will bring in a non-diverse party, and the joinder rules of the state are liberal enough to allow that claim to be joined, the plaintiff can defeat diversity.

b. **Federal question cases:** Section 1441(c) does apply to allow removal of the entire controversy where one of the "separate and independent" claims is based on *federal question* jurisdiction.

Example: P and D1 are both citizens of Kentucky. P brings an action in Kentucky state court asserting that D1 has violated the federal antitrust laws. P adds to that claim a claim against both D1 and D2 (D2 is a citizen of Kentucky) asserting that D1 and D2 have acted in a way that violates Kentucky unfair competition laws. There is, of course, no independent federal jurisdiction over P's state-law claim against D1 and D2. But §1441(c) will allow D1 and D2 to remove to federal court anyway, assuming that the judge concludes that the antitrust claim is "separate and independent" from the state unfair competition claim.

i. **Probably unnecessary:** However, §1441(c) is probably *unnecessary* in most of the very federal-question situations where it is usable. It will almost always be the case that the court's §1367 "supplemental" jurisdiction (of the sort that, before 1990, was referred to as "pendent" jurisdiction) will apply; if so, §1441(c) does not need to be used at all.

Example: Consider the facts of the prior example. If P brought both of his claims (antitrust and state unfair competition) in a federal action, the court would almost certainly conclude that the state claim fell within the supplemental ("pendent" under the old language) jurisdiction of the federal court. See *supra*, p. 112. Therefore, §1441(*a*) will be all that is needed for removal, since that section says that "any civil action ... of which the district courts of the United States have original jurisdiction, may be removed. ..."

ii. **Completely unrelated claims:** Of course, if the state-law claim was *completely unrelated* to the federal-question claim, then there would not be supplemental/ pendent jurisdiction, and §1441(c) might seem to be both applicable and useful. But in this situation, it is not clear that as a *constitutional* matter, the court could hear the state-law case anyway (since the constitutional basis for supplemental jurisdiction is that the two claims arise from a "common nucleus of operative fact," as *UMW v. Gibbs, supra*, p. 113, puts it).

iii. Other defendants don't join in removal petition: One rare instance in which §1441(c) may be both applicable and useful is where only *one* of multiple defendants *signs* the removal petition. Where removal occurs under §1441*(a)*, *all defendants* must join (or at least, all must support the removal, and if all do not sign, the absent signatures must be satisfactorally explained.) But under §1441*(c)*, only the defendant or defendants to the separate and independent federal claim need to seek removal. Thus, if P brings a state court action against D1 and D2, lodging state-law claims against both, but a federal-question claim against only D1, then only D1 needs to sign the removal petition under §1441(c). See *Alexander v. Goldome Credit Corp.*, 772 F.Supp. 1217 (M.D.Ala. 1991), in which this occurred.

c.   Remand: If §1441(c) does apply, and the entire case is removed to federal court, the federal judge is not necessarily required to hear the entire matter. Observe that by the last clause of §1441(c), the district court "may determine all issues therein, or in its discretion, may *remand all matters* in which *State law predominates*." So in those relatively rare instance where a defendant actually relies on §1441(c), plaintiff may score a partial victory by getting the state claim sent back to state court. This would probably then mean that defendant would have to defend two separate actions, one federal and one state, which might be even worse for defendant than having the whole case remain in state court.

i.   Remand even the federal claim: In fact, some courts and commentators have held that the federal judge, after determining that removal is proper, may remand *all claims* — even the properly-removed federal claim — if state law predominates in the whole controversy. See, e.g., *Alexander v. Goldome Credit Corp.*, *supra*.

I.   Remand: If the federal judge concludes that the removal did not satisfy the statutory requirements, he must *remand* the case to the state court from which it came. For instance, if in a diversity case it turns out that one or more of the defendants was a citizen of the state in which the suit was commenced, the federal judge must send the case back to the state court where it was commenced. §1447(c).

1.   Discretion to remand: The federal court also has *discretion* to remand to the state courts if a federal trial of the case would be jurisdictionally proper but unwise. This is most likely to happen if a federal question claim and a *supplemental* state claim are both removed, and the federal claim is *dismissed before trial*. *Carnegie-Mellon Univ. v. Cohill*, 484 U.S. 343 (1988).

Note: The principle that the federal court has discretion to decline to hear the supplemental state claim if the federal claim has been dismissed before trial is now codified in 28 U.S.C. §1367(c)(3). See *supra*, p. 121. (§1367(c)(3) apparently contemplates that the federal judge will dismiss the action, rather than remanding it to the state court, in this event.)

J.   Waiver: The defendant may be held to have *waived* his right of removal if he takes extensive action on the merits in state court. But federal judges have usually been *reluctant* to find such a waiver, even in cases where the defendant did such things as taking depositions in the state suit. Wr., 218.

K. Mechanics of removal: (see 28 U.S.C. §§1446-50)

   1. Filing: Defendant must usually file for removal within 30 days of the time he receives service of the complaint.

   2. Where filed: Defendant files by submitting to the district court a "notice of removal," setting out the facts that entitle him to remove.

   3. Stay: Once the notice has been filed, the state court may take no further proceedings until and unless the district court finds that no removal jurisdiction exists, and remands to the state court.

   4. *All defendants* except purely nominal ones must *join* in the notice of removal.

      a. Exceptions: The only exceptions are those defendants not served, and those in cases invoking §1441(c) who are not involved in the "separate and independent" claim.

      Note: Certain aspects of removal jurisdiction are handled in other sections. See, for example, the Sections on Amount in Controversy, Devices to Destroy Diversity, and Venue in Federal Actions.

Quiz Yourself on
REMOVAL OF CASES TO THE FEDERAL COURTS

31. P is a citizen of Ohio. D is a citizen of Kentucky. P has brought suit in the Ohio state courts, asserting that D drove his car negligently, thereby injuring P. P has incurred $48,000 of medical bills, plus significant pain and suffering. If P prevails at all, the likely award will be at least $80,000. Nonetheless, in the state court action P seeks only $45,000. (P is aware that under Ohio law, the jury is not limited to the sum demanded in the complaint.) D has filed a timely notice of removal with the federal district court for Ohio. P has made a timely motion to have the case remanded to the Ohio state courts due to the federal court's lack of removal jurisdiction. Should P's motion for remand be granted? _____

32. P is an individual who is a citizen of Pennsylvania. D is a corporation with its principal place of business in New Jersey, but incorporated in Delaware. P has sued D in the New Jersey state courts for breach of contract. P's claim seeks $100,000. D has filed a prompt notice of removal with the federal district court for New Jersey. P has moved to have the case remanded to the New Jersey state courts, on the grounds that removal was improper. Should P's motion be granted? _____

33. P is a citizen of Arizona. D is a citizen of New Mexico. P has sued D in the New Mexico state courts for violation of a federally-registered trademark held by P. Suits alleging violation of the federal trademark laws may be brought in either state or federal court. D has filed a timely petition removing the case to federal court for the District of New Mexico. P moves to have the case dismissed for lack of subject matter jurisdiction. Should P's motion be granted? _____

34. P, a citizen of North Carolina, has brought a state-law products liability suit against D1, D2, and D3, all citizens of South Carolina. P's suit has been brought in the North Carolina state courts. $1 million is at stake. D1 and D2 have signed and filed a notice of removal with the Eastern District of North Carolina (embracing the area where the state courthouse handling P's suit is located). D3 does not care whether the suit is removed or not, and has not signed the notice of removal. P moves to have the case remanded for lack of subject matter jurisdiction. Should P's motion be granted? _____

Answers

31. Yes. The federal courts only have removal jurisdiction of a case which could have been brought as an original action in the federal courts. For this purpose, "could have been brought" includes all requirements of federal subject matter jurisdiction, including any applicable amount in controversy requirement. Since P's claim could only have been brought as a diversity action (no federal question is present), that claim must be for more than $50,000 to satisfy the amount in controversy requirement. P is deemed to be *master of her complaint*, and if she seeks less than $50,000, that is dispositive even though her claim could quite properly have been for more than the jurisdictional amount. So the federal judge, as in any situation where removal is not proper, should remand the case to state court.

32. Yes. The most important single fact to remember about federal removal jurisdiction is that where a case is based solely on diversity, the defendant *may not remove if he is a citizen of the state where the action is pending*. (This restricts removal and diversity cases to situations in which the defendant would suffer from having to litigate "away" rather than "at home" if removal were not allowed.) Since a corporation is deemed to be a citizen of the state where it has its principal place of business as well as the state where it is incorporated, D is deemed a citizen of both New Jersey and Delaware, and may therefore not remove an action pending in the New Jersey courts.

33. No. Where the plaintiff's claim raises a federal question, the defendant may remove even though the state court suit is pending in the state of which the defendant is a citizen. This is the principal difference between removal jurisdiction in federal-question actions and removal in diversity suits (where a defendant may not remove if the suit is pending in his home state, as shown by the prior question).

34. Yes. Where there are multiple defendants, *all* defendants, not just a majority, must sign the notice of removal. See Wr., p. 227.

VIII. POWER TO PUNISH DISOBEDIENCE OF A COURT ORDER

A. **Court orders founded on invalid jurisdiction:** Each court has the power to determine that it has jurisdiction over the subject matter and parties to a suit. If a court finds that it has such jurisdiction, and makes certain orders based on this finding, what happens if a higher court finds that jurisdiction was lacking? When money damages are all that is involved, the issue is not too serious generally, since any money which has been paid over can be returned, just as it would be if the appellate court reversed for any other reason. But if an equitable order, such as an injunction, has been issued, and the person to whom it is addressed has violated it, may he still be punished for contempt after the appellate court decides that the trial court acted without jurisdiction?

1. **Traditional answer:** The traditional answer to this question was *"no,"* until a 1947 Supreme Court decision.

2. **Modern rule (*Mine Workers* case):** In that decision, *U.S. v. United Mine Workers of America*, 330 U.S. 258 (1947), the Court held that a contempt citation could be *valid, even*

though the order upon whose violation the citation was based (a temporary injunction) *was made without jurisdiction*. A five-Justice majority wrote that "It is for the court of first instance to determine the question of the validity of the law, and *until its decision is reversed for error by orderly review, either by itself or by a higher court, its orders based on its decision are to be respected*, and disobedience of them is contempt of its lawful authority, to be punished."

    a. Scope unclear: It is unclear whether the *Mine Workers* decision applies only to orders, like the temporary injunction there, that are given to *preserve the status quo during adjudication*, or whether it applies to more substantive relief as well. Wr., 87.

B. Citations based on unconstitutional order: If a court order is disobeyed, and later held to have been void because *unconstitutional*, a contempt citation based on the disobedience seems to be *enforceable*, just as *Mine Workers* held that it would be if the order had been void for lack of jurisdiction. *Walker v. City of Birmingham*, 388 U.S. 307 (1967).

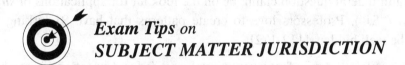

Exam Tips on
SUBJECT MATTER JURISDICTION

In any fact pattern involving a federal suit, you must check to make sure that the requirements of subject matter jurisdiction are satisfied. Here are some particular things to check for:

☛ First, check to see whether *diversity* can serve as the basis for subject matter jurisdiction. [96-102]

    ☞ Most important of all, make sure diversity is *complete.* Professors love to make fact patterns that include "incomplete" diversity (e.g., P1 from NY, P2 from CA, D1 from MA and D2 from CA). Remember that the requirement of complete diversity means that *no plaintiff may be a citizen of the same state as any defendant.* [96-97]

        ☞ Also, remember that a *corporation* is deemed to be a citizen of *both* the state where it is incorporated, and the state where it has its principal place of business, so no opposing party can be a citizen of *either* of these states. (Under the "nerve center" test, the principal place of business is the corporate headquarters; under the "muscle" test, it's the state where most plants or other company assets are located.) [100-101]

    ☞ Make sure the *amount in controversy* requirement is satisfied. More than *$50,000* must be at stake. [106-110]

        ☞ Professors frequently test *aggregation* issues. [108-110] You can spot such an issue when you see either: (1) several claims totalling more than $50,000, with no single claim equalling $50,000; or (2) one (or more) claims exceeding $50,000, plus one (or more) claims for less than $50,000. The rules on aggregation are too tricky to summarize here, but in general: (1) a P may combine several claims against a single D to get to $50,000; (2) a P may not bring in an additional D against whom all claims total less than $50,000; and (3) multiple P's can't combine their claims against a single D if no P has a claim for more than $50,000.

☛ Whether there's diversity or not, check on whether there's a ***federal question*** present. The existence of a federal question means, of course, that the case can go forward even if there's no diversity. [104-106]

   ☞ Remember that a "federal question" is one "arising under the Constitution, laws or treaties of the United States." Usually, your fact pattern will involve a constitutional issue or a federal statute if the professor is trying to see whether you can spot a federal question. [105]

   ☞ In general, look only to P's claim, not D's possible defenses, to determine whether there's a federal question.

   ☞ You don't have to worry about the amount in controversy if a federal question is present.

☛ Once you've determined that your fact pattern contains a valid diversity claim between two or more parties, or a valid federal question claim, be on the lookout for applications of ***supplemental jurisdiction*** ("SJ"). Professors love to create patterns that have SJ lurking in them, because SJ can be well hidden. [112-122]

   ☞ If the "core" (basic) claim in your fact pattern involves a ***federal question***, remember that SJ lets ***state-law claims*** be added to the suit. So anytime a P wants to assert both a federal-statutory claim and a state-law (perhaps common-law) claim, and there is not diversity between P and D, "Think SJ". [112-116}

      ☞ Also, recall that SJ lets ***additional parties*** be added to the state-law claim. So look for patterns where P has both federal and state-law claims against D1, and state-law-only claims against D2; if P is a citizen of the same state as either D1 or D2, SJ is the way that the entire suit can go forward. [112, 116-121].

   ☞ If the "core" claim is state-law-only, but is supported by ***diversity***, look to see whether SJ is available to cover ***new claims*** or ***new parties*** that would otherwise destroy diversity or would fail to satisfy amount-in-controversy.

      ☞ These types of situations are ***covered*** by SJ: (1) compulsory counterclaims; (2) joinder of additional parties to compulsory counterclaims; (3) cross-claims; (4) impleader claims by third-party plaintiffs (TPP's) against third-party defendants (TPD's); (5) any claims by TPP's or TPD's against anyone.

      ☞ These types of situations are ***not covered*** by SJ: (1) claims by a P against a TPD; (2) claims by a P against a person who is to be "joined if feasible"; (3) claims by a P against multiple Ds; and (4) claims by would-be intervenors who want to enter on the Plaintiff side of the suit.

      ☞ If you can't remember all this, just remember the rule of ***"defensive posture"***: in a diversity case, SJ helps only those in a defensive posture. So SJ applies to additional claims by defendants (including TPDs and TPPs), but ***not*** to additional claims asserted by plaintiffs. [p. 115}

☞ Remember that SJ *never affects* the requirements of *personal* jurisdiction. So if a D (even a TPD) does not have minimum contacts with the forum state, the fact that the claim is of a type to which SJ applies is not enough to allow D to be joined.

☛ Whenever your pattern involves a D who is sued in *state* court, and you're asked about the options available to D, consider *removal* of the suit to the federal courts. In general, any action brought in state court which P could have brought in federal court may be removed. [126-131]

☞ But remember that in a *diversity* case (not in federal question cases), there's a key additional requirement: the case may be removed only if *no D is a citizen of the state in which the action is pending*. Professors love to test on this exception, because it's easy to slip into the fact pattern and easy for the student to miss.

CHAPTER 4

PLEADING

ChapterScope

This Chapter covers pleading, the process by which the parties to a litigation spell out their claims and defenses. The emphasis in this chapter is on the pleading provisions of the ***Federal Rules***. These exemplify the modern, non-technical approach to pleading, and have served as the model for the pleading provisions of many states. The most important concepts in this Chapter are:

- **Two types:** In most instances, there are only two types of pleadings in a federal action. These are the ***complaint*** and the ***answer***. The complaint is the document by which the plaintiff begins the case. The answer is the defendant's response to the complaint.

  - ❏ **Reply:** In some circumstances, there will be a third document, called the ***reply***. The reply is, in effect, an "answer to the answer." Most often, a reply is allowable if the answer contains a ***counterclaim*** (in which case a reply is ***required***).

- **Elements of complaint:** There are three essential elements which a complaint must have:

  - ❏ **Jurisdiction:** A short and plain statement of the grounds upon which the court's ***jurisdiction*** depends;

  - ❏ **Statement of the claim:** A ***short and plain statement of the claim*** showing that the pleader is entitled to relief; and

  - ❏ **Relief:** A demand for judgment for the ***relief*** (e.g., money damages, injunction, etc.) which the pleader seeks.

- **Defenses against validity of complaint:** Either in the ***answer***, or by separate ***motion***, defendant may attack the validity of the complaint in a number of respects. Grounds for attack include lack of ***jurisdiction,*** insufficiency of ***service of process***, and failure to ***state a claim upon which relief may be granted***.

- **Affirmative defenses:** There are certain defenses which must be ***explicitly pleaded*** in the ***answer***, if D is to raise them at trial. These are so-called *"affirmative defenses."* (Examples: ***contributory negligence***, ***fraud***, ***res judicata***, ***statute of limitations***, and ***illegality***.)

- **Counterclaim:** In addition to defenses, if D has a claim against P, he may (in all cases) and must (in some cases) plead that claim as a ***counterclaim***. If the counterclaim is one which D is ***required*** to plead, it is called a ***compulsory*** counterclaim. If it is one which D has the option of pleading or not, it is called a ***permissive*** counterclaim. A counterclaim is compulsory if it "arises out of the transaction or occurrence that is the subject matter of the [plaintiff's] claim."

- **Variance of proof from pleading:** The Federal Rules allow substantial ***deviation*** of the proof at trial from the pleadings, so long as the variance does not seriously prejudice the other side.

I. HISTORY AND GENERAL PRINCIPLES

A. Three forms: Pleading evolved through three major forms:

1. *common law*, which is of largely historical interest;

2. *codes*, which are still in effect in a number of states; and

3. *the Federal Rules*, which are imitated in an increasing majority of jurisdictions.

B. Three purposes: Each of these three forms of pleading is characterized by a distinct overall purpose:

1. **Common law:** The object of pleading at *common law* was to *formulate the issues for trial.*

2. **Codes:** Pleading under the *codes* was designed to *reveal the underlying facts on which the claim rested.*

3. **Federal Rules:** The primary purpose of *federal* pleading is to *give notice* of the claim (or defense) to the adversary, so that he may make effective *discovery* requests and *trial preparation.*

II. PLEADING AT COMMON LAW

A. Aim of common-law pleading: Production of a *single issue in dispute* was the overall goal of common law pleading. This goal was rarely reached; when it was, it often resulted in one party's being unfairly thrown out of court, or otherwise denied substantial justice.

B. Sole pre-trial procedure: At common law, pleadings constituted the *sole pre-trial procedure.*

1. **Modern distribution of functions:** Many of the functions of common-law pleading are now distributed among various other pre-trial procedures (notably *discovery, pre-trial conference*, and *summary judgment*).

C. Technical: Common law pleading was highly technical, and required a different form of pleading for each kind of cause of action. These rigid categories of claims were known as *forms of action.*

> **Example:** The common law distinguished between "trespass" and "action on the case." The distinction depended solely on when the injury caused by the act occurred — if the injury was immediate, then the action was for trespass, whereas if the injury was somewhat delayed, then the proper action was "on the case." See *Scott v. Shepard*, 96 Eng. Rep. 525 (C.P. 1773). If the plaintiff labeled his action as one for trespass, but then proved facts constituting an action on the case, plaintiff was denied recovery, under the general rule that the proof could not vary from the pleading.

III. CODE PLEADING

A. **Field Code:** The 1848 New York Code of Civil Procedure (known as the *Field Code* after its author) was the first integrated set of rules for civil procedure in the United States. It merged law and equity, abolished the forms of action, and greatly simplified pleading.

B. **Fact pleading:** The Field Code and others like it emphasized that it was *facts*, not conclusions of law, that were to be pleaded.

   1. **Evidence:** The facts to be pleaded did not include "evidence," which was considered too specific for pleading.

   2. **Much litigation:** The difficulty of distinguishing "facts" from "evidence" on the one hand and "conclusions of law" on the other, led to tremendous amounts of litigation regarding the adequacy of particular pleadings. The Federal Rules have therefore carefully avoided use of the term "facts" in the description of what must be pleaded. (Rule 8)

C. **Limited:** Code pleadings were generally limited to (1) plaintiff's *complaint*; (2) defendant's *answer*; and (3) plaintiff's *reply*.

D. **Liberal construction:** The Codes mandated *liberal construction* of the pleadings, to do "substantial justice" between the parties.

   1. **Technical errors ignored:** The Codes attempted to eliminate dismissal or reversal for purely *technical* errors.

E. **Theory of the pleadings:** Some courts in Code states attempted to find a single legal theory (known as the *"theory of the pleadings"*) upon which the plaintiff's complaint relied. The court then decided whether or not the facts alleged were sufficient to support that legal theory, or cause of action. F,K&C, 473-76.

   1. **Conflict of aims:** This "theory of the pleadings" doctrine was at odds with the objective of doing substantial justice between the parties, and of eliminating dismissal for purely technical errors. If plaintiff cited certain facts, relying on one theory, and then during trial sought to shift to a different theory, the court frequently did not allow him to do so, claiming that the "theory of the pleadings" doctrine would be violated. Thus the plaintiff was thrown out of court, even though he would have, if allowed, proven facts entitling him to relief.

IV. MODERN FEDERAL PLEADING GENERALLY

A. **Purpose:** The guiding principle of pleading under the Federal Rules is that the pleadings should give *notice* to all parties of the nature of the lawsuit, sufficient to allow the other parties to make *pre-trial and trial preparation.*

   1. **Functions of pleadings revised:** At common law, and to some extent under the Codes, pleadings served a number of functions: (1) stating the facts underlying the case; (2) formulating the issues for trial; (3) weeding out sham claims; and (4) notifying the parties so that they could prepare for trial. The first three of these functions are not performed primarily by the pleadings under the Federal Rules:

a. **Fact stating:** The setting out of the facts underlying the claim is now accomplished by the use of extensive *discovery* procedures, which compel each side to state the facts of the case as it believes them to be.

b. **Definition of issues:** Issues are defined through discovery, and also through the *pretrial conference* — Rule 16 provides for such a conference to consider, among other things, "the simplification of the issues."

c. **Sham claims:** Meritless claims are now disposed of primarily through *summary judgment* under Rule 56. This is a more effective means of rejecting unmerited claims, since not only affidavits, but also all the fruits of discovery, may be introduced at the hearing on the summary judgment motion.

2. **Notice-giving:** Therefore, "The only function left to be performed by the pleadings alone is that of notice. For [this] reason, pleadings under the [Federal rules] may properly be a *generalized summary of the party's position*, sufficient to advise the party *for which incident he is being sued*, sufficient to show *what was decided for purposes of res judicata*, and sufficient to indicate whether the case should be tried *to the court or to a jury*. No more is demanded of pleadings than this; history shows that no more can be successfully performed by pleadings." Wr., 439.

B. General Principles

1. **No fact pleading:** Unlike the Codes, the Federal Rules do not require the pleading of "facts" upon which the claim is based. "No distinction is to be drawn between 'evidence,' 'ultimate facts,' and 'conclusions.' " Wr., 441.

2. **No "theory of pleadings":** The Federal Rules do not require, as many Codes do, that the plaintiff confine himself to one particular "theory of the pleadings." If plaintiff is entitled to relief, he is not to be thrown out of court because his lawyer chose an incorrect legal theory when drafting the pleadings. The ease with which pleadings may be amended, even during trial (see *infra*, pp. 159-162) is one indication of the abandonment of the "theory of the pleadings" requirement.

3. **Substantial justice:** The pleadings are to be "so construed as to do substantial justice." Rule 8(f). This replaces the common law principle that the pleadings are to be construed "most strongly against the pleader." Wr., 442.

4. **Dismissal:** A complaint should not be dismissed for "failure to state a claim on which relief may be granted" (Rule 12(b)(6)) *"unless it appears beyond doubt that the plaintiff can prove no set of facts in support of his claim which would entitle him to relief." Conley v. Gibson*, 355 U.S. 41 (1957).

C. Mechanics of pleadings

1. **Kinds of pleadings:** In most instances, only two pleadings, a *complaint* and an *answer*, are allowed. This represents a change from the common law system, in which the parties traded pleadings *ad infinitum*, until a single issue for trial was formulated.

a. **Reply:** A *reply*, which is an "answer to the answer," is allowable in two circumstances: (Rule 7(a))

   i. where the answer contains a *counterclaim* which is identified as such (in which case a reply is required);

   ii. by *order* of the court.

   Note: Where the answer contains a counterclaim, the reply must address itself solely to the allegations of the counterclaim, and must not discuss the defensive allegations contained in the answer. Wr., 426.

2. Verification of pleadings: Whereas the Codes often required that the pleadings be *verified*, or sworn to, Rule 11 states that the pleadings need not be verified unless this is required by statute or rule.

   a. Where verification required: The Federal Rules requiring verification in certain circumstances include:

     i. Rule 23.1, dealing with *stockholders' derivative suits;*

     ii. Rule 27(a), allowing the taking of certain *depositions before an action has been commenced*; and

     iii. Rule 65(b), permitting *temporary* restraining orders on a verified complaint showing that the petitioner will suffer "immediate and irreparable injury, loss or damage" if the restraining order is not granted.

   b. Relaxation of requirement: The verification requirement is sometimes relaxed where hardship would result. This occurred, for instance, in *Surowitz v. Hilton Hotels Corp.*, 383 U.S. 363 (1966), which was a stockholders' derivative suit brought by an elderly Polish immigrant with very limited understanding of the English language.

     i. The complaint was prepared by the plaintiff's son-in-law, and plaintiff verified it (as Rule 23.1 requires) only on faith in her son-in-law's advice.

     ii. Defendant, having shown by oral deposition of plaintiff that she could not have sworn to the accuracy of the complaint, moved to dismiss it as sham, and the District Court granted the motion.

     iii. Held sufficient: Justice Black held for the Supreme Court that the verification was *sufficient* and that trial should proceed. He found no evidence that Ms. Surowitz was pursuing the type of *strike suit* that the verification requirement was designed to foreclose. Further, he cited the policy of Federal Rules to "get away from some of the old procedural booby traps which common-law pleaders could set to prevent unsophisticated litigants from ever having their day in court."

     iv. Justice Harlan concurred on the narrower ground that verification by plaintiff's attorney satisfied 23.1.

3. Attorney must not file frivolous pleading (Rule 11): The non-lawyer commonly thinks that "you can say anything you want in a lawsuit." But in fact, at least in federal suits, it is the lawyer's job to make sure that a pleading (or any other paper submitted to the court) is *not frivolous*, and not issued to *harass* or *delay* the adversary. Rule 11 imposes this requirement, and provides that a lawyer who fails in this duty may be *fined* or otherwise sanctioned.

Note: The 1993 amendments to the FRCP included a major restructuring — and, most people feel, weakening — of Rule 11.

a. **Lawyer's obligation:** The pleader herself does *not* need to swear to the pleading in most instances. But the pleader's *lawyer* must sign the pleading, and is responsible for its contents in some important ways. When the lawyer files a pleading, the lawyer is thereby "*certifying* that to the best of the [lawyer's] knowledge, information, and belief, formed after an *inquiry reasonable under the circumstances*, —

(1) the pleading "is not being presented for any *improper purpose*, such as to *harass* or to cause *unnecessary delay* or needless *increase in the cost* of litigation";

(2) "the claims, defenses, and other legal contentions therein are *warranted by existing law* or by a *nonfrivolous argument for the extension, modification, or reversal* of existing law or the establishment of new law;

(3) "the allegations and other factual contentions have *evidentiary support*, or if specifically so identified, are likely to have evidentiary support after a reasonable opportunity for further investigation or discovery"; and

(4) "the *denials* of factual contentions are *warranted on the evidence* or, if specifically so identified, are reasonably based on a lack of information or belief."

See generally Rule 11(b).

i. **1993 Amendments:** The language quoted above is from the new version of Rule 11, enacted in 1993. The biggest change is that the role of *factual assertions or denials* is greatly expanded. For instance, where the plaintiff's complaint contains allegations that the plaintiff cannot yet prove (but believes he will be able to prove in the future), the complaint must *specially identify* these assertions (e.g., "Plaintiff believes that, after a reasonable opportunity for discovery, plaintiff will be able to prove that defendant negligently injured plaintiff. ...").

b. **Purpose of rule:** Rule 11 applies to all papers filed with the court, whether these are complaints, answers, motions, etc. But the main real-world consequence of the rule has been to deter lawyers for *plaintiffs* from asserting claims that have no basis in law or fact, and to prevent them from bringing to a multi-party action peripheral defendants (the "join 'em all" strategy).

i. **Important litigation area:** Since Rule 11 was strengthened in 1983 in order to better deter delay and other abuses, litigation seeking or opposing Rule 11 sanctions has grown into one of the most important aspects of federal practice.

c. **Nature of sanctions:** Rule 11 allows the court to impose a number of *sanctions* on lawyers or parties who violate the rule. However, the sanctions are somewhat weaker than they were before the 1993 changes. Thus Rule 11(c)(2) provides that sanctions "shall be limited to what is sufficient to deter repetition of such conduct or comparable conduct by others similarly situated." In any event, sanctions can include non-monetary measures such as *censuring* the offending lawyer, *striking* the offending pleading, etc. See 1993 Advisory Committee Notes to Rule 11(c).

i. **Monetary sanctions:** The most common sanction, however, is a monetary *fine*. In a big change from pre-1993 law, any monetary penalty will now normally be paid *to the court*, and will be paid to the other party only if "warranted for effective deterrence." Rule 11(c)(2). This of course deprives the party who is complaining of a Rule 11 violation of much of the financial incentive for doing so, and will thus probably result in fewer Rule 11 motions.

ii. **Discretionary:** Rule 11 sanctions are now *discretionary* with the court: if the court concludes that Rule 11 has been violated, it *"may ... impose an appropriate sanction. ..."* (Under pre-1993 law, sanctions were mandatory if the court concluded that Rule 11 had been violated.)

d. **What is "reasonable inquiry":** The lawyer must make *"reasonable inquiry"* before signing the pleading. What constitutes "reasonable inquiry" will, of course, vary from case to case. If the claim is one which, if true, should logically be supported by evidence already available to the plaintiff, the plaintiff's lawyer probably cannot blindly accept the client's word for what happened, and must at least question the client about his story. But if the only likely evidence in support of the proposed claim lies with the defendant, plaintiff's lawyer probably may sign the complaint without detailed inquiry, on the theory that she can obtain evidence through discovery after filing the action (though under the new Rule 11(b)(3), the allegations for which there is a lack of present evidence must be "specifically so identified" in the pleading.)

i. **Duty not to reaffirm bad pleading:** Suppose a lawyer makes a "reasonable inquiry" before filing the pleading, then *later learns* that the pleading is not meritorious. Must the lawyer *withdraw* the pleading or face sanctions? As the result of the 1993 changes to Rule 11, the answer now seems to be *"yes."* Under new 11(b), the certifications being made by the lawyer are triggered not only by the signing, filing, and submitting of a document, but also by the lawyer's *"later advocating"* that document. The Advisory Committee's notes to Rule 11 illustrate the "later advocating" rule by saying that if an attorney *orally insists* on preserving a claim or defense during a *pretrial conference*, he should be viewed as "presenting to the court" that contention and can be sanctioned if, based on his present (as opposed to original) state of knowledge, he is using it to delay/harass or without basis in existing law, etc.

Note: Observe that this "later advocating" change is likely to have at least as much, maybe more, impact on *defendants* as on plaintiffs — a defendant who denies a claim based on lack of knowledge or information sufficient to form a belief as to the claim's truth (see Rule 8(b)), for instance, will now not be able to continue to assert the defense if developments since his filing of an answer show him that the claim has substantial merit.

ii. **Bad faith not required:** Also, sanctions can be awarded without a showing that the lawyer (or the party signing the pleading) behaved in *bad faith*. If the lawyer honestly believes that the complaint is true, but a reasonable person would have made inquiries that would have shown the complaint to be false, sanctions may be imposed. See *Business Guides, Inc. v. Chromatic Communications Enterprises,*

Inc. (discussed further *infra*, p. 143), holding that this "objective standard of reasonable inquiry" applies.

e. Procedure for invoking Rule 11: Normally, proceedings to impose a sanction for violation of Rule 11 will come about because the opposing party has made a **motion** to impose the sanctions. But the court may also impose sanctions on its own initiative. Rule 11(c)(1)(B).

i. "Safe harbor" provision: The 1993 amendments to Rule 11 changed the procedure for invoking sanctions in one very important way. Under new 11(c)(1)(A), the party seeking sanctions serves a motion on the other party, but is not allowed to *file* the motion with the court "unless, within 21 days after service of the motion … the challenged paper, claim, defense … is not *withdrawn* or appropriately corrected." In other words, an offending party gets a 21-day *"safe-harbor"* in which to withdraw or correct any bad pleading, and if he does so, there can be no sanctions no matter how outrageous the original misconduct. Justice Scalia, dissenting from the Supreme Court's adoption of the 1993 changes to Rule 11, asserted that under the safe-harbor provision, "parties will be able to file thoughtless, reckless, and harassing pleadings, secure in the knowledge that they have nothing to lose; if objection is raised, they can retreat without penalty."

f. No sanctions on signer's firm: What happens if the lawyer purports to sign the pleadings on behalf of her law firm (e.g., "Janet Jones, on behalf of Smith, Brown & Jones, P.C.")? May Rule 11 sanctions be awarded against the entire law firm?

i. Old law: Under pre-1993 law, the answer was *"no."* In *Pavelic & Leflore v. Marvel Entertainment Group*, 493 U.S. 120 (1989), the Supreme Court held that Rule 11 requires the **individual** lawyer to sign, and that the consequences of this signature (including sanctions) apply **only to her**, even if she purports to sign on behalf of colleagues.

ii. Present law: But again, the 1993 amendment to Rule 11 changed this result. New Rule 11(c)(1)(A) effectively overrules *Pavelic* — and changes the answer to the above question to "yes" — by stating that "absent exceptional circumstances, a law firm should be held **jointly responsible** for violations committed by its partners, associates, and employees."

g. Sanctions against party: Normally, the **pleader herself** does **not sign** the pleadings. But even without signing the pleadings, the pleader can be **liable** for Rule 11 sanctions if the court finds that the party, not just the lawyer, was responsible for the Rule 11 violations (as where the pleader lies to her lawyer, leading the lawyer to believe that a claim or defense has merit when it does not.) See Rule 11(c) (court may impose sanctions upon "parties that have violated [Rule 11] or are responsible for the violation.")

i. Party signs: If the pleader *does* sign the pleadings (either without being required to, or because the situation is one of the rare ones requiring such a signature, such as where verification is required, or where the party is not represented by counsel) then the pleader is treated essentially like a lawyer for Rule 11 purposes. For instance, in *Business Guides, Inc. v. Chromatic Communications Enterprises, Inc.*, 498 U.S. 533 (1991), P, a corporation, had its officers sign the pleadings, because

P was seeking a Temporary Restraining Order, for which FRCP 65(b) requires a party's verification or signed affidavit. The Supreme Court held that once the officer signed, P as a corporation became liable for Rule 11 sanctions. Had P made reasonable inquiry into the facts, it would have known that the statements it made in the complaint were not true; therefore, P was assessed sanctions, which the Court upheld.

   ii. **1993 changes:** The 1993 amendments to Rule 11 make it harder to gain *monetary sanctions* against the party as opposed to the attorney. Under new 11(c)(2)(A), monetary sanctions are not allowed against a party where the violation consists essentially of frivolous *legal* arguments (i.e., use of claims or defenses that are not warranted by existing law or by nonfrivolous argument for changing the law). But a party can still be assessed monetary sanctions for causing pleadings or motions to be made for purposes of harassment or delay, or for making *factual contentions* that are without evidentiary support. So the actual result in *Business Guides, Inc., supra*, would apparently be the same under new Rule 11.

h. **Applicable where case voluntarily dismissed:** A standard technique among some over-aggressive litigators is to file a complaint first, then investigate. Such litigators may reason, "If my post-filing investigation shows that the complaint has no chance of winning, I can always take a voluntary dismissal under Rule 41(a)(1)(i), and there won't be any pending action in which the court can award Rule 11 sanctions against me." However, as a result of a Supreme Court decision, this strategy will not work. In *Cooter & Gell v. Hartmarx Corp.*, 496 U.S. 384 (1990), the Court held that even where the complaint has already been *voluntarily dismissed* by P, the court retains jurisdiction to award Rule 11 sanctions, including attorney's fees, if it finds that the complaint was filed without reasonable inquiry.

i. **Applicable where court has no subject matter jurisdiction:** Suppose that the federal court is eventually found to have been *without subject matter jurisdiction* over the controversy. The case, of course, must be immediately dismissed (see *supra*, p. 94) no matter how far the proceedings have gone. Does the district court lose its right to impose Rule 11 sanctions for conduct by the litigants which occurred before the dismissal? The Supreme Court has answered *"no"* to this question. In *Willy v. Coastal Corp.*, 112 S.Ct. 1076 (1992), the Court observed that the imposition of Rule 11 sanctions is not a judgment on the merits, but rather, the determination of a collateral issue — whether the attorney has abused the judicial process. There is no constitutional (or other) problem with allowing the district court to make such a finding of abuse of process, even though the abuse occurred during the course of a case over which the court did not have jurisdiction.

j. **Applicability to discovery abuses:** The 1993 amendments to Rule 11 made Rule 11 *inapplicable* to discovery. Therefore, the special discovery-specific sanctions contained in Rules 26 through 37 are now the only ones used in the discovery context. See Rule 11(d).

k. **Court has inherent sanction power apart from Rule:** Federal courts also have *"inherent power"* to sanction conduct that is in contempt of the court, whether or not this conduct is covered by Rule 11. That is, where a litigant abuses the judicial process, the court may use its general power to punish contempt in order to punish the litigant by fines or other sanctions, without using the procedures of Rule 11 at all. This is true even if the type of conduct being punished consists of the filing of harassing pleadings or motions (which would make Rule 11 sanctions applicable). The Supreme Court so held, in *Chambers v. NASCO*, 501 U.S. 32 (1991), a 5-4 decision.

    i.   **Facts of *Chambers:***   In Chambers, D, who had contracted to sell his television station to P, fraudulently conveyed the station to a family trust, made numerous misrepresentations to the courts, and otherwise abused the litigation process.

    ii.   **Holding:**   The Supreme Court held that the federal district court hearing the case had "inherent authority" to fine D for the entire litigation cost borne by P in bringing its specific performance suit (nearly $1 million), even though the court did not purport to be issuing the sanctions under Rule 11, and even though some of the conduct being punished was conduct that could have been reached by Rule 11. If a party's conduct falls squarely within the conduct that Rule 11 is designed to reach, the district court should *ordinarily* just use Rule 11. But if the district court concludes that because of the widespread scope of misconduct, the Rule 11 sanctions are not adequate to fully punish the abusive behavior, the court may use its inherent power and devise its own system of punishment, the Supreme Court held.

4. Pleading in the alternative: The pleader, whether he is plaintiff or defendant, may plead "*in the alternative*." That is, by Rule 8(e), "A party may set forth two or more statements of a claim or defense alternately or hypothetically. ..." This rule also provides that "a party may ... state as many separate claims or defenses as he has regardless of consistency and whether based on legal, equitable, or maritime grounds."

> **Example:** P performed certain work for D, for which he has not been paid. P can allege in one count that the work was done under a valid written contract, and that the measure of damages includes lost profits. P can then also allege, in a second count, that if the contract was not valid, P rendered value to D, and is thus entitled to recover in *quantum meruit* for the value of his performance. The two theories are obviously inconsistent, and are in fact phrased in the alternative. Such alternative pleading is allowed by Rule 8(e).

V. THE COMPLAINT

A. Definition of complaint: The complaint is the initial pleading in a lawsuit, and is filed by the plaintiff.

  1. Commencement of action: The action is deemed to have been "commenced" by the filing of the complaint with the court. See Rule 3.

    a. Effect on statute of limitations: In diversity cases, this filing, although "commencing" the action, does not satisfy or toll a state statute of limitations requiring actual service of process. Federal courts in diversity cases are required to follow the statute of limitations in the state where they sit. See *Guaranty Trust v. York, infra* p. 228, and *Ragan v. Merchants Transfer & Warehouse Co., infra,* p. 228.

B. Elements of complaint: Rule 8(a) sets out three essential elements which a complaint must contain:

1. **Jurisdiction:** "a short and plain statement of the grounds upon which the court's *jurisdiction* depends. ...";

2. **Statement of claim:** "a short and plain *statement of the claim* showing that the pleader is entitled to relief";

3. **Relief:** "a demand for judgment for the *relief* the pleader seeks."

   Note: The three elements above required by Rule 8(a) apply not only to a plaintiff's original complaint, but also to a defendant's *counterclaim*, to any party's *third-party claim*, and to any party's *cross-claim*. The nature of these other kinds of claims will be treated in the chapter on Multi-Party and Multi-Claim Litigation.

C. Jurisdictional allegation: The requirement that the complaint contain jurisdictional allegations stems from the U.S. Constitution's limitation of the subject matter jurisdiction of the federal courts. The requirements of federal subject matter jurisdiction are treated in the previous chapter.

1. **Diversity suit:** In a diversity suit, the jurisdictional allegation might read as follows: "Jurisdiction is founded upon diversity of citizenship, plaintiff being a citizen of State A and defendant being a citizen of State B. The amount in controversy, exclusive of interest and court costs, is in excess of $50,000.00."

2. **Federal question:** If the plaintiff asserts federal question jurisdiction, a reference is normally made to the federal statute or constitutional provision relied upon.

D. Degree of specificity required: Rule 8(a)'s requirement of a *"short and plain statement of the claim showing that the pleader is entitled to relief"* has generally been construed so as to place the *fewest possible technical requirements on the pleader*. The level of factual detail required has not been high; gaps in the facts are usually remedied through *discovery* or other pre-trial procedures.

   Example: P's federal complaint asserts that D has "falsely and slanderously" accused P of facilitating prostitution. The complaint does not expressly state that D ever "published" these allegations, i.e., made them to someone other than P. Since publication is a prima facie element of the tort of slander, D moves to have the complaint dismissed under FRCP 12(b)(6) for failure to state a valid claim.

   Held, D's motion is denied. Although P did not expressly allege publication, the context makes it clear that P was in fact asserting publication, and that D understood that P was so asserting. *Garcia v. Hilton Hotels International, Inc.*, 97 F.Supp. 5 (D.P.R. 1951).

   Note: One of the reasons for not insisting on extreme specificity in pleadings is that when a complaint is dismissed for failure to plead a valid cause of action, the plaintiff normally has the right to amend the pleading. Therefore, the dismissal-plus-repleading may have the effect of teaching P's lawyer how to plead better, but it doesn't eliminate any lawsuits. If the problem is actually a substantive one — i.e., P cannot in reality prove facts establishing a claim — the better way to handle the situation is by a motion prove facts establishing a claim — the better way to handle the situation is by a motion for summary judgment (see *infra*, p. 252), perhaps after discovery has been completed.

1. **Legal theory not required:** The plaintiff need state only facts, not the **legal theory** he is relying on. Thus in *Dioguardi v. Durning*, 139 F.2d 774 (2d Cir. 1944), an importer whose goods were sold at auction by the Collector of Customs filed a *pro se* complaint against the Collector alleging that the latter "sold my merchandise to another bidder with my price of $110, and not of his price of $120." The complaint also alleged that "three weeks before the sale, two cases of 19 bottles each case disappeared."

   a. **Holding:** The court held that plaintiff had stated enough to withstand a motion to dismiss the pleadings. Plaintiff did not have to state his legal theory (e.g., that the law recognizes a private right of action for a person aggrieved by a civil servant's breach of the duty to conduct a fair auction). It is sufficient that the plaintiff gives his adversary enough information about the claim to allow the latter to frame an answer and to commence discovery.

2. **Conclusory statement not enough:** The pleader must, however, state at least the basic facts of his claim, and may not simply **recite his conclusion** that he is entitled to relief.

   Example: Suppose that P sues his employer, D, for racial discrimination. P's complaint states solely that "D has discriminated against me on the basis of my race." This complaint is so completely conclusory — so lacking in even the basic facts surrounding the transaction at issue — that the court will almost certainly dismiss it for failure to state a valid claim. See, e.g., *Martin v. N.Y.S. Dept. Mental Hygiene*, 588 F.2d 371 (2d Cir. 1978), dismissing P's claim on essentially these facts.

3. **The "big case":** Some commentators have suggested that the pleading requirements should be stricter in a *"big case,"* such as an antitrust suit or stockholders' derivative suit. But the courts have **not** generally agreed. Most decisions have held that the federal pleading rules must be interpreted in the same liberal manner with respect to a large case likely to go on for a decade, as for a small automobile negligence suit. Wr., 446.

E. **Single or separate counts:** Rule 10(b) provides that each individual claim should be set forth in a *separate count*, and that the counts should in turn be broken into numbered paragraphs, each of which is limited to the statement of a "single set of circumstances."

F. **Demand for judgment:** Under Rule 8(a), each complaint (as well as each counterclaim and cross-claim) must contain "a demand for judgment for the relief to which [the pleader] deems himself entitled."

1. **Contents:** Generally, this demand for relief (sometimes called the *"prayer"*), will be for one or more of the following three things:

   a. *money damages;*

   b. *injunctive* or other equitable relief;

   c. a *declaratory judgment* as to the parties' rights and liabilities.

2. **Wrong relief requested:** If the trial makes it clear that the demand for relief was inappropriate, the court must nonetheless grant "the relief to which the party in whose favor

[judgment] is rendered is entitled, even if the party has not demanded such relief in his pleadings." Rule 54(c).

   a.   Default judgment: But this rule does not apply to *default judgments*, i.e., judgments entered against a defendant who never answers the complaint. Rule 54(c) states that "a judgment by default shall not be different in kind from or exceed in amount that prayed for in the demand for judgment."

G. Special matters: In addition to the general requirement of a "short and plain statement of the claim" imposed by Rule 8(a), certain *"special matters"* must be pleaded with *particularity* if they are to be raised at trial. These "special matters" are ones notice of which is thought to be necessary in order for the opponent to be able to prepare for trial. They are typically claims which the adversary will *not be expecting* unless his attention is specifically called to them.

   1.   Catalogue of matters: These special matters, which are listed in Rule 9, include the following:

      a.   any denial of any party's *legal capacity* to sue or be sued (9(a));

      b.   the circumstances giving rise to any allegation of *fraud or mistake* (9(b));

      c.   any denial of the performance or occurrence of a *condition precedent (9(c));*

      d.   the existence of *judgments* or *official documents* and acts, on which the pleader plans to rely (9(d) and (e), respectively);

      e.   material facts of *time* and *place*;

      f.   *special damages* (9(g));

      g.   certain aspects of *admiralty and maritime* jurisdiction (9(h)).

   2.   Effect of failure to plead special matter: Plaintiff's failure to specially plead one of the items listed in Rule 9 may prevent him from recovering at all, or from recovering particular items of damage.

      Example 1: P brings an action against D for false arrest and imprisonment. His complaint does not contain any allegation of "special damages." At trial, P testifies that as a result of the false imprisonment, P missed a meeting with a contractor relating to the remodeling of a building bought by P, and that this missed meeting caused P large losses. *Held*, because P did not plead special damages, he cannot recover for any items of loss which are not "natural consequences" of D's tort. Although P may recover nominal damages for the false imprisonment itself, he may not recover the increased remodeling costs, since these are not "natural consequences" of the imprisonment. *Burlington Transportation v. Josephson*, 153 F.2d 372 (8th Cir. 1946).

      Example 2: P brings a class action against D, a large corporation, alleging that D has disseminated false and misleading information to stockholders in D's annual reports and SEC filings. The complaint recites each of numerous statements made by D in these documents, then asserts that each was false, without giving further information. (For example, the complaint quotes D's statement that D has adopted advanced technology to solve distribution problems; then the complaint asserts that D does not in fact operate at the level of technological sophistication stated.)

Held, most of P's complaint must be dismissed for failure to follow Rule 9(b)'s requirement that "the circumstances constituting fraud ... shall be stated with particularity." "Generalized allegations such as these are completely inadequate. ... There must be allegations of facts amounting to deception in one form or another." (However, a few of the many allegations are sufficiently specific to withstand dismissal, and may go to trial.) *Decker v. Massey-Ferguson, Ltd.*, 681 F.2d 111 (2d Cir. 1982).

3. **If item not listed in Rule 9, no heightened pleading required:** If a particular matter is *not* listed in Rule 9, its exclusion means that the court may *not* require the party to plead that matter with particularity. *Leatherman v. Tarrant County Narcotics Intelligence & Coordination Unit*, 113 S.Ct. 1160 (1993)

> **Example:** P sues D, a governmental body, under 42 U.S.C. §1983, alleging that D has violated P's rights "under color of law." *Held*, since §1983 actions are not listed in Rule 9, a §1983 complaint does not need to plead with particularity, and merely needs to contain a "short and plain statement of the claim." *Leatherman, supra*.

VI. MOTIONS AGAINST THE COMPLAINT

A. **Motions generally:** Motions are met throughout litigation. Typically, they are contained in papers that are separate from the pleadings. They may be heard orally, or submitted to the court on briefs, from one or both sides. They may be heard and/or decided separately from the merits of the case, or on certain occasions heard at the time of trial and disposed of then. They typically relate to a particular point of law. The following discussion concerns one broad category of motions, those made by a defendant asserting the *invalidity of the plaintiff's claim or pleading.*

1. **Defenses which may be raised in motion:** Certain defenses may be raised either in the answer, or by motion. These defenses are listed in Rule 12(b):

   a. lack of *jurisdiction over the subject matter*;

   b. lack of *jurisdiction over the person*;

   c. improper *venue*;

   d. insufficiency of *process*;

   e. insufficiency of *service of process*;

   f. failure to *state a claim upon which relief may be granted*, see *infra*, p. 150; or

   g. failure to *join a necessary party* under Rule 19, see *infra*, p. 300.

2. **Time to move:** The time period in which each of these motions must be made varies.

   a. The defenses listed in (b) through (e) above must generally be made *before trial;* the precise time requirements are set out in Rule 12(h)(1).

   b. Defenses (f) and (g) may be made *at any time* before and during the trial. See Rule 12(h)(2).

c. The defense of lack of subject matter jurisdiction may be made *even after the trial*, and may be raised by the trial or appeals court if neither party raises it. See Rule 12(h)(3).

3. Based solely on pleadings: The motions referred to in Rule 12(b) are directed *solely at the pleadings*, and must be decided solely by reference to them. If either party raises contentions or introduces evidence not contained in the pleadings, the motion is treated as a motion for summary judgment under Rule 56, and not as a Rule 12 motion. See Rules 12(b) and 12(c). See the discussion of summary judgment, *infra*, p. 252.

> **Example:** P sues D on a contract. D signs an affidavit that the contract was never put in writing, and contends that the contract is therefore unenforceable under the statute of frauds. Even though D makes his motion in the form of a 12(b)(6) motion to dismiss for failure to state a claim on which relief may be granted, the motion must be treated as a Rule 56 motion for summary judgment, since items outside the pleading (e.g., the affidavit) have been introduced by the motion. Under the provisions of Rule 56, P will have a chance to produce affidavits and any relevant discovery to show that the contract was written, as well as the chance to argue that no writing was required.

B. 12(b)(6) motion to dismiss for failure to state claim: If the defendant believes that plaintiff's complaint does not state a legally sufficient claim, he can make a Rule 12(b)(6) motion to dismiss for *"failure to state a claim upon which relief can be granted."* The motion should assert that on the facts as indicated in the plaintiff's complaint, no recovery is possible *under any legal theory*.

> **Example:** P, a former patient in D Hospital, a state hospital, sues the hospital for malpractice. A state statute provides that sovereign immunity is a bar to state hospitals being held liable in tort. D's 12(b)(6) motion to dismiss should demonstrate that P can prove *no set of facts* which would entitle him to relief. Therefore, the motion should assert that on the facts as stated by P in his complaint, sovereign immunity makes any recovery, on any theory, impossible.

1. Standard for granting: The 12(b)(6) motion must not be granted "unless it appears *beyond doubt* that the plaintiff can prove *no set of facts in support of his claim* which would entitle him to relief." *Conley v. Gibson*, 355 U.S. 41 (1957).

a. Policy: The strict test of *Conley v. Gibson* reflects the great reluctance of most courts to dismiss the plaintiff's claim without giving him any chance to demonstrate it on the merits. Therefore, only when it is completely clear that trial on the merits would be fruitless will a 12(b)(6) motion be granted.

2. Amendment: If the complaint is dismissed under 12(b)(6), the plaintiff will almost always have the opportunity to *amend it*. The dismissal in such a situation is said to be *"without prejudice"* to plaintiff's right to replead.

a. Amendment as of right: Rule 15(a) allows amendment *without leave of court* any time *before a responsive pleading is served*. A 12(b)(6) motion is not itself a responsive pleading. Thus if the 12(b)(6) motion is made and granted, before the defendant has served an answer, plaintiff does not even need leave of court to amend his pleading.

b. Amendment by leave: If a responsive pleading, such as an answer, has been served by the defendant prior to the 12(b)(6) motion, permission to amend must be given by the court. Such leave to amend is almost always given following a 12(b)(6) dismissal, in line with Rule 15(a)'s statement that such leave "shall be freely given when justice so requires." Amendment of the pleadings is discussed further *infra*, p. 159.

3. **Effect of grant of motion:** If the motion to dismiss under 12(b)(6) is granted, plaintiff will have to choose between (a) continuing the action in the trial court by amending his pleading, as he is almost always allowed to do; and (b) appealing the decision on the motion.

    a. Consequences of amending: If the plaintiff exercises leave to amend his complaint and the amendment is merely a technical one, most courts will not allow the plaintiff to argue on appeal that the dismissal of his earlier pleading was erroneous. But if the amendment required by the court is so serious that it strikes "a *vital blow* to a substantial part of [the plaintiff's] cause of action," most courts will allow the plaintiff to argue on appeal that the dismissal of the first pleading was erroneous. See *Williamson v. Liverpool & London & Globe Insur. Co.*, 141 F. 54 (8th Cir. 1905).

    Example: The plaintiff's initial claim asserts that the defendant is strictly liable to him for an injury which he has suffered. The defendant succeeds in having plaintiff's claim dismissed under Rule 12(b)(6), but plaintiff is given leave to amend. He does so, this time pleading negligence. If he loses at trial on the negligence issue, he will probably be allowed to argue on appeal that the dismissal of the strict liability claim was in error. The reason for allowing him to do so is that the dismissal, insofar as it required him to assert a much harder-to-prove negligence claim, struck a "vital blow to a substantial part of [his] cause of action."

    b. Effect of appealing: If the plaintiff does not wish to replead, and insists on validity of his original pleading, a judgment will be entered on the judge's 12(b)(6) dismissal order; the plaintiff can then *immediately appeal* this judgment, since it is a "final judgment." (See 28 U.S.C.§1291.) If he loses on appeal, the appellate court may grant leave to replead under 28 U.S.C. §2106, or it may remand with discretion left to the trial court whether to allow repleading. Such leave to replead is not automatic, and the criteria for allowing it are stricter than those applied by a trial court immediately after a 12(b)(6) dismissal. (Neither an appellate nor a trial court would be likely to be too sympathetic to a plaintiff who had "gambled" on an appeal in lieu of a repleading.)

       i. Interlocutory appeal: Allowing the plaintiff to amend, after he has stood on his pleading, appealed, and lost, seems to circumvent the federal policy of not allowing interlocutory appeals (see *infra*, p. 319). But the fundamental policy against disposition of a case on technical grounds is probably more important than the policy against interlocutory appeals. (Also, the policy against interlocutory appeals is subject to waiver at the court's discretion, under 28 U.S.C. §1292(b) — see *infra*, p. 320).

4. **Effect of denial:** If the defendant *loses* on his 12(b)(6) motion, he may choose between (a) continuing the action in the trial court by answering, and (b) allowing a default judgment to be entered against him and then appealing the decision on the 12(b)(6) motion.

(He may not appeal without taking the default judgment, because the denial of his motion is not a "final judgment" under 28 U.S.C. §1291.)

   a. Effect of answer: If defendant answers and loses at trial, the appellate court may or may not end up reviewing the denial of the 12(b)(6) motion on appeal. Even if it does not, however, the same *legal issue* is likely to have arisen in one or more other guises during the trial, and the trial court's disposition of that issue is likely to be reviewable.

      i. Repeated as summary judgment motion: For instance, the defendant may rely on the same grounds that were unsuccessful in the 12(b)(6) motion in a subsequent motion for *summary judgment* before trial. Similarly, the legal issue may be reasserted as a motion for a directed verdict at the close of the evidence, or as a motion for judgment notwithstanding the verdict (JNOV) after the adverse verdict.

      ii. Appellate Review: The denial of any one of these later motions is then likely to be reviewed on appeal, so that the defendant will probably, one way or the other, get a chance at appellate review of the legal argument he first made in the 12(b)(6) motion. See F,K&C, pp. 536-37.

   b. Effect of default: If the defendant does not answer, and then loses his appeal from the default judgment, an appeals court might remand with leave to answer, though it may be unsympathetic to his "gamble" on an appeal rather than an answer. If the denial of the 12(b)(6) motion is reversed on appeal, leave to the plaintiff to replead will virtually always be granted.

C. Motion for judgment on the pleadings: A Rule 12(b)(6) motion to dismiss is generally made *before* the defendant files his answer. *After* the defendant files his answer, and the pleadings are complete, defendant can challenge the sufficiency of the complaint by a *Rule 12(c) motion for judgment on the pleadings.*

   1. Substance: The substance of a Rule 12(c) motion is exactly the same as that of a 12(b)(6) motion, except that the former is made only after the pleadings are completed, while the latter can be made as soon as the complaint is served.

D. Motion for more definite statement: If the complaint is "so vague or ambiguous that [the defendant] cannot reasonably be required to frame a responsive pleading," under Rule 12(e) the defendant may move for a *more definite statement*. If the motion is granted, the plaintiff will be required to replead his complaint in a more detailed or clearer manner. If the motion is not granted, the denial is not appealable and the defendant must file his responsive pleading.

   1. Plaintiff's motion: The plaintiff also may make a similar motion with respect to the defendant's counterclaim.

   2. Courts reluctant to grant: Motions for a more definite statement are not readily granted by the courts, since discovery is always available to tell the defendant more about the plaintiff's contentions.

      a. Test for granting: The test for whether a motion for a more definite statement should be granted is not whether plaintiff's complaint gives defendant enough information about the claim to go to trial, but merely whether it gives the defendant *enough information from which to draft his answer*, and to *commence discovery*.

E. Motion to strike: Rule 12(f) allows matter which is "redundant, immaterial, impertinent, or scandalous ..." to be *stricken* from a pleading. Such material can be stricken from any kind of pleading, whether a complaint, answer, counterclaim, or other pleading.

1. **Reluctance to grant:** Most courts are reluctant to strike material from a pleading. Most judges feel that the pleader should be given an opportunity to show on the merits that the material in question is founded in fact, and is not immaterial, scandalous or otherwise violative of Rule 12(f).

2. **Pruning:** If a pleading is grossly complicated, and Rule 8(e)'s requirement of "simple, concise and direct" averments is clearly violated, the court may sometimes *"prune"* the pleading without affecting its substance.

3. **Prejudicial material:** If the pleading contains material which is *prejudicial* to the other side, it may sometimes be stricken.

   a. **Where pleadings shown to jury:** In cases tried to a jury, the trial judge does not usually allow the jurors to see the pleadings. For this reason, there is little danger that material in the pleadings will be prejudicial to the other side, and material will generally not be stricken. But in those few jurisdictions where the pleadings are shown or read to the jury, the striking of material on the grounds of possible prejudice is not uncommon.

F. Suits brought *"in forma pauperis"*: There is another mechanism, completely outside the Federal Rules, for a certain class of cases to be dismissed by federal courts. A person who is *unable to pay costs and fees* is permitted under a federal statute (28 U.S.C. §1915) to bring a suit *"in forma pauperis."* The litigant makes an affidavit stating that he cannot pay the costs, and stating the nature of the action; the court can then allow the action to proceed without payment of costs, and can even request that a government-paid lawyer be appointed to represent the plaintiff. But there is an important limit to the plaintiff's *in forma pauperis* rights: §1915(d) allows the court to dismiss the case "if satisfied that the action is *frivolous* or *malicious*."

1. **Distinguished from 12(b)(6) motion:** There are some important differences between the court's ability to dismiss the action under §1915(d) and its regular right to dismiss ordinary civil actions under Rule 12(b)(6): (1) Most important, the *in forma pauperis* suit may be dismissed because the court does not believe the *factual allegations* in the complaint. By contrast, a 12(b)(6) motion takes the factual allegations as true, and examines only the legal adequacy of the complaint. (2) In an *in forma pauperis* suit, the court may dismiss "sua sponte," i.e., "on its own," with no advance notice to the plaintiff. By contrast, notice to the plaintiff, with an opportunity to amend the complaint, is required before a case is dismissed under 12(b)(6).

   a. **Consequence:** Consequently, if the court believes that P in an *in forma pauperis* suit is or may be stating true facts, but these facts do not state a legal claim, the court probably may not use the streamlined procedure of §1915(d). It must instead proceed under Rule 12(b)(6), thus giving P a chance to oppose dismissal or to amend before the ruling. See *Neitzke v. Williams*, 490 U.S. 319 (1989), to this effect.

Quiz Yourself on

PLEADING GENERALLY, THE COMPLAINT AND MOTIONS AGAINST IT

35. One day, Paul called Larry, a lawyer whom Paul had never met. Paul said to Larry, "Larry, I've been in a terrible car accident. I was a passenger in a car driven by Dave. Dave ran a stop sign, plowed into another car, and I was badly injured. I've been in the hospital for two months, I've got severe lower back damage, and the doctors say I'll never be able to work again. I'd like to sue Dave." Larry accepted the truth of Paul's statements, asked only a few questions about how the accident occurred, and then prepared a complaint stating that Paul had been permanently injured, had lost the ability ever to work again, and was entitled to $1 million in damages. Who, if anyone, must sign this complaint before it is served on Dave in a federal court action based on diversity? _____

36. Same facts as prior question. Assume that Larry honestly and in good faith believed everything that Paul told him. Larry did not ask for a copy of the police report. The actual police report showed that the driver was Dennis, not Dave. The case then went to trial. At trial, it turned out that Dennis, not Dave, was the driver, and that the suit was just Paul's attempt to find a "deeper pocket" to sue, since Dennis was judgment-proof. It also turned out at trial that Paul had only minor injuries, and had already been back at work at the time he made the telephone call to Larry. Dave has now finally won the case, but only after spending $10,000 in attorney's fees to defend the case. What, if any, action should Dave's lawyer take now that Dave has prevailed at trial? _____

37. P was injured in an automobile accident when his car was hit by a car driven by D. P has brought a negligence suit in federal court for the district in which P resides. The complaint states that P is a citizen of New York and that D is a citizen of New Jersey. The complaint also recites the facts of the collision, asserts that D was negligent, and asserts that P has suffered serious injuries (in an amount not specified). Nothing else in the complaint refers to any dollar amount. Is P's complaint a sufficient one?

_____

38. P and D entered into a contract. The contract turned out to be very unfavorable to P. P has uncovered evidence suggesting that D misrepresented certain major facts about the proposed contractual arrangement in order to induce P to enter into the contract. Therefore, P has brought a federal court action, based on diversity, against D. P's complaint recites the date and general subject matter of the contract, and then states, "D fraudulently induced P to enter into this contract." On account of this fraud, P asks the court to grant the equitable relief of rescinding the contract.

(a) Putting aside the correctness of the complaint's jurisdictional allegations and the adequacy of its demand for judgment, does the complaint satisfy the pleading requirements of the Federal Rules?

_____

(b) In light of your answer to (a), what procedural steps should D take? _____

39. P, an individual, brought a federal diversity action for libel against D, a television station. Before filing an answer, D made a timely motion under Federal Rule 12(b)(6) for dismissal for failure to state a claim upon which relief can be granted. The essence of D's motion was that under applicable substantive law, a statement made over the airwaves by a television station cannot be libel, and is at most slander. The federal judge agreed with D, and ordered P's claim dismissed. P now wishes to amend his pleading to allege slander rather than libel. Must P get the court's permission to amend his pleading in this manner?

_____

Answers

35. **Larry.** Federal Rule 11, first sentence, provides that "every pleading ... of a party represented by an attorney shall be signed by at least one attorney of record in the attorney's individual name. ... "

36. **Move for Rule 11 sanctions against Paul and/or Larry.** Rule 11 states that "by presenting [a pleading] to the court ... an attorney or unrepresented party is certifying that to the best of the person's knowledge, information, and belief, formed after an *inquiry reasonable under the circumstances* ... (3) the allegations and other factual contentions have *evidentiary support*." The rule goes on to say that if there is a violation, "the court may ... impose an appropriate sanction." Possible sanctions include "an order to pay a penalty to the court."

   Although Larry acted in good faith in signing the pleading, he almost certainly did not have a belief, made after a "reasonable inquiry," that there was evidentiary support for the proposition that Dave was the driver. For instance, reasonable inquiry would probably have included getting a copy of the police report, which would have led Larry to realize that Dennis, not Dave, should be the defendant. Assuming that the court agrees that Larry acted without making reasonable inquiries, the court could award sanctions against either Larry or Paul. Since Paul is the more guilty of the two (his wrongdoing was deliberate), the court will almost certainly award sanctions against Paul, and possibly against Larry as well. The court should probably order Paul and/or Larry to pay Dave the $10,000 that Dave has spent in attorney's fees defending the suit.

37. **No.** Observe that nothing in the complaint states that P has been injured to the extent of more than $50,000. Since the case is brought in diversity, the $50,000 amount in controversy requirement must be met. A federal court complaint is required to include "a short and plain statement of the grounds upon which the court's jurisdiction depends. ..." Federal Rule 8(a)(1). This is interpreted to require, in the case of a diversity suit, a statement that more than $50,000 is at stake. Consequently, P must amend her complaint to state something like, "As the result of D's negligence, P has suffered injuries aggregating more than $50,000."

38. (a) **No.** Federal Rule 9 sets out certain matters that must be pleaded in extra detail, called "special matters." One of these is fraud, as detailed in Rule 9(b): "In all averments of fraud or mistake, the circumstances constituting fraud or mistake shall be stated with particularity." P's conclusory statement that D fraudulently induced him to enter into the contract (without a statement of what the fraudulent misrepresentations were, or how D knew that these representations were false) seems not to satisfy this requirement of particularity.

   (b) **Make a Rule 12(e) motion for more definite statement.** If this motions fails, then at the least, D would be entitled in discovery to probe the details of how P thinks D behaved fraudulently.

39. **No.** Rule 15(a) provides that "a party may amend the party's pleading once as a matter of course at any time before a responsive pleading is served. ..." Since D has not yet served his responsive pleading (i.e., his answer), P has the right to make one amendment even without permission of the court or of his adversary. (D's filing of a motion against the complaint is not deemed to be a "responsive pleading" for this purpose.) But if D had already served his answer, then P would have to get the court's permission to amend or else get the written consent of the adverse party. (But even in this situation, Rule 15(a) states that "leave [to amend] shall be freely given when justice so requires," so the court would almost certainly give P such leave.)

VII. THE ANSWER

A. **The answer generally:** The defendant's response to the plaintiff's complaint is called an answer. Just as the plaintiff, in his complaint, must make a "short and plain statement of the claim," so the defendant in his answer "shall state in short and plain terms his defenses to each claim asserted and shall admit or deny the averments upon which the adverse party relies." Rule 8(b).

1. **Answer to counterclaim:** The language of Rule 8(b), quoted above, applies not only to a defendant's answer to a plaintiff's claim, but also to a plaintiff's answer to a defendant's counterclaim, to the answer of a third-party defendant to a third-party claim, and other such pleadings.

2. **Liberal rules:** The liberal rules of pleading, described above with respect to the complaint, are equally applicable to the answer. Thus answers, like complaints, must be "so construed as to do substantial justice."

3. **Alternative pleading:** Defenses, like claims, may be pleaded in the *alternative*. The defendant may even make defenses which are incompatible with each other.

   Example: In a breach of contract suit brought by P, D can in count 1 of his answer state that no contract ever existed, and in count 2 state that if such a contract did exist, it was breached by P, not D.

B. **Denials:** The defendant will seldom wish to concede, in his answer, the truth of all of the plaintiff's allegations. He is, therefore, permitted to make various kinds of *denials*, depending on how much of the plaintiff's complaint he wishes to deny, and on the state of his knowledge regarding the truth of the plaintiff's claims.

1. **Where not denied:** Averments in a complaint, other than those concerning the *amount of damage*, are "*admitted when not denied* … in the [answer]." Rule 8(d).

2. **Kinds of denials:** There are five kinds of denials in federal practice, four of which are set out in Rule 8(b), and the fifth of which is a judge-made extrapolation from Rule 11.

   a. **General denial:** Rule 8(b) permits the defendant to say that he "denies *each and every allegation* in plaintiff's complaint." This is a *"general denial."* 8(b) tries to restrict the general denial to situations where the defendant intends in good faith to contest *all of the plaintiff's allegations*, including the complaint's jurisdictional grounds: "When a pleader intends in good faith to deny only a *part* or a *qualification* of an averment, the pleader shall specify so much of it as is true and material and shall deny only the remainder." That is, unless the defendant is prepared to contest every single allegation in the complaint, one of the other types of denials listed below (e.g., specific denial or qualified denial) must be used rather than general denial. See, e.g., *Zielinski v. Philadelphia Piers, Inc.*, 139 F.Supp. 408 (E.D.Pa. 1956) (penalizing a defendant who improperly used a general denial when the defendant was really only contesting only one aspect of the complaint).

b. Specific denial: A denial may be made of all the allegations of a specific paragraph or averment of the complaint. This is a "*specific* denial."

c. Qualified denial: A denial may be made of a particular portion of a particular allegation. This is a "*qualified* denial."

d. Denial of knowledge or information (DKI): Defendant may "deny *knowledge or information*" if he does not have knowledge or information sufficient to form a belief as to the truth of plaintiff's complaint. This has the effect of a full denial, and is subject to the requirement of good faith.

e. Denial based on information and belief: The "denial based on *information and belief*" is not specifically set forth in 8(b). The courts have allowed a defendant without *first-hand knowledge*, but with enough information to believe in good faith that the complaint is false, to deny it on that ground. This kind of denial is usually used by *large corporate defendants*, on whom the burden of obtaining information may be great.

C. Signed by defendant's attorney: The answer must be *signed* by the defendant's lawyer. Rule 11 requires that every pleading be signed by an attorney representing the pleader, and provides that the signature "constitutes a certificate by the signer that the signer has read the pleading …; that to the best of the signer's knowledge, information, and belief formed after reasonable inquiry it is well grounded in fact and is warranted by existing law or a good faith argument for the extension, modification, or reversal of existing law, and that it is not interposed for any improper purpose, such as to harass or to cause unnecessary delay or needless increase in the cost of litigation." See *supra*, p. 140, for more about Rule 11.

1. Theoretical good faith requirement: This "reasonable inquiry" requirement in theory at least prevents the defendant's attorney from denying allegations which he knows to be truthful, and from denying knowledge or information about the allegation if he knows it to be truthful. If the lawyer violates Rule 11, sanctions may be used by the court. See *supra*, p. 140.

D. Affirmative defenses: Rule 8(c) lists 19 specific defenses which must be explicitly pleaded in the answer, if the defendant is to raise them at trial. Among the more important of these "*affirmative defenses*" are contributory negligence, fraud, *res judicata*, statute of limitations, and illegality.

1. Test for affirmative defense: In addition to the 19 items specifically listed in Rule 8(c), that Rule requires the defendant to plead affirmatively "any other matter constituting an avoidance or affirmative defense." The essential criterion for deciding whether a defense is an affirmative one is roughly as follows: *any new matter or issue not embraced by the complaint should be pleaded as an affirmative defense.*

2. Rationale: The justification for requiring the pleading of affirmative defenses derives from the notice-giving function of pleadings in federal practice. Affirmative defenses are those which the plaintiff may not be anticipating. This is so because they involve new issues not contained in the complaint. Therefore, the defendant must plead these new matters in order to put the plaintiff on his guard.

a. Facts within defendant's knowledge: Furthermore, affirmative defenses often involve facts that are peculiarly within the ***defendant's knowledge***. For this reason as well, it seems fair to put the burden upon the defendant, rather than the plaintiff, to allege these factual matters. See, e.g., *Gomez v. Toledo*, 446 U.S. 635 (1980), in which P sued D, a public official, for damages under §1983 of the Civil Rights Act. A public official's qualified immunity from damages liability was held to be an affirmative defense, and therefore up to D to plead, because it "depends on facts peculiarly within the knowledge and control of the defendant" (e.g., his good faith belief that his conduct was lawful, based upon "state or local law, advice of counsel, administrative practice, or some other factor of which the official alone is aware").

3. Amendment: A defendant who has neglected to plead an affirmative defense may use Rule 15(a)'s liberal amendment mechanism. In most instances, 15(a) gives the defendant 20 days from the service of the original answer in which to amend. After that, leave of court is necessary, but "leave shall be freely given when justice so requires." Even in the early stages of trial, when pleading may be presumed to be completed, leave to plead an affirmative defense will almost invariably be granted.

4. Allocation of pleading burden: Generally, in state courts, the allocation of the burden of pleading parallels the allocation of the ***burden of proof***. In diversity actions, however, the Supreme Court has held (*Palmer v. Hoffman*, 318 U.S. 109, 1943) that state law of pleading must be ***ignored*** in distributing the federal burden of pleading, even though state allocation of burden of proof controls at trial. Therefore, a defense which is listed in Rule 8(c) must be affirmatively pleaded, even though the state law, which will control as to burden of proof, holds that the defense is not an affirmative one.

a. State law consulted where 8(c) silent: "If Rule 8(c) is silent about a particular defense, state law, though not controlling, is frequently looked to in deciding whether it is an affirmative defense." Wr., 435, fn. 61.

E. Counterclaims: In addition to defenses, if the defendant has a claim against the plaintiff, he may, in all cases, and must, in some cases, plead that claim as a ***counterclaim***. If the counterclaim is one which the defendant is required to plead, it is called a ***compulsory*** counterclaim. If it is one which the defendant has the option of pleading or not, it is called a ***permissive*** counterclaim. Counterclaims, which are treated by Federal Rule 13, are discussed more extensively *infra*, p. 289.

VIII. TIME FOR VARIOUS PLEADINGS

A. Timetable: The timetable for various pleading steps is given by Rule 12(a), and is as follows:

1. Complaint: Filing of the complaint will normally occur before it is served. Service must then normally occur within 120 days (Rule 4(m)).

2. Answer: The ***answer*** must be served within ***20 days*** after service of the complaint, except that:

    a. **Different state rule:** If the plaintiff has served the defendant *out of state*, by using the long arm statute of the state where the district court sits (as allowed by Rule 4(k)(1)(A) — see *supra*, p. 41), the time to answer allowed under that state rule governs (typically a longer period).

    b. **Rule 12 motion:** if defendant makes a Rule 12 motion against the complaint, and loses, he has 10 days after the court denies the motion to answer. (If he wins, the plaintiff will usually replead.)

    c. **60 days if D waives formal service:** Under a 1993 amendment to Rule 12, if the defendant agrees to the plaintiff's request for *waiver of formal service* of the summons, then the defendant gets *60 days*, rather than 20 days, to answer. See Rule 12(a)(1)(B). The time runs from the date the request for waiver was sent by the plaintiff. This additional time is meant as an incentive to the defendant to accept "service by mail" in lieu of formal service. See *supra*, p. 45.

  3. **Reply to counterclaim:** If the answer contains a *counterclaim*, the plaintiff must serve his *reply* within *20 days* after the service of the answer.

IX. AMENDMENT OF THE PLEADINGS

A. Liberal policy: Rule 15 sets forth an extremely liberal policy on the amendment of pleadings.

B. Amendment as of right: A pleading may be amended once *as a matter of course* (i.e., without leave of court) in the following circumstances: (Rule 15(a)).

  1. **Responsive pleading required:** If the pleading is one to which the adversary must make a *response* (e.g., a complaint must be responded to by an answer — Rule 7(a)), the pleading may be amended *any time before the responsive pleading is served*.

    a. **Motions:** Motions are not considered responsive pleadings for this purpose, so the fact that an adversary has made, say, a 12(b)(6) motion, does not preclude amendment as a matter of course. Wr., 428.

  2. **Response not required:** If the pleading is one to which a responsive pleading is *not* required (e.g., an answer does not require a response, unless it contains a counterclaim), it may be amended within *20 days* after it is served.

C. Amendment by leave of court: If the requirements for amendment as of course are not met, the pleading may be amended only by *leave of court*, or by *consent of the other side*.

  1. **Leave freely given:** Leave by the court to amend "shall be freely given when justice so requires." Rule 15(a).

    a. **"Actual prejudice" usually required:** Normally, leave to amend should be denied only if it would cause *actual prejudice* to the other party.

    Example: P, who has been injured using a water slide, brings a personal injury action against D. D initially admits that it manufactured the slide. More than a year after this admission (and after the statute of limitations has apparently passed on any personal injury claim by P arising out of this accident), D discovers that it did not manufacture the slide, and moves to amend its answer to deny manufacture. The trial judge allows the amendment, a jury finds that D did not manufacture the slide, and P appeals the judge's grant of the amendment.

Held, the trial court did not abuse its discretion in allowing D to amend. Leave to amend will generally be denied only where granting it would result in actual prejudice to the other party, and the burden is on that other party to show such prejudice. Here, P did not show such prejudice, since he did not establish that if D were allowed to amend, D would prevail on the factual issue of manufacture of the slide; nor did P demonstrate that he would not be able to sue other parties because of the statue of limitations. Since disallowing the amendment would have been clearly prejudicial to D, and since there was no evidence that D's delay in moving to amend was motivated by bad faith, the trial court's ruling was not an abuse of discretion. *Beeck v. Aquaslide 'N' Dive Corp.*, 562 F.2d 537 (8th Cir. 1977).

    i. Belated amendment: Despite the rule that actual prejudice must generally be shown for an amendment to be denied, "a busy court does not abuse its discretion if it protects itself from being imposed on by the presentation of theories seriatim, and may deny a belated application to amend that makes a ***drastic change*** in the case in the absence of some good reason why the amendment is offered at a late stage." Wr. 429.

  b. Amendment at trial: In addition to the general principle that leave to amend shall be freely given if justice requires (see Rule 15(a)), amendment is generally allowed at trial when the evidence is objected to as being outside the scope of the pleadings. See Rule 15(b). See also the discussion of variance, below.

D. Relation back: Where a pleading has been amended, if the claim or defenses asserted in the amended pleading "arose out of the conduct, transaction or occurrence set forth or attempted to be set forth in the original pleading," the amendment ***relates back*** to the date of the original pleading. Rule 15(c).

1. Utility: The utility of this provision is in meeting ***statutes of limitation*** that have run between the filing of the original complaint and the amendment. Without such a provision, a plaintiff whose original complaint met the statute of limitations might find himself barred by the statute, even though his amended pleading was only slightly different from the original one, and even though the defendant had received fair notice of the general nature of the plaintiff's claim before the statute of limitations had run. Wr., 429-30.

2. When action is deemed "commenced": According to Rule 3, an action is deemed commenced as of the date on which the complaint is filed. In federal question cases, it is to this date that the amendment presumably relates back. In ***diversity cases***, by contrast, it will sometimes be the case that state law recognizes a different date (e.g., the date on which the complaint is ***served*** on the defendant) as being the commencement of the action for statute of limitations purposes. In this situation, it is probably the state commencement date, not the date of filing, to which the amendment of the pleading relates back. *Cf. Ragan v. Merchants Transfer and Warehouse Co, infra*, p. 228.

3. Easier state "relation back" rule followed: In a ***diversity*** case, the pleader gets the benefit of any more ***liberal state rule*** for deciding whether the amended complaint relates closely enough to the original complaint to qualify for relation back, if such a rule exists. In fact, the pleader gets the choice of the federal "same transaction or occurrence" standard or the state standard, whichever is more favorable. FRCP 15(c)(1) allows relation back if this "is permitted by the law that provides the statute of limitations applicable to the action. ..."

> **Example 1:** On Jan. 1, 1990, P serves D in a federal diversity action based on a 1989 contract between the two parties. On March 1, P realizes that D has also breached a 1988 contract between the parties, relating to a different but similar transaction. Therefore, on March 1 P amends to include the 1988 claim. The statute of limitations ran on the 1988 claim on Feb. 1, 1990. Assume that under *Erie* principles (see *infra*, p. 222), the applicable substantive state law is that of North Carolina, where the contract was signed. Under North Carolina's very liberal "relation back" law, the 1990 filing of the 1988 claim would relate back to the filing date of the original 1989 claim, because the two involved the same parties and a related, but different, transaction. Under the ordinary federal principles stated in Rule 15(c), the 1988 claim would not relate back, because it is not part of the same transaction as the earlier-filed claim. But under FRCP 15(c)(1), the fact that P could use the "relation back" doctrine under North Carolina law means that P *may also use that doctrine in her federal case.* Therefore, service of the amended complaint relates back to Jan. 1, 1990, and the filing will be deemed timely even though D does not learn of the 1988 claim until after the statute of limitations has run.

> **Example 2:** P brings a diversity action against D, asserting that a machine sold by D to P violated an implied warranty given by P to D, and caused personal injury to P. P's suit is filed on Jan. 1, 1990. On March 1, P realizes that on these facts, the better claim against D is a tort claim for strict product liability. That day, therefore, P amends his complaint to change the claim to tort. The statute of limitations on a tort action for this transaction ran on Feb. 1, 1990. Under Idaho law (the law that would govern the transaction, under *Erie* principles, since both P and D are based in Idaho), the "relation back" doctrine is very narrowly construed, and would not apply here, since P has changed his fundamental legal theory even though the same transaction is at issue in the amendment. In his federal action, P will get the benefit of relation back, under FRCP 15(c)(2), even though state law would not recognize the doctrine. In other words, under FRCP 15(c), P gets the benefit of "relation back" if *either* state law would grant the doctrine or 15(c)(2)'s "same conduct, transaction, or occurrence" test is satisfied.

4. **Change of party:** Suppose that the amendment to a pleading *changes the party* against whom the claim is asserted. In this situation, the amendment "relates back" only if, in addition to the "same transaction or occurrence" rule discussed above, it is the case that "within the period provided by Rule 4(m) for service of the summons and complaint, the party to be brought in by amendment (A) has received such notice of the institution of the action that the party will not be prejudiced in maintaining a defense on the merits, and (B) knew or should have known that, but for a mistake concerning the identity of the proper party, the action would have been brought against the party." Rule 15(c)(3).

a. **Illustration:** Suppose a complaint names D1, and is filed prior to the expiration of the statute of limitations. Suppose further that after the running of the statute, P discovers that the complaint really should have named D2, amends the complaint, and serves D2 sufficiently quickly that service is timely within Rule 4(m) (i.e., within 120 days after filing). Does the amendment as to D2 "relate back" to the original, timely filing? The answer is *"yes."* Rule 15(c)(3).

Example: The Ps file complaints for libel near the end of the applicable (state) statute of limitations. The complaints name "Fortune" as defendant. "Fortune," however, lacks the capacity to be sued, because it is only the name of a magazine and a division of Time, Inc., the magazine's publisher. After the statute of limitations has run, but within the 120-day period allowed for service of process under Rule 4(m), the Ps amend the complaints to name Time, Inc., and serve them on Time. Time argues that since no complaint properly naming it as defendant was served on it prior to the running of the statute, the Ps' action is now time-barred.

As a result of a 1991 amendment to 15(c)(3), Time, Inc. would lose with this argument. Since Time, Inc. was served "within the period provided by Rule 4(m) for service of the summons and complaint. ..." relation back would occur even though the service on Time did not take place until after the statute of limitations ran.

Note: The facts of the above example illustrate exactly the situation which motivated the 1991 amendment to 15(c)(3). On these facts, the Supreme Court, interpreting the pre-1991 version of 15(c)(3), held that Time, Inc. had *not* been timely served. *Schiavone v. Fortune*, 477 U.S. 21 (1986). (The prior version of 15(c)(3) required that the defendant receive actual notice of the suit "within the period provided by law for commencing an action against him." The Court held in *Schiavone* that this language meant that notice must be received before the statute of limitations has run, not before the expiration of the time for service of a timely-filed complaint.)

X. VARIANCE OF PROOF FROM PLEADINGS

A. **Common law and Code rules:** At common law, and under the Codes, a party was generally *barred* from proving material which he had not pleaded. If the court allowed such a *variance* of the proof from the pleadings, judgment was frequently reversed on appeal.

Example: P, a young woman, sues D, the magnate of Loew's theatres, for breach of a contract to "put your name in lights." The complaint alleges that the consideration for this was P's promise to accompany D and to devote herself to him as he should require. At trial, P testifies that she promised to "be like a daughter" to D. *Held* (on appeal), this "like a daughter" testimony was at variance with the pleading. Therefore, the trial court correctly issued a directed verdict for D. *Manning v. Loew*, 46 N.E.2d 1022 (Mass. 1943)

B. **Federal practice:** The Federal Rules are quite tolerant of deviation of proof from pleadings, so long as the variance does not unduly prejudice the other side.

1. **Tolerance:** The federal policy of tolerance toward variance is demonstrated by Rule 15(b), which provides that "If evidence is objected to at the trial on the grounds that it is

not within the issues made by the pleadings, the court may allow the pleadings to be *amended* and *shall do so freely* when the presentation of the merits of the action will be subserved thereby, and the objecting party fails to satisfy the court that the admission of such evidence would prejudice him in maintaining his action or defense upon the merits." 15(b) then provides that "The court may grant a *continuance* to enable the objecting party to meet such evidence."

2. **Effect:** The effect of Rule 15(b) is that an objection at the trial that proffered evidence is outside the scope of the pleadings, will seldom be sustained. The objecting party's best chance is to show that the omission of the issue from the adversary's pleading was *intentional*, and was designed to lead the objecting party into *wasted preparation*.

    a. **Objection after trial:** If variance is not objected to until *after* the trial, the objection is even less likely to be successful. The reason for this is that, by Rule 15(b), "When issues not raised by the pleadings are tried by express or implied consent of the parties, they shall be treated in all respects as if they had been raised in the pleadings." The objecting party's failure to speak up during the trial will generally be held to be an *implied consent* to trial of the issue, and the issue will be treated as if it had been originally pleaded.

    Example: P's complaint, brought under the Federal Tort Claims Act, does not allege special damages. At trial, P introduces evidence of such special damages. D does not object that such evidence is beyond the scope of the pleadings, and in fact cross-examines P's witness as to the special damages. D loses at trial and appeals.

    Held, D has *waived*, for purpose of appeal, the contention that special damages are not allowable when not pleaded. By his cross-examination, D has "impliedly consented" to the trial of the special damages issue, and Rule 15(b) applies. *Niedland v. U.S.*, 388 F.2d 254 (3rd Cir. 1964).

    b. **Evidence on two issues:** But if evidence is relevant to two issues, only one of which is pleaded, the adversary's failure to object to the evidence does not amount to an implied consent to trial of the issue not contained in the pleadings.

    Example: P sues D on a breach of contract claim, but does not make a *quantum meruit* claim. P introduces evidence at trial that he substantially performed the contract, and D produces evidence that there was not substantial performance. After trial, P argues in his brief that he is entitled to recover in *quantum meruit*, despite the absence of such a claim in his complaint. He contends that D introduced evidence on the substantial performance question, a question relevant to *quantum meruit*, and that D has therefore impliedly consented to the trial of the *quantum meruit* issue. P's argument should *not* succeed, because D's evidence on substantial performance was also relevant to the contract claim, and D has therefore not impliedly consented to trial of the *quantum meruit* claim.

Quiz Yourself on

THE ANSWER, TIMING, AMENDMENTS AND VARIANCE

40. P brought a federal diversity action against D, alleging that D breached an oral agreement to employ P for a five-year period. D, in his answer, denied each and every allegation of P, as permitted by Federal Rule 8(b). In what respect, if any, could D's answer have been improved? _____

41. P began a diversity suit against D by filing a complaint with the court on July 1. Service was made upon D on July 5. (D was served within the state in which the action is pending.) Assuming that D has not made any motion against the complaint, what is the last day upon which D may serve his answer? _____

42. On July 1, P filed with the federal court a complaint alleging that D violated a particular patent belonging to P; the complaint alleged that D imported a certain machine into the United States on a particular day, thereby committing the patent violation. According to federal trademark statutes, P's time for commencing the action expired on July 5. On July 10, P made personal service of the complaint upon D. On July 25, P, after realizing that it had cited the wrong patent number in its complaint, served upon D an amended complaint listing the correct patent number. All other aspects of the complaint are the same. Is P's amended complaint time-barred? _____

43. Pedestrian was severely injured when a car driven by Driver and owned by Owner struck him. Pedestrian brought a diversity action alleging negligence; the complaint was filed on July 1, and listed Driver as the sole defendant. According to applicable state law, the statute of limitations would be satisfied only if Pedestrian commenced the action no later than July 5; under state law, the filing of a complaint with the court is deemed to commence the action (as it is under Federal Rule 3). On July 10, Pedestrian made personal service upon Driver. That same day, Driver gave a copy of the suit to Owner, saying, "I'm surprised they didn't bring you into the suit as well." On July 11, Pedestrian filed an amended complaint listing Owner as a co-defendant. On July 12, this complaint was served on both Driver and Owner. Owner now moves to dismiss the amended complaint as being time-barred, at least as against him. Should Owner's motion be granted? _____

44. P, while standing on the sidewalk, was injured when a car driven by Driver and manufactured by Carco suddenly swerved in the street and struck her. P brought a federal court diversity action against Carco. Her complaint asserted that Carco had produced a dangerously defective product, and that Carco is strictly liable for P's injuries. At trial, P offered evidence that Carco was negligent in not ascertaining that the design of the car produced a significant likelihood of a sudden swerve to the right. Carco's lawyer did not object to this proof of negligence. The judge (the case was tried to a judge rather than to a jury) found that strict product liability does not apply to injuries caused to a bystander such as P, but also found that Carco is liable to P because of Carco's negligence in designing the car. Carco now moves to have the trial judge's verdict set aside, on the grounds that it is based upon a claim (negligence) that was not contained in P's complaint. How should the trial judge respond to this motion? _____

Answers

40. By asserting the affirmative defense of Statute of Frauds. Rule 8(c) states that a party shall "set forth affirmatively" a number of defenses, including Statute of Frauds. A defendant who does not specifically plead an affirmative defense may be held at trial to have waived the right to present evidence on that defense.

41. July 25. Even though the case is deemed commenced by filing the complaint with the court (see Federal Rule 3), D's time to answer does not start to run until he receives service. Under Rule 12(a) D generally has 20 days from receipt of summons and complaint within which to answer.

42. No. First, understand that in cases in which the Plaintiff's claim arises under the federal Constitution or a federal statute (i.e., federal-question cases), the action is deemed commenced, for statute of limitations purposes, by the filing of a complaint with the court. (Rule 3.) (In a diversity suit, state law determines what constitutes the commencement of the action for statute of limitations purposes.) Therefore, at least as to P's original complaint, P satisfied the statute of limitations by filing before July 5, even though service was not made on D until after this date.

Second, when P served the amended complaint on July 25, P got the benefit of Rule 15(c)(2), which provides that "whenever the claim or defense asserted in the amended pleading arose out of the conduct, transaction, or occurrence set forth or attempted to be set forth in the original pleading, the amendment *relates back* to the date of the original pleading." The same transaction (importation of a particular machine violating P's patents) is charged in both complaints, despite the fact that the patent number changed. Therefore, the amended complaint relates back to the original July 1 complaint filing, and is timely.

43. No. If there is a change of party, relation back (see previous question) may still help the plaintiff. But for the amended complaint to relate back in this changed-party situation, the plaintiff must pass three obstacles: (1) the claim must arise out of the same conduct, transaction or occurrence as the original complaint; (2) before the time for service of the summons and complaint has expired, the new defendant must have "received such notice of the institution of the action that the party will not be prejudiced in maintaining a defense on the merits"; and (3) before the time for serving the complaint and summons has expired, it must be the case that the new defendant "knew or should have known that, but for a mistake concerning the identity of the proper party, the action would have been brought against the party." Federal Rule 15(c)(3). Since requirement (1) is clearly satisfied, the issue is whether (2) and (3) are.

According to Rule 4(m), the time limit for service of the summons and complaint is 120 days after the complaint is filed. Since Owner was indeed served before this time expired (on July 12), and since Owner should have known that the action would be brought against him (from the conversation on July 10), the action is not time-barred and Owner's motion should not be granted.

Before the 1991 amendment to Rule 15(c), Pedestrian was required to serve notice on Owner before the statute of limitations had run (July 5), and therefore service would not have been timely. As this fact pattern demonstrates, the 1991 change allows for a more liberal amendment procedure (120 days as opposed to 5) than old Rule 15(c).

44. Deny it. The first sentence of Rule 15(b) provides that "when issues not raised by the pleadings are tried by express or implied consent of the parties, they shall be treated in all respects as if they had been raised in the pleadings." When Carco remained silent in the face of P's presentation of evidence on negligence, Carco was implicitly consenting to the trial of this issue, so the court will treat the case as if the complaint alleged negligence by Carco.

Exam Tips *on*
PLEADING

Be alert to Pleadings issues whenever the fact pattern gives you information about either (1) *when* a pleading was served or filed (whether it's a complaint, answer or reply), or (2) the *contents* of the pleading. Here are some particular things to check for:

☞ If the pleading you are given is a federal complaint, make sure that it contains the requisite *jurisdictional* allegations. [146] Professors sometimes give you the text of a complaint, and expect you to notice that the jurisdictional allegations are missing. If so, state that D can move to dismiss for lack of jurisdiction (since the burden is on P to make the jurisdictional allegations explicitly.)

☞ Again in a federal complaint, make sure that any *"special matter"* is pleaded with *particularity*. If it is not, have the defendant make a motion for a more definite statement. [148-149]

☞ Thus be on the lookout for allegations of *fraud*, *mistake*, etc., that are stated conclusorally. Also, if the complaint claims damages that are in fact *"special" damages* (i.e., ones which would not normally be expected to flow from the kind of injury P is claiming), make sure these special damages are pleaded in detail. For instance, damages for intangible torts like slander and false imprisonment, or consequential damages in contracts cases, will often be "special."

☞ Remember that pleading in the *alternative* is *allowable* under the FRCP (and in most states), so don't fall for assertions that a complaint should be dismissed because the allegations are inconsistent or mutually exclusive. [145]

☞ Scrutinize any *motions* made by D, to determine whether the rules governing motions have been satisfied. For instance, a Rule 12(b)(6) motion for "failure to state a claim upon which relief can be granted" must be made *before* D answers (though after the answer, D can move under 12(c) for "judgment on the pleadings.")[149-153]

☞ Keep in mind that in a 12(b)(6) motion, the motion can be granted only if there is *no set of facts that P could prove* that would entitle her to relief. It's not enough that the judge thinks that P is very unlikely to be able to prove the allegations contained in the complaint.

☞ If the pattern indicates that at trial D has tried to prove facts that amount to an *affirmative defense*, check back to make sure that the answer contained the affirmative defense. This applies to defenses like contributory negligence, fraud, res judicata, statute of limitations and illegality. If the trial is already well along before this failure-to-plead surfaces, have P move to dismiss the affirmative defense, or in the alternative to postpone the trial while P prepares to rebut the affirmative defense. [157-158]

☞ Be alert to whether pleadings are served and filed in a *timely* manner. [158-159] In a federal suit:

☞   D has *20 days* after service to answer, but if he has been served out of state by use of the state's long-arm, any *longer* period to answer allowed by that long-arm controls.

☞   If D *waives* formal service, then he gets *60 days* from the date the request for waiver was sent to him by P.

☞   If the answer contains a *counterclaim*, P gets *20 days* after service to reply.

☛ Know when *amendment* is allowed of right, and when it must be granted by leave of court. For instance, P gets to amend once by right prior to D's service of an answer. [159-160]

☛ If there seems to be a question whether a statute of limitations (S/L) is satisfied, and the complaint was originally served before expiration of the S/L, but amended after expiration, look for a *"relation back"* issue. [160-162]. In general, the amended complaint "relates back" to the date the action was originally commenced (but special limits apply where the amendment changes the party against whom the complaint is asserted.)

CHAPTER 5

DISCOVERY AND PRETRIAL CONFERENCE

Introductory Note: The main emphasis of this chapter is on the discovery procedures set forth in the *Federal Rules*. More states have adopted the Federal Rules for discovery than have adopted any other set of provisions of the Federal Rules, and these provisions give a good indication of the trends of modern discovery. The federal procedures for conducting pretrial conferences are also discussed.

The Federal Rules governing discovery were amended more profoundly in 1993 than at any time since their enactment. The 1993 revisions made certain types of disclosure automatic and compulsory early on in the lawsuit (see *infra*, p. 182), limited the number of interrogatories and depositions each side could issue or take (*infra*, p. 194 and p. 196, respectively), allowed videotaping of depositions in lieu of stenography (*infra*, p. 193), and otherwise changed the discovery landscape.

ChapterScope

This Chapter covers discovery, the process by which each party to a litigation reveals to her adversaries facts, documents, and other aspects of her claims or defenses. The emphasis in this chapter, as noted, is on the discovery provisions of the Federal Rules. The most important concepts in this Chapter are:

■ **Forms of discovery:** Discovery under the Federal Rules includes six main types:

❑ *Automatic disclosure*, in which each party must disclose in writing the names of occurrence witnesses, facts about documents, etc., early on in the litigation without a request from the other side.

❑ *Depositions*, in which a lawyer asks questions to a party or to a non-party witness. (Usually depositions are *oral*, i.e., both questions and answers are spoken and recorded.)

❑ *Interrogatories* addressed to a party. An interrogatory is a set of written questions, which is also answered in writing.

❑ Requests to *inspect* documents or property;

❑ Requests for *admission* of facts;

❑ Requests for physical or mental *examination*.

■ **Scope generally:** FRE 26(b), which applies to all forms of discovery, provides that the parties "may obtain discovery regarding *any matter, not privileged, which is relevant to the subject matter involved in the pending action*." So the two principal requirements for discoverability of material are that it is: (1) *not privileged*; and (2) *relevant* to the subject matter of the suit.

■ **Relevant but inadmissible:** To be discoverable, it is *not required* that the information necessarily be *admissible*.

■ **Privilege:** Only material which is *not privileged* may be discovered.

■ **Trial preparation immunity:** Certain immunity from discovery is given to the *materials prepared by counsel for trial purposes*, and to the *opinions of experts* whom counsel has consulted in trial preparation. This immunity is often referred to as *"work-product"* immunity.

❏ **Qualified immunity:** *"Qualified"* immunity is given to documents prepared *"in anticipation of litigation"* or for trial, by a party or that party's *representative*.

❏ **Absolute immunity:** *"Absolute"* immunity from discovery is given to the *"mental impressions, conclusions, opinions, or legal theories* of an attorney or other representative of a party concerning the litigation."

■ **Use at trial:** The rules for determining whether the fruits of discovery can be *introduced at trial* vary depending on the type of discovery.

❏ **Easily admissible:** Interrogatory answers, admissions and the results of physical and mental examinations are almost always admissible.

❏ **Depositions:** Answers to deposition questions are sometimes admissible, but a multi-part test must be applied to each answer to determine its admissibility.

I. GENERAL PRINCIPLES

A. Liberalization: The Federal Rules of discovery represent a great *liberalization* of the older common law and Code discovery provisions.

B. Forms: Discovery under the Federal Rules takes several forms:

1. *Automatic disclosure*, furnished by one side to the other early on in the litigation

2. *Depositions*, taken from both written and oral questions;

3. *Interrogatories* addressed to a party;

4. Requests to *inspect* documents or property;

5. Requests for *admission* of facts;

6. Requests for physical or mental *examination*.

C. Scope: *Any relevant material which is not privileged may be discovered.*

D. Objectives: The basic objectives of federal discovery are:

1. **Evidence not later obtainable:** To obtain evidence that might *not be obtainable at the time of trial.*

   a. **When used:** This is especially the case with respect to the testimony of individuals who are *ill, old, or about to leave the jurisdiction.*

2. **Issue formulation:** To *isolate and narrow the issues for trial.*

3. **New leads:**   To obtain information about the *existence of additional evidence* that may be admissible at the trial, and to obtain *leads* that will allow the discovering party to find further evidence on his own.

    a. **Rationale:**   The uncovering of material through discovery leads to more just trials, because *unfair surprise* is reduced. Hopefully the trial will become a contest that is in part a search for truth, and not solely a battle of wits between opposing counsel, with victory going to the more agile.

4. **Automatic disclosure:**   The traditional federal approach to discovery assumed that discovery would almost *never be self-executing*. That is, a party had to *request* a particular type of discovery, as to a particular issue, from her adversary. But the 1993 FRCP amendments added a new Rule 26(a), which calls for *automatic disclosure* of certain items by each party to the other early in the litigation, without any request needed from the adversary. This wide-sweeping change (which is discussed extensively *infra*, p. 182), has been extremely controversial.

II. SCOPE OF DISCOVERY

A. **Scope covered by Rule 26(b):**   Rule 26(b), which applies to all forms of discovery, provides generally that the parties "may obtain discovery regarding *any matter not privileged, which is relevant to the subject matter involved in the pending action.*"

B. **General scheme:**   Determining whether material falls within the scope of discovery can be accomplished by a seven question process to which each potentially discoverable item should be subjected:

1. *Is the material sought the existence or contents of an **insurance agreement**?*

    a. If so, it is discoverable regardless of the answer to the following questions. Rule 26(a)(1)(D).

    b. If not, go to step 2.

2. *Is the material **relevant** to the subject matter involved in the pending action?*

    a. If so, go to step 3.

    b. If not, discovery will not be allowed.

3. *Will the material be **admissible at trial**?*

    a. If so, go to step 4.

    b. If not, discovery will not be allowed unless the information sought appears *reasonably calculated to lead to the discovery of admissible evidence*. If so, go to step 4.

4. *Is the information sought **privileged**?*

    a. If the information is privileged, it is not discoverable, unless the privilege is waived.

    b. If the material is not privileged, go to step 5.

5. *Is the information outside of the **work product immunity**?*

a. If so, go to step 6.

b.   If the material is within the *qualified* work product immunity, discovery is allowed only if there is showing of *substantial need* of the material, and an *inability to acquire it by other means* without undue hardship. If the showing can be made, go to step 6.

c.   If the material falls under the *absolute* work product immunity (covering *counsel's mental impressions*) it is generally not discoverable at all.

6. *Is the material composed of facts and/or opinions held by experts?*

   a. If so, discovery may or may not be allowed depending on the factors discussed in the section on Discovery Concerning Experts, *infra*, p. 179.

   b. If not, go to 7.

7. *Is the material sought for the purpose of discovering whether the other party has evidence designed to impeach the discovering party's credibility?*

   a. If so, the material may or may not be discoverable depending on the factors discussed in the section on Impeachment Material, *infra*, p. 181.

   b. If this point has been reached without the material having been disqualified for discovery, it is probably discoverable.

C. Relevance: Rule 26(b)(1) requires that the information sought be *relevant to the subject matter* involved in the pending action.

1. Broader than trial requirement: This requirement that only relevant material may be discovered is much more lenient than the relevance requirement at trial.

   a. Contrast: Material is not admissible at trial unless it is relevant to the issues in the trial. By contrast, it is sufficient for discovery purposes that the material will be relevant to the subject matter of the action, and not to the precise issues which will arise at trial.

   i. Admissibility irrelevant: In fact, 26(b)(1) specifically states that "the information sought need not be *admissible* at the trial if the information sought appears *reasonably calculated to lead* to the discovery of admissible evidence."

2. Relevant non-admissible information: Material which itself will be admissible at trial is always discoverable if it is not privileged. In addition, there are at least three kinds of *inadmissible* information which meet the relevancy standard of 26(b)(1) and which therefore may be discovered:

   a. Leads: material which will serve as a *lead* to admissible evidence;

   Example: At a deposition, A, the deponent, is asked, "What did B tell you about C?" A's response, since it is hearsay, would not be admissible at trial. But since A's response may lead the discovering party to B, who will himself probably have admissible evidence, the question to A is within the scope of discovery under Rule 26(b)(1).

   b. Legal theories: material relating to *legal theories* on which the responding party expects to rely at trial; Rule 33(c) allows interrogatories which "relate to ... the application of law to fact. ..."

c. Witnesses: the identity and whereabouts of any *witness* who is thought to have discoverable information. See Rule 26(b)(1). Not only is the testimony of such a witness relevant, but it is also not privileged, and is outside the work-product immunity rule. Wr., 545.

D. Privilege: Rule 26(b)(1) allows discovery "regarding any matter, *not privileged.* ..."

1. Test: Material is privileged against discovery if it would be protected against disclosure *at trial*. In other words, if a person who has knowledge or who has a document could refuse to relate or produce it at trial on the grounds that he was protected by a privilege, such as the attorney-client privilege, that knowledge or document may not be the subject of discovery.

2. Who may assert: An attempt to obtain discovery of privileged material may be resisted only by the *person who could assert the privilege at trial.*

> **Example:** In a tort case, P sues D1 and D2 for conversion of his property. P asks D1 questions relating to the alleged theft at D1's deposition. D1 knows the answer, and is willing to respond, but D2's lawyer objects on the grounds that the questions may violate D1's privilege against self-incrimination. The existence of the privilege does not bar the deposition questioning, since the privilege, in order to block discovery, must be asserted by the person whom the privilege protects, D1.

3. Test in federal cases: In federal cases, the existence of privileges is determined under Federal Rule of Evidence 501. That Rule provides basically that with respect to a claim or defense "as to which state law supplies the rule of decision," state law of privileges shall be looked to.

a. Other federal cases: As to matters where state law does not supply the rule of decision, the court shall apply "the principles of the common law as they may be interpreted by the courts of the United States in the light of reason and experience."

b. Difficult distinction: The distinction between state and federal claims or defenses is often a difficult one, and is to be determined by reference to the body of case law stemming out of *Erie v. Tompkins*. See *Byrd v. Blue Ridge Rural Electric Cooperative, infra*, p. 230.

E. Trial preparation immunity: Certain immunity from discovery is given to the *materials prepared by counsel for trial purposes*, and to the *opinions of experts* that counsel has consulted in trial preparation. This immunity is granted by Rule 26(b)(3) (material) and 26(b)(4) (expert opinions). This immunity is often referred to as *"work-product"* immunity, since it is the lawyer's work-product which is in question.

1. Conflict: The work-product immunity rule represents an attempt to reconcile the basic conflict between the *purpose of discovery* (i.e., extensive pre-trial *issue formulation* and *fact-revelation*) and the *adversary model* (i.e., truth through lawyerly combat at trial.) A widely defined work-product immunity would thwart the aims of discovery; a too narrowly-defined immunity rule might lead to the situation where lawyers either kept everything in their heads, or failed to prepare and investigate, knowing that they would have to turn over the fruits of their labor to their adversaries.

2. **Distinction:** The *work-product immunity* must be distinguished from the *attorney-client privilege*. The attorney-client privilege governs only confidences made *by the client to the lawyer*, and allows these to be protected against discovery. It does not extend to materials that the attorney has acquired and *passed on* to the client; nor does it cover communications which were made for purposes other than the communication of legal advice. The work-product immunity, on the other hand, governs *all preparation for trial done by the lawyer*, or by any other representative of the party.

3. **Absolute or qualified:** The work-product immunity in a particular instance may be either *qualified* or *absolute*.

   a. **Absolute immunity:** Documents containing the *subjective thoughts (legal theories, conclusions, opinions, mental impressions)* of a party's lawyer or other representative are given what is usually called *"absolute"* immunity from discovery, an immunity which is almost impossible to overcome.

   b. **Qualified immunity:** All other documents prepared for litigation purposes by either a party or his representative (e.g., notes taken on what prospective witnesses said when interviewed) are only given *"qualified"* immunity. This immunity may be overcome by a strong showing that the discovering party has a *substantial need* for the materials, and that their equivalent is *not available through other means.*

4. *Hickman v. Taylor:* The leading case discussing the work-product immunity is *Hickman v. Taylor*, 329 U.S. 495 (1947).

   a. **Facts:** The general facts of *Hickman:*

      i. The tug "J.M. Taylor" sank while towing a car float across a river, drowning most of the crew-members (including plaintiff's decedent).

      ii. Counsel for the tug owners interviewed each survivor privately and obtained signed statements from each.

      iii. Plaintiff requested that the tug owner's lawyer "attach exact copies of all statements [by the survivors] if in writing, and if oral, set forth in detail the exact provisions of such oral statements or reports."

      iv. **Objection:** The lawyer refused the discovery request on the grounds that it called for "privileged matter obtained in preparation for litigation," and was an "attempt to obtain indirectly counsel's private files." He argued that answering such a request "would involve practically turning over not only the complete files, but also the telephone records, and, almost, the thoughts of counsel."

   b. **Holding:** The Supreme Court held the discovery request to be *improper* because it violated the trial-preparation or "work-product" immunity of defendant's counsel.

      i. **But not within attorney-client privilege:** The Court found, however, that the material sought was *not* within the attorney-client privilege (as distinguished from the work-product immunity). The Court implied that the scope of a privilege in discovery was equivalent to that of the privilege at trial. Since the latter only covers communications from client to lawyer, the privilege was not applicable here.

c. **Absolute vs. qualified immunity:** The Court held that the attorney's *mental impressions* (i.e. his recollections of what witnesses had told him in oral statements) were *absolutely privileged*. But existing transcriptions of the interviews and signed statements were only *qualifiedly* privileged.

   i. **Rationale for qualified privilege:** With respect to qualifiedly privileged material, "the general policy against invading the privacy of an attorney's course of preparation is so well recognized and so essential to an orderly working of our system of legal procedure that a burden rests on the one who would invade that privacy to establish *adequate reasons* to justify production ... [of the material sought to be discovered.]"

   ii. **Where other sources available:** If the discovering party can obtain the desired qualifiedly privileged information *elsewhere*, he has *not* met the burden of showing the kind of special circumstances required to overcome a qualified privilege. In *Hickman*, direct interviews with the witnesses by the plaintiff himself would have yielded substantially the information sought through discovery.

   iii. **Absolute privilege:** With respect to the absolutely privileged *mental impressions of counsel*, "forcing an attorney to repeat or write out all that witnesses have told him and to deliver the account to his adversary gives rise to grave dangers of *inaccuracy and untrustworthiness*. ... The standards of the [legal] profession would thereby suffer." Therefore, discovery of such absolutely privileged mental impressions will be possible only in *exceptionally rare* circumstances. Such circumstances are, in the *Hickman* analysis, presumably much rarer than those sufficing for the discovery of qualifiedly privileged material, for which merely "adequate reasons" are required by *Hickman*.

5. **Rules not adequate:** After *Hickman* was decided, the Supreme Court chose to develop the work-product rule suggested by that case on a case-by-case basis, rather than by amendment to the Federal Rules. The areas of confusion which resulted were numerous.

6. **Revision of Rules:** The Federal Discovery Rules were greatly revised in 1970. The rules relating to trial preparation (or "work-product") material are now covered by Rule 26(b)(3), which roughly codifies *Hickman v. Taylor*, maintaining the distinction between qualified and absolute immunity.

7. **Qualified immunity:** Qualified immunity is given by 26(b)(3) as follows: "A party may obtain discovery of documents and tangible things otherwise discoverable under subdivision (b)(1) of this rule and prepared *in anticipation of litigation* or *for trial* by or for another party or by or for that other party's *representative* (including his attorney, consultant, surety, indemnitor, insurer, or agent) only upon a showing that the party seeking discovery has *substantial need of the materials in the preparation of his case* and that he is *unable without undue hardship* to obtain the substantial equivalent of the materials by other means."

   a. **Non-legal representatives:** Thus the qualified immunity given by Rule 26(b)(3) applies to trial preparation materials produced not only by a party's lawyer, but by any other representative of the party, and even by the party himself.

b. Test for hardship: In determining whether the party seeking discovery of qualifiedly privileged material is "unable without undue hardship to obtain the substantial equivalent of the materials by other means," the following factors have been considered:

i. the *cost* of obtaining the desired information through means other than discovery of the qualifiedly privileged material;

ii. the *finances* of the party seeking discovery;

iii. the *hostility* of the witness to the discovering party in situations where a transcript of a witness's statement is sought.

Example 1: After an accident involving a train run by D Railway, D's claim agent interviews members of the train crew, and writes down their statements. P, an injured passenger, seeks a copy of the crew's statements, and is met with the objection that this material is covered by a qualified work-product immunity.

Held, the transcripts of the crew's statements are similar to the transcripts sought in *Hickman* which the Supreme Court found to be qualifiedly privileged. This qualified privilege can be overcome if P can show that the crew is likely to be *hostile* to any attempt by P's lawyer to interview them directly, because the crew does not want to displease their boss, D Railway. By such showing, P will have demonstrated that he is unable to obtain the "substantial equivalent" of the statements without "undue hardship." *Southern Railway v. Lanham*, 403 F.2d 119 (5th Cir. 1968).

Example 2: P sues D for automobile negligence in a diversity action. P serves a Rule 34 request to produce documents which show the length of the skidmarks of D's auto at the scene of the accident. The documents were made shortly after the accident by D's insurance company.

A court in this situation found that while the skidmark report was subject to 26(b)(3) qualified immunity, P had shown that (a) he had substantial need of the direct skidmark measurements, because they were material to the issue of negligence; and (b) he was unable to obtain the substantial equivalent of the report by other means. His own recollections were not reliable, and the report of a state patrolman was probably inaccurate. Therefore, the insurance report was indispensable, and discovery was allowed in spite of the qualified work-product immunity. *Rackers v. Siegfried*, 54 F.R.D. 243 (W.D. Mo. 1971).

8. Absolute immunity: In addition to the qualified work-product immunity discussed above, Rule 26(b)(3) also provides for what is sometimes called *"absolute"* immunity. The rule states that even where the required showing has been made to overcome qualified immunity, "the court shall *protect against disclosure of the mental impressions, conclusions, opinions, or legal theories of an attorney or other representative of a party concerning the litigation.*"

Example: Suppose that in the insurance claims report described in *Rackers, supra,* the claims agent has written his impressions of who he thinks was at fault in the accident. The court will allow discovery of the portion of the report containing the skid measurements since this material is qualifiedly privileged material as to which the necessary showing of speed has been made. But discovery will not be allowed of the portion containing the agent's conclusions about liability, since these conclusions fall under the absolute immunity given to "mental impressions, conclusions, opinions, or legal theories of an attorney or other representative of a party concerning the litigation." To permit the discovery of such conclusions would be to permit the plaintiff to benefit from the agent's expertise, and would undermine the adversary nature of the litigation process.

a. May not be "absolute": As noted, the immunity against disclosure given for "mental impressions, conclusions [etc.]" is sometimes referred to as "absolute" immunity. However, it is not clear that this immunity is truly absolute. What is clear is that at the very least a *substantially stronger showing of need* must be made in order to discover such mental impressions, conclusions, etc. than must be made to overcome the ordinary qualified work-product immunity.

Example: D, a corporation, conducts an investigation to determine whether any of its officials have made illegal bribes to foreign officials. D's legal department conducts interviews with company officials, and the lawyers take notes; the lawyers also write memos about the case. In a tax proceeding, the government seeks discovery of the notes and memos. D argues that disclosure should not be required because (apart from the attorney-client privilege) the materials reveal the attorneys' mental processes.

Held, by the Supreme Court, for D. The documents "reveal the attorneys' mental processes in evaluating the communications [between employees and company lawyers]. … [S]uch work product cannot be disclosed simply on a showing of substantial need and inability to obtain the equivalent without undue hardship. While we are not prepared at this juncture to say that such material is always protected by the work-product rule, we think a far stronger showing of necessity and unavailability by other means than was made by the Government … would be necessary to compel disclosure." *Upjohn Co. v. U.S.*, 449 U.S. 383 (1981).

Note: *Upjohn* seems to establish that an attorney's handwritten notes on a meeting, interview, etc. will fall within the "absolute" protection given to attorneys' "mental impressions, conclusions. …" The lawyer in such a position is not a mere stenographer; he is making judgments about what is important (and thus worth writing down) and what is not. He is also choosing the language in which to express concepts, and these language choices themselves may reflect "mental impressions, conclusions, opinions, or legal theories. …"

b. Discovery of legal claims or defenses: Although the discovery of documents containing conclusions of law is barred by the "absolute" work-product immunity rule, there is nothing to prevent the discovering party from directly asking, in an *interrogatory* or *request to admit*, what the other party's legal claims or defenses in the case are.

    i. Interrogatory: Rule 33(c) thus provides that "An interrogatory otherwise proper is not necessarily objectionable merely because an answer to the interrogatory involves an opinion or contention that relates to … the application of law to fact. …"

    ii. Request to admit: A request for admission, made under Rule 16, may similarly relate to "the application of law to fact." See Rule 36(a).

iii. Pure conclusions of law: However, even in the interrogatory or request to admit, the discovering party may only ask about matters that involve **both facts and law**, not about matters that involve **only** legal theories.

Example: P, a union member, is charged by the union with distributing information detrimental to it. The union conducts a hearing, finds him guilty, and imposes a fine; P sues the union to have its actions overturned as a violation of federal law. In interrogatories, P asks two sorts of questions: (1) questions asking what statements made by P D objected to, what provisions of the union's constitution these statements violated, and the manner in which these provisions were violated; and (2) questions asking why these union constitutional provisions are not nullified by a particular provision of federal labor law. The union refuses to answer, arguing that all of these questions seek to discover "legal theories," which it asserts are undiscoverable.

Held, P's questions falling into the first category are properly discoverable, but those in the second are not. Questions in the first category ask the union to tell how the law relates to the central facts in the case, and are therefore permitted under Federal Rule of Civil Procedure 33(b). But questions in the second category seek "pure legal conclusions which are [not] related … to the facts," and are therefore not allowable. *O'Brien v. International Brotherhood of Electrical Workers*, 443 F.Supp. 1182 (N.D. Ga. 1977).

c. Difficult distinction: It is sometimes difficult to distinguish between the rules applying to documents, which may be subject to the work-product immunity rule, and those applying to concepts not reduced to paper, which are usually not subject to this immunity. Pre-existing documents containing the legal theories, opinions, and conclusions of counsel, are given "absolute" work-product immunity. Interrogatory questions asking for legal/factual theories and conclusions by the witness, on the other hand, are not protected, as *O'Brien*, *supra*, shows.

d. Attorney's document selection: Suppose that out of many thousands of documents that are potentially relevant to a litigation, a lawyer for one of the parties **focuses on certain ones**, and uses them to prepare the case (perhaps by reviewing them with prospective witnesses). May the other party obtain discovery as to which documents his opponent has singled out for this special review? At least one case, *Sporck v. Peil*, 759 F.2d 312 (3d Cir. 1985), has answered this question in the negative. "The selection and compilation of documents by counsel in preparation for pre-trial discovery falls within the highly-protected category of opinion work product. In selecting and ordering a few documents out of thousands, counsel could not help but reveal the important aspects of his understanding of the case. The process of selection and distillation is often more critical than pure legal research."

e. Status in subsequent litigation: Material entitled to absolute work-product immunity in one litigation will also generally have that status in **subsequent litigation**. See, e.g., *Duplan Corp. v. Moulinage et Retorderie de Chavanoz*, 509 F.2d 730 (4th Cir. 1974).

9. Statements by witnesses: If a party makes a *statement* to another party or that other party's lawyer or representative, the maker of the statement may obtain a *copy* of his statement without being required to overcome the work-product immunity. Rule 26(b)(3), Para. 2, provides that "A party may obtain without the required showing a statement concerning the action or its subject matter previously made by that party."

    a. Effect: Thus the maker of a statement, if he is party to the lawsuit, can obtain a copy of his statement without showing that he has substantial need of it, or that he is unable to obtain its equivalent by other means.

        i. Right to depose first: Although a party is automatically entitled to obtain his own statement, many federal courts allow the party in possession of a statement made by an opposing party to *depose* the maker of the statement before turning it over to him. The purpose of this deposition is to prevent the maker of the statement from doctoring his deposition testimony to accord with the statement if the statement is false.

    b. Non-party: A person who is not a party may, like a party, automatically obtain a copy of any statement concerning the action that he made previously. See Rule 26(b)(3). This automatic right to receive his own statement applies even if there is evidence that he is friendly to the party opposing the party that took his statement, and will turn it over to the former.

    c. Non-maker's right to obtain: But a party to an action may obtain from his opponent the statement of a non-party witness only if the qualified work-product immunity is overcome.

10. Names of witnesses: Rule 26(b)(1) allows discovery of *"the identity and location of persons having knowledge of any discoverable matter."*

    a. Eye-witnesses: This category includes persons who were *eye-witnesses* to the events of the lawsuit, sometimes called "occurrence witnesses."

        i. 1993 change makes disclosure automatic: The 1993 amendments to Rule 26 made disclosure of the name and address of any occurrence witness *automatically* disclosable (even without a specific request from the adversary), early on in the litigation. See new Rule 26(a)(1)(A), discussed further *infra*, p. 183.

    b. Experts to be called at trial: The identity of *experts who will be called at trial* is discoverable in the same way as are the names and locations of occurrence witnesses. See Rule 26(b)(4)(A)(i). Discovery of the names of such experts will allow all parties to present a full case, based on all relevant expert opinions.

        i. Proposed amendment: As with occurrence witness, the identity of experts who will be called at trial is now subject to *mandatory, automatic* disclosure under the 1993 amendments to Rule 26. See new Rule 26(a)(2)(A), discussed *infra*, p. 186.

    c. Experts not to be called at trial: Usually courts will *not* allow discovery concerning the identity and whereabouts of experts who have been retained by a party but who will *not be called at trial*. See *infra*, p. 180.

F. Discovery concerning experts: The basic rule dealing with *experts*, Rule 26(b)(4), treats those experts to be used at trial in Section A of the Rule, and those not expected to be called in Section B. However, it is more useful to break the subject down even further. The classification below depends not only upon whether the experts will be used at trial, but also upon whether they were retained by opposing counsel, and upon whether they have personal knowledge of actual events relevant to the case.

1. The following classes of experts are each considered separately below:

    a. experts who will be *called at trial;*

    b. experts who have been *retained by counsel*, but who will *not be called at trial;*

    c. experts who have *not been retained*, and who will *not be called at trial;*

    d. *participant* experts; and

    e. *parties* who are themselves experts.

2. Experts to be called at trial: It is comparatively easy to get discovery concerning experts who the other party expects to *call at trial*. The 1993 changes to Rule 26 make this even easier than it had been.

    a. Identity: First, a party must furnish a list *identifying* each such "expert who may be called at trial" *automatically*, i.e., even without a request from the other side. See Rule 26(a)(2)(A). Normally this disclosure must occur at least 90 days prior to trial. Rule 26(a)(2)(C).

    b. Report: Second, the party who intends to call an expert witness must have the expert *prepare* and sign a *report* containing:

        i. all of the expert's *opinions,* and the basis for them;

        ii. the *data* considered by the expert in forming the opinion;

        iii. any *exhibits* to be used by her;

        iv. her *qualifications* (including a list of all publications authored by her within the preceding ten years);

        v. the *compensation* she is receiving; and

        vi. a listing of any *other cases* in which she has testified as an expert within the preceding 4 years.

    See new 26(a)(2)(B), discussed further *infra*, p. 186.

    So regardless of what report an expert to be called for trial has already prepared for the calling party's own use (a report that may be protected by the work-product immunity rules, see *infra*, pp. 172-181), the expert must also prepare a special "discovery" report just for purposes of complying with the mandatory disclosure provisions of new 26(a)(2)(B).

    c. Employee as expert: The written report described above is not just required from *independent* experts retained by a party. Such a report must also be supplied by an expert who is already an *employee* of the party, if his *regular duties* involve giving expert testimony. (For instance, in a product liability suit against an automobile manufacturer, the head design engineer employed by the company would come under this provision, if in past suits he had been frequently designated to give this type of testimony by the manufacturer).

d. **Deposition of expert:** A party also has the right to take the *deposition* of the other side's expert-to-be-called-at-trial. See Rule 26(b)(4)(A). This, too, is a change from pre-1993 law, under which one party could depose the other's expert only after a motion and a strong showing of need. However, the deposition may not take place until the other side has furnished the mandatory report by the expert (described above). Also, the party taking the deposition must normally pay a *"reasonable fee"* to the expert for the time spent preparing for and undergoing the deposition. Rule 26(b)(4)(C).

3. **Experts retained by counsel, but not to be called at trial:** Rule 26(b)(4)(B) makes it quite difficult to obtain discovery of an expert who has been retained by the other side, but who will *not* be called at trial.

a. **Physician's report:** Discovery of a *physician's report* made pursuant to a Rule 35 physical examination may be discovered as provided in 35(b), whose provisions are discussed below.

b. **Other reports:** Facts or opinions held by any other retained expert who will *not be called at trial*, as well as reports procured from such experts in anticipation of litigation, may be discovered only "upon a showing of *exceptional circumstances* under which it is impracticable for the party seeking discovery to obtain facts or opinions on the same subject by other means." See Rule 26(b)(4)(B).

i. **Only one expert available:** One situation in which discovery under the "exceptional circumstances" provision of 26(b)(4)(B) might be allowed is where there is only *one expert available* in the field, and where the side resisting discovery has retained him for the sole purpose of keeping him out of the discovering party's hands, without intending to call him at trial.

Note: There are two main reasons for distinguishing between discovery of experts to be called at trial, and discovery of those not to be called: (1) *parasitism* — generally, a party will use at trial only those experts favorable to him, and will not use those who will not be helpful. If non-trial experts were routinely subject to discovery, opposing counsel would be induced to simply sit back and let the other side do all the work of finding out the expert's opinion; (2) *inhibition* — if non-trial experts were easily subject to discovery, full preparation for trial might be inhibited. A party might be reluctant to consult with an expert prior to trial when there was a good chance that the expert would express an opinion contrary to the party's interest, and then become available through discovery to the other side.

4. **Unretained experts not to be called at trial:** There is virtually no way to discover the opinions of an expert who was *consulted, but not retained,* by the other side.

Example: An expert's opinion is asked by one party, who then decides not to call him, since his opinion is unfavorable. The other party cannot obtain discovery of this expert's opinions. The Advisory Committee Note on Rule 26(b)(4)(B) states that that rule "precludes discovery against experts who were informally consulted in preparation for trial, but not retained or specially employed."

5. **Participant experts:** Rule 26(b)(4)(B) "does not address itself to the expert whose information was not acquired in preparation for trial but rather because he was an actor or viewer with respect to transactions or occurrences that are part of the subject matter of the lawsuit. Such an expert should be treated as an ordinary witness." Advisory Committee Note to Rule 26(b)(4). Such *participant* experts are apparently to be treated as ordinary witnesses, whether or not they have been retained by the opposing side. They may therefore be deposed with respect to the occurrences which they witnessed.

G. **Impeachment material:** A party may wish to discover what *impeaching information* the adversary has obtained about the discovering party's own testimony, or the testimony of the moving party's witnesses. No uniform federal policy has emerged concerning the right to discover such impeachment material.

> **Example:** P claims total disability in a tort suit. D spies on P to determine whether P is really laid up. The courts are split as to whether P can get discovery of the results of D's spying.

1. **Law confused:** The law on discovery of impeachment evidence is confused, and there is no definitive Federal Rule covering the matter. Wr., 544.

a. **Relevance:** Where evidence has not only impeachment value, but also *relevance to the merits*, most courts have allowed discovery.

> **Example:** A party has evidence that the opposing party was drunk on the night of the automobile accident on which the suit is based. This evidence is not only of impeachment value, but is relevant to the substantive matter of contributory negligence. Most courts would allow it to be discovered.

b. **No substantive value:** Where impeaching evidence is *not relevant to the substantive merits*, the courts have been less willing to allow discovery. See, e.g., *Bogotay v. Montour R. Co.*, 177 F.Supp. 269 (W.D.Pa. 1959).

> **Example:** D has surveillance evidence concerning P's injuries, in a personal injury case. If the only issue at trial is D's liability, and not the extent of P's damages, the evidence is of only impeachment value, and not of substantive relevance. Most courts would not allow it to be discovered.

> **Note:** A party can always obtain discovery of information which would impeach an *opposing* witness' testimony. The courts are split only as to whether a party can discover material damaging to *his own*, or his own witness', credibility.

2. **1993 amendments:** The 1993 amendments to Rule 26 do not resolve this issue of whether a party may obtain discovery of evidence whose sole value is impeaching his own (or his witness') credibility. However, these changes suggest that such evidence will *not* be discoverable.

a. **Text of rule:** Rule 26(a)(3)(A) now requires a party to automatically disclose (i.e., without even a request by the other side) the name and address of every witness that party expects to present at trial, but witness names do not have to be provided for evidence that is expected to be "solely for impeachment purposes."

    b. Consequence: Nothing in new Rule 26 states whether one party can, by *interrogatories* or *depositions*, discover the names of witnesses who will give impeachment testimony, or the substance of the impeachment. But the careful carving out of impeachment-only witnesses from the mandatory ID provision suggests that courts should continue to be reluctant to allow a party to discover information whose only value is that it is damaging to the party's own, or that party's witness', credibility.

H. Insurance agreements: Under Rule 26(a)(1)(D), a party may obtain discovery of the existence and contents of "any *insurance agreement* under which any person carrying on an insurance business may be liable to satisfy part or all of a judgment which may be entered in the action or to indemnify or reimburse for payments made to satisfy the judgment.."

    1. Automatic discovery: This discovery of the existence and contents of insurance policies is automatic. The discovering party does *not* have to show that the policy is *relevant* to the lawsuit, as long as he shows that the insurer may be liable for some possible judgment that might be entered in the action. (In fact, discovery of insurance information became even *more* automatic under the 1993 amendments to Rule 26; under 26(a)(1)(D), information about insurance coverage now has to be disclosed by the party having the coverage early on in the suit, and without even a request for it from the adversary. This provision is discussed further *infra*, p. 183.)

    2. Not necessarily admissible: The fact that information concerning the insurance agreement is discoverable does not imply that it is admissible in evidence at trial. In fact, under the Federal Rules of Evidence, such information is not admissible, since the existence of insurance is not relevant to the issue of liability in most cases.

    3. General financial condition: The general *financial condition* of a party, other than its insurance policies, is *not discoverable* under the insurance contract provision of 26(b)(2).

        a. Use of general provision: Under some circumstances, financial status would seem to be discoverable under the broad provisions of 26(b)(1). For instance, if a store burns down, the store-owner's financial condition would be relevant in a suit against him for fraud by his insurance company. Discovery would therefore seem reasonably likely to lead to admissible evidence of motive, and would presumably be allowed. But questions designed to elicit the financial arrangements made between the plaintiff and his lawyer (e.g., the presence or absence of a contingent fee) are likely to be found irrelevant to the suit, and therefore not the proper subject of discovery. See, e.g., *Bogosian v. Gulf Oil Corp.*, 337 F. Supp. 1228 (E.D. Pa. 1971), refusing to permit discovery of such arrangements, even though defendant claimed that they might show an unethical fee arrangement.

I. Mandatory disclosure: The biggest changes made to Rule 26 in 1993 were ones that attempted to reduce the expense and delay of litigation by making various kinds of disclosure *automatic* and *mandatory*. These "mandatory disclosure" provisions were a departure from the traditional principle that one party essentially never had a duty to disclose anything unless the other party first asked for that disclosure in the form of an interrogatory, deposition, etc.

The changes impose "the functional equivalent of *court-ordered interrogatories*." Advisory Committee's Notes to 26(a)(1).

There are three types of mandatory disclosure imposed by new Rule 26: (1) automatic disclosure early in the case, before discovery has begun; (2) automatic disclosure later in the case of proposed expert testimony; and (3) automatic disclosure just before trial of witnesses and exhibits expected to be used at trial. We consider each of these in turn.

1. **Automatic pre-discovery disclosure:** The most far-reaching change to Rule 26 is embodied in Rule 26(a)(1). Under that Rule, "a party shall, *without awaiting a discovery request*, provide to other parties ..." various types of information early in the case.

   a. **Four categories:** The information which must be automatically provided early on in the lawsuit falls into *four categories*:

      i. "The name and, if known, the address and telephone number of *each individual* likely to have *discoverable information* relevant to disputed facts *alleged with particularity* in the pleadings, identifying the subjects of the information." (26(a)(1)(A).) So a party must identify all *"occurrence witnesses."*

      ii. "A *copy* of, or a *description* by category and location of, all *documents*, data compilations, and *tangible things* in the possession, custody, or control of the party that are relevant to disputed facts alleged with particularity in the pleadings." (26(a)(1)(B).)

      iii. "A *computation* of any category of *damages* claimed by the disclosing party, making available for inspection and copying as under Rule 34 the documents or other evidentiary material, *not privileged* or *protected* from disclosure, on which such computation is based, including materials bearing on the nature and extent of injuries suffered." (26(a)(1)(C).)

      iv. "For inspection and copying as under Rule 34 any *insurance* agreement under which any person carrying on an insurance business may be liable to satisfy part or all of a judgment which may be entered in the action or to indemnify or reimburse for payments made to satisfy the judgment." (26(a)(1)(D)).

   b. **Only applies to facts alleged with "particularity":** Observe that for the first two of these categories, only "disputed facts *alleged with particularity* in the pleadings" will trigger the disclosure obligation. Thus the more specific the complaint, the more things the defendant will have to disclose. For instance, if P asserts that D "released a defective car into the stream of interstate commerce, thus injuring D," it may well be that nothing has been alleged with sufficient particularity, and that nothing must therefore be disclosed by D. If, by contrast, P asserts that "D, acting through its dealer XYZ Motors Inc., sold plaintiff a 1989 Whizbang automobile, serial number 12345678, whose airbag failed to deploy in a front-end collision in which the vehicle was involved," then presumably D will have to disclose much more, including the names of the people at D who designed the airbag, the names of the people at the airbag manufacturer, a description of documents relating to the airbag design and to its test performance, etc.

c. Merely need to describe documents: Observe that when it comes to *documents*, 26(a)(1)(B) gives the defendant a *choice* between furnishing copies of the documents themselves, or just a "*description* by category and location" of the documents. Where there will be a large number of documents, presumably the defendant will find it cheaper and easier to furnish merely the description rather than the documents themselves.

d. No change in scope: Probably every item listed in the above four categories would have had to be disclosed, upon suitable request, under the pre-1993 federal discovery rules. To cite one example, insurance agreements already had to be disclosed under old 26(b)(2). So the significance of new 26(a) lies in the fact that: (1) the new provision requires disclosure *even in the absence of any request* by the other side for the information; and (2) the disclosure must come quite *early* on in the suit (as is discussed immediately below).

e. Timing: The automatic pre-discovery disclosure will ordinarily take place quite *early* in the case. The disclosures must be made no more than 10 days after the parties hold a discovery-related meeting required by new 26(f); this meeting must take place at least 14 days before a "scheduling conference" with the judge takes place, as required by both old and new Rule 16(b). The scheduling conference will normally have to occur within 90 days of when the defendant either answers or makes a Rule 12 motion. The net result of all these inter-related timetables is that the pre-discovery disclosures will ordinarily be due no later than *85 days after the defendant first moves or answers.* See Advisory Committee's Notes to Rule 26(a)(1). Indeed, one of the criticisms of the automatic disclosure scheme of new 26(a)(1) is that it forces the parties to spend lots of effort on disclosure very early on in the case, even though the case may well have settled without the need of disclosure had more time been given.

f. Local court's right to opt out: A court may *"opt out"* of the mandatory pre-discovery disclosures, by enacting a "local rule" so providing. Typically, the local rule is enacted by an *entire judicial district* (see *supra*, p. 2). The "opt out" can be for all cases, or just for a particular class of cases (e.g., Social Security cases). See 26(a)(1) and Advisory Committee's Notes thereto. Similarly, an individual judge may grant an "opt out" in a particular case, and the parties may stipulate with each other that the disclosure will not occur.

   i. Large use of opt out: In fact, courts are taking heavy advantage of the "opt out" provision. According to one survey, by mid-April, 1994 (less than five months after the 1993 changes went into effect), 53 of the 94 federal judicial districts in the nation had already opted out of the mandatory disclosure rules. (Some of these had local rules providing for some other sort of mandatory disclosure, though usually less sweeping than Rule 26(a)(1)'s provisions.) See *Chicago Daily Law Bull.*, April 23, 1994, p. 17.

   ii. Balkanization risk: Observe that with this right to opt out, there is a risk of *"Balkanization"* — instead of the uniform national federal civil procedure system Congress envisioned in enacting the FRCP, we could end up with different discovery rules in each district or even in each individual judge's court. This would make it hard to develop clear precedents, and hard to practice in multiple districts, as many lawyers (and most large law firms) do.

g. Arguments in favor: Proponents of the automatic early disclosure (mostly federal District Court judges) make several arguments in its *favor*. These include:

    i. Suits will move forward *faster*, because "core information" will be brought out on the table earlier. One of the ways this will happen is that a party seeking to resist making disclosure will not be able to stall the discovery process by arguing about the suitability of particular document-production or interrogatory requests — new 26(a)(1) sets a clearer standard for what must be disclosed, and the party opposing discovery will not have a particular request by his adversary to snipe at;

    ii. The change will lead to less costly litigation because there will be less, rather than more, *total discovery* — getting core information out early will prevent the adversary from engaging in "fishing expeditions" seeking information that does not exist or that is completely irrelevant to the issues in the case;

    iii. Parties — both plaintiffs and defendants — will have a strong incentive to *plead more specifically*, so as to get the benefits from the mandatory disclosure (since, as noted above, only items relevant to "disputed facts alleged with particularity in the pleadings" must be disclosed);

    iv. No piece of information is required to be disclosed that would not eventually have to be disclosed anyway under existing law, provided that the adversary made a request for it. All the change is doing is speeding up the process, not expanding the universe of disclosable materials.

h. Arguments against: The mandatory automatic early-disclosure proposal has been met with a firestorm of opposition, more so probably than any proposed change to the Federal Rules in recent decades. This opposition has come from lawyers of all types (e.g., defense lawyers and plaintiff's tort lawyers), and from all types of clients including corporations who are usually defendants and ones who are usually plaintiffs. The opponents also include three Justices who dissented from the Supreme Court's approval of 26(a)(1) (Justice Scalia, joined on this point by Justices Thomas and Souter), more than the number who dissented on any other 1993 change. The opponents make the following arguments, among others:

    i. There will be a large amount of *unnecessary* disclosure. A party who is found to have, "without substantial justification" failed to make disclosure that should have been made under Rule 26(a) "shall not, unless such failure is harmless, be permitted to use as evidence any witness or information not so disclosed" (37(c)(1)), so a party will over-disclose in order to be safe rather than sorry.

    ii. The disclosure is being required *too early* in the lawsuit. In particular, there are many small-stakes, relatively uncomplicated, suits filed in federal court. These would eventually settle (well before trial) with little or no discovery. Mandatory early disclosure — typically during the first three months of the suit will thus in these types of suits lead to a lot of disclosure that never would or should have happened at all without the proposed changes.

iii. The automatic process will spawn more *satellite litigation* than it is worth. As Justice Scalia argued in his dissent from the Supreme Court's approval of the Rules, parties will litigate "about what is 'relevant' to 'disputed facts,' whether those facts have been alleged with sufficient particularity, whether the opposing side has adequately disclosed the required information, and whether it has fulfilled its continuing obligation to supplement the initial disclosure."

iv. The *attorney-client relationship* will be *undermined*. It is one thing to ask a lawyer to respond to another party's request for particular types of documents or information. To ask a lawyer on her own to figure out what must be disclosed requires her to *use her professional skills in the service of the adversary.* As Justice Scalia put it, "by placing upon lawyers the obligation to disclose information damaging to their clients — on their own initiative, and in a context where the lines between what must be disclosed and what need not be disclosed are not clear but require the exercise of considerable judgment — the Rule would place intolerable strain upon lawyers' ethical duty to represent their clients and not to assist the opposing side."

i. **Opt-outs in response:** These criticisms help explain why most judicial districts have already opted out of the mandatory disclosure requirements, as described *supra*, p. 184.

2. **Disclosure of expert testimony:** Apart from the early mandatory disclosures required by paragraph 26(a)(1), 26(a)(2) would require each side to make major new types of disclosures regarding any *expert* who will be called at trial.

a. **Types of disclosure:** The things that must be disclosed regarding any witness are:

i. **Names of witnesses:** The *name* of the expert witness. 26(a)(2)(A). (There is nothing much new about this — old Rule 26(b)(4)(A)(i) already required this disclosure, though old law required the adversary to send an interrogatory, whereas the new rule would make the obligation to disclose the name automatic.)

ii. **Report:** For any expert who is "*retained* or *specially employed* to provide expert testimony ...," the party who will call that witness must furnish a *written report* prepared and signed by the witness. 26(a)(2)(B). See *supra*, p. 179, for a description of what this report must contain.

3. **Trial witnesses and exhibits:** New Rule 26 also calls for automatic disclosure concerning *non-expert witnesses and exhibits* to be used at trial. Under new 26(a)(3), the party must supply the name of each witness who may be presented at trial (separately identifying those whom the party "expects" to call at trial from those whom the party "may call if the need arises"). Also, each witness whose testimony is to be presented by means of their deposition must be identified, and each document or other exhibit to be introduced must be furnished to the other side. These disclosures are normally to be made at least 30 days before trial.

4. **Exclusion at trial:** The court may punish a party who fails to comply with mandatory disclosure by preventing that party from *offering certain evidence*, or proving certain claims or defenses. In fact, new 37(c)(1) makes this sanction *mandatory* in many instances: "A party that without substantial justification fails to disclose information required by Rule 26(a) or 26(e)(1) [the various types of mandatory disclosure summarized above, plus the duty to supplement, described below] *shall not*, unless such failure is *harmless*, be permitted to use as evidence at a trial … *any witness or information not so disclosed*." (This sanction is in addition to other more traditional sanctions such as the award of attorneys fees.)

   a.   **Favorable vs. unfavorable evidence:** Observe that this sanction only gives a party an incentive to disclose evidence favorable to her case, so that other sanctions will still be needed to make sure that a party will disclose unfavorable information (the kind of disclosure that parties are more likely to fail to make).

J.   Duty to supplement: Suppose a party makes a disclosure that is accurate when made, but later discovers that the disclosure is no longer accurate. Or suppose the party is honestly mistaken about some fact at the time of disclosure, but then learns of her mistake. In either of these situations, must the party *amend* or *supplement* her disclosure?

   1.   **Old law:** Under pre-1993 law, the answer was usually "no." A party who made a disclosure in discovery normally did *not* have any duty to supplement that response if the party learned that the prior disclosure was not accurate when made, or if later developments made a disclosure that was accurate when made no longer accurate.

   2.   **New law:** But the duty to supplement is greatly expanded under the 1993 amendments to the FRCP:

   a.   **Automatic disclosures:** First, any mandatory automatic disclosure required under 26(a) (i.e., all the material discussed in section I. above) must be supplemented "at appropriate intervals" if the party "learns that in some material respect the information disclosed is incomplete or incorrect and if the additional or corrective information has not otherwise been made known to the other parties during the discovery process or in writing." 26(e)(1).

   Example 1: P is suing D regarding an auto accident in which P was injured. As part of the mandatory disclosures required by Rule 26(a)(1)(A), P gives D a list of persons that witnessed the accident. Three months later, P learns, through work done by a private detective hired by P's lawyer, that X, a person not on this list, in fact saw the accident. P must promptly disclose to D X's existence.

   Example 2: In a product liability case, D describes or copies all documents that D knows of bearing on the design of the allegedly defective product. (This is now automatically required under Rule 26(a)(1)(B). Six months later, D learns of additional documents that are relevant to this issue. D must come forward with copies or descriptions of these documents, even if P does not ask for these documents or even suspect their existence.

   b.   **Expert:** Second, a party must supplement any disclosure made by that party's *expert(s)* who will be called at trial. So if the expert changes any opinion or other aspect expressed in the expert's report (see *supra*, p. 179), the party sponsoring that expert must disclose the change.

    c. Interrogatory and requests: Third, a party has a similar broad duty to supplement with respect to a response to an *interrogatory*, a request for *production*, or a request for *admission*. Rule 26(e)(2).

K. Privilege log: Suppose a party realizes that certain documents come within the other party's discovery request, or within the scope of mandatory disclosure under Rule 26(a)(1)(B), but the party also believes that the documents are immune from discovery because they are either *privileged* or *attorney work-product*. Does the party have to disclose to her adversary the fact that such a claim of non-discoverability is being made, or may the party just keep silent, fail to disclose the documents, and hope for the best?

    1. Pre-1993 law: Under pre-1993 law, a party could generally keep *silent* about both the fact that such a claim was being made and the nature of the documents as to which it was being made. Of course, this approach meant that the discovering party would never even know there was an issue of privilege, and would thus never get the chance to litigate the question of whether the privilege was in fact applicable.

    2. Change of law: But new 26(b)(5), as amended in 1993, changes this general approach. 26(b)(5) provides: "When a party withholds information otherwise discoverable under these rules by claiming that it is privileged or subject to protection as trial preparation material, the party shall make the claim *expressly* and shall *describe* the nature of the documents, communications, or things not produced or disclosed in a manner that, without revealing information itself privileged or protected, will enable other parties to assess the applicability of the privilege or protection." Thus, a party must in effect compile a *"privilege log"* and show it to the other party. The latter can then, if he disagrees with the claim of privilege, litigate the issue.

L. Required meetings: New 26(f), added in 1993, requires the parties to *meet* to "discuss the nature and basis of their claims and defenses and the possibilities for a prompt settlement or resolution of the case," as well as to make or arrange for the mandatory pre-discovery disclosures required by 26(a)(1), and to schedule other discovery. This meeting must take place at least 14 days before a scheduling conference with the judge occurs, so that the meeting will generally occur within the first two or at most three months of the case.

Quiz Yourself on
SCOPE OF DISCOVERY

45. P was injured in an auto accident involving a car driven by D. P's lawyer deposed D. During this deposition, the fact emerged that D stood by the car after the accident, and watched while W, an eyewitness to the accident, gave a statement to the police. P's lawyer asked D during the deposition, "What was the substance of W's statement to the police about what occurred?" D's lawyer objected on the grounds that any answer would be hearsay, and instructs D not to answer. (Assume that it would indeed be hearsay for D to testify at trial regarding W's statement.) P now moves for an order compelling D to answer this question. Should the court grant the order sought by P? _____

46. P brought a federal court diversity action against D. P's claim was that D willfully breached a contract with P. D raised the defense that the contract is unenforceable due to the Statute of Frauds. During a deposition of D conducted by P's lawyer, L, L ascertained that D had consulted with his own lawyer, X, before signing the contract. L then asked D, "Did you discuss with X the enforceability of the contract before you signed it?" D objected to the question on the grounds of attorney-client privilege. (This matter would indeed be privileged under the law of the state where the district court sits, if the question were asked of D at trial.) P now moves to compel D to answer the question. Should the court grant P's motion, and issue an order compelling an answer? _____

47. P was injured in an automobile accident involving a car driven by D. P brought a federal diversity suit against D on a negligence theory. After commencement of the suit, D's lawyer, L, conducted an interview with an eyewitness to the accident, W. L wrote down those aspects of W's account of the accident that seemed most interesting to L. P's lawyer, after learning about this interview, submitted to D a Rule 34 Request for Production of Documents, requesting "any notes taken by L of any interviews with W." D and L refused to comply, so P made a motion to compel discovery. Should the court grant P's motion to compel production of the notes? _____

48. P and D were involved in an automobile accident. P sued D in federal court based on diversity; the suit alleges that D behaved negligently. Shortly after the accident and before P filed his lawsuit, P furnished a statement to D's insurance company, at the insurer's request. At the time of the interview, P was not given a copy of the statement (which was in the form of a tape recording that was later transcribed). P's lawyer now submits, pursuant to Federal Rule 34, a request that D give P a copy of the transcript of P's statement. Is D obligated to give P a copy of this statement, assuming that P makes no showing of special need for this statement? _____

49. P, driving one car, was injured by a collision with a car driven by D. (P believes that the accident occurred because D went through a stop sign.) P sued D for negligence in federal court based on diversity. P's lawyer hired an expert accident reconstructionist, Rufus T. Firefly, to: (1) examine the skid marks, the damage to the two automobiles, and any other physical evidence of how fast each car was going at the time of the accident; and (2) determine whether this speed proves that D definitely did not stop at the stop sign. As a result of his investigation, Firefly has formed an opinion that D definitely did not stop at the stop sign. P plans to call Firefly to testify at trial to this effect.

   (a) How, if at all, can D learn that will be calling Firefly at trial? _____

   (b) How, if at all, can D get details of what Firefly will say at trial? _____

   (c) Assume that D has learned of Firefly's identity and the fact that he will be called to testify at trial about the results of his investigation. If D wishes to take the deposition of Firefly to hear in detail Firefly's conclusions about what caused the accident, is D entitled to do so? If so, when? _____

50. In a federal court action for antitrust, P, a corporation, claimed that D's predatory conduct had caused X to terminate a contract with P that was valuable to P. In a set of interrogatories, D asked P to state when and how the alleged interference by D with the P-X contract had occurred. P, in a set of answers signed by Prexy, P's president, responded that the interference had been in the form of a phone call by D's chairman, Charm, to X, on Sept. 15, 1989, in which Charm told X that P was preparing to breach the contract. Subsequent to the filing of this interrogatory answer, Prexy has learned that the conversation between Charm and X was a face-to-face one, and that it took place on Sept. 18, not Sept. 15. What obligation, if any, does P have to amend its interrogatory answer? _____

51. D, a plastic surgeon, performed cosmetic surgery on P's face to reduce the size of her chin. P was mildly displeased with the results, and found a lawyer, L, willing to bring a malpractice action (in federal court based on diversity) against D. L has commenced the action, and now would like to know whether D is covered by malpractice insurance for any verdict that P might recover here. L would also like to know the

limits of the policy, if one does exist. How may L get this information? _____

Answers

45. Yes. Even though it is true that the answer would consist solely of hearsay material, which would be inadmissible at trial, Rule 26(b)(1), last sentence, states that "the information sought need not be admissible at the trial if the information sought appears reasonably calculated to lead to the discovery of admissible evidence." Here, D's answer to the question will at least tell P whether it is worthwhile to conduct discovery of W (which may in turn produce admissible evidence), and may lead to admissible evidence in other not easily foreseen ways. Therefore, the court will almost certainly hold that the defendant must answer the question.

46. No. According to Federal Rule 26(b)(1), first sentence, parties may obtain discovery "regarding any matter, ***not privileged***, which is relevant to the subject matter involved in the pending action. ..." In diversity actions the rules of privilege are those of the state whose substantive law controls the action. The facts tell us that according to state law here, the question asked by L would require D to divulge information protected by the attorney-client privilege. Therefore, the court will not order D to answer the question.

47. No. The notes clearly fall within the ***work-product immunity*** of Federal Rule 26(b)(3). In fact, the notes probably come within the "absolute" protection given by the second sentence of 26(b)(3): "In ordering discovery of [work product] materials when the required showing [of need] has been made, the court shall protect against disclosure of the mental impressions, conclusions, opinions, or legal theories of an attorney. ..." Since L has written down only what he thinks is important, his notes of necessity contain his "mental impressions" and probably his "opinions." Therefore, the court is almost certain to reject discovery of those notes even if P needs them very badly (e.g., because W has died).

48. Yes. Rule 26(b)(3), first sentence of second paragraph, provides that even though a party's statement made to the other party is technically work product, it is still discoverable: "A party may obtain without the required showing [of need] a statement concerning the action or its subject matter previously made by that party." So P is entitled to the transcript even without any showing of special need.

49. (a) D need not do anything; P has an obligation to automatically disclose this information. Under Rule 26(a)(2)(A), as revised in 1993, "A party shall disclose to other parties the identity of any person who may be used at trial to present [expert] evidence. ..." This disclosure is "automatic," in the sense that the adversary does not have to ask for it. The disclosure must be made at least 90 days before trial; Rule 26(a)(2)(C).

(b) **Again, D need not do anything; P has an obligation to provide a report prepared by Firefly.** Under 26(a)(2)(B), the party preparing to call a retained expert must automatically provide to the other party "a written report prepared and signed by the [expert] witness." The report must contain "a complete statement of all opinions to be expressed and the basis and reasons therefor," as well as the data relied on, any exhibits to be used, the witness' qualifications and publications, the compensation to be paid the witness for testifying, and even a list of all cases in which the witness has testified as an expert in the previous four years. *Id.*

(c) **Yes, after the report is provided.** FRCP 26(b)(4)(A) says that a party may "depose any person who has been identified as an expert whose opinions may be presented at trial." The rule goes on to specify that where a report is to be provided by the expert, as Firefly would have to do here (see (b) above), the deposition may not be conducted until after the report has been provided.

50. P must amend its response unless the error has already been called to D's attention. Before 1993, parties usually did not have to supplement or amend discovery responses that were later found to be wrong or misleading. But under Rule 26(e)(2) as amended in 1993, "A party is under a duty seasonably to amend a prior response to an interrogatory, request for production, or request for admission if the party learns that the response is in some material respect incomplete or incorrect and if the additional or corrective information has not otherwise been made known to the other parties during the discovery process or in writing." Since P has now learned that its answer was materially incorrect (the place and date of this key conversation would surely be material), P must file an amended response, so long as D has not learned of the error in some other way.

51. L does not need to do anything; D's lawyer must disclose this information automatically. Automatic disclosure regarding liability insurance was made mandatory as part of the 1993 FRCP Amendments. Under Rule 26(a)(1), "[A] party shall, without awaiting a discovery request, provide to other parties: … (D) for inspection and copying … any insurance agreement under which any person carrying on an insurance business may be liable to satisfy part or all of a judgment which may be entered in the action or to indemnify or reimburse for payments made to satisfy the judgment." This mandatory disclosure must occur early on in the case.

III. METHODS OF DISCOVERY

A. General characteristics: The various forms of discovery (including *depositions, interrogatories* and *requests to produce documents*) are set out in Rules 30, 31, 33, 34, and 36. With the exception of Rule 35 requests for physical examination (discussed below), each of these forms has several important characteristics common to all. Among these common attributes are the following:

1. **Extrajudicial:** Each of these modes of discovery is designed to operate *extrajudicially*, that is, without the intervention of the court. It is only where one party refuses to comply fully with the other's discovery request that the court intervenes.

2. **Scope:** The scope of discovery, as discussed above, is the same for all of these forms of discovery. In general, the material sought to be discovered by any of these modes must simply be relevant to the subject matter of the lawsuit, and unprivileged.

3. **Signature required:** Every request for discovery of any type, and any response or objection to discovery, must be *signed* by the lawyer preparing it. Rule 26(g).

   a. **Certification:** The signature constitutes a certification by the lawyer that the request, response or objection is consistent with the Federal Rules, is not imposed for the purpose of harassing the adversary, causing unnecessary delay or needless increase in the cost of litigation, or other improper purpose, and that it is not "unreasonable or unduly burdensome or expensive, given the needs of the case, the discovery already had in the case, the amount in controversy, and the importance of the issues at stake in the litigation." Rule 26(g), including 26(g)(2)(C).

> **b. Sanctions:** If the court later finds that the certification was false, it may issue sanctions, including an order to pay the "amount of the reasonable expenses incurred because of the violation, including a reasonable attorney's fee." Rule 26(g)(3)

> **4. Court orders:** Upon motion by a person from whom any of these forms of discovery is sought, the court may make any order necessary to protect the discoveree from undue annoyance, embarrassment, or harassment. Such an order, called a ***protective order***, may limit the scope, terms, method, or use of discovery. See Rule 26(c); see also Wr., 560-66.

B. Persons affected: There are differences among the forms of discovery with respect to the ***persons from whom discovery may be taken.***

> **1. Depositions:** Depositions upon oral (Rule 30) or written (Rule 31) questions can be held of ***either party, or of non-parties*** who are thought to have information relevant to the case. In a deposition, the responses are given orally.

> **2. Other forms:** The other forms of discovery, by contrast, interrogatories (Rule 33), requests to produce or inspect tangible property (Rule 34) and requests for admissions (Rule 36) can be addressed ***only to parties***, not to non-party witnesses.

C. Times usable: Before 1993, there was no limit to the ***number of times*** a particular method of discovery could be used, or a person discovered.

> **1. Amendments:** But the 1993 amendments to the FRCP added some ***"presumptive limits"*** to the number of times certain discovery devices may be used. Unless the court orders otherwise, or the parties so stipulate, each side is limited to ***10 depositions*** and ***25 interrogatories*** (not ***sets*** of interrogatories, but individual interrogatory questions). See Rules 30(a)(2)(A) and 33(a), discussed *infra*, p. 194 and p. 196, respectively.

> **2. Protection against abuse:** Also, rule 26(b)(2) explicitly directs the court to limit the ***"frequency or extent of use"*** of discovery methods, under certain circumstances. Among the situations in which the court must limit discovery are where: (1) the discovery sought is "unreasonably ***cumulative*** or ***duplicative***," or is "obtainable from ***some other source*** that is more convenient, less burdensome, or less expensive"; (2) the party seeking the discovery has already had, through prior discovery in the case, ***"ample opportunity"*** to obtain the desired information; and (3) the ***"burden or expense*** of the proposed discovery ***outweighs its likely benefit***, taking into account "the needs of the case, the amount in controversy, ***the parties' resources***, the importance of the issue at stake in the litigation, and the importance of the proposed discovery in resolving the issues."

> > **a. Rationale:** These provisions for eliminating the abuse of discovery are directed at two main situations: (1) where a lawyer tries to force a favorable settlement by driving up the litigation costs of his less-affluent adversary; and (2) where the lawyer fears that if he loses and is shown to have missed a fact which might have been discoverable, he may be sued for malpractice. See Advisory Committee's comments to 1983 amendment of Rule 26.

D. Oral depositions (Rule 30): After the beginning of an action any party may take the ***oral testimony*** of any person (party or non-party) thought to have information within the scope of discovery, by asking oral questions.

1. **Leave not required:** Except for certain oral depositions taken within 30 days after service of the complaint, leave of the court is ***not required***. (Rule 20(a)).

2. **Notice:** The deposing party must give ***reasonable notice not only to the deponent, but also to every other party*** in the action. Notice should state the time, place, and person to be deposed. (Rule 30(b)(1)).

   a. **No subpoena for party:** If a *party* is to be deposed, a *subpoena* is not used, because non-compliance with the notice can be followed up by the discovering party with motions to compel discovery or impose sanctions under Rule 37.

   b. **Subpoena for non-party optional:** If a ***non-party*** is to be deposed, then the discovering party may subpoena the person to attend. The price of using a subpoena rather than a simple request is that the party must (1) pay witness fees; and (2) risk antagonizing the deponent. However, if no subpoena is used, the deponent cannot be compelled to attend. If he does not attend, the deposing party may have to pay the costs set forth in Rule 30(g).

      i. **Range of subpoena:** If the discovering party decides to use a subpoena, that subpoena is valid only if it requires the deposition to be held at a place within a 100 mile radius of "the place where [the] person [to be deposed] resides, is employed or regularly transacts business in person. …" Rule 45(c)(3)(A)(ii).

   c. **Answers by corporation:** Where the deponent named in the notice or subpoena is a corporation or partnership, the onus falls upon the business to *appoint* an appropriate person to answer the questions. Rules 30(b)(6), 31(a).

3. **Documents:** If the deponent is a party, Rule 30(b)(5) provides that the discovering party may attach a Rule 34 ***request to produce*** to the notice to the party. If the deponent is a non-party, the discovering party must serve the non-party with a subpoena *duces tecum* (since Rule 34 applies only to parties.)

4. **Mechanics of deposition:** Typically the deposition is held in a lawyer's office with every party (and often non-party deponents) represented by counsel. The deponent is sworn, interrogated by counsel for the discovering party, and possibly cross-examined by the other parties' counsel. Rule 30 provides that "Examination and cross-examination of witnesses may proceed as permitted at the trial under the provisions of the Federal Rules of Evidence."

   a. **Presiding officer:** A presiding officer appointed by the court must be present unless the parties stipulate, as they usually do, that his presence is waived. (In fact, most of the mechanics of discovery can be varied by agreement of the parties — see Rule 29).

   b. **Transcription:** The depositions so taken are then transcribed, and read and signed by the deponent. Under certain circumstances described below, these depositions may then be introduced as evidence at trial.

   c. **Method of recording:** Traditionally, depositions have been recorded manually by a stenographer (court reporter) who is present at the deposition, and who then transcribes his notes. But ***sound***, or ***sound-and-video***, are now the preferred recording methods as the result of 1993 changes.

    i. **Party's option:** Under new Rule 30(b)(2), "the party taking the deposition shall state in the notice the method by which the testimony shall be recorded. Unless the court orders otherwise, it may be recorded by sound, sound-and-visual, or stenographic means, and the party taking the deposition shall bear the cost of the recording." So the party ordering the deposition can arrange to have it recorded by audio tape recorder, or video recorder; either of these is likely to be significantly cheaper than the use of a court reporter. (But whatever method is chosen by the person conducting the deposition, another party may arrange for a different method to be used as well. Thus, if the plaintiff notices a deposition to be conducted by audio tape recording, the defense may order a stenographic record as well, but the defense will then have to pay for the stenography.)

    ii. **Transcript for testimony to be introduced at trial:** If a non-stenographic (e.g., video or audio recording) method is used, the party may use that non-stenographic version *at trial*. Rule 32(c). However, in that event the party must also *prepare a transcript*, and must give the transcript in advance of trial to the other parties (Rule 26(a)(3)(B)) and to the court (Rule 32(c)).

    iii. **Preference for non-stenographic version:** The 1993 changes actually show a *preference* for video or audio recording as opposed to stenographic reporting, in the case of a *jury trial*: "On request of any party in a case tried before a jury, deposition testimony offered other than for impeachment purposes shall be presented in *non-stenographic form*, if available, unless the court for good cause orders otherwise." Rule 32(c). So a party who notices a deposition and specifies that it should be recorded in video or audio form takes the risk that his adversary can require that this version (rather than the dryer stenographic version) be introduced in the jury trial.

5. **Coaching by lawyer:** Suppose the lawyer conducting a deposition asks a question that the deponent and the lawyer "defending" the deposition (i.e., the deponent's lawyer) don't expect. A crafty defending lawyer will often *coach* the deponent, by making a spurious objection that intentionally includes extraneous information suggesting to the deponent how the question should be answered. Rule 30 now tries to prevent this type of coaching: "Any objection to evidence during a deposition shall be stated concisely and in a non-argumentative and *non-suggestive* manner." Rule 30(d)(1).

6. **Presumptive limit of 10:** Each "side" (plaintiff and defense) is *limited* to a total of *10 depositions*, unless the adversary agrees to more or the court issues an order allowing more. See Rule 30(a)(2)(A), as revised in 1993. In a multi-party situation, this limit applies to all of the plaintiffs, or all of the defendants, taken as a whole; therefore, there are likely to be disputes among co-parties about how the 10 deposition opportunities should be used.

E. **Depositions upon written questions:** After the beginning of an action, any party may take the oral responses to *questions written prior to the deposition*, of any person (party or non-party) thought to have discoverable information. Rule 31.

1. **Distant non-party witnesses:** The main utility of Rule 31 depositions on written questions is for deposing *distant non-party witnesses* who cannot be served with Rule 33 interrogatories (since these are limited to parties). The discovering party's counsel is saved the expense of the journey.

2. **Similarity:** Deposition upon written questions is similar to deposition upon oral questions in all respects, except that a list of questions to be asked at the deposition is sent to the presiding officer, who then poses them to the deponent.

3. **Lack of flexibility:** The major disadvantage of depositions upon written questions is that the discovering party has much less flexibility, because he obviously does not have the ability to rephrase a question based upon the response to an earlier question. For this reason, depositions upon written questions have been little used in the federal system, except for distant witnesses.

4. **Cross-examination:** Copies of the questions to be asked are sent not only to the presiding officer who will pose them, but also to the other parties. These other parties may in turn serve *written cross-questions*, which will be posed by the presiding officer to the witness after the questions of the initial discovering party. See Rule 31(a), Para. 3.

> **Note:** During the course of a deposition, whether upon oral or written questions, either the deponent or a party may *object* to a particular question as being outside the scope of discovery. The presiding officer or the stenographer then notes the objection upon the transcript. Although the objecting party has the right to *suspend the deposition* for the time needed to make a Rule 30(d) motion to terminate or limit the deposition, generally the parties save up all their objections and go to the judge for rulings on all of them at the same time. Objections to deposition questions will be considered further in the treatment of abuse and sanctions relating to discovery generally, below.

F. **Interrogatories to the parties:** An interrogatory is a set of *written questions* to be answered in writing by the person to whom they are addressed. Interrogatories may be addressed *only to a party*. Rule 33(a).

1. **Under oath:** Answers to interrogatories are made under oath by the party, usually in close consultation with his counsel.

   a. **Who signs:** Answers are signed by the person making them, but objections to questions are signed by the attorney.

   b. **Objection:** If the interrogatory question is objected to (e.g., on the grounds that the question is outside the scope of Rule 26(b)(1)), the discoveree does not answer the question until the objection is ruled on by the court.

2. **Answer in records:** Where the answer to the interrogatory is in *business records* accessible only to the party served, it is a sufficient answer to the interrogatory for the deponent to specify which records contain the answers and to afford the discovering party an opportunity to examine the records and ascertain the answer. (Rule 33(c)). This procedure enables the party served to shift the cost of ascertaining the answer from himself to the discovering party.

   a. **Burden of searching records:** The court will generally only allow this type of 'answer' where the record examination burden is about equal for both parties. If the discoveree's familiarity with the records would enable him to find the answer more easily than the discoveror could, the burden will generally remain on the former.

   b. Harassment: If the discoveror's request seems to be a harassment of the discoveree, the court may prevent discovery, or may shift costs under Rule 37(d).

3. Limit of 25 questions: Each party is now limited to *25 interrogatory questions* directed to any other party, unless the parties stipulate otherwise or the court orders *otherwise*. Rule 33(a) (as revised in 1993).

   a. What is a "question": Furthermore, a party cannot get around this limit by clever drafting, since each "discrete subpart" of a question counts as though it were a separate question, if it seeks information about a "discrete separate subject". Advisory Committee Notes to 1993 Amendments to Rule 33(a).

G. Requests for admission (Rule 36): A party may serve upon any other party (but not upon non-parties) a written request for the *admission, for the purposes of the pending action only, of the truth of any matters within the scope of Rule 26(b). The statements the admission of whose genuineness may be requested include statements or opinions of fact*, or of the application of law to fact. An admission of the *genuineness of any documents* described in the request may also be sought. Wr., 592-95.

1. Utility: A request for an admission is not used primarily to obtain information, but to *narrow the disputed issues* and remove the necessity of *proving at trial* the fact whose admission is sought.

2. Answers and objections to requests to admit: If the party does not answer the request to admit at all within 30 days after its service (except that a defendant has at least 45 days after service of the complaint in which to answer), the matter is taken as *admitted.*

   a. Answer: The party may answer by:

      i. *admitting* the truth of the matter;

      ii. *denying* the matter in whole or in part (there is a specific requirement of *good faith* with respect to qualified admissions or partial denials — Rule 36(a), second paragraph); or

      iii. setting forth the *reasons why he cannot truthfully admit or deny* the matter. *Lack of information* is not an acceptable reason for this, unless the party states that he has made reasonable inquiries and does not have enough information to admit or deny honestly.

   b. Triable issue: It is *not* grounds for objection to a request to admit that the discoveree feels that the matter is a *genuine issue for trial.* However, a party can object on the ground that the question encompasses too many issues, some of which the party can admit and others which cannot be admitted.

   c. Sufficiency of the objection: If the answering party has objected to a request, the requesting party may move to determine the sufficiency of the objection. He may also move to determine the sufficiency of the answers which have been given. Rule 36(a), third paragraph.

3. Expenses for failure to admit: If a party fails to admit the truth of any matter requested for admission under Rule 36(a), and if the party making the request *proves* the truth of the matter at trial, the court upon motion by the discovering party may require the party who refused to admit to pay *reasonable expenses sustained by the movant in proving the matter.* (Rule 37(c)). These expenses may not be levied if (1) the request to admit was successfully objected to; (2) the admission sought was not of substantial importance; (3) the party who failed to admit had reasonable grounds to think he might prevail on the issue at trial; or (4) there was other good reason for the failure to admit.

    a. Rule 37(b) and (d) sanctions not applicable: The sanctions and orders of Rule 37(b) and (d) (contempt, striking of pleadings, etc.) do *not* apply to requests to admit, since to do so would in effect infringe upon the party's right to his day in court by coercing him into making involuntary admissions. Of course, even the 37(c) imposition of costs is coercive to a certain extent, but probably to a lesser one than, for example, a contempt citation.

4. Effect at trial: If a party makes an admission under Rule 36, the matter is *conclusively established at trial*, unless the court grants a motion to withdraw or amend the admission. The court may permit withdrawal or amendment only if two conditions are met:

    a. Presentation of merits: It must be the case that "the presentation of the merits of the action will be subserved [by amendment or withdrawal of the admission]", and

    b. Lack of prejudice: The party who obtained the admission must "fail … to satisfy the court that withdrawal or amendment will prejudice him in maintaining his action or defense on the merits." See Rule 36(b).

H. Requests to produce documents and to inspect land: A party may, by Rule 34, require any other party to *produce documents and things*. Thus any papers, photographs, and objects relevant to the subject matter of the case may be obtained by the discovering party from any other party, but *not from a non-party.*

1. Inspection of land: Rule 34 also allows a party to demand the right to inspect, photograph, and survey any *land* within the control of another party.

2. No requirement of "good cause": It is not necessary for the party seeking production or inspection to demonstrate "good cause" for his request. Therefore, the scope of discovery under Rule 34 is the same as for interrogatories and depositions. The material must simply meet the test of Rule 26(b)(1), i.e., it must be not privileged and relevant to the subject matter of the pending action.

3. Party's control: A party may be required to produce only those documents and other objects which are in his *"possession, custody or control"*. Rule 34(a). If the party who is requested to produce a document does not have actual possession of it, but is legally entitled to obtain possession or a copy, the request must be honored. Therefore, a party cannot escape discovery by turning the document or object over to his attorney, or to a third person. See Wright, p. 585.

4. Requests to produce: Rule 34 requests to produce, like Rule 33 interrogatories, can be addressed *only to parties*.

a. **Use of subpoena against non-parties:** Since non-parties cannot be made the subject of a Rule 34 request to produce, the only way to force a non-party to produce documents is to serve a *subpoena duces tecum* upon him, pursuant to Rule 45. (See Rule 34(c), providing that the Rule 45 subpoena procedure may be used for non-parties.) If the non-party fails to comply with such a subpoena, he is subject to a citation for contempt of court, pursuant to Rule 45(e).

I. **Physical and mental examinations (Rule 35):** When the mental or physical condition of a party (but *not non-parties*) or of a person in the custody or under the legal control of a party (e.g. a ward), is *in controversy*, the court in which the action is pending may order the party to submit to a *physical or mental examination* by a physician or other examiner, or to produce for examination the person under his custody or legal control. The order may be made only on motion; *good cause* must be shown, and *notice* must be given to the person to be examined and to all other parties.

1. **Difference from other discovery:** There are two important differences between Rule 35 orders for examination and the other discovery devices discussed above:

   a. **Motion required:** Rule 35 does not operate *extrajudicially*; the discovering party must make a motion showing good cause. The other discovery devices can be initiated by the parties themselves.

      i. **Agreement:** If the parties agree by themselves to allow a physical examination of one of them, Rule 35 does not come into play at all, and the court is never involved. This often happens where the parties are interested in an out-of-court settlement.

      ii. **Good cause:** Generally, good cause can be shown where the information can be acquired through no other means, and is relevant to the issues expected to be tried.

   b. **Controversy:** Rule 35 requires that the mental or physical condition of the party be *in controversy*. This means that the scope of discovery under Rule 35 is somewhat narrower than that governing the other modes of discovery under Rule 26(b), where the material simply has to be relevant to the *subject matter* in the pending action, and not *necessarily related to an actual issue in controversy* at trial.

      i. **Not formality:** The Supreme Court in *Schlagenhauf v. Holder*, 379 U.S. 104 (1964), emphasized that the "good cause" and "in controversy" requirements were not mere formalities, but "require an affirmative showing by the movant that each condition as to which the exam is sought is really and genuinely in controversy and that good cause exists for ordering each particular exam." In some cases, however, the pleadings alone will be sufficient to meet these requirements — this would be the case, for example, where plaintiff alleges personal injury in a negligence action.

      ii. **Interest in privacy:** The chief reason for the closer judicial supervision and narrower scope of Rule 35 examinations is the growing public, judicial, and constitutional concern for the right to privacy.

   c. **Rule 35 valid under Enabling Act:** In *Sibbach v. Wilson*, 312 U.S. 1 (1941), the Supreme Court held that Rule 35 was *valid* under the Rules Enabling Act of 1934. The

Court held that although the right to be free of a compulsory physical examination might be a substan*tial* right, the right was not substan*tive* in the sense of the Enabling Act. Therefore, the Rule was upheld. (See the fuller discussion of *Sibbach*, *infra*, p. 226). See also *Schlagenhauf v. Holder*, *supra*, similarly upholding Rule 35.

2. **Reports of examiner:** Rule 35(b) allows discovery of the ***actual medical report*** produced through a Rule 35 examination. This is an important exception to the rule that expert's reports are not generally discoverable.

   a. **Who may receive:** *A party against whom an order is made* under Rule 35(a), or the ***person examined***, may request and have delivered from the party causing the exam to be made, a copy of a written report of the examiner detailing his findings.

   b. **Other examinations:** After delivery of the report, the party who caused the examination is entitled on request to receive from the party against whom the order was made a report of any other examination made for the same condition at the requestee's behest.

   c. **Waiver of objection:** By requesting and obtaining a report of the examination ordered or by deposing the examiner, the party examined *waives any privilege* he may have in that action or any other involving the same controversy, regarding the testimony of *everyone who has examined or will examine him*. (Rule 35(b)(2)).

   d. **Where examination made by agreement:** (a), (b), and (c) above apply also to an examination made by agreement of the parties without court intervention, unless the agreement expressly provides otherwise.

Quiz Yourself on
METHODS OF DISCOVERY

52. P brought a federal court action against D in connection with an automobile accident. P learned that the accident was personally observed by W. P served upon W a set of interrogatories asking W to describe the accident as he saw it. Must W answer the interrogatories? _____

53. P brought a diversity-based negligence action against D in federal district court for the Southern District of New York. One of the witnesses to the accident in question was W (who is not a party). W is an individual who was visiting in New York at the time of the accident, but who resides in the Southern District of Florida. P's lawyer wished to take W's deposition, but P's lawyer did not wish to travel to Florida to do so. Consequently, P served upon W at W's residence in Miami a notice of deposition, together with a notice stating that W's reasonable travel and lodging expenses for a trip to New York (where the deposition was to be held) would be paid by P. W has indicated that she will not submit to any deposition unless subpoenaed to do so. If P is ready to bear W's travel and lodging expenses to New York, may W be subpoenaed to appear in New York for her deposition? _____

54. P and D were involved in an automobile accident. P sued D for negligence in federal court, based on diversity. P discovered the existence of a police report, issued by the police department of the City of Langdell (where the accident occurred). P served upon that police department a Rule 34 Request to Produce Documents, listing the police report as the document to be produced. Assuming that the City of Langdell is within the district where the action is pending, must the police department comply with the request? _____

55. P was hit by an automobile driven by D. P brought a federal diversity action against D alleging negligence. P claimed that he suffered serious whiplash in the accident, and that he has been physically disabled from working. D's lawyer had doubts about whether P was as severely disabled as he claims. Therefore, D's lawyer served upon P a notice to undergo physical examination, which stated, "Please present yourself at any time within the next two weeks at the office of Dr. John Smith, who will conduct a physical examination of you to determine the degree of your disability." Must P comply with this request?

Answers

52. No. Only *parties* may be served with, and required to respond to, interrogatories. See Federal Rule 33(a). If a party wishes to get discovery from a non-party witness, this must usually be done by taking the witness' deposition.

53. No. Federal Rule 45(c)(3)(A)(ii), which protects persons subject to subpoenas, states that a court shall quash a subpoena "if it requires a person who is not a party to travel to a place more than 100 miles from the place where that person resides, is employed or regularly transacts business in person. ..." Since a 1,300 mile trip from Miami to New York goes far beyond the 100 miles ordinarily contemplated for a subpoena, it is highly unlikely that a court would uphold the necessary subpoena. (But if P's lawyer is willing to travel to Miami to conduct the deposition, the lawyer can serve the subpoena for deposition on W at W's residence. See Rule 45(a)(3)(B), authorizing an attorney as an officer of the court to issue a subpoena for a deposition in another district, "if the deposition pertains to an action pending in a court in which the attorney is authorized to practice." Prior to the 1991 Amendment to FRCP 45, only the Florida district court could have issued a subpoena for a deposition at P's residence.)

54. No. A Rule 34 request to produce documents may be served *only on a party*. To compel the police department to deliver the report, P must cause the clerk of the court to issue a subpoena duces tecum on the department, pursuant to Rule 45(b).

55. No. Unlike nearly all the other discovery tools, the right to require another party to undergo a physical examination may be accomplished only by *obtaining a court order*. According to Rule 35(a), if the mental or physical condition of a party is "in controversy," the court where the action is pending may order that party to submit to a physical or mental examination. The order may only be made upon a showing of "good cause." Here, if D makes a motion to have P subjected to a physical examination, the court will almost certainly grant D's motion, since P's physical condition is clearly in controversy, and there is no other good way to ascertain the truth of P's claim of disability.

IV. ORDERS AND SANCTIONS

A. General availability of sanctions: Several types of orders and sanctions are available to the parties to enforce the discovery process. The type of sanction applied by the court depends both upon the *seriousness* of the violation, and whether a prior court order *compelling discovery* has been administered. Wr., 595-601.

B. Abuse of discovery: A party may sometimes use discovery in such a way as to harass his adversaries as, for example, by scheduling depositions for inconvenient places, or by requesting that the discoveree reveal trade secrets. There are two distinct ways in which the discoveree may resist such abuse: (1) he may simply object to a particular request, whether it is in the form of a deposition, an interrogatory, or a request to produce; or (2) he may seek a Rule 26(c) *protective order.*

1. **Objection:** An objection may be raised to a discovery request in the same way that a question at trial may be objected to. The usual ground for such an objection is that it is not within the scope of discovery under Rule 26(b)(1), or that it is privileged.

   a. **Interrogatory objection:** An objection to an interrogatory question is written down, and must be signed by the attorney making it. See Rule 33(b)(1) and (2).

      i. **Burdensome interrogatories:** Where objections are raised to interrogatory questions, the court will normally evaluate each of the challenged questions. But if they are extremely voluminous, the court may simply conclude that the entire set of questions is burdensome and sustain the objections as a whole, relieving the interrogee from having to respond.

   b. **Request to admit:** An objection to a request to admit may be signed by either the party or his lawyer, and the objection must include "the reasons therefor." See Rule 36(a).

   c. **Deposition:** If an objection is made to a deposition question, the stenographer simply notes the objection, the question is usually not answered, and the deposition continues. All of the objections are then usually disposed of at once by the judge.

2. **Protective order:** A party or other person against whom discovery is sought may, instead of raising a particular objection, seek a judicial order known as a *"protective order,"* pursuant to Rule 26(c). Such a protective order generally deals with a much broader range of material than does a simple objection. Whereas an objection generally relates to a single question, a protective order may be issued to prohibit an entire line of questioning, the use of a particular form of discovery, or the examination of a particular witness. Rule 26(c) allows the judge to make "any order which justice requires to protect a party or person from annoyance, embarrassment, oppression, or undue burden or expense. …" Certain specific reasons for concluding that a discovery request is unduly burdensome or expensive are now supplied in the last paragraph of Rule 26(b)(1) (e.g., the information is available from some other, more convenient, source).

   a. **Where sought:** A party may always seek a protective order from the court in which the action is *pending*. Furthermore, in the case of a deposition, the protective order may be sought from the court in the district where the deposition is to be taken as well as in the district where the action is pending. See Rule 26(c).

   Example: P sues D in the Southern District of New York. P deposes X, a competitor of D and a stranger to the action, in Los Angeles. X may seek a protective order from either the Southern District of New York, or the Central District of California.

b. Kinds of orders: Rule 26(c) lists eight particular kinds of protective orders which a judge may issue in order to protect a party from embarrassment or oppression. Among the more important possibilities are the following:

i. he may order that discovery or disclosure *not be had at all;*

ii. he may order that it be only held at a *certain time or place;*

iii. he may order that a *method* of discovery other than that sought by the discovering party be used;

iv. he may *restrict the scope* of discovery or disclosure (e.g., by prohibiting questions about certain subject areas);

v. he may order that a deposition be *sealed*, and opened only by court order; or

vi. he may limit or altogether bar the revealing of *trade secrets or other commercial information.*

c. Prohibition of public disclosure: As the above listing indicates, one of the common functions of a protective order is to allow trade secrets or other information to be discovered, but then to *bar the public disclosure* of the information by the discovering litigant. Discovering parties faced with such anti-disclosure orders have sometimes argued that the orders violate their *First Amendment right of free speech*. However, the Supreme Court has made it clear that only rarely will a protective order barring disclosure violate the First Amendment. The Court laid down the rules for evaluating such free speech claims in *Seattle Times Co. v. Rhinehart*, 467 U.S. 20 (1984).

i. *Seattle Times* **test:** Under the Court's test in *Seattle Times*, a protective order barring disclosure of discovered materials will *not violate* the First Amendment if it meets the following criteria: (1) there is a showing of *"good cause,"* as is required of any protective order by Federal Rule 26(c); (2) the order is limited to the context of *pretrial* discovery in *civil* cases (so that anti-disclosure orders in criminal cases are not necessarily immune from free speech claims, and so that material *introduced at trial* may not normally be ordered concealed); and (3) the order does not bar the dissemination of the discovered information if it is also *independently gained from other, non-discovery, sources.*

ii. Disclosure allowed where no "good cause" shown: Conversely, if the party opposing disclosure does *not* show "good cause" for keeping the discovered materials secret, Rule 26(c) implies, and most courts have held, that the court must *permit* public disclosure of that material. And even if the court bars pre-trial disclosure to guarantee a fair trial, it may (perhaps must) allow that disclosure once the trial passes and the need for secrecy no longer exists. For instance, in *Public Citizen v. Liggett Group*, 858 F.2d 775 (1st Cir. 1988), Ps brought a tort suit against D, a cigarette manufacturer. The trial court ordered Ps not to disclose before trial the documents discovered from D. But after the trial, the court modified its protective order to allow a public-interest group to publicize the documents, since the purpose of the protective order — to promote a fair trial — no longer applied. The appellate court held that the trial court had acted appropriately.

d. Use in deposition: If a protective order under Rule 26(c) is to be sought in the case of a deposition, the order is generally sought before the deposition is conducted. If, however, a deposition is commenced and is being conducted "in bad faith or in such a manner as unreasonably to annoy, embarrass or oppress the deponent or party," any party or the deponent may go to the judge on a *motion to terminate or limit examination* under Rule 30(d). The judge may either terminate the deposition completely, or limit the "scope and manner" of the deposition just as he could do under Rule 26(c).

C. Compelling discovery: A party seeking discovery may seek an *order compelling discovery* under Rule 37(a). Such an order is sought when the discoveree *refuses*, in the first instance, to divulge the requested information. Thus just as a discoveree may seek court protection against an unfair discovery request, so a person seeking discovery may enlist the court's help when the discoveree refuses to comply.

1. From whom sought: If the discovering party wishes to compel *another party* to grant discovery, he can seek an order compelling discovery from the *court in which the action is pending.*

    a. Deposition: If the form of discovery is a *deposition*, the party seeking discovery from another party may seek an order compelling discovery *either* in the court where the action is pending or in the court in the district where the deposition is being taken.

    b. Non-party deposition: If the order that is being sought is an order to compel discovery from a *non-party deponent*, the order *must* be sought from the court in the district where the *deposition is being taken.*

2. When available: An order to compel discovery may be granted if the discoveree fails to do any of the following things:

    a. answer a *written or oral deposition* question under Rules 30 or 31,

    b. answer an *interrogatory* submitted under Rule 33,

    c. allow a *request for inspection* or a *request to produce documents*, under Rule 34,

    d. *designate an officer* to answer deposition questions as required by Rules 30(b)(6) or 31(a)(3), if the discoveree is a *corporation.*

    Note: The Federal Rules use the word "failure" throughout the enforcement and sanction sections of the discovery provisions to denote both *intentional* and *innocent* non-compliances with the rules and/or court-orders. However, since the court has wide *discretion* in applying sanctions, the innocence or guilt of the delinquent party is usually taken into account.

3. Failure to answer deposition question: If a deponent fails to answer a question in oral deposition, the discovering party can choose either to adjourn the examination in order to seek an order compelling discovery, or go on to other questions, and seek the order to compel at the end of the examination.

4. Partial response: The discovering party may seek an order to compel discovery not only if the discoveree refuses to answer a question entirely, but also if he makes *"an evasive or incomplete answer"*; such an evasive answer is to be treated as a failure to answer. See Rule 37(a)(3).

5. **Sanctions:** If an order compelling discovery is obtained and the discoveree still refuses to divulge the information, certain Rule 37(b) *sanctions*, discussed below, may be imposed by the court.

6. **No right to make party conduct discovery:** The trial court has, as noted, the power to make a party submit to discovery. But it is not clear whether the court may similarly compel a party to *conduct* discovery of his adversary, in order to simplify the issues for trial.

   a. **Compulsion not permitted:** At least one Court of Appeals has answered *"no"* to this question. In *Identiseal Corp. v. Positive Identification Systems, Inc.*, 560 F.2d 298 (7th Cir. 1977), the trial judge was of the opinion that plaintiff could only try its case in an efficient manner if it conducted certain types of discovery first. When plaintiff's counsel stated that he preferred to try the case without discovery, the court dismissed the action for want of prosecution. The appeals court held that the trial court had *no power* to do this — the plaintiff could be required to give serious consideration to conducting discovery and obtaining admissions, but could not be compelled to actually follow the court's discovery suggestions.

D. **Sanctions:** Rule 37(b) provides a number of *sanctions* against parties who behave unreasonably during discovery.

1. **Financial sanctions:** If a discovering party seeks an order compelling discovery under Rule 37(a), and the court grants the order, the court may require the discoveree to pay to the discovering party the *reasonable expenses* he incurred in obtaining the order compelling discovery.

   a. **Lawyers' fees:** The expenses of procuring such an order may include the *cost of the lawyer's time* in making the motion for the order, and the damages suffered by the party in having the litigation delayed until the order was procured. But the costs of conducting the *discovery itself* (e.g., the cost of taking the deposition) may *not* be awarded under Rule 37(a).

   b. **Exceptions:** The court *must* grant the successful discovering party his expenses of procuring the order unless it finds either: (i) that the opposition to the discovering party's motion was *"substantially justified;"* (ii) that the party seeking the expenses failed to make a *good faith effort* to resolve the dispute *without court intervention*; or (iii) that "other circumstances make an award of expenses *unjust*." See Rule 37(a)(4)(A).

   c. **Expenses following denial:** Conversely, if a Rule 37 motion for an order compelling discovery is *denied*, the court may award expenses to the *discoveree*. Again, these expenses may include *attorneys' fees*, and must be awarded unless the court finds that the discovering party's motion was substantially justified or that there are other circumstances which make an award of expenses to the discoveree unjust. Rule 37(a)(4)(B).

   d. **Expenses after protective order:** If the *discoveree* seeks a Rule 26(c) *protective order* against discovery, the court may similarly award expenses to the winner, under the same standards as those set out in Rule 37(a)(4) and summarized in (a) through (c) above. See Rule 26(c), last sentence.

e. Refusal to admit: A party who *refuses to admit* on a matter which is later proved at trial may be required to pay *his adversary's cost of proving the matter.* Rule 37(c).

2. Other sanctions: If the discoveree does not furnish the discovery requested of him by the discoveror, the first step the latter must generally take to force disclosure is to seek a Rule 37(a) order compelling discovery. If he obtains such an order, and the discoveree *persists in his refusal* to grant discovery, then Rule 37(b)(2) allows the court a choice of coercive sanctions. The court may take the following actions, among others:

a. Facts established: It may order that "the matters regarding which the order was made or any other designated facts shall be taken to be *established* for the purposes of the action in accordance with the claim of the party obtaining the order".

    i. Personal jurisdiction: Even *personal jurisdiction* over the defendant may be taken to be established, if the defendant refuses to comply with a court order requiring him to furnish discovery of facts related to the existence of such jurisdiction. *Insurance Corp. of Ireland v. Compagnie des Bauxites de Guinee*, 456 U.S. 694 (1982).

b. Claims or defenses barred: The court may prevent the disobedient party from *making certain claims or defenses* in the case, or prevent him from introducing certain matters in evidence.

c. Entry of judgment: The court may *dismiss the action*, or enter a *default judgment*, or *strike* any portion of the pleadings.

    i. Drastic sanctions: However, these sanctions of dismissal/default judgment are the most *drastic* ones in the trial judge's arsenal, and even where the judge is convinced that there has been a major breach of discovery rules, she will use these sanctions only if others are inadequate. For instance, in *Coca-Cola Bottling Co. v. Coca-Cola Co.*, 110 F.R.D. 363 (D.Del. 1986), Coca-Cola flatly refused to comply with a court order compelling it to produce its secret formula. Even though the refusal was an unambiguous, intentional and serious breach of the discovery rules, the court refused to enter a default judgment against Coke (and instead ordered that most facts as to which the documents would be relevant should be taken as established against Coke, a lesser sanction described above).

d. Contempt: Lastly, the court may hold the disobedient party in *contempt of court.*

e. Mandatory sanctions for failure to disclose: The above sanctions are all essentially discretionary with the court. But the 1993 amendments to Rule 37 impose *mandatory* sanctions for a party's failure to comply with the new automatic *early disclosure* provisions of Rule 26(a) (see supra, p. 183) or with the *duty-to-supplement* obligations of 26(e)(1) (see *supra*, p. 187). Under new 37(c)(1), "A party that without substantial justification fails to disclose information required by Rule 26(a) or 26(e)(1) *shall not*, unless such failure is *harmless*, be permitted to use as evidence at a trial ... *any witness* or *information* not so disclosed."

Example: Suppose D fails, at the outset of the case, to list X as a person having knowledge of an event pertaining to the suit. Under new 37(c)(1), the court is required to prevent D from calling X to testify unless D had substantial justification or the failure was harmless (as it might be if P already knew about X or learned about X's existence later on during discovery.)

3. **Wilfulness usually required:** Rule 37(b) does not say anything about the **degree of culpability** necessary before the various sanction measures may be used. Generally, courts have not used sanctions — at least the more serious ones, such as dismissal or contempt — except on a showing that the offender has *wilfully*, rather than merely negligently, failed to follow the discovery rules. But courts have sometimes allowed some sort of sanction even for non-wilful violations.

   a. **Gross negligence suffices:** Courts have sometimes distinguished between "ordinary" negligence and "gross" negligence. For instance, in *Cine Forty-Second Street Theatre Corp. v. Allied Artists*, 602 F.2d 1062 (2d Cir. 1979), the Second Circuit held that a severe sanction (the preclusion of the discoveree's right to introduce evidence on matters that were the subject of the discovery order) was appropriate where the discoveree's failure to comply with the discovery order was *grossly negligent.*

      i. **Rationale:** The court noted that gross professional incompetence can and does delay litigation just as much as intentional disregard of court discovery orders.

      ii. **Final compliance insufficient:** The court also held that the fact that the discoveree finally filed the required interrogatory answers was not enough to relieve it of the sanctions; "any other conclusion would encourage dilatory tactics, and compliance with discovery orders would come only when the backs of counsel and the litigants were against the wall."

4. **Which court may issue:** The sanctions listed in subsections (a), (b), and (c) of paragraph 2 above may be applied only by the court in which the action is pending, and not by the court in which the deposition was held, if it was held outside of the district of the lawsuit. See Rule 37(b)(1).

   a. **Refusal to obey other judge:** These sanctions by the judge of the case may, however, be in response to the discoveree's refusal to obey an order compelling discovery made by the judge where the deposition was taken.

   b. **Contempt:** Either the judge of the case or the judge where the deposition was taken may hold the discoveree in *contempt* for refusing to obey an order compelling discovery. See Rules 37(b)(1) and 37(b)(2)(D).

5. **Physical exam:** Where the order which has been disobeyed is a Rule 35(a) order to submit to a *physical or mental examination*, the sanctions outlined above are applicable, except that the disobedient party may **not be held in contempt of court**. See Rule 37(b)(2)(D). This exception was apparently the product of a concern that it might be unconstitutional to imprison a party for refusing to submit to an examination of his person.

6. **Where allowed:** The sanctions listed in (2) above may be used in the following situations:

   a. in the case of *refusal to answer deposition questions,*

   b. against a *party* who *fails to attend* his own deposition,

   c. against one who *fails to answer interrogatories,* and

    d. against one who *fails to answer a request for inspection.*

       Note: A party who does any of these things may *not* defend himself on the ground that the discovery sought is *objectionable*, unless the discoveree has previously applied for a Rule 26(c) protective order.

  7. **Sanctions prior to issuance of order:** As noted, sanctions (other than the costs of making a motion) may generally be imposed only where the discoveror has procured an order compelling discovery, and this order has been disobeyed. But there are a few exceptions: where a party *fails to attend his own deposition* called by an opposing party, *fails to answer interrogatories*, or *fails to answer a request for inspection*, these violations generally occur before an order to compel discovery has been made, and are the only kinds of violations for which sanctions are meted out *prior to the issuing of an order compelling discovery.* Rule 37(d).

    a. **Failure must be complete:** The violations referred to in the previous paragraph are deemed to have occurred only where the party *completely* fails to respond to discovery. If he responds to discovery with an objection, the discovering party will have to make a motion for an order to compel discovery, rather than seeking the stronger sanctions of Rule 37(d). Then, if the order compelling discovery is disobeyed, the Rule 37(d) sanctions will become available.

V. USE OF DISCOVERY RESULTS AT TRIAL

  A. **Use of results generally:** Once a party has obtained information through discovery, he may wish to put that information into *evidence* at the trial. Yet the introduction of discovery results may sometimes conflict with the rules of evidence, particularly since inadmissible material is sometimes discoverable.

  B. **Rules on use:** To deal with such conflicts, certain rules with respect to the admissibility of various forms of discovery at trial have been set forth in the Federal Rules.

  C. **Rule 34 requests to produce:** Documents and reports which have been obtained through *Rule 34 requests to produce* pose little problem, because their admissibility does not depend on the unavailability at trial of the person who created them (as the admissibility of the depositions of non-party witnesses does — see *infra*). The admissibility of such tangibles is determined *without regard* to the fact that these items were obtained through discovery. They will therefore be admissible unless their contents constitute prejudicial, hearsay, or other objectionable material.

  D. **Depositions:** The admissibility of *depositions* is determined through a *two-part* test, *both* parts of which must be satisfied:

  1. **Test 1:** First, it must be determined whether the deposition statement sought to be introduced would be admissible *if the deponent were giving live testimony*. If not, the statement is automatically inadmissible. See Rule 32(a).

    Example: At his deposition, the deponent stated "X told me that D went through the red light." The deponent would probably not be permitted to make that statement on behalf of P at the trial of P's civil suit against D for auto negligence, because of the hearsay rule. Since the statement would not be admissible if made at trial, the deposition testimony is not admissible.

2. **Test 2:** Use of a deposition statement, rather than live testimony, is itself a form of hearsay. Therefore, even if the testimony would be admissible if given live, it will be allowed in its deposition form only if it falls within one of the three following categories, which are in effect exceptions to the hearsay rule:

   a. **Adverse party:** The deposition of an ***adverse party***, or of a ***director or officer*** of an adverse ***corporate*** party, may be admitted for ***any purpose at all***; see Rule 32(a)(2).

   b. **Impeachment:** The deposition of any witness, ***party or non-party***, may be used to ***impeach the witness' credibility***; see Rule 32(a)(1).

      Example: In an automobile accident case brought in diversity by P against D, W, a witness friendly to P, takes the stand. W testifies that the accident happened when D drove through a red light. In cross-examination, D's lawyer introduces a transcript of W's testimony from a deposition take during the case. In the transcript, W admits having once falsified a job application. Even though W is not a party, this deposition testimony is admissible, because it is used to impeach W's credibility.

   c. **Use for substantive purposes where conflicts with trial testimony:** Deposition testimony that ***conflicts*** with a witness' trial testimony may be used even for ***substantive*** purposes. This result is not contained directly in the Federal Rules, but is instead incorporated from the Federal Rules of Evidence. FRE 801(d)(1) allows admission of a witness' out-of-court statement if "the declarant testifies at the trial or hearing and is subject to cross-examination concerning the statement, and the statement is (a) inconsistent with the declarant's testimony, and was given under oath … in a deposition. …" FRCP 32(a)(1) then allows use of "any deposition … for any … purpose permitted by the Federal Rules of Evidence."

      Example: P brings a diversity action against D for automobile negligence. During D's case, D calls to the stand W, a non-party witness, who testifies that D was blameless and that P caused the accident by failing to stop at a stop sign. P's lawyer, in cross-examination of W, introduces W's deposition testimony, in which W said that P did stop at the stop sign in question. This statement from the deposition — that P stopped — is admissible as ***substantive*** evidence of whether P stopped at the stop sign.

   d. **Other circumstances:** The deposition of any person, party or non-party, can be used for any purpose if any one of the following ***"deponent unavailable"*** conditions exists:

      i. the deponent is ***dead***;

      ii. the deponent is ***100 or more miles from the trial*** (and the absence is not due to the conduct of the party introducing the deposition);

      iii. the deponent is ***too ill*** to testify;

      iv. the deponent is ***not obtainable by subpoena***; or

v. there are *exceptional circumstances* that make it desirable to dispense with the deponent's live testimony.

See Rule 32(a)(3).

e. **Sometimes not allowed:** The above categories are not all-inclusive — there remain circumstances where a deposition may *not* be used. For instance, a party may ordinarily not introduce her own deposition to buttress her case. Nor may a party normally introduce the deposition of a witness for substantive purposes, or to bolster that witness' credibility, if the witness is testifying at trial or is available to testify at trial. (But F.R.E. 801(d)(1)(b) makes an exception where the deposition or other out-of-court statement is "consistent with the declarant's testimony and is offered to rebut an express or implied charge against the declarant of recent fabrication or improper influence or motive. …")

Example 1 (Deponent is party): P brings a diversity suit against D, arising out of an auto accident. In a deposition taken during the course of the suit, P testifies that D went through a red light. At trial, P may not introduce his own deposition for any purpose, because the situation does not fall within any of the special cases described above (e.g., use by an adverse party, use to impeach a deponent unavailable to testify, etc.) However, if D's lawyer expressly or impliedly charges at trial that P has recently changed his story (e.g., by asking P on cross-examination, "Isn't this the first time you've said that D went through a red light?"), P may now use his deposition to rebut this charge of recent fabrication.

Example 2 (Use of non-party witness' deposition): P sues D in diversity relating to an automobile accident. D takes the deposition of W, who was in P's car and who is friendly to P. In that deposition, W testifies that D went through a red light. At trial, P elects not to call W as a witness, even though W is available, because P thinks W has shifty eyes and maybe perceived by the jury as being untruthful. P may not introduce W's deposition testimony on the red-light issue, because that testimony does not fall within any of the exceptions discussed above. The fact that the deposition was taken by D, and that D had a right to cross-examine at the time, is irrelevant. (But if W was now *unavailable*, because she was, for instance, ill, or located more than 100 miles away from the trial for reasons not due to P's conduct, P could use the deposition in lieu of W's live testimony.)

3. **Partial offering:** If only *part* of a deposition is offered into evidence by a party, an adverse party may introduce *any other parts* of the deposition which in *fairness* ought to be considered with the part introduced. See Rule 32(a)(4). This rule of fairness will almost always require that if only part of a particular deposition answer is offered by one party, the rest of the answer may be read in by any other party.

E. **Interrogatories:** The *interrogatory answer* of a party can be used by an *adverse party* for *any purpose*, including substantive as well as impeaching purposes. Since interrogatories may be addressed only to the parties, the rule allowing an interrogatory answer to be introduced by a party against the respondent is the same as the rule allowing the use of a deposition given by an adverse party. See Rule 33(b).

1. **Not binding:** Statements made in *depositions* and *interrogatories* are *not irrefutably binding* upon the maker. He may contradict them in court, and the trier of fact will weigh all relevant evidence in determining the issue. Of course, the credibility of a party who changes his story will suffer, but he is not legally bound by his interrogatory answer.

> **Example:** A party states in his deposition that a particular fact is so, "to the best of his recollection." After the deposition, he checks his records, and finds that he was mistaken. At trial, he may assert that his deposition answer was erroneous, and he will not be bound by that answer. The jury will, however, be entitled to conclude that the party's explanation of his change of response lacks credibility.

F. **Admissions:** *Admissions* obtained under Rule 36 are held to *conclusively establish* the matter admitted, except for an occasional right of rebuttal or amendment granted by Rule 36(b); see *supra*, p. 197.

G. **Physical and mental examinations:** The results of *physical and mental examinations* made under Rule 35 are almost always *admissible at trial*. Since such examinations are only conducted after a court has found that the physical or mental condition of the party to be examined is in controversy, the requirement of relevance has virtually always been satisfied. Only if the legal theories underlying the lawsuit have changed between the time of the examination and the time at which its results are to be introduced, might the examination be irrelevant.

1. **Waiver as to report:** The admissibility of the report is rendered even more probable by the fact that *if the examined party requests and obtains a report of the examiner*, that party is held to *waive any privilege* (e.g., doctor/patient) he may have in that action or in "any other involving the same controversy regarding the testimony of every other person who has examined" or may examine him. See Rule 35(b)(2). Since in most cases, the examined party will request a copy of the physician's request, the question of admissibility never even arises.

H. **Use in subsequent proceedings:** The above discussion relates to use of discovery materials in the action during which they were acquired. A separate issue is whether these results are usable in *subsequent actions*.

1. **Depositions:** If a *deposition* meets the above requirements for admissibility with respect to the action pursuant to which it was given, it may also be admissible in a subsequent proceeding. In federal civil trials, the admissibility of a deposition from a prior proceeding is governed by a combination of the FRCP and the Federal Rules of Evidence.

a. **Adverse party:** A *party's* own deposition may be admitted *against him* for any purpose at all, even if it comes from a prior proceeding. See FRE 801(d)(2)(A); FRCP 32(a)(1).

> **Example:** P believes that she has been injured by a prescription drug she has taken. She believes that the drug was manufactured by D1 and thus sues D1. She gives a deposition in that action, in which she says that her symptoms did not begin until 1985. P loses that suit. P then sues D2, another drug manufacturer, on a similar claim. In this trial, D2 may introduce, against P, P's deposition from the P-D1 case, just as D1 could have introduced that deposition in the original action — this is because FRCP 32(a)(1)

allows use of a deposition "for any ... purpose permitted by Federal Rules of Evidence," and FRE 801(d)(2) makes a party's own statement non-hearsay (and thus admissible) if offered against that party. (FRE 801(d)(2) is not limited to statements made during the course of the present proceeding.)

b. Impeachment: Similarly, the deposition of any witness, *party or non-party*, may be used to *impeach* that witness' credibility, even though the deposition was taken in a prior action. See FRE 801(d)(1)(A).

c. Deponent unavailable: The tricky question comes when the deponent in the first action is not a party to the current action, and is not a witness either. In this situation, the Federal Rules of Evidence try to guarantee that the deposition will be used only if this is *fair* to the party against whom the deposition is offered. Under FRE 804(b)(1), the deposition may only be offered if *both* of the following conditions are satisfied: (1) the deponent is now *unavailable* to give testimony (e.g., W is dead, not available by subpoena, or otherwise unavailable for the reasons summarized on p. 208 *supra*); and (2) the party against whom the deposition is now sought to be admitted, or that party's *"predecessor in interest,"* had the opportunity to *cross-examine* the deponent at the time of the earlier deposition.

i. Significance: Requirement (2) means that if the deposition is not offered against a person who was a *party* to the earlier action, then at least a person who was *similarly situated* to the person now opposing the deposition's use (in terms of posture in the suit and incentive to cross-examine) must have been present at the deposition.

Example: P sues D1, a drug manufacturer, alleging that a drug manufactured by D1 injured P when she took it. D1 takes the deposition of W, P's mother, during which W says that P took the drug only during the year 1985. P then loses the suit against D1, because the jury believes that the drug was not made by D1. W dies. P now brings an action against D2, a manufacturer of a similar drug, alleging that in fact it was D2 who made the drug in question. P seeks to introduce W's deposition testimony to prove that P took the drug in 1985 (not, as D2 is now asserting, 1984, before D2 was producing the type of drug in question).

Unless the court in the P-D2 action is convinced that D1 was *situated similarly* to D2 (in the sense that D1 was motivated to cross-examine W in the same way as D2 would have been), the court will *not* allow the deposition to be used against D2. This is because D2 is in effect deprived of its opportunity to cross-examine W and to show that she may be mistaken about the date. So if the year of P's ingestion was not an issue in the first suit, and was not in fact the subject of cross-examination by D1 during the deposition, P will probably be unable to use the deposition now against D2. (In terms of FRE 804(b)(1), the issue is whether D1 is D2's "predecessor in interest." The courts have interpreted this term somewhat loosely to mean "person with an incentive to cross-examine in the same manner." See *Lloyd v. American Export Lines, Inc.*, 580 F.2d 1179 (3d Cir. 1978).)

2. **Admissions:** Rule 36 explicitly states that *admissions* are for the purposes of the ***pending action only***. Admissions, unlike interrogatory or deposition answers, thus cannot be used against the admitting party in any other proceeding.

3. **Medical report:** The courts have not agreed on whether a **medical report** obtained under Rule 35 is generally admissible in subsequent proceedings. However, if the examinee requests a copy of the report, he waives any claim of privilege in any action "involving the same controversy." See Rule 35(b)(2). In that case, the report is admissible if relevant to the subsequent controversy.

Quiz Yourself on
ORDERS AND SANCTIONS; USE OF DISCOVERY RESULTS AT TRIAL

56. P and D are each corporations engaged in the pharmaceutical business; they compete with each other. P has brought a federal patent infringement suit against D, and has added to it a pendent state claim alleging that D, by hiring a former employee of P, effectively stole certain trade secrets belonging to P. During the discovery phase, P has served upon D a Rule 34 document production request seeking documents containing details of certain secret manufacturing processes used by D, so that P can determine whether these are derived from P's own trade secrets. D is afraid that if it complies, two bad results may occur: (1) P may use the information, including the trade secrets, to compete with D; and (2) P may disclose those trade secrets to the world, thus stripping D's competitive advantage. What should D do to deal with these problems? _____

57. P brought a product liability suit (based on diversity) against D. D is a corporation. P served D with a notice of deposition, which stated that D or its representative would be asked questions concerning how the product in question was designed. D designated Smith to be deposed on its behalf. Smith was D's Director of Product Safety at the time the product in question was designed, but had since left D's employ. Now, at trial, P seeks to introduce in evidence answers given by Smith in the deposition. The answers are offered for substantive purposes, and are offered even though Smith is available to testify at trial. Are the deposition answers admissible under these circumstances? _____

58. P and D were involved in an auto accident while each was driving a car. P brought a diversity action against D for negligence. D took the deposition of W, a bystander who observed the accident. W is available (indeed eager) to testify at trial, but neither party has called her. D now offers a portion of W's deposition testimony as evidence. Will this testimony be admitted if objected to by P? _____

59. Same facts as prior question. Now, however, assume that W was called to the stand by P and gave live testimony. D now seeks to offer into evidence portions of W's deposition testimony which would cast doubt upon the accuracy of W's statements made at trial. Is this deposition material admissible? _____

60. Cars driven by P and D were in an accident. P sued D in federal court for negligence. During the discovery process, P served upon D an interrogatory containing the following question: "State what, if anything, you told the police officer investigating the accident regarding whether you stopped at the stop sign located at the corner of Main and 21st Street just before the accident." D submitted the following response to this question: "I told the police officer that I did not stop at the stop sign."

(a) Suppose that at trial, D does not take the stand. May P introduce D's interrogatory statement for the purpose of proving that D did not in fact stop at the stop sign? _____

(b) Assume that at trial, (i) D testifies that he did stop at the stop sign; and (ii) P is permitted to introduce the interrogatory answer to impeach D's testimony. Will a properly-instructed jury be permitted to conclude that D stopped at the stop sign? _____

Answers

56. **Seek a protective order limiting how the information can be used.** Federal Rule 26(c) allows the federal court to issue, on motion by a party from whom discovery is sought, a protective order protecting the requesting party from annoyance, embarrassment, oppression, etc. One of the steps the court can order is "that a trade secret or other confidential research, development, or commercial information not be disclosed or be disclosed only in a designated way." D should seek an order that the information sought be used by P only for purposes of the litigation, that it not be used in P's business operations, and that it not be disclosed to any third parties. The Supreme Court has held that such an anti-disclosure protective order will generally not violate the First Amendment free speech rights of the other party (here, P). See *Seattle Times Co. v. Rhinehart* 467 U.S. 20 (1984).

57. **Yes.** Federal Rule 32(a)(2) states, "The deposition of a party or of anyone who at the time of taking the deposition was an officer, director, or managing agent, or a person designated under Rule 30(b)(6) … to testify on behalf of a … corporation … which is a party may be used by an adverse party for any purpose." Here, at the time of deposition, Smith was a person designated under Rule 30(b)(6) (by which the deposing party serves a notice of deposition on the corporation without naming an individual, and the corporation designates the person to answer the questions). Therefore, Smith's answers can be used against D even though Smith was no longer in D's employ at the time of the deposition. This is true even if Smith is available to testify at trial.

58. **No.** A non-party deponent's deposition testimony may be admitted for substantive purposes only under narrowly-defined circumstances, relating to the witness' unavailability to give live testimony. See Federal Rule 32(a)(3).

59. **Yes.** "Any deposition may be used by any party for the purpose of contradicting or impeaching the testimony of deponent as a witness. …" Federal Rule 32(a)(1).

60. **(a) Yes.** Federal Rule 33(b) states that "answers [to interrogatories] may be used to the extent permitted by the rules of evidence." Since an interrogatory may only be addressed to a party, and since by Federal Rule of Evidence 801(d)(2)(A), a party's statement is not classified as hearsay and is admissible against him for any purpose, an interrogatory answer will always be admissible against the party who made it. Therefore, D's interrogatory answer may be used substantively against him.

(b) Yes. Although a party's interrogatory answer is always admissible against him (whether for substantive or impeachment purposes), that answer is not "binding" on him. That is, the party who has given the interrogatory answer is always free at trial to state that his answer was wrong, and it is up to the jury to decide whether to believe what the defendant says at trial or what he said in the interrogatory. (Contrast this with the response to a Rule 36 request to admit, which *is* binding on the party making the admission.)

VI. PRETRIAL CONFERENCE

A. **Pretrial conference generally:** Many states, and the federal system, give the judge authority to conduct a *pretrial conference*. Typically, the judge will use such a conference to simplify or formulate the issues in the case, to keep the case moving, to identify witnesses to be presented at trial, and perhaps to facilitate a *settlement*. See Federal Rule 16(a) and 16(c).

1. **Scheduling:** Rule 16, although it leaves to the discretion of the judge whether to conduct a pretrial conference, *requires* in most cases that the judge issue a *"scheduling order"* within 120 days after filing of the complaint. This scheduling order must set a time limit for joinder of additional parties, amendment of the pleadings, filing of motions, and completion of discovery. Rule 16(b).

2. **Pretrial order:** If a pretrial conference is held, the judge must then enter a *pretrial order* reciting the actions taken in the conference. Such an order might summarize admissions of fact made by the lawyers, list the witnesses to be presented, narrow the issues to be litigated (perhaps by eliminating "frivolous claims or defenses"), etc. Rule 16(c), (e). This pretrial order is *binding* during the rest of the litigation, unless the court modifies it; but if the order is issued following the *final* pretrial conference, it may be modified *"only to prevent manifest injustice."* Rule 16(e).

3. **Sanctions:** If a party or his lawyer fails to participate in the pretrial conference, fails to do so "in good faith", or fails to comply with the scheduling or pretrial order, the judge may apply whatever *sanctions* are "just". Rule 16(f). 16(f) gives the trial judge explicit authority to use the sanctions imposed in Rule 37(b)(2)(B), (C), and (D) for failure to comply with discovery orders (striking of claims or defenses, barring of the submission of matters into evidence, dismissal of the action, issuance of a contempt citation, etc.)

   a. **Promoting settlement:** One of the key functions of the pretrial conference is to *promote settlement*. Some judges, anxious to clear their dockets, use "persuasion" that verges on coercion in trying to bring about a settlement. If the judge goes too far in trying to get the parties to settle, she may find herself reversed on appeal.

   Example: P brings a medical malpractice action against D. At a pretrial conference, the trial judge: (1) directs counsel for both sides to conduct settlement negotiations; (2) recommends that the case be settled for between $20,000 and $30,000; and (3) warns the parties that, if they settle for a comparable figure after the trial begins, he will impose sanctions against the "dilatory party." D offers $5,000 before trial, but this offer is rejected. The trial begins, and the case is settled for $20,000 after one day of trial. The trial judge then imposes $2,500 of sanctions on D (but not P) for waiting until after the start of trial to settle for a sum that was within the range urged earlier by the judge.

   Held (on appeal), the sanction was an abuse of the trial judge's power under Rule 16(f). The sanctions for failure to act in good faith at a settlement conference were "not designed as a means for clubbing the parties — or one of them — into an involuntary compromise." Here, at the time of the settlement conference, D had no reason to believe that P might be satisfied with a settlement as low as $20,000 (P was asking $50,000 at the time); since D had already made an offer of $5,000, he was not required to "bid against himself." Also, D and his lawyer were within their rights in changing their opinion once the trial started, since P's performance on the witness stand was an important new fact not available at the time of the settlement conference. *Kothe v. Smith*, 771 F.2d 667 (2d Cir. 1985).

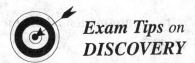

Exam Tips *on* DISCOVERY

The good news about Discovery on exams is that you'll almost always be able to recognize that you are indeed dealing with a discovery issue — you'll be told about a deposition, a request for document production, etc. The bad news is that discovery issues are extremely technical and based on the precise working of the FRCP — you can't rely on general reasoning or on "On the one hand, on the other hand …" analysis. Here are some particular things to check for:

☞ Be alert to *privileges*. [172, 188] Remember that information protected by a privilege may not be subjected to discovery. Also, remember that on federal-question issues, federal common law determines what is privileged, but on state-law issues, state law of privilege controls.

☞ Be alert to *work-product immunity* issues. Any time one litigant seeks from the other information that was prepared in anticipation of litigation, either the qualified or the absolute w.p. immunity will apply. So be on the lookout for attempts to get a lawyer's notes or memos, an investigator's report, etc. [172-178]

   ☞ Be sure to distinguish between *qualified* and *absolute* immunity. The latter applies only to *"mental impressions, conclusions, opinions or legal theories."* So documents that are entirely fact-based (e.g., what caused the accident?) will generally get merely qualified protection. If the immunity is qualified, it can be overcome by a showing of "substantial need" and an inability to obtain the equivalent materials without "undue hardship." [173-177]

   ☞ Before you conclude that something is w.p., make sure it was "prepared in anticipation of litigation." Even a document written by or to a lawyer won't be w.p. if it wasn't prepared at least partly in anticipation of litigation (so that, for instance, a document prepared to comply with a statute or government regulation won't be covered, though it might be covered by attorney-client privilege.)

   ☞ Remember that documents prepared by a *non-lawyer* (e.g., a private investigator) who is assisting in preparing for litigation will be covered.

   ☞ If the document in question was prepared by an *expert*, special rules governing experts (discussed below), not the work-product immunity rules, apply.

☞ Remember that if a person (whether party or non-party) makes a statement concerning the litigation to a party, the maker of the *statement* may automatically get a copy, *supra* p. 178. This rule overrides any work product immunity.

☞ Remember that names of *"occurrence witnesses"* are automatically discoverable. [178]

☞ Keep in mind that special rules apply to *experts*. [179-181] Professors are likely to test this area, because it changed greatly in 1993. Now, if a party plans to call an expert at trial, the party must have the expert prepare and sign a *report* containing his opinions and other information; the report is automatically given to the other side.

☛ Look out for any disclosure duties added in 1993. Thus parties must now disclose *automatically,* (i.e., without a specific request by the other side), early in the case:

☞   *Names and addresses* of each person having discoverable information relating to disputed facts alleged with particularity in the pleadings; and

☞   Copies or descriptions of all *documents* and tangible things relating to particularly-pleaded disputed facts. [182-188]

☛ Always keep in mind the distinction between parties and non-parties. For instance, an *interrogatory* can only be addressed to a *party*; disclosure relating to non-parties must occur through *depositions*. [191-198]

☞   Also, beware of the limits on the use of subpoenas for depositions. A subpoena to force a non-party to be deposed must set the deposition for no more than *100 miles* from the deponent's residence or place of business, *supra* p. 208.

☛ Remember that *medical exams,* are even more limited: only a party may be forced to undergo an exam, and then only if the party's condition is *in controversy* and the discovering party convinces the court that there is *good cause* for the exam. [198]

☛ Professors like to test the *admissibility* of discovery results at trial. [207-212] Use of *deposition* transcripts is the most-frequently-tested area. Use the two-part test:

☞   First, ask whether the deposition statement would be admissible if the deponent were giving *live testimony*.

☞   Second, make sure the statement falls into one of these *four categories*: (i) it was made by an *adverse party*, or by an officer or director of an adverse corporate party (in which case it is admissible for any purpose); (ii) it is used to *impeach* the deponent's credibility while the deponent is testifying (in which case it doesn't matter whether the deponent is a party); (iii) it *conflicts* with the deponent's trial testimony, if the interests of the deponent and the questioner are adverse (in which case it may even be used for substantive purposes); or (iv) various circumstances make the deponent *unavailable* to testify at trial (e.g., she is dead, or is located 100 or miles from the trial site).

CHAPTER 6

ASCERTAINING
APPLICABLE LAW

ChapterScope

This chapter is concerned with how federal and state courts determine what law to follow. For instance, in a diversity case, is the federal judge required to apply the law of the state in which she sits, or is he free to decide on her own, following other federal cases, what the law should be? In a state case involving a subject of federal concern (e.g., U.S. government bonds), to what extent is the state court obligated to apply principles formulated in federal cases?

The bulk of this chapter is concerned with the choice of law in *diversity* cases. The choice of law in federal question cases, and in state cases involving matters of federal interest, is treated at the end of the chapter.

Key concepts in this Chapter are:

■ *Erie v. Tompkins:* Under *Erie Railroad v. Tompkins,* in *diversity* cases the federal courts must apply *state judge-made law* ("common law") on any *substantive* issue where there is no federal statute on point.

❏ **"Forum shopping":** A key reason for this rule is to prevent *"forum shopping."* "Forum shopping" occurs where a plaintiff chooses between federal and state court based on which system is more favorable to her substantive case. Applying state substantive law in federal diversity cases thus removes the benefits of forum shopping.

■ **Determining state law:** When the federal court tries to apply state law, the standard is, *How would the state's highest court determine the issue if the case arose today?*

❏ The federal court must also apply state law governing *conflict of laws*. In other words, the conflict of laws rules of the state *where the federal court sits* must be followed.

■ **Procedure/substance distinction:** *Erie v. Tompkins* says that state common law controls in "substantive" matters. But federal rules and policies generally control on matters that are essentially "procedural." It is thus vital to distinguish between *procedure and substance.* As to procedural issues:

❏ **Federal Rules take precedence:** *Erie* is only applicable where there is no controlling federal statute. Since the Federal Rules of Civil Procedure are adopted pursuant to a congressional statute, *the FRCP take precedence over state policy when applicable*.

❏ **Federal statute on point:** Similarly, where there is a federal procedural *statute* (as distinct from a Federal Rule) that is directly on point, that statute will *control* over any state law or policy, even though this may promote "forum shopping."

❏ **Case not covered by a Federal Rule or statute:** If the issue at hand is *not* covered by anything in the FRCP or in a federal statute, but the issue is nonetheless arguably "procedural," the federal court *balances* the state and federal policies against each other. *Where the state interest in having its policy followed is fairly weak, and the federal interest strong, the court is likely to hold that the federal procedural policy should be followed*.

■ **Federal question cases:** In *federal question* cases, *federal common law, not state common law, usually applies*.

I.   NATURE OF PROBLEM

A. Concurrent jurisdiction: The jurisdiction of federal courts is, in most cases, *concurrent* with that of the state courts. That is, a particular controversy that is litigable in federal court may also, in most situations, be brought in state court. Since the decision whether to use state or federal court is left to the litigants, it becomes important to know whether these two courts will apply the same legal principles.

  1. Who chooses: Where jurisdiction of a particular claim is concurrent, the plaintiff makes the initial decision whether to use state or federal court. If he chooses state court, the defendant may sometimes remove the action to federal court.

  2. Choosing favorable forum: If jurisdiction in a particular situation is concurrent, and the state courts would apply rules of law different from those which would be applied by the federal court, the plaintiff, and in situations where removal is possible, the defendant, will have an incentive to *choose the court more favorable to his case.*

  a. Forum-shopping: This process of selecting the more favorable court is generally called *"forum-shopping."* The undesirability of forum-shopping plays a large role in the cases discussed throughout this chapter.

II.   THE *ERIE* DECISION AND OTHER FUNDAMENTALS

A. Rules of Decision Act: The Rules of Decision Act, 28 U.S.C. §1652, states that in civil actions, the federal courts must apply the "law of the *several states*, except where the Constitution or treaties of the United States or Acts of Congress otherwise require or provide." This Act has been in effect (with occasional changes of terminology) since 1789; (Wr., 347). Its interpretation, however, has changed drastically with the decision in *Erie Railroad v. Tompkins*, discussed extensively below.

  1. Interpretation: The Rules of Decision Act, together with Article VI of the Constitution, means and *has always been taken to mean* that the federal *Constitution, treaties*, and constitutional *Acts of Congress* always take precedence, where relevant, over all *state* provisions. *This rule applies to proceedings in federal and state courts alike.*

  2. State statutes: The Act has also *always* been taken to mean that in the absence of controlling federal provisions, the federal courts will be bound to follow *state constitutions and statutes*.

  3. Dispute about common law: There has been much dispute, however, about what law the federal courts should apply where there is *no controlling constitutional or statutory provision*, federal *or* state; that is, where the "law" in question is the so-called *"common," or judge-made, law.*

a. ***Swift v. Tyson:*** For many years the definitive Supreme Court opinion on the subject was contained in ***Swift v. Tyson***, 16 Pet. (41 U.S.) 1 (1842). There, the Court held that:

i. the federal courts were bound by state court opinions which construed the state's ***constitution or statutes***, or which pertained to ***real estate*** or other essentially ***local***, immobile matters;

ii. in all other questions, such as "general commercial law" (which was what was at issue in *Swift*) the federal courts were free to evolve their ***own common law*** irrespective of what state courts were doing. In other words, the phrase "laws of the several states" in the Rules of Decision Act ***did not encompass "general" common law.***

b. ***Swift* in disfavor:** During the first decades of this century, the *Swift* doctrine gradually fell into disfavor.

i. **Ideal theory rejected:** The legal philosophy which seemed to justify *Swift* — the view that the common law was an ***ideal entity*** which judges could not "create" but only try to ***"discover"*** — had been rejected by the best legal minds. Wr., 349-50. This "ideal entity" theory formed the foundation of the *Swift v. Tyson* doctrine; it was because judges do not "make" law but only "discover" the true common law that the federal courts should be free to engage on their own search for that truth. When legal writers began to express the view that judges "make" common law in much the same way that legislatures make statutory law, common law came to be seen as a "law of the state" just as statutes are laws of the state. *Swift's* distinction between statutory and common law therefore had less meaning.

ii. **Forum-shopping:** On a more pragmatic plane, the practice of ***"forum-shopping"*** was becoming notorious. "Forum-shopping" was the process by which a party tried to maneuver into a federal court in order to evade a state body of law that he found unfavorable, or into a state court to avoid the application of unfavorable federal common-law principles. The party (often the plaintiff, but sometimes the defendant using his right to remove to federal court) was said to be "shopping" for the most favorable forum in which to try his claim.

c. ***Black and White Taxicab:*** The disadvantages of allowing federal courts to determine their own common law became extremely apparent to many in the case of *Black and White Taxicab v. Brown and Yellow Taxicab*, 276 U.S. 518 (1928).

i. **Facts of *Black and White Taxicab*:** A Kentucky cab company, in order to form a monopolistic arrangement with a Kentucky railroad which it knew the state courts of Kentucky would not enforce, reincorporated in Tennessee to create diversity so as to be able to sue its Kentucky competitors in federal court.

ii. ***Swift* cited:** A majority of the Supreme Court, citing *Swift*, agreed that the monopoly was enforceable at general federal common law, and that state law should be ignored.

iii. **Holmes' dissent:** Justice Holmes, dissenting, articulated the new "realist" doctrine that no "transcendent body of law outside of any particular state" exists, that ***the common law of a state is as much a creation of the state's sovereign power as***

the statutory law, and that therefore the federal courts under the Rules of Decision Act should be *bound to follow state common law*. To refuse to follow state law, Holmes argued, insofar as this refusal permitted the federal courts to exceed the powers granted to the federal government, was "an *unconstitutional assumption of powers* by the Courts of the United States."

    iv. Practical result: Many observers were appalled by the practical effects of the *Taxicab* decision — a corporation, by undergoing a new incorporation for the sole purpose of establishing diversity, had succeeded in completely thwarting the state common law policy against monopoly. Most observers felt that this policy against monopoly was a substantive state law in a very real sense, and ought to be respected by the federal courts under the Rules of Decision Act.

4. *Erie v. Tompkins:* The decision in *Erie Railroad v. Tompkins*, 304 U.S. 64 (1938), transformed Holmes' dissent in *Taxicab*, *supra*, into the law of the land.

  a. Facts of *Erie:* The facts of *Erie* were as follows:

    i. Subject of suit: The suit was brought by a Pennsylvania citizen, for damages sustained as a result of being struck while walking along the railroad's right of way in Pennsylvania, by "something ... projecting" from a moving railroad car.

    ii. Suit in New York: The railroad was incorporated in New York, so plaintiff Tompkins filed suit in a federal district court there.

    iii. Pennsylvania common-law rule: Pennsylvania common law favored the railroad, holding that it had no duty or liability toward people walking along the right of way (these being deemed "trespassers") unless its negligence was "wanton or willful."

    iv. General federal common law used by District Court: The federal court in New York, following *Swift*, decided to interpret general common law on its own, and found against the railroad.

  b. Supreme Court's holding in *Erie:* The Supreme Court reversed, in an opinion by Brandeis. The opinion agreed with the Holmes *Taxicab* dissent that *the Rules of Decision Act applies to common law* as well as to constitutional and statutory provisions. The *Swift* doctrine was held *unconstitutional*, as it allowed the federal courts to *make* law in areas where the power to do so had never been granted to the federal government by the Constitution. The Court made three distinct arguments:

    i. Historical evidence: First, the Court claimed that new evidence had been produced demonstrating that the Rules of Decision Act was *intended by its authors* to include state common law.

    ii. Discrimination: Second, the practical results of *Swift v. Tyson* were undesirable: "*Swift v. Tyson* introduced *grave discrimination by non-citizens against citizens*. It made rights enjoyed under the unwritten 'general law' vary according to whether enforcement was sought in the state or federal court; and the privilege of selecting the court in which the right should be determined was conferred upon the non-citizen." In other words, the *Swift* doctrine gave the non-citizen the ability to *"forum-shop"* for the forum most favorable to him.

Note: The requirements of jurisdiction, venue, and removal, taken together, produce the result that it is generally the ***non-citizen*** of the forum state who chooses whether state or federal court will serve as the forum.

iii. **Unconstitutional:** Discrimination against citizens by itself would not have been enough to induce the Court to abandon *Swift*; "but the ***unconstitutionality*** of the course pursued … compels us to do so. … ***There is no federal general common law. Congress has no power to declare substantive rules of common law applicable in a state***, whether they be local in their nature or 'general,' be they commercial law or a part of the law of torts. And no clause in the Constitution purports to confer such a power upon the federal courts."

c. **Concurrence:** Justice Reed, concurring, argued that the case should be decided solely on the grounds that the *Swift* interpretation of the Rules of Decision Act was erroneous, without discussing the Constitutionality of the *Swift* view. Reed stated that he was "not at all sure whether, in the absence of federal statutory direction, federal courts would be [constitutionally] compelled to follow state decisions."

d. **Constitutional basis confusing:** The Constitutional basis of the Brandeis *Erie* opinion has confused commentators for years. Subsequent interpretations of *Erie* have tended to focus on the ***policy*** considerations expressed in the decision (e.g. the policy against forum-shopping) more than on its Constitutional basis. Cf. *Guaranty Trust v. York* (*infra*, p. 228), where the Court stated that "*Erie* expressed a ***policy*** that touches vitally the proper distribution of judicial powers between State and federal courts." Wr., 360-61.

5. **Certain federal common law matters remain:** Just as under *Swift* there was still a binding state common law in matters closely related to state sovereignty, such as real estate, similarly under *Erie* there remains a federal common law in matters ***related to clear federal questions***. See *infra*, p. 235.

Example: An example of federal common law, related to a federal question case, was given in a decision made by the Supreme Court the same day as *Erie*; the apportionment of the waters of an ***interstate stream*** was held to be a matter of federal, not state, common law. Wr., 387-88. It is only ***general*** federal common law that was held not to exist by the *Erie* decision.

B. **Federal procedural law:** The Rules of Decision Act, *Swift*, and *Erie*, all have to do with ***substantive*** law. Federal ***procedure*** has a separate history:

1. **Conformity Act:** Formerly, under the Conformity Act of 1872, 28 U.S.C. §724, a federal court had to apply the procedures of the courts of the state in which it was sitting, if no federal statute governed.

a. **Theory illusory:** "The theory [that state procedures would be followed] was largely illusory. The state practice was required to give way to any federal statute in point." Wr., 401. There were in fact federal statutes controlling most of the important aspects of procedure, so the Conformity Act was given little scope.

2. **Enabling Act:** In 1934, the Congress passed an "Enabling Act," 28 U.S.C. §2072, which allowed the Supreme Court to "prescribe, by general rules … the forms of process, writs,

pleadings, and motions, and the *practice and procedure in civil actions* at law" for the federal courts.

a. **Substantive rights not affected:** The Enabling Act provided that the rules so enacted must not *"abridge, enlarge, nor modify the substantive rights of any litigant."*

b. **Federal Rules:** Pursuant to the Enabling Act, the Court promulgated the Federal Rules of Civil Procedure in the same 1938 term in which it handed down the *Erie* decision.

III. *ERIE* PROBLEMS

A. **Ascertaining state law:** If the federal courts are to apply the "laws of the various states," they must be able to determine what these "laws" are. Statutes and constitutions are relatively easy to look up; but the determination of "case law" presents special problems. Perhaps no holding on point by the highest state court exists; or perhaps there is a holding which any reasonable observer would regard as obsolete and subject to change as soon as the court in question has a chance to reconsider.

1. **Intermediate-court decisions:** If there is no holding by the highest state court, the federal court looking for a state law to apply should consider *intermediate-court* decisions, and apply them unless there are "persuasive data" indicating "that the highest court of the state would decide otherwise." *West v. American Telephone and Telegraph Co.*, 311 U.S. 223 (1940). Wr. 370.

   a. **Trend reversed:** Prior to 1948, the Supreme Court tended to respect even *minor, unreported*, state decisions. But that year, this trend began to be reversed, when the Court held that the decisions of the Court of Common Pleas of South Carolina were by state practice so utterly *lacking in precedential value* that no federal court sitting in South Carolina was bound to follow them, although these decisions were entitled to "some weight." *King v. Order of United Commercial Travelers of America*, 333 U.S. 153 (1948). Wr. 372.

   b. **Where no court has spoken:** If no court in the state has ever considered the issue of law in question, the practice of other states, and the position of the Restatements and other authorities, may be consulted. But the issue is still *what the state's highest court would do* if confronted with the question, *not* what the federal court thinks is the proper holding. Wr., 375.

      i. **Other federal decision:** There are cases in which decisions in *prior federal diversity cases* dealing with the same issue of state law are *binding* on the federal court hearing the subsequent diversity case. This is likely to be the case if the prior federal decision comes from the district or circuit encompassing the state whose law is at issue, and the subsequent federal suit is in a different district or circuit.

         Example: A federal court sitting in New York is required to decide whether, under Tennessee law, the "right of publicity" survives the death of the person to be publicized (in this case, Elvis Presley). There are no Tennessee decisions on point.

There is, however, a decision by the Sixth Circuit (the circuit of which Tennessee is a part). *Held* (by the Second Circuit on appeal), since the Sixth Circuit has greater familiarity with Tennessee law because of the greater frequency with which it is required to apply that law, the Sixth Circuit decision is **binding** on the New York federal court. *Factors Etc., Inc. v. Pro Arts, Inc.*, 652 F.2d 278 (2d Cir. 1981).

2. **State decision obsolete:** Where there exists an *old* determination of state law by the highest state court, it is open to the federal courts to conclude that the state court would decide otherwise if confronted with the present case, and that therefore *the old ruling is not binding. Bernhardt v. Polygraphic Co. of America*, 350 U.S. 198 (1956). Wr., 372.

> **Example:** P, a woman who has used birth control pills made by D, sues D for personal injuries in Pennsylvania state court. D removes to Pennsylvania federal district court. Because the cause of action arose in Ohio, a Pennsylvania statute requires that the Ohio statute of limitations be applied, and all parties therefore agree that the federal court must apply Ohio limitations law. D asserts that under Ohio law, P's cause of action is time-barred. P counters that the Ohio Supreme Court would, if it had to decide the issue today, hold that P's claim is timely because the running of the statute of limitations was tolled until P discovered, or should reasonably have discovered, the actionable conduct.
>
> *Held*, for P. It is true that the only opinion on point by the Ohio Supreme Court, a nine-year-old case, appears not to grant P any relief from the statute of limitations, on the grounds that any change of law should be done by the legislature. However, a 1980 Ohio Supreme Court opinion tolls the statute in medical malpractice cases where a foreign object has been left inside the body. This granting of relief in an analogous instance suggests that if the matter were to arise today, the Ohio Supreme Court would toll the statute on these facts. *McKenna v. Ortho Pharmaceutical Corp.*, 622 F.2d 657 (3d Cir. 1980). (A dissent contended that the Ohio Supreme Court would not reverse itself were the issue to arise today, and that the majority was simply ignoring the relevant Ohio law because it found that law was "unenlightened.")

3. **Certification:** In some states, questions of law may be "certified" to the highest court in the state. In such cases, a federal court in doubt as to what the state "law" is can simply ask the state courts. Other states, however, will not allow this; their courts can only decide questions actually in controversy before them. F,K&C, pp. 241-42.

4. **Change to conform with new state decision:** Under *Erie*, it is **never too late** to change a federal decision in order to conform with a new pronouncement of state law, until the **final appeal** has been disposed of. A federal appellate court must rely on a new decision of a state's highest court even if handed down *after* the federal district court action was completed. Wr., 272.

   a. *De novo* **review by appellate court:** Also, the federal appellate court must make its **own de novo determination** about what state law would provide — the appellate court should not give deference to the federal trial judge's determination on this issue (deference that would be given, for instance, to factual findings by the trial judge — see *infra*, p. 258). See *Salve Regina College v. Russell*, 499 U.S. 225 (1991).

B. Conflict of laws: The Rule of Decision Act does not specify *which* state's law is controlling if, for example, the state in which a federal court is sitting is different from the state where the cause of action arose, and the laws of the two states (*lex fori* and *lex loci delicti* respectively) happen to differ.

1. *Swift* **rule:** Under *Swift v. Tyson*, a question of this sort was a "matter of general jurisprudence" and it was therefore up to the federal court to decide which state's law to apply, if one or both states had statutes covering the matter. If there were no state statutes, then of course the federal court did not have to refer to state law at all, unless the action were local.

2. *Erie* **rule:** But under *Erie*, the federal court should ask itself *which state's law would be applied by the courts of the state where the federal court sits*. In other words, the *conflict of laws rules* of the state where the federal court sits must be followed. *Klaxon Co. v. Stentor Electric Mfg. Co.*, 313 U.S. 487 (1941). If this were not the case, the Court said in *Klaxon*, "the accident of diversity would constantly disturb equal administration of justice in coordinate state and federal courts sitting side by side. ..."

   a. *Klaxon* **still good law:** The "follow the local state conflicts law" rule was applied by the Supreme Court in *Day & Zimmermann, Inc. v. Challoner*, 423 U.S. 3 (1975).

      i. **Facts of *Day & Zimmermann*:** The plaintiffs were soldiers who were wounded or killed in Cambodia when a shell manufactured by the defendant exploded prematurely. They brought a products liability diversity suit in Texas federal court, and obtained a recovery based on Texas tort law (which allows strict liability).

      ii. **Defendant's contention:** The defendant claimed that under Texas conflict of laws rules, the Texas state courts would have applied the tort law of the place where the accident occurred (Cambodia), and that under Cambodian law, there is no liability without fault.

      iii. **Court's holding:** The Supreme Court agreed with the defendant that *since Texas courts would apply Cambodian tort law, so must the federal court sitting in Texas*. The Court rejected the lower courts' ruling that the federal court was free to reject the mechanical Texas conflicts rule in factor of a more modern rule: "A federal court in a diversity case is not free to engraft onto [state conflicts] rules exceptions or modifications which may commend themselves to the federal court, but which have not commended themselves to the State in which the federal court sits."

   Note: The conflicts question was not discussed in *Erie* itself, even though a Pennsylvania cause of action was tried in a New York federal court. The Supreme Court never explained why Pennsylvania, rather than New York, law was applied. The New York conflicts rule would have applied the *lex loci delicti* (Pennsylvania law). The Court may have determined *sub silentio* that the New York courts should be followed in their policy of applying the *lex loci delicti*. But it is also possible that the Court decided on its own to follow Pennsylvania law, without regard for what the New York conflicts rule was. Wr., 364-65. If the latter, this is no longer the way a federal court would treat the matter today. A modern federal court, following *Klaxon* and *Day & Zimmermann*, would explicitly follow the conflicts rule of the state where the court sits.

C. Burden of proof: The federal court must also follow the ***rules governing the allocation of the burden of proof*** in force in the state where it is sitting. *Palmer v. Hoffman*, 318 U.S. 109 (1943). Cf. *Cities Service Oil Co. v. Dunlap*, 308 U.S. 208 (1939).

> **Example:** Suppose that the hypothetical state of Ames has an unusual policy governing the allocation of the burden of proof in products liability cases. Under this unusual approach, once P has shown some evidence that she was harmed in some way by a product manufactured by D, it is up to D to come forward with evidence sufficient to make it more probable than not that D's product was not "defective." (This is in contrast to the rule applied in all other states that the burden of proving a defect is on P.) A federal district court sitting in Ames, in a diversity products liability suit, must follow the Ames rule, and must require D to prove non-defectiveness. This is true even if the federal court believes that the Ames policy is completely illogical and misguided.

D. Procedure/substance problems: The most difficult set of *Erie* problems is that which arises out of the distinction between *"procedural"* and *"substantive"* matters. State common law, under *Erie*, is controlling in "substantive" matters, but "procedure" in federal courts is regulated by the Federal Rules, promulgated by the Supreme Court in the same 1938 term as the *Erie* decision was handed down. The relationship between *Erie* and the Federal Rules has caused considerable confusion.

1. Federal Rules always take precedence: *Erie* is only applicable where there is ***no controlling federal statute.*** Since the Federal Rules were adopted pursuant to a valid statute (the Enabling Act), the Rules take precedence over state policy according to the Rules of Decision Act. ***Erie doctrine is thus irrelevant to this supremacy of the Federal Rules.*** Cf. Ely, "The Irresistible Myth of *Erie*," 87 Harv. L. Rev. 693.

2. Rule's validity under Enabling Act: The only question, in deciding whether a Federal Rule takes precedence over a conflicting state policy, is ***whether that Rule is valid under the Enabling Act.*** To be valid, a Rule must:

a. fit into the list in the first sentence of the Enabling Act ("forms of process, writs, pleadings, and motions, and the practice and procedure in civil actions at law") ***and***

b. *not "abridge, enlarge, nor modify* the substantive rights of any litigant." The reference to "substantive rights" was intended to include rights created by both state and federal law.

   i. Meaning of "substantive": There has been much confusion about whether the term "substantive" in the Enabling Act means the same thing as the word "substantive" in *Erie* doctrine. If the two mean exactly the same thing, it would make no difference whether the dominance of a Rule over state policy were determined by reference to the Enabling Act or to *Erie* doctrine. If the Rule violated the "substantive right of litigants" provision of the Enabling Act, the Rule would not control over state policy, since it would not have been promulgated according to a U.S. statute. If the Rule were one which affected a substantive right under *Erie* doctrine, then state law would control (at least under the early *Erie* cases, which leaned extremely heavily towards the following of state law.)

ii. Hanna's distinction: But a 1965 Supreme Court decision, *Hanna v. Plumer* (discussed more fully below) suggests that the two uses of the term "substantive" are *not* the same: "The line between 'substance' and 'procedure' shifts as the legal context changes. ... It is true that both the Enabling Act and the *Erie* rule say, roughly, that federal courts are to apply state 'substantive' law and federal 'procedural' law, but from that it need not follow that the tests are identical. For they were designed to control very different sorts of decisions. When a situation is covered by one of the Federal Rules, the question facing the court is a far cry from the typical, relatively unguided *Erie* choice: the court has been instructed to apply the Federal Rule, and can refuse to do so only if the Advisory Committee, this Court, and the Congress erred in their prima facie judgment that the Rule in question transgresses neither the terms of the Enabling Act nor constitutional restrictions." Thus the term "substantive rights" in the Enabling Act is to be taken to cover fewer rights than this same term when used in the *Erie* context. But exactly how narrow the definition of substantive rights under the Enabling Act is remains to be seen; *no Federal Rule has yet been found to violate the "substantive" term of the Act.*

3. *Sibbach v. Wilson:* The initial construction of the "substantive rights" term of the Enabling Act was so narrow that state substantive law was not effectively protected against alteration by Federal Rule. In *Sibbach v. Wilson*, 312 U.S. 1 (1941), the Supreme Court found that a state policy forbidding compulsory physical examinations did *not involve a substantive right.* The Court therefore held that Federal Rule 35, allowing such examinations to be ordered, was not invalid under the Enabling Act.

a. Facts: The facts of *Sibbach:*

i. Plaintiff sued in an Illinois District Court for damages suffered in an accident occurring in Indiana.

ii. Defendant, in accordance with Federal Rule 35, obtained an order requiring plaintiff to submit to a physical examination to "determine the nature and extent of her injuries."

iii. Plaintiff refused to undergo the examination, claiming that her right to privacy was violated by the order. She was adjudged guilty of civil contempt.

b. Examination order valid: The Supreme Court reversed the contempt finding, holding it specifically prohibited by Rule 37. It held, however, that *the original order to submit to examination was valid* under the Rules and the Enabling Act.

c. No substantive right: Plaintiff's argument that the order, although it regulated procedure, abridged her "substantive right," was rejected.

i. State common law: Neither Indiana nor Illinois had a statute relevant to the court's ability to order a physical examination. But Indiana common law allowed such examination orders, and Illinois common law prohibited them.

ii. The Supreme Court held that if the right to be free of such an order were actually one of "substantive law," the Rules of Decision Act would require the court to apply *Indiana* law, which allowed the order. (But see par. (d) below.)

iii. **Plaintiff's dilemma:** Plaintiff was therefore in a dilemma. If she claimed that the right to be free of an order of examination was substantive, then the Rules of Decision Act would force application, the Court held, of Indiana law, and plaintiff would have to undergo the examination. But if she claimed that the matter was one of procedure, then Rule 35 would be a valid rule promulgated according to a statute, and thus entitled to be observed pursuant to the Enabling Act.

iv. **Plaintiff's argument:** To escape from her dilemma, plaintiff in *Sibbach* maintained that the Rule 35 provision and the court order pursuant to it were not matters of substantive *law* (for then she would have to undergo the physical exam according to Indiana law) but that the Rule and order did abridge her substantive *rights*, violating the Enabling Act.

v. **Enabling Act not violated:** The Court refused to recognize that a Rule which regulated procedure (as plaintiff admitted that it did) could so affect substantive rights as to violate the Enabling Act. The Court seemed to hold that "substan*tive*" was not the same thing as "substan*tial*"; a Rule could affect substantial rights without violating the Enabling Act. As long as the Rule was procedural, however, it could not affect substantive rights, and could not violate the Act.

d. **If *Sibbach* arose today:** If *Sibbach* arose today, plaintiff's dilemma, as described in (iii.) above, would be different. The decision in *Klaxon v. Stentor, supra*, p. 224, that the conflict of laws rule of the forum state should be applied in *Erie* cases, would have meant that Illinois conflict of laws should be looked to to determine whether Illinois or Indiana law on physical examination orders is to be observed. Since it is unlikely that Illinois would follow Indiana law and allow physical examinations in accidents arising in Indiana, when it did not allow them in Illinois accidents, probably Illinois would apply its own examination rule here.

i. **Result:** Thus, *if the matter were held to be substantive*, and state law were to control, Mrs. Sibbach would probably win her case. But it is unlikely that the Court today would find that the question is one of substantive law; the decision in *Hanna v. Plumer, infra*, p. 232, implies that a fair amount of interference with state-created rights is permissible without violating the Enabling Act. And as long as the Rule 35 provision is valid under the Act, it takes precedence. Thus, all in all, Mrs. Sibbach would not be in a dilemma (she could claim wholeheartedly that the matter was one of substantive right, and that state law should control) but she would probably lose.

4. **Reliance on *Erie* to construe Rules:** Since state-created substantive rights found little protection in *Sibbach's* narrow construction of the "no modification of substantive rights" provision of the Enabling Act, the Court came to rely instead directly on *Erie* doctrine to determine the scope and validity of the Federal Rules. Although no Rule was ever actually found to be unenforceable as against the state common law because of *Erie*, the *scope* of many Rules was limited by a kind of *Erie* analysis. Cf. *Ragan v. Merchants Transfer*, dis-

cussed *infra*, p. 228. The use of *Erie* for testing the validity and scope of the Federal Rules was aided by the Supreme Court's decision in ***Guaranty Trust Co. v. York***, 326 U.S. 99 (1945).

a. ***Guaranty Trust:*** *Guaranty Trust* involved the applicability of a ***state statute of limitations*** to a right of action arising under state law, but tried in federal court.

    i. **Federal courts must follow state statute of limitations:** The *Guaranty* opinion, by Frankfurter, first rearticulated the "realist" view of common law as something made by men, not discovered by them. He then held that this realist view, in the context of *Erie*, required that the federal courts obey the state statute of limitations.

    ii. ***Erie* applies to equitable rights:** Even though the right sought to be enforced in federal court in *Guaranty* was essentially ***equitable***, and the state statute of limitations applied only to actions at ***law***, the state statute still had to be respected. The basis of this holding seems to be that the state action, which would have been one at law, and not at equity, was barred by the statute, and that the federal court must therefore ***not give it longer life.***

    iii. **Meaning of "procedure":** Even though a statute of limitations might be "procedural" ***in some uses of the word***, for the purposes of *Erie* doctrine it was substantive. "[T]he question is not whether a statute of limitations is deemed a matter of 'procedure' in some sense. The question is whether such a statute concerns merely the manner and the means by which a right to recover, as recognized by the State, is enforced, or whether such statutory limitation is a ***matter of substance*** in the aspect that alone is relevant to our problem, namely ***does it significantly affect the result of a litigation for a federal court to disregard a law of a State that would be controlling in an action upon the same claim by the same parties in a State court?***"

    iv. **Outcome-determinative test:** A statute of limitations was substantive by the above definition — it affected the result of the litigation in the sense that the plaintiff could not sue ***at all*** in state court; he had at least a chance of winning in the federal court if the statute were ignored. The test of affecting the result of the litigation came to be known as the ***"outcome-determinative"*** test.

5. **Outcome-determination and the Federal Rules:** In *Guaranty Trust*, no Federal Rule was involved at all. In later cases, however, the outcome-determinative test did come to affect the Federal Rules.

    a. ***Ragan v. Merchants Transfer:*** In ***Ragan v. Merchants Transfer and Warehouse Co.***, 337 U.S. 530 (1949), the issue was not whether a state statute of limitations was applicable at all, but ***whether it was satisfied by the mere filing of the complaint with the court*** within the designated period, or on the other hand, required ***service on the defendant*** within the period. The state law held the latter, but Federal Rule 3 says that "a civil action is commenced by filing a complaint with the Court." The Supreme Court held that the ***state rule was controlling.***

i.   **Basis for holding unclear:**   The basis for following state law in *Ragan* is unclear. The holding might have rested solely on the ground that the Rule 3 provision *simply doesn't speak to statute of limitations problems at all*, that it was made part of the Rules to serve as a starting time against which the time limits for other acts described in the Rules are to be measured. Thus under this view, Rule 3 was simply *not applicable* to these facts; the *Erie* doctrine did not override the Rule, but simply applied state policy where no federal policy existed.

ii.   **Probable rationale:**   The Court seemed to imply, however, that since the state rule was "substantive" (in the sense that it might affect the outcome of the suit), it would take precedence *even over a Rule that was clearly applicable*. If this was the Court's *ratio decidendi*, it is no longer a valid one, since *Hanna v. Plumer*, discussed *infra*, p. 232.

b.   ***Ragan* still valid law:**   *Ragan v. Merchants Transfer* was expressly held *still to be valid law*, in *Walker v. Armco Steel Corp.*, 446 U.S. 740 (1980). The case involved virtually identical facts to *Ragan*, i.e., whether in a diversity action the federal court should follow state law, or alternatively, Federal Rule 3, in determining when an action is "commenced" for the purpose of satisfying the *statute of limitations*.

i.   **Holding:**   The Court held that *Hanna v. Plumer* does not apply to this question, because Federal Rule 3 simply does not speak to the issue of when a state statute of limitations is tolled; rather, Rule 3's statement that a civil action is commenced by the filing of the complaint is merely designed to give a starting point for the measurement of various time periods in the federal suit. Since there is no conflict between Rule 3 and the state law on tolling, the Court stated, a conventional *Erie* analysis must be done. As *Ragan* concluded, *state law* should clearly be chosen on this question.

ii.   **Rationale:**   The Court conceded that use of a federal rule tolling the statute of limitations by the filing of the complaint, would probably not lead to forum shopping. (Here, for instance, there was no evidence that P chose federal court because he didn't think he could comply with state service of process requirements before the statute of limitations had run.) However, use of such a federal principle would lead to *inequitable administration of the laws*. This is because the liability of the defendant would depend on the fortuity of whether he had been sued in federal or in state court.

6.   **Other outcome-determinative cases:**   On the same day as it decided *Ragan*, the Court held that:

a.   **Suit by foreign corporations:**   a plaintiff corporation, barred from bringing suit in a Mississippi state court by its failure to comply with a local statute governing out-of-state corporations, was equally barred from bringing suit in a federal court in Mississippi. *Woods v. Interstate Realty Co.*, 337 U.S. 535 (1949) and

b.   **Security in stockholder's derivative suit:**   a New Jersey statute requiring plaintiff in a stockholder derivative action to give security for the costs of litigation, was binding on the federal courts sitting in diversity. *Cohen v. Beneficial Industrial Loan Corp.*, 337 U.S. 541 (1949).

i.   **Rationale:** A dissent in *Cohen* by 3 Justices asserted that the N.J. statute was purely procedural; the majority held it to be *"outcome-determinative"* and thus binding under *Guaranty Trust.*

7. *Byrd v. Blue Ridge:* Finally, in *Byrd v. Blue Ridge Rural Electric Coop., Inc.*, 356 U.S. 525 (1958), the Court began to *retreat from its complete acceptance of the "outcome-determinative" test.*

a. **Facts:** Plaintiff sued for negligence in a federal court in South Carolina. The defense argued that the plaintiff was a "statutory employee" of the defendant, rather than an independent contractor, and that therefore workmen's compensation benefits were his sole remedy.

b. **Decision by judge:** Under a South Carolina decision, the question whether plaintiff was a "statutory employee," rather than an independent contractor, was to be determined by the *judge*, not the *jury.*

c. **Holding:** The Supreme Court held that the *federal policy* of having factual matters decided by a jury, not the state approach of having the judge decide the issue, must be followed. The Court reasoned as follows:

i.   **Outcome-determinative:** On one hand, the state policy *might* be outcome-determinative, and therefore *"in the absence of other considerations,"* the federal courts should follow it.

ii. **Federal policy:** On the other hand, the *federal policy* requiring jury trial of such "factual" issues was a very strong one and could *override the state policy*. "It cannot be gainsaid that there is a very strong federal policy against allowing state rules to disrupt the judge-jury relationship in the federal courts."

iii. **Weak state interest:** Also, the *state interest* in having the trial judge decide the question of employee status did not seem to be a strong one; it was *"not a rule intended to be bound up with the definition of the rights and obligations of the parties."*

iv. **Probability of outcome-determination:** In any case, the decision between judge- and jury-adjudication was *less likely* to "determine" the outcome of the suit than would be a choice, say, between an already expired state statute of limitations and no statute of limitations at all. The decision here *might* influence the outcome, but it was less likely to make a decisive difference than in most of the other cases where the Court had applied outcome-determination.

d. **Effect of *Byrd:*** The overall importance of *Byrd* is that it showed that state decisions that are basically procedural (though they may, of course, *affect* substantive rights) are *not necessarily controlling even if they are outcome-determinative*. The federal interest in the proper maintenance of the federal judiciary has to be given some respect, and controls if the federal policy is significantly stronger than the state policy. The test seems to be one of rough "balancing."

e. **Illustration of *Byrd's* effect:** The change made by *Byrd* is illustrated by *Szantay v. Beech Aircraft*, 349 F.2d 60 (4th Cir. 1965), which involved a state "door-closing" provision similar, though not identical, to the one in *Woods v. Interstate Realty Co.* (*supra*, p. 229).

i. **Facts of *Szantay*:** In *Szantay*, Illinois plaintiffs sued a South Carolina corporation and a Delaware corporation in South Carolina federal court. The cause of action arose in Tennessee. One of the defendants moved to dismiss on the grounds that a South Carolina procedural rule prevented suits in South Carolina by non-residents against foreign corporations unless the cause of action arose in South Carolina.

ii. **State rule not followed:** But the Court of Appeals, affirming the trial court, held that the South Carolina "door-closing" rule need *not* be followed. The court conceded that the choice of whether or not to follow the state rule was somewhat "outcome-determinative," and that rejection of the South Carolina rule in the federal court would promote some forum-shopping. But the state interest being served (probably prevention of congestion in the state courts) was irrelevant to the *Erie* question, and rejection of state law would not discriminate against South Carolina's citizens (since it would merely give to non-residents what residents already enjoyed, i.e., a South Carolina forum for a case against a foreign corporation.)

iii. **Countervailing federal interests:** Conversely, the federal interests were strong ones. These included the prevention of discrimination against non-residents (the very purpose of diversity jurisdiction); the interest in providing a convenient forum for federal litigants; and the use of efficient multi-party actions (since one of the defendants could be served only in South Carolina), among other factors. These interests supporting the federal principle of allowing non-residents in this situation to sue clearly outweighed the weak state interest.

iv. **Contrasted with *Woods*:** The decision in *Szantay* seems clearly inconsistent with the pre-*Byrd* decision in *Woods*, where a Mississippi rule preventing foreign corporations from suing if they had not complied with local licensing regulations was followed by the federal court, on the grounds of outcome-determinativeness. Thus the *Byrd* balancing of state interests against federal ones made the difference in *Szantay*.

f. **Unanimity for jury trials:** *Byrd* was similarly relied upon in a decision holding that the federal policy (not embodied in any Rule or statute, at the time) of requiring a *unanimous jury verdict*, not a state rule allowing a verdict based upon a *5/6ths majority*, must be followed in a diversity suit. *Masino v. Outboard Marine Corp.*, 652 F.2d 330 (3d Cir. 1982). The court relied on the following factors:

i. **Lack of strong state policy:** There was *no strong state interest* militating in favor of applying the state rule. The motivation behind the 5/6ths statute was simply to reduce the number of deadlocked juries, and thus increase the efficiency of the state court system. This interest was irrelevant to the *Erie* question, since the state had no interest in the administration of the *federal* judicial system.

ii. **Federal interest:** The federal interest in unanimous verdicts, by contrast, was a strong one, supported by a long tradition.

iii. **Not heavily outcome-determinative:**   Finally, the choice of rule would *not* be *heavily outcome-determinative*. Certainly, it would be unlikely that a plaintiff's choice of forum would be governed by the availability of a non-unanimous verdict. And "it is improbable that a party who has lost a verdict unanimously would have prevailed had he been required to persuade only seven, rather than eight, jurors to vote the other way." (Local federal district court rules provided for eight-person rather than twelve-person juries.

Note: If the question involved in *Masino* arose today, the result would be the same but the rationale would be different. Today, a Federal Rule (FRCP 48) specifies that a jury verdict must be unanimous unless the parties stipulate otherwise. A validly-enacted Federal Rule always prevails automatically over a contradictory state rule or policy, and *Erie* doctrine does not come into play — see the discussion of *Hanna v. Plumer, infra.*

g. *Forum non conveniens:*   Similarly, federal policies on when a case should be dismissed for *forum non conveniens* should be followed, rather than state policies, even though the choice of policies may be outcome determinative. Thus in *Sibaja v. Dow Chemical Co.*, 757 F.2d 1215 (11th Cir. 1985), a federal court sitting in Florida had to decide whether to dismiss for *forum non conveniens* product liability suits brought by Costa Rican agricultural workers against several American chemical companies.

i. **Facts:**   Florida would not have dismissed for *forum non conveniens*, because of a rule that precludes such dismissal where either party is a state resident (as the defendants were here). General federal principles dictated that the case be dismissed for *forum non conveniens* and litigated in the Costa Rican courts.

ii. **Federal policy chosen:**   Even though the choice of rule might affect the outcome (since the plaintiffs would not even get to the merits in their American lawsuit if the federal approach were chosen, but could bring and possibly win an American action if the state rule were chosen), the Federal Court of Appeals held that *Erie did not require application of the state rule.* The choice of policy on *forum non conveniens* "was not a decision going to the character and result of the controversy. Rather, it was a decision that occurred before, and completely apart from, any application of state substantive law."

8. *Hanna v. Plumer:*   *Hanna v. Plumer*, 380 U.S. 460 (1965), *removed the Federal Rules of Civil Procedure entirely from the scope of the Erie decision.*

a. **Facts:**   Plaintiff filed a diversity suit in federal court in Massachusetts, serving process on the wife of the defendant-executor, according to Rule 4(d)(1) (now 4(e)(2)), by leaving copies of the summons and complaint with her at his dwelling-place. Defendant claimed that this service conflicted with a Massachusetts statute making special provision for service upon the executor of an estate.

b. **Holding:**   The Supreme Court held that Rule 4(d)(1) was "in harmony with the Enabling Act," and that Rules thus valid are *not overridden by state policies or laws. Erie* doctrine is not controlling when a valid Federal Rule is in conflict with state common-law policy.

i. **Rationale:** To hold otherwise, the Court argued, would be to render the Federal Rules unworkable. "Thus, though a court, in measuring a Federal Rule against the standards contained in the Enabling Act and the Constitution, need not wholly blind itself to the degree to which the Rule makes the character and result of the federal litigation stray from the course it would follow in state courts [the Court then cited *Sibbach*], it cannot be forgotten that the *Erie* rule, and the guidelines suggested in *York*, were created to serve another purpose altogether. To hold that a Federal Rule of Civil Procedure must cease to function whenever it alters the mode of enforcing state-created rights would be to disembowel either the Constitution's grant of power over federal procedure or Congress' attempt to exercise that power in the Enabling Act."

c. **Rejection of outcome-determination:** The Court further claimed that *even in the absence of a Federal Rule* applicable to the question before it, state policy on service to executors might still not control. " 'Outcome-determination' analysis was never intended to serve as a talisman. ... *The 'outcome-determination' test ... cannot be read without reference to the twin aims of the Erie rule: discouragement of forum-shopping and avoidance of inequitable administration of the laws.*"

i. **No forum-shopping in *Hanna*:** In *Hanna*, the Court noted, it was almost inconceivable that plaintiff chose the federal, rather than state, forum, merely because the manner of service of process was slightly different. Thus, no forum-shopping considerations were really involved.

ii. **No discrimination:** Neither was discrimination against residents really at issue: "It is difficult to argue that permitting service of defendant's wife to take the place of in-hand service of defendant himself alters the mode of enforcement of state-created rights in a fashion sufficiently 'substantial' to raise the sort of equal protection problems to which the *Erie* opinion alluded."

d. **Harlan's concurrence:** Justice Harlan, in a very well-known concurrence, proposed a new test for determining when state law should be deferred to:

i. **Stricter test of Federal Rule:** A Federal Rule should not be automatically deferred to, Harlan argued. The majority had held that a Rule was constitutionally valid when it "regulate[d] matters which though falling within the uncertain area between substance and procedure, are rationally capable of classification as either." Harlan answered that "[s]o long as a reasonable man could characterize any duly adopted federal rule as 'procedural,' the Court, unless I misapprehend what it said, would have it apply *no matter how seriously it frustrated a State's substantive regulation of the primary conduct and affairs of its citizens*. ... Whereas the unadulterated outcome and forum-shopping tests may err too far toward honoring state rules, I submit that the Court's 'arguably procedural, ergo constitutional' test moves too fast and far in the other direction."

ii. **Primary decision test:** Harlan's test would thus "inquire ... if the choice of rule would substantially affect those *primary decisions respecting human conduct* which our constitutional system leaves to state regulation." If it would, state law must be applied even in the face of a Federal Rule to the contrary. Harlan cited

Ragan and the present case as examples where the state rule did *not* substantially affect primary decisions, but rather affected only behavior *after the cause of action arose*. He cited *Cohen, supra,* p. 229, however, as an example of a state rule that did in fact regulate primary human conduct; the statute requiring a bond in stockholder derivative suits "was meant to inhibit small stockholders from instituting 'strike suits,' and thus it was designed and could be expected to have a substantial impact on private primary activity."

e. Validity of rule: *Hanna v. Plumer* does not by itself immunize a Federal Rule against being found to be invalid under the Rules Enabling Act. It remains today the case that a Federal Rule must not "abridge, enlarge or modify any substantive right. ..." But the standard for judging the validity of a Rule is far more forgiving than the standard for determining whether a federal policy not embodied in a Rule abridges a state-created substantive right. "Rules which *incidentally* affect litigants' substantive rights do not violate this provision if *reasonably necessary* to maintain the *integrity of that system* of rules." *Burlington Northern Railroad Co. v. Woods,* 467 U.S. 1230 (1987). Furthermore, because any proposed Rule is scrutinized and approved by an Advisory Committee, a federal Judicial Conference, and the Supreme Court, plus subjected to a possible Congressional veto, any Rule that passes through this process is entitled to *"presumptive validity." Id. No Federal Rule has ever been found invalid under the Rules Enabling Act.* See Wr. p. 406.

9. Conflict must exist: *Hanna v. Plumer* only authorizes the federal court to disregard state procedural law and follow a Federal Rule if there is a *conflict* between the two. This conflict might be of two sorts. First, the Federal Rule and the state law (whether the state law is statutory or judge-made) may be in *direct collision*, in the sense that they cannot both be simultaneously satisfied. Alternatively, the Federal Rule and its legislative history may indicate an intent to *"occupy the field of operation"* of the state law, so that state law should be disregarded even though it would be theoretically possible for the two to be simultaneously followed. See *Burlington Northern Railroad Co. v. Woods,* 476 U.S. 1230 (1987) (where the Federal Rule gives the court discretion about whether to award damages to the non-appellant when the appellant takes a frivolous appeal, and where a state rule requires plaintiff to pay a 10% penalty after taking any appeal that loses, the state rule should not be followed because the Federal Rule was intended to occupy the entire field of penalties for frivolous appeals.)

a. No conflict found: Conversely, it will sometimes be the case that a Federal Rule and a state procedural rule will cover similar ground but be found *not* to be in conflict. That is, the court may decide that the federal rule *simply does not cover* the issue in question. If the court so concludes, it will then conduct a conventional *Erie/Byrd* analysis, balancing the state and federal interests against each other.

Example: P is injured in a fall on business premises. He sues, in a federal diversity action in Massachusetts, the persons listed on a public filing as being the owners of the property. But these turn out to be no longer the owners. After the local Massachusetts statute of limitations has run, P learns the true facts and sues the Ds, who are presently the owners. Federal Rule 15(c) would allow relation back to the time of the original suit only if the Ds had received notice before the statute of limitations had run (which they did not). But the Massachusetts rule would allow relation back in this situation, and would thus prevent the statute of limitations from barring the action.

Held, Hanna v. Plumer does not require the application of the Federal Rule; instead, the Massachusetts common-law rule, allowing relation back, should be followed (so that the suit can proceed). *Hanna* states only a "principle for resolving a direct conflict between two strictly procedural rules," and does not require that the Federal Rules "be woodenly applied irrespective of a discoverable substantive, as distinguished from a merely procedural, state purpose." Here, the state substantive purpose was a strong one, and outweighed whatever federal interest was embodied in the Federal Rule (especially in view of the strongly outcome-determinative nature of the choice.) *Marshall v. Mulrenin*, 508 F.2d 39 (1st Cir. 1974).

Note: The conflict that was at the center of *Marshall* would not arise today. In 1991, FRCP 15(c) was amended to allow relation back wherever state law would allow relation back. See *supra*, p. 160.

10. Conflict between congressional statute and state policy: So far, we have assumed that the federal-state conflict is either between a federal policy and a state statute or policy (the standard *Erie* situation), or between one of the Federal Rules and a state statute or policy (the *Hanna v. Plumer* situation). But there is at least one other interesting type of federal-state conflict: that between a *federal statute* directly enacted by Congress, and a state policy or statute. If a valid congressionally-enacted procedural statute outside of the Federal Rules conflicts with a state law or policy, the federal statute will control *even though this may promote forum shopping.*

a. *Stewart* **case:** A case involving transfer of venue illustrates how a federal procedural statute will prevail over even a strong state policy. In *Stewart Organization, Inc. v. Ricoh Corp.*, 487 U.S. 22 (1988), a contract between P and D contained a "forum selection" clause, which provided that any dispute arising out of the contract would be litigated only in a court in Manhattan. P sued in Alabama district court. D moved to have the case transferred to Manhattan. Alabama, as a matter of public policy, refuses to enforce, or even attach weight to, a contractual forum-selection clause, so the Alabama courts would have heard P's suit. In the federal system, recall that 28 U.S.C. §1404(a) (*supra*, p. 89) allows the district court to transfer the case to a different district court for the convenience of the parties. Section 1404(a) has long been interpreted in a way that gives considerable weight to any forum-selection clause in a contract between the litigants, so a federal court interpreting that clause might well (though would not necessarily) grant the transfer. So the question became: Should the district court follow the policy behind §1404(a) (thus giving weight to the forum-selection clause), or should it follow the policy of Alabama (and thus ignore the clause completely)?

i. **Federal law supreme:** The Supreme Court held that the *federal statute* must be followed. "When the federal law sought to be applied is a congressional statute, the first and chief question ... is whether the statute is 'sufficiently broad to control the issue before the Court.' ... If the District Court determines that a federal statute covers the point in dispute, it proceeds to inquire whether the statute represents a valid exercise of Congress' authority under the Constitution. ... If Congress intended to reach the issue before the District Court, and if it enacted its intention in a manner that abides with the Constitution, that is the end of the matter." Here, the statute did cover the point in dispute (by requiring the court to consider the parties' contractually-expressed venue preferences), and the section was clearly a valid exercise of Congress' constitutionally-granted power to run a federal judiciary. Therefore, federal statutory law controlled over the state policy.

Quiz Yourself on
ERIE *PROBLEMS*

61. P has brought a negligence action against D (based on diversity) in federal district court for the District of Iowa. P's complaint alleges that P was a social guest in D's house, that P fell when a wooden step on a stairway inside the house broke, and that had D used ordinary reasonable care in keeping his house safe, he would have discovered the danger and avoided it. (The complaint does not claim that D knew of the defect, merely that a reasonable person in D's position would have learned of the defect and fixed it.) A five-year-old decision of the Iowa Supreme Court holds that a social guest is only a "licensee," not an "invitee," and that a property owner owes a licensee no duty of inspection. A number of courts in other states have in the last few years abolished the licensee/invitee distinction, and have held that a property owner owes a duty of reasonable inspection to a licensee as well as an invitee. The federal district judge in whose court P's action is pending believes that these newer decisions represent the much better view. However, there is no evidence that the Iowa Supreme Court would change its attitude on this issue, since the court has on more recent occasions rejected other chances to expand tort liability. Should the federal judge impose upon D the duty of making reasonable inspection of his premises? _____

62. Same basic fact pattern as the prior question. Now, however, assume that the only Iowa case on the issue of whether a property owner owes a duty of inspection to a licensee is a 50-year-old decision by the Iowa Supreme Court, in which the court refused to impose any such duty of inspection. Since the courts of most states that have considered the matter within the past five years have rejected the traditional rule and imposed a duty of inspection on behalf of a licensee, the federal judge believes that the Iowa Supreme Court would probably follow this modern trend if it heard the case today. Should the federal court impose a duty of inspection on D? _____

63. P has sued D in federal district court for the Central District of California. The suit is based on diversity (since P is a citizen of California and D is a citizen of Arizona). P claims that D negligently drove an automobile, thus injuring P in an accident. The accident took place in Arizona. Under California state court decisions, any suit brought in the California state courts arising out of an auto accident is to be decided under California law if the plaintiff is a California resident, even if the accident took place in another state. This California approach is a minority and old-fashioned one; nearly every other state applies the rule of "lex locus delicti," whereby in auto accident cases the law of the state where the accident took place is the law that is used. The federal judge hearing the P-D suit believes that the majority "lex locus delicti" approach is much the sounder one. In the P-D suit the issue arises whether California state substantive law (under which contributory negligence is not a defense) or Arizona law (under which contributory negligence is still a defense) should be applied. The federal judge hearing the case believes that the California (no contributory negligence defense) is the better approach. Which state's substantive law of negligence, California's or Arizona's, should be applied by the federal judge? _____

64. P has sued D in diversity in federal court for the Northern District of Georgia. P seeks to assert against D a tort claim relating to an accident, as well as a breach of contract claim arising from a prior business rela-

tionship between P and D, having nothing to do with the accident. Under a Georgia statute, a tort claim may not be joined with a contract claim against the same defendant in state court, if the two claims relate to different transactions. However, joinder of unrelated contract and tort claims against a single defendant is expressly allowed by FRCP 18(a). In the federal action, may P join his contract and tort claims against D in a single action? _____

65. P and D signed a contract whereby P was to perform personal services for D. Almost immediately, it became clear to P that D was not living up to his part of the bargain, with respect to the duties that P was to be given. However, P tried to work things out with D for a long time (reasonable conduct by P in the circumstances), and therefore took no legal action for more than two years. He then brought a diversity action against D in federal district court for the District of Kansas, the state in which the contract was signed and was being performed. Under Kansas law, any action (whether legal or equitable) related to performance of a contract must be brought within two years of the performance or non-performance complained of. P does not seek damages in his federal suit; instead, he seeks to have the contract declared rescinded on account of D's nonperformance.

The federal courts have traditionally regarded actions to rescind a contract as being primarily equitable, and they apply the equitable doctrine of laches rather than any strict statute of limitations doctrine when the action is primarily equitable. Thus under general federal principles, P's suit will not be time-barred so long as P has acted within a "reasonable" period of time considering the circumstances. Should the federal court for the District of Kansas regard P's action as time-barred? _____

66. P has brought a diversity suit against D in federal district court for Montana; the suit alleges negligence. In both the Montana state trial courts and the federal district court of Montana, the applicable rules provide for a six-person jury. By Montana statute, the verdict in a civil case needs to be by only a 5/6's majority. The state rule allowing a 5/6's majority was adopted to reduce the number of hung juries and re-trials, thus reducing court congestion. By a long-standing federal policy a federal civil jury must reach a unanimous verdict. (There is no federal statute or Rule of Civil Procedure which directly requires unanimity.) Should the federal district judge recognize a verdict on which five out of the six juror agree? _____

Answers

61. **No.** This is a classic *Erie* situation. There is neither a state nor a federal statute on the matter. State common law creates the right being sued upon. Therefore, the federal court in diversity **must apply the common law (judge-made law) of the state where the federal court sits**, and may not apply the federal judge's own opinion of what a desirable rule would be. Since all the evidence is that the Iowa Supreme Court would not impose any duty of inspection on D here, the federal court may not impose any such duty either.

62. **Yes.** Again, the only issue is what the highest court of the state where the federal court sits would do if it heard the issue *today*. Since the facts indicate that the Iowa Supreme Court would probably overturn its 50-year-old ruling today, the federal court is not bound by that old ruling, and is instead required to behave as it thinks the Iowa court would behave today, by imposing the duty on D.

63. **California's.** In deciding an *Erie* case, the federal judge must apply the law of the state where the federal court sits. This principle includes the forum state's **conflict-of-laws principles** as well as its substantive principles. Therefore, the federal judge must apply California's conflicts rules. Since California's conflicts rules would make California rather than Arizona law applicable, the court must follow California's

substantive rules as well. One way to remember this is to apply the general principle that the federal court must *reach the same underlying decision* as the court of the state where the federal judge sits. (Observe that if California would apply Arizona law, then the task for the federal judge is not to apply what it thinks Arizona's state courts would decide, but rather, to apply what it thinks California's courts would think that Arizona's laws are!) See *Klaxon Co. v. Stentor Electric Mfg. Co.*, 313 U.S. 487 (1941).

64. **Yes.** This is an instance in which the federal policy is embodied in a Federal Rule of Civil Procedure that is exactly on point, and that is in direct conflict with the relevant state rule. In situations involving such a direct conflict, *Erie* doctrine (and the avoidance of forum shopping) does not apply at all. Instead, the sole question is *whether the federal rule is a valid one*. See *Hanna v. Plumer*, 380 U.S. 460 (1965). Since no Federal Rule of Civil Procedure has ever been found invalid under the Rules Enabling Act (i.e., no rule has ever been found to violate the Enabling Act's ban on the abridgement or enlargement of a litigant's substantive rights), Rule 18(a)'s rule of permissive joinder is certainly valid. Therefore, the federal court must follow Rule 18(a), and must disregard the policy behind the conflicting state rule. See *Har-Pen Truck Lines, Inc. v. Mills*, 378 F.2d 705 (5th Cir. 1967).

65. **Yes.** In diversity suits, the federal court must *apply the state-law statute of limitations*. Even though a statute of limitations has a "procedural" aspect, the choice of statute of limitations is heavily outcome-determinative. For example, here P will be allowed to maintain his suit if the federal laches approach is used, but will not be allowed to maintain suit at all if the state statute of limitations is used — the choice of law, therefore, is *completely* outcome determinative. The doctrine that state statutes of limitations control in diversity actions is the central holding of one of the most important *Erie* cases of all, *Guaranty Trust Co. v. York*, 326 U.S. 99 (1945). See also *Lipsky v. Commonwealth United Corp.*, 551 F.2d 887 (2d Cir. 1976).

66. **No.** Here, as in the previous question, we have a conflict between a federal policy not embodied specifically in a Federal Rule or statute, and a state policy or statute. Therefore, we must balance the two. The state interest here is relatively weak, and is in any event not thwarted by following the federal policy (since the number of hung juries and thus re-trials in state court will probably not be increased if the federal court has a hung jury). Conversely, the federal policy is a long-standing and apparently strong one — it is related to the Seventh Amendment's policy of giving maximum weight to the jury system, for instance. Similarly, there is a strong federal interest in having a treatment of the unanimity issue that is the same from one federal courtroom to another. Also, the choice of law is quite unlikely to be outcome determinative — it is hard to say, for instance, whether having a less-than-unanimous jury verdict would help P or D, since it is unclear who would get five but not six votes. And the choice of law is unlikely to promote forum shopping — it is hard to imagine that P will sue in state rather than federal court because juries in the former don't have to be unanimous.

All in all, the federal interests seem so much stronger than the state interests, and the risk of forum shopping so small, that the court will probably decide to follow the federal policy requiring unanimity. See, e.g., *Masino v. Outboard Marine Corp.*, 652 F.2d 330 (3d Cir. 1981), in which the court so decided.

IV. FEDERAL COMMON LAW

A. **Federal common law still exists:** Even though the *Erie* case makes it clear that there is no *general* federal common law, there are still *particular instances* in which federal common law is applied. That is, there are instances in which the federal court is free to disregard state law in making judicial interpretations.

1. **Federal question cases:** Most such instances arise in cases in which federal jurisdiction is founded on something other than diversity, such as *federal question cases*, cases in which the U.S. is a party, cases between a state and citizens of another state, or admiralty cases.

2. **General rule:** In most federal question cases, federal common law, not state common law, applies.

   a. **Statutory construction:** When the precise meaning of a federal statute is at issue, the federal court is of course free to follow federal decisions, and to ignore state constructions of the statute. This is not really even federal "common law" so much as pure statutory interpretation.

   b. **Right to ignore state precedents:** Even if the statute serving as the basis for federal question jurisdiction does not treat a particular problem at all, the federal court will still, in many instances, be free to disregard state decisions on point.

      Example: A check issued by the W.P.A., a federal agency, is stolen from the payee; an endorsement is forged, and the check is cashed by Clearfield Trust. *Held*, in a suit between Clearfield Trust and the Federal Reserve about whether there was timely notice of the forgery, federal, not state, common law must be consulted. "The issuance of commercial paper by the United States is on a vast scale and transactions in that paper from issuance to payment will commonly occur in several states. The application of state law, even without the conflict of laws rules of the forum, would subject the rights and duties of the United States to exceptional uncertainty. It would lead to great diversity in results by making identical transactions subject to the vagaries of the laws of the several states. The desirability of a uniform rule is plain." Thus all federal courts may follow each other's cases as precedent, so that a uniform body of law regarding federal commercial paper will emerge. *Clearfield Trust Co. v. United States*, 318 U.S. 363 (1943).

   c. **U.S. as party:** In the great majority of cases in which the *U.S.* is a *party*, federal common law will be applied, as it was in *Clearfield, supra.*

   d. **State as party:** Federal common law principles have also sometimes been applied in suits in which a *state is a party*. *Illinois v. City of Milwaukee,* 406 U.S. 91 (1972), for instance, applied a federal common law of nuisance to a claim by Illinois against several cities for pollution of Lake Michigan.

   e. **Private litigants:** Where a federal question case is between two *private litigants*, federal common law will usually, but not always, be applied to the federal question issues. If a particular issue in such a case is not one with which the federal courts have *expertise*, state law may be *deferred to.*

      i. **Meaning of "children":** Thus in *De Sylva v. Ballentine*, 351 U.S. 570 (1956), state law was consulted in determining whether an illegitimate child is one of the "children" of the copyright owner as that term is used in the federal copyright act.

Note: The federal court construing a federal question claim is always free to follow state law if it feels that this course is desirable. An example of this is the common situation of a federal statute which creates a right of action without setting a limit on the *time* within which such action shall be brought (e.g. Rule 10(b)(5) under the federal securities laws).

"The usual rule in such situations is to apply whatever statute of limitations the state has for analogous suits. If the case were subject to the *Erie* doctrine, then the state limitations doctrine would have to be applied in its full force. The *Erie* doctrine does not apply, and the federal court has much more freedom, where the state rule has merely been absorbed as the relevant federal rule." Wr., 394. Here the federal court is permitted, but not required, to follow state law if it thinks it wise to do so. *Id.*

B. **Federal common law in diversity cases:** Federal common law is in some instances applied even where the basis for federal jurisdiction is *diversity.*

   1. **Defense based on federal law:** This may be the case, for instance, where plaintiff's claim does not raise issues of federal law, but a claim by the *defendant* does.

      Example: A patent owner sues his licensee, in a diversity action, for unpaid royalties. The licensee raises the defense that the patents are invalid under the federal patent statutes. The validity of the defense is to be determined by resort to federal case law, not state case law. *Sola Electric Co. v. Jefferson Electric Co.*, 317 U.S. 173 (1942).

   2. **No formula:** There is no simple rule for determining when federal common law applies in a diversity case. However, these often-quoted words are helpful: "It is the *source* of the right sued upon, and not the ground on which federal jurisdiction is founded, which determines the governing law." *Maternally Yours, Inc. v. Your Maternity Shop, Inc..* 234 F.2d 538 (2d Cir. 1956).

   3. **Balancing test:** In determining whether to apply federal common law in diversity cases whose subject matter bears some relation to a federal statute, courts employ roughly the same kind of balancing between state and federal interests as was used in *Byrd v. Blue Ridge.*

C. **Federal common law in state courts:** Federal jurisdiction with respect to most federal question claims is concurrent with state jurisdiction. If concurrent jurisdiction exists with respect to a particular claim, and the suit is brought in *state court*, federal common law applies there if it would apply in federal court.

   1. **Binding on state court:** Thus in the kinds of cases described in the preceding sections, a state court would be compelled to apply earlier federal precedents, and to ignore state decisions, just as a federal court would. Wr., 392.

   2. **Procedural questions:** The application of federal common law to state court suits on federally-created rights may even extend to certain "procedural" matters.

      Example: The Ps bring an FELA (Federal Employer's Liability Act) suit against D, a railroad, in Ohio state court. (The FELA is a federal statute giving injured railroad employees the right to sue the railroad for personal injury damages in state court.) D defends on the grounds that the Ps have previously signed a release of all claims against D. The Ps assert that D committed fraud in obtaining the release, and that the fraud should vitiate the release. Under Ohio procedural law, the existence of fraud is to be determined by the judge. Under federal case law, all fact-based aspects of an FELA claim (including the existence of fraud as to a release) are to be determined by the jury.

Held (by the U.S. Supreme Court), federal law is binding on the judge/jury allocation, so the issue of fraud should have been heard by the jury. The federal right to a jury trial on all factual matters is "part and parcel of the remedy" offered by the FELA, and cannot be overridden by a "mere local rule of procedure." *Dice v. Akron, Canton & Youngstown R.R.*, 342 U.S. 359 (1952).

a. **Impact on federal policies:** This does not mean that federal procedure must be followed in every state case dealing with federally-created claims, but simply that local procedure must give way if it *substantially infringes on a federal policy.*

Example: Wisconsin procedural law provides that, before a tort suit may be brought against any city, plaintiff must give defendant notice of the claim within 120 days of the injury. P brings a state court action against Milwaukee under a federal statute (42 U.S.C. §1983), alleging that police officers of the city violated P's civil rights by their police brutality. The state court dismissed P's claim because he did not give the required notice in time.

Held (by the U.S. Supreme Court), enforcement of this state procedural rule in actions based on the federal §1983 statute "so interferes with and frustrates the substantive right Congress created that, under the Supremacy Clause, it must yield to the federal interest. ... Wisconsin ... may not alter the outcome of federal claims it chooses to entertain in its courts by demanding compliance with outcome-determinative rules that are inapplicable when such claims are brought in federal court. ..." *Felder v. Casey*, 487 U.S. 131 (1988).

Flow Chart for Analyzing *Erie* Problems

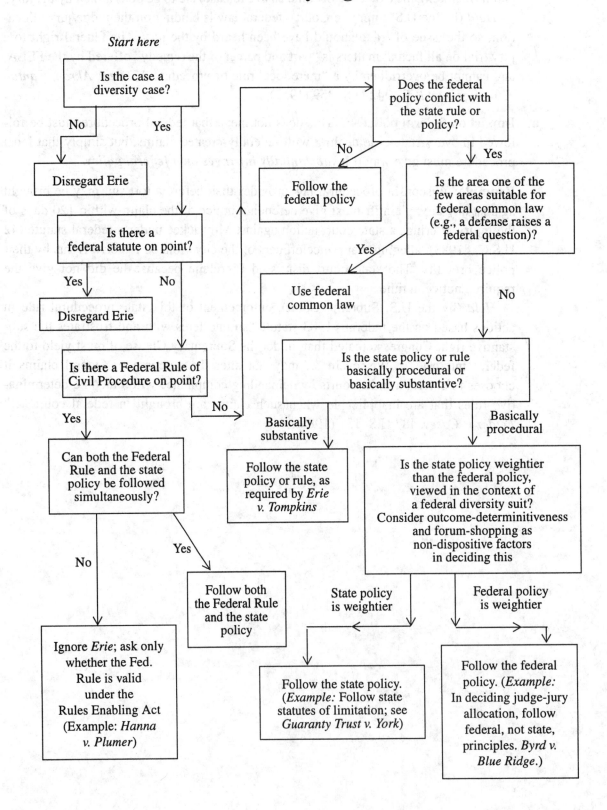

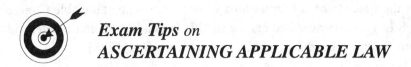

Exam Tips on
ASCERTAINING APPLICABLE LAW

Whenever your facts involve a *diversity* suit, you must be alert to *Erie* problems. Look for any suggestion that there is (or may be) a conflict between federal law and state law. Here are some particular things to check for:

☛ The most important thing is to *categorize* the problem accurately. [222-236] Decide which of the following categories the facts belong to:

    ☞ Category **1**: A *conflict* between state law (whether embodied in a statute, court rule or judge-made, i.e., common, law) and a federal policy *not embodied in any statute or in the FRCP*. In this instance, use *Erie* analysis: If the state law is basically substantive, *Erie* dictates that the state law must be followed. If the state law is basically procedural, balance the strength of the state and federal policies (considering outcome-determinitiveness and the likelihood of forum-shopping as factors.)

    ☞ Category **2**: A *direct conflict* between state law (statute, court rule or judge-made law) and a federal policy *embodied in a federal statute or in the FRCP*. Here, under the Supremacy Clause, the *federal statute/Rule must be followed* no matter how "substantive" the state law is (and no matter how outcome-determinative the issue is), and *Erie* principles *never come into play*. (This assumes, of course, that the federal statute or Rule is valid, which every FRCP has always been found to be, and which you should assume to be the case in your answer.) If you find that the fact pattern fits into this category, you should cite to *Hanna v. Plumer*.

    ☞ Category **3**: An *overlap* (i.e., coverage of the same subject area), but *not direct conflict*, between state law (statute, court rule or judge-made law) and a federal statute or FRCP Rule. Here, if the state policy can be followed without violating the federal statute/rule, follow the state policy.

☛ Many if not most exam questions involve Categories 2 and 3, not 1. That is, the professor wants to see that you can recognize that not every federal-state choice-of-law problem involves *Erie*. So anytime the federal law that governs the precise issue before you is spelled out by a statute or Federal Rule, be sure *not* to use *Erie*.

☛ If you have what you decide is a true *Erie* problem, *balance* between the state and federal interests by giving heavy weight to:

    ☞ whether the choice of which policy to follow is heavily *outcome-determinitive*. (If so, choose the state rule);

    ☞ whether using the federal policy is likely to induce the plaintiff to *forum-shop,* i.e., to choose between state and federal court based on whose law is more favorable to her. (If so, choose the state rule).

    ☞ whether using the state rule is likely to *thwart an important federal policy* governing the procedures to be used in federal trials. (If so, choose the federal rule). [230-236]

☛ Some of the common situations that *are* true Erie problems are:

☞   whether to follow the state *statute of limitations* where there is no applicable Congressionally-enacted S/L, (*yes*, because the choice of S/L is heavily outcome-determinative, and important federal procedural policies aren't implicated) [228]

☞   whether to follow the state *conflict-of-law*s provision, (*yes*, for the same reason) [224]

☞   whether to follow the state allocation of the *burden of proof* (*yes*) [225]

☞   whether to follow the state rules allocating issues between *judge and jury* (*no*, because this is not heavily outcome-determinitive, and will not induce forum shopping) [230]

☛ If you do decide that *Erie* applies, remember that the issue is **what the state's highest court would do now** if it heard the issue fresh. (Thus the fact that there is a precedent on the books from some time ago does not bind the federal court, if it thinks that the state highest court would overrule that precedent today.) [222-223]

☛ Consult the flow chart on p. 242.

CHAPTER 7

TRIAL PROCEDURE

ChapterScope

This Chapter examines the mechanics of trials, both jury and non-jury. The most important concepts in this Chapter are:

- **Two meanings of "burden of proof":** There are two kinds of *"burden of proof"* which a party may have to bear. Assuming that the issue is called *A*:

  - **Burden of production:** The party bears the "burden of *production*" if the following is true: unless the party produces *some* evidence that *A* exists, the judge must **direct the jury** to find that *A* does not exist.

  - **Burden of persuasion:** The party bears the "burden of *persuasion*" if the following is true: at the close of the evidence, if the jury cannot decide whether *A* exists or not, the jury must find that *A* does not exist.

- **"Preponderance" standard generally:** The usual standard of proof in civil actions is the *"preponderance of the evidence"* standard. A proposition is proved by a preponderance of the evidence if the jury is convinced that it is *"more likely than not"* that the proposition is true.

- **Summary judgment:** If one party can show that there is *no "genuine issue of material fact"* in the lawsuit, and that she is "entitled to judgment as a matter of law," she can win the case without going to trial. Such a victory without trial is called a *"summary judgment."*

- **Trial without jury:** A case will be tried without a jury if *either* of the two following conditions exists: (1) *No right to a jury trial* exists; or (2) *All parties* have *waived* the right to a jury trial.

  - **Appellate review:** When a case is tried to the judge (who thus acts as fact-finder), the trial judge's findings of fact will be set aside on appeal only if they are *"clearly erroneous."*

- **Jury trials:**

  - **Unanimity:** The verdict of a *federal* civil jury must be *unanimous*, unless the parties stipulate otherwise. FRCP 48. But most states allow a *less-than-unanimous* civil jury verdict.

  - **Jury selection:** The process by which the jury is selected is called the *"voir dire."* Any juror who is shown through the voir dire to be biased or connected to the case must be dismissed upon motion by a party (dismissal *"for cause"*). In addition to the jurors dismissed for cause, each party may dismiss a certain number of other prospective jurors *without showing cause* for their dismissal (*"peremptory challenges"*).

- **Directed verdict:** In both state and federal trials, either party may move for a *directed verdict*. Such a verdict *takes the case away from the jury, and determines the outcome as a matter of law*. (In federal trials, the phrase "directed verdict" is no longer used — instead, a party moves for "judgment as a matter of law.")

  - **Standard for granting:** Generally, the court will direct a verdict if the evidence is such that *reasonable people could not differ* as to the result.

■ **New trial:** The trial court, in both state and federal courts, may grant a *new trial*.

❑ **Harmless error:** A new trial may not be granted except for errors in the trial which are serious enough that they affect the substantial rights of the parties. FRCP 61. This is the so-called *"harmless error"* doctrine.

■ **JNOV:** Most states allow the judge to set aside the jury's verdict, and enter judgment for the verdict-loser. This is called a Judgment Notwithstanding the Verdict, or *JNOV*. In federal practice, the device is called *"judgment as a matter of law"* (JML).

■ **Constitutional right to jury trial:** The Seventh Amendment provides that "in suits at *common law* ... the right of *trial by jury* shall be preserved." This means that there is a federal jury trial right as to "legal" claims.

❑ **No state application:** The Seventh Amendment does not apply to *state* trials, only federal ones. So states may abolish jury trials in some or all civil cases.

❑ **Equitable claim:** Even in a federal case, there is no jury trial right as to *"equitable"* claims (e.g., a claim for injunction).

I. BURDEN OF PROOF

A. Two meanings of "burden of proof": To say that a party bears the "burden of proof" with respect to a particular issue, A, can mean either of two very different things:

1. **Burden of production:** It can mean that unless he produces *some* evidence that A exists, the judge must direct the jury to find that A does not exist. The party in such a situation is said to bear the "burden of *production*." James & Hazard, p. 340.

2. **Burden of persuasion:** Or, it can mean that if at the close of the evidence, the jury cannot decide whether A exists or not, it must find that A does not exist. The party seeking to prove A in this situation is said to bear the "burden of *persuasion*," or the risk of non-persuasion. James & Hazard, p. 314.

B. Factors in allocation: The allocation of both burdens to one side or the other depends on many factors — there is no simple test. Among the factors considered are (1) who has "the better *access* to the fact in question", and (2) who is alleging something that *"departs from what would be expected* in the light of ordinary human experience." James & Hazard, p. 324.

1. **Both burdens not always on same party:** The burden of production is not necessarily placed on the same party as the burden of persuasion. F,K&C, pp. 642-43. Indeed, the burden of production may itself shift throughout the course of the trial.

> **Example:** A trial consists of only one issue, A, which P asserts and D denies. P starts out bearing initially the burden of producing some evidence of A. If he produces just enough evidence so that the judge finds that a reasonable jury *might* find that A exists, P has met his burden of *production*. If P produces so much evidence that he is, in the absence of evidence from D, entitled to a directed verdict, P has *shifted* the burden of production to D. If D now produces evidence, he can either make a jury issue of A (in

which case neither P nor D bears the production burden anymore) or he can produce enough evidence so that P must once more meet the production burden, or suffer a directed verdict against him. See the diagram in F,K&C, p. 641.

C. What meets burden: In general, a party has met his burden of *production* on an issue, A, if he has given enough evidence to *send that issue to the jury*. He has met his burden of *persuasion* with respect to A if he has produced enough evidence to lead the jury "to believe that the existence of [A] is *more probable than its non-existence*." J & H (3d ed.), pp. 316-17. Or as the persuasion burden idea is often put, a party bearing that burden with respect to proving A's existence must demonstrate "by a *preponderance of the evidence*" that A exists. *Id.*, at 243.

II. PRESUMPTIONS

A. Definition: A presumption, in the sense of the word relevant here, is a "convention that when a designated basic fact exists, another fact, called the presumed fact, *must* be taken to exist in the absence of adequate rebuttal." F,K&C, p. 650. We shall refer to the designated basic fact as *B* and the fact presumed from *B*'s existence as *P*.

B. Assumptions for discussion: Assume in the following that the only disputed fact in a case is P, and that existence of the basic fact, *B*, is agreed to by both sides. Assume also that there is a statutory or common law presumption that where *B* exists, *P* exists. Plaintiff seeks to prove the existence of *P*. Assume that if there were no presumption, plaintiff would bear the *burden of persuading* the jury that *P* exists.

1. Burden of production: If no evidence is offered at all as to *P*, but *B* exists beyond dispute, plaintiff is entitled to a *directed verdict*. The party against whom the presumption is directed (in this case the defendant) bears the initial burden of producing evidence of non-*P*. If he produces no evidence, he suffers a directed verdict.

2. Burden of persuasion: If defendant offers enough evidence of non-*P* that a reasonable jury might find non-*P*, it is clear that he has met his production burden. *But who bears the burden of persuasion*? Courts and commentators are in complete dispute about whether the presumption of *P* from *B* changes the allocation of the persuasion burden from where it would be if no presumption existed. Three important different positions exist:

a. "Bursting bubble" approach: Under the so-called *"bursting bubble"* approach, the presumption affects *only* the production burden. Once the party bearing the burden (in our ongoing hypothetical, the defendant) satisfies that burden by producing evidence of non-*P*, and the case goes to the jury, the persuasion burden is allocated *exactly as if there were no presumption* — in this case, on the plaintiff. This approach is called the "bursting bubble" approach because once evidence tending to show the non-existence of the presumed fact is introduced, the presumption bursts like a bubble.

i. Federal Rules of Evidence: This "bursting bubble" approach is used by the *Federal Rules of Evidence* in civil suits. Under FRE 301, "A presumption imposes on the party against whom it is directed the burden of going forward with evidence to rebut or meet the presumption, but *does not shift to such party the burden of proof in the sense of the risk of non-persuasion*, which remains throughout the trial upon the party on whom it was originally cast." (But FRE 302 provides that if *state law* provides the rule of decision as to the claim or defense to which the presumed fact relates, the law of that state will determine the effect of the presumption. Thus if the presumed fact relates to a claim or defense under which *Erie principles* (*supra*, p. 222) require that state law be followed, state law will also determine whether the presumption can shift the burden of non-persuasion.)

  b. Uniform Rules of Evidence approach: A second approach is exemplified by the Uniform Rules of Evidence:

  i. Rational connection: If there is a *rational connection* between *B* and *P*, the existence of the presumption places the burden of persuasion as to *P* on the party against whom the presumption is directed — in this case, defendant.

  ii. No rational connection: If there is no logical or rational connection between *B* and *P*, the persuasion burden is unaffected by the existence of the presumption, the same as in the Thayer approach.

  c. Originally-proposed Federal Rules of Evidence approach: The Federal Rules of Evidence as they were originally proposed to the Supreme Court (but not as finally enacted; see *supra*, Paragraph 2(a)(i)) took a third position. They gave a presumption the effect of *completely shifting the burden of persuasion*. That is, the mere existence of the presumption placed the burden of persuasion as to *P* on the party against whom the presumption was directed. In other words, this approach treated *all* presumptions, logical or not, the way the Uniform Rules treated logical presumptions.

  Example of the three approaches: A statute states that where a railroad locomotive causes damage, there is a presumption that the railroad was negligent. *B* = damage by locomotive. *P* = railroad's negligence. The railroad offers enough evidence of its own due care to send the case to the jury (but not enough to obtain a directed verdict). The three approaches would work as follows:

  Federal Rules of Evidence: The presumption has no effect on the persuasion burden. Therefore, plaintiff must affirmatively convince the jury that the railroad was negligent.

  Uniform Rules: There is no logical connection between the fact of damage by a locomotive, and the negligence of the railroad — some other cause could explain the damage just as easily. Therefore, the persuasion burden is placed on plaintiff.

  Originally-proposed Federal Evidence Rules: Existence of the presumption against the railroad places the burden of persuasion on it. It must therefore affirmatively convince the jury that it exercised due care.

3. Illustration: By way of illustrating the way in which the burdens of production and persuasion work where a presumption is present, consider *Texas Dept. of Community Affairs v. Burdine*, 450 U.S. 248 (1981). In that case, P claimed that D, a public agency, had refused to promote her, and had then fired her, because she was a woman. P sued under Title VII of the 1964 Civil Rights Act.

  a. Presumption: The Supreme Court analyzed the burdens of production and persuasion, and the existence of presumptions, as follows: P had the burden of producing evidence that D intentionally discriminated against her. She also had the burden of persuading the trier of fact that such discrimination occurred. However, she had the benefit of a *presumption*: upon showing the basic fact (that she was qualified, that she was rejected, and that the position remained open for some time after the rejection, until it was filled by a male), she was entitled to a presumption that there had been unlawful discrimination against her.

    i. **Production burden shifts:** Thus once P established the basic fact, the presumption meant that she had satisfied the burden of producing evidence of intentional discrimination. The burden then shifted to D to produce evidence of non-discrimination. This burden of production could be (and was) satisfied by D's production of evidence "which would allow the trier of fact rationally to conclude that the employment decision had not been motivated by discriminatory animus." D satisfied its burden of production by articulating "lawful reasons for the action" (in this case, evidence that P and two female co-workers were terminated because they did not work well together).

    ii. **Persuasion burden does not shift:** Under the Federal Rules of Evidence, the existence of the presumption affected only the initial burden of production, ***not the burden of persuasion***, which remained on P, not D. Therefore, if the trier of fact had been unsure about whether there had been intentional discrimination, D would have won the case. P could have met this burden of persuasion by convincing the trier of fact that a discriminatory reason more likely than not motivated D, or by showing that D's contention that it was motivated by non-discriminatory reasons was unworthy of credence.

  b. **Holding:** The Supreme Court's actual holding in the case was that the Court of Appeals had been incorrect when it ruled that D should lose unless it came forward with evidence that would *persuade* the trier of fact that it acted for lawful motives — since the presumption only affected the burden of production, not the burden of persuasion, all D was required to do was to come forward with evidence that a reasonable trier of fact ***could rationally believe***, not evidence that would "persuade" the trier of fact.

    i. **Reformulation:** That is, phrased in the terms in which we have been speaking, the Court of Appeals erred by following the approach of the originally-proposed Federal Rules of Evidence, rather than FRE 301 as actually enacted.

III. PREPONDERANCE OF THE EVIDENCE

  A. **Definition of preponderance:** The usual standard of proof in civil actions is the ***preponderance*** standard. A proposition is proved by a preponderance of the evidence if the jury is convinced that it is ***"more likely than not"*** that the proposition is true.

    1. **Utility:** The preponderance standard is a measure of how much evidence the party bearing the ***burden of persuasion*** as to an issue must present in order to meet that burden. "If ... the burden is upon a party to prove a specified fact by the preponderance of the evidence, ... this means that [the jury] must find that the fact does not exist unless the evidence convinces them that its existence is more probable than its non-existence." F,K&C, p. 656.

B. Test for measuring probability: How is a jury to evaluate whether the existence of a fact is more "probable" than not? It is often said that it is "not enough that *mathematically* the chances somewhat favor a proposition to be proved." *Sargent v. Massachusetts Accident Co.*, 29 N.E.2d 825 (Mass. 1940). Thus, "the fact that colored automobiles made in the current year outnumber black ones would not warrant a finding that an undescribed automobile of the current year is colored and not black." *Id*. The belief in the truth of the proposition must be *"actual,"* not *"speculative."*

C. Adversary's denials: A party who has the burden of proving a fact by a preponderance of the evidence may *not rely solely on the jury's disbelief of his adversary's denials of that fact*.

> **Example:** A brakeman is killed while climbing down the side of a train. His estate sues the railroad, alleging negligence, but producing no evidence to that effect. Several witnesses for the railroad assert that the railroad exercised due care. D moves for a directed verdict, which the court denies. *Held* (on appeal), P has not met its production burden, even though the jury might have disbelieved the railroad's witnesses. Therefore, the trial judge should have granted a directed verdict. "Mere disbelief of denials of facts which must be proved is not the equivalent of affirmative evidence in support of those facts." *Cruzan v. N.Y. Central Ry.*, 116 N.E. 879 (Mass. 1917).

1. Rationale: There is a good reason for this doctrine. If it were otherwise, a party could never successfully *appeal* a judge's *refusal to direct a verdict*. For no matter how overwhelming in the trial record was the evidence for the party seeking the directed verdict, and no matter how non-existent the evidence for the other side, an appeals court would still have to conclude that "a reasonable jury might have disbelieved all the witnesses, based on their demeanor, which we cannot evaluate on appeal. Therefore, the trial judge rightly sent the case to the jury." See *Dyer v. MacDougall*, 201 F.2d 265 (2d Cir. 1952). See also, James & Hazard, p. 362, n. 27.

Quiz Yourself on
BURDEN OF PROOF AND PRESUMPTIONS

67. D, driving her car, struck and injured P, a pedestrian. P sued D in the courts of the state of Ames, which follows the Federal Rules of Civil Procedure and the Federal Rules of Evidence. P's suit charged that D drove negligently. The substantive law of the state of Ames imposes on P both the burden of production as to negligence and the burden of persuasion (by a preponderance of the evidence) on this issue. The case was tried to a jury. As part of P's case, P showed that shortly after the accident, D was stopped by the police, asked to take a breathalyzer exam, and refused to do so. According to the substantive law of Ames, refusal to take a breathalyzer upon request by the police gives rise to a presumption of intoxication (which under state law is a form of negligence when the person is the driver). During his case, P came up with no evidence of D's negligence other than the refusal to take a breathalyzer exam. At the close of P's case, D made a motion for a directed verdict, based on P's failure to prove negligence. Should the trial judge grant D's motion? _____

68. Same facts as prior question. Now, however, assume that the trial judge allowed the case to go forward, and D came up with some evidence indicating that she was not in fact intoxicated despite her refusal to take the breathalyzer exam. At the close of D's case, the judge instructed the jury as follows: "Under our law, the defendant's refusal to take a breathalyzer exam when asked to do so by the police gives rise to a presumption of intoxication. If you find that D refused to take the breathalyzer, then you must find that D was intoxicated unless D persuades you by a preponderance of the evidence that she was not intoxicated." Are the judge's instructions appropriate? _____

Answers

67. **No.** The trial judge should grant D's motion for directed verdict only if the judge believes that P has not carried his burden of production, that is, his burden of producing some credible evidence (evidence that might be believed by a reasonable jury) that D behaved negligently. The presumption (failure to take a breathalyzer equals intoxication and thus negligence) is enough to get P past this burden of production — by proving that D did not take the breathalyzer (the basic fact), P will be deemed to have met the burden of producing evidence that D was negligent (the presumed fact). Unless D comes up with credible evidence of her non-negligence, the court will in fact have to instruct the jury at the end of D's case that it should find for P on this issue.

68. **No.** Under the "bursting bubble" approach to presumptions imposed by Federal Rule of Evidence 301, "a presumption imposes on the party against whom it is directed the burden of going forward with evidence to rebut or meet the presumption, but does not shift to such party the burden of proof in the sense of the risk of non-persuasion, which remains throughout the trial upon the party on whom it was originally cast." Thus although the presumption "refusal to take breathalyzer equals intoxication" meant that once P showed such refusal, the burden of *production* as to intoxication shifted to D (see answer to prior question), this presumption did not help P get rid of the burden of *persuasion*. At the end of the trial, just as at the beginning, the burden remained on P to show by a preponderance of the evidence that D was in fact intoxicated. Thus if the jury believed that there was exactly a 50 chance that D was intoxicated, P loses, just as if there had been no presumption at all. To the extent that the judge's instructions indicate that D loses where the jury is completely undecided, those instructions are wrong.

IV. ADJUDICATION WITHOUT TRIAL

A. **Trial sometimes unnecessary:** Not all cases end in a full-scale trial. For instance, as was stated in the chapter on Pleading, a complaint can sometimes be dismissed under Rule 12(b)(6), for failure to state a claim upon which relief can be granted.

   1. **Other means of disposition:** Treated in this section are some of the other means by which a case may be disposed of *without* a full-scale trial with both parties presenting evidence.

B. **Voluntary dismissal by plaintiff:** A plaintiff in federal court may *voluntarily dismiss* his complaint *without prejudice* any time *before the defendant serves an answer or moves for summary judgment*. The plaintiff may do this without leave of court. The fact that the dismissal is "without prejudice" means that he may *bring the suit again*. See Rule 41(a)(1).

   1. **Only one dismissal:** Only the *first* dismissal of a claim is without prejudice. If a plaintiff has already once before dismissed a claim in either state or federal court, his second dis-

missal operates as an *"adjudication on the merits,"* i.e., he is barred from bringing the claim a third time by *res judicata* just as if the claim had been fully litigated and decided against him. See Rule 41(a)(1). This is sometimes called the *"two dismissal"* rule.

2. **After answer or motion:** After the defendant has answered or moved for summary judgment, plaintiff may voluntarily dismiss only with the court's approval, and on the court's terms. See Rule 41(a)(2).

3. **Payment of expenses:** If a claim has been voluntarily dismissed once before, the second time it is brought the court can order that the plaintiff pay the *court costs* of the first action before allowing the second one to go forward. See Rule 41(d).

C. **Involuntary dismissal:** The plaintiff's claim may also be *involuntarily* dismissed, by court order.

1. **Grounds:** An involuntary dismissal under Rule 41(b) may be ordered by the court, on motion, for:

   a. **Failure to prosecute:** failure to *prosecute* (failure of claimant to pursue the action);

   b. **Disobedience:** failure of complainant to *obey court orders* (e.g., discovery or pre-trial conference orders);

   c. **Other:** any of the reasons listed as defenses in Rule 12(b).

2. **With prejudice:** Normally an involuntary dismissal is *with prejudice*, and thus has the effect of an adjudication on the merits. *Exceptions* to this are dismissals for:

   a. *lack of jurisdiction* (of both the *parties* and the *subject matter*, and for *insufficient service*);

   b. improper *venue*; and

   c. *failure to join an indispensable party* under Rule 19. See Rule 41(b).

3. **Judgment on partial findings:** If the plaintiff puts on her case and fails to show that she is entitled to relief, the judge can dismiss the case before the defendant puts on his case.

   a. **Non-jury case:** In a *non-jury* case, if the plaintiff does not prove facts entitling her to relief, the defendant can make a motion for *"judgment on partial findings,"* pursuant to FRCP 52(c). The judge makes the findings of fact as if the case had been fully tried, since by hypothesis the plaintiff has been given a chance to establish all facts which she needs to sustain her case and has failed to do so.

   b. **Jury case:** In a *jury* case, defendant's motion at the close of plaintiff's case is called a motion "for judgment as a matter of law," a topic treated *infra*, p. 264.

D. **Summary judgment:** If one party can show that there is *no "genuine issue of material fact"* in the lawsuit, and that he is "entitled to judgment as a matter of law," he can win the case without going to trial. Such a victory without trial is called *"summary judgment,"* and is provided for by Rule 56.

1. **Court goes behind pleadings:** In deciding a motion for summary judgment, the court will go *"behind the pleadings."* That is, even if it appears from the pleadings that the parties are in dispute on some material issue of fact, the summary judgment motion may be

granted if the movant can show that the disputed factual issues presented by the pleadings are *illusory.*

2. How shown: The movant (the person seeking summary judgment) can show the lack of a genuine issue of fact by two main means:

a. Affidavits: First, he may submit *affidavits.*

i. Contents of affidavits: These affidavits must recite only matters as to which the affiant has *personal knowledge*, must state only matters which would be *admissible at trial*, and must "show affirmatively that the affiant is competent to testify to the matters stated therein." See Rule 56(e).

b. Discovery materials: Second, he may submit the fruits of *discovery* (e.g., depositions, interrogatory answers, etc.), no matter which side they were obtained from. See Rule 56(e).

3. Showing by movant: Regardless of who will have the burden of persuasion on an issue at trial, the *movant* bears the initial burden of *production* on that issue. That is, as part of his summary judgment papers, he bears the burden of coming forward with information that "clearly establishes that there is no factual dispute regarding the matter upon which summary judgment is sought." F,K&M, p. 444.

a. How to do this: Normally, the movant will, as noted, do this by presenting affidavits, depositions, etc. However, the Supreme Court has made it clear that at least in those situations in which the responding party will bear the burden of *persuasion* at trial, the movant will not necessarily have to come up with affidavits, depositions, or other evidentiary materials. Instead, he may be entitled to summary judgment merely by showing that *the existing record contains no evidence that the other side* (which will bear the burden of persuasion at trial) *will be able to prove an essential element of its case. Celotex Corp. v. Catrett*, 477 U.S. 317 (1986).

i. Facts of *Celotex*: The facts of *Celotex* indicate how this can happen. P claimed to have been injured by exposure to asbestos manufactured by D. After discovery, D moved for summary judgment on the grounds that there was no evidence in the record that any of D's products caused the injury, an issue on which P would clearly have the burden of persuasion at trial. D did not produce affidavits, depositions, or any other independent information in support of the proposition that its products were *not* the ones that caused P's injury — it simply pointed out to the court that P had no evidence implicating D's products.

ii. Holding: The Supreme Court held that in this situation, summary judgment could properly be given for D. "We find no express or implied requirement in Rule 56 that the moving party support its motion with affidavits or other similar materials negating the opponent's claim."

iii. How shown: Even under *Celotex*, however, it seems apparent that the moving party must do more than merely state in a conclusory fashion that there is no evidence for an essential element of the other party's claim. The moving party must review all affidavits, depositions, and other parts of the record, and must explain to the court in some detail why these materials fail to establish the existence of an element of the other side's case.

4. **Opposition:**   The party *opposing* the summary judgment motion may also submit affidavits, depositions, and other materials, which must meet the same standards as those prescribed for materials submitted by the movant. See Rule 56(e).

   a. **Opponent can't rest on pleadings:**   If the affidavits of the movant show that there is no genuine material issue of fact for trial, the opposing party cannot avoid summary judgment merely by repeating his pleadings' denial of the allegations of the movant's affidavits. "When a motion for summary judgment is made and supported as provided in this rule, an adverse party *may not rest upon the mere allegations or denials of the adverse party's pleading*, but the adverse party's response, by affidavits or as otherwise provided in this rule, must set forth *specific facts showing that there is a genuine issue for trial."* Rule 56(e).

   Example: P sues D on a promissory note. P's claim states that the note was validly executed by D. D's answer denies that D signed the note. P moves for a Rule 56 summary judgment, and submits an affidavit by X stating that X saw D sign the note. D cannot avoid summary judgment by merely repeating his answer's general denial of the signature. He must instead submit something more, perhaps an affidavit (even if only his own), asserting that the signature is a forgery, or that it was obtained by duress, etc. D's affidavit must, in the words of Rule 56(e), "set forth specific facts showing that there is a genuine issue for trial."

5. **Construction most favorable to non-movant:**   The party opposing summary judgment is not required to make an evidentiary showing unless the movant clearly demonstrates the lack of a triable issue of fact. In any event, the non-movant receives the *benefit of the doubt*. "The matter presented in connection with the motion must be construed *most favorably to the party opposing the motion*. That it may be surmised that the non-moving party is unlikely to prevail at the trial is not sufficient to authorize summary judgment against him." Wr., 668.

6. **Payment of costs:**   If the court decides, at any time, that affidavits presented for or against a summary judgment motion were made in bad faith or "solely for the purpose of delay," the trial judge may order the party who submitted the affidavits to pay to the other side the *costs* of presenting opposing affidavits, including attorney's fees. The court may also hold the offending party or attorney in contempt of court. See Rule 56(g).

7. **Partial summary judgment:**   Summary judgment may be granted with respect to *certain claims* in a lawsuit even when it is not granted with respect to all claims. If this occurs, the court may order the entry of judgment on the claims as to which summary judgment has been granted if there is "no just reason for delay" in the entry of judgment. See Rule 54(b). This is called *partial summary judgment*. The losing party may then *appeal* the partial summary judgment, while the undisposed-of claims are being tried.

   a. **On issue of liability:**   Rule 56(c) permits the court to grant summary judgment on the issue of *liability alone*, where a genuine issue concerning damages remains. This type of "partial" summary judgment is "interlocutory" in nature. It is therefore not immediately appealable except at the discretion of the trial judge pursuant to the Interlocutory

Appeals Act, 28 U.S.C. §1292(b) (discussed *infra*, p. 319). *Liberty Mutual Insurance Co. v. Wetzel*, 424 U.S. 737 (1976).

8. **Order establishing facts:** It may be the case that although there is one genuine material issue of fact relating to a particular claim, there is no substantial controversy concerning other material *aspects* of the claim. In that event, summary judgment cannot be granted on the claim, but the court may make an *order stating that the undisputed facts are deemed established for trial*. Although such an order is sometimes called "partial summary judgment," the term is not accurate, since the order is not an appealable final judgment as to the claim. Wr., 669-70.

Quiz Yourself on

ADJUDICATION WITHOUT TRIAL

69. P has brought a medical malpractice suit against D, in federal court based on diversity. P's complaint asserts that D performed an operation upon P to reduce the size of P's nose, and that the results were disastrous. The complaint asserts that the operation took place on October 13, 1988. D has moved for summary judgment pursuant to Rule 56, and has submitted in support of that motion an affidavit stating that he was not in the U.S. on October 13, 1988. D's moving papers give much additional information, all of which tends to indicate that D could not have performed the operation on the date P said D performed it (e.g., an affidavit from D's travel agent stating that D was in the south of France that day, as well as charges on D's phone bill showing calls made from the south of France to D's office on that date).P, in opposition to D's motion, has submitted an affidavit that furnishes a couple of details about the alleged operation (e.g., "On October 13, 1988, I went to D's offices at 456 Main Street. D was a brown haired man of about 50 years of age who wore glasses, and he performed the surgery on me.") P has not submitted any other information in opposition to D's motion. In reviewing these moving papers, the federal judge concludes that there is about a 90% chance that P is either honestly mistaken or is lying when she asserts that D performed the operation on her on that date. Should the federal judge grant D's motion for summary judgment? _____

Answer

69. **No.** Federal Rule 56(c) states that the motion for summary judgment may be rendered only if all the materials submitted by both parties "show that there is no genuine issue as to any material fact. ..." It is not enough that the judge concludes that the moving party is very likely to win at trial — the judge must conclude that *as a matter of law* all issues must be decided in favor of the movant, before the judge may grant summary judgment. Here, there is some chance (although admittedly not a very good chance) that P will be able to come up with more evidence that D really did perform the operation on the day stated, or will be able to show that D's evidence was fraudulent. Alternatively, P may be able to show that D performed the operation on a different day. Since the issue of whether D performed the operation is very fact-bound, and there seems to be an honest dispute, the court should deny D's motion even though it appears very probable that D will prevail at trial.

V. TRIALS WITHOUT A JURY

A. **When tried to court:**   A case will be tried without a jury if one of the two following conditions exists:

1. *no right to a jury trial* exists, or

2. all parties have *waived* the right to jury trial.

> **Note:** The circumstances under which a right to jury trial exists are discussed *infra*, p. 275.

B. **Effect:**   If there is no jury, the trial judge serves as both the *finder of fact* and the decider of law.

C. **Evidence rules:**   The rules of evidence followed by the judge (in federal trials, the Federal Rules of Evidence) are officially the same in non-jury trials as in jury trials. However, in practice, judges tend to *relax the rules* more when there is no jury present which could be prejudiced by the admission of evidence of dubious reliability.

D. **Findings of fact:**   If an action is tried without a jury, Rule 52 requires the trial court to *"find the facts specially* and [to] state separately its conclusions of law thereon. ..."* This means that the trial judge must *set forth the facts* as she finds them with some *particularity*, and must in a separate section of her opinion state the law which she believes disposes of the case.

1. **Where separate findings required:**   The separate findings of fact and conclusions of law required by Rule 52 are obligatory not only in cases which are fully tried, but also in the following circumstances:

    a. where requests for interlocutory *injunctions* are made, whether they are granted or denied; and

    b. where *"judgment on partial findings"* is given pursuant to Rule 52(c). Thus if, at the end of plaintiff's case, the trial judge believes that plaintiff has not carried his burden of proof, the judge may throw plaintiff's case out without even hearing the defendant's case; if the judge does this, Rule 52(c) requires her to make separate findings of fact and conclusions of law.

2. **Where separate findings not required:**   The trial judge is *not* obligated to make findings of fact and conclusions of law pursuant to the disposition of any kind of *motion* except one under 52(c).

    a. **Summary judgment:**   Thus the *grant* or *denial* of a Rule 56 motion for *summary judgment* or of a Rule 12(b)(6) motion for dismissal for *failure to state a claim* need not be accompanied by findings of fact and conclusions of law.

3. **Judgment on partial findings:**   The trial judge is encouraged to conduct a *"mini-trial"* of just one issue, if the judge thinks that the party carrying the burden of proof on that issue may not be able to satisfy it, and that issue is dispositive of a claim or the whole case. If the judge then finds against the party bearing the burden of proof, the judge issues a *"judgment on partial findings."* See Rule 52(c).

a. Rationale: The Advisory Committee Note to Rule 52 says that "If the court in considering a motion for summary judgment under Rule 56(b) determines from the discovery materials that a crucial fact may be quickly resolved at trial, it may (pursuant to Rule 42(b)) order trial of that issue, hear the evidence and enter judgment in conformity with the requirements of Rule 52(a). The availability of this course should eliminate any temptation by the court to shortcut the process of trial by entering summary judgment on Rule 56 despite doubts about the availability of essential proof."

Example: Suppose that P sues D for automobile negligence in diversity. D pleads the 3-year statute of limitations. Because of D's defense, the key issue quickly becomes the date on which the accident occurred, and on this the parties come up with conflicting, and credible, affidavits. The trial judge should not try the whole case, since the trial may be unnecessary if the statute of limitations issue is resolved against P. Conversely, the trial judge should not stretch to find against P on summary judgment, if there is some chance that P will prevail on the limitations issue. Instead, the trial judge should conduct a "mini-trial," at which only evidence bearing on the date of the accident is examined. If P fails to prove that the accident occurred less than three years before the suit was filed, the trial judge should render judgment against P based on the partial findings concerning the accident date. The judge must issue findings of fact and conclusions of law about the accident date and the statute of limitations, but need not try the rest of the case.

E. Appellate review of findings of fact: If the loser of a non-jury trial appeals, the appellate court will generally accept the trial judge's findings of fact as the factual background against which to review the trial judge's conclusions of law. The judge's findings of fact will be set aside only if they are *"clearly erroneous."* See Rule 52(a).

1. Test for "clearly erroneous": A finding is "clearly erroneous," according to the Supreme Court, when "although there is evidence to support it, the reviewing court on the entire evidence is left with the definite and firm conviction that a mistake has been committed." *U.S. v. United States Gypsum Co.*, 333 U.S. 364 (1948).

2. Witness' credibility: Where the findings of fact relate to the trial testimony given by live witnesses, Rule 52(a) requires that the appellate court give "due regard ... to the *opportunity of the trial court to judge of the credibility of the witnesses.*" This implies that the appeals court should be particularly loath to overturn the trial judge's findings of fact regarding such testimony.

a. Rationale: This is so because the trial judge had the opportunity to judge the witnesses' credibility through observation of their *demeanor* at trial.

b. Standard: The Supreme Court has expressed the standard for appellate review of credibility determinations this way: "[W]hen a trial judge's finding is based on his decision to credit the testimony of one of two or more witnesses, each of whom has told a coherent and facially plausible story that is not contradicted by extrinsic evidence, that finding, if not internally inconsistent, *can virtually never be clear error.*" *Anderson v. Bessemer City*, 470 U.S. 564 (1985).

i. Exception: But where the witness's story is internally inconsistent, or is contradicted by documents or objective evidence, the fact that the trial judge has labeled his decision as being based upon credibility will not shield the finding from review. In this situation, the ordinary "clearly erroneous" standard applies. *Id.*

3. **Documentary evidence and inferences from undisputed facts:**   Sometimes findings of fact are based upon *documentary evidence*, or upon *inferences from undisputed facts*. In this situation, it can be argued that the appellate court has the same ability as the trial court to make findings of fact, since everything that is needed to make the finding is contained in the record. This argument implies that the appellate court need not be as hesitant to overturn the lower court's finding in this situation. Until 1985, courts were in great disagreement as to whether this approach should be followed.

   a. **Supreme Court view:** The Supreme Court then disposed of the issue, at least for the federal courts. In *Anderson v. Bessemer City*, 470 U.S. 564 (1985), the Court held that even where the federal district court's findings "do not rest on credibility determinations, but are based instead on physical or documentary evidence or inferences from other facts," the appeals court *may not make a de novo review of the evidence*. Instead, the "clearly erroneous" rule applies in this situation, just as in those involving credibility determinations.

      i. **Rule amendment:** The Court's holding in *Anderson* has led to a change in Rule 52(a), incorporating the *Anderson* result. The third sentence of 52(a) now reads, "Findings of fact, *whether based on oral or documentary evidence*, shall not be set aside unless clearly erroneous. ... "

4. **Not applicable to conclusions of law:** The "clearly erroneous" rule applies only to findings of fact, and *not to conclusions of law*. With respect to conclusions of law made by the district court, the appeals court considers the matter *de novo*, and gives little deference to the judgment of the trial court. Wr., 649-70.

5. **Mixed facts and law:** An issue will frequently involve a *mix* of facts and law. Therefore, it may sometimes be the case that the district court's finding of fact derives directly from his conclusion of law.

   Example: Although the trial court may find as a matter of fact that the defendant was negligent, this finding will be based upon the judge's legal conclusion as to what constitutes negligence.

   a. **Correct rule of law:** If in this "mixed law and fact" situation the trial court's finding of fact derives from a *correct rule of law*, the "clearly erroneous" rule applies to the finding of fact. Wr., 649-70.

   b. **Incorrect rule of law:** If in a mixed-law-and-fact situation the trial court's judgment on the facts derives from an *incorrect* rule of law, that finding must be reversed or remanded for a new determination. The finding of fact will not be judged by the "clearly erroneous" standard, but will instead be presumed incorrect because of the error of law. Wr., 649-70.

   Example: If a finding of negligence were based on an erroneous understanding of the duty of care owed by the defendant to the plaintiff, the appellate court would reverse and remand for further findings of fact consistent with its holding. The "clearly erroneous" standard would not be applied to the negligence finding.

i. **Remand for further findings:** In such a mixed-law-and-fact situation, the existence of an error of law does *not* normally give the appellate court the right to make its *own* finding of fact on the issue to which the trial court applied the wrong rule of law. Unless it is clear that only one resolution of the factual issue can result once the correct legal rule is applied, the appellate court *must remand*, rather than deciding the factual issue for itself. *Pullman-Standard v. Swint*, 456 U.S. 273 (1982).

6. **Defamation suits:** A special rule now applies to appellate review of certain facts in *defamation* suits. Because libel and slander suits threaten the First Amendment rights of the defendant, the Supreme Court has placed several limits on the right to recover in such actions. Most notably, a *"public figure"* may not recover for libel or slander unless he shows that the defendant made the defamatory statement with "actual malice" (a term of art meaning that the defendant either knew his statement was false or acted in reckless disregard of its truth or falsity). See Emanuel on *Constitutional Law*. The Supreme Court has held that the *actual issue* of whether the defendant acted with "actual malice" must be *carefully scrutinized* by the appellate court, and a judgment against the defendant must be reversed unless the appellate court concludes that there is *"clear and convincing proof"* of such malice. Therefore, on the issue of actual malice, *the "clearly erroneous" rule does not apply. Bose Corp. v. Consumers Union*, 466 U.S. 485 (1984).

Quiz Yourself on
TRIALS WITHOUT A JURY

70. P sued D in federal district court for employment discrimination. The case was tried to a judge. Both sides put on their case. The judge announced from the bench that she would decide the case within several weeks. After four weeks, the judge issued a written opinion, which read in its entirety as follows: "The judge finds for D, on the grounds that while P has proven that D did not hire P, P has not proven that this refusal was on account of D's race, as required by the federal civil rights statute under which P brought suit." The judge has not issued any other statements or documents in connection with the case. Has the judge complied with applicable procedural requirements? _____

71. P brought a federal suit against D for negligence relating to an automobile accident in which P was injured. The suit was based on diversity. The essence of P's claim was that D went through an intersection while the light was red, striking P's car. The case was tried without a jury. At trial, P presented a witness, W, who testified to having seen D go through the intersection when the light was red against D. P himself also testified that the light was green for him (and thus red for D) when D entered the intersection. The only witness or other evidence on behalf of D was D's own testimony, in which D asserted that the light was yellow when D passed through the intersection. The trial judge found in favor of D. The judge's findings of fact, after summarizing the testimony given by each of the witnesses, stated, "Although the only apparently objective witness supports P's account, I find that D's testimony was more credible, and I therefore conclude that the light was yellow at the time D entered the intersection. Accordingly, I find that D did not act negligently, and is therefore not liable."

   P appealed the case to the Court of Appeals. The three-judge panel hearing the appeal has concluded, after reading the entire trial transcript, that there is a 70% or so chance that the light was red against D at the time D entered the intersection. The only issue on the appeal is whether the trial judge's finding of fact as to the color of light was a correct one. Should the appeals court affirm the lower court judgment?

Answers

70. No. Federal Rule 52(a) provides, "In all actions tried upon the facts without a jury ... the court shall *find the facts specially* and state separately its conclusions of law thereon. ..." The judge has almost certainly failed to find the facts "specially" — this word indicates that the judge must state the facts with some particularity, so that a reviewing court will know whether the judge has conducted the trial in an adequate way and has reached a verdict in accord with the weight of the evidence. At a minimum, the judge should have summarized the evidence of intentional discrimination produced by P (if any), and should have described why she did not find this evidence sufficient. If P were to appeal this case, the appellate court would probably remand it to the district court for an opinion that recites the facts and conclusions of law much more specifically.

71. Yes. One of the most important sentences in the entire Federal Rules of Civil Procedure is the third sentence of Rule 52(a): "Findings of fact, whether based on oral or documentary evidence, shall not be set aside unless *clearly erroneous*, and due regard shall be given to the opportunity of the trial court to judge of the *credibility* of the witnesses." Here, each witness' testimony is internally consistent, and there are no documents that contradict any witness' story. Therefore, the case boils down completely to whether one believes P and W on the one hand, or D on the other. This is the very sort of credibility determination that the Federal Rules leave to the trial court. Thus even though the appellate court believes that there is a 70 chance that the trial judge made an error, the appellate court should not reverse or even order a new trial. (The main rationale for this deference to the trial judge's findings, especially on matters of credibility, is that the trial judge can *see* things in court that are not apparent from the trial transcript. For instance, both P and W may have appeared to be evasive, pausing a long time before answering questions, failing to look the questioner in the eye, etc.; by contrast, D might have appeared to be a quite straight shooter whose demeanor strongly suggested honesty.)

VI. THE JURY

A. Seventh Amendment: The Seventh Amendment to the U.S. Constitution provides that "in suits at common law ... the right of trial by jury shall be preserved. ..." As we discuss more fully *infra*, p. 275, this Amendment applies to *federal trials*, but does not apply to state trials.

B. Number of jurors: Traditionally, juries have been composed of 12 members. But the Seventh Amendment is no longer construed to require, even in federal civil cases, that the jury be composed of 12 members.

   1. Six-person jury: The Federal Rules provide that a federal jury must have *six or more* members participating in the verdict. FRCP 48 provides that "the court shall seat a jury of not fewer than six members. ..." Normally, the court will seat *more* than six jurors, so that even after illness of one or more jurors, at least six will be left to render the verdict. (Since 1991, federal juries no longer include "alternates"; see *infra*, p. 261.)

      a. Too few remaining: If the jury dwindles to fewer than six members by the time of deliberations and verdict, a *mistrial* must be declared unless the parties both agree to continue. See FRCP 48, last sentence ("unless the parties otherwise stipulate ... (2) no verdict shall be taken from a jury reduced in size to fewer than six members").

2. State trials: The number of jurors in *state* trials varies from state to state.

C. Unanimity: The verdict of a federal civil jury is still required to be *unanimous*, unless the parties stipulate otherwise. Rule 48. (But it is not clear whether unanimity in federal civil suits is required by the Seventh Amendment. See F,K&M, p. 530; Wr., p. 628, n. 5.)

1. States: More than half of the states allow a less-than-unanimous civil verdict. F,K&C, p. 703.

    a. New York: For example, in New York, a civil verdict is reached when five of the six jurors agree on it. CPLR, §4113.

D. Jury selection: The process by which the jury is selected is called the *"voir dire."* In most states the *voir dire* consists of oral questions by both sides' counsel to the prospective jurors. These questions are designed to discover whether a potential juror is biased, and whether he has connections with a party or with a prospective witness. See Rule 47(a).

1. Dismissal of juror: Any juror who is shown through the *voir dire* to be biased or connected to the case must be dismissed upon motion by a party. When a juror is dismissed for such bias or connections, his dismissal is said to be *"for cause."* There is no limit to the number of motions, or "challenges," that may be made to have jurors dismissed for cause.

2. Challenges without cause: In addition to the jurors dismissed for cause, each party may dismiss a certain number of other prospective jurors, *without showing cause* for their dismissal.

    a. Peremptory challenges: The right to dismiss a juror without cause is called a *"peremptory challenge"*.

    b. Federal practice: In federal civil trials, each party receives *three* peremptory challenges. See 28 U.S.C. §1870.

3. Balanced pool: The Seventh Amendment requires that the jury, and the pool from which it is drawn, must be roughly *representative of the overall community*. As Wright has stated, "the jury must be an impartial cross-section of the community, without systematic and intentional exclusion of any economic, social, religious, racial, political or geographical group." Wr., 627.

4. Alternates: After the members of the jury have been selected, in most states the court may order the selection of up to six *alternates*.

    a. Not used in federal practice: Under *federal* practice, alternates are *no longer used*, since the Rules were amended in 1991. The use of alternate jurors was rejected in 1991 "because of the burden it places on alternates who are required to listen to the evidence but denied the satisfaction of participating in its evaluation." Advisory Committee Notes to Rule 47. See FRCP 48, which now provides that "all jurors shall *participate* in the verdict unless excused from service by the court. ..." (Although six jurors is the minimum number needed for a federal verdict, the judge typically seats additional ones to allow for attrition due to sickness, etc.)

b. Minority approach: In a few jurisdictions, more than the required number of jurors are selected to sit in the jury box, and only after the case has been presented are some of them chosen to be jurors and the rest dismissed as alternates. This procedure avoids the danger that persons who know they are merely alternates will not pay attention during the trial.

E. Instructions: The judge must *instruct the jury* as to the law relevant to their finding of fact.

> **Example:** If plaintiff sues for negligence, the judge must instruct the jury that they should find for the plaintiff if the defendant's conduct was not that of a reasonable man, and was the "proximate cause" of the plaintiff's injuries.

1. Judge's right to comment: In federal courts, and in some but not all states, the judge retains the right to comment on the quality and weight of the evidence, Wr., 629.

2. Requests to charge: At the close of evidence, "any party may file written requests that the court instruct the jury on the law as set forth in the requests." Rule 51.

3. Objections: In order to raise the inadequacy of the instructions on appeal, a party must make an objection to them *before the jury retires*. In other words, he must give the trial judge a chance to reconsider, and to correct his mistake. This objection must be specific enough to allow the judge to see what is wrong and to correct it.

a. Where no objection made: In a very few cases, appellate courts exercise the right to review the instructions for *plain error*, even though no objection was timely made. This power is exercised "only to prevent a serious miscarriage of justice caused by the most palpable of errors." F,K&C, p. 703.

F. Juror misconduct: A jury verdict may be set aside, and a *new trial* ordered, for certain kinds of jury misconduct. These include subjecting themselves to *outside influence* (as by talking to a party, or by taking an unauthorized view of the scene of an accident), and concealing a *bias* or prejudice on *voir dire*.

1. Impeachment: The traditional rule, still followed in most states, has been that the jury may not *impeach its own verdict*. That is, a verdict will not be set aside because of a juror's testimony of his own or another juror's misconduct. A verdict, on this view, will only be set aside on evidence offered by a third party ("such as from persons having seen the transaction through a window." F,K&C, p. 709 fn. 5).

2. Federal Rules of Evidence: The Federal Rules of Evidence have modified this principle slightly for federal trials. Under Rule 606(b), the general principle is stated that "A juror may not testify as to any matter or statement occurring during the course of the jury's deliberations or to the effect of anything upon his or any other juror's mind or emotions as influencing him to assent to or dissent from the verdict ... or concerning his mental processes in connection therewith. ..."

a. Exception for extraneous information: However, that same Rule makes one exception: a juror may "testify on the question whether *extraneous prejudicial information* was improperly brought to the jury's attention or whether any *outside influence* was improperly brought to bear upon any juror." Thus a juror could testify that he or a fellow juror *read a newspaper article* about the case, or was bribed by one of the parties. But he would not be allowed to testify that he didn't really agree with the verdict but just went along with the others, or that he and/or the others failed to heed the judge's instructions.

3. **Bias discovered after trial:** Suppose that after the trial, one of the lawyers discovers that a juror *failed to disclose* information during *voir dire* that would have indicated possible bias. The lawyer may make a *motion for a new trial* (*infra*, p. 267). The Supreme Court has held that the lawyer must show the following in order to prevail on a new trial motion: (1) that the juror "failed to *answer honestly* a *material question*" during the *voir dire*; and (2) that a correct response "would have provided a valid basis for a challenge for *cause.*" *McDonough Power Equipment, Inc. v. Greenwood*, 464 U.S. 548 (1984).

   a. **Inadvertent error:** Under this standard, if the juror fails to disclose information because he *innocently misunderstands* the question, the new trial motion should not be granted.

   b. **Discretion of trial court:** In any event, a new trial motion based on subsequently-discovered bias, like new trial motions in general, is "committed to the *discretion* of the [trial] court" under the Federal Rules. See *McDonough*, *supra*. Therefore, if the district court denies the motion, it will only rarely be overturned on appeal.

Quiz Yourself on
THE JURY

72. P has sued D in a diversity action brought in the federal court for the District of Iowa. According to properly-adopted local court rules for the Iowa District Court, a civil jury shall consist of six members. P's claim against D was tried before a six-person jury, and the jury split 5-1 in favor of P. No aspects of the jury trial procedure have been agreed upon between the parties. May a verdict be entered in favor of P?

_____

73. Same facts as prior question. Now, however, assume that before the trial, P and D signed a stipulation providing that any verdict reached by four or more of the six jurors shall be taken as the verdict of the entire jury. The jury split by 4-2 in P's favor. Should the judge enter a verdict in favor of P?

_____

74. P sued D in federal court for the District of Colorado. The suit, which was based on diversity, alleged that D negligently injured P in an automobile accident. At the close of D's case, the judge instructed the jury that under Colorado law of comparative negligence (applicable here because of *Erie* doctrine) any contributory negligence by P would not bar P from recovery. However, the judge omitted to point out, as requested by D, that under Colorado law if P's fault was greater than D's, P may not recover at all. D's lawyer made no comment on the judge's jury instructions. The jury found in favor of P. On appeal, D now asserts that the trial judge's failure to give the requested "P more negligent than D" instruction constitutes reversible error. Assuming that the appellate court agrees that the judge's instruction was erroneous, should the appellate court affirm the verdict? _____

Answers

72. No. The six-person jury is allowable; see *Colgrove v. Battin*, 413 U.S. 149 (1973) (holding that a six-person jury does not violate the Seventh Amendment right to jury trial in civil cases, and allowing such a jury where provided by local court rules). But it *is* required in federal civil trials that the jury be unanimous. This result is reached by the negative implication of FRCP 48, which states, "The parties may stipulate that the jury shall consist of any number less than 12 or that a verdict or a finding of a stated majority of the jurors shall be taken as the verdict or finding of the jury." Since P and D did not stipulate that a less-than-unanimous verdict would suffice, the trial must be treated as a "hung jury" and the case retried.

73. **Yes.** Federal Rule 48 expressly allows a stipulation of the parties regarding what the majority shall control. See the language quoted in the answer to the prior question.

74. **Yes, probably.** The next to last sentence of Federal Rule 51 provides that "No party may assign as error the giving or the failure to give an instruction unless that party objects thereto before the jury retires to consider its verdict, stating distinctly the matter objected to and the grounds of the objection." A request for a particular instruction, made before the judge gives his instructions, is not a substitute for an after-the-instruction objection. Therefore, by the strict language of Rule 51, D waived his right to an instruction on this point by failing to object before the jury retired. There is some chance that the appellate court might conclude that this error was "plain error" which should be reversed despite the lack of an objection; however, most appellate courts in the federal system are reluctant to reverse even for plain error in instructions, on the theory that this wastes judicial resources (since a new trial is necessary, whereas with a timely objection the judge might have corrected his mistake and obtained a properly-instructed jury verdict the first time around). See *Platis v. Stockwell*, 630 F.2d 1202 (7th Cir. 1980), rejecting D's appeal on similar facts.

VII. DIRECTED VERDICT / JUDGMENT AS A MATTER OF LAW

A. **Effect:**   In both state and federal trials, either party may move for a ***directed verdict***. Such a verdict ***takes the case away from the jury, and determines the outcome as a matter of law***. (In federal trials, the party now moves for "judgment as a matter of law" rather than the more traditional "directed verdict." FRCP 50. We will continue to speak generally of "directed verdicts," but use the federal phrase "judgment as a matter of law" when speaking specifically of federal practice.)

1. **Federal trials:**   In federal trials, a party may move for ***"judgment as a matter of law"*** after the other party "has been ***fully heard*** on an issue. ..." FRCP 50(a)(1). Generally, this means that the defendant may move for a directed verdict at the ***close of plaintiff's case***. Either party may move for directed verdict after ***both sides*** have rested.

B. **Standard for granting directed verdict:**   As a general rule, "the court has the power to direct a verdict if the evidence is such that ***reasonable [persons] could not differ*** as to the result." Wr., 628.

1. **Federal standard:**   Federal Rule 50, as revised in 1991, now articulates a standard for granting ***"judgment as a matter of law"*** (the new federal term combining directed verdict and JNOV): "If during a trial by jury a party has been fully heard on an issue and there is ***no legally sufficient evidentiary basis for a reasonable jury to find for that party on that issue***, the court may determine the issue against that party and may grant a motion for judgment as a matter of law against that party with respect to any claim or defense that

cannot under the controlling law be maintained or defeated without a favorable finding on that issue." Rule 50(a)(1).

> **Example:** P is an inventor who has invented a two-deck VCR, which can be used to make copies of video tapes. P brings suit against D1 and D2, the two largest VCR manufacturers, asserting that they conspired to block her from manufacturing and selling her invention. In P's direct case, she shows that D1 and D2 both refused to manufacture her invention, but shows no evidence whatsoever that the Ds conferred with each other, or tried to influence any other manufacturer not to make P's device. At the close of P's case, the federal trial judge, either on his own motion or on a motion by D, should order judgment as a matter of law against P. That is, the trial judge should conclude that no reasonable jury could, based on the evidence produced by P, find that the asserted conspiracy existed.

2. **Distinction:** Some courts have distinguished between the amount of evidence needed to direct a verdict *against* the party bearing the burden of persuasion, and that needed to direct a verdict in *favor* of that party.

   a. **Stronger showing where burden against movant:** Clearly, a party seeking a directed verdict must make a stronger showing of evidence if he bears the burden of persuasion. But it is difficult to formulate a clear conceptual distinction between the two degrees of evidence required.

C. *Erie* **effect of directed verdict standards:** The Supreme Court has never decided whether the degree of evidence needed to issue a judgment as a matter of law in a diversity case is controlled by state or federal law. F,K&C, pp. 695-96. Most federal courts have followed what they perceive to be federal law.

   1. **Federal standard:** One case lists as the federal rule a standard somewhat more favorable to the movant than the usual "most favorable evidence" test (*supra*). That case, in which defendant sought a directed verdict (which today would be called in federal practice a judgment of a matter of law), held that the judge should consider *"only the evidence favorable* to plaintiff and the **uncontradicted, unimpeached** evidence **unfavorable** to him." If a reasonable person could not find for the plaintiff, a verdict must be directed against him by this standard. *Simblest v. Maynard*, 427 F.2d 1 (2d Cir. 1970).

D. **Use of JNOV:** A judge's grant of a directed verdict, thus taking the case from the jury, may be reversed on appeal. This will necessitate a new trial, and the original jury's work will be wasted. For this reason, most judges "reserve decision" on a directed verdict motion until after the jury has reached a verdict; the motion is then treated as one for a judgment notwithstanding the verdict (JNOV). This procedure is described more fully *infra*, pp. 273-274. (Federal Rule 50 now obliterates the difference between directed verdict and JNOV — both concepts are combined to "judgment as a matter of law.")

Quiz Yourself on

DIRECTED VERDICT; JUDGMENT AS A MATTER OF LAW

75. P has brought a diversity-based contract action against D in federal court. The sole issue in the case is whether D in fact signed the document that P has proffered as "the contract." At trial, the only witnesses were P and D. P testified that D signed the contract. D testified that he did not sign the contract. No documentary evidence was produced (except for the alleged contract document itself). After both sides rested, the judge instructed the jury, and the jury found in favor of P. D has now moved for judgment as a matter of law (after having complied with any procedural prerequisites for this motion). In considering the j.m.l. motion, the trial judge has a fairly strong belief that D told the truth and that P lied; however, the judge also recognizes that if P's testimony is believed rather than D's, P should win the case. The judge has also concluded that a person would not be completely irrational in concluding that it was D, rather than P, who had lied. Should the judge grant the j.m.l. motion? _____

76. P brought a negligence action against D in federal court, based on diversity. At the close of P's case, D immediately presented his first and only witness. The jury found in favor of P. D then made a motion for j.m.l. Assuming that the trial judge agrees with D's contention that a reasonable jury could not possibly have found in favor of P, should the trial judge grant D's j.m.l. motion? _____

Answers

75. **No.** When a judge decides a j.m.l. motion (as when she decides a motion for directed verdict), the judge's job is not to substitute herself for the jury. Instead, her task is to decide whether a reasonable juror could possibly find in favor of the non-movant; if the answer to this is "yes," the j.m.l. or directed verdict must be denied. Where the non-movant (here, P) presents testimony which if believed is adequate to make out a claim, the judge will rarely grant the motion even though the judge believes the contradicting testimony supporting the movant. On the other hand, if the trial judge believed that P's testimony was so implausible, so internally self-contradictory, or so completely contradicted by other evidence that no rational juror could believe it, then it would be proper for the judge to grant the motion.

76. **No.** According to Federal Rule 50(b), second sentence, a j.m.l. motion may only be granted if the movant has previously made a motion for a ***directed verdict***. Since on our facts, D never moved for a directed verdict, he has waived his right to seek a j.m.l. This means that the most D can get, either from the trial judge or on appeal, is a new trial, not an entry of judgment in his favor.

VIII. SPECIAL VERDICT AND INTERROGATORIES

A. **Special verdict:** A special verdict is a *specific finding of fact,* as opposed to a general verdict, which merely grants victory to one side or the other.

B. **Permitted by Federal Rules:** Rule 49(a) allows a court at its discretion to order a special verdict "in the form of a special written finding upon each issue of fact." This procedure has been little used, and has been attacked by Justices Black and Douglas as "but another means utilized by courts to weaken the constitutional power of juries and to vest judges with more power to decide cases according to their own judgments." 374 U.S. 865 (dissenting from the adoption of the 1963 amendments to the Federal Rules of Civil Procedure.) See *Columbia Horse and Mule Commission Co. v. American Insurance Co.*, 173 F.2d 773 (6th Cir. 1949).

1. **Judge's omission of issue:** If the judge fails to submit a question on a specific issue of fact when he gives his list of special verdict questions to the jury, the parties waive their right to a jury trial on that issue if they do not object before the jury retires. Rule 49(a).

C. General verdict with interrogatories: The judge may, instead of requiring a special verdict, require a general verdict supported by interrogatories as to specific findings of fact. Rule 49(b).

1. **Where consistent:** If these facts are consistent with the verdict, the verdict is entered.

2. **Where inconsistent:** If the findings of fact are inconsistent with the verdict, the judge may either enter a judgment consistent with the interrogatory answers, ignoring the jury's verdict, or he may order a new trial.

3. **Return to jury:** If the answers are inconsistent with *each other*, the judge must send the case back to the jury for further deliberation.

IX. NEW TRIAL

A. Judge's discretion: The trial court in both state and federal courts generally has wide discretion to grant a motion for a *new trial*, since such a motion runs less of a risk of abridging the Seventh Amendment than does a directed verdict or a JNOV.

B. Federal new trials: The Federal Rules set different standards for granting new trials in jury and non-jury cases.

1. **Grounds for new jury trial:** Where there has been a jury trial, the judge may order a new trial "for any of the reasons for which new trials have heretofore [before 1938] been granted in actions *at law*" in the U.S. Rule 59(a)(1).

2. **Grounds for new non-jury trial:** Where the action was tried without a jury, a new trial may be granted for any of the reasons an *equity court* would have granted rehearing. Rule 59(a)(2).

   a. **Evidence rulings in non-jury trials:** Judges conducting non-jury trials typically err on the side of admitting *too much*, rather than too little, evidence. This approach certainly lowers the risk that the judge will be reversed on appeal. It is highly unusual for a new trial to be ordered, even on appeal, because of the *admission* of incompetent evidence by a judge sitting without a jury. "On the other hand, a trial judge who, in the trial of a nonjury case, attempts to make strict rulings on the admissibility of evidence, can easily get his decision reversed by *excluding* evidence which is objected to, but which, on review, the appellate court believes should have been admitted." *Builders Steel Co. v. Commissioner*, 179 F.2d 377 (8th Cir. 1950).

3. **Harmless error:** A new trial may not be granted "unless refusal to [do so] appears to the court inconsistent with substantial justice." "The court ... must *disregard any error or defect in the proceeding which does not affect the substantial rights of the parties*." Rule 61. This doctrine that only an error affecting the substantial rights of the litigants is ground for a new trial is known as the *"harmless error"* doctrine.

4. **Objection required:** For most types of error at the trial court level, the party injured by the error must make a *timely objection*, in order to preserve the right to cite that error on appeal as a ground for a new trial. For instance, where evidence is erroneously admitted or excluded, this cannot serve as grounds for a new trial unless objection is immediately

made to the trial judge. See Federal Rule of Evidence 103(a)(1). (However, this rule requiring objection does not apply to "*plain errors* affecting substantial rights." Federal Rule of Evidence 103(d). See *Rojas v. Richardson, infra* p. 268, for an example of such "plain error.")

5. **Grounds for new trial:** Some of the more common grounds for granting a new trial are: (1) judicial error; (2) prejudicial conduct by party, witness or counsel; (3) juror misconduct; (4) verdict against the weight of the evidence; (5) excessive or inadequate verdict; and (6) newly discovered evidence. We consider each of these immediately below. (The discussion that follows assumes that the new trial motion is addressed to the trial judge. However, the appellate court can order a new trial on essentially the same grounds.)

C. New trial for judicial error

1. **Judge's correction of own errors:** The trial judge may order a new trial because of what the judge has concluded were *her own errors* committed during the trial. This is especially likely to occur in jury trials, where the judge believes that her errors have tainted the jury's verdict. "The trial judge may thereby correct its own errors in much the same way that an appellate court does." James & Hazard, p. 383.

   a. **Examples:** Thus, the trial judge may grant a new trial where she is convinced that she has improperly charged the jury, or where she believes that she has improperly excluded or admitted evidence.

D. New trial for prejudicial conduct by party, witness or counsel

1. **Improper conduct:** If a *party*, *witness*, or *counsel* conducts himself improperly, so that there is a substantial risk that an unfair verdict will result, the trial judge may grant a new trial.

   Example: P, who has worked for D as a ranchhand, sues for injuries he sustains when he is thrown by a horse. During the closing argument, D's lawyer refers to P as an "illegal alien" (although P's lawyer fails to object). After D wins the trial, P appeals and seeks a new trial.

   Held, P is entitled to a new trial. The remark was "highly prejudicial and a blatant appeal to jury bias." Furthermore, the prejudice to P is so clearly apparent that this is a "plain error," which may be redressed on appeal even though no objection was made at the time of trial; Fed. R. Evid. 103(d). *Rojas v. Richardson*, 703 F.2d 186 (5th Cir. 1983). (However, in a rehearing, D showed that P's lawyer had previously made the jurors aware, during the *voir dire*, that P was an "illegal alien." Therefore, the appeals court concluded that D's lawyer's remark was not so prejudicial as to constitute "plain error," and set aside its earlier decision. See 713 F.2d 116.)

E. New trial for jury misconduct

1. **Jury misconduct:** A new trial may under some circumstances be granted where there is evidence that the jury behaved improperly. The criteria for granting a new trial based on this are discussed *supra*, pp. 262-263.

F. New trial where verdict against the weight of the evidence

1. **State-to-state variation:** There is wide variation from jurisdiction to jurisdiction on what the state of the evidence must be for the trial judge to set aside a verdict as "*against the weight of the evidence*":

   a. **Unlimited discretion:** A *minority* of courts give the trial judge virtually **unlimited discretion** in deciding whether to grant a new trial on this ground. If he grants a new trial, he will not be reversed for abuse of discretion "where there is **any evidence** which would support a judgment in favor of the moving party." It has been said by one such court, "... the trial court shall exercise the function of a **thirteenth juror**. ... It is his duty to weigh the evidence and independently determine therefrom whether or not it is sufficient to sustain the verdict." *McLaughlin v. Broyles*, 255 S.W.2d 1020 (Tenn. 1952).

   b. **Strict test:** A different minority of courts are extremely strict about when a new trial may be granted. In these courts, the judge may *not* order a new trial if "on the evidence as presented and under the pleadings, the *jury could reasonably have found in accordance* with the verdict as rendered." This boils down to virtually the same test that is sometimes used in determining whether to allow a directed verdict. J & H (3d ed.), pp. 385-86. See *supra*, p. 264.

   c. **Federal standard:** The *federal courts,* and some state courts, have taken a *middle position*. The judge does not have unlimited discretion, but neither is he as restricted as on a motion for directed verdict. According to the classic formulation of the federal test, the judge must on motion order a new trial "if he is of the opinion that the verdict is against the *clear weight* of the evidence, or is based upon evidence which is *false,* or will result in a miscarriage of justice, *even though there may be substantial evidence which would prevent the direction of a verdict." Aetna Casualty & Surety v. Yeatts*, 122 F.2d 350 (1941). See also James & Hazard, p. 393.

      i. **No substitution of judgment:** The federal test emphasizes that the judge must *not substitute his own judgment* for that of the jury on matters of credibility of testimony and weight of evidence, unless the verdict is so obviously against the general trend of the evidence "that the court can clearly see that [the jury] has acted under some mistake, or from some improper motive, bias, or feeling." James & Hazard, 320. *It is not enough that the judge merely disagrees with the verdict, and would vote otherwise if he were a juror.*

      Note: *Granting of JML and new trial distinguished:* A new trial may be granted, under the federal test, even if there is substantial evidence to support the verdict (e.g., new trial because of excessive verdict or verdict against the weight of the evidence.) A motion for "judgment as a matter of law" (JML), on the other hand, may *not* be granted under such circumstances. (In the federal system, JML is the new term for both the JNOV and directed verdict motions. *Supra*, p. 264.) See the distinction drawn between JNOV (now JML) and new trial in *Montgomery Ward v. Duncan*, 311 U.S. 243 (1940).

G. **New trial where verdict is excessive or inadequate**

1. **Verdict excessive by law:** Where the damages allowable in an action are fixed as a *matter of law*, or are liquidated (e.g. an insurance policy with an upper amount), a verdict in

excess of this sum may be set aside as being wrong as a matter of law. James & Hazard, p. 394. Similarly, a verdict which gives plaintiff *less* than he is allowed by law, given that he is entitled to recovery, may be set aside.

2. **Where excess is matter of discretion:** But where the damages are set by the jury's discretion, as in the case of personal torts, trial judges are more hesitant to set aside a verdict as *excessive*. However, if the damages are completely out of line, the judge may order a new trial. Since the judge's power to do so dates back well beyond the enactment of the Bill of Rights, the Seventh Amendment is not in danger of violation — that Amendment allows re-examination of facts tried by jury "according to the rules of the common law."

3. **Inadequate:** Where the verdict is *inadequate*, but not fixed by law (as in a nominal recovery for a very serious tort injury), the judge also has some power to order a new trial. Where it is apparent that the inadequacy of the verdict is due to the jury's mixing of issues of liability and damages, courts differ. Some invariably set aside the verdict, on the grounds that as a matter of law, the jury must consider the two issues separately. Other courts allow such compromises to stand. James & Hazard, p. 394.

H. *Remittitur and Additur*

1. **Definition:** A judge may find the jury's verdict excessive or inadequate, but may wish to avoid, if possible, ordering a new trial. This is particularly the case where he is confident that the jury has decided the issue of liability properly, but has miscalculated the damages. He may therefore *conditionally order a new trial*, the new trial to occur *unless the plaintiff agrees to a reduction* of the damages to a specified amount (*remittitur*), or (where the damages are inadequate), the new trial to occur *unless the defendant consents to a raising* of the damages (*additur*).

2. **Validity:** The validity of the *remittitur* in federal practice is today firmly established. James & Hazard, 396. The *additur*, however, has been found by the U.S. Supreme Court to be in *violation of the Seventh Amendment*, and is therefore *not allowed in federal trials.* (The Seventh Amendment has not been applied to state trials). *Dimick v. Schiedt*, 293 U.S. 474 (1935).

3. **Allowed in many state trials:** Some *states allow* the trial judge to use the additur. States are free to do this, because the Seventh Amendment (the basis for the Supreme Court's *Dimick* decision banning the additur in federal trials), does not apply to state trials. See R,S&D, pp. 893-94.

4. **Amount of *remittitur:*** The usual test for determining the amount of the *remittitur* is that it should reduce the verdict only to the *highest amount that the jury could properly have awarded*. James & Hazard, p. 401. This seems to be established as the federal rule. *Id.* at 402, n. 52.

5. **Not appealable:** If the plaintiff accepts the *remittitur*, he may not thereafter *appeal* the trial court's *remittitur* order. *Donovan v. Penn Shipping Co.*, 429 U.S. 648 (1977).

I. Partial new trial

1. **New trial on damages:** It is sometimes apparent from the jury's verdict that they have reached an acceptable conclusion as to one issue, but an incorrect decision as to another. This most typically occurs with respect to the issues of liability and damages — the trial

judge finds the jury's conclusion that defendant is liable perfectly reasonable, but feels that the damages are either inadequate or excessive. Rather than using the *remittitur* or *additur*, he may grant a new trial ***on the issue of damages only.*** See *Gasoline Products v. Champlin Ref. Co.*, 283 U.S. 494 (1931).

J. New trial for newly discovered evidence

1. **Requirements:** Four criteria must generally be met before a judge will grant a motion for a new trial because of newly discovered evidence; (F,K&C, p. 744).

   a. **New discovery:** The evidence must clearly have been discovered since the end of the trial;

   b. **Diligence:** The movant must demonstrate that he was "reasonably diligent" in his search for evidence prior to and during trial, and that he could not reasonably have found the evidence in question before the trial's end.

   c. **Materiality:** The evidence must be ***material*** (not just cumulative or impeaching), and "of such character that on a new trial such evidence will probably produce a different result."

   d. **Injustice:** In addition to the above criteria, "[a]s a practical matter the motion is usually denied unless the trial judge has an abiding feeling that injustice has plainly resulted." F,K&C, p. 745.

K. Appealability of new trial order

1. **Not appealable:** An order for a new trial is ***not appealable***, at least in the federal system, because it is not a ***final judgment***. James & Hazard, p. 41. A party who wishes to raise on appeal the granting of a new trial must wait until the new trial has been carried out, and has yielded a final judgment. He may then appeal from the final judgment, and raise as an issue the new trial order.

   Note: The ***appealability*** of an order should be distinguished from the ***reviewability*** of that order. The former refers to timing — a case is normally not appealable until a final judgment has been rendered. (28 U.S.C. §1292, the Interlocutory Appeals Act, is an exception). An order is ***reviewable*** if it is something which the appellate court will examine when an appeal finally comes before it. The next section discusses such review. See F&K, 564, fn. p. See also Wr., 636-37.

Quiz Yourself on
NEW TRIAL

77. P has brought a diversity-based product liability action against D in federal court. The jury has awarded damages (compensatory only) of $3 million, a sum which the trial judge believes to be at least twice what a reasonable damage award would be. However, the judge agrees with the jury's finding that D should be liable. The judge does not want to waste the litigants' and court's time by ordering a new trial. What should the judge do? _____

Answer

77. Grant a remittitur. That is, the judge should conditionally order a new trial — the new trial will occur unless P agrees to a reduction of the damages to an amount set by the court, probably $1.5 million. It will then be up to P whether to accept this "deal" or not. If P accepts, he may not appeal the remittitur thereafter, and must be content with the $1.5 million. If P declines the remittitur, he must go through a new trial, which he may lose entirely.

X. REVIEW OF ORDERS GRANTING OR DENYING NEW TRIAL

A. Review generally: When a final judgment comes before an appellate court, the appellant may designate as error the judge's granting or denying of a new trial. The appellate court will examine this contention — the order is thus *reviewable*. But when, on review, such an order is considered, there is much dispute about the circumstances under which the court may reverse.

B. Review of errors of law

   1. New trial granted: When the *grant* of a new trial is an error of *law*, the appeals court may reverse the new trial order, and order the original verdict reinstated. (The appeals court almost never receives the case until the second trial has been carried out — the new trial order itself is not an appealable final judgment.)

   2. New trial denied: Similarly, where the *denial* of a new trial is an error of law, the appeals court may order a new trial. (Although the denial of a new trial is not itself a final judgment, it leads to a final judgment being entered in accord with the regular verdict. The latter is appealable, and the denial of a new trial may be raised as error on appeal.)

   > **Example:** A statute prevents the award of punitive damages in negligence cases. The judge is unaware of this, and charges the jury that they may grant such damages. They do, and D moves for a new trial based on the erroneous charge. The judge refuses, and final judgment is entered against D. On appeal, the denial of a new trial will be reversed, since that denial was the result of an error of law. *Fairmount Glass Works v. Cub Fork Coal Co.*, 287 U.S. 474 (1933).

   > But note that what the appeals court has done is not really to review the order denying the new trial, but rather reviewed the error of law itself.

C. Review of errors of fact: There is great dispute about the reviewability of a motion for new trial on *factual* grounds, e.g., excessiveness of the verdict, or verdict against the weight of the evidence.

   1. Trial judge's discretion: It is generally settled that the trial judge has a certain amount of *discretion* in this respect.

   a. No substitution of judgment: Thus the appellate court may not reverse simply because it would have decided the motion for new trial differently, if it had been sitting at trial.

   2. Abuse of discretion: However, some federal courts have held that there is power to reverse for *abuse of discretion* by the trial judge. If the trial judge's error in granting or denying new trial is *egregious* enough, it may be reversed on the evidence, but more is required than that the appeals court would have decided the motion differently. *Grunenthal v. Long Island Ry.*, 393 U.S. 156 (1968).

XI. JUDGMENT NOTWITHSTANDING VERDICT (JNOV) / JUDGMENT AS A MATTER OF LAW

A. **Dilemma:** A judge who is requested to direct a verdict is in a dilemma. If he grants the directed verdict, the appeals court may find that he erred, and a whole new trial will be necessary, wasting the original jury's work. But if he denies the motion, he may be sending a case to the jury that should be decided as a matter of law, and he risks being overturned on appeal.

1. **Use of JNOV:** Many judges avoid this problem by *reserving judgment* on a motion for a directed verdict, and submitting the case to the jury. Then if the jury decides against the movant, the judge can evaluate the legal sufficiency of the evidence on a motion for *judgment notwithstanding the verdict* (judgment *"non obstante veredicto"* in Latin, or *JNOV*). A JNOV results in the entry of *judgment for the party who lost the verdict;* it is a finding that the verdict had *no sufficient legal basis.*

   a. **Rationale:** The use of the JNOV avoids the need for a second trial if the appellate court holds, contrary to the trial court, that the evidence was not sufficient to take the case from the jury. The jury's verdict can simply be reinstated.

2. **Federal Rules change term:** In federal practice, the concept of JNOV no longer exists. Under a 1991 amendment to FRCP 50, the trial judge, even after the jury's verdict, grants *"judgment as a matter of law,"* rather than a JNOV. See FRCP 50(b).

   a. **Practice unchanged:** The underlying practice remains unchanged. Most importantly, the party seeking judgment as a matter of law must make a *motion* for that judgment *before the case is submitted to the jury.* The moving party must "specify the judgment sought and *the law and the facts* on which the moving party is entitled to the judgment." Rule 50(a)(2). Then, the judge submits the case to the jury, and waits for its verdict. Now, assume verdict goes against the movant. Assume further that the movant *renews* the motion after the verdict (as she must do under Rule 50(b), second sentence, if the judge is to reconsider the motion). If the judge agrees with the movant that no reasonable jury could have found against the movant, then the judge may effectively overturn the jury's verdict by granting judgment as a matter of law.

   Example: P brings an employment discrimination action against his former employer, D, alleging racial discrimination. The suit is brought in federal court. After both sides have presented their evidence, D believes that P has not made an evidentiary showing that would enable a reasonable jury to find that D discriminated against P on the basis of race. Before the case goes to the jury, D should make a "motion for judgment as a matter of law," pursuant to FRCP 50(a).

   Even if the judge agrees that no jury could find in P's favor on the core issue of whether there was racial discrimination against P, the judge will probably reserve decision on D's motion, and submit the case to the jury anyway. If the jury finds in favor of P, and the judge believes that the jury could not reasonably have done so, then the judge will belatedly grant judgment as a matter of law (or, alternatively, order a new trial). See FRCP 50(b). If D failed to make the judgment-as-a-matter-of-law motion before the case went to the jury, then the judge would *not* be authorized to grant the judgment as a matter of law. See FRCP 50(b). (The reason for requiring a motion before the case is sent to the jury is "to assure the responding party an opportunity to cure any deficiency in that party's proof that may have been overlooked. ..." Advisory Committee Notes to FRCP 50.)

3. **Applicable to defenses:** JNOV (or, under federal practice, Judgment as a Matter of Law) is usually entered on a claim. But some courts permit JNOV/JML to be entered on a *defense* as well. Thus, under a 1993 amendment to FRCP 50(a), the court is now authorized to issue JML on a defense, either for or against the party asserting the defense. (This corrects an ambiguity under existing law, where it seemed from the text of 50(a) that JML could be issued only on claims, not defenses.)

    Example: P brings a federal court diversity action against D for battery, alleging that D shot him. D raises a Rule 8(c) affirmative defense, claiming that the shooting was in self-defense. Under Rule 50(a), as it is proposed to be amended in 1993, if the judge concludes that no reasonable jury could find for D on the self-defense defense, the judge can prevent that defense from being submitted to the jury.

XII. REVIEW OF COMBINED NEW TRIAL AND JML MOTIONS

A. **Conditional ruling:** In federal practice, a motion for judgment as a matter of law (JML) may be joined with one for a new trial. Rule 50(b). If the JML motion is granted, the judge must also *rule conditionally* on the new trial motion. If the JML order is reversed on appeal, and the trial judge has conditionally *granted* the new trial motion, the new trial occurs automatically, unless the appeals court specifies otherwise. Rule 50(c)(1). If the trial judge conditionally *denies* the new trial motion, the *original verdict is reinstated* when the grant of JML is overturned on appeal.

1. **Utility:** This provision for conditional ruling saves time, because the appeals court is not obliged to remand for a determination of whether to award a new trial. (As seen in the previous section, the power of the appellate court to decide the new trial issue for itself is questionable, and rarely exercised.)

2. **Criticism:** However, the conditional ruling provision is often attacked for impracticality — "It is extremely unrealistic [to ask] the trial judge to make a conditional ruling on the assumption that, for reasons which he cannot know, his ruling on the [JML] motion is held to be erroneous." Wr., 644.

B. **Four possibilities:** If both JML and new trial motions are made, there are four possible responses the judge can make, each of which has different possibilities for review on appeal.

1. **Both motions denied:** Where the trial judge has denied both motions, the appeals court may order either JML or a new trial. But where the reason for attack on the verdict was *factual* (e.g. excessive verdict, or verdict against the weight of the evidence), JML is never granted where there is any *substantial evidence* in favor of the verdict winner. Nor is a new trial often granted on appeal in such circumstances. Where, on the other hand, an

error of *law* is the basis for attack on this verdict, appeals courts have substantial latitude in granting JML or a new trial.

    a. Dismissal: If plaintiff's case is found by the appeals court to have been insufficient to go to the jury as a matter of law, that court may on remand order the district court to *dismiss* it. *Neely v. Martin Eby Construction Co.*, 386 U.S. 317 (1967).

2. JML granted, new trial conditionally denied: In this situation, the verdict winner may appeal. The appeals court may either reinstate the verdict, or order a new trial (Rule 50(c)(1), last sentence.) If the appeals court reverses the JML, and doesn't specify a new trial, the verdict stands, and judgment is entered on it.

3. JML granted, new trial conditionally granted: In this situation, the verdict winner may appeal. JML is reversible. If JML is reversed, the judge's new trial order almost always controls.

4. JML denied, new trial granted: Here, there has been no final judgment, so appeal may not be taken until the new trial has been completed, and judgment entered on it. Appeal from the second trial's judgment may be taken, however. If the judgment is *against* the winner of the first verdict, he may claim that the award of a new trial was erroneous (but see preceding section for appellate reluctance to reverse such a grant where factual matters are at stake.) If the judgment is in *favor* of the winner of the first verdict, the loser may argue that the denial of both the new trial and JML motions was reversible error. But appeals courts in this situation are likely to be even more reluctant to reverse the new trial order for factual reasons, than where the judgment appealed from is *against* the winner of the first verdict.

> **Note:** The important thing to remember is that appellate courts do not hesitate to reverse decisions of JML motions, since these present questions of the *legal sufficiency* of plaintiff's case — the sufficiency of the evidence as a matter of law can be more or less judged from the appellate record. (Witness credibility is sometimes taken into account, but it is seldom crucial in determining legal sufficiency, since this involves taking the most favorable possible view of the verdict winner's case, according to most courts.)
>
> It is where a motion for *new trial*, based on the weight of the evidence, or the size of the verdict, is concerned, that appellate courts are reluctant to disturb the trial judge's disposition of the motion — to do so requires a much more comprehensive evaluation of the evidence than is required to evaluate legal sufficiency for JML, and is an evaluation that is best made by the trial judge, who has had opportunity to judge the credibility of the witnesses.

XIII. CONSTITUTIONAL RIGHT TO JURY TRIAL

A. Seventh Amendment: The Seventh Amendment provides that "in suits at *common law* ... the *right of trial by jury* shall be *preserved*. ..."

1. No state application: This provision clearly applies to federal trials. It has *never been held applicable to state trials*. We shall consider only the right to jury trial in federal actions in this section.

2. **Federal Rule protection:**   Federal Rule 38(a) provides that "the right of trial by jury as declared in the Seventh Amendment to the Constitution or as given by a statute of the United States shall be preserved to the parties inviolate."

    a. **Party must demand:**   This right is not self-executing. A party who wishes a jury trial on a particular issue must file a ***demand*** therefor to the other parties within 10 days after the service of the last pleading directed to that issue. (Rule 38(b)).

3. **Distinguished from equitable claim:**   But there is no jury trial as to "equitable" claims (e.g. a claim for injunction). The legal/equitable distinction is discussed further *infra*, p. 276.

B. **Federal law used:**   The right of jury trial in the federal courts is to be determined as a matter of ***federal law*** in ***diversity*** cases. Where the determination of the existence of this right requires the characterization of a claim as equitable or legal, this characterization must be made by a federal standard. (The scope of the substantive claim itself, however, is determined by general *Erie* principles, which often require the following of state law.)

C. **Meaning of suit "at common law":**   A claim will be "at common law", and therefore entitled to adjudication by trial, not only if it is the kind of claim which the law courts prior to adoption of the Seventh Amendment would have recognized, but also if it is based on a modern statute and is *"legal,"* rather than *"equitable,"* in nature.

1. **Fair Housing Act:**   Thus a claim for housing discrimination based on the 1968 Fair Housing Act has been found to be a "common law" claim, and either party has a right to jury trial on it. ***Curtis v. Loether***, 415 U.S. 189 (1974).

    a. **Rationale:**   The Court in *Curtis* pointed to the fact that the Fair Housing Act allows recovery of damages, and a claim brought under it is essentially a tort action (as to which there has always been a right to jury trial.) The Court distinguished actions for employment discrimination under the 1964 Civil Rights Act — these suits are essentially for equitable relief (e.g. injunction against further discrimination), and thus do not involve a right to jury trial.

D. **Pre-merger simplicity:**   Before the merger of law and equity, litigation at law was generally restricted to single action cases demanding single remedies. It was thus usually simple to determine whether a cause of action was "at common law," and therefore merited a jury trial as provided by the Seventh Amendment, or whether the action was equitable, and did not qualify for jury trial.

1. **Multi-party problems:**   Modern multi-party, multi-claim litigation, however, makes it very difficult at times to determine what is equitable and what is legal. It is therefore sometimes hard to determine to what cases and issues the right of jury trial applies.

    a. **Where all legal or all equitable:**   Where several claims or counterclaims are present in one lawsuit, it may be that all are legal, or that all are equitable. In such a case, there is no problem in determining whether there is a right to a jury trial — the entire lawsuit is tried to a jury, or none of it is.

    b. **Distinct issues:**   It may be the case that some of the claims in a specific lawsuit are legal, and some are equitable, but that the issues of fact involved are particular to each claim. There is then no problem in trying the equitable claims to the judge, and the legal claims to the jury — neither interferes with the other, and the order of hearing can be determined by considerations of judicial efficiency, since there are no common factual issues.

  c. **Issue of fact common to legal and equitable claim:** But where an *issue of fact is common to a legal and to an equitable claim*, problems arise. If the equitable claim is tried first, the judge's findings of fact will be **binding on the jury** which subsequently tries the legal claim, by the doctrine of "law of the case." Yet the case may be such that it is inefficient to try the legal claim first. For instance, if a party wishes to have a contract reformed for mutual mistake, and then to recover for breach of the reformed contract, it makes little sense to try the legal recovery issue before trying the equitable reformation issue.

  i. *Beacon* **solution:** In the kind of situation described in (c.) above, federal practice was in a confused state, until the Supreme Court handed down *Beacon Theatres v. Westover*, discussed immediately *infra*.

E. *Beacon Theatres:* *Beacon Theatres v. Westover*, 359 U.S. 500 (1959), was the first major Supreme Court case to deal with the right to jury trial where there are both legal and equitable claims.

  1. **The facts:** The facts of *Beacon Theatres* were as follows:

  a. Plaintiff Fox Theaters had certain contracts with movie distributors allowing it exclusive showing rights to films. A competitor, Beacon Theatres, threatened Fox with an antitrust suit, claiming that the contracts were in restraint of trade.

  b. Fox sought both an injunction preventing Beacon from instituting the antitrust suits, and also a declaratory judgment that its contracts with the distributors did not violate the antitrust laws.

  c. Beacon counterclaimed that the contracts were indeed in violation of the antitrust laws, and sought treble damages. It demanded a *jury trial* on the factual issues presented by its counterclaim.

  2. **Lower court's holding:** The district court held that even though certain factual issues were common to both Fox's claim and Beacon's counterclaim, it would hear Fox's claim for equitable relief first. The appeals court affirmed.

  3. **Supreme Court's reversal:** The Supreme Court held that the judge had *no authority to hear the equitable claim first*, against Beacon's wishes. To allow it to do so might "operate either by way of *res judicata* or collateral estoppel so as to conclude both parties with respect [to the issues involved in] the subsequent trial of the treble damage claim."

  a. **Summary of holding:** Thus *Beacon* stands for the proposition that *where there are both legal and equitable claims in the same case*, the trial judge must ordinarily *try the legal claims first*, so as to ensure the right of jury trial as to those claims (unless, of course, there has been a waiver of the jury trial right).

  b. **Legal claim rarely triable second:** The Court in *Beacon* did not absolutely forbid, in all situations, the trial of equitable claims before legal ones. But it held that only if the party asserting the equitable claims would be *irreparably harmed* by having these claims delayed till after hearing of the legal claims, could the court hear the equitable claims first (assuming that issues of fact common to the legal and equitable claims were involved.)

i. No problem in *Beacon:* This rare situation clearly did ***not*** exist in *Beacon* itself. The status quo could have been temporarily preserved by a temporary injunction preventing Beacon from starting other antitrust suits during the trial; this injunction would not have resolved any important fact issues. Then, the underlying issues germane to Fox's counterclaim (e.g., the issue of whether the distributor contracts violated the antitrust law) could have been tried by a jury. If the jury found that there was no antitrust violation, then a permanent injunction could have been issued by the trial court against further suits by Beacon, and a declaratory judgment could have been entered. In summary, the Federal Rules gave the trial judge in *Beacon*, as in nearly all cases, enough flexibility to ensure that equitable rights were preserved even though issues germane to a legal claim were tried first.

4. Significance of modern rules changes: As the *Beacon* court implied, one consequence of the ***merger of law and equity*** under the Federal Rules is that an underlying claim which, historically, might have been the proper subject for equitable relief, may no longer be.

a. Inadequacy of legal relief: It has always been held that equitable relief will be granted only where legal relief is ***inadequate***. If, because of procedural changes made by the Federal Rules, legal relief in a particular case would be adequate, ***there will be no right to equitable relief.***

i. Illustration: For instance, modern rules allowing ***joinder of defendants*** may facilitate an adequate legal suit for a plaintiff who has claims against multiple defendants, thus rendering unnecessary (and unavailable) the old equitable remedy of a "bill of peace."

ii. Injunctions: Similarly, while a suit for an ***injunction*** will always be equitable (and will thus not have a jury trial right), it may turn out that there are fewer and fewer situations where an injunction is the appropriate remedy (because of the broadened availability of legal remedies).

iii. Narrowed scope of equity: In a sense, therefore, the Federal Rules and other procedural improvements are ***narrowing the scope of equity.***

5. Declaratory judgment: Recall that the plaintiff in *Beacon* sought, among other things, a ***declaratory judgment*** that the distributor contracts were valid. Unlike a suit for injunction, a suit for declaratory judgment is, by itself, ***neither legal nor equitable***. Moore's Manual, §22.01[6]. Instead, it is the ***underlying issues*** which control whether there is a right to a jury trial in a declaratory judgment suit.

a. Contract action: Thus suppose an action were brought to obtain a declaratory judgment that a particular contract was valid. The facts underlying a counterclaim raised by the defendant might determine the extent to which there was a right to a jury trial; facts suggesting the right to have the contract reformed would not be triable before a jury (since reformation is equitable), but facts showing that there was a contract, which was breached by one side, would be triable before a jury (since actions for breach of contract are legal.)

F. *Dairy Queen:* Shortly after *Beacon Theatres*, the Supreme Court again gave a broad reading to the jury trial right, in ***Dairy Queen v. Wood***, 369 U.S. 469 (1962).

1. **Facts:** The facts of *Dairy Queen* were as follows:

    a. **Licensing:** Defendant had been licensed by plaintiff to use the latter's "Dairy Queen" trademark. The terms of the contract provided that defendant make certain payments for the use of the trademark.

    b. **Plaintiff's claims:** Defendant fell behind in payment, and plaintiff sought two kinds of relief: (1) an injunction preventing defendant from further use of the trademark, and (2) an "accounting" to determine the amount owed by defendant, and a judgment for that amount.

    c. **Defendant's jury trial motions:** Defendant moved for jury trial on the accounting demand, arguing that since it was a demand for a money judgment, it was clearly legal, not equitable.

    d. **Plaintiff's response:** Plaintiff countered that the demand was equitable, since it asked not for damages for but an "accounting."

2. **Lower courts deny jury trial:** Both the district court and the appeals court denied a jury trial on the money judgment claim.

3. **Supreme Court allows jury trial:** The Supreme Court held that a jury trial *must be allowed:*

    a. **Claim is legal:** No matter whether the claim was for damages for trademark infringement, or for the sum owed under the contract (it was not clear which was being sought), the claim was definitely *legal*.

        i. **Nature of claim not determined by pleadings:** The use of the word "accounting" in the complaint did not make the claim equitable — "the constitutional right of trial by jury cannot be made to depend on the choice of words used in the pleadings."

        ii. **Legal relief not inadequate:** The claim could only have been equitable if no adequate legal remedy was available. Where a money judgment is sought, the only reason legal relief might be inadequate is because the accounts between the parties are so complicated that a jury cannot understand them. But now that special masters are available under Rule 53(b) to assist the jury in understanding such complicated matters, it certainly cannot be said that legal relief is inadequate.

        iii. ***Beacon* repeated:** The rationale in (ii.) above reiterates the *Beacon* court's argument that procedural innovations at law will *constrict the scope of equity*, and therefore *increase the right of jury trial.*

G. *Ross v. Bernhard:* *Ross v. Bernhard*, 392 U.S. 531 (1970), further expands the idea that procedural modifications may broaden the right to jury trial.

1. **Stockholders' derivative suit:** In *Ross*, plaintiffs brought a stockholders' derivative suit under Rule 23.1.

   a. **Essence of derivative suit:** The basis for the stockholders' derivative suit is that the stockholders acquire the rights of the corporation as against third parties — if the corporation could sue a third party, the stockholders are allowed to sue on its behalf, if the directors refuse to sue.

   b. **Historically equitable:** Historically, the stockholders of a corporation had no right to sue on behalf of the corporation at law. Therefore, equity, following the rule that it would act where the legal remedy was inadequate, permitted the stockholders to sue.

      i. **Equitable suit allowable:** Since the corporation's right of action against third parties was often legal, the stockholders' suit meant that the equity court was trying legal issues. But this was permissible, since at that time there was no way such a suit could have been brought at law.

2. **Currently legal:** The Supreme Court held in *Ross* that under modern federal procedure, the stockholders' right (derived from the corporation's right) to sue third persons was *legal*, if the corporation's own suit would have been legal.

   a. **Underlying claim:** The determination that the stockholders have the right to sue on behalf of the corporation is still equitable. But once the judge has determined that they have this right, the actual suit, if it presents legal issues, merits a *jury trial*. "The heart of the action is the corporate claim. If it presents a *legal issue*, one entitling the corporation to a jury trial under the Seventh Amendment, *the right of a jury is not forfeited merely because the stockholders' right to sue must first be adjudicated as an equitable issue triable to the court. Beacon and Dairy Queen require no less.*"

3. **Dissent:** The dissent sought to distinguish *Ross* from *Beacon* and *Dairy Queen*, on the grounds that it did not involve two claims, one of which was equitable and the other legal. Rather, the dissent argued, the stockholders' derivative suit was historically "wholly a creature of equity." "And whatever else can be said of *Beacon Theater* and *Dairy Queen*, they did not cast aside altogether the historic division between equity and law."

H. **Other procedural devices:** The principle of *Ross* presumably applies to other devices which were historically available only in equity, such as interpleader and class actions. As the *Ross* court said, *"nothing now turns upon ... the procedural devices by which the parties happen to come before the court."*

I. **Limitations on jury trial right:** In several special situations the courts have considered whether there is a right to jury trial:

1. **Complex case:** In a footnote to *Ross*, the Supreme Court indicated that one factor to be considered in determining whether there was a right to jury trial is "the *practical abilities and limitations of juries."* Therefore, it may be that there are some cases that are *so complex* that their mere complexity makes them unsuitable for jury trial. However, while courts and commentators have hinted at this possibility, few if any cases have ever actually found that the case in question dictated a complexity exception to the right of jury trial. The argument for a "complexity exception" to the Seventh Amendment is strongest

in *securities and antitrust* cases, because of the large numbers of claims, and huge numbers of documents, that are often involved in such cases.

a. Complexity exception recognized: In one antitrust case, the Third Circuit stated that a case might be so exceedingly complex that the right to a jury trial would be lost. In *In re Japanese Electronic Products Antitrust Litigation*, 631 F.2d 1069 (3d Cir. 1980), a group of American television manufacturers sued Japanese manufacturers under the antitrust laws. The Court of Appeals held that if a case was too complex for jurors to decide by rational means, with a reasonable understanding of the evidence and of relevant law, a jury trial would violate the Due Process Clause of the Fifth Amendment; also, the court held, the Fifth Amendment right to due process would override the Seventh Amendment right to jury trial. The Court of Appeals therefore remanded the case for consideration of its complexity, though the court warned that "Due process should allow denials of jury trials only in exceptional cases."

b. Exception rejected: But an apparently exactly opposite conclusion was reached by the Ninth Circuit in a securities case. See *In re U.S. Financial Securities Litigation*, 609 F.2d 411 (9th Cir. 1979). That case would have required the factfinder to read over 100,000 pages during a two-year trial. But the Court of Appeals *rejected* a "complexity exception" to the Seventh Amendment. Nor did it concede that a jury trial in a complex case would deny due process: careful procedural control by the judge could reduce the complexity, and in any event jurors are as competent as a judge in factfinding, according to the court. Finally, the court suggested, the judge has power to grant a new trial or a JNOV, thereby protecting the parties from an irrational verdict. Thus the Seventh Amendment right to jury trial obtains "in even the most complex cases at law."

c. No Supreme Court case on point: The Supreme Court has never decided whether there should be such a "complexity exception" to the right to jury trial.

2. Bankruptcy: A claim's *close relation to an equitable proceeding* may prevent a right to jury trial. For instance, a *bankruptcy proceeding* has always been recognized to be equitable, and creditors therefore have no right to jury trial of their claims against the bankrupt estate. This principle was extended to require that where a creditor makes a claim, and the bankruptcy trustee counterclaims to recover a preferential transfer made by the bankrupt to the creditor, the creditor has no right to a non-bankruptcy jury trial (called a "plenary" trial) on this counterclaim, even though he would have had such a right if he had not entered the bankruptcy proceeding with his own claim. *Katchen v. Landy*, 382 U.S. 323 (1966).

3. Damages: Finally, the fact that a party has a Seventh Amendment right to a jury trial on the *liability* portion of his case does not mean that he has one on the *damages* portion. Indeed, the rule now seems to be that there is *never* a constitutional right to a jury trial on a damages issue. See *Tull v. U.S.*, 481 U.S. 412 (1987), holding that even though D was entitled to a jury trial on the liability aspects of the federal government's claim that D had violated the federal Clean Water Act, D did not have a right to jury trial on the issue of how much the *civil penalty* (analogous to a damage award) should be. The issue was whether the right to a jury trial on the civil penalty was "fundamental ... inherent in and of the essence of the system of trial by jury"; the Court concluded that it was not.

      a. **Scope of decision:**   It is possible that the Court's rationale in *Tull* applies only to cases involving a statutorily-authorized "civil penalty," not to the broader class of cases involving common-law damages. But the most obvious reading of the Court's language and rationale in *Tull* is that there is no Seventh Amendment right to have any issue of damages determined by a jury.

Quiz Yourself on

CONSTITUTIONAL RIGHT TO JURY TRIAL

78. P has sued D for negligence in Colorado state court. A recently-enacted Colorado statute provides, "In any civil suit in which the amount in controversy is less than $10,000, the case shall be tried before a judge sitting without a jury." P's claim is for $9,000. P asserts that the statute, insofar as it deprives him of the right to have his claim tried before a jury, violates the Seventh Amendment. Is P's contention correct?

_____

79. On July 1, P served on D a summons and complaint for a federal district court action alleging breach of contract. On July 15, D served an answer on P. There were no pleadings after the answer. At no time did P make a demand for a jury trial. On September 1, shortly before the case was to be tried, D served upon P a demand that the case be tried before a jury. Is D entitled to a jury trial? _____

80. P has brought a federal trademark infringement action against D. P seeks two types of relief: (1) an injunction prohibiting D from further violating P's trademark; and (2) money damages for the past violations. D seeks a jury trial on any issues for which he has a jury trial right.

    (a) On which, if either, of the two claims does D have a jury trial right? _____

    (b) What rule should the court follow with respect to the order in which the issues should be tried?

_____

81. Insurer wrote a $100,000 policy on the life of X. X, who owned the policy, notified Insurer that the beneficiary should be W, X's wife. Two years later, just before X died, he wrote to Insurer, "I wish to change the beneficiary from W to S, my son." After X's death, both W and S made a claim to the policy proceeds (W's claim was on the basis that X was not mentally competent at the time he purported to change the beneficiary). Insurer instituted a Rule 22 interpleader action in federal court, with W and S as the defendants. Insurer and S were content to have the case heard by a judge, but W demanded a jury trial. Is W entitled to a jury trial on the issue of whether she is the proper beneficiary? _____

Answer

78. No. The Seventh Amendment is one of the few Bill of Rights provisions that has never been "incorporated" into the Fourteenth Amendment's due process guarantees. Therefore, the Seventh Amendment applies only to federal, not state, civil trials. A state is free to deny juries entirely in civil trials if it wishes.

79. No. According to Federal Rule 38(b), "Any party may demand a trial by jury of any issue triable of right by a jury by serving upon the other parties a demand therefor in writing at any time after the commencement of the action and not later than 10 days after the service of the last pleading directed to such issue." This means that the last time D could demand a jury trial was 10 days after he served his answer, or July 25. After that, he waived his right, and only in very exceptional cases will the court relieve him from this waiver.

80. (a) Only the damages claim. Federal Rule 38(a) gives the right of jury trial "as declared by the Seventh Amendment to the Constitution." That Amendment applies only to suits "at common law." Therefore, there is only a right to a jury trial (unless Congress specifically otherwise provides) where the suit is one which is "legal" rather than "equitable." An injunction suit is always regarded as "equitable," so there is no right to a jury trial on an injunction claim. A claim for damages, by contrast, is virtually always "legal," so it does carry with it a right to a jury trial.

(b) The court should try the damages claim first. If the court tries the injunction claim (without a jury) first, this will probably bind the jury when the jury hears the damages claim later, because of the doctrine of "law of the case." Yet if the jury is not given comparatively free reign in deciding the damages claim, D's right to a jury trial is violated. Therefore, even though it may be somewhat inefficient, the federal judge should try the damages claim first, then the injunction claim, if there are significant issues in common between the two. (There are almost certainly such common issues here, e.g., the issue of whether P's trademark is valid and whether D has in fact infringed it.) See *Beacon Theatres v. Westover*, 359 U.S. 500 (1959).

81. Yes. The issue is whether the action is legal or equitable. It may well be that prior to the enactment of the Federal Rules of Civil Procedure in 1938, interpleader was regarded as an equitable action. But today, the court determines whether a claim is equitable or legal not by reference to the procedural device by which the parties come before the court (here, interpleader) but rather, by reference to the **underlying claim**. Here, the underlying issue is basically an issue of contract law (was X competent to change the policy beneficiary?), and such a contract-law issue will almost always be legal rather than equitable. Since the underlying issue is legal, each party has the right to demand a jury trial as to that issue (and if one party so demands, there will be a jury trial even though the other parties do not want one). See *Ross v. Bernhard*, 396 U.S. 531 (1970) (for determining whether the claim is legal or equitable, "nothing now turns upon ... the procedural devices by which the parties happen to come before the court").

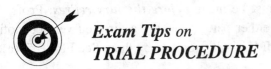

Exam Tips on
TRIAL PROCEDURE

Trial Procedure covers a welter of disparate issues. The professor will often be able to hide the issues from you by having the litigants state their requests and objectives cursorily and without much reasoning (e.g., "D moves for summary judgment"). Because you have to figure out what the reasoning could have been, issue-spotting can be unusually difficult in the trial context.

☛ Keep in mind the distinction between the burden of **"production"** and the burden of **"persuasion,"** — don't use the ambiguous phrase "burden of proof." [246-247]

    ☞ If the facts involve a **presumption**, remember these rules: the party against whom the presumption is directed bears the burden of **production** (if he produces no evidence to rebut the presumption, he suffers a directed verdict or judgment as a matter of law). But in the federal system and most states, the presumption has no effect on the burden of **persuasion** — once the production burden is met, the presumption disappears (**"bursting bubble"**). This is the most frequently-tested aspect of burden of proof / presumptions. [247-249]

☞ Where a party moves for *summary judgment*, remember the applicable standard: the movant wins only if there is *no "genuine issue of material fact"*. Typically, the facts will *not satisfy* this requirement, and you should conclude that s.j. is not appropriate. For instance, often there will be a genuine issue of material fact remaining either because:

   ☞ there is a dispositive issue as to which you may feel that one party is highly likely to prevail at trial, but the issue still turns on the *credibility* of the witnesses, or

   ☞ there are *multiple* sub-issues (one of which may be non-obvious), and although there's no genuine factual question as to some part(s), there *is* an issue as to one (probably a non-obvious) part. [252-255]

☞ If the case is *tried to a judge*, and is then *appealed*, be careful to distinguish between fact-based arguments for reversal and law-based ones. Remember that on appeal, the court is extremely *limited* in its ability to reverse for *fact-finding* errors: "Findings of fact, whether based on oral or documentary evidence, shall not be set aside unless *clearly erroneous*, and due regard shall be given to the opportunity of the trial court to judge of the *credibility* of the witnesses." FRCP 52(a). Normally you should conclude that the appeals court can't reverse, since the prof. probably can't make a fact-finding error seem egregious in a brief question without tipping off the "clearly erroneous" issue. [256-259]

☞ When the case is tried to a jury, be on the lookout for non-unanimity. In the federal system, the verdict must be *unanimous* unless the parties stipulate otherwise (and in the typical fact-pattern, they don't so stipulate). [261]

☞ If a party moves for *judgment as a matter of law* (in the federal system) or directed verdict / JNOV (some states), two points are most vital to remember [264-265]:

   ☞ The standard is essentially *whether reasonable jurors could differ* as to the result — if they could, the court shouldn't grant JML/directed verdict/JNOV.

   ☞ The motion (whatever it's called) must be made *before the jury retires*. Profs. frequently have the jury retire without either party's making a directed verdict motion, then have the verdict loser move for JML — it's too late by then. See FRCP 50(a)(2); 50(b).

☞ Professors frequently test on *juror misconduct*. The most important rule to remember is that generally, "the jury *may not impeach its own verdict*." That is, the verdict won't be set aside because of a juror's testimony about his own or another juror's misconduct — only evidence from a *third party* will suffice. [262-263]

   ☞ But under the FRCP, there is a limited *exception* — a juror may testify about whether *extraneous prejudicial information* was brought to the jury's attention, or whether any *outside influence* was improperly brought to bear. But a juror can't testify about how the jury conducted its deliberations, so that testimony that, say, the jurors ignored the judge's instructions will still not be allowed under the FRCP.

☞ Fact patterns often involve a party's efforts to obtain a new trial, either from the trial judge or on appeal. Some of the reasons for which the court (either the trial judge or the appellate court) can grant a new trial are [267-270]:

☞   Improper conduct by a *party*, *witness* or *counsel*

☞   *Jury* misconduct (see above)

☞   *Judicial error* (e.g., the judge charges the jury incorrectly)

☞   *Verdict against the weight of the evidence*. (In the federal system, the verdict must be against the "*clear* weight" of the evidence, but a new trial can be granted even if there is substantial evidence supporting the verdict, which would be enough to prevent the issuance of Judgment as a Matter of Law.)

☞   Verdict *excessive* or *inadequate*

   Note: Remember that to be grounds for a new trial, the error must "affect the substantial rights of the parties." FRCP 61. This is the *"harmless error"* doctrine. Whenever your fact pattern suggests to you that one of the above grounds for new trial exists, be sure to mention the possibility that the error might be "harmless" unless it's clear that it's not. [267]

☛ Instead of a new trial, state courts usually allow the judge to order a *remittitur* (new trial to occur unless the victorious plaintiff accepts a lower amount specified by the judge) or *additur* (new trial to occur unless the defendant agrees to pay a higher amount). But in federal trials, only remittitur is allowed — *additur has been held to violate the constitutional right to jury trial*. This last point is frequently tested. [270]

☛ Many essay questions involve the *constitutional right to jury trial*. [275-282] Here are the most important (and frequently-tested) points:

☞   The 7th Amendment (right to jury trial in civil cases) applies only to *federal*, not state, trials.

☞   The 7th Amendment applies only to *"legal,"* not *"equitable,"* issues. [276]

   ☞   Therefore, you must be on the lookout for claims or defenses that are equitable in nature, so you can point out that there's no right to jury trial on these. Thus attempts to procure an *injunction*, to *rescind* a contract, to receive an *accounting*, or to *reform* a contract for *mistake*, would all be claims for which there is no right to jury trial.

   ☞   A suit for *money damages* will almost always be "legal." (But a suit for a statutory penalty will not, necessarily.)

☞   If a case contains *both* legal and equitable claims, and there is an issue of fact common to both, the court must usually allow the *legal claims to be tried first* (to the jury). This is the single most frequently-tested aspect of right-to-jury-trial. You should cite to *Beacon Theatres v. Westover* if this "which claims to try first" issue arises. [277]

☞   In deciding whether something is legal or equitable, remember that it's not the procedural device by which the issue comes before the court, but the nature of the underlying claim, that counts. For instance, a declaratory judgment suit can be either legal or equitable, depending on the underlying issue.

   ☞   Professors sometimes want to know whether the fact that a particular case is *extremely complex* is enough to nullify the right to jury trial. Some courts have held that this is at least a factor to be considered in determining whether there is a right to jury trial. [280-281]

CHAPTER 8

MULTI-PARTY AND MULTI-CLAIM LITIGATION

ChapterScope

This Chapter examines various devices that either enlarge the number of claims between the existing parties to a litigation, or bring new parties into the litigation. Again, the emphasis is on the devices available under the Federal Rules. The most important concepts in this Chapter are:

■ **Counterclaims:** A *"counterclaim"* is a claim *by a defendant against a plaintiff*. The Federal Rules provide for both *"permissive"* and *"compulsory"* counterclaims. FRCP 13.

❑ **Compulsory counterclaim:** If D's counterclaim arises out of the *same transaction or occurrence* as P's claim, it is a *"compulsory"* counterclaim. If D does not assert her compulsory counterclaim, she will *lose* that claim in any future litigation.

❑ **Permissive:** Any claim that does *not* arise out of the same transaction or occurrence as P's claim is a *"permissive"* counterclaim. D does not lose her counterclaim in future litigation if she declines to assert it in the first suit.

■ **Joinder of claims:** Under the device of *"joinder of claims,"* once a party has made a claim against some other party, he may then make *any other claim he wishes against that party*. FRCP 18(a).

■ **Joinder of parties:** Under the device of *"joinder of parties,"* multiple plaintiffs may join together, or a plaintiff may sue multiple defendants.

❑ **Permissive joinder by plaintiffs:** Joinder done at the *discretion* of the plaintiff(s) is called *"permissive"* joinder. FRCP 20. Multiple plaintiffs may (but need not) join together in an action if they satisfy two tests (1) their claims for relief must arise from a *single "transaction, occurrence, or series of transactions or occurrences,"* and (2) there is a *question of law or fact common to all plaintiffs* which will arise in the action.

❑ **Permissive joinder of defendants:** If one or more plaintiffs have a claim against *multiple defendants*, these defendants may be joined based on the same two tests as plaintiff-joinder. That is, claims against the co-defendants must: (a) arise from a *single "transaction*, occurrence, or series of transactions or occurrences"; and (b) contain a *common question* of law or fact.

❑ **Compulsory joinder:** There are certain situations in which additional parties *must* be joined, assuming the requirements of jurisdiction can be met. Such joinder is called *"compulsory"* joinder. The basic idea is that a party must be joined if it would be *uneconomical* or *unfair* to litigate a claim without her. FRCP 19. (There are two sub-classes involving compulsory joinder: *"necessary"* parties and *"indispensable"* parties. Necessary parties must be joined where possible, but the action can go on without them if joinder is made impossible by jurisdictional problems; indispensable parties are ones so vital that the action must be dismissed if they cannot be joined.)

■ **Class action:** The *class action* is a procedure whereby a single person or small group of co-parties may *represent* a larger group, or *"class,"* of persons sharing a *common interest*. FRCP 23.

    ❑ **Binding on absentees:** The results of a class action are generally *binding on the absent members*. Therefore, all kinds of procedural rules exist to make sure that these absentees receive *due process* (e.g., they must receive notice of the action, and notice of any proposed settlement).

    ❑ **Defendant class:** The class may be composed *either* of plaintiffs or defendants. The vast majority of the time, the class will be composed of *plaintiffs*.

■ **Intervention:** By the doctrine of *"intervention,"* certain persons who are not initially part of a lawsuit may enter the suit *on their own initiative*. The person who intervenes is called an "intervenor." FRCP 24.

    ❑ **"Of right" vs. "permissive":** Intervention can be "of right" or "permissive". "Of right" means that no permission of the court is required; "permissive" means that the court has discretion whether to allow the intervention or not.

■ **Interpleader:** The device of *interpleader* allows a party who owes something to one of two or more other persons, but is not sure whom, to force the other parties to argue out their claims among themselves. The technique is designed to allow the "stakeholder" to avoid being made to pay the same claim twice.

■ **Impleader:** Under the device of *impleader*, a defendant who believes that a third person is *liable to him* for all or part of the plaintiff's claim against the defendant may *"implead"* such a person as a *"third-party defendant" ("TPD")*. FRCP 14(a). The defendant who is making the third-party impleader claims is called the *third-party plaintiff* ("TPP").

    ❑ **Additional claims:** Once a TPD has been impleaded, she may make *claims of her own*, including counterclaims against the TPP (either permissive or compulsory), cross-claims against any other TPDs, etc.

■ **Cross-claims:** A claim by a party against a *co-party* is called a *"cross-claim."* A cross-claim is made only against a party who is on the *same side* of an already-existing claim (e.g., a claim by one co-defendant against another, or by one co-plaintiff against another).

■ **Jurisdiction and venue:** When dealing with any of these multi-claim and multi-party devices, it's vital to examine the requirements of *personal jurisdiction*, *subject matter jurisdiction* and *venue*. The doctrine of *supplemental jurisdiction* will often (but not always) be available to negate the need for an additional party or claim to independently meet the requirements of federal subject matter jurisdiction.

I. BACKGROUND

    A. Common law: At common law, the prevailing policy was to prohibit any sort of action other than one involving a single plaintiff and a single defendant. Also, a lawsuit was generally limited to a single legal theory, or cause of action.

B. Equity: The courts of equity, however, were willing to entertain more complex sorts of actions, since they used no juries and all their proceedings were in writing. Many of the maneuvers to be discussed in this section had their origin in the willingness of equity courts, as contrasted with common law courts, to hear all possible aspects of a case at once.

1. Merger: The merger of law and equity, as represented by the Federal Rules and by the present rules of most states, resulted in the incorporation of multi-party, multi-claim suits into the unitary civil action.

> **Note:** The material in this chapter treats a number of devices which bring new parties into the action. These devices include ***compulsory and permissive joinder, class actions, intervention, interpleader***, and ***third-party complaints***. Before these joinder-of-party devices are considered, however, two devices which do not bring new parties to the lawsuit, but which enlarge the number of claims between the existing parties, are treated. These devices are the ***counterclaim***, and Rule 18(a) ***joinder of claims***.

II. COUNTERCLAIMS

A. Generally: Suppose the defendant has what he thinks is a valid cause of action against the plaintiff. May he bring this into the original suit, or must he file a separate action of his own?

1. Common law: At common law, there were two devices, both quite limited, by which a defendant could bring a claim against the plaintiff:

a. ***recoupment***, in which he could assert claims arising from the same transaction as the original complaint, but only for the purpose of reducing or cancelling out the plaintiff's recovery. That is, he could ***not*** win an ***affirmative recovery.***

b. ***set-off***, which was not limited to the "same transaction," but which had to be for liquidated damages or arise out of a contract or judgment. Like recoupment, set-off did not allow an affirmative recovery. See F,K&C, p. 541.

2. Codes: The codes, in general, combine these remedies into the "counterclaim." A typical code provision permits assertion as a counterclaim of any claim "arising out of the contract or transaction set forth in the complaint as the foundation of plaintiff's claim, or connected with the subject of the actions." F,K&C, p. 542. On such a counterclaim, however, there is the possibility of an affirmative recovery.

a. State practice: A number of states still follow the code rule that only claims related to the plaintiff's claim may be asserted by the defendant as counterclaims. Most states, however, follow the more liberal federal procedure, described in the following paragraphs.

B. Federal Rules: The Federal Rules, in order to promote judicial economy, have gone beyond the codes with respect to counterclaims. Rule 13 provides for both ***"permissive"*** and ***"compulsory"*** counterclaims.

1. Permissive counterclaim: Rule 13(b) allows assertion as a counterclaim at the defendant's ***discretion*** of "any claim ... ***not arising out of the transaction or occurrence*** that is the subject matter of the opposing party's claim." This means that ***no claim is too far***

removed from the subject of the plaintiff's claim to be allowed as a counterclaim. (Exceptions are indicated in Rule 13(d), and in the "presence of third parties" clause of 13(a), but these are minimal.)

2. **Compulsory counterclaim:** If a claim does arise "out of the *transaction or occurrence that is the subject matter of the opposing party's claim ...,*" its assertion is *compulsory*, under Rule 13(a). Such a counterclaim is, roughly speaking, the same sort of counterclaim which was permitted, but not required, under the codes.

   a. **Failure to state compulsory counterclaim:** The penalty for failing to state such a compulsory counterclaim is *loss of the claim in future litigation.* That is, if a compulsory counterclaim is not asserted, a later suit on that claim by the present defendant will be precluded by the rules of *res judicata*. This consequence is discussed further *infra*, p. 292.

   b. **Exceptions:** Rule 13 lists certain claims that are *not compulsory* even though they are within the same "transaction or occurrence" as the plaintiff's claim. These include:

      i.   claims by the defendant which for *"just adjudication"* require the presence of *additional parties* of whom the court *cannot get personal jurisdiction* (Rule 13(a)) and

      ii. claims in which the suit against defendant is *in rem* or *quasi in rem* (assuming that the defendant is not making any other counterclaim in the action) (Rule 13(a)(2)).

   Note: The reason why a counterclaim is not compulsory if the claim against the defendant is *quasi in rem* or *in rem* is as follows: *Quasi in rem* and *in rem* suits do not subject the defendant to personal liability; he can defend such a suit without risking anything more than the property which is under attachment. If a counterclaim by him against the plaintiff were compulsory, the defendant would be put to the harsh choice between: (1) losing his claim forever through failure to assert it, or (2) making his claim and thereby subjecting himself to unlimited personal liability. (According to most courts, personal liability results if a defendant makes a claim of his own.) Therefore, Rule 13(a)(2) gives the defendant a chance to avoid unlimited liability and at the same time preserve his claim for a separate suit.

   c. **Must be asserted in defendant's pleading:** If the defendant's counterclaim is a compulsory one, it must be brought in the defendant's *pleading*. See Rule 13(a). If an action is *dismissed* before it reaches the point where defendant must file an answer, then no compulsory counterclaim exists. See *Lawhorn v. Atlantic Ref. Co.*, 299 F.2d 353 (5th Cir. 1962).

   d. **Default by plaintiff:** If the defendant has asserted a counterclaim (whether compulsory or permissive), and the plaintiff neglects either to serve a reply or to move against the counterclaim, a *default judgment* may be entered against the plaintiff on the counterclaim. See Rule 55(d).

C. **"Transaction or occurrence":** A counterclaim is compulsory, under Rule 13(a), only if it arose out of the *same "transaction or occurrence"* as the plaintiff's claim. The meaning of the term "transaction or occurrence" is therefore of substantial importance. The courts have not agreed on a precise formula for determining what constitutes a "transaction or occurrence."

1. **Logical relation:** The most accepted verbal formula is that a claim arises out of the same "transaction or occurrence that is the subject matter of [P's] claim" (and is therefore a compulsory, rather than permissive, counterclaim) if it is *"logically related"* to P's claim. This is the test advocated by Wr., p. 529, but a definition of "logical relationship" seems necessary before the test is useful. Wright does not offer such a definition.

   a. **"But for" cause:** The tort-law notion of a *"but for"* cause may be relevant. That is, if the counterclaim would not have arisen but for the events which gave rise to the main claim (or vice versa), the court is somewhat more likely to find the requisite "logical relation" between the two, and therefore to find that the counterclaim is compulsory.

      Example: P sues D for assault, and D counterclaims for a libel published shortly before the assault, which D claims provoked the assault. *Held*, the libel counterclaim arose from the same transaction or occurrence as the assault. *Mulcahy v. Duggan*, 214 P. 1106 (Mont. 1923). Insofar as the assault would not have occurred without the libel (assuming that D's contention was correct), this result seems reasonable — there is a "logical relationship" between the two episodes.

2. **Rule of thumb:** Many courts, in deciding whether a counterclaim meets the "transaction or occurrence" test, are especially interested in whether there is a substantial amount of *evidence* that bears upon both the claim and the counterclaim, and which would therefore have to be considered twice if the counterclaim were not allowed (or, under the Federal Rules, if the defendant were allowed to keep it in reserve for another action, and chose to do so.)

D. Counterclaims by third parties

1. **Any party may make:** A counterclaim may be made by *any party* against "any opposing party." Rule 13(a), 13(b). The test for distinguishing between "compulsory" and "permissive" counterclaims in this context is the same as in the case of the single defendant counterclaiming against the single plaintiff.

   a. **Third-party defendant:** Thus a third-party defendant (see discussion of third-party Practice, *infra*, p. 343) may counterclaim against either the original defendant, or against the original plaintiff. (In the latter case, a claim by the plaintiff against the third-party defendant must first have been made.)

   b. **Plaintiff's counterclaim:** A plaintiff may have a counterclaim to a counterclaim. This "counter-counterclaim" will even be compulsory, if it arises from the same transaction or occurrence as the defendant's counterclaim. (This is true even if the defendant's counterclaim is itself permissive rather than compulsory.) The defendant's counterclaim is a "claim" under Rule 8(a), so any claim by any other "opposing party", arising out of the same transaction or occurrence, is a compulsory counterclaim under Rule 13(a).

   c. **New parties:** *New parties* to a counterclaim can be brought into a suit, as long as the joinder test of either Rule 19 or Rule 20 is satisfied. Rule 13(h).

Example: D's counterclaim against P requires for its just adjudication the joinder of a third party, X, as a defendant to the counterclaim. X may be joined under Rule 19(a) if to do so would not destroy diversity, and if personal jurisdiction over X may be obtained. Here, diversity is no problem, since the general rule is that a compulsory counterclaim need meet no independent subject matter jurisdictional requirements, since such a counterclaim is within a court's *supplemental jurisdiction*. But *personal* jurisdiction may be a problem — if service cannot be made on X, D's counterclaim is *not* considered compulsory, no matter what its relationship to P's claim. (Rule 13(a)).

    d. Cross-claims: A claim by a party against a *co-party* (someone joined *with* him as a co-defendant, co-plaintiff, or co-third-party) is a *cross-claim*, not a counterclaim. Cross-claims are *never compulsory*, and are discussed *infra*, at p. 349.

E. Failure to raise a compulsory counterclaim

1. Barred: Generally, a party who fails to assert a compulsory counterclaim in a federal action is then *forever barred* from suing on that claim in another federal action. Wr., 530.

    a. Basis unclear: It is not clear whether the basis for this rule is a general principle of "*res judicata*," or whether the bar is simply an implied provision of Rule 13.

    b. Lenient: In cases of *hardship*, where a party was not at the time of the first suit *aware* that he had a compulsory counterclaim, the federal courts have been lenient in waiving the bar against subsequent assertion of the claim in a new action. This provision is often invoked where the defense of an alleged tortfeasor is handled by his insurance company, and the tortfeasor himself only later discovers what turns out to be a compulsory counterclaim.

        i. Amendment: The need for such lenience is rendered less pressing by Rule 13(f), which allows the court to grant leave to a party who has overlooked a compulsory counterclaim, to assert that counterclaim by *amendment* during the original action, after trial has begun. Wr., 530.

2. State court: There has been dispute about whether a *state* court may entertain a claim that should have been asserted as a compulsory counterclaim in an earlier *federal* action. *Most state courts have barred such claims*. Wr., 531. See the discussion of *Horne v. Woolever*, *infra*, p. 367.

3. First suit in state court, second in federal: Where a claim should have been asserted as a counterclaim in a state court, and was not, it is possible that a *federal court* would dismiss it when brought as a separate action. But few if any federal courts have explicitly decided this question.

F. Jurisdictional requirements for counterclaims

1. Supplemental jurisdiction: A *compulsory* counterclaim to a federal action is within the federal court's *supplemental jurisdiction*, and requires *no independent subject matter jurisdictional grounds*. Wr., 535.

    Example: A, a N.Y. resident, sues B, a Massachusetts resident. B has a compulsory counterclaim against A for less than $50,000. The counterclaim is also against C, a Massachusetts resident not yet in the action, who is required for "just adjudication" as this term is used in Rule 19. B's counterclaim falls within the court's supplemental jurisdiction, and thus diversity is not affected, and the jurisdictional amount does not have to be satisfied.

Note: The concept of *supplemental jurisdiction* (formerly called "ancillary" jurisdiction in this context) is of the utmost importance to multi-claim litigation. Without it, the modern complex federal action would be virtually impossible. In reading this chapter, the reader should carefully observe to which joinder devices the supplemental doctrine applies, and thus for which parties and claims no independent subject matter jurisdictional grounds are required. See *supra*, p. 112.

2. **Permissive counterclaims not supplemental:** A permissive counterclaim is probably *not* within a court's supplemental jurisdiction, and must therefore satisfy the requirements of federal subject matter jurisdiction. Thus a permissive counterclaim may not be used to join a third party who is of the same citizenship as the party asserting the counterclaim against him. Similarly, it is generally held that a permissive counterclaim must *independently exceed the amount in controversy requirement*. Wr., 535.

G. **Pleading of counterclaims:** The party raising a counterclaim is, for the purpose of that claim, a "plaintiff" and his opponent a "defendant," whatever their positions are in the litigation as a whole. The rules of pleading relevant to the counterclaim correspond substantially to those for an ordinary plaintiff's claim, and an ordinary defendant's response. See Rule 8(a).

H. **Statutes of limitations for counterclaims:** Assertion of a counterclaim often raises issues concerning the *statute of limitations*.

1. **State rule:** If P's complaint is timely, but D's counterclaim would be barred by the statute of limitations if sued on alone, may D assert the counterclaim? The most common rule in *state* courts follows common-law precedent: counterclaims arising from the *same transaction* as P's claim may be asserted as *defenses against any timely claim, but may not yield an affirmative recovery*. A counterclaim *not* arising from the transaction on which P sues must generally be timely on its own.

2. **Federal diversity cases:** Where the case is a *federal* one based on *diversity*, D's right to bring an arguably time-barred counterclaim will depend in part on whether the statute of limitations ran before or after plaintiff brought the case:

   a. **Time-barred when P sued:** If D's counterclaim was *already time-barred* at the time P sued, few if any federal courts will allow D to assert the counterclaim as a means of making an affirmative recovery.

      i. **Allowed as defense:** However, a court might allow the "counterclaim" to be used as a *defense*, in the sense that it could reduce P's recovery but not yield an affirmative recovery for D. The court is far more likely to allow this limited use if the "counterclaim" is one that would be *compulsory* (related to the subject matter of P's complaint) than if it is one that would be "permissive."

   b. **Time-barred after P sues:** If the statute of limitations on the counterclaim ran *after* P commenced the suit, but before D asserted his counterclaim, D has a much better chance of getting the court to hear the counterclaim. Wright argues that "the counterclaim ought to be allowed for all purposes." Wr., p. 535.

Example: The Ps sue D in diversity on a claim relating to an automobile accident. At the moment the Ps file the action with the court (thus "commencing" it), a counterclaim by D based on the same accident has not yet become time-barred. However, by the time D is served in the action several months later, his would-be counterclaim has become time-barred. D nonetheless asserts the counterclaim, arguing that it should relate back to the commencement of the Ps' action.

Held, for D. D's counterclaim was the "same age" as the Ps' claim (since both arose out of the same automobile accident). Therefore, "the counterclaim is no more stale than the complaint. Simple justice dictates that if the plaintiffs are given an opportunity to present a claim for relief based on a particular automobile collision, the defendant should not be prevented from doing so by a mere technicality." *Azada v. Carson,* 252 F.Supp. 988 (D.Haw. 1966).

     i. Permissive counterclaim: Observe that in *Azada,* D's counterclaim was a compulsory one, thus allowing the court to make its "same age" argument. But if D's counterclaim is a *permissive* one, the "same age" argument will not necessarily apply; nor will the court's sense of justice be as offended by denying D his right to counterclaim. Therefore, the court is somewhat less likely to allow a counterclaim that became time-barred after P commenced his action, where the counterclaim is a permissive one.

     3. Federal question cases: Suppose now that the case is a *federal question* case. Where the main claim and the counterclaim are based on federal rights rather than state-created ones, state law on the statute of limitations issue becomes irrelevant. As in the diversity situation, if D's counterclaim was time barred before P sued, the federal courts will almost certainly not allow D to sue. If the counterclaim became time-barred after P commenced the action, federal courts are split. Most do *not* permit the counterclaim, even as a means of reducing P's recovery. See Wright, pp. 534-35.

Quiz Yourself on
COUNTERCLAIMS

82. P and D were each seriously injured when a car driven by P collided with a car driven by D. P sued D in federal district court on a negligence theory; the case was based on diversity. D submitted a general denial as his answer. The jury found in favor of D. D has now brought a separate federal diversity-based action against P relating to the same accident; D's suit asserts that P's negligence caused the accident. Will D's suit be permitted to go to trial? _____

83. Pedestrian was injured when she was struck by a delivery van driven by Worker. The van was owned by Boss, and was being driven by Worker as part of the job that Worker did for Boss. Pedestrian brought a federal court diversity-based action against Boss alleging that Worker drove negligently and that Boss was liable for that negligence under the doctrine of respondeat superior. Boss impleaded Worker as a third-party defendant under Federal Rule 14(a), on the theory that if Boss was liable to Pedestrian based on respondeat superior, Worker must indemnify Boss. The jury found against Pedestrian and thus in favor of Boss. Worker has now commenced a new federal action, alleging that Boss knowingly gave Worker a defective van to drive, thus preventing Worker from stopping, and contributing to injuries suffered by Worker in the same accident in which Pedestrian was injured. Should Worker's suit against Boss be allowed to go forward? _____

84. In Connecticut, a car driven by Alan collided with a car owned by Bob but driven by Carol. Bob has sued Alan for negligence in Connecticut federal district court; the case is based on diversity. Bob's claim is for $100,000. Alan and Carol are citizens of Massachusetts; Bob is a citizen of Connecticut. The Connecticut long arm allows out-of-state mail service on anyone who is involved in an accident which takes place inside the state. Now, Alan wishes to make a counterclaim (relating to the same accident) against Bob; Alan's claim is such that Carol must be made a co-defendant if it is feasible to do so (see FRCP 19(a)). Alan's claim is for $20,000 against Bob, and would be for another $20,000 against Carol if she is joined.

  (a) May Alan bring a counterclaim against Bob and Carol together? _____

  (b) If Alan does not bring his counterclaim against Bob or Carol, may he bring a later state-court suit against them both? (Ignore jurisdictional problems with this second suit.) _____

85. P has brought a tort action against D, arising out of an automobile accident. The case is pending in federal district court. The case is based on diversity, and P's claim is for $70,000. D now seeks to assert a counterclaim against P; the counterclaim is for $30,000, and alleges that P breached a contract with D entered into before (and unconnected with) the automobile accident.

  (a) Is D's counterclaim compulsory? _____

  (b) May D bring that counterclaim? _____

***

Answers

82. No. Since D's present claim arises out of the "same transaction or occurrence" that was the subject of P's claim in the first suit, D's claim was a ***compulsory*** counterclaim in the first action. That is, D was required to assert that claim as a Rule 13(a) compulsory counterclaim in the first action, or face losing it. Since D did not do so, he will be barred from bringing the claim as a separate suit now (even though the result in the first trial indicates that D is probably correct in asserting that the accident was caused by P's negligence).

83. No. The rule that compulsory counterclaims must be asserted in the initial action or waived applies not only to defendants, but to any other parties. Thus Federal Rule 13(a) does not refer to defendants specifically, but instead to any "pleading" by any "pleader" — the pleader is required to raise any claim against "any opposing party" if that claim arises out of the same transaction or occurrence that is the subject matter of the opposing party's claim. Since Worker's claim against Boss for injuries results from the same transaction or occurrence (the accident with Pedestrian) as Boss's third-party claim against Worker, Worker must assert his claim as a counterclaim against Boss, or lose it. Since he did not so assert it, he will be found to have waived it.

84. (a) Yes. Compulsory counterclaims fall within the ***supplemental jurisdiction*** of the court under 28 U.S.C. §1367. Since Alan's counterclaim arises out of the same transaction or occurrence as Bob's claim, Alan's counterclaim is compulsory and will satisfy the "same case or controversy" requirement of §1367. Since §1367(b), which excludes certain types of claims in diversity actions, does not mention counterclaims, Alan's claim will fall within supplemental jurisdiction, and it will not matter that Carol and Alan, opposing parties, are citizens of the same state. Nor does it matter that Alan's claim totals less than $50,000. (The supplemental jurisdiction statute, where it applies, obviates the need to meet the usual requirements of subject matter jurisdiction, such as complete diversity and amount in controversy.)

  (b) No. Alan's federal-court counterclaim was compulsory, so by not asserting it he lost it. If Alan had not been able to get ***personal*** jurisdiction over Carol, his counterclaim against Bob would not have been compulsory, because the last phrase of the first sentence of Federal Rule 13(a) makes a counterclaim permissive if it "require[s] for its adjudication the presence of third parties of whom the court cannot acquire jurisdiction." But since Carol had minimum contacts with Connecticut, and Connecticut had a long arm authorizing service out-of-state on Carol, jurisdiction was not a problem. The supplemental jurisdiction statute would have taken care of any subject matter jurisdictional problem. Therefore, Alan's claim was an ordinary compulsory counterclaim, even though it needs for just adjudication the presence of a third person not previously a party to the action. Since a state court will normally bar a claim that would have been a compulsory counterclaim in an earlier federal action, Alan will be barred.

85. (a) No. Since the two claims arise out of different transactions or occurrences, the counterclaim is permissive.

(b) No. Permissive counterclaims do not fall within the court's supplemental jurisdiction, because by definition they do not derive from a "common nucleus of operative fact." They must therefore satisfy the requirements of federal subject matter jurisdiction independently of the main claim. Consequently, most courts hold that a permissive counterclaim must independently exceed the amount-in-controversy requirement (i.e., the counterclaim cannot be aggregated with the main claim), which in diversity cases is $50,000.

III. JOINDER OF CLAIMS

A. Joinder of claims generally: Rule 18(a) provides that "a party asserting a claim to relief as an original claim, counterclaim, cross-claim, or third-party claim, may join, either as independent or as alternate claims, as many claims, legal, equitable, or maritime, as the party has against an opposing party."

1. **Rule:** In other words, *once a party has made a claim against some other party*, he may then make *any other claim he wishes against that party*. Wr., 526.

   Example: P sues D, claiming that D intentionally assaulted and battered him. Rule 18(a) allows P to join to this assault and battery claim a claim that D owes P money on a contract entirely unrelated to the alleged tort.

2. **Never required:** Joinder of claims is *never required* by Rule 18(a), but is left at the claimant's option. However, the rules of *res judicata*, particularly the rule against splitting a cause of action, will often as a practical matter induce the claimant to join claims. See *infra*, p. 360.

   Example: P is involved in a car collision with D, and suffers both personal injury and damage to his car. If P were to sue only for the bodily injury, the rule against splitting a cause of action might result in his losing his claim for property damage, whether he wins or loses the bodily injury suit.

3. **Subject matter jurisdiction not affected:** Rule 18(a) *does not affect the requirements of subject matter jurisdiction*, which must be *independently satisfied* by the joined claim. That is, *supplemental* jurisdiction does not apply to a claim joined with another under Rule 18(a).

Example: P sues D. D counterclaims against P, and brings in X as a co-defendant to his counterclaim, allowed by Rule 13(h). D may join to his claim against X any other claim against X that he cares to assert, but there must be diversity between D and X, or a federal question raised between them.

a. **Not usually restrictive:** As a practical matter, however, the subject matter jurisdiction requirements will not usually impede the use of Rule 18(a). Wr., 524.

i. **Diversity:** Diversity is not affected generally by Rule 18(a) joinder of claims. This is because no new parties are added when the Rule is used.

ii. **Amount in controversy:** *Aggregation* of the claims is possible to satisfy the *jurisdictional amount;* aggregation of all claims by a given plaintiff against a given defendant is allowed. See *supra*, p. 108.

iii. **Supplemental jurisdiction:** However, if the initial claim against a particular defendant is itself possible only because of the court's *supplemental jurisdiction*, there may be jurisdictional problems with joinder of other claims. For instance, in the previous example, suppose that D's claim against X is worth less than $50,000, and is allowed only because the counterclaim was compulsory and therefore within the court's supplemental jurisdiction. An additional claim against X, which together with the counterclaim does not aggregate to $50,000, is not joinable under Rule 18(a).

iv. **Federal question claim:** Similarly, if the original claim against a particular defendant was a *federal question* claim, a non-federal claim could not be joined to it under 18(a), unless either diversity exists, or the two claims are closely related so that the doctrine of supplemental jurisdiction (formerly called "pendent" jurisdiction in this context) applies. See *supra*, p. 112.

IV. JOINDER OF PARTIES

A. **Reason for joinder:** If every lawsuit were limited to the trial of one claim by one plaintiff against one defendant, much wasteful, repetitious litigation might ensue. For instance, if several persons share the same claim against one potential defendant, or if a particular person has a claim against several potential defendants, it would be highly inefficient to break up the litigation into several pieces, each consisting of one plaintiff, one defendant, and one claim.

1. **Rules 19 and 20:** Therefore, Rules 19 and 20 provide for the bringing in of multiple plaintiffs or defendants in certain circumstances, in federal actions. Most states have similar joinder provisions.

2. **Two kinds of joinder:** Two kinds of joinder of parties are provided by the Federal Rules: (a) *permissive joinder* (Rule 20), and (b) *compulsory joinder* (Rule 19). Each is considered separately below.

3. **Multiple plaintiffs or defendants:** Each of these two kinds of joinder can apply to *either multiple plaintiffs or multiple defendants*.

B. Permissive joinder: Rule 20 allows plaintiff in certain circumstances: (a) to join other *plaintiffs* with himself, or (b) to make several parties *co-defendants* to his claim.

1. **At plaintiff's option:** If the requirements for Rule 20 joinder are met, it is completely at the option of the *plaintiff* (or plaintiffs) whether to use this device or not. For this reason, Rule 20 joinder is known as *"permissive"* joinder, as distinguished from Rule 19 "compulsory" joinder.

2. **Requirements:** Plaintiffs may join together in an action if they satisfy two tests:

   a. **Single transaction or occurrence:** Their claims for relief must arise from a *single "transaction, occurrence, or series of transactions or occurrences,"* and

   b. **Common questions:** There must be a question of *law or fact common to all plaintiffs* which will arise in the action. See Rule 20(a).

3. **Test:** The test for determining whether all claims arise from a single "transaction or occurrence" is approximately the same as for determining whether a counterclaim is compulsory. (See *supra*, p. 291.) Thus the "logical relation" and "common evidence" tests have been suggested for determining whether all claims in question arise from the same transaction or occurrence, and may therefore be subject to permissive joinder.

4. **Common question must be substantial:** The "common question of law or fact" must be of *substantial importance* to all the claims. The existence of other questions *not shared* by all plaintiffs does *not*, however, bar joinder.

   Example: A car driven by Driver and containing Passenger is hit from the rear by Taxicab. Driver and Passenger can join together as plaintiffs in a suit against Taxicab, even though the damages suffered by the two plaintiffs are not the same, and even though contributory negligence may be an issue with respect to Driver's claim but not as to Passenger's. The "common question of law or fact" is the negligence of Taxicab. Wr., 466-67.

5. **Each plaintiff must be voluntary:** A person can be brought in as co-plaintiff under Rule 20 only if he so *agrees*. A potential plaintiff who does not want to be part of the suit cannot normally be forced to be. Under limited circumstances, however, he can be made an "involuntary plaintiff" under Rule 19(a).

6. **Joinder of defendants:** *Defendants*, as well as plaintiffs, may be joined under Rule 20, if the claims against them satisfy the same two-pronged test as for plaintiff-joinder. Rule 20(a). That is, claims against the co-defendants must: (a) arise from a single "transaction, occurrence, or series of transactions or occurrences," and (b) contain a common question of law or fact.

   a. **At plaintiff's option:** Joinder of multiple defendants is at the option of the plaintiff or plaintiffs.

7. **Judicial discretion:** Once joinder of plaintiffs or defendants has occurred, the court under Rule 20(b) has considerable discretion in arranging the proceedings so as not to cause undue inconvenience or prejudice to any party.

   a. **Separate trials:** For instance, the judge may order *separate trials*. Wr., 467-68.

C. Jurisdiction in permissive joinder cases: Permissive joinder under Rule 20 may raise problems of *personal jurisdiction, diversity,* and *venue.*

1. *In personam* **jurisdiction:** Where joinder of defendants is involved, the requirements of *in personam* jurisdiction must be met with regard to *each defendant individually.* This means that:

   a. **Service:** Each defendant must be *personally served.*

   b. **Contacts:** Each defendant must individually fall within the *in personam* jurisdictional limits of the court (e.g., by having *"minimum contacts"*).

   c. **Long-arm limits:** Since federal courts in diversity suits follow the *long-arm of the state in which they sit*, certain defendants may be out of joinder range even though personal jurisdiction could be constitutionally exercised over them. See *supra*, p. 45.

   Note: The requirements of personal jurisdiction must be met with respect not only to permissive-joinder defendants, but with respect to *any* defendant, no matter under what device he is brought into the action. Thus defendants to *impleader* and *interpleader* actions, and parties brought in to *defend against counterclaims*, must all be subject to the personal jurisdiction of the court.

   Two devices, however, neither of which applies to Rule 20 joinder, are sometimes available to make personal jurisdiction more easily obtained. First, the 100-mile bulge provision of Rule 4(k)(1)(B) makes service easier in certain multi-party cases, particularly impleader cases. See *supra*, p. 41. Secondly, nationwide service of process is allowed by federal statute in certain interpleader cases. In Rule 20 cases, however, the ordinary rules of personal jurisdiction apply.

2. **Subject matter jurisdiction:** In addition to the requirements of personal jurisdiction over defendants outlined above, all parties (whether plaintiffs or defendants) joined under Rule 20 must meet federal *subject matter jurisdiction* requirements. *Supplemental jurisdiction generally does not apply* to Rule 20 joinder. See 28 U.S.C. §1367(b), discussed *supra*, p. 117. Therefore, these subject matter jurisdiction requirements often prove fatal to Rule 20 joinder.

   a. **Complete diversity:** If the action is brought as a diversity action, the diversity must be *complete*, as 28 U.S.C. §1332 has been construed. That is, no state may be represented on both sides of an action.

   Example: In an action where no federal question is present, there are 12 plaintiffs, 11 from Connecticut and one from New York, and 12 defendants, 11 from New Jersey and one from New York. There is no diversity. Thus one of the New Yorkers must be dropped if the action is to proceed in federal court with complete diversity as required.

   b. **Aggregation:** It is not clear whether *multiple plaintiffs* are permitted to *aggregate* their claims to meet the *jurisdictional amount*. It is possible that 28 U.S.C. §1367, codifying supplemental jurisdiction, will apply to allow one or more plaintiffs who do not meet the jurisdictional amount to add their claim to a plaintiff who does. However, the fact that §1367(b) does not explicitly prohibit this, while prohibiting the use of supplemental jurisdiction in the case of Rule 20 joinder of co-*defendants*, may be just a drafting error that will be remedied shortly. Also, if courts do have such jurisdiction in the multiple-plaintiff situation, they may decline to *exercise* that jurisdiction. See *supra*, p. 121.

i. Each defendant must meet: Where the Rule 20 joinder involves *multiple defendants*, it is quite clear that supplemental jurisdiction does *not* apply, so that *each defendant* must have claims against him equal to the jurisdictional amount. See 28 U.S.C. § 1367(b).

Example: P1 has a diversity claim for $60,000 against D1, and a diversity claim for $6,000 against D2. P2 has a related diversity claim for $6,000 against D1, and $60,000 against D2. It is not clear that P1's claim against D2 and P2's claim against D1 can be part of the suit, although P1's claim against D1 and P2's claim against D2 may be joined together under Rule 20 (assuming they meet the "transaction or occurrence" and "common question" requirements). P1's claim against D2 may be ruled out because it is worth less than $50,000 — supplemental jurisdiction is clearly not permitted in the case of a single plaintiff's claims against multiple defendants, and might not be permitted in the case of multiple plaintiffs' claims against a single defendant (unless there is a common and undivided right being sued on by all plaintiffs — see *supra*, p. 108.) P2's claim against D1 may fall for the same reason.

3. Venue: In addition to the requirements of personal and subject matter jurisdiction, Rule 20 joinder must satisfy applicable *venue* requirements. In a case in which there are co-defendants who reside in different states, the easiest way to satisfy the venue requirements will be by bringing suit in a district in which a substantial part of the *events* giving rise to the claim occurred. (Such "place of events" venue is available in both diversity and federal question cases.) See 28 U.S.C. §1391(a) and (b), discussed *supra*, p. 83.

D. Compulsory joinder (Rule 19): The joinder discussed above is completely at the option of the plaintiff or plaintiffs. For this reason, it is called "permissive" joinder. In some circumstances, however, it would be uneconomical or unfair to litigate a claim between two parties without at the same time bringing in other claims and parties. Therefore, Rule 19(a) sets forth certain situations in which additional parties *must* be joined, if the requirements of jurisdiction are met. This Rule 19 joinder is said to be *"compulsory."*

1. Two categories: Rule 19(b) goes further, and sets forth situations in which, if joinder is not possible for jurisdictional reasons, the entire action must be dropped.

a. "Necessary" parties: Parties whose joinder, if possible, is required by Rule 19(a), are called *"necessary"* parties.

b. "Indispensable" parties: Parties who are so vital that if their joinder is impossible, the whole action must be dropped, are called *"indispensable" parties.* See Rule 19(b).

2. Distinguishing "necessary" from "indispensable": How does the court determine, then, whether a party is merely "necessary" (to be joined if possible), or truly "indispensable" (so that the whole action must be dropped if joinder is not possible)? The standard for distinguishing between these two classes is laid out in Rule 19.

a. "Necessary": Rule 19 first describes those parties who must be joined if (1) service can be validly made on them, and (2) their joinder would not destroy diversity. These are *"necessary"* parties. (Rule 19 does not actually use that term.) To be a "necessary" party, a person must meet one of the following two tests:

i. **Incomplete relief:** "in the person's absence complete relief cannot be accorded among those already parties." (19(a)(1)) *or*

ii. **Impaired interest:** a judgment in the person's absence will either (1) as a practical matter impair an interest the person has, or (2) impose on some of the existing parties "double, multiple, or otherwise inconsistent obligations." (19(a)(2))

b. **"Indispensable":** Assuming that the absentee meets the test of (i) or (ii) above, the court then determines whether that absentee is in fact *"indispensable"* — so vital that the action should be dropped if joinder is not possible — by considering the following additional factors, all laid out in Rule 19(b):

i. **Prejudice:** the extent of *prejudice* to the absentee, or to those already parties;

ii. **Framing of judgment:** the possibility of *framing the judgment* so as to mitigate *such* prejudice;

iii. **Adequacy of remedy:** the adequacy of the *remedy* that can be granted in his *absence*;

iv. **Result of dismissal:** whether the *plaintiff* will have an *adequate remedy* if the action is *dismissed*.

See Rule 19(b).

3. **Jurisdictional obstacles:** In determining whether joinder is jurisdictionally possible, and thus whether it is 19(a) or 19(b) which applies, personal jurisdiction, subject matter jurisdiction, and venue, must all be examined.

a. **Variety of difficulties:** There are thus several different reasons why the joinder of a particular party might be impossible. In the case of a potential defendant, these reasons might include:

i. his presence would *destroy diversity*, since he is a citizen of the same state as one plaintiff, and there is no federal question;

ii. the claim against him does not meet the *amount in controversy* requirement; or

iii. he is beyond the personal jurisdiction of the court, because the *local long-arm* would not reach him (since the local long-arm is what is relied on in diversity suits — see *supra*, pp. 48-49.)

b. **Supplemental jurisdiction:** If a person who is sought to be joined as a defendant under Rule 19(a) is not diverse with all plaintiffs, or if the claim against her does not meet the amount in controversy requirement, the doctrine of *supplemental jurisdiction* does *not* apply to overcome these defects. Therefore, joinder will not be allowed in this situation.

i. **Clarified by 1990 statute:** This result became clear in 1990, when Congress enacted 28 U.S.C. §1367. That section creates "supplemental" jurisdiction (combining the prior judge-made concepts of "ancillary" and "pendent" jurisdiction).

§1367 further provides, in subsection (b), that in diversity cases there will not be supplemental jurisdiction "over claims by plaintiffs against persons made parties under Rule ... 19 ..., or over claims by persons proposed to be joined as plaintiffs under Rule 19. ..."

   ii. Significance: So no matter how badly an absent prospective defendant is needed for carrying out the litigation in a sensible manner, if that defendant is not diverse with all plaintiffs (or if the claim against that defendant does not meet the jurisdictional amount), Rule 19(a) joinder may not occur.

4. *Provident Tradesmen's*: *Provident Tradesmen's Bank and Trust Co. v. Patterson*, 390 U.S. 102 (1968), illustrates the kind of fact pattern in which the absentee is at least "necessary," and perhaps "indispensable."

   a. Facts: The facts of *Provident* were as follows:

      i. The litigation arose from a traffic accident in which a car belonging to Dutcher and driven by Cionci collided with a truck. Cionci and one of his passengers, Lynch, were killed.

      ii. Provident Bank, the administrator of the estate of Lynch, the dead passenger, sued Cionci, the driver. The suit was settled for $50,000 which was never paid, due to the insolvency of Cionci's estate.

      iii. Dutcher, the owner, had an insurance policy that had a limit of $100,000 per accident. Provident sued for a declaratory judgment to the effect that Dutcher had given Cionci permission to use the car, and that therefore the insurance policy covered the accident and the $50,000 judgment.

      iv. The defendants in Provident's declaratory judgment suit were Cionci's estate, and Dutcher's insurance company. Dutcher was not joined as a defendant, since his presence would have destroyed diversity.

      v. Lower court holding: Judgment was given for Provident, and Dutcher's insurers appealed. Dutcher's indispensability as a defendant was never raised at trial or on appeal, but the Court of Appeals, on its own initiative, held that Dutcher was an ***indispensable party*** to the action, and that the judgment must be thrown out because of his absence.

   b. Absence not fatal: The Supreme Court held that under Rule 19(b), Dutcher's absence was not fatal, particularly since the trial had already been carried out.

      i. Absence possibly prejudicial: The Court acknowledged that Dutcher's absence might have been prejudicial to him, a possible reason for dismissal listed in 19(b). The possible prejudice was due to the fact that other suits arising from the same accident might be brought against Dutcher by other injured parties. Dutcher therefore had an interest in having it held that he had not given Cionci permission, and that the insurance policy did not cover the accident. That way, the $100,000 from the policy would all be available, in case future suits should decide the issue of permission against Dutcher, and grant judgments against him as the lender of the car.

ii. But prejudice unlikely: But the Court found that this possibility of future judgments was very unlikely, since the only suits on this accident which were not barred by the statute of limitations were two suits which had lain dormant in state court for ten years, and which seemed unlikely to be resumed. Also, Dutcher might be able to relitigate in these suits the permission issue — since he was not a party to the first suit, he could argue that he was not bound by the finding that permission had been given. The Court noted the possibility that Dutcher might be held to have *waived the right to intervene as of right* under Rule 24(a)(2). But the Court declined to decide whether the failure to intervene did in fact constitute such a waiver.

iii. Judgment not thrown out: All things considered, the Court concluded, the possibility of prejudice to Dutcher was not sufficiently great that the judgment should be *thrown out*, even though that possibility might have been enough to result in dismissal at the beginning of the suit. The case was remanded to the Court of Appeals, with orders that the judgment be adjusted to protect Dutcher's interests.

iv. Remand: On remand, the Third Circuit (411 F.2d 88, 1969) directed the trial court to amend its judgment so as to protect Dutcher's interests, by enjoining any payment out of the insurance fund until Dutcher had had the opportunity to litigate his assertion that the fund did not cover Cionci. Presumably this suit would be against Cionci for declaratory judgment.

5. *Haas v. Jefferson Bank:* A good illustration of an absentee who is truly "indispensable," and in whose absence the action must be dismissed, came in *Haas v. Jefferson National Bank of Miami Beach*, 442 F.2d 394 (5th Cir. 1971). The dispute centered on the ownership of certain bank stock.

a. Facts: Plaintiff alleged that he and Glueck, the unjoined party, had arranged to buy the stock jointly, but with Glueck to be the nominal owner.

b. Joinder impossible: In a suit against the bank to obtain the stock certificates representing his half interest, plaintiff failed to join Glueck as a defendant, because to do so would destroy diversity. The trial judge found that Glueck was an indispensable party, and therefore dismissed plaintiff's suit. Plaintiff then appealed.

c. Joinder if feasible: The appeals court first decided that Glueck was definitely a person who, under 19(a), must be *joined if feasible:*

i. Double obligation: His absence would expose the bank to the risk of double obligation (19(a)(2)(ii)), since a judgment that plaintiff owned the stock would not bind Glueck, who could later sue the bank for the whole amount.

ii. Interest affected: Also, a judgment ordering the issue of the stock to the plaintiff might adversely affect Glueck's interest, the court said. (This might be impossible as a legal matter, since Glueck would not be bound by anything that happened in his absence. But as a practical matter, if the bank obeyed a court order to give the stock to the plaintiff, Glueck would have to bring a new lawsuit to protect his interests.)

d. Indispensable: The appeals court then determined that Glueck's presence was so important that the trial court was right to have *dismissed* the action rather than proceed in his absence.

   i. Prejudice: The reasons given for finding him a party to be joined if feasible also applied to the first criterion for *dismissal* in 19(b) — the "extent [to which] a judgment rendered in the person's absence might be prejudicial to him or those already parties."

   ii. No adjustment of decree possible: Also, since title to the stock was what was really at issue, the court saw no way of adjusting the decree to protect either the bank or Glueck.

   iii. Remedy after dismissal: Furthermore, plaintiff still had another remedy if the suit was dismissed — he could sue Glueck in state court for a declaratory judgment as to the title to the stock, and then if he was successful, he could sue the bank in a new federal action. In the new federal action, there would be no possibility of *double obligation* for the bank, since Glueck would then be foreclosed by the state proceedings from making any claim against the bank, by the doctrine of *collateral estoppel*. Similarly, there would be no way in which Glueck's interest could be jeopardized by the proceedings — he would already have been found not to have title to the stock in question.

e. Factors weighed: Weighing all the factors listed in 19(b), the appeals court therefore determined that *dismissal* because of Glueck's absence was proper.

6. State-court suits: So far, we have considered the doctrine of necessary and indispensable parties only in the context of federal suits. But the concept of necessary/indispensable parties also exists in many *state* courts. For an illustration of a state-court suit that ultimately was not permitted to go forward because the state court did not have jurisdiction over what it considered to be an indispensable party, recall *Hanson v. Denckla*, discussed *supra*, p. 22. The Supreme Court in *Hanson* noted, "As we understand [Florida] law, the trustee is an indispensable party over whom the court must acquire jurisdiction before it is empowered to enter judgment in a proceeding affecting the validity of a trust."

E. Broadening of compulsory joinder: Recall that under Rule 19(a)(2), a person will be a "necessary" party (and must therefore be joined if possible) if he "claims an interest relating to the subject of the action," and he is so situated that if the suit goes ahead without him this may "(i) as a practical matter impair or impede [his] ability to protect that interest or (ii) leave any of the persons already parties subject to a substantial risk of incurring double, multiple, or otherwise inconsistent obligations. ...." The Supreme Court has applied this definition in an affirmative action context, in a way that suggests that third parties will now *more frequently be found to be "necessary"* than formerly.

1. *Martin* case: In *Martin v. Wilks*, 490 U.S. 755 (1989), white firefighters sued the city of Birmingham, Alabama, claiming that the city was illegally discriminating against them in favor of black firefighters. The city defended on the grounds that any special treatment it was giving to the black firefighters was required by an earlier settlement that the city and the black firefighters had made to resolve a discrimination suit that the black firefighters had brought.

a. **Holding:** The Supreme Court (by a 5-4 vote) held that the city and the black fire-fighters ***should have joined all white firefighters as Rule 19 necessary parties*** during the original suit. The majority's theory was that the result of the suit between the blacks and the city was likely to "as a practical matter impair or impede [the whites'] ability to protect [their] interest" with respect to job conditions. Since the city did not join the whites, the whites could now argue that the settlement should not be allowed to have any substantial impact on them, and the whites' discrimination claims must be considered from scratch.

b. **Significance:** *Martin* seems to mean that any time a racial or other group argues that an employer is discriminating against it, the employer (and/or the plaintiffs) should join all the workers who are ***not*** part of the plaintiffs' racial or other group as Rule 19 "necessary" parties. If the employer and the plaintiffs do not do this, then these third-party workers may be able to undermine any settlement or court ruling — even many years after the original suit is finished — by claiming that the ruling or settlement unfairly impacts on their own rights.

Quiz Yourself on
JOINDER OF CLAIMS AND JOINDER OF PARTIES

86. P brought, in federal court, an action against D for violation of P's federally-registered copyrights. (The suit alleged that D plagiarized language in a novel written by P.) Before D's time to answer ran, P amended his suit to add a second claim, that D libelled P by calling P a "dishonest writer." The alleged libel has nothing to do with the alleged copyright violation. Putting aside questions of personal and subject matter jurisdiction, is P entitled, procedurally, to add this second claim to his action? _____

87. Same basic fact pattern as prior question. Now, however, assume that P and D are citizens of the same state. Assume also that both the copyright claim and the libel claim are for more than $50,000. May the federal court hear the libel claim? _____

88. P and D were both injured in a car accident, when the cars driven by each collided. P brought a federal court diversity action against D for negligence, seeking $100,000 of damages. D brought a counterclaim against P for negligence (relating to the same accident) in that same action; D joined to that counterclaim a second person, X (the owner of the car driven by P). D claimed that P and X each owed $30,000 on D's counterclaim. D then joined a second claim against X, for breach of contract, in an unrelated transaction; this claim was for $15,000. P is a citizen of Alabama, D is a citizen of Georgia, and X is a citizen of Florida.

    (a) May the court hear D's claim against X for damages from the car accident? _____

    (b) May the court hear D's claim against X for breach of contract? _____

89. P, a motion picture company, is the owner of the "Richie Rat" cartoon character. Because of Richie Rat's enormous popularity, a number of small entrepreneurs produce teeshirts, sweatshirts, dolls, and other objects with the Richie Rat character on them, without authorization from P. P has brought a federal district court action against D1 and D2, alleging federal copyright violation. D1 and D2 have no connection with each other or with P, except that P claims that D1 has put Richie Rat on a series of teeshirts, and that D2 has put the character on a series of dolls, both without authorization. Is P justified in joining D1 and

D2 in a single action? _____

90. P1 and P2 were both passengers in a twin-engine aircraft owned and operated by D1 (a commuter airline) and manufactured by D2. Both P1 and P2 were seriously injured when the plane caught fire while landing. P1 and P2 are both citizens of New York. D1 is incorporated in Delware and has its principal place of business in New York. D2 is both incorporated in, and has its principal place of business in, Kansas. P1 and P2 have brought a single federal court diversity action, in which D1 is charged with negligent inspection and operation, and D2 is charged with strict products liability. P1 and P2 each meet the amount in controversy requirement. Is the joinder of all parties proper? _____

91. X, shortly before dying, signed a contract in which he promised to leave P $100,000 in his will, in consideration for services performed for him by P. X then died, and his will did not mention P. P has brought a federal court diversity action against D1 (X's estate), seeking to enforce this contract to make a will. P's suit does not list as defendants D2 and D3 (X's children, who are his beneficiaries under the will). Neither P nor D1 seems troubled by the absence from the suit of D2 and D3. Assuming that D2 and D3 can be subjected to the personal jurisdiction of the federal court, and that they are not citizens of the same state as P, what if any action should the federal judge hearing the suit take? _____

92. X, a wealthy citizen of New York, in 1980 gave possession of a valuable Van Gogh painting to P, a museum located in Florida. X assured P that she wanted P to have the painting forever, and that this would be confirmed in X's will. In 1990, X died. X's will left all of X's property (including, specifically, the Van Gogh) to Y, X's daughter, who is a citizen of Florida. (Y has no contacts with New York.) P has brought a diversity suit against D (X's estate) in New York federal district court, seeking a judgment that the 1980 transfer of possession of the Van Gogh to P was a completed gift, and that the painting now belongs to P. (X's estate is deemed a citizen of New York.) P has not joined Y as a co-defendant, because Y's presence would destroy diversity of citizenship and because the court could not get personal jurisdiction over Y. Y is afraid that if the action proceeds without her, and P wins, P may sell the painting, lend it to a museum outside the U.S., or otherwise put the painting beyond Y's reach. Assuming that there is no way for Y to become part of the pending action, should the New York federal district court dismiss the action on account of Y's absence? _____

93. Same facts as the prior question. Now, however, assume that Y, because of regular business dealings with New York, has such minimum contacts with the state of New York as to make it constitutional for Y to be subjected to the personal jurisdiction of the New York courts (and, by extension, to the personal jurisdiction of the New York federal district court sitting in diversity). Also, the New York long-arm would reach Y in a New York state-court action. Should the New York federal court order Y to be joined, order the action to go on without Y, or dismiss the action because Y cannot be joined? _____

Answers

86. **Yes.** Federal Rule 18(a) provides, "A party asserting a claim to relief … may join, either as independent or as alternate claims, as many claims, legal, equitable, or maritime, as the party has against an opposing party." Since P and D are opposing parties based on P's initial copyright claim, P has the right to add whatever claims against D he wishes, even if these other claims have nothing to do with the original copyright claim.

87. **Probably not.** Since P and D are citizens of the same state, there is no diversity jurisdiction. This is not a problem for the copyright claim, since that is founded upon federal law. But the libel claim is based upon state law. If the libel claim were closely related to the copyright claim (e.g., both related to the same trans-

action or occurrence), the libel claim could be heard together with the copyright claim under the doctrine of supplemental (formerly pendent) jurisdiction. The supplemental jurisdiction statute, 28 U.S.C. §1367, allows parties to join claims that are so related as to form part of the "same case or controversy" in the same suit. But since the two claims have nothing to do with each other, supplemental jurisdiction does not apply here. Therefore, there is no federal subject matter jurisdiction over the libel claim, and it cannot be heard by the federal court.

88. (a) Yes. D's claim against X for the car accident is a compulsory counterclaim. (That is, D's claim against P is a garden-variety compulsory counterclaim, and X is an additional party to that counterclaim joined pursuant to Rule 13(h).) Compulsory counterclaims, and the joinder of additional parties to compulsory counterclaims, fall within the court's supplemental jurisdiction under 28 U.S.C. §1367 because they concern a "common nucleus of operative fact." Consequently, it does not matter that D's claim against X fails by itself to meet the amount in controversy requirement; supplemental jurisdiction obviates the need for the usual diversity jurisdiction in this case. (In fact, it wouldn't even matter that D and X were citizens of the same state.)

(b) No. This second claim by D against X is allowed procedurally only because of Rule 18(a)'s joinder of claims provision (which allows any party, not just the plaintiff, to join additional claims against an opposing party who is already in the action). But Rule 18(a) joinder of claims does not fall within the court's supplemental jurisdiction unless the claims are so related as to form part of the same case or controversy (the "common nucleus of operative fact" standard). We are told that the breach of contract claim is based on an unrelated transaction. Since it does not fall under supplemental jurisdiction, the unrelated claim must independently meet federal subject matter jurisdictional requirements. Because D's second claim against X is not for more than $50,000, that second claim cannot be heard.

89. No, probably. The circumstances under which a plaintiff may join two or more defendants are governed by Federal Rule 20(a)'s "permissive joinder" provision: "All persons … may be joined in one action as defendants if there is asserted against them jointly, severally, or in the alternative, any right to relief in respect of or arising out of the *same transaction*, occurrence, or series of transactions or occurrences and if any question of law or fact common to all defendants will arise in the action."

Here, there is a good chance that P could meet the second of these tests (common question of law or fact), since identical questions as to what constitutes federal copyright infringement, or whether Richie Rat is copyrightable, are likely to be involved in the case against D1 and D2. But the first test — that all claims involve the "same transaction, occurrence, or series of transactions or occurrences …" — probably is not satisfied. It is true that the transactions are roughly similar, but they are not the *same*. Just as a plaintiff probably cannot join in one federal action all defendants who owe him money where each defendant is liable under a separate contract, so it is probably the case that P cannot join independent copyright violators.

90. No. In general, multiple plaintiffs may join together, and may join multiple defendants, provided that (1) the claims arise out of the "same transaction, occurrence, or series of transactions or occurrences" and (2) there is at least one question of law or fact in common. FRCP 20. Since all claims involve a single occurrence (the accident) and a single question of law or fact (who caused that accident?), this two-part test is easily satisfied.

However, the *usual requirements of subject matter matter jurisdiction* (as well as personal jurisdiction) *apply to joinder of parties.* Since D1 has its principal place of business in New York, it is deemed to be a citizen of New York (as well as of Delaware, its state of incorporation.) This means that there is not the required complete diversity of citizenship (i.e., it is not the case that no plaintiff is a citizen of the same state as any defendant.) Since the action involves no federal question, and there is no diversity, the action could go forward as pleaded only if supplemental jurisdiction somehow eliminated the requirement of complete diversity. But the supplemental jurisdiction statute, 28 U.S.C. §1367, states in subsection (b) that in diversity actions the district courts shall ***not*** have supplemental jurisdiction over claims by plaintiffs (like P1 and P2) against persons made parties under Rule 20 (such as D1) if the result would be inconsistent with the requirements of diversity. Because §1367 does not apply in this case, each claim and each party must independently meet federal subject matter jurisdictional requirements. Consequently, D1 will have to be dropped from the action (though the action may proceed as a suit by P1 and P2 against D2).

91. Order that D2 and D3 be joined as defendants. Federal Rule 19(a) provides that if any of the three criteria stated there are satisfied by a person who not currently a party to the action, that person must be joined if feasible. One of these criteria is that the person "claims an interest relating to the subject of the action and is so situated that the disposition of the action in the person's absence may ... as a practical matter impair or impede the person's ability to protect that interest. ..." If D2 is not made a party to the action, and P prevails against the estate, then the estate will pay out the $100,000 to P immediately. In a strictly legal sense, D2's legal rights cannot be affected by a suit to which D2 is not a party — D2 is free to sue P and/or D1, and to re-litigate the issue of whether the contract to make a will was enforceable. But as a ***practical*** matter, D2's interest will be impaired — D1 will already have laid out the money to P, and it will be harder for D2 to get this money back (since the estate will no longer have the money and P may spend it immediately) than if D2 were a party to the original P-D1 suit. The same analysis is true of D3. Therefore, even though neither P nor D1 moves to have D2 and D3 joined to the action, the court should on its own order that they be joined since joinder is (by the hypothesized facts) available.

92. Yes, probably. Y is clearly a person who should be joined if feasible (Federal Rule 19(a)), but the facts make it clear that it is not "feasible" to join Y. Therefore, we have to look at Rule 19(b) to determine whether Y's presence is so indispensable that it is better to dismiss the action entirely than to proceed in Y's absence. Rule 19(b) lists four factors to be considered by the court on this issue of indispensability. One of these factors is "to what extent a judgment rendered in the person's absence might be prejudicial to the person or those already parties." On this factor, Y's claim to have the action dismissed is very strong — a judgment entered in P's favor (especially since P already has possession) might make it very difficult indeed for Y to ever get her own day in court, since P might sell the property, lend it abroad, or otherwise effectively put it outside the court's jurisdiction.

Another factor also cuts in Y's favor — "whether the plaintiff will have an adequate remedy if the action is dismissed for non-joinder." Since P and Y are both Florida residents, and D (the estate) owns property currently located in Florida, it is almost certain that the Florida courts would have jurisdiction over an action by P against D and Y jointly; therefore, P would have an adequate remedy if the federal judge dismissed for non-joinder.

Cutting the other way is still another factor listed in Rule 19(b): "the extent to which, by protective provisions in the judgment, by the shaping of relief, or other measures, the prejudice can be lessened or avoided. ..." That is, the federal court could find in favor of P, but could simultaneously instruct P to hold the painting without disposing of it for, say, one year to permit Y to bring a separate action. However, this method only avoids prejudice by allowing a complete re-litigation of the merits, a very wasteful approach.

So putting it all together, the court will probably conclude that it is better to dismiss the action (and let P bring a Florida state court action or D bring a federal statutory interpleader action joining both P and Y) than to let the action proceed in Y's absence. See *Haas v. Jefferson National Bank of Miami Beach*, 442 F.2d 394 (5th Cir. 1971), finding the absentee to be an indispensable party, on analogous facts.

93. **Dismiss the action because Y cannot be joined.** Y's minimum contacts with New York take care of the problem of personal jurisdiction over her. But the problem of lack of diversity persists. Before 1991, there was some chance that the federal court might have applied ancillary jurisdiction to this situation (which would have the effect that complete diversity as between Y and P would not be needed). But the new supplemental jurisdiction statute, 28 U.S.C. §1367, would *definitely not* allow jurisdiction in this case, thus preserving the policy established in *Owen Equipment v. Kroger*, 437 U.S. 365 (1978). *Kroger* only granted supplemental-type jurisdiction to parties in a *defensive* posture. Similarly, §1367(b) specifically excludes claims by plaintiffs against persons joined under Rule 19 if the result would destroy diversity. All Rule 19 parties, whether indispensable or not, must therefore each meet the usual subject matter jurisdiction requirements.

V. CLASS ACTIONS

A. Background

1. **Definition:** The class action is a procedure whereby a single person or small group of co-parties may *represent* a larger group, or "*class*," of persons sharing a *common interest*. It may be used where joinder of all the potential co-parties is not feasible, either because the class is simply too *large* (numbering possibly in the millions) or because of insuperable difficulties of personal jurisdiction, venue, or diversity.

   a. **Jurisdiction:** In the class action, *only the representative(s)* must satisfy the requirements of personal jurisdiction, subject matter jurisdiction, and venue. As to jurisdictional amount, see *infra*, p. 318.

2. **Bill of Peace:** The English ancestor of the class action was the "bill of peace," an equitable procedure whereby a large number of potential legal actions involving common questions of law or fact could be settled.

3. **Due process:** One factor tending to limit the use of the class action is the necessity of insuring *due process* to the "represented" members. If a class action is to be of any use in curtailing massive litigation, its results must be *binding on the absent members*; therefore steps have to be taken so that these absentees are not deprived of their day in court. See *infra*, pp. 316-318, for guarantees found in the present Federal Rule for class actions.

4. **Federal and state:** The class action is available in both the federal courts and in most state courts. This discussion focuses on the federal class action, the requirements for which are set out in Federal Rule 23.

5. **Defendant class:** In federal practice, as well as in states which permit class actions, the class may be either plaintiffs or defendants. The vast majority of the time, the class will be composed of plaintiffs. However, defendant class suits, in which the class is designated by the plaintiff, have been brought.

Example: A patentee alleges that numerous persons have infringed his patent. He brings suit against the class of all persons alleged to have committed acts of infringement, and he names only a few of these class members to be "representatives" of the class, for purposes of defending the suit. If he can persuade the court that these representatives will do an adequate job of presenting a defense applicable to the other, unnamed, infringers, and meets all the other requirements of Rule 23, the court may allow the suit to proceed as a class action against the defendant class. See *Dale Electronics v. R.C.L. Electronics*, 53 F.R.D. 531 (D.N.H. 1971).

B. **Rule 23 generally:** The Federal Rules as originally promulgated in 1938 contained a provision for class actions, designated as Rule 23. This Rule was, however, found to be very confusing in its application, and in 1966 was extensively revised.

1. **Present Rule 23:** The present Rule 23(a), as amended in 1966, states four *prerequisites* which must be met before there is any possibility of a class action:

   a. **Size:** The class must be *so large* that joinder of all the members is *not feasible;*

   b. **Common questions:** There must be *"questions of law or fact common to the class";*

   c. **Typical claims:** The claims or defenses of the representatives must be *"typical"* of those of the class;

   d. **Representation:** The representatives must *"fairly and adequately represent the interests of the class."*

2. **Three categories:** In addition, once these prerequisites are met, a class action will still not be allowed unless the action fits into one of three categories. These categories are represented by 23(b)(1), 23(b)(2), and 23(b)(3), each of which is treated in a separate section beginning with (D) below.

C. **Rule 23(a)'s prerequisites for class actions**

1. **Size:** No consensus has emerged with respect to how *large* the class must be in order to be "so numerous that joinder of all members is impracticable." Rule 23(a)(1). A class of only 25 members has been held large enough, and one of 350 held not large enough. Wr., 473.

   a. **Geographical dispersion:** The *geographical dispersion* of the class members has been taken into account as well as their precise number. See *Dale Electronics v. R.C.L. Electronics*, 53 F.R.D 531 (D.N.H. 1971).

2. **"Common questions" and "typical claims":** The requirements that there be "questions of law or fact common to the class" (23(a)(2)) and that the claims and defenses of the representatives be "typical" of those of the class (23(a)(3)) have given little difficulty.

   a. **Little practical effect:** Wright suggests that the "common question" test will always be met if the case fits within one of the categories of 23(b), which it must in order to proceed. Wr., 473, fn. 14. He also argues that the requirement that the representatives' claims be "typical" is "only a further particularization of the requirement that the named representatives will adequately represent the entire class." *Id.*

b. Some bite: Nonetheless, the "common questions" and "typical claims" requirements do have some bite. This was illustrated by a Supreme Court case, *General Telephone Co. v. Falcon*, 457 U.S. 147 (1982), an employment discrimination case where the plaintiff sought to have the case certified as a 23(b)(2)-type class action (for cases in which injunctive or declaratory relief is the principal object of the suit; see *infra*, p. 314.)

    i. Facts: P claimed that D had violated the principal federal fair employment statute (Title VII of the 1964 Civil Rights Act) by refusing to promote him on the grounds of his Mexican-American ancestry. P sought to have the case certified as a class action in which the class would consist of all Mexican-Americans against whom D had discriminated by refusing to hire them, or by refusing to promote them.

    ii. Certification reversed: But the Supreme Court held that P had not made a sufficient showing to entitle him to certification. Whereas the Court of Appeals had held that P could properly represent a class defined as all persons discriminated against on account of national origin by one defendant at one place of operations, the Supreme Court held that such a broad certification *violated* the requirements of "common questions of law or fact" and "typical claims." Here, for instance, P had not shown that the claims of those who were not hired had anything significant in common with the claims of those who were hired, but denied promotion. (The Court did not say that no such showing could be made, merely that it had not been. It indicated, for instance, that a showing that D had applied to both groups a biased testing procedure, or an "entirely subjective decision making process," would have sufficed to meet the "commonality" and "typicality" requirements. But P had merely made a generalized claim of racial discrimination.)

3. Fair representation: The requirement that the representatives *"fairly and adequately protect the interests of the class"* has often been seized upon by the defendant in a plaintiff class action to show why the class action should not be allowed. The representatives must not have any *conflict of interest* with the absent class members, and they must furnish *competent legal counsel* to fight the suit. "The quality of the representation is more important than numbers, and ... even a single representative of the class may be enough." Wr., 475.

4. *Hansberry v. Lee:* The first important interpretation of "fair representation" was in *Hansberry v. Lee*, 311 U.S. 32 (1940). In that case, a *restrictive covenant* among a neighborhood's landowners was sued on for enforcement. By the terms of the agreement, which was to take force when the owners of 95% of the neighborhood's property had signed it, none of the land was to be sold to Negroes.

a. Previous action: In an earlier action, four defendants attempting to sell to a Negro were sued in the name of the rest of the landowners. It was stipulated by the parties that 95% of the landowners had signed the agreement, and that it therefore took effect. Since at that time, such agreements were not regarded as illegal or unconstitutional, an injunction was issued against the sale.

b. ***Hansberry claim:*** In *Hansberry*, another defendant was sued for attempting to sell a lot to a Negro. He alleged that in fact only 55% of the owners had signed the agreement, and that therefore the covenant had not taken effect.

c. **State court finding of estoppel:** The Illinois courts held that defendant, as a member of the class of landowners, had been vicariously a plaintiff in the prior action. He was therefore prevented by ***collateral estoppel*** from claiming that fewer than 95% of the owners had signed, since this issue had been disposed of by stipulation in the first action. The Illinois court also found that this stipulation had not been fraudulent.

d. **Supreme Court finds no estoppel:** The U.S. Supreme Court reversed, holding that the defendant in *Hansberry* was ***not bound*** by the prior determination that 95% had signed. He was ***not a member of the same class as the plaintiffs in the first action***, even though he and they were both land-owners.

    i. **Opposition of interests:** This was because his interests were fundamentally opposed to those of the class of plaintiffs in the first suit — they sought to have the agreement enforced; he sought to resist enforcement. "Because of the dual and potentially conflicting interests of those who are putative parties to the agreement in compelling or resisting its performance, it is impossible to say, solely because they are parties to it, that any two of them are of the same class."

    ii. **Due process:** Therefore, to bind the defendant by the prior finding would be to deny him due process of law, in violation of the 14th Amendment. Due process requires that for a party to be found a member of the class, and therefore bound by a judgment respecting that class, ***his interests must be adequately protected by members of that class who are actual parties*** to the action leading to the judgment.

    Note 1: The Supreme Court appears to have had fears that the first lawsuit, in which it was falsely stipulated that 95% of the owners had signed the agreement, was brought in ***collusion*** between the two sides, for the sole purpose of preventing all the other owners from violating the agreement in the future. Although the Court never explicitly stated this, Wright refers to the earlier suit as "collusive." Wr., 474.

    Note 2: *Hansberry* was not a federal suit, and thus did not involve Rule 23. It is, however, illustrative of the constitutional due process requirement that the representatives in a class action adequately represent the class members. If the plaintiffs suing to have the covenant enforced in the first *Hansberry* suit sought to have all neighborhood landowners declared members of a Rule 23 class action, the request would almost certainly be denied. The denial could be based either on the ground that the representatives, since they sought enforcement, did not adequately represent those absentees who did not want enforcement, or on the grounds that the representatives' claims were not "typical" of those of the class as a whole. Rule 23(a)(3), 23(a)(4).

5. **Time when adequate representation measured:** The adequacy of representation is measured at two different times. First, prior to certifying the action as a class action, the judge must believe that the named plaintiff will furnish an adequate representation of the class members. Secondly, once the suit is over, if the defendant argues that a non-named plaintiff is bound by the result, the court in the new action by the non-named plaintiff will evaluate whether the representation was *in fact* adequate in the first suit. If not, the non-named plaintiff will not be bound.

a. *Gonzales* **case:** For example, in *Gonzales v. Cassidy*, 474 F.2d 67 (5th Cir. 1973), a class action was brought on behalf of all Texas uninsured motorists whose licenses had been suspended, pursuant to statute, when they were involved in accidents and were unable to furnish security for the damages allegedly caused to others. The court ruled in that action that the statute was unconstitutional, but gave retroactive effect to its decision only as to the named plaintiff; as to all other persons, the decision prevented only those suspensions occurring after the decision.

    i. **Second suit:** A new suit was then begun by a non-named (or "absent") plaintiff in the first suit, Gonzales, whose suspension had occurred prior to the first decision, and who was therefore denied relief. The defendant (Chairman of the Texas Motor Vehicles Dept.) argued that Gonzales was bound by the prospective-only decision in the first suit. Gonzales contended, however, that the named plaintiff in the first suit had not appealed from the prospective-only aspect of the first decision (he had no incentive to do so, since it was made retroactive as to him), and that he had therefore failed to give fair and adequate representation.

    ii. **Court agrees:** The Court of Appeals agreed with Gonzales that the named plaintiff's failure to appeal the non-retroactivity "rendered his representation [of plaintiff and others similarly situated] inadequate."

    iii. **No duty to intervene:** The court also rejected the defendant's contention that since Gonzales knew about the non-retroactivity decision as soon as it was handed down, he had an obligation to *intervene*, and to appeal on behalf of the class. The court stated that "The purpose of Rule 23 would be subverted by requiring a class member who learns of a pending suit involving a class of which he is a part to monitor that litigation to make certain that his interests are being protected."

    iv. **Not bound:** Therefore, Gonzales, and others whose suspension occurred before the first decision, were not bound by that decision, and could bring their own suit.

D. **23(b)(1) actions:** In addition to the prerequisites of Rule 23(a), a class action will not be permitted unless the case fits into one of the three categories of Rule 23(b). The first of these categories, *23(b)(1)*, applies to situations that are similar to the circumstances requiring the joinder of necessary parties under Rule 19, treated *supra*, p. 300.

1. **Test for 23(b)(1):** A class action is allowed under Rule 23(b)(1) if individual actions by or against members of the class would create a risk of either:

    a. *inconsistent decisions* forcing an opponent of the class to observe *incompatible standards of conduct;* Rule 23(b)(1)(A); or

    b. the *impairment of the interests* of members of the class who are not actually a party to the individual actions; Rule 23(b)(1)(B).

2. **Typical cases:** The risk of inconsistent standards is illustrated by Example (a) below; the risk that individual actions would impair the interests of members of the proposed class is illustrated by Example (b):

> **Example (a):** A number of taxpayers wish to have a municipal bond issue declared invalid, and others wish to have the terms of the issue changed. If the taxpayers bring individual actions, the municipality may as the result of one suit be required to refrain from floating the bond issue altogether, but as the result of another suit merely be forced to limit the size of the issue, or to change the prospectus. There would thus be a risk that the municipality would be forced to observe incompatible standards of conduct, if individual actions were required. A court would therefore hold that this fact situation met the requirement of Rule 23(b)(1)(A), and would allow a class action, providing that 23(a) had been satisfied. See the Advisory Committee's Notes to present Rule 23(b)(1), Clause A.

> **Example (b):** Members of an association wish to prevent a financial reorganization of the association. If one member sues individually and loses, the reorganization will proceed, since its validity will have been determined by a court. The reorganization's effect will thus spread to all the other members who wished to prevent it, without these others having had their day in court. A court would therefore hold that the requirement of 23(b)(1)(B) is satisfied and a class action would be permitted. See Advisory Committee's Notes to present Rule 23(b)(1), Clause B.

> **Note:** If individual suits are brought instead of a class action, a person who is not present at one of the individual suits can never be *legally* bound by that suit. (The principles of *res judicata* prevent a person from being adversely bound by a judgment in a suit to which he was not a party.) Clause B of Rule 23(b)(1) is directed to the *practical*, rather than the *legal*, effects of an adverse judgment on an absentee. In Example (b) above, for instance, the reorganization might be vindicated by the first individual suit, and other association members would for practical purposes be too late to stop it, even though they would not be legally barred from doing so.

3. **No opting out:** A key aspect of the Rule 23(b)(1) type of class action (in contrast to the more common 23(b)(3) action, discussed below) is that members of the 23(b)(1) class *may not "opt out"* of the class, and will therefore *necessarily be bound* by the disposition. See Rule 23(c)(3).

4. **Mass tort claims:** The 23(b)(1) device has begun to be used for the joint litigation of *mass tort claims*. Typically, these efforts have involved 23(b)(1)(B), on the theory that if there is no class certification, individual plaintiffs whose cases are not among the first tried may find their interests impaired, especially with respect to the recovery of *damages* from a defendant with *limited financial resources*. The topic is more extensively discussed *infra*, p. 320.

E. **23(b)(2) actions:** Rule 23(b)(2) allows the use of a class action if "the party opposing the class has acted or refused to act on *grounds generally applicable to the class*, thereby making appropriate final injunctive relief or corresponding declaratory relief with respect to the class as a whole."

1. **Civil rights cases:** The main utility of Rule 23(b)(2) has been for *civil rights cases*, where discrimination against a whole class is alleged, and an *injunction* prohibiting further discrimination is sought.

2. **Other uses:** Rule 23(b)(2) is not limited to civil rights actions. For instance, the first suit in *Gonzales, supra*, p. 313, for an order declaring the Texas uninsured motorist statute unconstitutional, was a 23(b)(2) action.

3. **Not for money damages:** Rule 23(b)(2) does *not* apply where *money damages* are the sole or primary relief sought. *Injunctive or declaratory relief* must be the chief goal of the suit. Wr., 478.

4. **"Commonality" and "typicality" requirements:** Remember that the class in a 23(b)(2) suit, like those in (b)(1) and (b)(3) suits, must still satisfy the general requirements of Rule 23(a) (*supra*, p. 310). For instance, a proposed class action claiming that the defendant employer has racially discriminated against prospective and actual employees, and seeking an injunction against continuation of such conduct, might always seem to satisfy the requirement that the defendant have "acted ... on grounds generally applicable to the class." Yet there may not be sufficient issues of law or fact common to the members of the class, and the named plaintiff's claim may not be sufficiently typical of those of the class. This was the result in *General Telephone Co. v. Falcon*, 457 U.S. 147 (1982), discussed *supra*, p. 311.

5. **No opting out:** Members of a 23(b)(2) class, like those who belong to a 23(b)(1) class, *may not "opt out"* of the class. See Rule 23(c)(3).

F. **23(b)(3) actions:** The final type of class action, and the most common, is provided for by Rule *23(b)(3)*.

1. **Two requirements:** Rule 23(b)(3) allows a class action if the court makes two findings:

   a. **Common questions:** "that the questions of law or fact *common* to members of the class *predominate* over any questions affecting only individual members"; and

   b. **Superior method:** "that a class action is *superior to other available methods* for the fair and efficient adjudication of the controversy."

2. **Most popular form:** This is the famous "b(3)" class action, into which category have fallen "the great bulk of reported cases in which class actions have been allowed under the revised rule." Wr., 480. This is so in part because the requirements imposed by b(3) are less restrictive than those imposed by b(1) and b(2).

3. **Factors:** To aid the court in determining whether a class action is "superior" to other forms of adjudication, and whether common questions predominate, Rule 23(b)(3) lists four factors to be considered:

   a. **Interest in individual control:** "the interest of members of the class in *individually controlling* the prosecution or defense of separate actions";

   b. **Existing litigation:** "the extent and nature of any litigation concerning the controversy *already commenced* by or against members of the class";

   c. Concentration in one forum: "the desirability or undesirability of *concentrating the litigation* of the claims in the *particular forum*";

   d. Difficulties of management: "the difficulties likely to be encountered in the *management* of a class action."

4. Likelihood of victory: Some courts have held that, in determining whether to allow a class action, the *likelihood that the class will win on the merits* may be considered. The Supreme Court's decision in *Eisen v. Carlisle & Jacquelin*, below, however, appears to *prevent* such consideration, insofar as it disallowed such analysis for the purpose of allocating costs of notice.

5. Securities cases: Rule 23(b)(3) class actions have been found particularly useful in *securities fraud* cases, where it is impractical for most investors who have been harmed to sue individually, since the amount lost is often too small to justify the costs of a suit. It has also frequently been used in *antitrust* cases.

6. Mass tort claims: Some litigants have tried to use section b(3) for *mass tort actions*, such as *airline crashes* and mass drug-related *product liability* suits. But in general, courts have been slower to allow the use of (b)(3) than they have been to permit (b)(1) actions, in the mass tort context. See *infra*, p. 324.

G. Requirement of notice: The members of a class, other than the representatives, do not necessarily know that the suit has been commenced. Therefore, the court will normally require that these class members be given *notice* of the fact that the suit is pending.

1. When required: The Federal Rules explicitly require the giving of notice of the suit only where it is a 23(b)(3) class action. Rule 23(c)(2) requires the giving of "the best notice practicable under the circumstances" to all b(3) class members.

   a. Individual notice: Individual notice, almost always by mail, must be given to all those class members whose names and addresses can be obtained *with reasonable effort*, even if the class numbers in the millions.

   b. Plaintiff unwilling: If the plaintiff is unwilling to pay the cost of mail notice to each such member, the class action must be *dismissed*. See *Eisen v. Carlisle & Jacquelin*, discussed extensively *infra*, pp. 327-328.

2. Contents of notice: The notice provided for in Rule 23(c)(2) must advise the class member that:

   a. Right of exclusion: the court will *exclude* him from the class if he so requests, so that the judgment will not affect him;

   b. Binding effect: the judgment will affect him, whether it is favorable or not, unless he excludes himself; and

   c. Right to lawyer: if he does not exclude himself, he may *appear, with a lawyer*, in the class suit.

3. b(1) and b(2) actions: Even though the notice provisions of Rule 23(c)(2) apply only to Rule b(3) class actions, it has been held that due process requires adequate notice in *b(1) and b(2)* class actions as well. See *Eisen v. Carlisle & Jacquelin*, 391 F.2d 555 (2d Cir.

1968) ("*Eisen II*"), discussed below. It is unclear whether publication notice can suffice in such a case, or whether mail notice is necessary.

   a. **Mass tort cases:** In *mass tort* class actions, which are often brought under b(1), court have typically required mail notice to all identifiable class members. See, e.g., *In re Joint Eastern and Southern District Asbestos Litigation*, 129 Bankr. 710 (E. & S.D.N.Y., 1991), vacated on other grounds, 982 F.2d 721 (1992), where the court held that because class members would not be permitted to opt out, and because members' practical ability to recover money damages was being affected, the stringent notice requirements of *Eisen* (including mail notice to all claimants identifiable with reasonable effort) must be followed even though the case was brought under b(1).

4. **Cost of identifying class members:** *Eisen* established that the plaintiff must bear the cost of notifying the class members, but did not address the question of who should bear the cost of *identifying* them. In *Oppenheimer Fund v. Sanders*, 437 U.S. 340 (1978), the Supreme Court held that in most circumstances, this burden must also be borne by the named *plaintiff*.

   a. **Facts:** In *Oppenheimer*, the proposed class consisted of all persons who had held shares in the Oppenheimer Investment Fund during certain years. Because this group did not match the group of present shareholders of the Fund, it was estimated that it would cost about $16,000 to compile a list of class members. This work could not be done directly by the defendant, but would have to be done by the Fund's Transfer Agent (which keeps records of the company's shareholders).

   b. **Holding:** The Supreme Court held that since the cost of the compilation would be about the same whether the work was paid for by the plaintiff or the defendant, the plaintiff must pay. The Court indicated, however, that if the cost had been *"insubstantial"*, or if the task had been one the defendant would have had to do during the ordinary course of its business, the cost might be placed on the defendant.

H. **Binding effect of class action decision:** Judgment in a Rule 23(b)(3) class action is *binding*, whether it is *for or against* the class, on all those whom the court finds to be members of the class. Rule 23(c)(3).

1. **Exclusion:** However, any person has the right to *exclude himself* from the class in a b(3) action, if he notifies the court to that effect prior to a date specified in the notice of the action sent to him. 23(c)(2)(A). One of the reasons for which notice to all known members of the class must be sent is to give each member the chance to "*opt out*," and to bring his own suit.

   a. **Consequence of exclusion:** A person who excludes himself from the action will not be bound by an adverse judgment. But conversely, he may not *assert collateral estoppel* in his own action, if the judgment turns out to be favorable to the class. Wr., 483.

   b. **b(1) and b(2) actions:** Apparently absent class members in Rule *23(b)(1) and b(2)* actions do *not* have the right to "opt out" of the class and bring their own suits.

      i. **b(1):** To allow exclusion in b(1) cases would give rise to exactly the kind of inconsistent adjudication that the Rule is designed to prevent.

ii. b(2): Similarly, opting out of a b(2) action would make no sense, since the declaratory or injunctive relief to which b(2) addresses itself generally applies to the whole class.

Example: A restaurant enjoined from discriminating would hardly make a point of continuing to discriminate against those class members who excluded themselves from the class suit. Thus there is no reason to permit members of the class to opt out of the 23(b)(2) class suit.

2. **Minimum contacts not required:** An absent plaintiff who does not "opt out" will be bound by the decision, ***even if he lacked "minimum contacts" with the forum state*** (and thus could not have been bound had he been a *defendant*). The Supreme Court so held in *Phillips Petroleum Co. v. Shutts*, 472 U.S. 797 (1985), discussed more extensively *supra*, p. 35.

   a. **Due process problem:** As noted above, absent class members in a b(1) or b(2) action apparently do not have the right to "opt out" of the class and bring their own suits. Where a plaintiff does not have minimum contacts with the forum state, ***and*** is not permitted to opt out because the action is a b(1) or b(2) action, the absent member could plausibly argue that his ***due process*** rights have been infringed. It is not clear whether a federal court that refuses to allow an absentee plaintiff to opt out of a b(1) or b(2) action, where the absentee lacks minimum contacts with the state where the federal court sits, has violated due process — this issue is discussed further *infra*, p. 325, in the context of mass tort litigation.

I. Amount in controversy: Only the named representatives of a class have to meet the requirements of ***diversity and venue***. The Supreme Court has held, however, that ***every member of the class*** must satisfy the applicable ***jurisdictional amount***. See *Zahn v. International Paper Co.*, discussed *supra*, pp. 108-110.

1. **Effect of *Zahn*:** The *Zahn* decision makes it much tougher to bring a federal class action based on ***diversity***. The amount in controversy in such cases must exceed $50,000, and in many instances it will not be the case that all members of the class can reasonably claim such damages.

   a. **Use in mass tort cases:** But in one important kind of case, *Zahn* has proven ***not*** to be a problem: where plaintiffs have tried to get class certification for a ***mass tort*** case, in which each member of the class has suffered physical injury, courts have typically held that it cannot be said that "to a legal certainty" individual class members have failed to suffer the requisite $50,000 in damages. Therefore, courts have typically allowed such actions to proceed (assuming other requirements for class action status are satisfied) without requiring any members to be dropped, and without requiring any particulars as to each member's claim. See the further discussion of this point *infra*, p. 325.

2. **b(1) and b(2) actions:** Although *Zahn* was a Rule 23(b)(3) suit, most lower courts have held that it applies to b(1) and b(2) class actions as well. However, in many b(1) actions, plaintiffs will be suing on a "joint" right, and therefore entitled to aggregate their claims; see *supra*, p. 109. See also Wr., 485.

3. Federal question cases: In *federal question* cases, however, Congress has abolished the amount in controversy requirement. The feasibility of federal-question class actions is thus unaffected by *Zahn*.

J. Determination that no valid class action exists: Rule 23(c)(1) provides that "as soon as practicable after the commencement of an action brought as a class action, the court shall determine by order *whether it is to be so maintained*." The court is said to *"certify"* the class, if it decides a class action is appropriate. The certification requirement applies to Rule b(1) and b(2) suits as well as to those brought under b(3).

1. Consequence of denial: If the court finds that no class action is possible, the suit may be continued by the "representatives," but with *no res judicata* effect for or against the absent would-be class members.

2. Sub-class: Alternatively, the suit may be continued by a *sub-class* of the original class, as the Supreme Court implied in a footnote to *Eisen*, below. In that event, no *res judicata* effect extends to those original class members not included in the new sub-class.

3. No right to appeal: If the trial court finds that the action should not proceed as a class action, this finding is not a *final order*, and consequently an *immediate appeal may not be taken*. The named plaintiffs must try the case as a non-class action (or with a smaller class), and only on appeal from the judgment on the merits will the correctness of the trial court's refusal to certify the class be reviewed.

    a. "Death knell" doctrine: A number of courts of appeal had allowed an immediate appeal from a refusal to allow a class action, at least where the claims of the individual plaintiffs were so small that it was clearly uneconomical for the action to continue on their behalf alone. These courts reasoned that the refusal to allow class certification sounded the *"death knell"* of the action, and was in effect really a final judgment. The doctrine thus became known as the *"death knell"* doctrine.

    b. Doctrine rejected: But the entire death knell doctrine was rejected by the Supreme Court, in *Coopers & Lybrand v. Livesay*, 437 U.S. 463 (1978). The Court pointed out that to apply the doctrine properly, the trial court and appeals court would both have to make an extensive evaluation of the merits and size of all the claims in the suit, in order to determine whether a refusal to allow class action treatment really would induce an abandonment of the claim. Also, the doctrine is discriminatory, since it never applies to allow defendants to appeal a grant of class status, even though such a grant is often of equal significance to them.

    c. Interlocutory Appeals Act: On rare occasions, plaintiffs may be able to take an immediate appeal under the *Interlocutory Appeals Act*, 28 U.S.C. §1292. The Act has two sections, one covering situations where an appeal is allowed as of right, and the other where an appeal is discretionary.

        i. Appeal as of right: §1292(a) lists several situations where an interlocutory appeal is allowed *as of right*. The most important of these is given by §1292(a)(1): interlocutory appeal is allowed of orders "granting, continuing, modifying, refusing or dissolving *injunctions*, or refusing to dissolve or modify injunctions. ..." Observe that a decision denying class action status will virtually never fall within this subsection. (But for an example of the subsection's use, see *Carson v. American Brands, Inc.*, 450 U.S. 79 (1981), holding that a trial court's **refusal to approve a settlement** in a class action suit had the practical effect of "refusing an injunction," since the settlement itself would have enjoined the defendant from continued employment discrimination.)

    ii. Discretionary appeal: §1292(b) governs interlocutory appeals which may be heard **upon judicial discretion**. The section applies where: (1) the district judge who makes the interlocutory order is "of the opinion that such an order involves a controlling question of law as to which there is substantial ground for difference of opinion ..." and also believes that "an immediate appeal from the order may materially advance the ultimate termination of the litigation ..."; **and** (2) the court of appeals then (also in its discretion) agrees to take the case. The odds are that the required discretion by both district court and court of appeals will **not** be exercised in the typical denial-of-class-certification situation.

K. Settlements: Any **settlement of a class action** must be **approved by the court**. F.R.C.P. 23(e). This requirement is not consistent with the general rule that parties to an action are free to settle or end their case. The purpose of the approval requirement is principally to ensure that the **interests of the absent class members** are **adequately protected**. (For instance, the court will want to be sure that the defendants are not "buying off" the plaintiffs' contingent fee lawyers, at the expense of the plaintiff class members.)

    1. Notice requirement: In addition, at least if a class has already been certified, **notice** of a **proposed settlement** must also be given under Rule 23(e).

        a. Court approval before certification of class: Suppose, however, that some or all of the named plaintiffs wish to settle the case **before** the class has been certified; are notice to the putative class members, and a decision on whether the case is a valid class action, necessary? Courts are split on the answer; some have required notice and a judicial finding that the class would be certifiable, whereas others have merely checked for the basic fairness of the settlement. F,K&M, p. 756.

    2. Financial condition: It has been held that the **financial condition of the defendant** may be taken into account in determining whether the settlement is fair. Thus in *Grunin v. International House of Pancakes*, 513 F.2d 114 (8th Cir. 1975), which was a suit by IHOP franchisees against the parent company/franchisor, the court relied on the defendant's weak financial condition in approving a settlement that might otherwise have been disapproved as too small.

L. Attorneys' fees: If the class is victorious (or receives a settlement), courts often award **reasonable attorneys' fees** to the class' lawyers. These fees are generally added to the sum awarded, and serve as an incentive to the bringing of actions where no single class member could afford to hire a lawyer. The granting of attorneys' fees thus encourages a kind of "private enforcement" against legal wrongs which the government does not have the resources to police itself.

    1. Alyeska Pipeline case: In suits brought under **federal statutes**, attorneys' fees may be awarded **only if a federal statute so provides**. See *Alyeska Pipeline Service Co. v. Wilderness Society*, 421 U.S. 240 (1975). Congress has passed such statutes for a few kinds of federal actions. For instance, attorney's fees have been allowed by Congress in a wide range of *civil rights* cases; see 42 U.S.C. §1988.

2. **Court supervision of fees:** Most class actions that result in the award of attorneys fees are *settled* rather than litigated to their conclusion. Even in the case of a settlement, however, courts exercise substantial authority to approve or disapprove of the amount of attorneys fees agreed upon between the parties. In fact, courts closely scrutinize such agreements, for fear that the defendant will "buy off" the plaintiffs' lawyers, enriching those lawyers at the expense of the members of the plaintiff class.

M. **Mass tort cases:** So-called *"mass tort"* cases have become an increasingly important aspect of modern litigation. Starting in the late 1980s, the federal diversity class action has begun to be an important way of dealing with mass tort problems. Therefore, it is worth exploring in some detail how federal courts have handled some of the problems in using federal class action procedures to deal with these kinds of cases.

1. **Definition of "mass tort":** To begin with, what do we mean by *"mass tort"*? In reality, there are two different kinds of situations covered by the term. These sub-types are often referred to as "mass accidents" and "mass product liability" respectively.

    a. **"Mass accident" suits:** In a *"mass accident,"* a large number of persons are injured as the result of a *single accident*. Examples of such accidents include an *airplane crash*, the collapse of a building, or the explosion of a factory accompanied by the release of toxic substances (e.g., Bhopal).

    b. **"Mass product liability" cases:** A *"mass product liability"* case arises out of the sale of a *defective product* to thousands of buyers, who are thereby injured. Whereas even a very large "mass accident" case tends to involve a few thousand claimants, a mass product liability "case" can involve hundreds of thousands of people. Examples of products which have given rise to mass product liability scenarios include *asbestos*, IUDs such as the Dalkon Shield, prescription drugs such as DES (to prevent miscarriages) and medical devices such as breast implants or heart valves.

2. **The problem to be solved:** Both mass accident and mass product liability scenarios are hard for the conventional "bilateral" (two-party) traditional tort litigation model to handle. In the traditional model, an individual litigant, represented by a lawyer for whom that claim presents a unique set of facts (and with the client's approval on such matters as pleading, discovery tactics, trial tactics and settling), builds a case from scratch. Discovery, trial, appeal, and/or settlement negotiations, are all conducted as if no other case has presented closely-similar issues, and as if there were no opportunities for economies of scale in the litigation process.

    a. **Mass torts overwhelm the system:** This traditional model works very poorly, if at all, in the mass tort situation. Consider the problems of *asbestos* litigation, for instance. Let's examine a somewhat typical, mostly hypothetical, asbestos litigation.

        i. **Facts:** Suppose that our particular plaintiff, P, was a shipyard worker who was exposed to the substance while working in a government shipyard during WWII. P has now contracted mesothelioma, a uniformly fatal form of cancer. P is one of 3,000 workers who all worked in the same Navy shipyard during the same period, all of whom have contracted diseases which they believe to be due to their asbestos exposure. D is the principal, but not sole, manufacturer of the asbestos to which P and his co-workers were exposed.

ii. **Discovery and trial:** Now, observe what is likely to happen if P conducts his case according to the traditional two-party tort litigation model, and following traditional tort doctrine. P will need to carry out discovery, as well as a trial, in which P will try to establish: (1) that D was one of the manufacturers of the asbestos to which P and his co-workers were exposed; (2) that D knew at the time of manufacture that asbestos was defective and dangerous, but concealed this information from P and his co-workers; (3) that asbestos is in fact defective and dangerous; (4) that P's condition of mesothelioma (a universally fatal cancer which hundreds or thousands of the co-workers have also contracted) is frequently caused by asbestos exposure, and almost never caused by exposure to any other kind of substance; and (5) that in addition to compensatory damages, D's conduct is so outrageous that punitive damages ought to be awarded to P.

iii. **Difficulties:** Obviously, discovering and proving all these facts is a tremendously time-consuming business, not only for P and his lawyer, but for D, for other potential co-defendants (such as other manufacturers who may also have made asbestos to which P was exposed), and for the court system as a whole. If 5,000 workers each insist on conducting extensive discovery and then having a full-dress trial on their claim, the transaction costs will be enormous, and the court system may well be paralyzed (as has indeed happened in those federal judicial districts where many asbestos claimants live).

iv. **Common issues:** At the same time, many of the issues listed above for P's suit are probably ***common*** to many or all of the similarly-situated plaintiffs: whether asbestos is indeed defective and dangerous; whether D manufactured it; whether the workers at a particular place were exposed to it; whether D knew of the dangers at a particular moment; whether a particular disease such as mesothelioma is always caused by asbestos; whether D's conduct in concealing its knowledge and selling the product anyway was so outrageous as to justify punitive damages, etc. Clearly a way of litigating these issues ***once*** or a few times, rather than thousands of times, seems sensible both economically, and in terms of expediting compensation to those who have been injured in a way that deserves redress.

3. **Suitability of class actions:** The federal class action, on its face, seems like a potentially good way of handling these problems. A class action could be certified for the purpose of disposing of the common questions of fact (e.g., defectiveness) while reserving for separate actions the individualized questions (e.g., causation and damages). But the federal courts have been slow to allow the class action procedure of Rule 23 to be used in this way.

a. **Advisory Committee Notes:** Much of courts' initial reluctance to allow class actions in mass tort cases stems from the original Advisory Committee Notes, written in 1966, to the present version of the FRCP 23. These Notes state that "a 'mass accident' resulting in injuries to numerous persons is ordinarily ***not appropriate*** for a class action because of the likelihood that significant questions, not only of damages but liability, would be present, ***affecting the individuals in different ways.*** In these circumstances, an action conducted nominally as a class action would degenerate in practice into multiple law suits separately tried."

4. **Early cases reject:** Thus most of the district court decisions, and nearly all the court of appeals decisions, up until the late 1980s ***refused to allow class certification*** in mass tort cases, especially mass product liability actions.

a. **IUD litigation:** The best known appellate decision rejecting class status in the mass product liability scenario is *In re Northern District of California, Dalkon Shield IUD Products Liability Litigation*, 693 F.2d 847 (9th Cir. 1982). The case involved many claims by women who had used IUDs manufactured by D, and who had allegedly suffered various physical injuries as a result. The claims were based on a variety of theories, including strict products liability, negligence, and warranty. The Ninth Circuit Court of Appeals reversed the trial judge's certification of a (b)(3) class action that was limited to the issue of D's *liability*. Even with this limitation, the Court of Appeals held, a class action was a poor way to handle the case because:

   i. **No "commonality" or "typicality":** The Rule 23(a) prerequisites of "commonality" and "typicality" would be very hard to satisfy, since not all injuries complained of could have had the same proximate cause, nor would the same affirmative defenses (e.g., assumption of risk, failure to follow instructions, statute of limitations) apply to all claims.

   ii. **Predominance of common issues:** Similarly, the 23(b)(3) requirement that "questions of law or fact common to the members of the class predominate over any questions affecting only individual members" was not met for the same reasons. Also, the plaintiffs were using varying theories of recovery (e.g., strict liability vs. breach of warranty), and the proof required for one theory would not be the same as for another.

   iii. **Special considerations:** Finally, the four individual factors listed in 23(b)(3) as ones which must be considered in determining whether common questions of law or fact predominate, and whether a class action is the ***superior vehicle***, militated against class status. For instance, many of the clients, and their lawyers, wanted to pursue individual actions rather than be part of the class, so these would probably "opt out." (Apparently neither a majority of the claimants nor the defendant wanted the cases to proceed as a class action.)

b. **Punitive damages:** The Court of Appeals in the Dalkon Shield case (*supra*) also refused to allow certification of a related nationwide class for litigating the issue of whether D should be required to pay ***punitive damages***. This proposed class action was a (b)(1) class action, the theory for which was that if individual actions were allowed, and early claimants recovered punitive damages against D, D might be rendered ***insolvent*** so that there would be nothing left to satisfy even compensatory damages earned by later claimants. This would have been a "mandatory" nationwide class action, in the sense that individual claimants would not have been permitted to opt out. But the Court of Appeals rejected this certification as well, arguing, *inter alia*, that: (1) the 50 jurisdictions in which the cases arose do not apply the same punitive damages standards, so that there would not be "questions of law or fact common to the class" as required by 23(a); and (2) there had been no showing that separate early punitive awards would "inescapably affect later awards," which the Court of Appeals asserted to be the correct standard for determining whether the rights of later claimants would be impaired in the absence of a class action.

5. **Modern trend towards accepting class status:** But in the late 1980s, several types of mass tort cases so overwhelmed the federal judicial system that the tide turned, with more district courts certifying class actions, and more courts of appeal agreeing.

   a. **b(1) mandatory class actions:** Probably the most significant aspect of these new decisions allowing class actions in mass tort cases is that they have tended to certify actions as *b(1) "mandatory" class actions*, rather than b(3) "common question" optional class actions. Courts are most likely to certify a class action where there are so many thousands of claimants that there is reason to believe that the defendant (or even all defendants taken collectively) will be *insolvent* before the last claimants have recovered, and that what is at issue is thus a *"limited fund."* Recall that under 23(b)(1)(B), a "mandatory" (i.e., non-opt-out) class action can be certified if individual actions would create a risk of "impairment of the interests of members of the class who are not actually a party to the individual actions. ..." Where there is a limited fund, and later claimants may receive their judgments only after the fund has been exhausted, courts have frequently held that this requirement of "impairment of the interests of [absent] members" is satisfied. Since these actions are certified as b(1) actions, claimants tend not to be allowed to "opt out" (though this is not a completely black-or-white issue, as discussed below, p. 293).

6. **The 4th Circuit Dalkon Shield litigation:** Perhaps the most important case to allow class action certification in a mass tort case is *In re A.H. Robins Co.*, 880 F.2d 709 (4th Cir., 1989). This was one of the first cases in which a Court of Appeals upheld a class certification in a mass tort case. The case is also noteworthy because it involved very much the same issue — liability for the manufacture and sale of the Dalkon Shield IUD — as had the earlier 9th Circuit case disallowing class action certification (see *supra*, p. 323). (The class action certified by the 4th Circuit was against Aetna Insurance Company, the insurer of A.H. Robins Co., the manufacturer of the Dalkon Shield. By then, Robins was bankrupt, and had set up a trust to pay claimants. But the issues posed by the case, and the identity of the claimants, were quite similar to that in the earlier 9th Circuit case where class action status was disallowed.)

   a. **Class certified:** In *Robins*, the 4th Circuit upheld the certification of a class. The class was to consist of all claimants nationwide who alleged that Aetna was a joint tortfeasor with Robins and was thus liable along with Robins for any Dalkon Shield-related injury. The action was allowed to go forward as a *b(1)* action, principally on the theory that having hundreds or thousands of potentially *inconsistent determinations* of whether Aetna was a joint tortfeasor would subject Aetna to "inconsistent or varying adjudications ... which would establish incompatible standards of conduct for the party opposing the class ... ," as stated in 23(b)(1)(A).

   b. **Not a limited fund:** One interesting aspect of the 4th Circuit decision is that the class action was permitted to go forward even without a showing that there was a *lim-*

ited fund. Aetna was a very rich company, and there was no showing made that even if all claimants established that Aetna was a joint tortfeasor and was thus liable for Dalkon Shield injuries, Aetna would become insolvent. Instead, it was the risk to Aetna of *inconsistent adjudications* on the issue of whether Aetna was a joint tortfeasor, that qualified the case as a b(1) case. And this certification was based on (b)(1)(A) ("inconsistent adjudications") rather than (b)(1)(B) ("impairment of absentees' interests").

7. **Punitive damages:** The fact that the defendant's assets form a limited fund that may be insufficient to satisfy all claimants, is an important factor in gaining class certification of the b(1) "mandatory" variety. Where early claimants seek *punitive* damages, the case for b(1)(B) certification is especially strong. The outrageousness of the defendant's conduct is usually a "common" factor (as opposed to the questions bearing on causality and compensatory damages), making the class action vehicle especially suitable. Also, the size of a punitive damage award bears no foreseeable relation to the size of a compensatory damage award, so that just a few very successful early punitive-damage claimants can wipe out a small or mid-sized defendant. (This is what happened, for instance, in the early litigation involving A.H. Robins and the Dalkon Shield.)

8. **Opting out:** Recall that the major difference between a b(1) and b(3) action is that in the latter, claimants must clearly be given the right to opt out, whereas in the former, no specific requirement in FRCP 23 requires an opt-out. However, there may be *due process* problems with certifying an action as a b(1) action and disallowing absent claimants the right to opt out. The Supreme Court in *Phillips Petroleum Co. v. Shutts*, 472 U.S. 797 (1985) (other aspects of which are discussed *supra*, p. 35) said in dictum that a state court could bind absent class plaintiffs to a judgment for money damages "if it provides the absent parties with the minimal procedural protections of adequate representation, notice of the action, and an opportunity to opt out of the litigation." Some courts and commentators have argued that in a mass tort case where plaintiffs are seeking monetary damages, due process as interpreted by *Shutts* is violated where the claimants are bound to the class procedure and not given an opportunity to opt out. The Supreme Court has not yet spoken specifically on the question of when an opt-out must be given.

    a. **Use of sub-classes required:** One Court of Appeals has held that a 23b(1) action may go forward without an opt-out, but only if individual *sub-classes* are certified by the court, with each sub-class consisting of people having a common interest. Then, only if representatives for each sub-class have the opportunity to litigate the case (or approve settlement) will the absent members be bound without having had the opportunity to opt out. See *In re Eastern & Southern District Asbestos Litigation*, 982 F.2d 721 (2d Cir. 1992) (Where settlement of suits against large asbestos manufacturer was certified as a b(1) class action, and settled, the settlement could not be valid unless physically-injured individual claimants were placed in a separate sub-class from co-defendant manufacturers, with each sub-class voting to approve the settlement).

9. **Amount in controversy:** Nearly all mass tort actions are brought as diversity, rather than federal question, cases (since they are based upon state tort law). Recall that under *Zahn* (*supra*, pp. 108-110), each claimant in a federal diversity class action must have a claim of at least $50,000. When a mass tort class action is filed, the class representatives and their

lawyers will often not even know the identity of all claimants, let alone the size of their injuries. Therefore, people opposing class certification have frequently argued that the amount in controversy requirement is not met by every member of the class, and that the action may not proceed.

    a. Argument rejected: However, most courts have responded by holding that the amount in controversy requirement is deemed satisfied unless it appears to a *"legal certainty"* that the amount is not in issue; where a claimant seeks redress for personal injury, courts have held, this is an "unliquidated" claim that can never be said, as a matter of legal certainty, to be worth less than the statutory amount.

10. Partial certification: In considering the use of a class action in a mass tort case, keep in mind the possibility of *partial* class certification, that is, certification as to a *single issue*. This is expressly allowed by Rule 23(c)(4)(A). Thus certification will frequently be appropriate as to *liability*, or at least portions of liability (e.g., was the product "defective"?) even where it is not appropriate for damages. If the court grants a partial certification along these lines, then there will be a single trial on the certified issues. Each claimant would then have her own conventional trial or hearing on the non-class issues, such as damages (assuming that the class action was decided favorably to the class on the certified issues.)

11. Other techniques: In addition to the class action, courts have begun to use other special techniques for dealing with mass tort cases. Here are two important ones:

    a. Consolidation for pretrial proceedings: Cases from across the nation may be *consolidated* into a single district, for *pretrial* purposes. Under this approach, authorized by 28 U.S.C. §1407, the Judicial Panel on Multidistrict Litigation (consisting of seven circuit and district judges from around the country) can order all related cases pending nationwide to be transferred to a single district for pretrial proceedings. The district judge who receives the cases coordinates *discovery* and, possibly, settlement discussions. The cases are then sent back to their original districts for trial.

        i. Use in asbestos cases: Such a consolidation has occurred, for example, in asbestos litigation: all federal claims for personal injuries resulting from asbestos exposure, regardless of who the defendant is, are now being supervised for discovery, settlement, class action certification and other pretrial procedures, in a single judicial district, the Eastern District of Pennsylvania. See *In re Asbestos Products Liability Litigation*, 771 F.Supp. 415 (Jud.Pan.Mult.Lit. 1991).

    b. Aggregation and sampling: In mass tort cases, there will be important issues that are *not* common to the entire group of victims. Most dramatically, *damages* will typically vary greatly from claimant to claimant. If a full-dress trial has to be had on the damages issue, then much of the benefits from class-action certification will be lost. A few courts have dealt with this problem by the method of *"aggregation and sampling."* Under this procedure, for each type of injury or for each relatively narrow fact setting, a few *"representative"* claimants try their cases before a jury. The results of these "test cases" are then *averaged out*, and each of the claimants who did not have an individual trial gets the average verdict attributable to his group.

i. **Illustration:** For instance, in the principal case to have tried the technique so far, *Cimino v. Raymark Industries*, 751 F.Supp. 649 (E.D.Tex. 1990), a group of over 2,000 asbestos plaintiffs agreed to participate in the sampling process. For each of the common diseases that can be caused by asbestos (e.g., mesothelioma, asbestosis, etc.), somewhere between 15 and 50 claimants were selected to try the damage aspect of their claim to a jury. The resulting jury verdicts were averaged, and each of the remaining claimants who had not tried his case received the average for that disease (e.g., $50,000 for mesothelioma).

ii. **Due process:** Probably this technique of "sampling and aggregation" is permissible in terms of *due process* only if the plaintiff *voluntarily* agrees to participate.

N. **The *Eisen* case:** Perhaps the most important Supreme Court case on class actions, at least (b)(3) class actions, is *Eisen v. Carlisle & Jacquelin*, 417 U.S. 156 (1974). The case is most significant today for its holding that *individualized notice* in a (b)(3) class action must be given to *each member* who can be identified through reasonable effort, and that this notice must be paid for by the plaintiff.

1. **Facts:** Plaintiff Eisen filed suit as "representative" for some 3,750,000 purchasers and sellers of "odd-lots" on the New York Stock Exchange. He alleged that two brokerage firms had conspired to monopolize the odd-lot (less than 100 shares) trade, and had fixed prices in violation of the Sherman Act.

2. **District court:** The district court hearing the case (after a lot of intermediate procedural litigation) certified the case as a (b)(3) action. The trial court also made the following rulings:

   a. **Notice:** Individual notice was to be supplied to the *largest* potential claimants, and to a *random sample* of the identifiable smaller ones. The rest would be notified only through *advertisements* in certain key newspapers.

   b. **Mini-hearing:** A preliminary hearing, or *"mini-hearing,"* showed that the plaintiff would probably succeed on the merits. Defendants were therefore ordered to *bear 90% of the cost of notice.*

3. **Supreme Court rejects certification:** The Supreme Court then held that the case should *not* proceed as a class action, at least as structured by the district court. The most important aspects of the Court's opinion were as follows:

   a. **Notice to all identifiable members:** The Court rejected the district court's plan for having just all large purchasers, and a random sampling of small purchasers, be notified. This plan did not meet the requirements of Rule 23(c)(2), which provides for "the best notice practicable under the circumstances, *including individual notice to all members who can be identified through reasonable effort."* Since the names and addresses of over 2 million members of the class could be easily ascertained, these people *must* be individually notified.

      i. **Rationale:** The Court rejected plaintiff's assertion that since a possibly meritorious action would be ended by this requirement (plaintiff couldn't pay the cost of notice, since he had only $70 at stake in the litigation) the individual notice requirement should be waived in this instance. It also rejected the argument that the only purpose for notice was to allow class members to "opt out" and bring their own suits, something that no class member in this case would do because of the small sums involved. The Court wrote, "the short answer to these arguments is that individual notice to identifiable class members is not a discretionary consideration to be waived in a particular case. It is, rather, an unambiguous requirement of Rule 23 ... *There is nothing in Rule 23 to suggest that the notice requirements can be tailored to fit the pocketbooks of particular plaintiffs.*"

b. **"Mini-hearing" disallowed:** The district court had conducted a preliminary "mini-hearing" and had determined that plaintiff would probably win on the merits. It therefore imposed 90% of the cost of notifying class members on the defendants. The Supreme Court found such a preliminary hearing unsupported by Rule 23, and stated that it might "result in *substantial prejudice* to a defendant, since it is not accompanied by the traditional rules and procedures applicable to civil trials."

c. **Cost of notice:** The Supreme Court also rejected the imposition of notice costs on the defendant. "Where, as here, the relationship between the parties is truly adversarial [as opposed to the case where plaintiff and defendant are in a fiduciary relationship, as in a stockholder derivative suit], *the plaintiff must pay for the cost of notice* as part of the ordinary burden of financing his own suit."

d. **Sub-class:** The Court observed in a footnote that its dismissal of the overall class action was without prejudice to any effort plaintiff might make to define a *"sub-class"* with respect to which notice requirements might be met. A partial dissent by Justice Douglas noted that Rule 23(c)(4)(B) allows the division of a class into sub-classes, each of which could then be treated as a class for purposes of a new lawsuit. Douglas suggested that a sub-class of all those buying odd-lots within a short time-span, or all those buying odd-lots through a payroll deductions plan, might be feasible sub-classes for purposes of a new lawsuit.

Quiz Yourself on
CLASS ACTIONS

94. A cooperative located in the City of Langdell has 16 apartments, and thus 16 shareholders. The members of the co-op wish to bring a federal court securities action against the prior owner of the building; the suit would allege that the prior landlord created a false prospectus (concealing defects in the building's structure known to him), and then sold shares in the corporation holding title to the building, in violation of a federal securities law provision. Each of the 16 members has a claim worth in excess of $100,000. The co-op members would like to bring their suit as a class action. Are they likely to be able to do so?

95. P1 and P2 are individuals whose applications to live in a particular federally-subsidized housing project were rejected by D, the state agency that administers the project. P1 and P2 brought a federal action alleging that D's refusal to furnish them with a statement of reasons for their rejection constituted a deprivation of their right to due process, in violation of a federal civil rights statute. P1 and P2 now seek to certify as a plaintiff class all individuals whose applications for this project were rejected where the rejection was not accompanied by a statement of reasons. They seek a declaratory judgment that D violated the civil rights of each class member, and an injunction against further violations. (They don't seek damages.) The

identities of the would-be class members can be compiled quite readily from the records of D; there are approximately 700 such individuals. Assuming that the trial judge believes that the lawyers for P1 and P2, and P1 and P2 themselves, can adequately represent the interests of the 700 absent members, should the judge permit the action to go forward as a class action? If so, under what subdivision of Rule 23(b)?

_____

96. Same basic fact pattern as prior question. Assuming that the federal judge certifies the plaintiff class as requested by P1 and P2, must P1 and P2 pay for notice to all 700 absent class members?

_____

97. D operates a chemical plant in the Town of Pound. Late one night, an explosion occurred in the plant, and a cloud of toxic gas was released. The cloud drifted for several miles before dispersing, and hundreds of people appeared to be injured by it in various ways. One year after the explosion, P1, a resident of Pound who claimed to have been seriously injured by his exposure to the toxic cloud, filed suit against D for violation of federal environmental protection statutes. P seeks certification of a class consisting of all individuals residing within five miles of the plant who were or may have been injured by the toxic substance released. The suit seeks compensatory damages on behalf of each class member. Assuming that P can adequately represent the absent class members, should class certification be granted? If so, under what subdivision of Rule 23(b)? _____

98. P1 instituted a federal class action against D. D is a large investment banking firm, and P1's suit alleged that D broke federal securities laws when it sold stock on behalf of Z Corporation. D and Z are both Delaware corporations with their principal place of business in New York. The suit took place in New York federal district court. The court certified as a class all persons who purchased Z Corp. stock during a certain time period. One of these individuals was X, a California resident with no significant contacts with either Delaware or New York. X ignored the notice telling him he had the right to opt out. The class action was decided in favor of D. X then instituted his own individual suit against D in California federal district court. D now argues that X should be bound by the prior class action results. X points out in rebuttal that he, X, had no minimum contacts with New York, and argues that he should not be bound by the results in the New York class action suit given this lack of minimum contacts. Is X's contention correct?

_____

99. P1 and P2 have instituted a federal suit against D, a large bank that issues many credit cards. The suit contends that credit cards issued by D were misleadingly advertised, in violation of the law of New York (the state where the federal action is pending). P1's claim is for $60,000 and P2's claim is for $70,000. P1 and P2 are both citizens of New Jersey. D is a citizen of New York. No federal question is present. P1 and P2 seek certification of a class consisting of all those who ordered credit cards from D in reliance on the misleading advertising, regardless of the amount of damage suffered by that person. (All these others have damages of at most $20,000 each.) Assuming that the requirements of Federal Rule 23(a) and 23(b)(3) are satisfied, should the court grant certification of the proposed class? _____

100. Biff is the publisher of Biff's Notes, a series of study aids sold to college and high school students. Each year, Biff's acquires about one million new customers for its study aids, which cost an average of $3 each. P, a college student who is a customer of Biff's Notes, brought a federal antitrust suit against Biff, accusing him of price fixing, predatory tactics, and other Congressionally-forbidden tactics to maintain a dominant share of the study aid market. P has asked the court to certify a class consisting of all customers who have bought any study aids from Biff during the last four years. (Of the approximately four million Biff's customers during this period, the names and addresses of about 800,000 are identifiable by Biff's from its records, because they have sent in a card requesting free updates.) The court has certified this class under

Rule 23(b)(3).

   (a) Which, if any, of these customers must receive individualized notice of the pendency of the class action? _____

   (b) Assuming that at least some customers must receive such notice, who must pay for it? _____

   (c) What if anything can the person who must pay for notice pursuant to (b) do to reduce the cost? _____

101. Same facts as prior question. Assume that after the court has certified the action as a class action, P's lawyer and the lawyers for Biff work out a proposed settlement, by which a $1 discount coupon will be sent to each identifiable class member, and Biff's will reduce its prices by 10% for the next two years. What procedural steps, if any, must be taken? _____

Answers

94. No. One of the requirements for a federal class action, according to Rule 23(a)(1), is that the class be "so ***numerous*** that joinder of all members is impracticable. ..." Sixteen is such a small number that it is hard to see why the individual co-op members cannot simply join together as co-plaintiffs under Rule 20(a). Twenty-five seems to be about the smallest group that has been granted class action status.

95. Yes, under Rule 23(b)(2). First, a proposed class action must meet the four requirements of Rule 23(a): numerosity, common questions of law or fact, typicality of claims or defenses, and adequate representation. Seven hundred members seems sufficiently numerous. There are certainly questions of law or fact common to the class — for instance, each class member's claim presents the issue of whether due process is owed to a rejected housing applicant. The claims of P1 and P2 seem quite typical of the claims of other class members, since all are rejected applicants claiming a due process right. Finally, the facts tell us to assume that there is adequate representation.

Now that Rule 23(a) is satisfied, we must still find some subdivision of Rule 23(b) that is satisfied. The most likely candidate is (b)(2): "The party opposing the class has acted or refused to act on grounds generally applicable to the class, thereby making appropriate final injunctive relief or corresponding declaratory relief with respect to the class as a whole. ..." Here, the plaintiffs are seeking a declaratory judgment that due process is owed to a housing applicant, and an injunction against denying due process to future applicants. Since D is apparently treating all rejected applicants the same way (by not giving them a statement of reasons for the rejection, or other trappings of due process), the "generally applicable to the class" requirement seems satisfied.

96. No. In a (b)(1) or (b)(2) class action, notice is not required by Rule 23 (in contrast to (b)(3) actions). See Rule 23(c)(2), first sentence. Instead, Rule 23(d)(2) leaves it up to the discretion of the judge whether to order notice to some or all members of a (b)(2) class action. The reason for this is that if the suit is successful, it will result in an injunction or declaratory judgment applicable to ***all*** members of the class, whether notified or not, and class members will not be able to opt out, so that no good would probably come of class-wide notice. On these facts, it is unlikely that the judge will order notice given to each individual (though the judge might order publication notice, or notice sent to a small sample).

97. Unclear, but probably not. Even assuming that the four requirements of 23(a) can be satisfied, P's only chance of certification would be as a (b)(3) action. (A Rule 23(b)(1) action is out, because there is no risk of inconsistent or varying adjudications, or prejudice to the absentees — even if D was ordered to pay damages to P and not to some absentee, or vice versa, there would be no inconsistency or prejudice. Similarly, (b)(2) is out, because the suit does not seek declaratory or injunctive relief.)

For a (b)(3) action to be certified, the court must find that "questions of law or fact common to the members of the class predominate over any questions affecting only individual members." This requirement seems not to be met here: while there is a common question of liability, the more interesting and time-consuming questions will probably relate to causation (given that a particular class member was sick or injured, was this because of the toxic cloud?) and damages, issues which are not common. Similarly, it is unclear that the court should conclude that "a class action is superior to other available methods for the fair and efficient adjudication of the controversy," as required by Rule 23(b)(3). Individual suits by each injured resident may be a superior way to proceed, because of the causation and damage issues. However, such suits may be less efficient and more costly in terms of legal fees. (The court might certify a class action only as to D's general liability, rather than as to causation and damages. But see *In re Northern District of California, Dalkon Shield I.U.D. Products Liability Litigation*, 693 F.2d 847 (9th Cir. 1982), refusing to allow even a liability-only class certification in a mass tort suit.)

98. **No.** In *Phillips Petroleum Co. v. Shutts*, 472 U.S. 797 (1985), the Supreme Court held that an "absent" member of the plaintiff class (i.e., one who does not participate in the suit, but who also does not opt out) will nonetheless be bound by the results of the case, even if the absent member does not have minimum contacts with the state where the class action is pending. Thus even though X had absolutely no contacts with New York, where the class action took place, he is bound by the results since he did not opt out.

99. **No, probably.** The Supreme Court has held that *each member* of a federal class action founded on diversity of citizenship must *independently* meet the amount in controversy requirement ($50,000). See *Zahn v. International Paper Co.*, 414 U.S. 291 (1973). That is, it is not enough that the named plaintiffs each meet the jurisdictional amount. Consequently, the diversity class action is probably basically dead, since it will be a very rare class as to which each member will meet the $50,000 amount in controversy requirement. (*Zahn* is not a problem for class actions involving federal questions, since there is generally no amount in controversy requirement for federal-question cases.)

The 1990 supplemental jurisdiction statute, 28 U.S.C. §1367, does not appear to change this analysis. It is possible that the named plaintiffs can argue that since the court has original jurisdiction over them, §1367(a)'s grant of supplemental jurisdiction over all other claims in the action that are "part of the same case or controversy" should mean that the non-named plaintiffs' claims fall within supplemental jurisdiction and thus need not independently satisfy the amount in controversy requirement. This argument could be buttressed by the fact that §1367(b) removes certain claims (those asserted by certain types of plaintiffs) from supplemental jurisdiction, and does not mention non-named class action plaintiffs among the exclusions. However, this seems to be a very stretched reading of §1367, so probably a court will hold that *Zahn v. Int'l Paper Co.* remains in force, and that each member of a federal class action founded on diversity of citizenship must thus still independently meet the amount in controversy requirement.

100. **(a) All 800,000 identifiable members.** Individual notice must be given (usually by mail) to any class member who can be "identified through reasonable effort." *Eisen v. Carlisle & Jacquelin*, 417 U.S. 156 (1974). Thus the 800,000 customers whose names and addresses are on file at Biff's offices must each be sent notice by mail. This is true even though the average Biff's Notes costs $3, and thus even though the cost of notice is large, if not prohibitive, compared with the possible recovery. Additionally, the court may order publication notice to reach the approximately 3,200,000 customers whose names are not on file.

(b) P must pay the entire cost. This is true even if the court concludes that P would probably prevail at trial, and even if the court concludes that the cost of notice is so great relative to P's possible recovery that imposing the cost of notice on P will effectively kill the action.

(c) P could define a sub-class, and give notice only to that class. For instance, P could restrict his suit only to those who bought during the most recent year, or only to those who bought more than a certain quantity of books, or to those who bought only certain titles. The advantage would be that P's costs of notice diminish. The disadvantage, of course, would be that any recovery would be reduced, and the fees awarded by the court to P's lawyer in the event of victory would be correspondingly reduced.

101. Notice of the proposed settlement to absent class members, and judicial approval of the settlement. Rule 23(e) provides, "A class action shall not be dismissed or compromised without the approval of the court, and notice of the proposed dismissal or compromise shall be given to all members of the class in such manner as the court directs." In the case of a large class, each member of which has very small claims, the court will probably not order notice by mail to anyone, but will instead probably permit publication notice. In deciding whether to approve the settlement, the court will consider principally whether it is fair to the absent class members (since there is a danger that P's lawyer and Biff will collude, by agreeing to pay P's lawyer a large amount and paying smaller damages to class members than would be appropriate based on the strength of P's case).

VI. INTERVENTION

A. **Intervention generally:** Rule 24 allows certain persons who are not initially part of a lawsuit to enter the suit *on their own initiative*. Such an entry is called "intervention," and the person who intervenes is called an "intervenor".

  1. **Two forms:** Rule 24 recognizes two forms of intervention:

     a. *"intervention of right"*; see Rule 24(a), and

     b. *"permissive intervention"*; see Rule 24(b)

  2. **Distinction:** Where the intervenor is permitted to intervene "of right," no leave of court is required for his entry into the case. Where the facts are such that only "permissive" intervention is possible, it is left to the court's discretion whether to allow intervention.

B. **Intervention as of right**

  1. **Who may intervene as of right:** A stranger to an existing action has an automatic *right* of intervention, under Rule 24(a), if he meets all of the following criteria:

     a. **Interest in subject matter:** he must "claim an interest relating to the *property or transaction* which is the *subject* of the action."

     b. **Impaired interest:** he must be "so situated that the disposition of the action may as a *practical matter impair or impede his ability to protect that interest"*; and

     c. **Inadequate representation:** he must show that this interest is not *"adequately represented* by existing parties."

2. **Statute:** If the outsider cannot meet the criteria of (1) above, he may nonetheless automatically intervene under Rule 24(a) if a federal *statute* gives him such a right.

   a. **Intervention by U.S.:** Of the federal statutes giving certain outsiders the right to intervene, the most common are those which allow the *U.S.* to intervene. Of this latter group of statutes, the most important is 28 U.S.C. §2403, which allows federal intervention of right in actions involving the *constitutionality of an act of Congress.*

3. **Practical impairment:** Rule 24(a)'s reference to the outsider's ability to protect his interest is not concerned with the danger that the non-party will be legally bound by a judgment entered in his absence; the principles of *res judicata* prevent this. As a *practical* matter, however, his interest may be compromised.

   Example: Company A has a subsidiary, Gas Company. A is sued by the government for antitrust violations, and as a settlement agrees to divest itself of Gas Company. Company X, which distributes natural gas, depends solely on Gas Company for its supply. It fears that its supply will be interrupted because of the divestiture, and seeks to intervene as of right in the antitrust suit, and prevent the settlement.

   Held (by the Supreme Court), X's interests are not adequately represented by the existing parties, since all of these parties want the settlement. Although X would not be bound in any legal sense by the settlement agreement, X's supply of gas would effectively be cut off by the divestiture. Therefore, X has a right to intervene without leave of court. *Cascade Natural Gas Corp. v. El Paso Natural Gas Co.*, 386 U.S. 129 (1967).

   Note: The *Cascade* case has been given very limited effect in subsequent cases, which have tended to require a stronger showing of interest and inadequate representation before allowing intervention of right.

4. *Stare decisis* **effect:** Rule 24(a) has in one case even been stretched to the point of requiring the intervention of right of a party who is interested in the litigation only because it may set an *adverse precedent* whose *stare decisis* effect may later hamper him.

   a. **Facts:** This unusual result occurred in *Atlantis Development Corp. v. U.S.*, 379 F.2d 818 (5th Cir. 1967). The case involved the "Atlantis group," a series of uninhabited coral reefs. Defendant, a general contractor, began work on the reefs without permission from the U.S.; the Government sued, alleging that the reefs are federal property. Atlantis Development Corp., claiming that it bought the rights to the reefs from the latters' discoveror, sought to intervene of right.

   b. **Holding:** The Fifth Circuit held that Atlantis Development did indeed have the kind of interest which "as practical matter" would be impaired by the adjudication of the suit in its absence. The court noted that any later suit between the U.S. and Atlantis would, like the present suit, be litigated in the Fifth Circuit. The court then observed that if the first suit reached the conclusion that the reefs belonged to the U.S., the court was almost certain to follow that holding, as a matter of *stare decisis* (not *res judicata*) in any later U.S.-Atlantis suit. Therefore, the court concluded, Atlantis could intervene of right.

Note: Most courts would probably not go as far as *Atlantis*, and would not recognize the outsider's interest in avoiding an adverse precedent as being sufficient for intervention of right. It is probable, however, that the great majority of trial courts would grant the outsider *permissive* intervention in this situation.

5. **Comparison to necessary joinder:** The criteria which allow a person to intervene as of right are the same as those which require that he be *"joined if feasible"* under Rule 19(a)(2)(i). As the Advisory Committee's Notes to Rule 24(a) put it, "where, upon motion of a party in an action, an absentee should be joined so that he may protect his interest which as a practical matter may be substantially impaired by the disposition of the action, he ought to have a right to intervene in the action on his own motion."

6. **Jurisdiction:** Independent *subject matter* jurisdictional grounds are *required* for an intervention of right in a diversity case. In other words, such intervention does *not* fall within the court's *supplemental* jurisdiction.

> **Example:** A, a citizen of New York, and B, a citizen of California, have closely related interests that they would like to assert in a diversity suit against D, a citizen of New York. If A and B join as plaintiffs from the outset, they will of course not have complete diversity as against D. Now, suppose that B sues D by himself, and A seeks to intervene as of right. Because there is no diversity as between A and D, A's intervention will not be allowed. See 28 U.S.C. §1367(b).

> a. **Tightening:** This represents a tightening of the law, compared to federal practice prior to 1990. Before Congress codified supplemental jurisdiction in 28 U.S.C. §1367, the case law generally held that intervention of right fell within the court's ancillary jurisdiction; thus on pre-1990 law, A would have been able to intervene as of right in the above example.

C. **Permissive intervention:** A person who has a "claim or defense" involving a *"question of law or fact in common"* with a pending action may be allowed to intervene at the *discretion of the court*. See Rule 24(b). Such intervention, since it requires the court's permission, is called *"permissive intervention."*

1. **Discretion:** Since the granting of permissive intervention is left to the trial court's discretion, the trial court's decision, whichever way it goes, is *unlikely to be reversed on appeal*. Since appeal of a refusal to allow permissive intervention is seldom fruitful, most appeals concerning intervention therefore relate to Rule 24(a) intervention of right.

2. **Jurisdiction:** An outsider given permission to intervene in a diversity case under Rule 24(b) must meet federal *subject matter jurisdictional* requirements independently (as in the intervention-of-right situation). See 28 U.S.C. §1367(b).

Quiz Yourself on
INTERVENTION

102. P and X were passengers aboard an airplane owned and operated by D. The plane caught fire while landing, and P and X were both seriously injured. P filed a diversity suit against D in federal district for the Southern District of Michigan, arguing that D flew the plane in a negligent manner. X now plans a separate suit against D. Before filing that suit, X has learned that P and he are both planning to use the same

expert witness at trial, Edward, who will testify that D's pilot did not land the plane in accordance with the manufacturer's instructions. X's lawyer fears that if P tries his suit first, and does not properly prepare Edward for testimony, Edward will be seriously attacked in cross-examination, and will be a less useful witness in X's own later action against D. In this situation, what tactical step should X consider?

103. Same facts as prior question. Assume that P is a citizen of Michigan, D is a citizen of Ohio, and X is a citizen of Ohio. Will the tactic you suggested in your answer to the prior question still work?

104. Same facts as prior question. Now, however, assume that the federal district court rules that X is entitled to intervene as of right in the action. Does X's presence in the action satisfy the requirements of federal subject matter jurisdiction? _____

105. The United States government (represented by the Justice Department) has brought a federal court suit against the Ames Board of Education, charging that Ames is administering its public schools in a racially discriminatory manner. The essence of the complaint is that intra-district boundaries are being intentionally drawn on racial lines, and that predominantly-black schools within Ames are receiving fewer resources than predominantly-white schools. P is the parent of a black Ames public school student, who wishes to intervene as of right in the action, as a co-plaintiff. Should such intervention be granted?

Answers

102. **Seek the court's permission to intervene under Federal Rule 24(b).** Since X's proposed claim and P's existing action have a "question of law or fact in common," X can move the Michigan federal court for leave to intervene as a co-plaintiff in P's suit. Clearly there is one major question of law/fact that the two claims have in common: whether D flew the plane in a negligent manner. The fact that there is also at least one non-common question of fact (each plaintiff's damages) should be irrelevant. It will be up to the district court's discretion whether to allow the intervention. (The requirements for intervention of right under Rule 24(a) do not seem to be satisfied — X is not really "so situated that the disposition of the [main] action may as a practical matter impair or impede [X's] ability to protect that interest ...," since X ought to be able to find a different expert witness, or to improve Edward's testimony even if he gives poor testimony in P's action.)

103. **No.** The action is in diversity, which means that there must be complete diversity (no plaintiff from the same state as any defendant). If X's motion for permissive intervention is allowed, X will be treated as a plaintiff. Since he will then be a citizen of the same state (Ohio) as D, diversity will be ruined. Supplemental jurisdiction would not apply for permissive intervention — 28 U.S.C §1367(b) provides that intervenors under Rule 24 must meet jurisdictional requirements for diversity actions and cannot rely on the court's supplemental jurisdiction. The statute thus treats permissive intervenors in the same way as the judge-made "ancillary" doctrine did.

104. **No.** The supplemental jurisdiction statute makes no distinction between intervention as of right and permissive intervention. 28 U.S.C. §1367(b) clearly states that persons seeking to intervene under Rule 24 will not be allowed if their presence would destroy diversity (as it would here).

105. **Yes, probably.** For a person to be entitled to intervention as of right, Rule 24(a) requires that "the applicant claims an interest relating to the property or transaction which is the subject of the action and the applicant is so situated that the disposition of the action may as a practical matter impair or impede the

applicant's ability to protect that interest, unless the applicant's interest is adequately represented by existing parties." P certainly has an interest relating to the same transaction as the main action: the procedure by which Ames draws district boundaries and administers its schools. There is also a danger to P that his ability to bring a successful action in the future might be compromised by a poor result in the U.S.'s action — if the Justice Department does a lackluster job and loses the case (e.g., the court finds that there was no racially discriminatory intent on Ames' part), a subsequent court is unlikely to permit the issue of intentional discrimination to be completely relitigated (even though the rules of collateral estoppel do not formally bind P, since P was an absentee to the U.S.-Ames original action).

The toughest question is whether "the applicant's interest is adequately represented by existing parties" — either the U.S. or Ames can make a plausible argument that the Justice Department is adequate to represent P's interests. But P can argue in turn that the U.S. government may be pursuing other interests (e.g., a desire to settle such suits in return for partial relief, rather than litigating them to the fullest extent to get complete compliance with the law), and that P's interests are therefore not completely congruent with the U.S.'s.

On balance, the court will probably rule that P is entitled to intervene as of right (and will almost certainly at least allow P to intervene permissively). See *Smuck v. Hobson*, 408 F.2d 175 (D.C.Cir. 1969), allowing parents to intervene as of right in a similar litigation.

VII. INTERPLEADER

A. **Definition:** Interpleader is a technique whereby a party who owes something to one of two or more other persons, but isn't sure which, may force them to argue out their claims among themselves before coming to sue him. It is designed to ***prevent the party from being made to pay the same claim twice.***

> **Example:** X and Y both claim a bank account at Bank. Y alleges that it was assigned to him by X; X denies the assignment, claiming that a document Y offers as evidence was a forgery. Y demands the money from Bank.
>
> If there were no interpleader, Bank could not avoid the possibility of having to pay both X and Y:
>
> (1) If Bank chose to pay Y, X could come in with his own demand, sue, and prove his allegation of forgery. Bank has to pay X, and practical factors may prevent it from getting the amount back from Y.
>
> (2) Bank could refuse to pay Y in the first place, let Y sue, and then raise the issue of forgery. But if Y wins, and Bank pays, this result is in no way binding on X, who may still sue Bank, allege the forgery and, free of any estoppel, win. Bank not only has paid twice; it is worse off than in (1), since it is now legally impossible for it to get back the money from Y, who is armed with a judgment which is binding on Bank, though not on X.
>
> Interpleader allows Bank to avoid this dilemma, by forcing X and Y to litigate between themselves as to the ownership of the account. Bank need pay only the winner.

1. **Federal and state:** Interpleader is allowed in both the federal courts and most state courts, in situations where it is necessary to prevent double liability.

2. **Federal practice:** In federal practice, two sorts of interpleader are allowed:

   a. *"statutory interpleader"* pursuant to 28 U.S.C. §1335, and

   b. *"rule interpleader"* permitted by Federal Rule of Civil Procedure 22. Both of these forms are discussed below. The chief differences between them concern personal and subject matter jurisdiction.

B. **Need for jurisdiction over both claimants:** Interpleader only works well if the court has *jurisdiction* over both (or all) claimants. If one or more claimants are absent from the proceedings, then the whole purpose of an interpleader — to relieve the stakeholder of the possibility of having to pay the same claim twice — is likely to be thwarted, since the absentee will not be bound and can bring her own suit later. An early Supreme Court case, *New York Life Insurance Co. v. Dunlevy*, 241 U.S. 518 (1916), illustrates how this may happen.

   1. **Facts:** The facts of *Dunlevy* were as follows:

      a. Gould, and his daughter Ms. Dunlevy, were at the outset both residents of Pennsylvania. Gould held a life insurance policy, the surrender value of which was $2,479. Ms. Dunlevy claimed that her father had assigned the policy to her.

      b. Boggs and Buhl held a valid personal judgment against Ms. Dunlevy. They sued in Pennsylvania state court to garnish the policy, which Ms. Dunlevy claimed to own. Gould, however, denied the assignment, and claimed the money owed under the policy for himself. Meanwhile, Ms. Dunlevy had moved to California.

      c. New York Life, the insurer on the policy, wanted the Pennsylvania court to establish which of the parties, Gould, Ms. Dunlevy or Boggs and Buhl (through their claim against Dunlevy), had the valid claim on the policy. The insurer therefore moved for interpleader. The Pennsylvania court was not able to obtain *in personam* jurisdiction over Ms. Dunlevy in California, due to the fact that Pennsylvania, like most states at the time, had no long-arm statute. Therefore, although Ms. Dunlevy was notified of the suit, she failed to respond or to submit herself to the Pennsylvania court's jurisdiction. All other parties appeared.

   2. **Holding in Pennsylvania action:** The Pennsylvania court held that the assignment was not valid. N.Y. Life was ordered to pay the $2,479 to Gould.

   3. **Removal of California claim:** Afterwards, Ms. Dunlevy sued N.Y. Life in California state court for the $2,479. The insurance company removed to federal court, and claimed that Ms. Dunlevy was estopped by the Pennsylvania interpleader proceeding from claiming that the policy was hers.

      a. **Federal court holding:** The federal district court found in Ms. Dunlevy's favor, holding that the Pennsylvania court had had *no jurisdiction* over her, and that therefore she could not be bound.

   4. **Supreme Court affirms:** The U.S. Supreme Court affirmed the district court's decision, agreeing that the Pennsylvania interpleader proceeding *did not bind* Ms. Dunlevy.

a. **Distinguished from garnishment:** The Supreme Court distinguished between the garnishment proceedings and the interpleader proceeding. With respect to the former, the Pennsylvania court had every right to determine whether Ms. Dunlevy owned the policy (that is, whether the insurer had a debt to her) even though the court did not have jurisdiction over her person. But the interpleader proceeding was ruled to have been an *in personam*, not a *quasi in rem*, proceeding, and was therefore invalid without personal jurisdiction over Ms. Dunlevy.

   i. **Effect:** The end result of this distinction between garnishment and interpleader was that the Pennsylvania court had the right to say that Ms. Dunlevy *did* own the policy (and thus to allow its garnishment), but that it did not have the right to say that she *did not* own it, and to order its payment to Gould.

b. **Double obligation:** Ms. Dunlevy was therefore not bound by the interpleader finding that her father, not she, owned the policy. She could thus sue the insurance company for the amount of the policy. As a result, the insurer ended up *paying the policy amount twice.*

C. **Federal statutory interpleader:** 28 U.S.C. §1335 allows a person holding property which is claimed or may be claimed by two or more adverse claimants to interplead those claimants.

1. **Jurisdictional problems:** Were it not for problems of personal and subject matter jurisdiction, a stakeholder could in most cases avoid double liability without interpleader, simply by joining (under Rule 20) all potential claimants as defendants to a declaratory judgment suit concerning title to the property. Three major jurisdictional difficulties may prevent such joinder:

a. **Personal jurisdiction:** The claimants may be so dispersed geographically that no federal district court (all of which follow local long-arms in diversity actions) could obtain *personal jurisdiction* over them.

b. **Diversity:** *Diversity* might be impossible, as would be the case if one claimant was a citizen of the same state as the stakeholder.

c. **Amount in controversy:** The *amount in controversy* requirement may not be satisfied. The claim in an ordinary diversity case must be in excess of $50,000.

2. **Solution:** 28 U.S.C. §1335's main utility is that it simplifies these jurisdictional problems in the following ways:

a. **Nationwide service:** *Nationwide service of process* in a §1335 interpleader action is permitted by 28 U.S.C. §2361. That is, a court in which the stakeholder has filed a §1335 suit may serve its process on any claimant, no matter where in the U.S. that claimant resides or is found.

   Note: The nationwide service of process provision would have meant that if the original suit in *Dunlevy* had been brought in (or removed to) federal court, Ms. Dunlevy would have been served, and therefore bound by judgment, no matter where in the U.S. she resided.

b. **Diversity:** Diversity is satisfied as long as *some two claimants are citizens of different states*. See 28 U.S.C. §1335(a)(1).

Example: Two New York residents and a Californian all claim the proceeds of a particular insurance policy. Since either New Yorker and the Californian form a diverse pair, the diversity requirement for statutory interpleader is satisfied. The citizenship of the insurance company is irrelevant.

c. **Amount in controversy:** The property which is the subject of the suit must merely exceed *$500* in value, not $50,000 as is required for ordinary diversity actions. See 28 U.S.C. §1335(a).

d. **Venue:** The requirements of *venue* are also simplified in §1335 interpleader actions. 28 U.S.C. §1397 allows suit to be brought "in the judicial district in which *one or more of the claimants reside.*"

3. **How commenced:** A §1335 suit is commenced by the *stakeholder*, who is referred to as the "plaintiff" in 28 U.S.C. §1335. The stakeholder must, to begin the suit, *deposit into court* the amount of the property in question, or post a bond for that amount.

4. **Right to deny debt:** Even though the stakeholder must deposit the amount of the property with the court, he is not estopped from claiming at trial that he does *not owe the money to any claimant at all*. Wr., 498-99.

5. **Other suits restrained:** To further the goal of protecting the stakeholder from double liability, 28 U.S.C. §2361 allows a court hearing a §1335 action to *enjoin (prohibit) all claimants* from *starting or continuing any other action*, in any state or federal court, which would affect the property.

Example: Insurance Co. is sued in state court by the son of a recently deceased policy-holder; the son asserts that he is entitled to the policy's proceeds. The widow of the policy-holder also files a claim, in federal court. Insurance Co. may bring an interpleader action in the federal court of the district in which either the son or the widow resides, as long as the two are citizens of different states. The federal judge will then enjoin both the son's suit and the widow's suit, and will decide the matter himself.

a. **Must concern property:** The trial court's power to enjoin other lawsuits applies *only* to suits concerning the *property held by the stakeholder* and deposited with the court. This is illustrated by *State Farm Fire and Casualty Co. v. Tashire*, 386 U.S. 523 (1967). In that case, a collision between a truck and a Greyhound bus in California resulted in two deaths and thirty-six injuries, of persons from five states and one foreign country. Suits were filed in California against Greyhound, the truck owner, and the two drivers.

i. **Interpleader sought:** State Farm, the truck-driver's insurer, filed for interpleader in federal court in Oregon (residence of both drivers), claiming it had a limited $20,000 fund available under the driver's policy and wanted all claims against the driver or the fund to be worked out in one proceeding. Alternatively, it claimed that the policy did not cover this particular accident at all.

ii. **Injunction:** An order was issued, restraining all other suits against the truck-driver or against State Farm. Proper service on all claimants was made as specified in 28 U.S.C. §2361.

iii. **Broadening of injunction:** Greyhound then successfully sought a broadening of the order to prevent the prosecution in any other court of *any suits against it arising from the accident.*

iv. **Supreme Court limits injunction:** The U.S. Supreme Court found that the interpleader was proper, but that the restraining order could *only* bar suits against the *$20,000 fund*, and could not bar suits against the insured, or against Greyhound and its driver.

(1) **Effect on insurer:** The insurer could therefore make sure that its $20,000 fund could not be reached in any other action outside the interpleader, but it could not stop all suits against the insured himself.

(2) **Rationale:** The Court emphasized that interpleader was not a "bill of peace," and could *not be used to bring together all potential litigation arising from an occurrence.* "The circumstance that one of the prospective defendants happens to have an insurance policy is a fortuitous event which should not of itself shape the nature of the ensuing litigation. For example, a resident of California, injured in California aboard a bus owned by a California corporation, should not be forced to sue that corporation anywhere but in California simply because another prospective defendant carried an insurance policy."

D. **Federal Rule interpleader:** *Federal Rule 22* provides an interpleader remedy much the same as that of 28 U.S.C. §1335. By the Rule, whenever a person "is or may be exposed to double or multiple liability," he may demand interpleader. A person may do this by coming into court on his own initiative, as plaintiff, or by counterclaiming or cross-claiming as defendant in an action already commenced against him.

1. **Distinguished from statutory interpleader:** The chief difference between interpleader under the statute and interpleader under Rule 22 is that *Rule 22 interpleader has no effect on ordinary jurisdictional and venue requirements.*

a. **Complete diversity:** Diversity must be complete between the stakeholder on one hand and all the claimants on the other (or else there must be a federal question, but this is rare). Wr., 497.

b. **Service of process:** Service of process must be carried out as in any other civil diversity action — that is, within the state where the district court sits, or pursuant to the long-arm of the state. *Supra*, p. 44.

c. **Amount in controversy:** The $50,000 amount in controversy requirement must be met.

2. **No deposit:** The stakeholder is *not required*, as he is in statutory interpleader, to *deposit* the property or money into the court.

3. **Denial of liability:** Rule 22 specifically allows the stakeholder to "aver that he is not liable in whole or in part to any or all of the claimants."

Comparison: Statutory and Rule Interpleader

	Statutory	Rule 22
When there is no federal question, what kind of diversity must exist?	Some pair of claimants must be diverse with each other.	The stakeholder must not have the same citizenship as any claimant.
Where may service of process be made?	Anywhere in the U.S.	Ordinary rules for federal civil suits must be followed.
How much money must be in controversy?	More than $500	More than $50,000 (unless a federal question is present).
Must the stakeholder deposit the amount in dispute in court?	Yes	No
May the stakeholder claim that he is not liable to any of the claimants?	Yes	Yes

Quiz Yourself on
INTERPLEADER

106. A car driven by Xavier hit and injured two pedestrians, Al and Betty. The only insurance policy on Xavier's car was issued by Insurer, and has a $30,000 policy limit. Al is a citizen of the Southern District of New York; Betty is a citizen of the Western District of Oklahoma; Insurer is a citizen of the Western District of New York. Insurer is worried that it will have to defend Xavier in two distinct actions (one brought by Al and the other brought by Betty), and that defense costs plus judgments may total more than $30,000. Also, Insurer is worried that Al, Betty or both may sue in states allowing a direct action against the defendant's insurer. Insurer wants to be sure that it doesn't have to pay out more than $30,000 as the result of this accident. No suit has been commenced yet by either Al or Betty. Tactically, what should Insurer do? _____

107. Same fact pattern as prior question. Can Insurer bring an action pursuant to federal Rule 22 on these facts? _____

108. H and W, a married couple, jointly applied for a homeowner's insurance policy from Insurer. They then got entangled in a nasty divorce proceeding. While this proceeding was pending (and when the status of the marital home was still in doubt), a hurricane destroyed the home. H now asserts that he is entitled to the entire proceeds by virtue of a prenuptial agreement signed between H and W; W asserts that she is entitled to the sole proceeds because she is the sole occupant of the house at the moment. W is a citizen of Indiana, where the home is located; H has now moved to Ohio, of which he is currently a citizen. Insurer is a citizen of Kentucky. Insurer's assets are heavily invested in junk bonds, which are relatively illiquid at the moment. Therefore, Insurer would like to delay as long as possible having to pay out the claim or even deposit the $500,000 policy proceeds in court during an interpleader proceeding. Assuming that none of the three states involved (Ohio, Kentucky and Indiana) has helpful interpleader laws, what tactical step should Insurer take? _____

Answers

106. **Bring a federal statutory interpleader proceeding, under 28 U.S.C. §1335.** That section allows a person holding property claimed by two or more adverse claimants to interplead those claimants. Thus Insurer can commence a federal proceeding "against" both Al and Betty, and say in effect to the court, "Here's the $30,000; you decide how this should be split among Al and Betty. Return any excess to us." Even though this is a suit brought, in essence, in diversity, the amount in controversy requirement is only $500 (not $50,000). Also, the requirement of complete diversity is cancelled, and all that is required is that some two claimants be citizens of different states (satisfied here since Al is a citizen of New York and Betty is a citizen of Oklahoma).

107. **No.** Federal Rule 22 does allow an interpleader action to be brought by a stakeholder (whether the stakeholder acts as plaintiff, or is already a defendant in an existing proceeding brought by one or more claimants). But Rule 22 interpleader, unlike statutory interpleader, does not give any relief from the normal requirements of personal jurisdiction, subject matter jurisdiction, and venue. In a Rule 22 interpleader action, there must be complete diversity between the stakeholder on the one hand and all of the claimants on the other hand. Since Insurer and Al are both citizens of New York, the required complete diversity is not present. Also, a Rule 22 interpleader action must satisfy the ordinary $50,000 amount in controversy requirement for diversity actions, which the controversy here does not. (What counts for a Rule 22 action is the size of the stake, not the aggregated sizes of the various claims against the fund.)

108. **Use Federal Rule 22 interpleader.** The most promising place for Insurer to start such a proceeding is in federal court for the District of Indiana where the home is located; H, as a former resident of Indiana and one who still asserts a property interest in Indiana real estate, certainly has minimum contacts with Indiana and is therefore subject to personal jurisdiction (assuming that the Indiana long arm allows him to be served, which is quite likely). Although Rule 22 suits require complete diversity (in the sense that the stakeholder not be a citizen of the same state as any of the claimants), this requirement is satisfied here, since neither H nor W is a citizen of Insurer's home state of Kentucky. The amount-in-controversy requirement is satisfied, since more than $50,000 is at stake. The district where the home is located suffices for venue also, since that is the district where a "substantial part of property that is the subject of the action is situated." 28 U.S.C. §1391(a)(2).

The big advantage for Insurer of Rule 22 interpleader versus statutory interpleader is that under Rule 22 interpleader, Insurer does not have to deposit the "stake" (the $500,000 policy proceeds) with the court at the outset of the proceeding, or post a bond in that amount, as it would for statutory interpleader. Therefore, Insurer gets the use of the money while the suit is pending.

VIII. REAL PARTY IN INTEREST

    A. Assignment: A plaintiff or potential plaintiff may *assign* his claim or "chose in action" to some other party. This assignee may then maintain the suit. At common law, the assignee had to sue in the name of the original claimant; in equity, he could sue in his own name.

B. Suit in assignee's name: Modern codes, and Federal Rule 17, require that a complaint be in the name of the *"real party in interest."* This means that the *assignee must sue in his own name*, since it is he who will benefit from the judgment.

1. **Subrogation:** The same rule covers *subrogation.* Suppose an insurer has already compensated its insured, who is a tort victim. The insurer is said to be *subrogated* to the rights of the insured, and may sue the tortfeasor just as the insured himself could. Subrogee insurers have been held to be "real parties in interest" under Rule 17, and must therefore *sue in their own name*, not in the name of the insured. Wr., 454-55. (One reason why a subrogee might prefer, if allowed, to sue in the name of the subrogor, is that juries are likely to be more sympathetic to a plaintiff who has actually been injured than to the large insurance company which stands behind him and which is in the very business of sustaining such losses.)

2. **Diversity:** The citizenship of the real party in interest (the assignee or subrogee) controls for diversity purposes.

3. **Rationale:** The reason for requiring the real party in interest to be named relates to the *res judicata* effects of the judgment.

   Example: Insurance Company pays off claimant, the victim of a tort allegedly committed by Tortfeasor. Insurance Company is, by the usual common-law rules of subrogation, entitled to sue Tortfeasor just as Claimant could have. If Insurance Company is permitted to sue in the name of Claimant, and loses, it might try to sue again in its own name. Since *res judicata* is often determined, at least preliminarily, from the pleadings, Tortfeasor might have difficulty showing that Insurance Company had already had its day in court, and lost. Therefore, Rule 17(a) requires Insurance Company to sue in its own name. See Advisory Committee's Notes to Rule 17(a).

C. Representative: Executors, administrators, bailees, and other types of persons listed in Rule 17(a), are considered as being themselves "real parties in interest," and do not need to bring suit in the name of the person they represent. Wr., 452-53.

1. **Citizenship of representative controls:** But the citizenship of the represented party (e.g., the estate) generally controls for diversity purposes. *Supra*, p. 98.

IX. THIRD-PARTY PRACTICE (IMPLEADER)

A. Third-party defendant: A defendant alleging that a third person is *liable to him* "for all or part of the plaintiff's claim against him" may *"implead* such a person as a *'third-party defendant.'* " Rule 14(a).

   Example: An employer who is sued on the theory of vicarious liability wishes to recover from his allegedly negligent employee on an indemnity theory. Rather than wait for a judgment against himself, and then bring a separate action against the employee (and risk losing the second suit as well as the first, since the employee is not bound by collateral estoppel), the employer may choose to bring the employee into the original action. The employer is called a "third-party plaintiff," and the employee is a "third-party defendant."

B. Claim must be derivative: For a third-party claim to be valid, the third-party plaintiff may not claim that the third-party defendant is the *only* one liable to the plaintiff, and that he himself is not liable at all. The third-party plaintiff's theory must be one that has the third-party plaintiff's own liability as a *prerequisite* for throwing liability on the third-party defendant. Thus, the chief purpose of impleader is to assert claims for *indemnity, subrogation, contribution*, and *breach of warranty*. Wr., 510.

    1. Alternative pleading: However, the third-party plaintiff is not precluded from claiming in an *alternative* pleading that neither he nor the third-party defendant is liable.

    2. Partial claim: Also, the third-party plaintiff does not have to claim that the third-party defendant is liable for all of the recovery against the third-party plaintiff. He may instead allege that only a *portion* of the recovery is due from the third-party defendant.

        Example: Contractors Co. is a partnership composed of two handymen, A and B. The two get drunk one day, and while they are working on repairs at the house of a customer, they cause damage to the property. The customer sues A alone, alleging that he is jointly and severally liable for torts committed by the partnership. A can implead B as a Rule 14(a) third-party defendant, in order to obtain *contribution* from him. A will not recover from B the full amount of the tort liability under a contribution theory, as would be the case if B had agreed to indemnify A. Instead, B will pay over to A one-half of the customer's recovery, so that A and B will end up splitting the cost.

C. When leave of court not needed: If an original defendant serves a third-party summons and complaint upon the third-party defendant within *10 days* of the time the original defendant served his answer to the plaintiff's claim, no leave of court is necessary for the impleader. Rule 14(a), second sentence.

    1. Leave necessary: After this 10-day period, however, the court's permission to implead is necessary. Wright argues that such permission should be given liberally, and that the court's power to order *separate trials* of separate issues pursuant to Rule 42(b) is enough to eliminate any confusion which might result from impleader. Wr., 509.

D. Impleader by plaintiff: Just as a defendant may implead a third-party defendant, so a *plaintiff* against whom a *counterclaim* is filed may implead a third person who is liable to him for the counterclaim. See Rule 14(b).

E. Jurisdictional requirements relaxed: Both personal and subject matter jurisdictional requirements are relaxed with respect to the third-party claim.

    1. 100-mile bulge: Rule 4(k)(1)(B) allows service of third-party complaints anywhere within the *100-mile bulge* surrounding the courthouse, even if the place of service is outside the state, and is beyond the scope of the local long-arm. See *supra*, pp. 41-42.

        Example: P sues D in the Southern District of New York, the courthouse for which is located in Manhattan. D wishes to implead X, who lives in Newark, N.J. Since Newark is within 100 miles of the courthouse, X may be served there, even if the New York state long-arm would not reach him.

    2. Supplemental jurisdiction: A third-party claim falls within the court's *supplemental jurisdiction*. Thus, "there need be no independent jurisdictional grounds for such claim if there was diversity between the original parties, or if plaintiff's claim against the original defendant raised a federal question." Wr., 515.

> **Example:** P sues D in diversity. D impleads X, a resident of the same state as D, as a third-party defendant. D's third-party claim against X is for less than $50,000. As long as jurisdictional requirements between P and D are met (diversity and amount in controversy) it does not matter that D and X are from the same state, and that the jurisdictional amount is not met by D's third-party claim.

3. **Venue:** Similarly, if *venue* is proper between the original parties, it remains valid no matter what the residence of the third-party defendant. However, if this would result in very great inconvenience to a third-party defendant, the court may refuse to allow the impleader at all. Wr., 516.

F. **Claims involving third-party defendant:** The presence of a third-party defendant may give rise to a welter of different types of claims.

1. **Claim by third-party defendant:** Once a third-party defendant has been impleaded, he may make certain claims of his own. Rule 14(a) allows him to make the following kinds of claims:

    a. *counterclaims* against the third-party plaintiff, which are either permissive or compulsory depending on whether they arise out of the same transaction or occurrence as the third-party plaintiff's claim against the third-party defendant;

    b. *cross claims* (discussed below) against any other third-party defendants;

    c. any claim against the *original plaintiff* "arising out of the transaction or occurrence that is the subject matter of the plaintiff's claim against the third-party plaintiff;"

    d. any *counterclaim* against the *original* plaintiff, if the original plaintiff has made a claim against the third-party defendant (which can occur in circumstances discussed below);

    e. *impleader claims* against persons not previously part of the suit, if these persons may be liable to the third-party defendant for all or part of the third-party plaintiff's claim against him.

2. **Supplemental jurisdiction:** *All of the above kinds of claims*, except *permissive counterclaims, fall within the court's supplemental jurisdiction*, and thus need no independent federal subject matter jurisdictional grounds.

3. **Defenses:** A third-party defendant may also raise against the original plaintiff the same *defenses* that the original defendant could have raised. See Rule 14(a). "This protects the third-party defendant if the original defendant fails or neglects to assert a proper defense to the plaintiff's claim on which the third party may be liable over." Wr., 513.

    a. **Defenses against third-party plaintiff:** Also, the third-party defendant may of course raise defenses against the third-party plaintiff. He may, for instance, show that no duty of indemnification exists.

4. **Claims by original plaintiff:** The *original plaintiff* may "assert any claims against the third party defendant arising out of the transaction or occurrence that is the subject matter of the plaintiff's claim against the third-party plaintiff." Rule 14(a).

   a. **Jurisdiction:** A claim by a plaintiff against a third-party defendant does not fall within the court's supplemental jurisdiction, and thus must *independently satisfy jurisdictional requirements*. The court will not allow the possibility of *collusion* between plaintiff and defendant, whereby a plaintiff who could not sue the third-party defendant directly could sue him indirectly by having the defendant implead him. This means that there must be diversity between the plaintiff and the third-party defendant, or a federal question between them, and also that the jurisdictional amount must be met by plaintiff's claim against the third-party defendant. See 28 U.S.C. §1367(b), discussed *supra*, p. 117; see also *Owen Equipment Co. v. Kroger, supra*, p. 115.

      i. **Venue:** Such a claim by plaintiff against third-party defendant is not required to meet the *venue* provisions that would be applicable if the claim were an original, separate, action. Wr., 516-17.

   Note: Observe that "supplementality" is not symmetrical. Although a claim by the original plaintiff against the third-party defendant is not supplemental, a claim by the third-party defendant against the original plaintiff is, since there is no reason to fear collusion between the third-party defendant and the original defendant.

5. **Joinder of claims:** The original defendant may *join* to his third-party claim *any other claims* he has against the third-party defendant. Such joinder falls within Rule 18(a) which, as discussed above, allows a party to join "as many claims ... as he has against an opposing party."

6. **Illustration:** The many different claims which may arise when a third-party defendant is brought into a suit are illustrated by the following example.

   Example: Servant, on business for Master and driving Master's car, has an accident with a car owned and driven by P. Both drivers are injured, both cars are damaged, and one or both of the drivers was negligent. Master is sued by P. Some of the possible claims are as follows:

   (1) P may allege against Master that Master is vicariously liable for Servant's negligence, that P himself was not negligent, and that P therefore has a right to recover for both personal injury and property damage.

   (2) Master must allege against P, as a compulsory counterclaim, that P was negligent, that Servant was not (Servant's non-negligence is an integral part of Master's counterclaim, assuming a jurisdiction where contributory negligence is a complete bar, and where it is imputed to the master), and that he, Master, may therefore recover for the damage to his own car.

   (3) Master may then implead Servant as a third-party defendant, alleging that if Servant's negligence (and P's non-negligence) results in a judgment against Master, Servant is liable for an indemnity.

   (4) Master may join with this an allegation that Servant has been negligent and is therefore liable for the damage to Master's car; he may maintain this claim regardless of the outcome of P's original action, as it has nothing to do with possible negligence

by P. On the other hand, under the prevailing tort rule, if Servant is found negligent, Master cannot recover against P on his counterclaim.

(5) Once Servant is in the picture as a third-party defendant, P may choose to file his own complaint for negligence against him.

(6) In that case, Servant must file as a compulsory counterclaim his own claim for injuries against P.

(7) P may then allege contributory negligence as a defense to Servant's counter-claim.

7. **Dismissal of main claim:** If the main claim is *dismissed* before or during trial, the court still has the authority to hear the third-party claims based on it, if these are applicable, and if they are within the court's supplemental jurisdiction. Whether to exercise this authority is generally left to the trial court's discretion. See 28 U.S.C. §1367(c)(3).

> **Example:** A third-party claim for indemnity would be meaningless if the original claim for which indemnity is sought is dismissed. If the third-party plaintiff added to his indemnity claim a damage claim against the original plaintiff, however, this claim could be tried after dismissal of the main claim, since it is within the court's supplemental jurisdiction. The court might, however, decide as a matter of discretion (as 28 U.S.C. §1367(c)(3) allows it to do) that a new action meeting all the requirements of jurisdiction would be preferable.

Quiz Yourself on
THIRD-PARTY PRACTICE (IMPLEADER)

109. A commercial aircraft owned and operated by Airline, Inc. crashed into the tip of a peak in the Himalayas while en route from San Francisco to Nepal. Investigation of the "black box" and other instruments found in the wreckage indicated that the pilot believed that he was flying at 20,000 feet above sea level when he was in fact flying at only 9,000 above (less than the height of the mountain). The estate of P, one of the passengers killed in the accident, has sued Airline and Doeing (the plane's manufacturer) in a single federal court diversity action. The suit alleges that Airline was negligent in not discovering the altimeter problem, and that Doeing breached the implied warranty of merchantability by delivering a plane containing an altimeter that would fail.

Doeing's lawyer realizes that if the altimeter was defective, Doeing will be liable even if it behaved without negligence. The lawyer also realizes that if Doeing has breached the implied warranty of merchantability with respect to the altimeter, that warranty has also been breached by Altimeters R Us, the manufacturer of the altimeter (which is not a defendant thus far). What tactical step should Doeing take to ensure that Doeing does not get unfairly saddled with liability for an act (manufacture and delivery of a defective altimeter) that is really the fault of Altimeters R Us? _____

110. Paula, a citizen of Ohio, wished to have a house constructed for her on land she owned in Ohio. She contracted with Dave, a builder who is a citizen of Kentucky; the contract stated that Dave would build a house according to Paula's specifications on Paula's land, for a total construction price of $200,000. Because the capital and risk associated with this project were too much for Dave to deal with alone, he entered into a side-contract with Ted, a financier, whereby Ted agreed to put up half the capital needed for the project, in return for half the profits from the job. This side-contract also provided that the two would share equally in any losses or liabilities that might result from the project. Ted did not contract directly with Paula in any way. Dave is a citizen of Kentucky, and lives in the town of Covington. Ted is a citizen of Ohio, and lives in Cincinnati (about 50 miles from Covington).

Dave constructed the house; Paula paid for it, and moved in. Paula then discovered certain latent defects, which rendered the house substantially less valuable. Paula has brought a suit against Dave in federal court for the Eastern District of Kentucky (where Covington is located); the suit is based in diversity, and seeks $80,000 damages for breach of contract. Paula has not joined Ted in the suit. Dave would now like to bring Ted into the suit somehow, so that if Dave is required to pay up to $80,000 damages, Ted, in the same action, will be required to pay half of this amount over to Dave (so that they will end up having to pay equal shares of any damage award). Although Ted has minimum contacts with Kentucky, the Kentucky long-arm statute is a very limited one which would not allow service on Ted in an action by Paula or Dave concerning either the Paula-Dave or the Dave-Ted contract.

(a) What can Dave do to bring Ted into this action? _____

(b) Describe any procedural intricacies associated with your answer to (a). _____

(c) What special FRCP provision will help you solve a problem relating to jurisdiction? _____

111. Same basic fact pattern as the prior question. Assume that Ted now wishes to file a claim against Paula, alleging that Paula libeled him by writing a letter to the local newspaper, which stated, "Ted secretly and crookedly induced Dave to save them both a few bucks by building my house in a sloppy and dangerous way." Ted's claim is for $100,000. Will the court hear Ted's claim against Paula? _____

112. Same basic fact pattern as the prior two questions. Now, assume that after Paula has sued Dave, Dave has impleaded Ted, and Ted has made a claim against Paula for libel, Paula wishes to make a claim against Ted for deceit — she alleges that Ted conspired with Dave to induce her to pay for an improperly-constructed house. The claim does not involve a federal question, and is for $70,000. Will the court hear Paula's claim against Ted? _____

Answers

109. **Doeing should implead Altimeters pursuant to Federal Rule 14(a).** A defendant may, as a third-party plaintiff, cause a summons and complaint to be served "upon a person not a party to the action who is or may be liable to the third-party plaintiff for all or part of the plaintiff's claim against the third-party plaintiff." Rule 14(a), first sentence. By impleading Altimeters, Doeing is stating that if it is liable for breach of warranty, Altimeters must be derivatively liable to it. (This is a correct statement of warranty law.)

110. **(a) Dave can implead Ted pursuant to Federal Rule 14(a).** Since Ted will be liable over to Dave for half of anything that Dave is required to pay Paula, Ted's liability is derivative. Therefore, it is appropriate for Dave to bring a third-party action against Ted, even though Paula has not made any claims against Ted directly.

(b) Dave has to solve three problems: (1) diversity; (2) amount in controversy; and (3) personal jurisdiction. As to (1), a claim by a third-party plaintiff against a third-party defendant will come within the court's *supplemental* (formerly ancillary) jurisdiction, provided that it and the main claim concern a "common nucleus of operative fact." The supplemental jurisdiction statute, 28 U.S.C. §1367, does not specifically exclude claims by third-party plaintiffs under Rule 14, as it excludes some claims made by plaintiffs. Thus the fact that Paula and Ted are both citizens of Ohio, and are in a very general sense opposing parties (theoretically nullifying the complete diversity usually required) doesn't matter — so long as Paula and Dave, the original parties, are diverse, the citizenship of the third-party defendant is ignored. As to (2), similarly, the fact that Dave's third-party claim against Ted gets supplemental treatment means that amount in controversy is ignored as to the third-party claim. Therefore, the fact that Dave's claim against Ted is for only $40,000 (half of the up-to-$80,000 claim by Paula) is irrelevant — since Paula's claim against Dave, the original claim, is for more than $50,000, that's all that matters. As to (3), see the answer to (c).

(c) FRCP 4(k)(1)(B)'s "100-mile-bulge" provision. Under ordinary principles, Dave would not be able to get personal jurisdiction over Ted, because he would not be able to make service on him — the federal court sitting in diversity only allows service on out-of-staters to the extent that the long arm of the state in which the federal court sits would so allow. Here, since Kentucky would not allow service over Ted, the federal court would not normally be permitted to allow such service either (even though Ted has minimum contacts with Kentucky). But the special "100 mile bulge" provision of Federal Rule 4(k)(1)(B) comes to Dave's rescue: according to that Rule, anyone who is brought in as a third-party defendant pursuant to Rule 14 may be served in a place that is "not more than 100 miles from the place from which the summons issues. ..." Since Cincinnati is within 100 miles of Covington (where the action is pending), Ted may be served at his residence.

111. Yes. Rule 14(a) provides that "the third-party defendant may also assert any claim against the plaintiff arising out of the transaction or occurrence that is the subject matter of the plaintiff's claim against the third-party plaintiff." Since Paula's claim against Dave and Ted's claim against Paula both relate to construction of Paula's house, Ted's claim against Paula will presumably be found to meet this "same transaction or occurrence" test. The bigger potential problem is that Ted and Paula are both citizens of Ohio, and all claims are based solely on diversity. There would thus not seem to be the complete diversity required. However, a claim by a third-party defendant against the original plaintiff falls within the court's supplemental jurisdiction, under 28 U.S.C. §1367, since the claim is closely related to the original claim. Since §1367(b) does not exclude claims by third-party defendants against original plaintiffs, the lack of diversity doesn't matter.

112. No. A claim by the original plaintiff against the third-party defendant does ***not*** fall within the court's supplemental jurisdiction. The supplemental jurisdiction statute, in 28 U.S.C. §1367(b), specifically bars claims made by the original plaintiff against "persons made parties under Rule 14, 19, 20, or 24." This provision codifies the result of *Owen Equipment Co. v. Kroger*, 437 U.S. 365 (1978). Paula's claim against Ted would have to be brought under Rule 14(b). Therefore, that claim must independently meet the requirements of federal subject matter jurisdiction. Since Paula and Ted are both citizens of Ohio, the requisite diversity is not present, so the claim cannot be heard. (Similarly, Paula's claim against Ted must independently meet the amount in controversy requirement of $50,000, which it does.)

X. CROSS-CLAIMS

A. Definition of cross-claim: Rule 13(g) allows a party to make, in certain situations, a claim against a *co-party*, such as a co-defendant or co-plaintiff. Such a claim against a co-party is called, in federal practice, a ***cross-claim***. It is to be distinguished from a counterclaim, which is a claim made against an opposing party. A cross-claim is made only against a party who is on the same side of an already-existing claim as is the cross-claimant.

1. **Use by co-plaintiff:** Some courts hold that one *co-plaintiff* may cross-claim against another only if there is an *existing claim against both* (e.g., a counterclaim, or a claim by a third-party defendant). Wr., 396. See, e.g., *Danner v. Anskis*, 256 F.2d 123 (3d Cir. 1958).

B. **Requirements:** There are two principal requirements which a claim must meet before it may be asserted as a cross-claim.

1. **Transaction or occurrence:** First, it must have arisen out of *"the transaction or occurrence* that is the subject matter of the original action or of a counterclaim therein," or else relate to property that is the subject matter of the original action. See Rule 13(g).

> **Example:** Cabdriver is in an accident with a car driven by Driver and owned by Owner. Cabdriver sues both Driver and Owner, alleging that each is liable for the accident. Owner may bring a cross-claim against Driver for the damage to his car, since Owner and Driver are co-defendants to Cabdriver's initial claim, and since Owner's claim arises from the same occurrence, the accident, as Cabdriver's.

     a. **Compared to compulsory counterclaim:** Observe that the test for allowing a cross-claim is basically the same as that for determining whether a counterclaim is compulsory. But a cross-claim, no matter how closely related to the subject of the existing action, is *never compulsory*. Wr., 537.

2. **Actual relief:** Second, the cross-claim must ask for *actual relief* from the co-party against whom it is directed. Thus, where one defendant claims that he is *blameless* and that the other defendant is liable, no cross-claim can be made. (This is simply a complete defense.)

C. **Jurisdiction:** Cross-claims are within the *supplemental jurisdiction* of the court, and therefore need no independent jurisdictional grounds. Nor can a cross-claim affect venue. Wr., 539.

Quiz Yourself on
CROSS-CLAIMS

113. Deborah and Dell, each driving a separate car, decided to drag-race one day. While doing so, one or both of them (this is not clear) collided with a car driven by Pete, injuring him. Pete has brought a federal diversity action against both Deborah and Dell, alleging that each, because of negligence, is jointly and severally responsible for his injuries. Pete is a citizen of Michigan; Deborah and Dell are both citizens of Wisconsin. Deborah would like to be able to make a claim against Dell for damage to her car, suffered in the same accident. However, Deborah does not want to make the claim in the current action, because she thinks that the federal judge assigned to this case is hostile to women drag-racers. If Deborah does not assert her claim against Dell in the present action, will she be able to bring a separate suit against Dell in Wisconsin state court after Pete's case is completed? _____

114. Same facts as prior question. Suppose that Deborah does bring a claim against Dell as part of Pete's original action. Assume that Deborah's claim is for $30,000. Will the federal court take jurisdiction over Deborah's claim against Dell? _____

115. Same basic fact pattern as prior two questions. Now, assume that Deborah does not want to make any claim against Dell for injuries arising from the accident. Instead, Deborah wishes to assert against Dell a

claim for breach of contract. This claim asserts that Dell agreed to sell Deborah his house, and refused to do so when Deborah tendered the purchase price. The claim is for $60,000. Putting aside any problems relating to lack of diversity, may Deborah assert this claim against Dell as part of the action brought by Pete? _____

Answers

113. **Yes.** If Deborah were to make a claim against Dell as part of Pete's existing action, Deborah's claim would be a ***cross-claim*** under Rule 13(g). However, Deborah is ***not required*** to make this cross-claim against Dell — cross-claims under the Federal Rules are always optional, never compulsory (in contrast to counterclaims, which are compulsory if they arise out of the same transaction or occurrence as the original claim). Thus Deborah will not be barred from bringing a separate state-court action against Dell later on (though the doctrine of collateral estoppel will probably prevent her from relitigating issues that were actually litigated by her in the original action).

114. **Yes.** As discussed in the prior answer, Deborah's claim against Dell would be a cross-claim, asserted pursuant to Rule 13(g). Cross-claims fall within the court's supplemental jurisdiction, under 28 U.S.C. §1367, since they are by definition closely related to the original action and since they are not excluded by subsection (b). Therefore, the ordinary requirements of federal subject matter jurisdiction are ignored. It does not matter that Deborah and Dell are both citizens of the same state, or that Deborah's claim is for less than the $50,000 amount in controversy ordinarily required for diversity suits.

115. **No.** Since Deborah and Dell are co-defendants, Deborah's claim against Dell must be a cross-claim, asserted pursuant to Rule 13(g). However, Rule 13(g) allows a cross-claim only if it "aris[es] out of the transaction or occurrence that is the subject matter either of the original action or of a counterclaim therein or relating to any property that is the subject matter of the original action." Since the Deborah-Dell contract has nothing whatsoever to do with the drag-racing, it does not satisfy this requirement of relatedness, so it cannot be asserted by Deborah even if Dell is willing to have it heard in the basic action.

Exam Tips *on* MULTI-PARTY AND MULTI-CLAIM LITIGATION

This area is a welter of individual procedural devices, and is usually tested from a federal perspective. The one overarching principle is that you must always worry about subject matter jurisdiction and personal jurisdiction; remember that the need for the former will often be eliminated by supplemental jurisdiction. Here are some particular things to watch for:

☞ If the facts involve a ***counterclaim*** ("cc"), be sure to distinguish between permissive cc's and compulsory ones. Remember that a compulsory cc is one that arises out of the *same "transaction or occurrence"* that is the subject matter of the opposing party's claim. Rule 13(a). [289-294]

  ☞ The need to distinguish between the two types of cc arises most often because you have to decide whether a claim that could have been asserted as a cc in an earlier action is now barred. Remember that a litigant *loses* an unasserted compulsory cc but not an unasserted permissive cc.

☞ A sometimes-tested issue is whether, in the second suit, a federal court sitting in diversity must *follow the counterclaim rules of the state* where the district court sits, especially whether the federal court must decline to hear a claim that state law would regard as compulsory (and thus refuse to hear because not asserted in an earlier action), even though the cc would be permissive under the FRCP. Because of the heavy outcome-determinativeness of the issue, the answer is probably that the federal court must follow the state rule.

☞ Remember that a *compulsory* cc falls within *supplemental jurisdiction* ("SJ"). Therefore, it does not need to independently involve $50,000. Furthermore, SJ means that D can bring in additional parties to the compulsory cc with whom D is not diverse. (But there probably is *not* SJ for *permissive* cc's, so these must meet the amount-in-controversy and complete-diversity requirements.)

☛ *Joinder of claims* raises few testable issues. Just remember that once P has a valid claim against a particular D, he can add as many additional claims as he wishes against that D. These do not have to independently meet the amount in controversy requirement (since "aggregation" of all claims by one P against one D is allowed). [296-297]

☛ For *joinder of parties,* here are the most testable issues [297-305]:

☞ For both plaintiff-joinder and defendant-joinder, you'll need to know the two requirements imposed by FRCP 20: (1) the claims must arise from a *single "transaction, occurrence*, or series of transactions or occurrences"; and (2) there must be a question of law or fact *common* to all Ps or all Ds. You'll usually want to discuss exactly how these two tests are or are not satisfied by your fact pattern. The tests are both pretty easy to satisfy, so normally you should find that joinder is proper (assuming there are no jurisdiction problems.)

☞ Remember that the requirements of *subject matter* and *personal jurisdiction* must be met as to *each D*. Furthermore, there's no supplemental jurisdiction for each multi-plaintiff joinder or multi-defendant joinder. So check that:

☞ each D was properly served;

☞ each D has minimum contacts with the forum state

☞ no D is a citizen of the same state as any P (if it's a diversity case); and

☞ each D satisfies the amount in controversy (if diversity). (It's possible that if one D meets the $50,000 amount in controversy, others can "piggyback," but this is not clear.)

☞ Compulsory joinder is often tested. Distinguish between "necessary" parties and "indispensable" ones. [300]

☞ A party who is *"necessary"* (the "weaker" case for joinder) must be joined if jurisdictionally possible, but the action may go on without him if there are jurisdiction problems.

☞ A party who is *"indispensable"* (the stronger case for joinder) not only must be joined if jurisdictionally possible, but the action must be dismissed if she cannot be joined.

☞ Consult the text of FRCP 19 (and the capsule summary) for analysis of the standards for these two classifications. For a finding of indispensability, the key factors are the degree of *prejudice to the absentee* from proceeding without him, and the *adequacy of P's remedies* (e.g., state court ones) if the federal action is dismissed.

☞ Where there's a "necessary" or "indispensable" party (as with any other type of multi-defendant joinder), supplemental jurisdiction does *not* apply, so ordinary requirements of subject matter jurisdiction apply

☛ Here's what to look for if your fact pattern involves a *class action.* [309-328]:

☞ Sometimes the whole idea of a class action will be hidden. Anytime you see multiple (at least 15) people with similar "injuries," you should consider whether they might bring a plaintiff class action.

☞ The *amount in controversy* for a diversity class action is one of the most frequently-tested issues in all of Civil Procedure. Remember that *each member of a diversity class action must independently meet the $50,000 requirement*. Cite to *Zahn* on this point. [108-110]

   ☞ A sub-issue is often what kind of a showing each P must make to satisfy the $50,000 requirement. Remember that as long as it's not a "legal certainty" that some P can't meet the requirement, the requirement will be deemed met. This essentially means that if each P has suffered some sort of *physical injuries*, the amount requirement will usually be deemed satisfied. Another sub-issue is whether the possibility of *punitive* damages may be considered — the answer is unclear, but probably little weight should be given to this possibility.

☞ *"Numerosity"* and *"fair representation"* are frequently-tested elements. If there are more than 25 claimants, "numerosity" is probably satisfied, and if less than 15, it's probably not. To decide "fair representation," look to how much the named P's have in common with the unnamed P's. [310-313]

☞ The majority of the time, if there is to be a class action, it will be a *b(3)* action, not a b(1) or b(2) action. In the garden-variety situation of multiple claimants seeking money damages from a solvent defendant, the action will proceed under b(3) or not at all.

   ☞ For a b(3) action, make sure that (1) *common issues* of law or fact *predominate*; and (2) the class action is *superior* to other methods (e.g., individual actions). Thus if there are important issues on which each P varies (e.g., each claimant has a unique set of physical injuries), the class action is probably not superior. [315-319]

   ☞ You'll often have a *mass tort* fact pattern (e.g., an airplane crash or a toxic gas leak/explosion). Here, know that courts often *refuse* to allow b(3) class actions (and to require individual actions instead) because of causation issues and the variety of damages suffered. (If D might go broke from thousands of claims, consider the possibility of a b(1) action to preserve a limited fund.)

☞ Remember that absent class members must always be given *notice* (individual, where possible), and that this notice must be paid for by the named plaintiffs. Cite to *Eisen v. Carlisle* on this point. [327-328]

☞ Class actions questions often require you to say who is *bound* by the judgment. In the usual b(3) action, each class member must be given a chance to *opt out*; if she does so, she's not bound by an adverse judgment or settlement (and can bring her own suit), but conversely, she doesn't get any benefit (including collateral estoppel) from any favorable judgment. ***One who doesn't opt out (even if she never got notice) is bound by the judgment.*** [317]

     ☞ There's no right to opt out in b(1) or b(2) actions.

☞ Before a c.a. can go to trial, it must be "certified" as a c.a. by the court — i.e., the court declares that the requirements for a c.a. have been satisfied.

     ☞ If on particular facts you conclude that the entire proposed class does not satisfy the requirements (e.g., the named Ps' claims aren't typical, or the named Ps can't fairly represent everyone), consider the possibility that the court could certify a *sub-class* (just one group of Ps), which could go forward.

☞ Remember that any proposed *settlement* must be approved by the court, and, if the action has been certified, *notice* of the proposed settlement must be given to absent class members. [320]

☛ For *intervention*, here are the key points [332-334]:

☞ Sometimes the intervention issue is hidden. Look for a fact pattern in which persons who are not parties might be affected by the outcome, and you're asked how they can protect their interests. For instance, questions sometimes involve a non-party who might someday face a similar lawsuit, and would like to help prevent an adverse precedent that wouldn't be binding on him by collateral estoppel but that would pose *stare decisis* problems. (In this situation, say that permissive intervention is justified but intervention of right is not).

☞ Always distinguish between *permissive* intervention (FRCP 24(b)) and intervention of *right* (24(a)). Of-right requires much tighter ties to the subject matter of the litigation, among other things. [332]

     ☞ The main consequence of the distinction is that a trial court's denial of permissive intervention is almost never reversed on appeal, but a denial of intervention of right will often be reversed.

☞ Remember that the usual requirements of *subject matter jurisdiction* apply to both types of intervention, i.e., there's no supplemental jurisdiction. Be alert to diversity situations where the would-be intervenor is a citizen of the same state as an opposing party — intervention can't occur no matter how heavily implicated the intervenor's interests are. (Also, in this situation, consider whether the would-be intervenor is an "indispensable" party in whose absence the action must be dismissed.)

☞ Here's what to watch for concerning *interpleader.* [336-341]:

☞ Interpleader issues are often hidden. Look for someone in possession of a *"stake,"* where the stakeholder doesn't know **which of two people is entitled** to that stake. Examples: banks that hold bank accounts, insurance companies that hold policy proceeds, contest sponsors that hold prizes, estates that hold assets. Typically, it will be up to you to notice that the stakeholder faces the possibility of double/inconsistent adjudications, and up to you to say that the stakeholder should interplead the competing claimants.

☞ If you decide that the stakeholder should use interpleader, always specify whether he should use statutory interpleader or FRCP Rule 22 interpleader. Here are the main differences:

☞ Statutory interpleader (s.i.) affects personal jurisdiction and subject matter jurisdiction; Rule interpleader (r.i.) does not. So nationwide service of process in allowed for s.i. (but not for r.i.). Similarly, diversity is satisfied for s.i. as long as some two claimants are citizens of different states (whereas for r.i. the stakeholder may not be a citizen of the same state as any claimant). And the amount in controversy has to be merely $500 for s.i. (compared with the usual $50,000 for r.i.)

☞ On the other hand, the stakeholder has to deposit the property in court (or post a bond) to use s.i., but does not for r.i.

☞ *Impleader* (third-party practice) issues are very common. [343-347] Here's what to look for:

☞ Impleader issues are sometimes hidden. Look for any situation in which an existing party may want to say, in effect, "If I'm liable to so-and-so, then you're liable to me in whole or in part for anything I have to pay to so-and-so." In general, you're looking for claims of *"indemnity"* (whole reimbursement) and *"contribution"* (partial reimbursement). This means that you should think "impleader" in these types of situations (D is the original defendant, and X is a person not yet a party, who D should consider impleading):

☞ D is accused of a tort, and X is D's *insurer.* (X has agreed by contract to indemnify D.)

☞ P is a tort victim, D made the *product* that injured P, and X made a *component* of that product (e.g., D made the aircraft that crashed and X made the possibly-defective engine).

☞ P is a tort victim injured by a product, D sold it to P, and X is *"upstream" in the chain of sale.* P sues only D, on an implied warranty theory. (E.g., P sues D, the retailer, and D impleads X, the manufacturer or wholesaler.)

☞ P is a tort victim, D and X were *separately-acting tortfeasors* who have potentially joint-and-several liability and P has chosen to sue only D, not X. (D has a common-law right of contribution from X in this situation.) Example: P is a patient injured while in D, a hospital, and while under the care of X, a doctor not employed by the hospital. P sues only D.

☞ The third-party plaintiff, or TPP (P in the above examples) may *not* claim that the third-party defendant, or TPD (X above) is the *only one* liable to P. The TPD's liability must be "derivative" of the TPP's liability. (On the other hand, TPP doesn't have to prove at the outset that TPD definitely or even probably has derivative liability; it's enough that TPD "may be" liable to TPP is TPP is liable to P.) [344]

☞ When impleader claims are part of the fact pattern, be hyper-alert to *personal and subject matter jurisdiction* issues, which are very frequently present. You'll typically see a TPP and TPD who are both citizens of the same state, for instance. Remember that both types of jurisdictional requirements are relaxed in impleader cases:

  ☞ Most important, impleader claims come within the court's *supplemental jurisdiction*. This means that TPP and TPD *don't have to be diverse* to each other (and TPD doesn't have to be diverse to P), and TPP's claim against TPD doesn't have to be worth $50,000. (The third-party claim can be a *partial* claim, such as a claim for contribution, so this amount-in-controversy relaxation can be important.)[344]

  ☞ Also, *personal jurisdiction* can be relaxed because service of the third-party complaint can occur anywhere within a *100-mile bulge* of the federal courthouse, even if TPD has no contacts with the state where the federal court sits. (Therefore, be on the lookout for service on TPD that takes place in a city close to the courthouse but in another state; the facts will often state the distance between courthouse and point of service, which should tip you to the presence of a "bulge" issue.) [344]

  ☞ You don't have to worry about *venue* for the third-party complaint.

☞ Remember that once a party has been impleaded, there can be additional claims involving the TPD (e.g., TPD against P, P against TPD, TPD against TPP, etc.) Generally, *supplemental jurisdiction will apply* to these, *except* for: (1) P's claim vs. TPD; and (2) TPD's permissive counterclaims against TPP or against P.

☛ Where two people are *already* parties, and are on the *same side* (both Ps or both Ds), one may make a *cross-claim* against the other. [349] Things to remember:

☞ The cross-claim must arise out of the *same "transaction or occurrence"* as the original action;

☞ A cross-claim is *never compulsory* (i.e., it's not lost if not asserted in the present action);

☞ Cross-claims come within *supplemental* jurisdiction (so D1 doesn't need to be diverse with D2 to cross-claim against him).

CHAPTER 9

FORMER ADJUDICATION

ChapterScope

This Chapter examines the rules that prevent re-litigation of claims and issues that have already been contested (or, in some situations, could have been contested) in an earlier lawsuit. The most important concepts in this Chapter are:

- **"Res judicata":** There is a set of rules that prevents re-litigation of claims and issues; the set is sometimes collectively called the doctrine of *"res judicata."* There are two main categories of rules governing re-litigation: the rules of "claim preclusion" and the rules of "collateral estoppel."

- **Claim preclusion:** The rules of *"claim preclusion"* prevent a *claim* (or "cause of action") from being re-litigated. They break down into two sub-rules:

  - ❑ **Merger:** Under the rule of *"merger,"* if P *wins* the first action, his claim is "merged" into his judgment. He cannot later sue the same D on the same cause of action for higher damages.

  - ❑ **Bar:** Under the doctrine of *"bar,"* if P *loses* his first action, his claim is extinguished, and he is barred from suing again on that cause of action.

- **Collateral estoppel:** The rules of *"collateral estoppel"* prevent re-litigation of a particular *issue of fact or law*. When a particular issue of fact or law has been determined in one proceeding, then in a subsequent proceeding between the same parties, *even on a different cause of action*, each party is *"collaterally estopped"* from claiming that that issue should have been decided differently than it was in the first action. A synonym for "collateral estoppel" is *"issue preclusion."*

  - ❑ **Issues covered:** For an issue to be subject to collateral estoppel, three requirements concerning that issue must be satisfied: (1) the issue must be the *same* as one that was *fully and fairly litigated* in the first action; (2) it must have been actually *decided* by the first court; and (3) the first court's decision on this issue must have been *necessary* to the outcome in the first suit.

  - ❑ **Persons who can be estopped:** Generally, only the *actual parties* to the first action can be *bound* by the finding on an issue.

  - ❑ **Persons who can benefit from estoppel:** But even one who was *not a party* to the first action (a *"stranger"* to the first action") may in some circumstances *benefit* from estoppel. That is, the stranger to the first action may assert in the second suit that her adversary, who *was* a party to the first action, is collaterally estopped from re-litigating an issue of fact or law decided in that first action. (Courts are *more willing* to allow the *"defensive"* use of collateral estoppel by a stranger than they are to allow the *"offensive"* use. "Offensive" use refers to use by a stranger who is a *plaintiff* in the second action; "defensive" use refers to use by a stranger who is a *defendant* in the second action.)

■ **Full Faith and Credit:** Where the first and second suits are in different jurisdictions, the second jurisdiction must generally *enforce* the first jurisdiction's judgment (including that judgment's *res judicata* effect), under the doctrine of *"Full Faith and Credit."*

I. GENERAL PRINCIPLES

A. Scope: All courts agree on the principle that where two parties have fully litigated a particular *claim*, and a final judgment has resulted, that claim may not later be *relitigated* by the loser. All courts are similarly in agreement that if a particular finding of *fact* has been made in the course of a lawsuit between two parties, that issue of fact may not later be retried by the loser, even though the cause of action is different in the second suit. The entire set of rules that prevent re-litigation of claims and issues is often collectively referred to as the doctrine of *"res judicata"* (Latin for "things which have been decided").

1. **Merger and bar:** The rules that prevent a *claim* (or as it is sometimes called, a *cause of action*) from being relitigated are called the rules of *claim preclusion*. Two separate but closely related rules, the rule of *"merger"* and the rule of *"bar,"* make up the doctrine of claim preclusion.

   a. **Merger:** If plaintiff wins the first action, his claim is *"merged"* into his judgment. He cannot later sue the same defendant on the same cause of action for higher damages.

   b. **Bar:** If the plaintiff in the first action loses, his claim is extinguished, and he is *"barred"* from suing again on that cause of action.

   Note: The term *"res judicata"* is sometimes used to refer solely to the rules of claim preclusion. But we use that term in this chapter in its more general sense, to encompass both the rules of claim preclusion and the rules (summarized immediately below) of collateral estoppel.

2. **Collateral estoppel:** If a particular *issue of fact or law* has been determined in one proceeding, then in a subsequent proceeding between the same parties (even on a different cause of action), each party is *"collaterally estopped"* from claiming that that issue should be decided differently than it was in the first action. Thus the doctrine is usually called *collateral estoppel.*

   a. **"Issue preclusion":** The doctrine generally referred to as collateral estoppel is sometimes also called *"issue preclusion,"* to reflect the fact that what is being prevented from relitigation is an issue. The phrase "issue preclusion" has the advantage of contrasting sharply with its opposite, "claim preclusion." Partly for this reason, the Second Restatement of Judgments favors the terms "claim preclusion" and "issue preclusion." See Rest. 2d, Introduction to Chapter 1. Notwithstanding the growing use of the term "issue preclusion," we use the more traditional "collateral estoppel" here.

   b. **Mutuality:** Most courts, until about twenty years ago, applied the doctrine of collateral estoppel only where the parties in the second action had *both* been present in the first action. A stranger to the first action could not in the second action assert that his adversary (who had been a party in the first action) was collaterally estopped from relitigating an issue decided in the first action — the reason for this was that the stranger could not have been *bound* by a finding of fact in the first action unfavorable to him (the requirements of due process prevent binding a party without giving him a day in court.) Therefore, courts reasoned, it was unfair to give the stranger the *benefit* of the first action, where he could not have been saddled with the *burden* of that action. The rule that a stranger to the first action could not assert collateral estoppel against one who had been a party to that first action is known as the doctrine of *mutuality.*

   i. Demise of mutuality: Most courts have discarded the general doctrine of mutuality. Many courts, however, still prevent a stranger to the first action from asserting, in certain situations, collateral estoppel against a party to the first action.

B. Privies: The rules of claim preclusion and collateral estoppel generally apply to certain persons who are said to be in *privity* with the litigants in the earlier action. These persons include a *successor in interest* (e.g., the purchaser of property which has been the subject of an earlier quiet-title action), and an *indemnitor* whose indemnitee was a party to the earlier action.

C. Full Faith and Credit: The Constitutional requirement of Full Faith and Credit compels the courts of each state to give to a judgment of a sister state the same effect that that judgment would have in the state which rendered it. This requires each state to apply the same rules of merger, bar, and collateral estoppel as the state which rendered the earlier judgment would apply. A statute, 28 U.S.C. §1738, compels the federal courts to give Full Faith and Credit to the judgments of state courts.

D. Applicable only to new actions: The rules discussed in this chapter apply only to *new actions* subsequent to the action in which the original judgment was rendered — they do not apply to *further proceedings* in the same action in which the original judgment was rendered. Thus, these rules do not apply to a party who is seeking a *new trial* (in which he hopes the first judgment will be replaced by one of different effect), or to a party who is seeking to have the judgment reversed on *appeal.*

E. Rationale: The rules discussed in this chapter are based on the principle that *a party who has been given one fair opportunity to litigate a claim or an issue, should not be given a second chance.* This principle is in turn based on two policy considerations: (1) *fairness to the victor* requires that he not be required to relitigate the claim or issue on which he has been victorious; and (2) *judicial economy* requires that litigation arising from a particular controversy not be continued indefinitely.

II. CLAIM PRECLUSION (MERGER AND BAR)

A. Definition: If a judgment is rendered for the plaintiff, his claim is *"merged"* into the judgment; that is, it is extinguished and a new claim to enforce the judgment is created. If judgment is for the defendant on the merits, the claim is extinguished and nothing new is created; plaintiff is *"barred"* from raising the claim again. Rest. 2d Judgments, §§18, 19; James & Hazard, p. 589. Some illustrations of the operation of merger and bar:

1. P sues D for $1000 damages resulting from an automobile accident. The verdict and judgment grant P only $500. His claim, or cause of action, is "merged," meaning that P cannot initiate a new suit for the other $500.

2. Same suit as (1), but D is found not to be liable at all. P is "barred" from making the same claim in a second suit against D.

3. P sues D and wins the full $1000, but finds that D has no property within the state upon which execution can be levied. His remedy is to bring an action "on the judgment" in the courts of whatever state he can find where D does have property. This action will be governed by the rules of Full Faith and Credit; unless D defaulted in the first action and the first court had no jurisdiction over him, the court of the second state must duplicate the judgment of the first court. The two judgments do not merge, and P can levy (or sue in yet a third state) on *either* of them. Cf. *Moore v. Justices of the Municipal Court of Boston*, 197 N.E. 487 (Mass. 1935).

B. Scope of claim: Since through claim preclusion a judgment is conclusive with respect to the entire "claim" which it adjudicates, it is essential to determine exactly what the dimensions of a claim are.

   1. **Rule against splitting of claim:** A claim can include much *more* than plaintiff actually chose to state in his complaint. Plaintiff cannot *"split"* his claim — if he sues upon *any portion* of a claim, the other aspects of that claim are merged in his judgment if he wins, and barred if he loses.

      Example: Plaintiff claims $1000 due under a single indivisible contract. He thinks there is a three in ten chance that a judge will find in his favor, and so he files ten separate suits, for $100 each, in the hope of winning at least a few of them. He has violated the rule against splitting a claim — the first judgment of the ten will merge with the others if he wins, in which case he has lost the other $900; if the first judgment comes out against him, it bars the others, and he has lost the entire $1000.

      a. **Strict application:** The rule against splitting a claim can have very harsh results for a plaintiff who does not realize the full scope of her possible claim. Consider, for instance, *Jacobson v. Mutual Benefit Health & Accident Assoc.*, 11 N.W.2d 442 (N.D. 1943). In *Jacobson*, P was the insured under an insurance policy, Part A of which entitled P to $2000. Part B of the policy, of which P's lawyer was unaware, entitled P to an additional $1800. P sued only for the $2000. She won, and later discovered the $1800 clause. Suit on the latter clause was not allowed; it had been *"merged"* in the first judgment.

      Note: Where the splitting of a claim occurs through the gross incompetence of counsel, courts will sometimes refuse to strictly apply the rule against splitting, and will permit plaintiff to bring a new suit for the remainder of the claim.

      b. **Installment contracts:** Suppose that the claim relates to payments due under a *lease* or *installment contract*. The general rule is that a plaintiff must sue at the same time for *all payments* due at the time the suit is filed, in this lease or installment-contract situation. See James & Hazard, p. 597.

Example: Defendant has made monthly lease payments in January and February, has skipped March, paid for April, and then skipped every month through September. If plaintiff sues in September, he **must** sue for March and May-September at once, or else forfeit whatever months he omits, since all the monthly payments are part of the same claim. October's payment, not being due yet, is not part of the same cause of action — if defendant also defaults on it, plaintiff can sue for it at a later date.

  i. **Acceleration clauses:** Many installment contracts contain *acceleration clauses*, providing that whenever defendant defaults on one payment, the whole balance becomes due. The courts have disagreed as to whether plaintiff **must** sue for the whole balance at once, or whether he may sue for just those months which have actually elapsed. A strict application of the splitting rule would require that plaintiff sue for the entire amount. But such a result is likely to drive the defendant into bankruptcy.

  ii. **Running account:** The same rule requiring suit for all payments due at the time of suit applies where there is a *"running account"* between creditor and debtor. For instance, if Merchant sells goods on credit to Consumer, any suit against Consumer must be for the entire amount which Consumer owes Merchant at the time the suit is brought, even though that debt arises out of separate transactions involving separate items. See Rest. 2d, Judgments §24, Comment d.

  iii. **Promissory notes:** But where a debt is represented by *promissory notes*, a separate suit may be brought upon each note. James and Hazard, p. 607.

2. **Multi-theory actions:** In each of the above instances, plaintiff's claims involved a single contract and a single legal theory. The splitting rule is, however, also applicable to a lawsuit which contains several claims, all arising from the same set of facts and all alleging a violation of the same legal right, but involving a *variety of theories or remedies.*

  a. **Common law:** At common law, "causes of action" were narrowly construed, and a single act could lead to actions of, say, trespass and trespass on the case, which could not be joined in a single pleading. Claim preclusion was invoked only in such relatively simple cases as those described above. Since plaintiff could not join trespass and case, then the outcome of one action did not "merge" or "bar" the other. (The doctrine of "inconsistent remedies" might have prevented plaintiff's second suit, but that doctrine had nothing to do with claim preclusion, and will not be discussed here.)

  b. **Extension of claim concept:** Procedural reforms within the last century, such as the Federal Rules, have greatly increased a plaintiff's freedom to join several legal theories and remedies in a single pleading. These reforms have correspondingly *increased the scope of claim preclusion.*

  i. **Transactional test:** The modern approach is to define "cause of action" by a *"transactional"* definition. Thus the Restatement Second of Judgments, §24, provides that there will be merger or bar of all of the plaintiff's rights against the defendant "with respect to all or any part of the *transaction*, or *series of connected transactions*, out of which the [initial] action arose." What constitutes a "transaction" or "series of transactions" is to be determined pragmatically, giving weight to such considerations as whether the facts are *related in time, space, origin, or* *motivation*, whether they form a *convenient trial unit*, and whether their treatment as a unit conforms to the *parties' expectations* or *business understanding or usage*." See, e.g., *Harrington v. Vandalia-Butler Board of Education, infra*, p. 363(where plaintiff has claims under two different federal anti-discrimination statutes, there is only one cause of action, since both claims arise out of the same discriminatory action by defendant.)

Example: Plaintiff files two suits against defendant, each for violation of the anti-trust laws. Suit 1, which is against defendant as a sole tortfeasor, alleges violations of the Clayton Act. P loses, then brings Suit 2. Suit 2 charges defendant with conspiring with unnamed persons, and is brought under the Sherman Act.

Held, "the wrongful acts alleged on the part of the defendant and the damages alleged to have been sustained by the plaintiff are practically identical in both suits." Suit 2 is barred by the judgment against plaintiff in Suit 1. "The plaintiff having alleged *operative facts* which state a cause of action because he tells of defendant's misconduct and his own harm has had his day in court. He does not get another day after the first lawsuit is concluded by giving a different reason than he gave in the first for recovery of damages for the same invasion of his rights." *Williamson v. Columbia Gas & Electric Corp.*, 186 F.2d 464 (3rd Cir. 1950).

c. **Second claim not valid at time of first suit:**   Modern courts' broad definition of "claim" is, of course, designed to encourage a litigant to advance all legal theories relating to a given set of facts in one, rather than multiple, proceedings. Suppose that at the time the first suit is brought, there is only one legal theory on which the plaintiff can reasonably proceed, but that *after the first* suit, a *change in law* makes a *second legal theory* available. In this situation, the main rationale behind the rule preventing the splitting of a claim would seem not to have any weight. Nonetheless, at least some courts hold that if the claim which subsequently becomes available arises out of the same transaction as the claim litigated in the first action, the newly-available claim will be barred or merged.

Example: P brings an employment sex-discrimination suit under Title VII of the 1964 Civil Rights Act against D (a municipal board of education). Although she is found to have been discriminated against, she is found as a matter of statutory interpretation not to be entitled to compensatory damages or attorney's fees. P does not, as part of this first suit, allege a violation of another federal statute, 42 U.S.C. §1983 (which allows compensatory damages to be recovered against any "person" who, under "color of law" violates the plaintiff's constitutional rights) because, at the time of the first suit, the established law is that municipalities are not "persons" subject to liability under §1983. After the first suit has been completely resolved, the Supreme Court reverses prior law, and concludes that municipalities may now be sued under §1983. P starts a new suit against D alleging a violation of §1983; she relies upon the same discriminatory acts as in the first suit.

Held, P is barred by the doctrine of *claim preclusion* from litigating the §1983 claim. While it is true that P reasonably believed that no §1983 claim against D was available to her at the time of the first suit, she could have challenged the then-applicable case law that prevented §1983 actions against municipalities, so that the §1983 claim was not completely "unavailable" to her at the time of the first suit. In any event, application of *res judicata* here is no more unfair to P than are other consequences of the finality of judgments; for instance, after the conclusion of the first suit, had the Supreme Court reinterpreted Title VII to allow compensatory damages for attorney's fees, P would not have been entitled to the benefits of that change of law. (The rules of *res judicata* need not be strictly applied if "their application would contravene an overriding public policy or result in manifest injustice." But the result of *res judicata* here, although it contains "an element of injustice," does not involve either a sufficiently overriding public policy or a sufficiently large injustice that the usual principle of finality should be dispensed with.) *Harrington v. Vandalia-Butler Board of Education*, 649 F.2d 434 (6th Cir. 1981).

3. **Personal and property damage from accident:** Where a person suffers both ***personal injuries*** and ***property damage*** from the same accident (typically, an auto accident), most states today follow the rule that plaintiff has a ***single claim***, not distinct claims for personal injuries on the one hand and property damage on the other. J&H, p. 601. The rationale for this majority view is that a single tortious act has caused all of the injuries, so they should all be litigated together. (The promotion of ***judicial efficiency*** also argues in favor of this rule.) See *Rush v. City of Maple Heights*, 147 N.E.2d 599 (Ohio 1958) (Ohio follows majority rule). But a handful of states allow the plaintiff to litigate separately her claims for personal injuries and for property damage arising out of a single accident.

4. **Application to equitable remedies:** The merger of law and equity has resulted in the application of the rules of merger and bar to ***equitable*** remedies as well as to legal ones. In fact, it will not infrequently be the case that a demand for legal relief (generally, money damages) and a demand for equitable relief (e.g., an injunction) will both be deemed to be part of the same "claim," so that both demands must be made in the same action. See Rest. 2d, Judgments, §25, Comment i.

   a. **Reformation:** For example, in *Hennepin Paper Co. v. Fort Wayne Corrugated Paper Co.*, 153 F.2d 822 (7th Cir. 1946), a plaintiff who had previously sued on a contract and lost due to the parol evidence rule, brought an equitable action for ***reformation*** of the contract.

      i. **Holding:** The court held that the reformation action was barred by the judgment in the contract action. The court emphasized that the plaintiff could have, under the Federal Rules, sought reformation at the same time it sought recovery on the contract as written. (Rule 8(e)(2) allows a party to state "as many separate claims or defenses as he has regardless of consistency and whether based on legal, equitable, or maritime grounds.") Since the plaintiff had this right of joinder, it was obliged to exercise it, or lose the reformation claim forever.

      ii. **Limitation:** The court indicated that this principle applied *only* where the law court in the first action had the power to grant the equitable relief sought in the second action. If the first court did not have this power, then plaintiff would not be barred from seeking equitable relief subsequently.

b. Legal claim following equitable claim: Just as *Hennepin* illustrates the principle that an equitable claim may be barred by a previous legal judgment, it is also the case that a legal claim may be barred by or merged into an earlier equitable judgment.

Example: Plaintiff, an Iowa law student, claims to have been a resident of Iowa since 1964. In 1966 he successfully seeks an injunction against the enforcement of nonresident tuition rates against him. Later, he seeks to recover the excess tuition that he paid from 1964 to 1966.

Held, P's claim to tuition was **merged** into the injunction, and has thus been lost. "The judgment is conclusive, not only as to matters which were decided, but also as to all matters which **might have been decided.**" *Clarke v. Redeker,* 406 F.2d 883 (8th Cir. 1969).

5. Exception to claim preclusion rules: There nevertheless remain instances where two possible legal theories relating to the same incident cannot be joined in any forum, and where as a result claim preclusion is not applicable. Such cases often arise due to statutory *jurisdictional* requirements — if the court trying the first action would not have had subject matter jurisdiction of the theory used in the second action, there will be no bar or merger. Rest. 2d, Judgments, §26(1)(c).

Example: P sues D in state court under a state antitrust law, and loses on the merits. P then sues D in federal court alleging the same facts, and charging a violation of the federal antitrust laws. Because the federal courts have exclusive jurisdiction of antitrust claims, the state court could not have heard the federal claim. Therefore, the second (federal court) action is not barred. Rest. 2d, Judgments, §26, Illustr. 2. See also *Cream Top Creamery v. Dean Milk Co.,* 383 F.2d 358 (6th Cir. 1967). (The federal court hearing the second suit should look to the claim preclusion rules of the *state* court that entered the earlier judgment, which will ordinarily not preclude the later federal suit — see *infra.*)

6. Suits in two different jurisdictions: Where Suit 1 and Suit 2 are in *two different jurisdictions,* the court hearing Suit 2 must normally apply not its own rules of claim preclusion, but *those of the court that heard Suit 1.*

a. State suit followed by federal suit: This is true not only where Suit 1 and Suit 2 are in two different states, but also where Suit 1 is in state court and Suit 2 is in federal court, and vice versa. The rule that it is the first court's claim preclusion rules which apply is a corollary to the more general requirement that each court must render "Full Faith and Credit" to the judgments of other jurisdictions. See *infra,* p. 388, for a fuller discussion of this principle.

Example: The Ps are orthopedic surgeons whose applications for membership in D (the American Academy of Orthopaedic Surgeons) are denied. The Ps bring an Illinois state court suit claiming that D's action violated associational rights protected by Illinois common law. (They do not assert a cause of action under the Illinois Antitrust Act, which is very similar to the federal Sherman Antitrust Act.) The Ps lose in state court. They then start a federal action based on the Sherman Antitrust Act. D argues that since the state and federal suits involve the same facts, and since the Ps could have brought a state antitrust claim highly similar to the present federal claim, claim preclusion should bar the federal suit.

Held (by the U.S. Supreme Court), the federal court should not have made its own independent analysis based on general federal common law principles. Instead, it should have determined what rule of claim preclusion the Illinois state courts would apply in this type of situation. If the Illinois courts would not preclude the subsequent suit (e.g., if they would apply the generally-accepted rule, discussed above, that there is no preclusion of a claim that would have been beyond the subject matter jurisdiction of the first court), then the federal court may not apply claim preclusion.

If the federal court concludes that the Illinois courts *would* preclude the later suit, the federal court should then determine whether Congress, in enacting the Sherman Act, intended an exception to 28 U.S.C. §1738's statutory full-faith-and-credit provision. (See *infra*, p. 389.) *Marrese v. American Academy of Orthopaedic Surgeons*, 470 U.S. 373 (1985).

C. Adjudication on the merits: For the rule of "bar" to take effect, the original adjudication for the defendant must have been *"on the merits."* This means that some of the many ways in which plaintiff can lose a case will **not bar future efforts** on his part to relitigate the same claim. See Rest. 2d, Judgments, §20.

1. **Rule 41(b):** Federal Rule 41(b) specifies the following as grounds for dismissal which *never* lead to bar:

   a. *lack of jurisdiction;*

   b. *improper venue;*

   c. *failure to join an indispensable party.*

   d. **Other:** Any other dismissal "operates as an adjudication on the merits" **unless the court specifies otherwise** in its order for dismissal.

   Note: Most states similarly regard the items listed in (a), (b) and (c) above as not leading to bar or merger. See Rest. 2d, Judgments, §20(1). Consequently, it should make no difference whether both actions are federal, both state, or one each — there will never be claim preclusion when the first action is disposed of in one of these three ways.

2. **Failure to prosecute or obey court:** A Federal Rule 41(b) dismissal for failure to **prosecute**, or for failure to **comply** with an order of the court, is apparently **with prejudice** unless the court specifies otherwise. Wright notes that "this is a drastic sanction, and though the courts have the power and must have the power if they are to discharge their responsibility to prevent undue delay in litigation, it is a power that should be exercised only in extreme situations." Wr., 655.

   a. **Abuse of discretion:** The failure of the trial judge to specify that such a dismissal is without prejudice is reviewable on appeal and may be reversed as an abuse of discretion.

3. **Failure to state a claim:** Formerly, courts were reluctant to declare a bar where the first trial was dismissed on a demurrer or for *failure to state a cause of action*, and plaintiff

corrected the defects in his pleadings in a second action (rather than through amending the pleadings in the first action). See, e.g., *Keidatz v. Albany*, 249 P.2d 264 (Cal. 1952), holding that dismissal on a demurrer was not a bar, regardless of whether plaintiff had had leave to amend and failed to use it, so long as the complaint in the new action remedied the defect. But in modern courts, a dismissal for failure to state a claim usually counts as an adjudication on the merits.

a. **Federal system:** Thus in the federal system, a dismissal for failure to state a claim counts as an adjudication on the merits unless the court specifies otherwise. FRCP 41(b). If the court does not specify otherwise, plaintiff must either amend his pleading (if given leave) or appeal; he may not commence a new action. See *Rinehart v. Locke*, 454 F.2d 313 (7th Cir. 1971).

   i. **Restatement in accord:** The same is usually true in state courts. Thus the Second Restatement of Judgments, §19, Comment d, provides that a state court adjudication that a complaint is legally insufficient precludes a second suit on the claims asserted in it.

D. **Counterclaims:** A defendant who pleads a counterclaim is, in effect, a plaintiff with respect to that claim. He is bound by the outcome, just as the plaintiff is bound by the outcome of his original claim.

1. **No splitting:** Every jurisdiction now permits a defendant to make a counterclaim on which he may obtain *affirmative recovery*. That is, if plaintiff sues defendant for $10,000, defendant can interpose a counterclaim for $100,000 and hope to win the difference of $90,000, or even the whole $100,000. In such a case, defendant *may not split his counterclaim* into two parts, using $10,000 to offset plaintiff's claim, and later suing for the remainder.

2. **Collateral estoppel danger:** A defendant with a claim against one who is suing him has the *option of not using his claim at all* in that action, preserving it for a separate action. He must be careful, however, for if in his *defense* at the first trial he attempts to prove facts which are essential to his own claim, and fails, he will be *collaterally estopped* from pursuing his own claim later on. (See *infra*, p. 369). If his own claim is much greater than the one against him, he may think it worthwhile to *default* at the first trial — no collateral estoppel effect will attach to a default judgment. *Lovejoy v. Ashworth.* 45 A.2d 218 (N.H. 1946).

   a. **Defendant wins:** If the defendant declines to assert his counterclaim, and *wins* as to the plaintiff's claim, he will be able to start a new suit based on the claim he could have asserted as a counterclaim (assuming it was not a compulsory counterclaim, discussed below). Thus in *Schwabe v. Chantilly Inc.*, 226 N.W.2d 452 (Wis. 1975), the defendants in the first action asserted fraud as an affirmative defense, but not as a counterclaim, and won. They were thereafter permitted to bring a fraud claim based on the same actions by their adversary.

3. **Compulsory counterclaims:** Under the Federal Rules, and many state counterparts, a counterclaim which arises from the same transaction as the plaintiff's claim is *compulsory*. Rule 13(a). If the defendant fails to raise it, he is *barred* from using it in a later

action. Note that this "transaction" test is similar to the transactional test which is gaining favor for the purpose of defining "cause of action."

a. State respects federal counterclaim rule: Most states respect the policy behind the federal compulsory counterclaim rule, and thus *bar an action* on a claim that should have been raised as a compulsory counterclaim in a prior federal action. See, e.g., *Horne v. Woolever*, 163 N.E.2d 378 (Ohio St. 1959). See also F,K&M, p. 354.

b. Settlement: Suppose D does not assert what should be a compulsory counterclaim, and the main action is then *settled*. Is D barred from bringing the claim in a later suit? Courts are split on the question. For a case holding that D should *not* be automatically barred, and holding that D's *awareness* that he had a counterclaim should be considered in deciding whether D should be allowed to bring the new claim, see *Dindo v. Whitney*, 451 F.2d 1 (1st Cir. 1971).

E. Change of law: Once a final judgment has been rendered (and either appealed, or the time for appeal passed), *not even a change in the applicable law* will prevent *res judicata* from operating. The fact that the losing party would, because of such an overruling of legal precedent, win the lawsuit if he were allowed to start it again, is irrelevant.

1. Appeals by co-parties: This principle was vividly demonstrated in *Federated Department Stores, Inc. v. Moitie*, 452 U.S. 394 (1981). Moitie was one of seven plaintiffs who filed suit against various department stores on price-fixing charges; although the suits were separate, they were all before the same judge, and all tracked the same U.S. antitrust suit against the department stores. The trial court dismissed all of the suits on technical antitrust grounds; most of the plaintiffs, but not Moitie, appealed. Moitie instead refiled with a different complaint (but which was found to involve really the same claims as the dismissed suit). While the other plaintiffs' appeal was pending, the Supreme Court, in a separate case, *reversed prior law* as to the technical antitrust issue. The other appealing plaintiffs in the department store suits were permitted to reinstitute their suit in the trial court. The question was, should Moitie's new suit be barred?

a. Claim preclusion applied: Notwithstanding the fact that the applicable substantive law had been changed, and that the other original plaintiffs were permitted to refile their suit, the Supreme Court held that claim preclusion *barred* Moitie from refiling her suit. The Court rejected the assertion that "non-appealing parties may benefit from a reversal when their position is closely interwoven with that of appealing parties."

2. Major constitutional change: But where there has been a *major change* in *constitutional law* between the first suit and the second suit, so that the litigant who lost the first time would win now, claim preclusion may *not* be strictly applied, especially if the issue has great public importance. For instance, suppose particular conduct by a school system were found not to constitute intentional (and thus illegal) racial segregation, but then the constitutional definition of forbidden segregation changed; the same plaintiff might be permitted to relitigate the issue of whether the system was illegally segregating. See F,K&M, p. 658.

F. Persons not party to first action: Thus far we have limited our discussion of *res judicata* to situations where one of the original parties to the first action is sought to be precluded from relitigation. Normally, *only* parties to the initial judgment will be subject to merger or bar.

1. **Privies:**   But in a few situations, a non-party may be *so closely related* to a party to the first judgment, that he will be both burdened and benefitted by that judgment as if he had been a party to it. He is said, in this case, to be a *"privy"* to the first judgment. A trustee and his beneficiary, and an indemnitor and his indemnitee, are examples of privity relationships. The subject of privies is discussed more fully *infra*, p. 375, in the treatment of collateral estoppel. See, e.g., *Fagnan v. Great Central Insur. Co.*, discussed *infra*, p. 377 (insurer may claim benefit of *res judicata* applicable to insured, since the two are privies.)

Quiz Yourself on

CLAIM PRECLUSION (MERGER AND BAR)

116. P and D, each driving a car, collided. P suffered serious personal injuries, and her car was totally demolished. P brought an action in Ames state court for damages for her personal injuries, but not for any loss of property. P won the suit. P then commenced a second action against D, for the damage to her car, in Ames state court. Will the court hear this second action? _____

117. Pauline and Doug, while each was driving, collided. Pauline suffered personal injuries and damage to her car. Pauline brought a federal court diversity action against Doug, for her personal injuries but not for her property damage. Suit was brought in Iowa federal district court. Doug made a motion under Rule 12(b)(6) for failure to state a cause of action; he asserted that Pauline's claim was barred by the statute of limitations. The federal judge agreed with this assertion, and dismissed the case. The order of dismissal did not say whether the dismissal was with prejudice. Pauline has then brought another action, again in federal court for Iowa, seeking to recover for the property damage she sustained in the accident (in contrast to the personal injury damages she sought in the first action). Should the federal judge hear Pauline's second claim on the merits? _____

118. Same basic fact pattern as the prior two questions. Now, assume that Pauline's claim in Iowa federal court proceeded to a decision on the merits. The judge applied Iowa state law, which is that contributory negligence by the plaintiff, no matter how small in degree, completely blocks plaintiff from recovering. The judge found in favor of Doug on the grounds that Pauline was slightly negligent. The judge entered a final judgment in favor of Doug. One month later, the Iowa Supreme Court reversed its prior decisions, and held that comparative negligence, rather than contributory negligence, will henceforth be the official doctrine of Iowa. Pauline has now brought a second suit against Doug in federal court for Iowa, for property damage from the original accident. Should the federal judge allow Pauline's action to go forward?

_____

Answers

116. **No, probably.** The twin doctrines of *merger* and *bar* (collectively known as *"claim preclusion"*) prevent a plaintiff from "splitting her cause of action" between two suits. If a plaintiff splits a cause of action and wins the first suit, her second claim is said to be "merged" into the favorable first judgment; if she loses the first suit, her second claim is held to be "barred" by the unfavorable first result.

Most courts today follow the "transaction" test for determining what constitutes a cause of action. By this test, both P's personal injury claim and her property damage claim formed a single cause of action, since they stemmed from a single transaction (the auto accident). Therefore, most courts would treat P as losing her property damage claim because it was merged into her previously-asserted personal injury claim. See F,K&M, p. 634-35.

117. No. Claim preclusion only applies where the first suit was resolved *"on the merits,"* so the question becomes whether the dismissal here was on the merits. Under Federal Rule 41(b), an order of dismissal is treated as being on the merits unless either the dismissal order specifies that it is without prejudice, or the dismissal is for lack of jurisdiction, improper venue, or failure to join an indispensable party. Since none of these exceptions applies here, the dismissal is treated as being on the merits. As such, the result is the same as if Pauline had tried her case through to, say, a jury verdict. Her property-damage claim is part of the same cause of action as her personal injury claim, so she is barred by the earlier dismissal from asserting the property damage claim here.

118. No. Once a final judgment has been rendered, not even a change in the applicable law will prevent res judicata from operating. The fact that Pauline would have won her original lawsuit if it were brought today, is irrelevant. Since the property damage claim being asserted now and the personal-injury claim asserted then are part of the same cause of action (see the answer to Question 230 above), Pauline's property damage claim will be barred just as if there had been no intervening change of law.

III. COLLATERAL ESTOPPEL

A. Effect: Regardless of which of the parties to an action is victorious, the judgment is "conclusive in a subsequent action between them *upon the issues actually litigated in the action.*" Rest. 2d, Judgments, §27; James & Hazard, p. 607. A party who seeks to relitigate one of the issues disposed of in the first trial is said to be *collaterally estopped* from doing so.

   1. Application: The principles of collateral estoppel always apply where *both* of the parties in the second action were present in the first action. These rules sometimes, but not always, apply where only the person against whom estoppel is sought to be used was present in the first action.

   2. Distinguished from merger and bar: Whereas claim preclusion applies only where the "claim" in the second action is the same as the one adjudicated in the first action, collateral estoppel applies as long as any *issue* is the same, even though the causes of action are different. Also, whereas claim preclusion prevents the second suit altogether, collateral estoppel does not prevent suit, but merely compels the court to make the same finding of fact on the identical issue that the first court made. (Sometimes, of course, this will as a practical matter bar suit, as in a negligence case like *Little, infra*, where the initial finding of plaintiff's non-negligence effectively disposes of a later suit by the defendant.)

   > **Example:** Blue Goose sues Little for damage to its bus resulting from a collision with Little's automobile. Damages of $139 are recovered. In a subsequent action, Little sues for his own personal injuries.
   >
   > *Held* (in the second suit), "the issue of negligence was necessarily determined" in the first action, and may not be relitigated. The fact that the negligence alleged by Little is 'wanton and willful' negligence (whereas only ordinary negligence was debated in the first action) is irrelevant. The judgment for Blue Goose was definitely a finding that it had not been either ordinarily or willfully negligent (the doctrine of contributory negligence would have barred recovery if it had been.) This finding of non-negligence

is binding on Little in the second action. *Little v. Blue Goose Motor Coach Co.*, 178 N.E. 496 (Ill. 1931).

B. Issues to which collateral estoppel applies: For an issue to be subject to collateral estoppel, three requirements must be satisfied: (1) the issue must be the *same* as one that was *fully and fairly litigated* in the first action; (2) the issue must have actually been *decided* by the first court; and (3) the first court's decision on this issue must have been *necessary to the outcome* in the first suit. Rest. 2d, Judgments, §27.

1. Same issue: For the relitigation of an issue to be collaterally estopped, that issue must be *identical* to an issue litigated in the earlier trial. However, this requirement of identity is not interpreted with the greatest possible strictness.

> **Example 1:** Suppose the first action involves X's negligence to Y's automobile. In a second action, Y will be collaterally estopped from relitigating X's negligence to Y's *person* for injuries arising from the same car accident — the two kinds of negligence will be held to be a single issue for collateral estoppel purposes. See *Fleischer v. Detroit Cadillac Motor Car Co.*, 165 N.Y.S. 245 (1st Dept. 1917).

> **Example 2:** The Ps (Berlitz School of Languages and Berlitz Publications) sue D (Charles Berlitz, grandson of the founder of the Ps) in state court. They claim that language books authored by D violate state unfair competition and trademark laws, in that the public will be confused into thinking that D has a relationship with the Ps. The state court determines that a disclaimer on the front of each of these books (stating that D is no longer associated with the Ps) suffices to avoid confusion. Some years later, D authors a new set of books, which include the same disclaimer on the cover. The Ps sue in federal court, alleging federal trademark infringement and unfair competition. D defends on the grounds that the factual issue of the disclaimer's ability to prevent the public from being confused was already decided in the first case, and should be given collateral estoppel effect. The Ps point out that the author's name is larger on the covers in the new series, and the disclaimer smaller, than in the old series.
>
> *Held*, for D. The size modifications on the author's name and the disclaimer are so small that the same factual issue is really involved in both proceedings, and the earlier finding must be given collateral estoppel effect. (But if in the future there are "substantially greater discrepancies" in the relative size of D's name in the disclaimer, the Ps will have a claim as to which there will be no collateral estoppel effect.) *Berlitz Schools of Languages of America v. Everest House*, 619 F.2d 211 (2d Cir. 1980).

2. Actually litigated and decided: For collateral estoppel to apply to an issue, the issue must have been *actually litigated* and *decided* at the first trial. A defendant is thus *not obligated to raise all of his defenses at one trial* if he knows that some of them may be relevant to future trials. He does not forfeit these defenses by not raising them as he would forfeit a compulsory counterclaim.

   a. Distinguished from merger and bar: This requirement of actual litigation is different from the rules of merger and bar, which can apply "not only as to matters which were decided, but also as to all matters which might have been decided." *Clarke v. Redeker*, 406 F.2d 883 (8th Cir. 1969).

Example: P sues D for an installment of rent under a lease, and wins. In a later suit for subsequent installments due on the same lease, D denies that the lease was ever executed.

Since D did not deny execution in the first action, he is not collaterally estopped from litigating the execution issue in the second action. Collateral estoppel applies only to issues which were actually litigated previously. *Jacobson v. Miller*, 1 N.W. 1013 (Mich. 1879).

b. "Full and fair" litigation: The party against whom collateral estoppel is sought to be used must have had a *"full and fair opportunity"* to litigate the claim. For instance, if he litigated the claim, but important evidence bearing on that issue was rejected by the court without good reason, he would not be bound, on the grounds that he lacked a "full and fair opportunity" to litigate the issue. See Rest. 2d, Judgments, §28(5)(c).

3. Issue essential to verdict: For relitigation of an issue to be precluded, that issue must not only have been litigated and decided in the first action, but the finding on that issue must have been *necessary to the judgment*. Rest. 2d, Judgments, §27.

Example: Jeffery sues Cambria, and loses. The court's findings of fact state that both parties were negligent, and recovery is denied on the grounds that Jeffery was contributorily negligent. Cambria then sues Jeffery, who claims that Cambria's (contributory) negligence was decided in the first action.

Collateral estoppel is *not* applied. Since the court in the first action based its verdict on the fact that Jeffery was contributorily negligent, its finding that Cambria was negligent has no effect in the second action. Collateral estoppel applies only to issues whose adjudication was *necessary* to the verdict in the first action. *Cambria v. Jeffery*, 29 N.E.2d 555 (Mass. 1940).

a. Alternate findings: Where a judgment rests upon *alternate* findings, either of which would be sufficient to sustain it, there has been much dispute about whether either finding should be given collateral estoppel effect. The Second Restatement of Judgments reasons that in this situation, it cannot be said that either of the findings was necessary to the judgment, and that therefore *neither should be given estoppel effect*. Rest. 2d, Judgments, §27, Comments h, i, j. Another rationale in support of not giving either finding collateral estoppel effect is that where there are alternative findings, the court may not be as careful in considering each, thus increasing the possibility of unfairness to the litigant who is bound by one of the findings. (But if both of the determinations are *upheld on appeal, each* will have estoppel effect. Id., §27, Comment o.)

i. Close question: The problem of alternative findings is a difficult and close one. Thus while the Second Restatement, as noted, provides that neither finding has estoppel effect, the First Restatement took the opposite view that *both* have effect; Rest. Judgments, §68, Comment n. The New York Court of Appeals has agreed with the First Restatement that both findings should be binding; see *Malloy v. Trombley*, 405 N.E.2d 213 (N.Y. 1980) (relying on evidence that the alternative ground in question was extensively litigated, and that the trial court carefully considered it).

4. Foreseeability of future litigation: There is an increasing tendency to apply collateral estoppel in a subsequent action only where that action was ***reasonably foreseeable*** at the time of the initial adjudication of the issue in question. This limitation was suggested by Learned Hand in dictum; he advocated that the estoppel effect of findings be restricted to "future controversies which could be thought reasonably in prospect when the first suit was tried." If this were not done, "Defeat in one suit might entail results beyond all calculation by either party; ***a trivial controversy might bring utter disaster in its train.***" *The Evergreens v. Nunan*, 141 F.2d 927 (2d Cir. 1944).

   a. Followed in Restatement: Hand's suggestion has been followed in the Second Restatement of Judgments, §28(5)(b) and Comment i — relitigation of an issue which was litigated and determined is permitted if it was "***not sufficiently foreseeable*** at the time of the initial action that the issue would arise in the context of a subsequent action."

5. Courts of limited jurisdiction: There is dispute as to whether a court of ***limited jurisdiction*** can, in deciding a case within its jurisdiction, make findings of fact which are binding in subsequent actions that would be beyond that jurisdiction. The Second Restatement of Judgments recognizes that it will not be appropriate to attach collateral estoppel effect if a redetermination of the issue is "warranted by differences in the ***quality or extensiveness*** of the ***procedures*** followed in the two courts or by factors relating to the ***allocation of jurisdiction*** between them." Rest. 2d, Judgments, §28(3).

   a. Jurisdictional amount: If the only difference between the two courts is that the first court had a ***maximum dollar limit*** on claims which it could adjudicate, so that the claim in the second action could not have been disposed of by the first court, this will usually ***not*** be enough of a reason to deny collateral estoppel effect to the first court's finding.

   Example: A brings a negligence action against B for property damage, in a court whose jurisdiction is limited to $2,000. The rules governing the court's trial procedures are essentially the same as in a court of general jurisdiction. A wins, because the court finds that B was negligent. B now brings a negligence action against A in a court of general jurisdiction, seeking $10,000 for personal injuries arising out of the same transaction. The first suit's finding that B was negligent will have collateral estoppel effect, thus barring B from recovery if the jurisdiction applies the doctrine of contributory negligence. Rest. 2d, Judgments, §28, Illustr. 6.

   b. Informal procedures: But if the first court not only has jurisdiction limited to a certain dollar amount, but also has ***informal procedures***, it will generally not be appropriate to give its finding collateral estoppel effect when the second suit is in a court of general jurisdiction. For instance, in most ***small claims courts***, there are no pleadings, no rules of evidence, and usually no counsel present; therefore, findings by such courts will generally not have collateral estoppel effect in a later action in a court of general jurisdiction. Thus on the facts of the above example, if the first suit was in such a court, B would still be able to claim in a second suit that he himself was not negligent. See Rest. 2d, Judgments, §28, Illustr. 7.

i. **Rationale:** The principle denying collateral estoppel effect to small claims court judgments seems reasonable. The purposes of a small claims court may be defeated if people are obliged to either default or to litigate their small claims or defenses to the hilt because of the possibility that large potential lawsuits might later be determined by the outcome.

c. **Surrogate's or probate court:** Sometimes the jurisdiction of the first court is limited not by dollar amount, but by the *subject matter* of the dispute. This is true, for instance, of *surrogate's* or *probate* courts. Generally, the procedures followed in these courts are of comparable rigor to those in courts of general jurisdiction. Therefore, findings made by these courts will generally be *binding* in a later general-court action. See, e.g., *U.S. v. Silliman*, 167 F.2d 607 (3d Cir. 1948) (surrogate court's findings concerning fraud are binding in a later fraud action in a court of general jurisdiction). See also Rest. 2d, Judgments, §28, Illustr. 8.

d. **Second action within exclusive federal jurisdiction:** So far in this chapter, we have generally assumed that both actions take place in the *same jurisdiction*. The rules are generally applicable, however, even if the actions are in the courts of two different states, or one action is brought in state court and the other in federal court. Suppose, however, that the first action is brought in state court, and the second is not only brought in federal court, but involves a *claim as to which the federal courts have exclusive subject matter jurisdiction*. In this situation, the federal court will nonetheless grant collateral estoppel effect to the state court's determination unless, as a matter of statutory interpretation, the court concludes that Congress, in establishing the federal right being sued upon, intended not to defer to the factual determinations of state courts. This issue is discussed more extensively *infra*, p. 389.

6. **Differences in burden of proof:** Differences in the *allocation of the burden of proof* between the first proceeding and the second may dictate that collateral estoppel not apply. If in the first action, the allocation of the burden of proof was more favorable to the party seeking to apply collateral estoppel than it was in the second action, collateral estoppel will not be allowed. Rest. 2d, Judgments, §28(4).

> **Example:** The first proceeding is an arbitration by a shipper of goods against the carrier of the goods. In that proceeding, the carrier is found at fault, under rules that place the burden of proof as to fault upon the carrier. The second proceeding is a lawsuit by the carrier against its insurance company.
>
> *Held*, the insurance company may not use collateral estoppel to avoid payment on the policy, even though the earlier proceeding made findings of fact (e.g., that the carrier concealed certain facts from the insurer) that were sufficient to void the insurance contract. The insurer has the burden of proof on the concealment issue in the second action, and may therefore not use collateral estoppel to take advantage of the earlier burden of proof that was less favorable to the carrier. *Steelmat, Inc. v. Caribe Towing Corp.*, 747 F.2d 689 (11th Cir. 1984).

7. **Settlement:** In most jurisdictions, the *settlement* of an action by consent of the parties has *no collateral estoppel effect*. See Rest. 2d, Judgments, §27 (issue must have been "actually litigated" for collateral estoppel to apply).

a. **Minority view:** In a minority of states, however, the settlement may be held to be binding on some or all of the issues which would have been litigated had the suit been tried. Such estoppel effect is of course in conflict with the general rule that only issues which have been fully and fairly litigated are subject to collateral estoppel — nonetheless, some jurisdictions attach collateral estoppel effect to settlements. The parties can avoid this possibility by specifying in the settlement that the agreement is to have no effect on any other cause of action. F,K&C, p. 1115.

8. **Findings of law:** Normally, the question of collateral estoppel arises with respect to findings of *fact*. However, a court's conclusion of *law* is also generally given collateral estoppel effect (assuming, of course, that the other requirements for that doctrine are met). In most situations, "it is unfair to the winning party and an unnecessary burden on the courts to allow repeated litigation of the same issue in what is essentially the same controversy, even if the issue is regarded as one of 'law.' " Rest. 2d, Judgments, §28, Comment b.

> **Example:** A federal statute provides that any naval officer who "served during the Civil War" shall upon retirement be given the next higher grade and pension. Moser, who was a cadet at the Naval Academy during the Civil War, sues at his retirement to have the statute applied to him. The government asserts that service at the Naval Academy is not "service during the Civil War" within the meaning of the statute, but the court rejects this defense and awards Moser the higher rank. In a later suit by a different cadet, Jasper, the government points to a different retirement statute, and the court denies Jasper the higher grade. In a subsequent suit by Moser for a later installment of pension, the government claims that the first Moser suit is not binding upon it because the determination was one of statutory interpretation, i.e., a finding of "law."
>
> *Held*, (by the U.S. Supreme Court), collateral estoppel applies, and the government is bound by the earlier finding that Moser's service at the Naval Academy falls within the statute. While it is true that collateral estoppel effect will not be given to "pure questions of law," such effect will be given to the determination of a "right," even though the determination may have been reached by an erroneous application of law to fact. *U.S. v. Moser*, 266 U.S. 236 (1924).

a. **Exceptions:** But the Restatement of Judgments recognizes two situations in which a conclusion of law should *not* be given collateral estoppel effect: (1) the two actions "involve claims that are *substantially unrelated*"; or (2) "a new determination is warranted in order to take account of an *intervening change in the applicable legal context* or otherwise to *avoid inequitable administration* of the laws." Rest. 2d, Judgments, §28(2)(a) and (b).

b. **"Substantially unrelated" claims:** The exception where the two claims are "substantially unrelated" seems to be another way of implementing the rule endorsed in *dictum* by the U.S. Supreme Court, in *Moser, supra*, that collateral estoppel does not apply to *"pure questions of law"* (in contrast to the application of a legal principle to a factual setting).

> **Example:** P sues D, a municipality, for injuries he claims D tortiously caused to him. D successfully defends on the grounds of sovereign immunity. Several years later, P sues D again, this time for a completely different injury. The first court's determina-

tion that sovereign immunity is a valid defense should not be given collateral estoppel effect, since the claims in the two actions arise out of different factual settings and are thus unrelated. (However, the doctrine of *stare decisis* may lead the court to conclude that it should not reconsider the validity of the sovereign immunity defense; but *stare decisis* is a completely different, and highly discretionary, principle.) See Rest. 2d, Judgments, §28, Illustr. 2.

    i.   **Constitutional adjudication:**   The "unrelated claims" exception is especially important where the legal issue is a ***constitutional*** one, and the party against whom collateral estoppel is sought to be used is the ***government*** or another party with an ***ongoing interest*** in the constitutional issue. If collateral estoppel were applied to pure conclusions of law in unrelated factual settings in this situation, the result might be to "freeze doctrine in areas of the law where responsiveness to changing patterns of conduct or social mores is critical." *Montana v. U.S.*, 440 U.S. 147 (1979).

  c.   **Change of legal climate:**   If, between the first and second suits, there has been a ***significant change in legal principles***, the court may as a discretionary matter decline to apply collateral estoppel. This is especially appropriate where use of collateral estoppel "would impose on one of the parties a ***significant disadvantage***, or confer on him a ***significant benefit***, with respect to his ***competitors***." Rest. 2d, Judgments, §28, Comment c. See also *Commissioner of Internal Revenue v. Sunnen*, 333 U.S. 591 (1948).

    Example: P, a state liquor licensing agency, sues to have D's wholesale liquor license revoked, on the grounds that D has violated the law governing such licenses by selling only to himself as a retailer. The court finds that D has not violated the law. P then sues X, whose conduct has been the same as D's; a higher court than decided the first case concludes that this conduct violates the statute, and orders X's license revoked. P then brings a second lower-court action against D for revocation. Collateral estoppel effect should not be given to the first P-vs.-D suit, since there has been an intervening change in legal principles, and since use of collateral estoppel would have given D a perpetual, and unfair, advantage over X and other similarly-situated competitors. See Rest. 2d, Judgments, §28, Illustr. 3.

9.   **Where second decision fails to apply estoppel:**   If for some reason collateral estoppel is not applied in an action where it should have been, and a new judgment results which decides an issue differently from the prior one, the ***second judgment receives binding effect by estoppel***. The original finding is thus in a sense "overruled", and will not be followed in a third action. *Donald v. J.J. White Lumber Co.*, 68 F.2d 441 (5th Cir. 1934).

C. **Persons bound by collateral estoppel:**   Where an issue which was litigated in one action reappears in a subsequent action, only certain parties in the second action will be estopped from relitigating the issue. James & Hazard, pp. 617-37.

1.   **Privies:**   All ***parties*** to the first action are bound by the finding on that issue. In addition, certain persons who are said to be ***"in privity"*** with parties to the first action are also bound. Following are some of the classes of persons likely to be held in privity with the original party:

a. **Successors in interest:** One who has purchased or otherwise succeeded to an *interest in real property* is in privity with all previous owners. He will thus be collaterally estopped from relitigating any issue with respect to the status of that property that was tried by any of the previous owners.

Example: P brings an action to *quiet title* to a piece of real estate. After the court finds that X is the rightful owner of the property, P conveys his interest (inferior as it may be) to S. S is collaterally estopped from relitigating the issue of title against X.

The estoppel effect would be the same if P had conveyed his interest to S *before* the entry of judgment in X's favor.

b. **Beneficiaries of trust:** If the trustee of a trust is, in his capacity as trustee, a party to the first action, the findings of fact made in that action will be binding on the *beneficiaries* — they are "in privity" with the trustee. This rule also applies to other kinds of persons who are represented by a party to the first action — for instance, *heirs* who were unborn or unascertained at the time of the first action are in privity with the party who represented them.

c. **Other representation:** Other kinds of representation which may lead to estoppel of a "privy" include *principal-agent* and *bailor-bailee.*

d. **Indemnitors:** Persons who are obligated by either law or contract to *indemnify* another may be in privity with their indemnitee. An example of indemnity-by-contract is a liability insurance policy, in which the insurer agrees to indemnify the policy-holder against any liability judgment which may be entered against him. An example of indemnity-by-law is the *employer-servant relationship*, in which the law of most states compels the employee to indemnify his employer for any judgment entered against the latter because of the employee's negligence.

   i. **Vouching in:** In either kind of indemnity, the indemnitee who is sued may "vouch in" his indemnitor, by giving him notice of the action, and granting him the opportunity to control the defense. If the indemnitor participates in the defense, he will of course be bound by all the results of the litigation. But even if the indemnitor *declines to participate*, he will (assuming he received notice of the suit) be bound as to the indemnitee's liability in a later suit by the indemnitee. (But he will not be bound as to the issue of whether an indemnitor-indemnitee relationship really exists.) James & Hazard, p. 636.

   Example: Cars driven by P and D collide. D notifies Insurance Co. (who D believes has written a valid policy on D's car) of the suit. Insurance Co. refuses to take part in the defense of the suit, claiming that it has not insured D. P establishes D's liability, and D pays the judgment. D then sues Insurance Co. to recover (on an indemnity theory) the amount paid to P.

   Insurance Co. is collaterally estopped from denying D's liability to P. But it may litigate the issue of whether it validly insured D. (In a state permitting an injured party to bring suit directly against the tortfeasor's insurer, Insurance Co. would be subject to the same limitations if sued by *P* following P's judgment against D.)

e. **Also applicable to claim preclusion:** The above rules of privity apply not only to collateral estoppel, but also to *claim preclusion*. A person who is in privity with a party to an earlier action will thus be barred not only from relitigating the issues of fact decided in the earlier suit, but also from even bringing a claim which would be barred to the original party. Thus if the original party had attempted to split his cause of action, the privy would be prevented by bar or merger from bringing the untried part of the claim, even though collateral estoppel would not by itself prevent relitigation. (Collateral estoppel, unlike claim preclusion, prevents relitigation only of matters which were *actually* litigated in the first action. Claim preclusion applies to those aspects of a claim which *could have been* litigated, even if they were not.)

Example: An automobile collision occurs between a car driven by Thompson (in which Harness is a passenger) and one driven by Fagnan. Thompson dies and Harness and Fagnan are injured. Harness sues Thompson's estate in federal court; the estate impleads Fagnan for contribution, and Harness then makes a claim against Fagnan under Rule 14(a). Fagnan crossclaims against the estate for contribution, but does not make any claim for his own injuries. All of the claims are settled. Fagnan then sues Thompson's insurance company in state court, seeking damages for his own injuries; the suit is brought under a state statute allowing tort actions against insurers. The insurer defends on the grounds that Fagnan's claim against it was a compulsory counterclaim under Federal Rule 13(a), and is therefore barred from being brought either against Thompson or against the insurance company.

Held, for the insurance company. Fagnan's claim against the estate was a compulsory counterclaim which was required to be brought in the first action, since it arose out of the same transaction or occurrence that was the subject of that suit. Since the insurance company's liability derives from the estate's liability, the extinction of the claim against the estate also extinguishes the claim against the insurer. *Fagnan v. Great Central Insurance Co.*, 577 F.2d 418 (7th Cir. 1978).

2. **Strangers to first action:** A person who is a complete *stranger* to the first action *can never be bound* by collateral estoppel. That is, a person who was neither a party nor a privy to the first action may, in a new action — whether he is the plaintiff or the defendant — litigate any issue, even if that issue was litigated in the first suit.

Example: A bus owned by Bus Company and a car driven by Driver collide. Driver sues Bus Company. In this suit, Bus Company is held to be the sole cause of the accident. Later, P, a passenger in the bus, sues both Driver and Bus Company in a separate action. Driver asserts that under the doctrine of collateral estoppel, the finding in the first suit that he was not negligent should be binding in the present suit. Therefore, Driver contends, P should be found not liable, so that P must recover (if from anyone) solely from Bus Company.

Held, for P. P was not a party to the earlier Driver-Bus Company action. Consequently, nothing decided in that action can have any collateral estoppel effect on P. Therefore, P is free to show in the present action that Driver was the sole negligent party, that Bus Company was, or that both were jointly negligent. *Neenan v. Woodside Astoria Transportation Co.*, 184 N.E. 744 (N.Y. 1933).

a.   **Collusion danger:**   One reason for this rule that a stranger can never be barred is the danger of *collusion*. For instance, on the facts of *Neenan, supra,* suppose that Driver had been indigent and thus judgment-proof. Bus Company and Driver might have conducted a collusive suit, in which they conspired to have the court find that Driver was the negligent one. Then, when P, the passenger, sought to recover, she would not be able to show Bus Company's negligence, yet would not be able to collect any judgment from Driver.

b.   **Due process:**   But apart from the possibility of collusion, there is an even more basic reason for not collaterally estopping a stranger to the first action. Such use of estoppel would *violate the stranger's due process rights*; he would be deprived of his *day in court*, by being bound by the results of a lawsuit in which he did not participate.

D.   Persons who can benefit from estoppel: Who may *benefit* from collateral estoppel? It is not the case that any litigant in the second action may automatically benefit from estoppel. Any person who was *present* as a litigant in the first action may benefit (assuming the general requirements for estoppel are satisfied). But a person who was a *stranger* to the first litigation may under certain circumstances be deprived of the benefit of estoppel in the second action. However, the limits on a stranger's use of estoppel are far narrower than they used to be.

1.   **Mutuality:**   It was once held that a party not *bound* by an earlier judgment (because not a party to it) could not use that judgment to bind his adversary who *had* been a party to the former action. The rule prohibiting a stranger's use of collateral estoppel was known as the doctrine of *mutuality.*

a.   **Rationale:**   The doctrine of mutuality was rationalized on the grounds that to do otherwise was a violation of the basic principles of fair play. If a litigant could not be burdened with the effect of a prior judgment, it seemed inequitable to allow him to benefit from it.

b.   **Historical exceptions:**   Exceptions to the mutuality doctrine were always recognized. For instance, in a master-servant situation where M was entitled to an indemnity from S, and T sued S, lost, and then tried to sue M, M (though not a party to the prior action, nor in privity — an indemnitor may be a privy but not an indemnitee) could use estoppel against T. Restatement of Judgments, §96 (1942). See also *Good Health Dairy Products Corp. v. Emery,* 9 N.E.2d 758 (N.Y. 1937).

2.   **Demise of mutuality:**   Most courts *no longer recognize the general principle of mutuality.* While many courts refuse in particular circumstances to allow the use of estoppel by one not a party to the first action, it is no longer a general rule that a stranger to the first action cannot benefit from findings of fact made against his adversary. See Rest. 2d, Judgments, §29.

a.   *Bernhard v. Bank of America:*   The first major assault on the mutuality doctrine came in *Bernhard v. Bank of America,* 122 P.2d 892 (Cal. 1942), a decision by Judge Traynor.

i.   **Facts:**   Ms. Bernhard sued the executor of an estate to which she was a beneficiary, claiming that he had wrongfully taken money from the deceased's bank account and placed it in his own. It was held that the executor had been the legitimate recipient of a gift from the deceased. Ms. Bernhard then tried to sue the bank for allowing this withdrawal. The bank succeeded in collaterally estopping her from relitigating the issue of whether the withdrawal was legitimate.

   ii. **Holding:** Judge Traynor's opinion stated that "no satisfactory rationalization has been advanced for the requirement of mutuality." The decision went on to state that only three questions are pertinent in deciding whether to allow collateral estoppel: "Was the issue decided in the prior adjudication identical with the one presented in the action in question? Was there a final judgment on the merits? Was the party against whom the plea is asserted a party or in privity with a party to the prior adjudication?" If the answer to each of these questions is "yes", then estoppel is to be allowed in spite of the absence of mutuality.

   b. **Other courts:** Other courts quickly followed *Bernhard's* rejection of the general principle of mutuality. See, e.g., *Israel v. Wood Dolson Co.*, 134 N.E.2d 97 (N.Y. 1956), preventing P, who had failed to prove a breach of contract by X in Suit 1, from relitigating the breach issue in Suit 2, brought by P against Y for having induced the alleged breach.

3. **Offensive/defensive distinction:** *Nearly all jurisdictions* (and the Second Restatement of Judgments — §29) have by now followed *Bernhard's* rejection of the general principle of mutuality. However, many courts have limited *Bernhard's* application so as to prevent results that appear unjust. Most importantly, some courts have distinguished between the *"offensive"* and the *"defensive"* use of estoppel, allowing the latter but not the former.

   a. **Nature of distinction:** This distinction, which was first set forth by Prof. Currie in "Mutuality of Collateral Estoppel: Limits of the *Bernhard* Doctrine," 9 Stan. L.R. 281 (1957), may be summarized as follows: (1) Where a *defendant* in the second action seeks to assert estoppel against the plaintiff, this use of estoppel is said to be *"defensive"* — estoppel is being used as a *"shield"* rather than as a *"sword."* (2) Where a *plaintiff* in the second action seeks to assert estoppel against the defendant, this use is *"offensive."*

   b. **Rationale for distinction:** The arguments for allowing defensive use of estoppel are stronger than those for allowing offensive use. In the defensive use case, plaintiff has chosen the second forum and the adversary — he is likely to have had the prospect of the second lawsuit in mind at the time of the first lawsuit, and it is not terribly unjust to hold him to the findings of fact made in that suit. Where the plaintiff in the second action was also a plaintiff in the first action, the arguments for collaterally estopping him are quite strong indeed. If the plaintiff in the second action was a defendant in the first action, and is seeking to assert estoppel, this is still "offensive" estoppel, but the arguments for estoppel are less compelling. Nonetheless, many courts would allow estoppel here.

   c. **Offensive use:** The arguments in favor of "offensive" estoppel, by contrast, are weaker. The defendant against whom estoppel is sought to be applied has not had the choice of either forum or adversary; furthermore, it may be assumed that at the time of the first action, he was less aware of the prospect of the second suit than he would have been of a suit which he contemplated bringing as plaintiff. The application of estoppel to bind him might therefore unfairly prejudice him. If the defendant in the second action, against whom estoppel is sought to be applied, was also a defendant in the first action, the case for estoppel is at its weakest.

Example: The best-known example of the injustice of allowing estoppel to be used against a party who was a defendant in both the first and second actions is called the *"multiple plaintiff anomaly."* Suppose D, a railroad company, is involved in a collision in which 50 passengers are injured. The injured persons, instead of consolidating their actions, sue one at a time. If P1 loses, then the other plaintiffs are of course not bound, since they were not parties to P1's action. But if P1 wins, then the application of offensive collateral estoppel will mean that *each of the subsequent plaintiffs automatically wins against the railroad*. If plaintiffs 1-29 lose, but then P30 wins, offensive collateral estoppel will mean that plaintiffs 31-50 all win, even though the railroad won 29 of the first 30 suits. The railroad is thus compelled to defend fully against every suit, or face the loss of all remaining suits. Furthermore, the 50 plaintiffs are likely to get together and agree that the most appealing plaintiff (perhaps the most severely injured, or the one with the most children) should sue first.

It does not take a very refined sense of justice to feel that the railroad is unfairly treated by a scheme which compels it to win each action or face total disaster in the remaining ones. This injustice is coupled with the *judicial inefficiency* inherent in a scheme which gives the plaintiffs a powerful incentive to avoid consolidating their cases, and to sue one at a time, hoping for a positive result in one case. Most courts would therefore probably deny the offensive use of estoppel in such circumstances. But see *Hart v. American Airlines*, 304 N.Y.S.2d 810 (N.Y. Sup. Ct. 1969), an airplane crash case in which the finding of liability of the airline in the first suit to be completed was given collateral estoppel effect in a subsequent case.

4. **Offensive estoppel approved by Supreme Court:** The Supreme Court has held that, in at least some federal cases, *offensive non-mutual estoppel is permissible. Parklane Hosiery Co. v. Shore*, 439 U.S. 322 (1979).

    a. **Facts of *Parklane:*** In *Parklane*, P brought a stockholders class action against D, based on an alleged false proxy statement issued by the latter. After the suit was started but before it was tried, the SEC brought a suit containing the same allegations, and the trial court found in the Commission's favor. P then sought to use the verdict in the SEC case to collaterally estop D from relitigating the issue of the falsity of the proxy statement.

    b. **Offensive use allowed:** The Supreme Court *permitted* this use of collateral estoppel, even though it was not only non-mutual but also *offensive* (in the sense that the use was sought by a plaintiff, rather than defendant, in the second action). The Court conceded that offensive collateral estoppel may create an incentive on the part of each plaintiff to adopt a "wait and see" attitude, in the hope that the first action by another plaintiff will result in a favorable judgment. Also, the Court acknowledged, offensive use of collateral estoppel may sometimes be unfair to the defendant; this might be the case, for instance, if the first suit was for such a small amount that the defendant had no reason to contest it vigorously, or if the second action "affords the defendant procedural opportunities unavailable in the first action that could readily cause a different result" (e.g., the first action was in a forum inconvenient for the defendant, preventing him from making full-scale discovery or calling witnesses.)

    i. **Case-by-case approach:** Nonetheless, the Court concluded, these difficulties should not be resolved by a ban on all non-mutual offensive use of collateral estoppel, but rather, by a *case-by-case* analysis of the wisdom of allowing such use. In this case, offensive use was reasonable; there was no evidence that P had an incentive to sit out the first litigation (he probably couldn't have joined the SEC suit even if he had wanted to.) Also, D had every incentive to litigate the SEC case vigorously (particularly since it knew about P's case, which had already been filed).

c. **Right to jury trial:** D also raised the serious objection that offensive use of collateral estoppel here *deprived it of its right to a jury trial in the second action*. (No jury trial was permissible in the SEC action, but would have been in the second suit.) Since mutuality was a requirement for collateral estoppel at common law (as it existed in 1791, the date of the enactment of the Seventh Amendment), allowing offensive collateral estoppel here restricted D's jury rights from what they would have been in 1791.

    i. **Not fatal objection:** The Court conceded that this represented an abridgment, but noted that many other procedural devices developed since 1791 have similarly diminished the civil jury's domain, without being found inconsistent with the Seventh Amendment. The abridgment here was no more severe than in the case of these other procedural modifications (e.g., the modern form of directed verdict, which may be used to take the case away from the jury in a situation where this could not have been done in 1791).

d. **Dissent:** Justice Rehnquist dissented, first on the grounds that D's Seventh Amendment rights were violated by offensive use of collateral estoppel here. Secondly, he argued, apart from the constitutional issue offensive use here was unfair to D, since the availability of a jury trial could easily lead to a different result from that obtained in the first action. Finally, he noted, a jury would have to be impaneled anyway to resolve other issues in the case (e.g., damages), so that the savings of court time and of litigants' resources would be minimal.

5. **Factors in case-by-case analysis:** As the result of *Parklane*, federal courts (and probably state courts as well, although these are not explicitly bound by *Parklane*) apply a case-by-case analysis in determining whether to allow offensive non-mutual estoppel. Courts should consider the following factors:

a. **Alignment in first suit:** Whether the party sought to be bound (the defendant in the second suit) was a *plaintiff* or a *defendant* in the first suit. If he was a defendant, this will militate against use of estoppel, since he was less likely to have had the choice of the forum in which the issue was to be litigated. See Rest. 2d, Judgments, §29, Comment d.

b. **Incentive to litigate:** Whether the person to be estopped had a reasonable *incentive* to litigate the issue fully in the first suit. For instance, as the *Parklane* court noted, the fact that the first suit was for a small amount might mean that the defendant had no reason to contest the issue vigorously. The degree to which the second suit was ***fore-seeable*** at the time of the first suit might also be considered in gauging whether there was an incentive to litigate fully in the first suit.

c. Discouraging "breakaway" suits: Whether the plaintiff in the second action could have joined in the first action, and ***"sat out"*** that first action in order to derive a tactical advantage (by which he would be able to use estoppel if his prospective adversary lost, and would not be bound by estoppel if that adversary won). See Rest. 2d, Judgments, §29(3).

d. Multiple plaintiff anomaly: Whether permitting offensive estoppel would present a danger of the ***"multiple plaintiff anomaly"*** (*supra*, p. 380.) That is, if there were numerous potential plaintiffs waiting in the wings, the court would be less likely to permit offensive estoppel, than where the second suit would probably be the last. The court also might look to whether the potential multiple plaintiffs had seemingly gotten together and selected the most appealing plaintiff to sue first.

e. Procedural opportunities: Whether there are ***procedural opportunities*** available to a party in the second action that were not present in the first, which might make a difference in the outcome. For instance, if the court in the second suit allows ***more extensive discovery*** than the first court, this might make a difference. Similarly, if the first case was tried to a judge, and the defendant in the second trial has a Seventh Amendment ***right to a jury trial*** which would be impeded by collateral estoppel, this may be a factor. (Although the Supreme Court in *Parklane* allowed use of offensive estoppel even though the defendant was deprived of his right to a jury trial on the issue, the Court did not say that the jury trial right could not be considered as a ***non-dispositive factor*** in deciding whether to allow such estoppel.)

f. Issue of law: Whether the issue is one of ***law*** or merely of "fact." Where the issue is one of "law" the more flexible doctrine of *stare decisis*, rather than collateral estoppel, should normally be applied. Otherwise, "the court is foreclosed from an opportunity to reconsider the applicable rule, and thus to perform its function of developing the law." Rest. 2d, Judgments, §29, Comment i.

g. Government is party: Whether the defendant in the second action is the ***government***. Non-mutual offensive use of collateral estoppel will ***virtually never be allowed against the government***. The Supreme Court so announced, as to the federal government, in *U.S. v. Mendoza*, 464 U.S. 154 (1984).

  i. Rationale: In announcing this rule, the Court reasoned that allowing non-mutual estoppel against the government "would substantially thwart the development of important questions of law by freezing the first final decision rendered on a particular legal issue." This would in turn mean that the Supreme Court would not get the chance to follow its current practice of frequently waiting for a conflict to develop between circuits before granting *certiorari*. Also, the federal government would come under pressure to appeal virtually every adverse trial court decision in order to avoid losing the opportunity for reconsideration in a different case presenting the same issue.

ii. **State and local governments:** The Court's rule in *Mendoza* only deals with the situation in which the party against whom estoppel is sought to be applied is the *federal* government, and the second suit is in federal court. However, the rationale of that decision also appears applicable to federal court cases in which a state or local government is the defendant, and may in addition be adopted by state courts deciding whether to grant non-mutual offensive estoppel against governmental bodies.

6. **Use of criminal conviction:** The courts are split on whether to allow estoppel effect to a previous *criminal conviction* of a party. In the heyday of mutuality, any use of a criminal conviction, even as evidence, was forbidden. Today, at least one state, California, has given full collateral estoppel effect to a previous criminal conviction. *Teitelbaum Furs, Inc. v. Dominion Insur. Co.*, 375 P.2d 439 (Cal. 1962). Other jurisdictions allow the conviction to be used only as *evidence*; it thus forms a rebuttable presumption. In some jurisdictions (e.g. New York), a conviction for a minor traffic violation may not even be used as evidence, let alone for estoppel.

a. **State conviction and federal §1983 suit:** The Supreme Court has allowed a state criminal conviction to have collateral effect in a subsequent *federal* case. For instance, the 1871 Civil Rights Act, in 42 U.S.C. §1983, gives a person the right to bring a federal suit against anyone who violates his constitutional rights "under color of" state law. The statute thus allows a federal civil damages suit against state officials who have violated the plaintiff's constitutional rights by false arrest, by search without probable cause or warrant, or by other official misconduct. The Supreme Court has held that a state court's finding in a criminal case that *no constitutional violation* of the criminal defendant's rights occurred may have collateral estoppel effect in a federal §1983 suit brought by that same defendant. *Allen v. McCurry*, 449 U.S. 90 (1983) (discussed more extensively *infra*, p. 390.)

Note: *Acquittal* in a criminal case *never becomes binding* in a subsequent civil action. First of all, to grant such estoppel effect would be to allow the criminal defendant to bind a non-party; non-parties may *never* be bound by earlier decisions, even though they may sometimes benefit from such decisions. Secondly, there is a discrepancy between the "beyond a reasonable doubt" standard of proof necessary for a criminal conviction, and the "preponderance of the evidence" standard in civil suits.

Quiz Yourself on
COLLATERAL ESTOPPEL

119. Phillip was injured when a car he was driving collided with a car driven by Doreen. Phillip sued Doreen for negligence in Ames state court. The case was tried before a jury, and the jury found for Phillip, awarding him substantial damages. Judgment was entered. Then, Doreen brought a negligence suit against Phillip for property damage arising from the same transaction. This suit, too, was brought in Ames state court. Ames follows traditional negligence law, by which even a small amount of contributory negligence on the part of the plaintiff prevents the plaintiff from recovering. Ames has no statute or judicial policy making any cause of action a compulsory counterclaim. In Doreen's suit, may she assert, and prove, that Phillip's negligence caused the accident? _____

120. Same basic fact pattern as the prior question. Now, assume that after Phillip sued Doreen in Ames state court for negligence, Doreen declined to answer. A default judgment was entered against her for $100,000 in damages. Doreen then instituted an action, in Ames, against Phillip for negligence. Will the court allow Doreen to assert and prove that Phillip was negligent? _____

121. Same basic fact pattern as the prior two questions. Now, assume that Phillip's suit against Doreen was actively litigated, with Phillip claiming that Doreen was negligent, and Doreen claiming that Phillip was contributorily negligent. The jury found in favor of Doreen. In response to two special interrogatories, the jury stated that Phillip was contributorily negligent and that Doreen was also negligent. (Remember that according to Ames law, even a small amount of contributory negligence bars recovery, even if the defendant was also negligent.) In a second Ames action, Doreen then sued Phillip for negligence. Will Doreen be collaterally estopped from denying her own contributory negligence in this second action? _____

122. Penny and Dan, each driving a car, were involved in what at first appeared to be a minor fender bender. Penny sued Dan for negligence in municipal court for the town of Langdell, a small claims court whose jurisdiction is limited to cases involving less than $5,000. This court has quite informal procedures; for instance, there is no right to jury trial, and there are no formal rules for the admissibility of evidence. The jurisdiction applies common-law contributory negligence. Penny sought $2,000 for property damage suffered by her. The judge found that Dan drove negligently and that Penny did not; he awarded the full $2,000 to Penny.

Dan shortly thereafter developed back trouble, which in the opinion of his doctor, stemmed from the collision with Penny. Dan sued in a court of general jurisdiction (in the state where Langdell is located) for $100,000 of compensatory damages for medical expense, and pain and suffering. Penny now asserts that Dan is collaterally estopped from either: (1) showing that Penny was negligent; or (2) denying that Dan himself was negligent. Which, if either, of these assertions is correct? _____

123. Perry sued Denise for negligence, arising out of an auto accident. Since Perry was seeking only a modest sum for actual medical expenses, Denise agreed to settle the case for a $2,000 payment to Perry. The settlement document recited these facts, and made no statement about what effect the settlement would have on any other litigation. A judgment was entered in accordance with this settlement. Shortly thereafter, Xavier, who was injured in the same accident, sued Denise. Putting aside the issue of whether the mutuality doctrine or Xavier's status as a stranger to the first action prevents him from using collateral estoppel, is Denise entitled to deny her negligence as part of her defense of the action brought by Xavier? _____

124. The Agriculture Department of the state of Ames bars any milk wholesaler from selling milk within Ames at a wholesale price of less than $1 per quart. Potter, an out-of-state wholesaler who wanted to sell milk at less than the $1 price, sued the Department of Agriculture in Ames state court. Potter's claim was that the price law discriminated against out-of-state commerce, in violation of the dormant Commerce Clause of the U.S. Constitution. The trial judge who heard the suit agreed with Potter's assertion. Potter, immediately after his victory, began selling milk at 90 cents per gallon. The Agriculture Department did not appeal. Instead, it actively defended a similar suit brought by Xavier, and lost that one at the trial level also. Subsequently, the Department appealed the loss to Xavier to the Ames Supreme Court (the highest court in the state), which found that the price floor was valid as a constitutional matter. Potter continued to sell 90 cent/gallon milk after the decision in Xavier's suit. The Agriculture Department then brought a suit to obtain an injunction against Potter's continuing to sell milk at less than $1 per gallon. Potter asserts that his victory in the earlier suit against him collaterally estops Ames from relitigating that issue with him now. Will Potter get the benefit of collateral estoppel on these facts? _____

125. Peter and Paul were neighbors who agreed to share a cab ride to the airport one night. The cab was driven by David. On a poorly lit city street, the cab smashed into an abandoned car (whose owner was never traced) and Peter and Paul were both seriously injured. Peter brought a suit against David in Ames state court. Peter's lawyer aggressively and expertly litigated the case, but the jury found in favor of David. Special interrogatories given to the jury made it clear that the jury simply believed that David used all due care, and could not have prevented the accident by ordinary precautions. After this verdict, Paul brought a suit against David in Ames state court, also alleging negligence relating to the same accident. Assuming that Paul has no evidence of David's negligence to put forth except evidence used by Peter in the first suit, may Paul nonetheless assert and prove that David drove negligently and caused the accident? _____

126. Parker was a lifelong smoker. The only two brands he ever smoked were Acme and Baker. On average, he smoked two packs of Acme per day, and one pack of Baker. He contracted lung cancer, and then brought a products liability suit against Acme in Ames state court, asserting that Acme was responsible for his lung cancer. Acme presented evidence that Parker's lung cancer was of a type not usually associated with cigarette smoking, that it was of a type usually associated with asbestos exposure, and that Parker had worked around asbestos for many years. The case was tried to a judge, who concluded that Parker had failed to prove by a preponderance of the evidence that cigarette smoking (regardless of brand) contributed substantially to his getting lung cancer. Parker then brought a suit against Baker, again in Ames state court, making the same type of allegations he had made against Acme. Baker now argues that Parker should be collaterally estopped from asserting that his lung cancer was caused by any brand of cigarette. Granting Baker's request will result in Parker's claim being dismissed before trial. Should Baker be permitted to use collateral estoppel to bar Parker from claiming that his lung cancer was caused by cigarettes? _____

127. Fred and Greg went one day to a diner operated by Dave. Fred ordered a bowl of clam chowder. The meal went uneventfully, and Fred and Greg left. One week later, Fred sued Dave for strict product liability, alleging that the chowder was dangerously defective, and caused Fred to undergo food poisoning. The suit was tried in a court of general jurisdiction of the state of Ames, and Fred sought $500 in damages. Dave defended by trying to show that Fred's illness was in fact the flu, but the judge found in Fred's favor, and awarded $500 in damages. Nowhere during the trial was Greg mentioned.

Shortly after Fred's verdict against Dave, Greg instituted a suit against Dave in Ames state court. His suit alleges that he drank some of Fred's order of clam chowder, and that he too was food poisoned. Greg's suit seeks $100,000 in damages, stating that while the hospital was treating him for food poisoning, it gave him a drug which caused him to go into convulsions, and that Dave must be liable for all of the resulting injury to Greg. At the trial, Greg seeks to collaterally estop Dave from denying that the clam chowder was dangerously defective (though he is willing to let Dave attempt to prove that the defectiveness was not the proximate cause of Greg's own injuries). Should Greg be allowed to use collateral estoppel in this manner? _____

128. A group of plaintiff lawyers decided that the time was ripe for bringing a serious strict product liability action against one or more of the leading cigarette companies. They singled out the Deadly Tobacco Co. as their primary defendant. They then advertised in consumer magazines for possible plaintiffs who had suffered cigarette-related illnesses. After interviewing dozens of potential plaintiffs, they finally settled upon Angie as their first plaintiff. They picked Angie because her case was especially appealing for several reasons: (1) she began smoking while she was still a minor, and did so in response to repeated televi-

sion advertising by Deadly and other cigarette companies (this was before the ban on televised cigarette advertising); (2) she tried repeatedly to stop smoking through methods such as hypnosis, but appears to be simply addicted; and (3) she would make a very appealing witness, in part because she has the most serious of all cigarette-related illnesses, lung cancer. Angie's case was tried to a jury in Ames state court. After a long trial, the jury found that cigarettes produced by Deadly were dangerously defective, that Deadly did not issue adequate warnings, and that Deadly should be liable to Angie for $200,000 (a higher figure was rejected since the jury believed that some of the fault was Angie's).

After this victory, the same group of lawyers selected Betty as the next plaintiff. Her case also seems to be strong, though not as strong as Angie's for several reasons (e.g., she did not start smoking until she was an adult, and never saw televised cigarette advertising). Betty's lawyers now propose that Deadly be collaterally estopped from denying that its cigarettes are a dangerously defective product, and from denying that its warning labels (at least during the years that were at issue in Angie's suit) were inadequate. Should this use of collateral estoppel be allowed? _____

Answers

119. No. Doreen is ***collaterally estopped*** from relitigating the issue of Phillip's negligence in the accident. This is because: (1) the issue of Phillip's negligence was ***fully and fairly litigated*** in the first action, (2) that issue was ***actually decided*** (since the finding in favor of Phillip, under the substantive law of Ames, was inconsistent with any negligence on Phillip's part); and (3) the finding was ***necessary*** to the verdict (since if Phillip had been negligent, he could not have recovered under Ames' law on contributory negligence).

120. Yes. Collateral estoppel does not apply here. For collateral estoppel to apply to an issue, that issue must have been actually litigated at the first trial. When a default judgment is entered, no issue is deemed to have been litigated.

121. No. For collateral estoppel to apply to an issue, the disposition of that issue must have been ***necessary*** to the first verdict. Here, once the first jury found that Phillip was contributorily negligent, it didn't matter whether Doreen was negligent (since Phillip couldn't recover even if Doreen were negligent). Since Doreen's negligence was not a necessary component of the first verdict, she will be permitted to relitigate the issue of whether she was (contributorily) negligent during the second suit. See *Cambria v. Jeffery*, 29 N.E.2d 555 (Mass. 1940).

122. Neither. Where the first trial takes place in a court that not only has very limited jurisdiction but also very informal procedures, the findings of that court will generally ***not*** be given collateral estoppel effect. The reason is that the findings of such a court are viewed as insufficiently trustworthy to determine the outcome of a much larger later controversy. (The mere fact that a jury trial was not available would not by itself be enough to deprive the first court's findings of collateral estoppel effect, but the absence of rules of evidence probably would be.) See F,K&M, p. 681-82.

123. Yes. A ***settlement*** normally has ***no collateral estoppel effect*** on other suits. Therefore, Xavier will not be able to treat the settlement as establishing Denise's negligence, even though a judgment against Denise was entered pursuant to that settlement. (Also, the rule against giving collateral estoppel effect to settlements can be viewed as a specific application of the general rule that collateral estoppel effect will only be given to issues that were litigated in the first action.)

124. No, probably. Collateral estoppel does not usually apply to "pure" issues of law, but does usually apply to "mixed" issues of law and fact, i.e., the application of a given legal principle to a particular fact situation. However, even if the first decision involves (as it does here) a mixed question of law and fact rather than a pure question of law, most courts believe that they have *discretion* to decline to apply collateral estoppel where there has been a *significant change in legal principles* between the first and second suits. Courts are especially likely to exercise that discretion where use of collateral estoppel would "impose on one of the parties a significant disadvantage, or confer on him a significant benefit, with respect to his competitors." Rest. 2d Judgments, §28, Comment c. Here, use of collateral estoppel would give Potter a perpetual advantage over his competitors (he can undercut their price slightly, and they cannot ever match him). The court is very unlikely to grant Potter, just because of the fortuity of his earlier victory, such a permanent advantage. This is especially true where, as here, the intervening decision was by a higher court than decided the original case in favor of the party now seeking collateral estoppel.

125. Yes. *A stranger to the first action will never be bound*, either for claim preclusion or collateral estoppel purposes, by the results of that first suit. Peter and Paul were not privies, since their cab-sharing relationship does not fall within any of the traditional relationships recognized as constituting privity by the common law (e.g., master/servant, insurer/insured, etc.). Thus Paul is entitled to get his "day in court," even if that amounts to merely trotting out the same evidence as already used by Peter against David.

126. Yes. Until the last 20 or 30 years, many courts might have automatically denied Baker's attempt to use collateral estoppel, on the now-discredited doctrine of mutuality (by which since Baker was a stranger to the first action, it could not claim the benefits of collateral estoppel in the second action). Today, virtually all jurisdictions reject the automatic principle of mutuality. Instead, most courts decide on a case-by-case basis whether to allow collateral estoppel use by a stranger. When it is the defendant in the second action who seeks to use collateral estoppel, and seeks to use it against a party who was a plaintiff in the first action, the case for allowing collateral estoppel is at its strongest. Thus here, Parker had the opportunity to fully and fairly litigate the causation issue during his first trial, and Baker is merely trying to use collateral estoppel as a shield rather than a sword in the second action. Nearly all courts would allow Baker to use collateral estoppel here. (This "use by the plaintiff in first action who is also plaintiff in second action" scenario matches the situation in *Bernhard v. Bank of America*, 122 P.2d 892 (Cal. 1942), the major case rejecting mutuality and allowing a stranger to use collateral estoppel.)

127. No. Greg is not only a stranger to the first action but is attempting an *offensive* use of collateral estoppel. (That is, he is a plaintiff in the second action.) Therefore, the court will do a case-by-case balancing (similar to that performed by the Supreme Court in *Parklane Hosiery v. Shore*) to decide whether to allow estoppel here. Two factors strongly militate against allowing estoppel here: (1) the first suit was for relatively little money ($500), so Dave did not have an incentive to litigate it to the hilt; and (2) the possibility of a later action by Greg (or anyone else relating to that particular serving of chowder) was quite unlikely from Dave's perspective, so Dave was not at all on notice that issues might be decided as to which collateral estoppel would later be possibly applicable. Together, these factors make it most unlikely that the court would estop Dave from attempting to disprove Greg's allegation of dangerously defective chowder.

128. No. Again, we have a situation where a stranger to the first action is proposing to make offensive use of collateral estoppel. Here, we have a stark case of the *"multiple plaintiff anomaly"* — if Deadly wins any given suit, it still has to completely relitigate the merits with the next plaintiff in line, yet under collateral estoppel one defeat by Deadly would cause it to lose against everyone later in line. The unfairness to Deadly from allowing collateral estoppel here is further exaggerated by: (1) the fact that the plaintiffs' lawyers have intentionally chosen the most appealing plaintiff to go first; and (2) the fact that the lawyers intentionally declined to join the additional victims as plaintiffs in the first suit, preferring to have them "wait in the wings." Therefore, it is unlikely that Deadly will be deprived of its chance to relitigate the issue of whether its cigarettes are dangerously defective or its warnings inadequate.

IV. FULL FAITH AND CREDIT

A. Scope: So far, we have generally assumed that both suits take place in the same jurisdiction. We turn now to the special problems that arise when the two suits occur in different jurisdictions. There may be two different states involved, or a state court and a federal court. In either situation, the principle generally referred to as *"full faith and credit"* comes into play.

B. Effect: The Full Faith and Credit clause of the U.S. Constitution (Art. IV, §1) requires each state to give to the judgment of any other state *the same effect that that judgment would have in the state which rendered it*. (A statute, 28 U.S.C. §1738, requires the federal courts to give Full Faith and Credit to state court decisions. See *infra*, p. 389.)

1. Utility: This provision is often applicable where a plaintiff has won a judgment in State X, but can find no property in X on which to levy. If he can locate property belonging to the defendant in State Y, he may levy on it by bringing a suit in Y "on the judgment". The courts of Y must accept this judgment at face value, and may not reconsider any issues which it concluded.

2. Collateral attack on jurisdiction: The court in which enforcement of the judgment is sought may examine one aspect of the original judgment: *jurisdiction* (either personal or subject matter), *provided that the jurisdictional question was not litigated or waived* in the first action. *Durfee v. Duke*, 375 U.S. 106 (1963). See the fuller discussion of collateral attack on jurisdiction, *supra*, pp. 75, 95.

a. Waiver: The jurisdictional question will be held to be *waived* if the defendant contests on the merits (as opposed to taking a default judgment), and does not raise the issue of jurisdiction. Thus in *Chicot County Drainage District v. Baxter State Bank*, 308 U.S. 371 (1940), parties to an action were held to have waived their objection to the fact that the court's eventual judgment was made under a federal statute subsequently determined unconstitutional; they were not permitted to collaterally attack the judgment.

C. Misinterpretation of another state's law: State A must give Full Faith and Credit to an adjudication of State B, even if that judgment was based on a *misinterpretation of the laws of State A.*

> **Example:** A gambling debt is contracted in Mississippi. The debt is sued on in Missouri, which holds that since the Mississippi courts would enforce such a debt, it will do likewise.
>
> The judgment is then sued on in a Mississippi court. Even if the Mississippi court knows that that state's highest court would not enforce the debt, and that the Missouri judgment was thus based on an erroneous construction of Mississippi law, it must still grant enforcement of the Missouri judgment. *Fauntleroy v. Lum*, 210 U.S. 230 (1908).

D. Later decision binding: If State A erroneously fails to give Full Faith and Credit to a decision of State B, and reaches a decision of its own which becomes final, this second judgment is in turn binding on State B. In other words, a "last in time" rule seems applicable to Full Faith and Credit. *Treinies v. Sunshine Mining Co.*, 308 U.S. 66 (1939).

E. No duty to decisions of other countries: There is no constitutional requirement that the judgments of *other nations* be accorded Full Faith and Credit. The federal courts, and most state courts, will give Full Faith and Credit to the adjudications of *common-law countries*. As to *civil law nations*, practice varies.

1. ***Hilton v. Guyot:*** In *Hilton v. Guyot*, 159 U.S. 113 (1895), the Supreme Court declined to give credit to a French judgment, on the grounds that the French courts did not give credit to our judgments.

F. Full Faith and Credit to *res judicata effect*: A state must give to the judgment of any other state at least the *res judicata effect* that that judgment would have in the state of its rendition.

> **Example:** A court of State A renders Judgment I, which by the laws of State A would act as a bar to certain subsequent actions. Action II, which is then brought in State B, would, if brought in State A, be barred by Judgment I.
>
> Even if Action II would not have been barred by Judgment I had both been brought in State B, Action II must nonetheless be barred. In other words, Full Faith and Credit must be given to the *res judicata* effects of a judgment rendered by a sister state — a judgment must be given the same effect, with respect to *res judicata*, that it would have in the state of its rendition.

1. **Greater effect:** Some courts have given a *greater* effect to another state's judgment than it would have in that other state. Thus in *Hart v. American Airlines*, 304 N.Y.S.2d 810 (N.Y. Sup. Ct. 1969), the court gave collateral estoppel effect to a Texas court's finding of the defendant airline's liability, even though Texas itself, since it required mutuality of estoppel, would not have given the earlier judgment such effect. The giving of greater effect to the first state's judgment does not violate the Full Faith and Credit clause, since that clause merely requires that a court give to a sister court's judgement *at least* the same effect it would have in the sister state, not that it be given no greater effect.

G. Federal suit follows state suit: Suppose that the first judgment is in a *state* court and the second one is in a *federal* court. Several Supreme Court decisions have established that, unless Congress has explicitly or implicitly provided otherwise in a particular context, *the federal court must grant the state court judgment the same res judicata effect it would have in that state*.

1. **§1738:** The general rule requiring federal courts to give state court judgments Full Faith and Credit is set forth in 28 U.S.C. §1738, which provides that "The records and judicial proceedings of any court [of] any State ... shall have the same full faith and credit in every court within the United States ... as they have by law or usage in the courts of [the] State ... from which they are taken." Since every federal court is a "court within the United States," the federal courts are bound by this statute to give state court judgments the same effect (including *res judicata*) as the state itself would give them. (But the statute does not say anything about the effect in state court of an earlier federal court judgment — however, the state court is clearly bound in this situation; see *infra*, p. 392.)

2. **Partial repeal by Congress:** Since §1738 is a statute rather than a constitutional principle, it is, of course, subject to repeal by Congress. Any statute may be partially repealed, and this partial repeal may be implied as well as express. Therefore, whenever Congress creates a new federal statutory right, it could be argued that this new federal statute implicitly repeals §1738 with respect to any state court determination relevant to the federal right; if this argument were accepted, the result would be that a federal court need not grant to a prior state court judgment the *res judicata* effect of that judgment if doing so would affect a federal right.

3. **View rejected:** But the Supreme Court has held that this argument will normally fail — unless Congress has made it *quite clear* that it wishes to deny the state court judgment *res judicata* effect in the federal court proceeding, the federal court must give the state court judgment the *same preclusive effect it would have in the state which rendered it.*

   a. *Allen v. McCurry:* Thus in *Allen v. McCurry,* 449 U.S. 90 (1980), the Court held that Congress did not intend a partial repeal of §1738 when it enacted 42 U.S.C. §1983, a post-Civil War statute giving a person the right to bring a federal suit for damages against anyone who violates his constitutional rights "under color of" state law. Therefore, a federal court hearing a §1983 action must give to any prior state court judgment the same claim preclusive and collateral estoppel effect as that judgment would have had in the state where it was issued.

      i. **First suit in *Allen:*** In *Allen,* McCurry claimed that police officers who arrested him on heroin charges had unconstitutionally searched his home and seized evidence. McCurry tried to get the evidence suppressed from the state criminal trial, but failed, and was convicted. The state criminal proceeding thus constituted a finding that, as a factual matter, the search and seizure was not unconstitutional.

      ii. **Federal suit:** McCurry then brought a federal §1983 action against the police, seeking damages for what he claimed was their violation of his Fourth Amendment rights by carrying out the search and seizure.

      iii. **Collateral estoppel applied:** The Supreme Court observed that 28 U.S.C. §1738 "require[s] all federal courts to give preclusive effect to state-court judgments whenever the courts of the State from which the judgments emerged would do so. …" While Congress could have implicitly repealed this requirement as it applies to §1983 suits, the Court concluded that Congress had *not intended to do so.* Therefore, collateral estoppel effect must be given to the state court's finding that the search and seizure were not unconstitutional, unless the state court would not impose such collateral estoppel effect.

      iv. **Lack of "full and fair opportunity":** The Supreme Court conceded that if McCurry had not received a "full and fair opportunity to litigate the claim" in the state court, the federal court need not grant the finding collateral estoppel effect. (The Court indicated that this result might well be reached as a matter of the interpretation of §1983, which after all was enacted to help federal courts enforce constitutional rights which state courts were often not prepared to enforce.) However, since McCurry had had such an opportunity in the state court, this exception was of no help to him.

v. No automatic opportunity to litigate in federal court: The Supreme Court rejected a lower court's principle "that every person asserting a federal right is entitled to one unencumbered opportunity to litigate that right in a federal district court, regardless of the legal posture in which the federal claim arises." This "rule" seemed to the Court to be motivated by "a general distrust of the capacity of the state courts to render correct decisions on constitutional issues," a distrust which the Court felt was unfounded and in any event irrelevant to the problem of interpreting §1738's requirement of Full Faith and Credit.

4. Administrative agency findings: What about state *administrative agency* determinations? Must the federal court give these administrative findings the same preclusive effect they would have in the state courts? Section 1738 does not directly require this result, since that section requires the federal courts to give full faith and credit to "judicial proceedings" of any state "court," with no mention of administrative decisions. But the Supreme Court has held that as a matter of federal common law, the *same result* should normally occur where a state administrative agency has made a judicial-type decision. See *University of Tennessee v. Elliott*, 478 U.S. 788 (1986), holding that "when a state agency acting in a judicial capacity ... resolves disputed issues of fact properly before it which the parties have had an adequate opportunity to litigate, federal courts must give the agency's fact finding the same preclusive effect to which it would be entitled in the State's courts."

a. Congress may indicate otherwise: But remember that this result — that state administrative decisions should normally be given the same preclusive effect in federal court as they would have in state court — is not required by any statute, and is merely judge-made. Therefore, the rule is not ironclad, and if the court decides that Congress' intent would be thwarted by giving a particular agency determination preclusive effect in federal court merely because it would have that effect in state court, then the preclusive effect will *not* be given.

Example: The federal Age Discrimination Act requires the plaintiff to use any available state agency to hear his age-employment-discrimination suit first, before suing. The Act does not specify what preclusive effect should be given to the agency's decision. *Held* (by the Supreme Court), since the federal statutory remedy here would be useless if the state agency decision were preclusive, no preclusive effect should be given to that decision even if it would be preclusive in state court. *Astoria Fed. Sav. & Loan Ass'n v. Solimino*, 501 U.S. 104 (1991).

5. Claim preclusion: *Allen* and *Elliott* involved collateral estoppel. But the Supreme Court has held that state *bar and merger* (i.e., claim preclusion) rules must similarly be applied in subsequent federal actions unless Congress has affirmatively indicated in creating the federal right that state bar and merger rules are to be ignored. See *Migra v. Warren City Bd. of Ed.*, 465 U.S. 75 (1984).

6. May not give greater effect to judgment: Suppose, as we have been doing, that a state suit is followed by a federal suit; suppose further that the facts of the second suit are such that the state court would *not* give preclusive effect to its own earlier judgment, but that general federal principles *would* dictate a preclusive effect. It is now clear that the federal court *may not give preclusive effect* to the prior state court judgment. That is, 28 U.S.C

§1738 requires that the federal court treat the state court judgment in the same way as would the state court that rendered it. *Migra v. Warren City Bd. of Ed.*, 465 U.S. 75 (1984) (Justice White, concurring). See also *Marrese v. American Academy of Orthopaedic Surgeons*, discussed *supra*, p. 365.

    a. **Illustration:** For instance, if the initial state judgment comes from a state that does not allow non-mutual offensive use of collateral estoppel, the federal court hearing the second suit *may not apply such collateral estoppel*, even if the situation is one which under the Supreme Court's *Parklane Hosiery* ruling (*supra*, p. 380) collateral estoppel would be appropriate.

    b. **Pros and cons:** This result can be criticized on the grounds that §1738's purpose is merely to make sure that state court judgments are given respect, and that this purpose is not impaired by giving greater effect to the judgment than the state itself would give. See Justice White's concurrence in *Migra*, so arguing. But it has been argued in rebuttal that "The interest of the federal court … in avoiding re-litigation is not sufficient to impose preclusion at the expense of the state court's interest in limiting the effect of its own proceedings." Wr., p. 691.

H. State suit follows federal suit: Suppose now that the *federal* suit comes *first*, and the *state* suit *second*. It is well-established that *the state court must give to the federal judgment the same res judicata effect that that federal court would give its own judgment*. This is not required by 28 U.S.C. §1738 (which by its terms applies only to the judgments of state, not federal, courts); nor is it expressly required by any other federal statute. It is probably the case that the Constitution's *Supremacy Clause* requires that the preclusive effect of federal judgments be honored in state courts. See Wright, pp. 694-95.

Quiz Yourself on
FULL FAITH AND CREDIT

129. In the courts of the state of Ames, Abel sued Baker for negligence arising out of an automobile accident. The judge concluded that Baker was negligent, and entered judgment in favor of Abel. Shortly thereafter, Conroy sued Baker for negligence arising out of the same auto accident; this suit is taking place in the courts of the state of Bates. The Ames Supreme Court allows broad offensive use of collateral estoppel, and would allow Conroy to make use of collateral estoppel against Baker on the issue of Baker's negligence in the accident, if Conroy's suit had been filed in Ames. The Supreme Court of Bates, by contrast, is a more old fashioned jurisdiction which almost never allows offensive use of collateral estoppel by a stranger to the first action. Conroy seeks to collaterally estop Baker from denying Baker's negligence in the accident.

    (a) Should Conroy be given the benefits of collateral estoppel here? _____

    (b) Is the answer left to the court's discretion, or is it imposed by some non-discretionary requirement? _____

130. Same basic fact pattern as prior question. Now, however, assume that the second action (by Conroy) was filed not in the state courts of Bates, but rather, in federal district court for the District of Bates. Should/must the federal judge give Conroy the benefit of collateral estoppel against Baker? _____

131. Same basic fact pattern as prior two questions. Now, however, assume that the first suit is in federal court for the District of Ames (sitting in diversity), and the second suit is in the state court of Bates. Assuming that the federal judge sitting in Ames would grant offensive use of collateral estoppel against Baker in this situation, must the state court of Bates do the same? _____

Answers

129. (a) **Yes.**

(b) **The answer is required by the Full Faith and Credit Clause of the U.S. Constitution.** The Full Faith and Credit Clause of the U.S. Constitution (Article IV, Section 1) requires each state to give to the judgment of any other state the same effect that that judgment would have in the state which rendered it. This requirement extends to the *res judicata effect* of the first state court's judgment. Here, therefore, Bates must give to the judgment of the Ames court the same effect that the Ames court system would give to that prior judgment. Since Ames would grant preclusive effect to the judgment against Baker (i.e., Ames would let Conroy collaterally estop Baker), Bates must do the same. This is true even though the Bates courts, if left to their own devices, would prefer not to give collateral estoppel effect to the judgment against Baker.

130. **Yes, the federal judge must do so.** A federal statute, 28 U.S.C. §1738, requires federal courts to give state court judgments the same effect (including res judicata effect) as the state itself would give them. Except in a very few instances where later, more specific, congressional statutes indicate that Congress does not want the federal courts to have to honor the preclusive effect of a state court judgment, the federal court is bound by §1738 to give the state court judgment the same effect the state itself would give it. Therefore, since no special congressional statute is at issue here, the federal judge must grant collateral estoppel against Baker solely on the grounds that the Ames court would do so.

131. **Yes.** No congressional statute, and no specific constitutional provision, requires the state court to follow the prior federal judgment's preclusive effect. However, state courts universally do so — it may be that this is required by the Supremacy Clause of the U.S. Constitution.

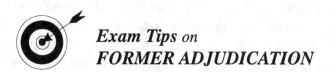

Exam Tips on
FORMER ADJUDICATION

You will almost always know when you have a Former Adjudication problem, because the fact pattern will have to clue you in to the existence of two suits, one of which has already resulted in a judgment. The trick, of course, is to determine what effect the first judgment should have on the second suit.

☛ Make sure to distinguish between *claim preclusion* (sometimes called by the ambiguous phrase "res judicata," which you should avoid unless your professor uses it, or by the preferable terms *"merger"* and *"bar"*) and *issue preclusion* (usually called *"collateral estoppel,"* which is the preferable phrase to use on exams.) [358]

    ☞ Where the first suit was between the *same parties* (or their privies) as the second suit, and involved the same *"claim,"* you're interested in *claim preclusion*. If you find that the requirements for claim preclusion have been met, the case is over — the claim in the second suit is *"merged"* into the earlier judgment (if P in the second suit won the first suit), and it's *"barred"* by the earlier judgment (if P in the second suit lost the first suit).

☞ Where the second suit involves at least one *different party* than the first suit, *or* where you conclude that the second suit involves a *different "claim"* than the first suit, then you're interested in issue preclusion / *collateral estoppel* (c.e.) If c.e. applies, it resolves a *particular issue*, but not necessarily the whole claim.

☞ Often, you'll want to examine the possibility of claim preclusion first, then go on to issue preclusion / c.e. if the requirements for claim preclusion aren't satisfied.

☛ For *claim preclusion*, here are the major sub-issues [359-368]:

☞ One tip-off for a claim-preclusion problem is *"claim splitting."* [360] Typically, P has an accident, and sues in Suit 1 for *property damage*, and then in Suit 2 sues the same defendant for *personal injuries* (or vice versa). In most states, this doesn't work — since both types of damages were suffered in the same incident, they're deemed to be a single "claim." If P won in the first suit, say his second claim is "merged" into the first; if P lost the first suit, say he's now "barred."

☞ Another situation involving claim splitting is the compulsory counterclaim context. When D in Suit 1 fails to assert what is (under the applicable federal or state proce- dural rules) a compulsory counterclaim, then the mechanism by which D loses the right to bring the claim later is the doctrine of merger and bar.

☞ Many questions involve *privies*. [368] Here, the relation between P1 (plaintiff in the first suit) and P2 (plaintiff in the second suit) is so close, legally speaking, that P2 will be treated as if he had been a claimant in the first suit, so that he can suffer claim pre- clusion even though he was not formally a party to the first suit. The same can happen for two Ds. Here are some common fact patterns posing an issue of privity:

☞ D1 is an *employee* charged with a tort, and D2 is D1's *employer* (liable for D1's torts under *respondeat superior*.) Here, D1 and D2 are definitely privies, so D2 is bound if D1 loses the first suit. (But the converse probably does not involve privity — if the employer is sued first, the employee is probably not bound as a privy.) If D1 is an *independent contractor*, D2 (who has engaged D1) is probably not a privy.

☞ P1 is a passenger in a car who suffers injuries from a different car driven by X, and P2 is the owner of the car containing P1. P1 and P2 might be held to be privies.

☞ P1 is an injured person, and P2 is P1's spouse, who has her own claim for, say, loss of consortium or (if P1 dies) wrongful death. Here, probably P1 and P2 are privies.

☛ For *collateral estoppel* (c.e.), here are the main things to look for [369-383]:

☞ Remember that c.e. applies only to issues that were *actually litigated and decided* in the first suit. Anytime you see a fact pattern that involves two suits, look for an issue decided in the first suit that may be relevant to the second suit, and determine whether c.e. may apply to compel the second court to use the first court's finding on that issue.

☞ Because the issue must have been actually litigated and decided, if the first suit ended in a ***default judgment***, it has ***no*** c.e. effect on the absent defendant.

☞ The issue must also have been ***necessary to the outcome*** of the first suit. So if the first suit would have come out the same way even if the issue had not been decided at all, or decided differently, then c.e. won't apply to that issue. [371]

☞ C.e. questions often involve "who can be ***bound***." [378-383] There are two main points to remember:

☞ A true ***stranger*** to the first action can ***never be bound*** by c.e., no matter how similar the fact issue, and even if the party who won in the first suit on the issue is now present in the second suit.

☞ However, as with claim preclusion, if a party in the second suit is found to be a ***privy*** to a party in the first suit, then the privy can be bound by the earlier finding. Example: If Employee loses in the first suit on an issue of whether he behaved negligently, Employer will be bound in a second suit as a privy.

☞ C.e. questions also often involve "who can ***benefit***" from c.e. Of course, one who was a party to the first action can benefit from c.e. But the key issue — which seems to surface in most c.e. fact patterns —is whether a true ***stranger*** to the first action can benefit from factual findings made there. Here are the key sub-issues/rules:

☞ Nearly all courts today have ***abandoned*** the rule of ***mutuality***, i.e., the old blanket rule that a stranger to the first action could never benefit from c.e. So when your fact pattern involves a stranger trying to use c.e., you should preface your discussion with something like "Assuming that the jurisdiction follows the majority approach of abandoning mutuality, X may be able to benefit from c.e. ..."

☞ Always distinguish between ***"offensive"*** and ***"defensive"*** use of c.e., and state which kind of use is proposed in your fact pattern. "Offensive" means use by a first-action-stranger who is the ***plaintiff*** in the second action; "defensive" means use by one who is a ***defendant*** in the second action. Remember that courts are ***more willing to allow "defensive" use*** (but they do sometimes allow offensive use as well.)

☞ If the facts involve offensive c.e., check whether P in the second suit ***"hung back,"*** i.e., declined to join the first suit even though he had a good opportunity to do so. If so, P is less likely to be allowed to use c.e., on fairness and judicial-efficiency grounds.

☞ Determine whether the person to be bound had an ***incentive to litigate*** the issue the first time. A key aspect is whether that person could reasonably have ***foreseen that the second suit would come along*** — the less foreseeable, the less incentive to litigate, and the less likely the second court is to allow c.e. Also, check whether the first suit was in a court of ***limited jurisdiction***, which would make it less likely that the party to be bound had the requisite incentive to litigate fully. [381]

☞ Check whether the facts involve a danger of the ***"multiple plaintiff anomaly"*** (a mass tort in which each P sues in turn; once D is found liable in one, c.e. would mean D would lose all subsequent suits.) In this m.p.a. situation, courts usually hold that c.e. is unfair. [382]

☛ Finally, look for *Full Faith & Credit* (FF&C) issues [388-392]:

☞ Any time you have a *judgment* in Suit 1, and Suit 2 takes place in a *different jurisdiction* than Suit 1, you have a potential FF&C issue. You need to ask, "Is the court in Suit 2 bound to follow the judgment issued in Suit 1?"

☞ If Suit 1 and Suit 2 were both in *state* courts, the FF&C clause of the *U.S. Constitution* requires that the Suit 2 court give to the Suit 1 judgment the same effect that that judgment would have in the state that decided it. So State 2 can't allow re-litigation of any factual or legal issues, even if the substantive law of State 2 would have produced a completely different result. Also, State 2 must *"enforce"* the State 1 judgment — it must let the winner of the State 1 judgment seize the loser's State 2 assets without any re-litigation of the merits.

☞ If Suit 1 is in state court and Suit 2 in federal court (or vice versa), FF&C principles similarly require the second court to honor the first court's judgment.

☞ The key exception — frequently tested — is that the second court can reconsider whether the first court had *jurisdiction* (either personal or subject matter), if the jurisdiction issue was *not litigated or waived* in the first suit. This is *"collateral attack."*

☞ FF&C means that the *res judicata* effect of the earlier judgment must also be enforced by the second jurisdiction. So if State 1 would allow, say, offensive use of c.e. by a stranger, State 2 must do the same.

ESSAY EXAM
QUESTIONS AND ANSWERS

The following questions were asked on Civil Procedure Examinations given at Harvard Law School. The sample answers are intended to show one possible approach to each question. Page references are to the main text of the outline.

QUESTION 1: Muenster Airways, Inc., is a small airline flying regularly scheduled flights between points in New Jersey, New York, and New England. It is incorporated in New Jersey and has its principal place of business there. Amos Stilton, a passenger on the ill-fated flight described below, is a citizen of Ames, a small midwestern state located between Indiana and Illinois.

In December 1988, Muenster conducted an advertising campaign in Ames and other midwestern states offering a special flying tour of New England in the spring of 1989, featuring stopovers in Tiverton, R.I., Worcester, Mass., and White River Junction, Vermont. Stilton, attracted by the advertisement, bought a round-trip ticket from an independent travel agent in Ames and was put into a group of Ames travelers who were leaving on the tour from Ames City on April 1. (Transportation to Newark, N.J., the starting point of the tour, was provided by another airline.)

Stilton and his fellow travelers arrived in Newark on the appointed day and boarded a Muenster plane for Tiverton, but the plane was forced to make an emergency landing in Bridgeport, Conn., and although no passengers were killed, many (including Stilton) were seriously injured.

One of the passengers, Charlene Cheddar, brought a diversity action for $75,000 damages against Muenster in a New Jersey federal court. The case went to trial and the jury found Muenster liable but awarded only $500 to Cheddar, apparently rejecting her claim of serious injury. No appeal was filed.

Stilton has now brought an action of his own against Muenster in an Ames federal court, seeking $100,000 damages. Service of process was made on Muenster by registered mail (without any acknowledgement-of-service or request-for-waiver-of-service form enclosed) at its home office in New Jersey. Ames has a jurisdiction statute identical to the Uniform Interstate and International Procedure Act (pp. 18-19). In addition, Stilton has sought to establish jurisdiction in the Ames federal court by attachment of an airplane owned by Muenster and currently under two-year lease to Gorgonzola Airways, a company doing business solely in Ames, at an annual rental of $20,000.

A. What are the arguments for and against Muenster's motion to dismiss the action in its entirety for lack of jurisdiction? How should the motion be decided?

B. Assume that all motions addressed to jurisdiction are denied and that Stilton, relying on the New Jersey decision, moves for summary judgment on the issue of liability. If the issue is one of first impression, what decision should be made on the motion and why?

QUESTION 2: Staley's Tire Store, Inc., a retail outfit located just across the Rancid River in Langdell City, Langdell, until recently was a franchise dealer for the Plastic Tire Company, Inc., a manufacturer whose principal place of business is here in Ames. Staley's just recently decided to carry a line of tires manufactured by our client, Vinyl Tire company, Inc., whose plant is also located in this state. Staley's has just brought suit under the federal antitrust laws against Plastic in the Langdell federal court, alleging that its franchise agreement with Plastic violated those laws and seeking rescission and damages. Plastic has filed an answer denying any violation of the antitrust laws, and has counterclaimed for damages for breach of the franchise agreement. Plastic has sought to add our client, Vinyl, as a party to the counterclaim, alleging that Vinyl induced the breach. Service of process was made by a federal marshal at Vinyl's home office here in Ames City. Can Vinyl be forced to litigate this case in Langdell, or is there some way we can have the action against it dismissed?

QUESTION 3: Our client, William Byer, entered an agreement with Stanley Cellar to purchase a parcel of Ames land from Cellar for $50,000. A down payment of $10,000 has been made by Byer and the transfer was to occur on May 1. Byer claims that he was induced to enter the contract by Cellar's fraud, and when Cellar refused to call the deal off, Byer brought suit in Ames federal court, on April 1, for cancellation of the contract and refund of the down payment. (Byer and Cellar are of diverse citizenship). Last week, after getting an extension of time to file his answer, Cellar interposed an answer denying the alleged fraud and counterclaiming for the remainder owing on the contract. He has demanded a jury on all issues triable as of right by a jury. So far as I can tell, the only contested issue in the case is the alleged fraud of Cellar. Does Cellar have a jury trial right on that issue?

QUESTION 4: Our client, Albert Hill, is suing Peter Dale in the Ames federal court for fraud under the federal securities acts. At the trial, there was evidence both ways on the fraud issue, although unfortunately one of our key witnesses was unable to testify because of illness. The judge's charge to the jury, in my view, imposed too heavy a burden of proof on the plaintiff but the jury still came in with a verdict for Hill, awarding substantial damages. After entry of judgment, Dale moved for judgment as a matter of law and, in the alternative, for a new trial, and both motions were denied. I understand that Dale plans to appeal in order to renew two arguments that were raised and rejected in the trial court — (1) that the federal securities acts do not apply to the transaction in controversy and (2) that the evidence was insufficient to take the case to the jury. What procedural steps, if any, should we take at this point? Dale apparently had moved for judgment as a matter of law before the case went to the jury.

QUESTION 5: We are defending a personal injury case and our client has been asked the following Rule 33 interrogatory. "Please give the name and address of all doctors whom you or your attorney have retained, specially employed, or informally consulted concerning the damage aspects of this action." The case is one in which the plaintiff is admittedly totally and permanently disabled by something called Pert's Disease. The issue is whether this condition is causally connected with the blow on the head the plaintiff received as a result of the defendant's alleged negligence. Our medical witness, whose report was made available to plaintiff's counsel two months ago, insists that Pert's Disease cannot be caused or aggravated by trauma and that plaintiff cannot possibly find an expert to support such an absurd claim. Last week I met Dr. Francis Pert, whose research led to the discovery of the disease that bears his name, at a cocktail party. I mentioned the pending lawsuit and asked whether our doctor's opinion was sound. Dr. Pert said that it reflected the general view and was confirmed by Dr. Pert's own published writings. He then added: "But I can tell you, in confidence of course, that my recent research, not yet published, convinces me that the disease can be precipitated by a blow such as you describe in this case." Dr. Pert's distaste for court proceedings is so great that he invariably refuses to appear as an expert witness. How should we answer the interrogatory consistently with the Federal Rules and our sense of professionalism?

QUESTION 6: The State of Ames has enacted the following statute: "No person engaged in the business of a contractor shall be permitted to present any judicial demand before any court of this state for the collection of compensation for performance of any act for which a license is required by the law of this state without alleging and proving that he was a duly licensed contractor at all times during the performance of such act." Dauntless Construction Co. is a Thayer corporation engaged in the business of installation and construction of telephone facilities. Dauntless contracted with Pacific Telephone Co., an Ames corporation, to construct certain facilities and install them in Ames. This was a contract for performance of which a license was required by Ames law. Dauntless was a duly licensed contractor in Thayer but neglected to obtain a license in Ames, apparently through ignorance of the Ames requirement. A dispute arose between the parties during the performance of the contract, and Pacific brought an action against Dauntless in the Ames Superior Court for breach of contract. Proper service of process was made. Dauntless removed the action to the U.S. District Court for Ames and filed an answer denying plaintiff's allegations, setting up certain affirmative defenses, and also asserted a counterclaim claiming damages for misrepresentation in the negotiation of the contract and breach of various conditions therein. Pacific has moved to dismiss the counterclaim because of noncompliance with the Ames licensing statute. There is an Ames decision, *McCord v. Dean Waterworks Co.*, 321 Ames 400 (1972), holding that an unlicensed contractor cannot maintain a counterclaim arising out of a contract performed in Ames. You are the law clerk to the federal judge who is about to hear the motion. He has asked you for a memorandum to aid him in dealing with the problem. Prepare the memorandum.

QUESTION 7: Your client, Peripheral Products, Inc., brought a treble damage action against Devious Corp., in the U.S. District Court for Ames under the Clayton Act for alleged antitrust violations. The defendant's answer included a defense based on the four-year statute of limitations provided by four-year statute of limitations provided by Congress for actions arising under the antitrust laws. After hearing on a motion for summary judgment based on that defense, the court entered this order: "It is ordered, adjudged and decreed that the defendant's motion for summary judgment be, and the same hereby is, granted with costs to be taxed." Peripheral has now brought another action in the Ames Superior Court, alleging virtually the same facts and claiming damages for unfair competition. The Ames statute of limitations allowing six years for such actions has not yet expired. Devious has pleaded *res judicata*. Prepare a memorandum on the problem.

ANSWERS

SAMPLE ANSWER TO QUESTION 1:

Part A: The most difficult jurisdictional questions in this case relate to jurisdiction over the parties. However, there are two preliminary subject matter jurisdictional issues which will be dealt with first: (1) Is there diversity? and (2) Is the amount in controversy requirement met?

Under 28 USC §1332(c), Muenster is a citizen of New Jersey, since that state is both the state of incorporation and the principal place of business. Stilton is a citizen of Ames, so diversity is established.

The satisfaction of the $50,000 amount in controversy requirement is clear, at least if the action proceeds *in personam* (rather than *quasi in rem*). Stilton has claimed damages of $100,000; under the *St. Paul Mercury* case (p. 107) this amount will control unless it appears to a legal certainty that Stilton cannot recover more than $50,000. Since Stilton's claim appears to be in good faith, and he is seriously injured, the amount in controversy requirement is satisfied.

However, if the attached airplane is to serve as a source of *quasi in rem* jurisdiction, the amount in controversy requirement may pose a problem. It is only if personal jurisdiction over Muenster turns out to be lacking that the issue of *quasi in rem* becomes important; in that event, the *quasi in rem* action must itself meet the jurisdictional amount. However, it is unclear exactly what it is that must exceed $50,000. Some courts have held that the value of the attached property controls; others have held that it is the value of the claim that matters (p. 62). If the latter measure alone is adopted, the requirement is clearly met. But if it is the value of the attached property that is relevant, a further complication arises. Is it the airplane itself that is being attached, or Gorgonzola's debt for it under the lease? Since the airplane is presumably worth more than the two years of lease payments, Stilton will probably seek *quasi in rem* jurisdiction over the plane itself — if he succeeds, amount in controversy is met as long as the value of the plane exceeds $50,000. But the Ames federal court may conclude that Gorgonzola's interest is unfairly violated by allowing Stilton to attach the plane and levy on it for a claim that has nothing to do with Gorgonzola. In that case, only Gorgonzola's debt to Muenster, $40,000, could serve as the *res* of a *quasi in rem* action (on the theory of *Harris v. Balk*, pp. 54-55) and this debt does not meet the $50,000 requirement.

Thus, the jurisdictional amount question is doubly complicated if the action turns out to be solely *quasi in rem* (which would be the case if personal jurisdiction over Muenster is lacking). It would depend first on whether the court views the amount of the attached property, or the amount of the claim, as controlling, and then on whether it is the airplane, or just Gorgonzola's debt, that is the *res*.

Turning to the question of *in personam* jurisdiction, UIIP §103(a)(1) may grant personal jurisdiction over Muenster. That section provides for jurisdiction over any person "who acts directly or by an agent," with respect to a "cause of action arising from the person's . . . transacting any business in this state." Muenster will undoubtedly argue that the travel agent who sold Stilton his ticket was not its agent, and that the UIIP therefore does not apply. Muenster might on this ground escape the decision in *Gelfand v. Tanner Motor Tours* (p. 25), which held that a company which advertised its tours in the forum state by means of a travel agent had the minimum contacts necessary for jurisdiction.

In determining whether the travel agent was Muenster's agent within the meaning of the UIIP, the amount of Muenster tickets the agent sold, and the existence of communication between Muenster and the agent, should be considered. Clearly if the agent sold so many tickets that had he not been in business, Muenster would have set up its own Ames office, the minimum contacts are present. *(Gelfand)*. Conversely, if the agent only very rarely sold a Muenster ticket, and few Ames residents took the Muenster tours, the necessary minimum contacts probably should be found lacking. Note that the UIIP only applies to those in-state contacts which are related to the particular cause of action in question. It is also possible that Muenster's other contacts with Ames, unrelated to the Conn. crash, may be sufficient to confer jurisdiction over Muenster. For instance, in *Asahi*, pp. 29-32, the Supreme Court suggested that advertising extensively might be enough to subject a defendant to the forum's personal jurisdiction. However, these unrelated contacts must be quite extensive for jurisdiction to be conferred (*Perkins v. Benguet*, p. 25.)

If it is held that personal jurisdiction over Muenster does not exist, *quasi in rem* jurisdiction may be present. *Quasi in rem* jurisdiction is allowed in federal actions only if: (a) the plaintiff cannot obtain personal jurisdiction over the defendant through reasonable efforts, and (b) the law of the state in which the federal court sits permits such jurisdiction. (FRCP 4(n), as amended in 1993). Requirement (a) would be satisfied if the Ames long-arm (the UIIP) is interpreted not to reach Muenster by virtue of the travel agent's acts (as discussed above). Requirement (b) raises questions: the UIIP is silent on the subject of *quasi in rem* jurisdiction. However, if Ames is like most states, it permits such jurisdiction to be exercised over either tangible property present in the state, or over a debt owed by a debtor who is present in the state. Thus the airplane might be treated as the *res*; alternatively, Gorgonzola's debt to Muenster may be the *res*, under the attachment-of-the debt theory of *Harris v. Balk*. (*Harris* allows *quasi in rem* jurisdiction if the forum state can obtain personal jurisdiction over the debtor). However, Muenster will have a good chance of arguing that under *Shaffer v. Heitner* (pp. 56-60), *quasi in rem* jurisdiction over it is unconstitutional, because Muenster lacks minimum contacts with Ames. This will certainly be the case if *in personam* jurisdiction over it is lacking, since under *Shaffer* the two tests are now the same.

An additional issue arises with respect to *notice*; was registered mail service a sufficient form of notice to Muenster? Federal Rule 4(e)(1) allows service by any method (e.g., registered mail) allowable under the law of the state in which the federal court sits. While the UIIP is silent on notice, Ames may have another statute allowing registered mail notice. If it does, registered mail service here is sufficient. If it does not, only personal service suffices, and Muenster can dismiss.

Part B: Summary judgment ought to be denied Stilton. He is seeking an offensive use of collateral estoppel. That is, he is, as a plaintiff, trying to apply the finding of liability in the Cheddar case against Muenster in this case. Such offensive use of collateral estoppel was allowed by the Supreme Court in *Parklane Hosiery* (pp. 380-383). But in *Parklane*, only two lawsuits were involved; here, there is the likelihood of not only the Cheddar and Stilton actions, but of actions by each of the other injured passengers as well. It seems unfair to require Muenster to play this "heads you win; tails I lose" game in each of the many possible suits. This is the "multiple plaintiff anomaly" situation (p. 382).

The issue becomes even more stark when one considers the possibility that the jury's finding in *Cheddar* was not really one of liability-but-no-serious-injury, but rather a finding of serious-injury-but-doubtful-liability. In other words, the jury may have mixed elements of liability and damages, and decided to give Cheddar something for her trouble (and save her from paying court costs) even though it didn't really think Muenster was liable. If this is what in fact happened, then there is all the more reason not to hold that the *Cheddar* litigation was conclusive on the negligence issue.

It is true, of course, that to deny the use of collateral estoppel in this instance may promote additional litigation — the negligence issue will be retried, perhaps many times over. But this prospect is somewhat offset by the likelihood that Muenster will not wage as long and desperate a defense. If estoppel were applied, then in the first of a string of suits, the defendant would drag out the litigation as long as possible, and defend as ardently as it could, even if only a few dollars were involved. If estoppel is not applied, then the defendant in Muenster's position can afford to defend a small claim half-heartedly — the amount of increased litigation may thus not be as great as might at first glance be feared.

A further injustice is implicit in allowing the use of collateral estoppel in this situation — Cheddar is effectively penalized for having gone first. Assuming that the jury did in fact render a compromise verdict because of its uncertainty on liability, Cheddar would have been better off waiting until someone else won against Muenster, and then using collateral estoppel. Thus each plaintiff has a powerful incentive to wait for someone else to go first, and to refuse to consolidate with other plaintiffs. When this judicial inefficiency is coupled with the likelihood that the plaintiffs will all agree to let the most appealing plaintiff sue first, it can be seen that Stilton's case for estoppel is about as poor as it could possibly be.

SAMPLE ANSWER TO QUESTION 2:

The question is a very close one, and involves many complexities. Vinyl may or may not be amenable to suit in Langdell federal court; if it is, service may or may not have been valid. If the requirements of personal jurisdiction are met, federal subject-matter jurisdiction is probably present, even though Plastic and Vinyl are citizens of the same state.

Personal jurisdiction: Two issues arise with respect to personal jurisdiction over Vinyl: (1) Is Vinyl *amenable* to suit in Langdell?; and (2) If it is, was service on Vinyl made within the geographical boundaries for service specified by the Federal Rules?

(1) Vinyl's amenability to suit: In federal question cases, the federal courts have generally held that a corporation is amenable to suit (i.e., suable) as long as it has minimum contacts with the state in which the district court sits sufficient to meet the *International Shoe* test (p. 20); in other words, local state law is ignored for purposes of amenability to suit. In diversity cases, however, *Arrowsmith* (pp. 48-49) holds that the Federal courts should allow only the jurisdiction that is exercised by the courts of the state in which the federal court sits, even if the state courts do not extend their jurisdiction as far as is Constitutionally permissible.

If the Langdell state courts would have exercised jurisdiction over Vinyl had the Plastic claim against it been brought there, the federal court here should clearly exercise jurisdiction. Such an exercise of jurisdiction appears to be within the limits of Constitutional due process, since the cause of action on which Vinyl is being sued is an alleged inducement to breach a contract made in the forum state — given that *Burger King* (pp. 32-35) establishes that a franchise contract closely related to the forum state furnishes minimum contacts, the inducement of a *breach* of that contract probably constitutes minimum contacts as well. If, on the other hand, the Langdell state courts would *not* exercise jurisdiction over Vinyl, the issue is more difficult. While it is true that, as stated above, the federal courts in federal question cases will generally go to the limits of due process in exercising personal jurisdiction, that general practice relates to *claims* which involve federal questions. Here, although this is a federal question *case*, the claim on which Vinyl is being sued is a state claim. The court should therefore probably treat the problem of amenability as if the case were purely in diversity. In that event, jurisdiction would not be exercised over Vinyl if the Langdell state courts would not do so.

(2) Geographical boundaries for service: If we conclude through the above reasoning that Vinyl is amenable to service, there is an additional requirement that service be carried out within the geographical limits specified in the Federal Rules. According to Rule 4(k)(1)(A), service on Vinyl may be made anywhere that the laws of Langdell permit. If the Langdell long-arm would permit service on Vinyl's Ames offices, then the federal service which occurred is valid. If Langdell law would not permit such service, the service may nonetheless be valid under the "100-mile-bulge" provision of 4(k)(1)(B). That provision allows service on persons who are brought in as additional parties to a counterclaim pursuant to Rule 19 at a place not more than 100 miles from the court where the action is pending. Thus, if Rule 19 allows Vinyl to be brought in as additional party to Plastic's counterclaim, and if Vinyl's Ames offices are within 100 miles of the Langdell federal courthouse, service was valid.

It is unclear whether Vinyl may be brought in pursuant to Rule 19. That Rule allows joinder of certain persons who are subject to service of process (is this circular?) and whose joinder will not destroy subject matter jurisdiction. Assuming for the moment that Vinyl meets these two tests (the subject matter question is discussed below), it is joinable under Rule 19 if it "claims an interest relating to the subject of the action and is so situated that the disposition of the action in [its] absence may . . . as a practical matter impair or impede [its] ability to protect that interest. . . . " Since Vinyl has an interest in having Staley stay in business so that it will continue to distribute Vinyl products, it is arguable that Vinyl satisfies the provision of Rule 19 just cited. If so, service within the 100-mile bulge is permitted.

Subject-matter jurisdiction (supplemental jurisdiction): Plastic and Vinyl are both citizens of Ames. Plastic's claim against Vinyl therefore fails to satisfy independently the requirements of diversity. Unless the claim can be "tacked on" through supplemental jurisdiction, the claim must be dismissed.

The doctrine of supplemental jurisdiction, recently codified in 28 U.S.C. §1367, allows a federal court which has jurisdiction over an initial claim to also hear a related claim, even though that related claim would not independently satisfy the requirements of federal subject-matter jurisdiction (diversity and amount in controversy). One of the ways supplemental jurisdiction can apply is to allow a court to hear a state-created claim closely related to a federal-question claim that is the "core" claim supplying original jurisdiction. (In other words, supplemental jurisdiction can be used to supply what was known before the 1990 enactment of §1367 as "pendent" jurisdiction).

For a court to exercise its supplemental jurisdiction, the two claims must form part of the "same case or controversy under Article III" of the Constitution. This test is usually deemed satisfied if the state-created claim and the federal claim derive from a "common nucleus of operative fact"; see *UMW v. Gibbs* (p. 113). Since both the federal claim (that the franchise agreement violated the antitrust laws) and the counterclaim against Staley and Vinyl (alleging that Vinyl induced Plastic to breach the franchise agreement) relate to the franchise agreement, probably the "common nucleus of operative fact" test would be satisfied. Therefore, supplemental jurisdiction would govern the counterclaim against both Staley and Vinyl.

Under pre-1990 law, the addition of Vinyl to the Staley-v.-Plastic counterclaim would probably ***not*** have been allowed under the doctrine of pendent jurisdiction. The Supreme Court's decision in *Finley v. U.S.*, (pp. 113-114), made it very difficult for ***additional parties*** to be brought in to defend a pendent state claim. But §1367(a), in effect since 1990, expressly overrules *Finley* — that section allows "claims that involve the joinder or intervention of additional parties." So Vinyl does not get any comfort from the subject matter jurisdiction aspect of the case — supplemental jurisdiction allows Vinyl to be brought into the counterclaim, even though a claim by Plastic against Vinyl would not independently meet federal subject matter jurisdictional requirements.

All of this assumes, of course, that there is something in the Federal Rules which allows the joinder of Vinyl to Plastic's counterclaim against Staley, apart from questions of jurisdiction. The operative Rule is 13(h), which allows additional parties to a counterclaim to be brought in "in accordance with the provisions of Rules 19 and 20." While there is some doubt as to whether Rule 19 would allow such joinder, Rule 20 almost certainly does. That rule allows joinder of persons as defendants "if there is asserted against them…any right to relief in respect of or arising out of the same transaction, occurrence, or series of transactions or occurrences and if any question of law or fact common to all defendants will arise in the action." (A defendant to a counterclaim is presumably a defendant for the purposes of Rule 20.) If the Staley claim and the claim against Vinyl are closely enough related so that the supplemental jurisdiction doctrine applies, then they are certainly close enough so that Rule 20 applies. In that case, Rule 13(h) joinder is allowable. Since such joinder is at the discretion of the counterclaimant, there is nothing Vinyl can do.

SAMPLE ANSWER TO QUESTION 3:

Cellar is raising a legal counterclaim (damages for breach of contract) to an equitable suit (rescission). The question of fraud is a factor affecting both claims, since it would be a defense to the counterclaim and is the basis for the original suit. In *Beacon Theatres*, (pp. 277-278), the U.S. Supreme Court held that a trial judge did not have discretion to order the trial of legal and equitable issues in such a way that the right to jury trial of the former would be lost. Since the issue of fraud will only be tried once (the rules of *res judicata* and "law of the case" require this), it must therefore be tried to a jury, in order to protect Cellar's right to jury trial of his legal counterclaim.

SAMPLE ANSWER TO QUESTION 4:

We should (1) file an answer to Dale's motions in the Appeals Court; and (2) request a new trial on burden of proof in the alternative. The conditional new trial request is necessary to protect ourselves; if the only thing we do is to attempt to refute Dale's arguments, and we fail, the Appeals Court will have no choice but to grant judgment as a matter of law for Dale. It will not be able to grant a new trial, since no party will have made this request on appeal. We should, therefore, specifically state that if the denial of *JML* is found to have been incorrect, we wish a new trial on the burden of proof issue. Such a contention on our part is specifically provided for by Rule 50(d), which allows the Appeals Court either to decide our new trial motion itself, or to remand for a determination of this issue by the trial court. (Of course, if the Appeals Court decides that the federal securities laws do not apply at all, they will dismiss for lack of subject-matter jurisdiction, and will not order a new trial. Our motion under 50(d) would thus make a difference only if the Court finds jurisdiction present, but rules for Dale on the sufficiency of the evidence.)

SAMPLE ANSWER TO QUESTION 5:

The issue is whether the name and address of an expert whom we informally consulted, but whom we did not retain and will not call at trial, is within the scope of discovery. There is virtually no way under Federal Rule 26 that such discovery may be obtained.

26(b)(1) does allow discovery of the "identity and location of persons having knowledge of any discoverable matter." However, this does not help plaintiff — Dr. Pert does not have "knowledge of any discoverable matter". It is true that he has an opinion which would be admissible at trial, and which thus falls within the general rule that material which would be admissible at trial is discoverable. However, *no* kind of discovery at all may be taken of Dr. Pert under any of the subsections of 26(b)(4); therefore, he does not have "knowledge of any discoverable matter," and his name and whereabouts are thus not discoverable under 26(b)(1).

Even though the Federal Rules don't compel us to divulge Pert's name or address, I suppose it might be argued that a well-developed sense of professionalism on our part would include the divulging of this information as a matter of courtesy. On the other hand, we do have an obligation to represent our client's interest, which in this case lies in not calling the other side's attention to Pert. It seems to me that if we seek an order preventing discovery, on the grounds that the Federal Rules don't allow discovery in this instance, we have not made any misrepresentation, and have not violated professional ethics.

SAMPLE ANSWER TO QUESTION 6:

This is a classic *Erie* problem, in which the federal interest in consolidation of litigation conflicts with a state interest in enforcing licensing requirements. An additional wrinkle is presented by the fact that it is a counterclaim, rather than an original claim, which is in question.

The *Erie* doctrine of course applies only where no statute, federal or state, directly governs the issue. Here, there is an Ames statute almost on point. However, that statute speaks of "present[ing] a judicial demand" — it is unclear whether this language includes the filing of a counterclaim, or applies only to original actions by plaintiffs. Ames common law, as evidenced by *McCord*, holds that the statute does apply to counterclaims as well as original actions. The decision whether to follow state common law is an *Erie* question — if the court decides to follow Ames law, the Dauntless counterclaim will be barred.

The "twin evils" to which the *Erie* decision was addressed are: (1) discrimination against the citizen of the forum state; and (2) forum-shopping (p. 218). Both of these evils would result to a certain extent if the court here refuses to follow Ames state law, and allows Dauntless to pursue its counterclaim. Dauntless, as non-citizen of Ames, has had the opportunity to select a federal forum by means of the right of removal. (Your honor is aware, of course, that a defendant may remove only if he is not a citizen of the state in which the action is originally brought). Dauntless has thus been able to "shop" for a forum which it hopes is the more likely to be hospitable to its claim — it knew that it would fail in Ames state court, so it chose to remove to federal court. If your honor permits Dauntless to prosecute its counterclaim in the face of Ames law, this "forum-shopping" will have paid off.

Prior to the Supreme Court's decision in *Byrd v. Blue Ridge* (pp. 230-232), the problem could have been easily disposed of by resort to the "outcome-determinative" test first espoused in *Guaranty Trust v. York* (p. 228). *Guaranty* held that state law must be followed if it would "significantly affect the result of a litigation for a federal court to disregard a law of a State that would be controlling" had the action been brought in state court. The effect of ignoring Ames law here is nearly the same as the effect would have been in *Guaranty* of ignoring the state statute of limitations. *Guaranty* held that it was "outcome-determinative" to ignore a statute of limitations, since this would be to allow prosecution in federal court of a claim which would be completely barred in state court. Here, similarly, the effect of ignoring the *McCord* decision would be to allow a claim in federal court which would be barred in Ames state court.

As *Byrd* indicates, however, (1) there are varying degrees of outcome-determinativeness, and (2) the fact that the decision of which law to apply will be somewhat outcome-determinative does not settle the matter — there may be stronger countervailing considerations. Thus, the decision whether to try an issue to a judge or to a jury is less likely to determine the outcome of a lawsuit than is the decision whether to bar an action as untimely. *Byrd* held that the former issue is so little outcome-determinative that strong countervailing federal policies may compel a refusal to follow state decisions on the allocation of judge/jury roles.

It might seem, at first glance, that there is not any strong federal interest in favor of allowing the Dauntless claim. However, there is a strong federal interest in *consolidating* all the related litigation between two parties into one single action. This interest in consolidation is not evident at first — one might argue that if the Dauntless claim is barred, then it can't be brought in either Ames state *or* federal court, and will not reappear to be litigated in a separate, judicially wasteful, action. However, this argument that no consolidation interest is present overlooks a crucial consideration: *the Dauntless claim may be triable as an original action in the state or federal court of some other jurisdiction, perhaps Thayer. If it is in fact* the case that the Dauntless claim can and will be tried elsewhere, then there is a strong federal interest in disposing of all claims between Pacific and Dauntless in one action. Thus, the situation is quite different from that in *Guaranty*, where the federal courts had no strong reason to try a claim time-barred in state court (assuming that no other state court would have allowed the *Guaranty* claim).

It is difficult to tell from the record as it has so far been developed whether the Thayer state courts would entertain the Dauntless claim. Personal jurisdiction over Pacific can be constitutionally exercised by Thayer courts — the making of a contract with a citizen of the forum state is generally a sufficient contact to permit jurisdiction in a suit arising out of that contract. (See *Burger King*, pp. 32-35.) Thus, if the state of Thayer has a long-arm which would reach Pacific, the Dauntless action might be maintainable in Thayer. It is possible, of course, that the Thayer court will defer to the Ames statute (and the *McCord* interpretation of it), and bar the Dauntless claim. This is a question of conflict of laws. If Dauntless would be allowed to sue in Thayer state court, then a federal court sitting in Thayer would have to allow the suit, under the rule of *Klaxon v. Stentor* (p. 224), which compels a federal court sitting in diversity to apply the conflicts rule of the state in which it sits.

It is therefore quite possible that if this court bars the Dauntless claim, it will later be brought in either the state or the federal court of Thayer. In that event, this court will have promoted a kind of "lateral forum-shopping"; defendants in the position of Dauntless will select a forum like Thayer instead of bringing their claims as counterclaims in Ames. Such an inducement to hold back from asserting a counterclaim promotes judicial inefficiency, as well as forum-shopping. This possibility indicates that Ames law should be disregarded, and the Dauntless claim allowed.

However, one additional possibility may negate the above reasoning — if the Dauntless counterclaim is *compulsory*, then it may be waived if it is not brought in this action. Since the counterclaim arises out of the same contract that is the subject of Pacific's claim for breach, it probably meets the "transaction or occurrence" test of Rule 13(a), and is thus compulsory. However, it is not clear whether Dauntless is barred from bringing the claim as an independent action in Thayer if it has done everything it could to assert the counterclaim in this case, and has failed. It would probably *not* be held to be barred from suing on the claim as plaintiff in Thayer state or federal court. Therefore, the fact that the counterclaim arises out of the same transaction or occurrence as the Pacific claim is irrelevant. The above argument for ignoring Ames law and letting Dauntless assert the counterclaim would thus still hold.

One difficulty with this argument, however, is that it compels a district court faced with the kind of problem presented in this case to examine the jurisdictional and conflicts policies of every other potential jurisdiction, in order to determine whether the action will be brought somewhere else if the present court dismisses it. Such an examination may be time-consuming and ineffective. Nonetheless, I think it would not be burdensome for this court to set forth a principle that where the federal court *knows* that there is some other jurisdiction, either state or federal, that will hear the claim, it should not give excessive weight to the door-closing rule of the state in which it sits.

Thus if your honor later determines that Thayer, or some other jurisdiction, would in fact permit the Dauntless claim as an original action, this court should allow the claim.

SAMPLE ANSWER TO QUESTION 7:

The basic prerequisites for the application of *bar* are the following: (1) The present and former suits must represent very similar "causes of action;" (2) The parties to both suits must have been the same; and (3) The former adjudication must have been "on the merits."

(1) Similarity of causes of action: I think our best hope of defeating the claim of *res judicata* lies in showing that the two claims are not sufficiently identical for bar to apply. While it was formerly the case that absolute identity of the two claims had to be shown, the courts have now adopted a looser test which

serves to bar a greater number of claims. Devious will be able to cite decisions like *Clarke v. Redeker*, (p. 364) which held that "the judgment is conclusive, not only as to matters which were decided, but also as to all matters which ***might have been decided***." Of course, decisions like *Clarke* do not mean that any claim which could have been asserted in the first action is barred — if that were the case, there would be no hope for us at all, since we could have asserted the unfair competition claim by the doctrine of supplemental jurisdiction (see discussion below). The test for determining whether the second cause of action is so closely related to the previously litigated claim as to be barred by it is a pragmatic one: if two actions allege very similar facts, and claim violation of the same legal right, bar will apply, even though two different legal theories for recovery are involved. The facts of our case are somewhat similar to those of *Williamson v. Columbia Gas*, (p. 362), in which it was held that a claim under the Sherman Act was so similar to a previously litigated Clayton Act claim that the latter bound the former. We should argue that the elements of unfair competition are different from those of antitrust violation, and that the protected legal right is not the same in both cases. However, I am not optimistic.

It should be noted that if the kind of relief we now seek was not available from the court in which we tried the previous action, we will not now be barred. (*Hennepin Paper*, p. 363). If we can, for instance, show that the unfair competition claim could not have met the requirements of federal subject matter jurisdiction, and could not therefore have been joined with the antitrust claim, we will be in the clear. Unfortunately, the doctrine of supplemental jurisdiction (p. 112 and pp. 116-122) would almost certainly have permitted the unfair competition claim to be joined to the antitrust claim, since the two claims involve a common nucleus of operative fact.

(2) Identity of parties: The parties to both actions are identical.

(3) Adjudication on the merits: Our only remaining hope for avoiding bar is to demonstrate that the original adjudication for untimeliness was not "on the merits." However, this approach is not promising. While a 12(b)(6) dismissal for failure to state a valid claim might arguably be considered not on the merits, a summary judgment is as final and dispositive of the issues as a jury trial. Therefore, I don't think we will get anywhere with this line of attack.

In my opinion, unless we can persuade the court that the two claims are not sufficiently identical for bar to be applied, we will be prevented from litigating the unfair competition claim.

This page intentionally left blank

TABLE OF CASES

Principal discussion of a case
is indicated by page numbers in italics.

FEDERAL RULES OF CIVIL PROCEDURE

REFERENCES TO TITLE 28, UNITED STATES CODE

SUBJECT MATTER INDEX

EMANUEL LAW OUTLINES
PRODUCTS FOR 1994-95 ACADEMIC YEAR

emanuel law outlines

Year after year, Steve Emanuel's *Outlines* have been the most popular in the country. Nineteen years of law graduates swear by them. In the 1993-94 school year, law students bought an average of 3.0 Emanuels each - that's 130,000 Emanuels.

Civil Procedure, *rev.* '94-95 Ed	$17.95
Constitutional Law, *rev.* '94-95. Ed	23.95
Contracts, '93-94 Ed	16.95
Corporations, '92-93 Ed	17.95
Criminal Law, '92-93 Ed	14.95
Criminal Procedure, *rev.* '94-95 Ed	14.95
Evidence, '91-92 Ed	16.95
Property, '93-94 Ed	16.95
Secured Transactions, '88-89 Ed	12.95
Torts (General Ed.), *rev.* '94-95 Ed	16.95
Torts (Casebook Ed.), *rev.* '94-95 Ed	16.95

Keyed to '94 Ed. Prosser, Wade & Schwartz

smith's review

All titles in this series are written by leading law professors. They follow the Emanuel style and format. They have big, easy-to-read type, extensive citations and notes, and clear, crisp writing. Most have capsule summaries and sample exam Q & A's.

Agency & Partnership, '88-89 Ed	$12.95
Bankruptcy, *new* '94-95 Title	14.95
Commercial Paper, '91-92 Ed	12.95
Family Law, '93-94 Ed	14.95
Fed. Income Taxation, *rev.* '94-95 Ed	14.95
Intellectual Property, '90-91 Ed	15.95
International Law, *new* '94-95 Title	14.95
Labor Law, '88-89 Ed	11.95
Products Liability, '93-94 Ed	12.95
Torts, '91-92 Ed	13.95
Wills & Trusts, '93-94 Ed	14.95

emanuel law tapes
Constitutional Law
'92-93 Edition
(11 90-Minute Cassettes)

Each set is attractively displayed in a shrink-wrapped distinctive Emanuel box. Features:
- mnemonics
- songs & skits
- Multi-State Bar Exam questions and answers
- a special night-before-the-exam review tape
- a printed supplement.

$37.95

socratutor software

A specially condensed version of the corresponding Emanuel outline on a computer disk for use on *DOS, Windows or Macintosh.* Let's you add your own comments and create your own outline.

Emanuel Outlines

Civil Procedure	Criminal Law
Constitutional Law	Evidence
Contracts	Property
Corporations	Torts

Smith's Review

Agency & Partnership	Labor Law
Family Law	Wills & Trusts

each title... $19.95

question & answer collections

siegel's
essay & multiple-choice Q & A's

Now published by Emanuel, each of these books contains 20-25 essay questions with model answers plus 90-100 Multi-state-format Q & A's. The objective is to acquaint the student with the techniques needed to successfully handle law school exams. Titles are:

Civil Procedure	Criminal Procedure
Constitutional Law	Evidence
Contracts	Real Property
Corporations	Torts
Criminal Law	Wills & Trusts

each title...$15.95

steve finz's
multistate method

967 MBE (Multistate Bar Exam)-style *multiple choice questions and answers covering* all six Multistate subjects - **Plus** a complete 200 question model MBE practice exam— perfect for law school exam review and for the BAR EXAM in all states.

'92-93 Title...$31.95

steve emanuel's
first year Q & A's

1,143 Objective-style questions & answers in first year subjects, as preparation for exams. A single volume covers Contracts, Torts, Civil Procedure, Property, Criminal Law & Procedure.

with

'92-93 Civil Procedure Supplement.................$17.95

For any titles not available at your local bookstore call us at (914) 834-7735.
Mastercard and Visa accepted.
Hours: 9-5:30 EST Monday-Friday

Law in a Flash

flashcards

Civil Procedure 1 ((New '94-95 Ed.)........	$16.95
Civil Procedure 2 (New '94-95 Ed.)	16.95
Constitutional Law......................................	16.95
Contracts	16.95
Corporations...	16.95
Criminal Law	16.95
Criminal Procedure	16.95
Evidence..	16.95
Future Interests	16.95
Professional Respon. (2 part set)	29.95
Real Property	16.95
Sales (UCC Art.2) (New '94-95 Ed.)..........	16.95
Torts	16.95
First Year Law Set..	95.00
Multistate Bar Review Set	165.00

software

Civil Procedure 1 (New '94-95 Ed.)	$24.95
Civil Procedure 2 (New '94-95 Ed.)	24.95
Constitutional Law......................................	24.95
Contracts	24.95
Corporations...	24.95
Criminal Law	24.95
Criminal Procedure	24.95
Evidence..	24.95
Future Interests	24.95
Professional Respon.....................................	39.95
Real Property	24.95
Sales (UCC Art. 2) (New '94-95 Ed.).........	24.95
Torts	24.95
California Baby Bar Set	95.00
First Year Law Set..	145.00
Multistate Bar Rev. Set	225.00
Multi-Year Set..	295.95

strategies & tactics books

Strategies & Tactics for First Year Law	$12.95
Strat. & Tact. for the MPRE (Multistate Prof. Respon. Exam)	19.95
Strat. & Tact. for the MBE (Multistate Bar Exam)	34.95

ABA Journal, ABC News Transcripts, Accounting Today, Across The Board, Adweek, Advertising Age, Aerospace Daily, Africa News, Agence France Press, Alabama Business Review, Alaska Business Monthly, Alert Country News, Alliance Alert, Alternative Energy Digests, American Banker, American Demographics, American Fitness, American Journal of Medicine, American Stock Exchange, AMEX Market Summary, Annual Reports, Appliance Manufacturer, APS Diplomat, Archives of Environmental Health, Arkansas Business, Art In America, Asian Wall Street Journal Weekly, Associated Press, Astronomy, Atlanta Constitution, Audubon, Automotive Marketing, Automotive News, AutoWeek, Aviation Daily, Baltimore Sun, The Banker, BBC Summary of World Broadcasts, Bear, Stearns & Co., Better Homes and Gardens, Beverage World, Bicycling, Billboard, Biotechnology Business News, Black Enterprise, BNA Banking Daily, Boating, The Boston Globe, Boston Herald, Boy's Life, British Medical Journal, Broadcasting & Cable, Builder, Building Supply Home Centers, Bulletin of Economic Research, Bulletin of the World Health Organization, The Bureau of National Affairs, Inc., Business Asia, Business Credit, Business Europe, Business Week, Business Wire, BYTE, CAD/CAM Update, California Business, Campaigns & Elections, Canadian Banker, Canadian Business, Cancer Research Weekly, The Capital Source, Car & Driver, Caribbean Update, The Catholic World, Cellular Marketing, Chemical Business, Chicago Tribune, Chief Executive, Children's Business, The China Business Review, The Christian Science Monitor, Cincinnati Enquirer, The Cleveland Plain Dealer, Columbia Business, Columbus Dispatch, Communications News, CommunicationsWeek, Conservationist, Consultant, Consumer Reports, The Cook Political Report, Corporate Computing, Corporate Legal Times, Cosmopolitan, Credit Card News, Daily Herald, The Daily Mail & Mail on Sunday, The Daily/Sunday Telegraph, The Dallas Morning News, Datamation, Delaware Business Review, Denver Business, The Denver Post, The Detroit News, Direct Marketing, Dow Jones Averages, Drug and Cosmetic Industry, Ebony Magazine, Economic Journal, EDGE, Electric Light & Power, Electronic Media, Electronics, Energy Alert, Enterprise, Environment, Environment Week, EPA Journal, Equity, Esquire, Essence Magazine, Euromarketing, Europe 2000 Newsletters, Evening News, Evening Standard, Executive Speaker, Export Control News, FCC Daily Digest, FDIC Watch, Federal News Service, Finance East Europe, Financial Executive, Financial Times, Flight International, Florida Library, Flying, Focus, Food & Beverage Marketing, Forbes, Foreign Policy, Fortune, Fusion Power Report, Futurist, Gannet News Service, The Gazette, Genetic Technology News, Georgetown Law Journal, Georgia Law Review, Good Housekeeping, Gorman's New Product News, Government Finance Review, Greater Cincinnati Business Record, Greater Lansing Business Monthly, Harford Business Ledger, Harper's Bazaar, Hartford Business, Harvard Business Review, Harvard Health Letter, Harvard Law Review, Hawaii Business, Hawaii Investor, Hazardous Waste Network Online Today, Health Industry Today, Health News, Health Services Research, Herald, History Today, Honolulu Advertiser, Hot Rod, Houston Business Journal, The Humanist, IBM System User, Idaho Falls Post Register, Illinois Business Review, Independent Living, Indiana Business Review, Industrial & Labor Relations Review, Industrial Computing, Industrial Finishing, The Information Advisor, InformationWeek, InfoWorld, Ingalls & Snyder, Ingram's, Inside Media, Insight, Intelligencer, Intercorp, Internal Revenue Bulletin, International Herald Tribune, International Journal, International Trade Forum, Investor's Business Daily, Iowa Law Review, The Irish Times, Israel Economist, Japan Computer Industry Scan, J.C. Bradford & Co., The Jerusalem Post, Jonesboro Sun, Journal of the American Medical Association, Kansas Business News, Kansas City Business Journal, Kentucky Business Ledger, Kentucky Law Journal, La Crosse City Business, Ladies Home Journal, Lane Report, Las Vegas Business Press, LatinFinance, Law Society's Gazette, The Legal Intelligencer, Library Trends, Long Island Business News, The Los Angeles Business Journal, Los Angeles Times, Machine Design, Maclean's, The MacNeil/Lehrer News Hour, Madison Capital Times, Managed Care Law Outlook, Manage, Marketing News, Martindale-Hubbell Law Directory, Mediaweek, Medical World News, Memphis Business Journal, Metropolitan Home, Metropolitan Toronto Business Journal, Miami Herald, Miami Review, Middle East News Network, Midwest Real Estate News, Minneapolis-St. Paul City Business, Minneapolis Star Tribune, Minnesota Business Journal, MIS Week, Modern Maturity, Montana Business Quarterly, Moscow News, Motor Trend, Nashville Business Journal, National Parks, National Public Radio, Natural History, NEA Today, Netline, The Network News, New China News Agency, New England Journal of Medicine, New Hampshire Business Review, New Jersey Business, The New Leader, New Mexico Business Journal, New Orleans Business, New Orleans Times-Picayune, New York Law Journal, New York Stock Exchange Market Summary, The New York Times, New Zealand Law Reports, Newsweek, Northern Ireland Law Reports, NTT Weekly, Nuclear News, Nursing Homes, Nutrition Today, Ocean State Business, O'Dwyer's PR Services Report, Official Kremlin International News Broadcasts, Ohio Business, Ohio Statehouse Journal, Oil Week, Omni, Oregon Business, Orlando Sentinel Tribune, PAC Summary Reports, Pacific Northwest Executive, Parks & Recreation, PC Magazine, PC Week, Pediatrics for Parents, Pennsylvania Business & Technology, Pennsylvania Law Journal, People, Pipeline Industry, Popular Science, Public Finance Quarterly, Quarterly Journal of Business and Finance, Radio & TV Reports, Real Estate Weekly, The Reuter Business Report, Rhode Island Public Utilities Report, Russian Press Digest, San Diego Business Journal, The San Francisco Chronicle, Saturday Evening Post, Software Industry Report, South Carolina Business Journal, South Dakota Business Journal, St. Louis Post-Dispatch, Standard & Poor's Daily News, Tech Street Journal, Texas Business Locator, Texas Law Review, Time, The Times and The Sunday Times, The Toronto Star, Tucson Business Journal, UCLA Law Review, UNESCO Courier, United Press International, United States Banker, United States Law Week, USA Today, USA Weekend, Vermont Business Magazine, Virion Marketing News, Virginia Environmental Law Journal, Wall Street Abstracts, The Washington Post, Washingtonian, The Writer, Yale Law Review, Working Woman, Worldwide Energy, The Writer, Xinhua (New China) News Agency, Yale Investment Research, and thousands more...

Have we got news for you.

It's all about competitive advantage. And while access to legal information is vital, it's not all that's needed to win. You could be missing some very critical information. News. Current news that could significantly affect your research.

LEXIS®/NEXIS® is the only online service that provides access to current legal and news sources. And public records. And international materials.

LEXIS/NEXIS even lets you automatically validate your cites using a special feature called CheckCite™ software.

Quite simply, if your current search system limits you to just legal sources...you're only getting half the picture. Call LEXIS/NEXIS today, at 1-800-543-6862 because we've got news for you.

LEXIS·NEXIS®
1-800-543-6862

LEXIS® and NEXIS® are registered trademarks of Mead Data Central. The WORLD IN YOUR HAND logo is a trademark of Mead Data Central, a division of The Mead Corporation.
©1994, Mead Data Central. All rights reserved. CheckCite is a trademark of Jurisoft Licensing Corporation.

"These days, law firms are watching the bottom line very closely. I have to find the best candidates, and not spend a lot of time doing it. The Martindale-Hubbell® & LEXIS® Student Directory helps me do just that."

Ann Ogburn,
Director of Recruiting & Client
Services, Baker & McKenzie
Washington, DC

Ann Ogburn has a big responsibility. Finding the right candidates for Baker & McKenzie. To do the job right, she chose the Martindale-Hubbell & LEXIS Student Directory. "Our focus is mostly tax law," states Ann, "It's hard to find people with that particular specialty. People who are really interested. This online service efficiently searches for candidates with specific experience or background. It's frustrating to think you've found the perfect resume in your files, only to find out they have already been hired. This service eliminates that problem because you only receive current resumes." Call your LEXIS representative or check the career library online and enter "RESUME" and see how the Martindale-Hubbell & LEXIS Student Directory service can help bring you the best candidates, while protecting your bottom line.

LEXIS® and NEXIS® are registered trademarks of Mead Data Central. The WORLD IN YOUR HAND logo is a trademark of Mead Data Central, a division of The Mead Corporation. Martindale-Hubbell® is a registered trademark of Reed Properties, Inc., used under license. ©1994, Mead Data Central. All rights reserved.

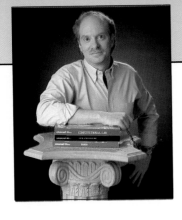

emanuel law outlines, inc.

1865 Palmer Avenue
Larchmont, NY 10538
914-834-7735

Dear Law Student:

Welcome to our 1994-95 Catalogue.

We published our first study aid 20 years ago — it was a typewritten manuscript on *Civil Procedure,* which I sold exclusively to my first-year classmates at Harvard. Needless to say, we've grown. We now sell over 150,000 study aids each year, not just books, but also tapes and computer software. The average American first-year student buys over two of our titles, with second- and third-year students not far behind.

You probably know us best for our **Emanuel Law Outlines**® series. These eleven titles — all written solely or mainly by me — are the bedrock of our business. But we also publish or distribute many other law study aids that I think you'll find useful, including:

- **The Smith's Review Series,** written by distinguished law professors, and covering mainly upper-year subjects.

- **Socratutor™ Software,** a computerized version of an Emanuel Law Outline,® or a Smith's Review — you can customize it until it becomes your own outline.

- **Siegel's Essay & Multiple Choice Q & A** series, for exam-writing practice in ten subjects.

- **Law In A Flash** flashcards, books and computer software.

We pride ourselves on keeping our materials meticulously up to date. This year, I've personally prepared new editions of the Emanuel Law Outlines in *Civil Procedure, Constitutional Law, Criminal Procedure* and *Torts* (General and Prosser editions).

I wish you the best of luck in your law school career and beyond. We'd love to hear your comments about any of our products, pro or con, so drop me a line, or send me E-mail at: 74224.3600@compuserve.com.

Very truly yours,

Steve

Steve Emanuel

Is Now Exclusively Distributed By

emanuel law outlines, inc.

For all **Law In A Flash** Products see pages 18-19

Contents

© 1994 Emanuel Law Outlines, Inc.

Comic art (including cover) by Neal Adams.

Anatomy of

Every Emanuel and Smith's has a slew of special features.

Capsule Summary, usually about 65-75 pages, for night-before-the-exam review.

c. **Prior conduct:** The *prior course of dealing* may make it reasonable for the offeree's silence to be construed as consent. (*Example*: Each time in the past, Seller responds to purchase orders from Buyer either by shipping, or by saying, "We don't have the item." If Seller now remains silent in the face of an order by Buyer for a particular item, Seller's silence will constitute an acceptance of the order.)

d. **Acceptance by dominion:** Where the offeree receives *goods*, and *keeps them*, this exercise of "dominion" is likely to be held to be an acceptance.

V. ACCEPTANCE VARYING FROM OFFER

A. **Common law "mirror image" rule:** Under the common law, the offeree's response operates as an acceptance only if it is the *precise mirror image* of the offer. If the response conflicts at all with the terms of the offer, or adds new terms, the purported acceptance is in fact a rejection and counter offer, not an acceptance. (*Example*: A writes to B, "I'll sell you my house for $100,000, closing to take place April 1." B writes back, "That's fine; let's close April 2, however." At common law, B's response is not an acceptance because it diverges slightly from the offer, so there is no contract.) [23]

B. **UCC view:** The UCC *rejects the "mirror image" rule*, and will often lead to a contract being formed even though the acceptance diverges from the offer. Wherever possible, the UCC tries to find a contract, so as to keep the parties from weaseling out (as they often try to do when the market changes). This entire "battle of the forms" is dealt with in UCC §2-207, probably the most important UCC provision for the Contracts student. [24]

CAPSULE SUMMARY

1. **General:** At the most general level, §2-207(1) provides that any *"expression of acceptance"* or *"written confirmation"* will *act as an acceptance* even though it states terms that are "additional to or different from" those contained in the offer. (*Example*: Buyer sends a "purchase order" containing a warranty. Seller responds with an "acknowledgement," containing a disclaimer of warranty. There will be a contract under the UCC, even though there would not have been one at common law.)

2. **Acceptance expressly conditional on assent to changes:** An "expression of acceptance" does *not* form a contact if it is *"expressly made conditional on assent to . . . additional or different terms."* §2-207(1). So if the purported "acceptance" contains additional or different terms from the offer, and also states something like, "This acceptance of your offer is effective only if you agree to all of the terms listed on the reverse side of this acceptance form," *there is no contract* formed by the exchange of documents. [26]

a. **Limited:** Courts are reluctant to find that this section applies. Only if the second party's form makes it clear that that party is *unwilling to proceed with the transaction* unless the first party agrees to the second party's changes, will the clause be applied so as to prevent a contract from forming.

3. **"Additional" term in acceptance:** Where the offeree's response contains an *"additional"* term (i.e., a clause taking a certain position on an issue with which the offer does not deal at all), the consequences depend on whether both parties are merchants. [28-30]

a. **At least one party not merchant:** If at least one party is *not a merchant*, the additional term does not prevent the offeree's response from giving rise to a contract, but the additional term becomes part of the contract only if the offeror *explicitly* assents to it.

Example: Consumer sends a purchase order to Seller, which does not mention how disputes are to be resolved. Seller sends an acknowledgement form back to Consumer, which correctly recites the basic terms of the deal (price, quantity, etc.), and then says, "All disputes are to be arbitrated." Even though the acknowledgement (the "acceptance") differed from the purchase order by introducing the arbitration term,

Page references to the full treatment in the body of the outline.

B. ***Hadley v. Baxendale:*** The rules limiting the kinds of damages for which the plaintiff may recover are derived from the famous English case of ***Hadley v. Baxendale***, 156 Eng. Rep. 145 (1854).

1. **Facts of Hadley:** Plaintiffs operated a mill which was forced to suspend operations because of a broken shaft. An employee of the plaintiffs took the shaft to the defendant carrier for shipment to another city for repairs. The carrier knew that the item to be carried was a shaft for the plaintiff's mill, but was not told that the mill was closed because the shaft was broken. The carrier negligently delayed delivery of the shaft, with the result that the mill was closed for several more days than it would have been had the carrier adequately performed the contract. Plaintiffs sued for the profits they lost during these extra days.

2. **Holding:** The court held that plaintiff could not recover for the lost profits. The loss of profits was not a consequence which "in the usual course of things" flows from a delay in the shipment of a shaft.

3. **The two rules of Hadley:** The court in deciding *Hadley* stated that a plaintiff suing for breach of contract may recover only damages which fall into one of two classes. These two classes are known today as the two "rules" of *Hadley v. Baxendale*. The damages must either:

a. arise "naturally, i.e., according to the ***usual course of things***, from [the] breach of contract itself. . . ." or

b. arise from "the ***special circumstances*** under which the contract was actually made" if and only if these special circumstances "were ***communicated*** by the plaintiff to the defendants. . . ."

4. **Reformulation of rule:** Another way to express the two classes of damages allowed in *Hadley* is as follows:

a. The court will "impute" foreseeability to the defendant as to those damages which any reasonable man should have foreseen, whether or not the defendant actually foresaw them; and

b. The court will also award damages as to remote or unusual consequences, but only if the defendant had ***actual*** notice of the possibility of these consequences.

5. **Application of facts of *Hadley:*** The lost profit sought by the plaintiffs in *Hadley* did not fall into either of these two categories. That an enterprise might be shut down for lack of a shaft would not normally be foreseen by one in the position of the defendant carrier; therefore, the damages did not fall in the first class of "general" or "ordinary" damages. Nor did the plaintiffs give the defendant notice of the possibility of the shutdown of the mill; therefore, the damages did not fall in the second class. (The official head-notes to the case state that the defendant was told that the mill was shut down, but the opinion itself assumes that such notice was not given).

Extensive discus[sion] of cases — not j[ust] citations, but the facts, the holding, the dissents, and most of all, the significance of th[e] case — Why is i[t in] the casebook? Where does it fit [in] the overall subje[ct]? Do other courts agree?

Detailed table of contents, to show you at a glance how the topics fit together.

E. **Acceptance expressly conditional on assent to changes:** §2-207(1) provides that any "expression of acceptance" or "written confirmation" acts as an acceptance even though it states terms that are "additional to or different from" those contained in the offer. (This is the general rule, which, as noted, overturns the common-law "mirror image" rule.) However, that subsection also contains one extremely important proviso: the "expression of acceptance" does *not* form a contract if it is ***"expressly made conditional on assent to the additional or different terms."***

1. **Significance of exception:** This exception means that if the purported "acceptance" contains additional or different terms from the offer, and also states something like "This acceptance of your offer is effective only if you agree to all of the terms listed on the reverse side of this acceptance form," ***there is no contract*** formed by the exchange of documents.

Example: Buyer sends a purchase order for steel coils to Seller. Seller sends back an acknowledgment form. The acknowledgment form contains the following clause: "Seller's acceptance is, however, expressly conditional on Buyer's assent to the additional or different terms and conditions set forth below and printed on the reverse side. If these terms and conditions are not acceptable, Buyer should notify Seller at once."

Held, no contract was formed by the exchange of purchase order and acknowledgment. The clause quoted above fell within §2-207(1)'s "expressly conditional" exception, thus preventing what would otherwise have been an acceptance from being one (since Buyer never did assent to the additional or different terms). Thus even after sending the form, Seller would have been free to decide not to ship and could have walked away from the deal with no liability. (However, Seller did in fact ship, and Buyer paid for the goods. Therefore, a contract by performance, under §2-207(3), came into existence; this aspect of the case is discussed *infra*, p. 34.) *C. Itoh (America), Inc. v. Jordan Int'l Co.*, 552 F.2d 1228 (7th Cir. 1977).

Hundreds of examples, so you can see how a legal rule applies on particular facts.

12. Grandfather, a wealthy landowner, was aware that the price of land near New York City had grown exorbitant. Although Grandfather then lived in California, he owned a one-half acre parcel in the New York suburbs. He said to his daughter's son, Grandson, "If you build a house on my land and live in it for two years, I will deed the land to you." Grandson spent $100,000 to construct a house on the parcel. The land itself was worth $200,000. Grandson then lived on the property for the required two years. At the end of that period, Grandfather refused to convey the property to Grandson. Grandson now sues to enforce the promise of a deed.

(a) May Grandson recover from Grandfather on the promise?

(b) If the promise is enforced, what amount should Grandson receive?

12. (a) **Yes.** The promise was not supported by consideration, so under ordinary contract principles it would not be enforceable. (There is no evidence that Grandfather "bargained for" Grandson's building of the house on Grandfather's property. For instance, the facts are such that Grandfather did not obtain the benefit of having Grandson live close to him, since Grandfather lived elsewhere.) But a court would probably apply the doctrine of ***"promissory estoppel"*** here. Grandfather should reasonably have expected that his promise of a deed would induce action by Grandson, and the promise did indeed induce that action (building of a house and living on the premises). Since Grandson foreseeably relied to his detriment on the promise, the court will probably enforce it. See Rest. 2d, §90(1).

(b) **$100,000.** Most courts, even when they apply the promissory estoppel doctrine, limit the remedy to what justice requires. Typically, this means that the damages awarded are not the full expectation "benefit of the bargain" measure, but merely reliance damages. Here, Grandson is only "out of pocket" $100,000, the amount he spent on building the house. Therefore, the court would probably only award him his $100,000, not the $200,000 value of the property (which would be what was required to put him in the position he would have been in had the promise been kept). See Rest. 2d, §90, Illustr. 12.

Short-answer Questions, toget[her] with Answers tha[t are] really "mini essa[ys]"

All selections taken from Emanuel on *Contracts,* reproduced at 35% of original size, except for the discussion of set-asides, which is from Emanuel on *Constitutional Law.*

an Outline

Here's just some of what you get in
a typical one:

Easy-to-read format, with every paragraph captioned to make the scanning simpler.

Key concepts shown in bold italic.

Clear statement of basic principles.

References to Hornbooks, Restatements, casebooks and other authorities.

Multistate-format Questions, together with extensive explanatory Answers

Essay Exam questions drawn from actual law school exams, plus our model answers

The latest cases and statutory changes — more rigorously up to date than any other outline series.

II. TOTAL AND PARTIAL INTEGRATION

A. The concept of "integration": A written document does not always represent a deal that the parties consider final. The writing may, for instance, be intended only as a tentative draft of their agreement. But if the parties do intend a document to represent the *final expression of their agreement*, the document is said to be an *"integration"* of their agreement. The parol evidence rule applies, as we shall see, only to documents which are integrations, i.e., final expressions of agreement.

B. "Partial" vs. "total" integrations: Once it is determined that a document is an integration (i.e., a final expression of agreement), it must be determined whether the parties intended that integration to contain all of the details of their agreement, or only some of these details. If the document is intended only as a memorandum of the agreement, it may state only the most important details, and leave the others to the parties' recollection.

1. **Partial integration:** If the document is not intended by the parties to include all details of their agreement, it is said to be a *"partial"* integration.

2. **Total integration:** If, on the other hand, the document is intended by the parties to include all the details of their agreement, it is called a *"total"* integration.

C. Statement of the parol evidence rule: Having defined the concepts of "partial integration" and "total integration," we are now ready to state the parol evidence rule. The rule has, in effect, two parts, one dealing with partial integrations, and the other with total integrations. The rule provides as follows:

1. **Partial integration:** *When a writing is a partial integration, no evidence of prior or contemporaneous agreements or negotiations (oral or written) may be admitted if this evidence would contradict a term of the writing.*

2. **Total integration:** *When a document is a total integration, no evidence of prior or contemporaneous agreements or negotiations may be admitted which would either contradict or even add to the writing.*

3. **Summary of rule:** In summary, the parol evidence rule provides that evidence of prior agreement may never be admitted to *contradict an integrated writing*, and may furthermore not even *supplement* an integration which is intended to be *complete*. See Rest. 2d, §213.

   Example: Seller and Buyer make an oral agreement for the sale of the Ardsley Acres Hotel, together with all the furniture in the hotel. They reach oral agreement as to the purchase price of the hotel, and also agree that Buyer shall have one year in which to complete payment of this price. The parties then employ a lawyer to prepare a written contract. He does so, and they sign it. It does not mention furniture, or make any reference to personal property. It also provides that Buyer shall only have six months in which to complete payment. If Seller can show that the written contract was intended as the final expression of the parties' agreement (i.e., that it is an integration), Buyer will not be allowed to show that the original oral agreement gave him a year, rather than six months, to pay. He would not be allowed to show this because

---

QUESTION: The General Construction Co. of Memphis, Tennessee decided to build for itself a new headquarters building of an original and striking design. It secured much publicity in journals read by architects and builders by printing artists' sketches of the building, located at a dramatic site at a bend in the Mississippi river. In the publicity was included the announcement of a self-imposed deadline for completion, a deadline that was very short by usual standards of the construction industry for a building of that size.

The Frank Corporation is a steel fabricator which buys steel ingots and transforms them into structural steel. On September 1, 1972 the General Construction Co. and the Frank Corporation executed a written contract under which Frank undertook to fabricate and deliver the structural steel called for by General's specifications, which were made part of the contract. The contract provided a delivery schedule with five lots to be delivered as follows:

Lot I   March 6, 1973
Lot II   March 27, 1973
Lot III April 10, 1973
Lot IV   April 24, 1973
Lot V   May 1, 1973

SAMPLE ANSWER: I will examine first whether General's cancellation of the contract constituted a breach, and will then discuss the question of damages.

The cancellation: I think General can make a fairly strong case that it was entitled to cancel the contract when it did. For a definite answer, a number of UCC sections, particularly those dealing with installment contracts, must be examined.

The contract was clearly an "installment contract," since it authorized in "separate lots", and since each lot would obviously be "separately accepted" (or rejected), due to the relatively long time periods between them. §2-612(1). The real crux of the breach issue is presented by §2-612(3): "Whenever non-conformity or default with respect to one or more installments substantially impairs the value of the whole contract there is a breach of the whole . . ." (pp. 201, 206-07).

Frank will undoubtedly argue that the delay with respect to Lot III did not "substantially impair the value of the whole contract," and that General therefore had no right to cancel. Frank will base this argument on the evidence that General could not have used the steel had it been delivered on time, since it would have been submerged by the flood, and would have cost $120,000 to clean. Thus, Frank will argue, the delay did not substantially impair the value of the contract, since it didn't make things any worse for General than they otherwise would have been.

I think General can make a fairly convincing response to this, to the effect that not only the delay on Lot III, but also the *uncertainty* about whether Frank could make a timely delivery (or any delivery at all) on Lots IV and V, must be considered in determining whether there was a "substantial impairment" of the whole contract (p. 207).

Frank in turn can respond that if it was anxious about Lots IV and V that induced General to cancel, General's proper remedy was to "demand assurances" pursuant to §2-609, and not to cancel (p. 221). However, I think that General can reply, successfully, that Frank's April 12th telegram was itself a failure to furnish reasonable assurances in response to General's request for assurances on April 9th. In that event, General had the right to treat the lack of assurance as a repudiation (§2-609(4)), thus allowing it to

---

6. On March 22, by a written memorandum signed by both parties, Varsey agreed to sell and Pantel agreed to buy a described parcel of realty. The contract called for closing of title on May 30, and fixed all other terms, but did not indicate the price to be paid. On May 30, Pantel tendered $60,000 cash, but Varsey refused to convey the realty. Pantel subsequently instituted an action against Varsey for specific performance of the contract, and offered evidence that $60,000 was the fair market value of the realty, both on March 22 and on May 30. In defense Varsey asserted that the memorandum failed to satisfy the requirements of the Statute of Frauds. Pantel's suit against Varsey should

(A) succeed, if Pantel and Varsey are both in the business of buying and selling real estate.

(B) succeed, because under the Uniform Commercial Code a contract which is silent as to price is presumed to call for payment of fair market value.

(C) fail, because the written contract did not fix the price to be paid.

(D) fail, unless the evidence establishes that the parties orally agreed that the price to be paid was the fair market value of the realty.

---

6.   C   Under the Statute of Frauds, a contract for the sale of any interest in real estate must be in writing, and the writing must contain all the essential terms. The price is an essential term in a contract for the sale of realty, since the court will be unable to fashion a remedy without it.

Although the UCC makes special provision for contracts between merchants, providing that a contract silent as to price is presumed to be for a reasonable price, these provisions do not apply to the sale of land, but only to the sale of goods. **A** and **B** are, therefore, incorrect. Since this contract does not satisfy the requirements of the Statute of Frauds regardless of which party tries to enforce it, it is unenforceable over the objection of either party, even though oral evidence might establish the intentions of the parties with respect to missing terms. **D** is, therefore, incorrect.

K. Set-asides by Congress: But the rules are very different for minority set-asides imposed by *Congress*. In the post-*Croson* case of *Metro Broadcasting, Inc. v. FCC*, 110 S.Ct. 2997 (1990), the Court upheld a congressionally-imposed scheme awarding preferences to minority-owned applicants for *broadcast licenses*. The Court held that benign race-conscious measures by Congress must merely satisfy *intermediate-level scrutiny*, not the strict scrutiny which *Croson* held must be satisfied by state and local governments.

1. **Facts:** *Metro Broadcasting* involved two FCC policies that favored minority applicants for broadcast licenses: (1) a policy whereby in awarding new radio or TV licenses, the FCC would consider minority ownership as *one factor* among several (including past broadcast record, "character," etc.); and (2) a plan whereby an existing licensee in danger of losing its license for wrongdoing could head off those proceedings by agreeing to make a *"distress sale"* of its license to a minority purchaser at a below-fair-market-value price. These two plans were initially adopted by the FCC on its own, but Congress later effectively required the Commission to maintain them.

2. **Holding:** By a 5-4 vote, the Court *upheld* the FCC preferences in *Metro*. The majority opinion, by Justice Brennan, stated that "benign race-conscious measures mandated by Congress — even if those measures are not 'remedial' in the sense of being designed to compensate victims of past governmental or societal discrimination — are constitutionally permissible to the extent that they serve important governmental objectives within the power of Congress and are substantially related to achievement of those objectives." This majority opinion thus established important new ground in two respects:

We'll get you through the *Civ Pro* Maze

Civil Procedure
New '94 Ed. $17.95

Civil Procedure was the first title we ever published. Since then, it's been thoroughly rewritten, through more than a dozen new editions. The book is suitable for use with any casebook, such as *Field, Kaplan & Clermont; Cound, Friedenthal, Miller & Sexton; Rosenberg, Smit, & Dreyfuss* and *Yeazell, Landers, & Martin.*

The current edition tracks Supreme Court and Federal Rule developments through July, 1994. This edition also features complete coverage of the new amendments to the Federal Rules that became effective December 1, 1993, including the new Rule 4 and the controversial Rule 11 and Rule 26(a) provisions.

Special Features:

New! Exam tips: at end of each chapter, special tips on how to spot the key issues, what's most frequently tested, how to structure and phrase your answers . . . and more.

- Capsule Summary
- Text Correlation Chart
- Essay Exam Q&A's
- Short-answer Q&A's
- Tables (Cases, FRCP, Refs. to U.S.C., Subject-Matter Index)

Summary of Contents

Jurisdiction Over the Parties. . . • Over Individuals • Over Corporations • Federal Jurisdiction Over the Parties • Over Things • Opportunity to be Heard • Defenses to Claims of Jurisdiction • Venue

Subject Matter Jurisdiction. . . • Federal Jurisdiction Generally • Diversity • Federal Question • Amount in Controversy • Supplemental • Removal to the Federal Courts • Power to Punish Disobedience

Pleading. . . • At Common Law • Code • Modern Federal Complaint • Motions Against Complaint • Answer • Time for Various Pleadings • Amendment • Variance of Proof

Discovery and Pretrial Conference. . . • Scope • Methods • Orders and Sanctions • Use of Results at Trial v. Appellate Review • Pretrial Conference

Ascertaining Applicable Law. . . • Nature of Problem • *Erie* and other Fundamentals • *Erie* problems • Federal Common Law

Trial Procedure. . . • Burden of Proof • Presumptions • Preponderance of the Evidence • Trials Without Jury • Jury • Adjudication Without Trial • Directed Verdict • Special Verdict and Interrogatories • Declaratory Judgments • New Trial • Review of Grant or Denial of New Trial • Judgment as a Matter of Law • Review of Combined New Trial and JML Motions • Constitutional Right to Jury Trial

Multi-Party and Multi-Claim Litigation. . . • Counterclaims • Joinder of Claims • Joinder of Parties • Class Actions • Intervention • Interpleader • Real Party in Interest • Third Party Practice • Cross-Claims

Former Adjudication. . . • Claim Preclusion • Collateral Estoppel • Full Faith and Credit

---

" *My only regret with the outline is that I did not purchase it earlier in the year...* "

I used the Civil Procedure law outline. It was my primary source of study and I found that I succeeded . . . as a result. I used the outline once a week to review a section just covered in class. My only regret is that I did not purchase it earlier in the year.

Matthew P. Hallisey, Franklin Pierce Law School

Q. What do a sperm and a lawyer have in common?
A. Each has a 1-in-1,000,000 chance of some day becoming a human being.

Con Law: Here's Why It's Our Best Seller

Constitutional Law
New '94 Ed. $23.95

Over many years *Constitutional Law* has been our best-selling title. During the 1993-94 school year, we sold almost 21,000 copies, more than one for every two students taking the course in the U.S.

Here's why:

- **Detailed treatment** of all major **cases** — facts, holding, and significance.

- **Clear statement of legal principles** — not just rules and exceptions, but an explanation of where and why the law is fuzzy for a rule to exist.

- Meticulous **up-to-dateness.** We wait until the Supreme Court term has closed in late June before we start writing so you won't miss anything.

- **Other authorities.** We read and refer to Hornbooks, Law Review articles, newspaper commentaries, and anything else that can help you understand better this most abstract and difficult of all subjects.

- An **Up-to date capsule summary** summarizing the entire subject for night-before-the-exam review.

New! **Exam tips:** at end of each chapter, special tips on how to spot the key issues, what's most frequently tested, how to structure and phrase your answer . . . and more.

Summary of Contents

Supreme Court's Authority. . . • Acts of Congress • State Court Decisions • Congress' Control of Federal Jurisdiction

Federalism and Federal Power Generally

Federal Commerce Clause. . . • Cases Prior to 1933 • Court Barriers to New Deal • Modern Trend • Tenth Amendment

Other National Powers. . . • Taxing • Spending • War, Treaty and Foreign Affairs • Other Powers

Two Limits on State Power: Commerce Clause and Congress. . . • Dormant Commerce Clause-Regulation • State Taxation of Interstate Commerce • Congressional Action-Preemption

Intergovernmental Immunities and Interstate Relations. . . • Tax Immunities • Federal Immunity from State Regulation • Interstate Relationship

Separation of Powers. . . • Domestic Policy • Foreign Affairs and Armed Forces • Appointment and Removal of Executive Personnel • Legislative and Executive Immunity

Due Process of Law. . . • Bill of Rights and

States • Substantive Due Process • "Taking" and "Contract" Clauses• Ex Post Facto Laws • Protection of Non-Economic Rights • Procedural Due Process

Equal Protection. . . • Economic and Social Laws-The "Mere Rationality" Test • Suspect Classifications, Especially Race • Affirmative Action and "Benign" Discrimination • Sex • Alienage • Illegitimacy • Middle-Level Scrutiny • Fundamental Rights

State Action

Congressional Enforcement of Civil Rights

Freedom of Expression. . . • Advocacy of Illegal Conduct • Regulation of Context • Symbolic Expression • Defamation and Invasion of Privacy • Obscenity • Commercial Speech • Freedom of Association, Denial of Public Jobs or Benefits, Unconstitutional Conditions • Special Problems Concerning the Media

Freedom of Religion. . . • Establishment Clause • Free Exercise Clause

Justiciability. . . • Advisory Opinions • Standing • Mootness • Ripeness • Declining Jurisdiction • Political Questions

Con Law Tapes... for those who prefer audio

Eleven 90-minute tapes on Constitutional Law, with Steve Emanuel as your lecturer.

13 1/2 hours covering the entire subject plus two 90-minute review tapes — for your night-before-exam listening. Steve reviews the key principles of the subject.

Not just an audio form of the Emanuel book on *Constitutional Law.* Steve Emanuel spent a whole year carefully scripting and delivering the lectures, so they work as a stand alone audio presentation. Here are some of the special features you get:

- **Mnemonics** for quick recall

- **Songs and skits** — professionally acted and sung — to dramatize the key principles and cases

- **Multistate Bar Exam** Questions and Answers, integrated into the lectures

- **Printed 64-page** supplement, containing a **capsule summary**

The tapes reflect all Supreme Court decisions through 1992.

'92 Ed. $37.95

BUY both the outline and the tape and get $6 REBATE

Redeem to Emanuel Law Outlines, Inc., 1865 Palmer Avenue., Larchmont, NY 10538 with proof of purchase. For outline, proof is retail receipt and copyright notice cut from title page; for tapes, proof is retail receipt and Steve Emanuel's photo cut from back of tape box. No Xerox or other mechanical reproduction accepted for any proof. Purchase must be dated after August 15, 1994.

Purchase of both items required. All coupons must be postmarked not later than December 15, 1994. We are not responsible for late, lost or mutilated mail. Only original coupon is accepted. Offer void where prohibited, taxed or restricted by law. No substitution of items allowed.

NAME

ADDRESS

CITY

ST   ZIP

SCHOOL

GRAD YEAR   TEL:

Rely on us for *Contracts*

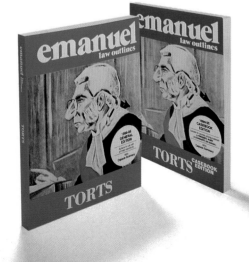

Contracts
'93 Ed. $16.95

One of our best sellers, now in its fifth edition.

Suitable for use with *Calamari; Farnsworth & Young; Fuller Eisenberg; Murphy & Spiedel;* and *Dawson, Harvey & Henderson* • Treats common-law principles and UCC Article 2 (sale of goods) • Analyzes all the major cases.

Special Features:

- Capsule Summary • Essay Exam Q&A's • Multistate-Style Q&A's
- Short-Answer Q&A's • Tables and Subject-Matter Index

Summary of Contents

Introduction. . . • Void, Voidable, and Unenforceable Contracts • Sources of Contract Law

Offer and Acceptance. . . • Intent • Offer and Acceptance • Validity • Acceptance Varying from Offer • Indefiniteness • Misunderstanding

Consideration. . . • Gift Promises • Past Consideration • "Detriment" element • Pre-Existing Duty Rule • Mutuality of Consideration • Illusory, Alternative, and Implied Promises • Requirements and Output Contracts

Promises Binding Without Consideration. . . • Past Debts • Benefits Received • Estoppel

Mistake. . . • Nature • General Rule • Mutual • Unilateral • Defenses and Remedies • Reformation as Remedy

Parol Evidence and Interpretation. . . • Rule • Total and Partial Integration • Judge and Jury • Rule not applicable • Interpretation • Trade Usage, Course of Performance, Course of Dealing • Omitted Terms Supplied by Court

Conditions. . . • Classification • Conditions and Promises Distinguished • Express • Constructive • Substantial Performance • Excuse • Repudiation & Prospective Inability to Perform

Anticipatory Repudiation; Other Aspects of Breach. . . • Total and Partial Breach • Anticipatory Repudiation • Other Aspects of Repudiation • Successive Actions

Statute of Frauds. . . • Suretyship Agreements • Marriage • Land Contracts • One-Year • Goods • Memorandum • Non-Compliance • Oral Rescission • Modification • Restitution, Reliance, Estoppel

Remedies. . . • Equitable • Damages • Expectation Damages • Reliance Damages • Restitution • Substantial Performance • Quasi-Contract • Foreseeability • Avoidable Damages • Nominal and Punitive Damages • Liquidated Damages • Sales Contracts

Contracts Involving More Than Two Parties. . . • Assignment • Delegation • Third Party Beneficiaries

Impossibility, Impracticality, and Frustration. . . • Impossibility • Impracticability • Frustration of Purpose • Restitution and Reliance Where Parties are Discharged

Miscellaneous Defenses. . . • Illegality • Duress • Misrepresentation • Unconscionability • Capacity

Warranties. . . • Express • Implied • Fitness for Particular Purpose • Title and Against Infringement • Privity • Disclaimers • Modifying Remedies

Discharge of Contracts. . . • Rescission • Accord and Satisfaction • Substituted Agreement • Novation • Account Stated • Release and Covenant Not to Sue

Torts: Two choices, take your pick

General Edition, New '94 Ed. $16.95

In Torts, Emanuel gives you two choices. One is our General Edition, suitable for use with all major casebooks, including *Dobbs; Epstein; Hendersen & Pearson;* and *Keeton, Keeton, Sargentich & Steiner.*

The other is a special Casebook Edition, geared specifically to the *Prosser, Wade*

& Schwartz casebook (9th Edition).

Special Features:

• **New! Exam tips:** at end of each chapter, special tips on how to spot the key issues, what's most frequently tested, how to structure and phrase your answers . . . and more.

Casebook Edition, New '94 Ed. $16.95

- Capsule Summary
- Essay Exam Q&A's
- Multistate-style Q&A's
- Short-Answer Q&A's
- Tables (Cases, Restatement References, Subject-Matter Index)

Summary of Contents

Intentional Torts Against the Person. . . • "Intent" Defined • Nominal and Punitive Damages • Scope of Liability • Battery • Assault • False Imprisonment • Mental Distress

Intentional Interference with Property. . . • Land Trespass • Trespass to Chattels • Conversion

Defenses to Intentional Torts. . . • Consent • Self-Defense • Defense of Others • Defense of Property • Arrest • Authority of Law • Justification

Negligence Generally. . . • Components • Unreasonable Risk • Reasonable Person • Rules Governing Behavior • Malpractice • Violation of Statutes • Jury Trials • Res Ipsa Loquitur

Actual & Proximate Cause. . . • Causation in Fact • Forseeability • Intervening Cause

Joint Tortfeasors. . . • Liability • Satisfaction • Release • Contribution • Indemnity

Duty. . . • Failure to Act • Effect of Contract • Mental Suffering • Unborn Children • Pure Economic Loss

Owners and Occupiers of Land. . . • Outside Premises • Injuries on Premises • Trespassers • Licensees • Invitees • Rejection of Categories • Lessors & Lessees • Vendor & Vendees

Damages. . . • Personal Injury • Punitive • Recovery by Spouse of Children • Wrongful Death Actions

Defenses in Negligence Actions. . . • Contributory • Comparative • Assumption of Risk • Immunities

Vicarious Liability . . . • Employer-Employee • Independent Contractors • Joint Enterprise

Strict Liability. . . • Animals • Abnormally Dangerous Activities • Limitations on Strict Liability • Worker's Compensation

Products Liability . . . • Negligence • Warranty • Strict Liability • Duty to Warn • Design Defects • Defenses • Statute of Limitations

Nuisance. . . • Public • Private

Misrepresentation

Defamation

Criminal Law: For Substance or Procedure

Criminal Law
'92 Ed. $14.95

Most first-year students think that the substantive side of Criminal Law is easy. But the subject can be very subtle indeed. Our *Criminal Law* book helps you spot and understand these subtleties. It's suitable for use with all leading casebooks, including *Johnson; Kadish, Schulhofer & Paulsen; LaFave; and Perkins & Boyce.* Virtually every Model Penal Code

---

Summary of Contents

Actus Reus and Mens Rea. . . • Actus Reus • Mens Rea • Concurrence

Causation. . . • Cause in Fact • Proximate Cause Generally • Unintended Victims • Unintended Manner of Harm

Responsibility. . . • The Insanity Defense • Diminished Responsibility Automatism • Intoxication • Infancy

Justification and Excuse. . . • Duress • Necessity • Self-Defense •Defense of Others • Defense of Property • Law Enforcement • Maintaining Authority • Consent • Entrapment

Attempt. . . • Mental State • Mere Preparation Impossibility • Renunciation • Attempt-Like Crimes

Conspiracy. . . • The Agreement • Mens Rea

• The Conspiratorial Objective • Multiple Objectives • Multiple Parties • Duration of Conspiracy • The Plurality Requirement

Accomplice Liability and Solicitation. . . • Parties to Crime • The Act Requirement • Mental State • Additional Crimes by Principal • Guilt of the Principal • With- drawal by the Accomplice • Victims as Accomplices • Post-Crime Assistance • Solicitation

Homicide and Other Crimes. . .

Against the Person. . . • Homicide Generally • Murder • Felony Murder • Degrees of Murder • Voluntary Manslaughter • Involuntary Manslaughter • Assault, Battery & Mayhem • Rape • Kidnapping

Theft Crimes. . . • Larceny • Embezzlement • False Pretenses • Consolidation of Theft Crimes • Burglary • Robbery • Blackmail and Extortion

---

provision is analyzed in detail. A capsule summary is included.

Special Features:

• Capsule Summary

• Essay Exam Q&A's

• Short-Answer Q&A's

• MBE-style Q&A's

• Tables (Cases, Model Penal Code Refs., Subject-Matter Index)

Criminal Procedure
New '94 Ed. $14.95

This book covers Constitutional Criminal Procedure, including Arrest, Searches, Electronic Surveillance, Confessions, Lineups, and other aspects of police work. In this subject, the law is what the Supreme Court says it is. So we meticulously cover the detailed facts, holding, concurrences and dissents of every major case. And we've tracked every Supreme Court development through July, 1994, especially vital in this fast-changing, politically controversial area.

Summary of Contents

Constitutional Criminal Procedure Generally...

Arrest, Search and Seizure. . . • Areas Protected by Fourth Amendment • Probable Cause • Particular Information Establishing Probable Cause • Search Warrants-Issuance and Execution • Arrest Warrants

Warrantless Arrests and Searches. . . • Search Incident to Arrest • Exigent Circumstances • "Plain View" Doctrine • Automobile Searches • Consent Searches • Consent by Third Persons • "Stop-and-Frisk" and Other Brief Detention • Inspections and Regulatory Searches

Electronic Surveillance and Secret Agents. . . • Fourth Amendment Protection of Katz • Constitutionality of Wiretapping Statutes • Use of Secret Agents • Entrapment

Confessions and Police Interrogation. . . • Pre-*Miranda* Confession Cases • *Escobedo* and the Right to Counsel • *Miranda* • What is a "Custodial" Interrogation • Minor Crimes • What Constitutes Interrogation • "Public Safety" Exception • Warnings Required Under *Miranda* • Waiver of *Miranda* Rights • *Miranda* Rights of Grand Jury Witnesses • Other Admissibility Issues Relating to *Miranda*

Lineups and Other Pre-Trial Identification Procedures. . . • Privilege Against Self-Incrimination • Right to Counsel • Exceptions to Right to Counsel • Due Process Limitations

Exclusionary Rule. . . • Standing to Assert the Rule • Derivative Evidence • Collateral Use Exceptions • "Good Faith" Exception

Right to Counsel. . . • Indigent's Right to Appointed Counsel • Proceeding in Which Right Applies • Stages at Which Right Attaches • Waiver • Entitlements of Right to Counsel

---

Two drunks are walking through a cemetery. They see a tombstone that reads, "Here lies a lawyer and an honest man." One drunk says to the other, "Gee, times are so tough they're planting them two to a grave."

New! Exam tips: at end of each chapter, special tips on how to spot the key issues, what's most frequently tested, how to structure and phrase your answers . . . and more.

Corporations
'92 Ed. $17.95

This book covers every facet of corporate law. It includes every major case from all of the major casebooks: *Cary & Eisenberg; Hamilton; Henn & Alexander;* and *Solomon, Schwartz & Bauman.*

Every topic of state corporate law is covered from the perspective of both Delaware and the RMBCA. The increasingly influential *ALI Principles of Corporate Governance* are also treated extensively. There is a generous treatment of federal securities laws where applicable (e.g., insider trading, mergers and acquisitions, and securities issuance.)

Summary of Contents

The Corporate Form. . . • Where and How to Incorporate • Ultra Vires and Corporate Powers • Pre-Incorporation Transactions • Defective Incorporation and Its Consequences • Piercing the Corporate Veil

Corporate Structure. . . • Allocation of Powers • Directors • Officers • Formalities for Shareholder Action

Shareholders' Rights and Proxy System. . . • Shareholder Inspection of Records • Reporting Requirements for Publicly Held Companies • Proxy Rules • Implied Private Actions Under Proxy Rules • Shareholder Communications • Proxy Contests

Close Corporations. . . • Shareholder Voting Agreements, Voting Trusts and Classified Stock • Agreements Restricting Board's Discretion • Super-Majority Voting and Quorum Requirements • Share Transfer Restrictions • Resolution of Disputes, Including Dissolution

Duty of Care & Business Judgment Rule. . . • Standard of Care • Business Judgment Rule • Statutory Modifications to Director Liability

Duty of Loyalty. . . • Fiduciary Status • Self-

Dealing • Executive Compensation • Corporate Opportunity Doctrine • Sale of Control

Insider Trading. . . • State Common-Law Approaches • SEC Rule 10b-5 and Insider Trading • Who is an "Insider" or "Tippee"? • Misrepresentations or Omissions Not Involving Insider Trading • Short-Swing Trading Profits and s. 16(b)

Shareholders' Suits. . . • Distinguishing Derivative from Direct Suits • Requirements for Derivative Suit • Demand on the Board; Early Termination • Security-for-Expenses Statutes • Settlement of Derivative Suits • Plaintiff's Attorney's Fees • Indemnification and D&O Insurance

Structural Changes-Mergers and Acquisitions . . . • Corporation Combinations • Protecting Shareholders • Recapitalizations-Hurting Preferred Shareholders • Freezeouts • Tender Offers, Hostile Takeovers

Dividends and Share Repurchases. . . • Dividends-Protection of Creditors • Protection of Shareholders • Stock Repurchases

Issuance of Securities

Case-law legislative developments through June, 1992 are reflected.

Special Features:
• Capsule Summary
• MBE-style Q&A's
• Tables (Cases; References to RMBCA, to *ALI Principles of Corporate Governance,* and to Delaware, New York and California corporation statutes; Subject-Matter Index)

Evidence
'91 Ed. $16.95

Our book on *Evidence* focuses on the Federal Rules of Evidence, now adopted not only for the federal system but in more than half the states. But you also get the common-law rules of Evidence — extensive treatment of the common-law approach to classic problems like hearsay and the various privileges.

The book gives detailed coverage of the

Summary of Contents

Basic Concepts. . . • First Principles • Organization of Trial • Making and Responding to Objections • Competency

Relevance. . . • Probative Value • Prejudice, Confusion and Waste of Time

Circumstantial Proof: Special Problems. . . • Character Evidence • Use of Character Evidence in Civil Cases • Other Crimes Evidence in Criminal Cases • Evidence of Criminal Defendant's Good Character • Character of Victim • Habit and Custom • Similar Happenings • Subsequent Remedial Measures • Liability Insurance • Compromises; Offers to Pay Medical Expenses

Examination and Impeachment. . . • Direct Examination • Cross-Examination • Redirect and Recross • Refreshing Recollection • Examination by the Court • Impeachment • Prior Criminal Convictions • Prior Bad Acts • Opinion and Reputation Regarding Character • Prior Inconsistent Statements • Bias • Sensory or Mental Defects • Contradiction; "Collateral Issue" Rule • Religious Beliefs • Rehabilitating the Impeached Witness

Hearsay and Exceptions. . . • Definitions

• Admissions • Availability Immaterial • Spontaneous, Excited, or Contemporaneous Utterances • Past Recollection Recorded • Business Records • Public Records and Reports • Former Testimony • Dying Declarations • Declarations Against Interest • Statements of Pedigree • Prior Statements of Available Witness • Residual Exception

Confrontation and Compulsory Process

Privileges. . . • Attorney-Client • Physician-Patient • Against Self-Incrimination • Marital • Miscellaneous

Real and Demonstrative Evidence. . . • Authentication • Foundation Requirements • "Best Evidence Rule" for Recorded Communications • Real and Demonstrative Evidence

Opinions, Experts and Scientific Evidence. . . • First-hand Knowledge and Lay Opinions • Expert Witness • Scientific Evidence

Burdens of Proof, Presumptions and Other Procedural Issues. . . • Presumptions • Judge-Jury Allocation • Appeals and "Harmless Error" Doctrine

Judicial Notice. . . Adjudicative Facts • Legislative Facts • Notice of Law

principal cases from all the major casebooks, including *Kaplan & Waltz; Lempert & Saltzburg;* and *Weinstein, Mansfield, Abrams & Berger.*

Legislative and Supreme Court developments through June, 1991.

Special Features:
• Capsule Summary
• Multistate-format Q&A's
• Actual past Multistate Q&A's
• Tables (Cases, FRE Refs., Subject-Matter Index)

Property
'93 Ed. $16.95

A sophisticated but clear treatment of this very technical subject. Our book is suitable for all of the major casebooks, and gives especially detailed consideration to every principal case in the Third Edition of *Dukeminier & Krier*. Personal property, future interests, landlord and tenant law, and zoning are just some of the special topics treated in

Summary of Contents

Possession and Transfer of Personal Property
• Rights of Possessors • Accession • Bona Fide Purchasers • Bailments • Gifts

Adverse Possession. . . . • Physical Requirements • Mental Requirements • Continuity of Possession • Length of Time Required • Rights of Adverse Possessor • Conflicts Between Possessors

Freehold Estates. . . . • Fee Simple • Fee Tail • Life Estates

Future Interests. . . . • Possibility of Reverter and Right of Entry • Reversions • Remainders • Rule in Shelley's Case • Doctrine of Worthier Title • Statute of Uses and Executory Interests • Waste • Rule Against Perpetuities • Restraints Upon Alienation

Marital Estates. . . . • Marital Right • Dower • Curtesy • Community Property • Homestead Exemptions

Concurrent Ownership. . . . • Joint Tenancy • Tenancy in Common • Tenancy by Entirety • Relations Between Co-Tenants • Tax Consequences

Landlord and Tenant. . . . • Various Tenancies

and Their Creation • Tenant's Right of Possession and Enjoyment • Condition of Premises • Tort Liability of Landlord and Tenant • Tenant's Duties • Landlord's Remedies • Transfer and Sale by Lessor; Assignment & Subletting by Lessee • Some Important Legislation

Easements and Promises Concerning Land. . . • Creation • Scope • Transfer and Subdivision • Termination • Licenses • Covenants-Running With Land • Covenants-Running of Burden and Benefit • Equitable Servitudes

Zoning and Other Public Land-Use Controls. . . • Taking Clause & Land-Use Controls as Takings • Zoning • Legal Limits • Administration • Exclusionary • Regulation of Subdivision and Growth • Historical and Environmental Preservation • Eminent Domain

Land Sale Contracts, Mortgages and Deeds. . . • Contracts • Mortgage and Installment Contracts • Deeds

Recording System and Title Assurance. . . • Common-Law Priorities • Recording Statutes • Title Registration • Method of Title Assurance

Rights Incident to Land. . . . • Nuisance • Lateral and Subjacent Support • Water Rights • Air Rights

detail in this book. (These are topics which are sometimes left out of competing "real property outlines.")

A carefully crafted **capsule summary**

boils the whole subject down into 57 pages — a real bonus for pre-exam review in this complex and technical subject where most questions have a clear right and wrong answer.

" *I felt overwhelmed. Then I found clarity and focus with the Emanuel Outline...* "

The class in *Property* in my first year of law school was an intricate and complicated area of law. There was so much material to learn, including covenants/easements, zoning laws and landlord-tenant issues, that I felt overwhelmed. Then I found clarity and focus with the Emanuel outline.
Stacey Kerr, Villanova Law School, Class of 1993

Secured Transactions
'88 Ed. $12.95

Just because a subject is extensively codified (in this case, in Article 9 of the UCC) doesn't mean it's necessarily easy to understand. Our *Secured Transactions* volume explains not only the legal principles but the business realities behind them — How do banks and finance companies make sure they get first crack at the collateral? How can a seller of goods take priority over pre-existing secured creditors? What happens to security interests in bankruptcy?

Contains Tables of Cases, UCC references, Bankruptcy Code references and Subject-Matter Index.

Summary of Contents

Scope and Purpose of Article 9. . . . • Nature of Security Interests • Scope of Article 9 Generally • Leases as Security Interests • Consignments as Security Interests

Formal Requisites of a Security Interest. . . • General Requirements • Use of Financing Statement as Security Agreement • Requirement that Collateral be Described • Other Requirements for Enforceability

Perfection. . . . • Various Means • By Filing • Special Perfection Rules for Particular Types of Collateral •Certificate of Title Acts • How Third Parties Can Get Details of Security Agreement

Perfection in Multi-State Transactions. . . • Documents, Instruments and Ordinary Goods • Mobile Goods and Intangibles • Vehicles Covered by Certificates of Title • Chattel Paper • Minerals

Priorities. . . . • Scope • Between Conflicting

Security Interests • Special Priority for Purchase-Money Security Interests • Rights of Unperfected Security Interests • Rights of Purchasers of Collateral • Proceeds • Future Advances • Subrogation

Fixtures. . . . • Priority Rules for Fixtures • Removal on Default

Bankruptcy. . . . • Scope • Secured Creditor's Right to Repossess • Trustee's Right to Debtor's Property • Trustee's Use of Actual Creditor's Rights • Security Interest Not Perfected on Date of Bankruptcy • Delayed Perfection as Preference • "Floating Lien" and Preferential Transfer Rule • Proceeds in Bankruptcy • Seller's Right of Reclamation in Bankruptcy

Default. . . . • Definition • Creditor's Options • Self-Help Repossession • Resale of Collateral • Debtor's Right to Redeem Collateral • Taking Collateral for Debt • Consequence of Creditor's Failure to Follow Rules

Special Features:
• Table of Cases   • UCC references

• Bankruptcy code references
• Subject matter index

The Finz Multistate Method – Bar Exam Questions for Graduate and Student

'92 Ed.   **$31.95**

The *Finz Multistate Method* is an amazing tool for both law school exams and the intricate Multistate Bar Examination (MBE). It contains:

- Multiple-choice questions in the MBE style and format, each with sophisticated fact patterns.

- A 200-question Practice Exam with corresponding answers and analyses.

- A 21-page guide to handling an MBE-type Question. How to break the Question down into its essential factual elements. How to recognize the issues. How to avoid the traps and pitfalls. And, of course, how to pick the right Answer.

Each of the 1167 Questions and Answers was personally prepared by Professor Steven Finz, Professor Finz is America's leading guide through the maze and morass of the MBE. He has written and lectured for Josephson/ BRC, BAR/BRI and PMBR.

1167 Q&A's:

146 on *Constitutional Law*

194 on *Contracts*

140 on *Criminal Law*

143 on *Evidence*

148 on *Property*

196 on *Torts*

Plus

200 in a *Practice-Exam* Format

Drill Yourself 1144 Times, with *Steve Emanuel's First Year Q&A's*

$17.95

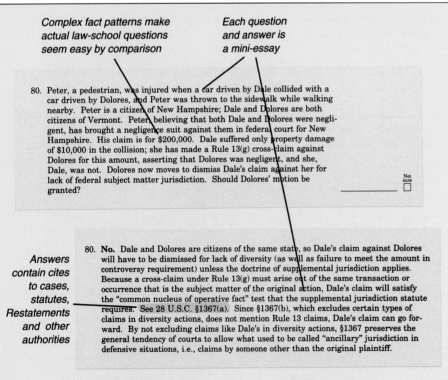

Complex fact patterns make actual law-school questions seem easy by comparison

Each question and answer is a mini-essay

80. Peter, a pedestrian, was injured when a car driven by Dale collided with a car driven by Dolores, and Peter was thrown to the sidewalk while walking nearby. Peter is a citizen of New Hampshire; Dale and Dolores are both citizens of Vermont. Peter, believing that both Dale and Dolores were negligent, has brought a negligence suit against them in federal court for New Hampshire. His claim is for $200,000. Dale suffered only property damage of $10,000 in the collision; she has made a Rule 13(g) cross-claim against Dolores for this amount, asserting that Dolores was negligent, and she, Dale, was not. Dolores now moves to dismiss Dale's claim against her for lack of federal subject matter jurisdiction. Should Dolores' motion be granted?

Not sure ☐

Answers contain cites to cases, statutes, Restatements and other authorities

80. **No.** Dale and Dolores are citizens of the same state, so Dale's claim against Dolores will have to be dismissed for lack of diversity (as well as failure to meet the amount in controversy requirement) unless the doctrine of supplemental jurisdiction applies. Because a cross-claim under Rule 13(g) must arise out of the same transaction or occurrence that is the subject matter of the original action, Dale's claim will satisfy the "common nucleus of operative fact" test that the supplemental jurisdiction statute requires. See 28 U.S.C. §1367(a). Since §1367(b), which excludes certain types of claims in diversity actions, does not mention Rule 13 claims, Dale's claim can go forward. By not excluding claims like Dale's in diversity actions, §1367 preserves the general tendency of courts to allow what used to be called "ancillary" jurisdiction in defensive situations, i.e., claims by someone other than the original plaintiff.

Table of Contents tells you what subject is covered by each question — quickly find all the Erie problems, for example

Subjects are arranged in the order they are covered in the Emanuel Law Outline Series

---

Many first-year law students walk into their first exams without ever having practiced their exam-taking skills.

Steve Emanuel's First Year Questions & Answers helps you avoid this pitfall. It gives you 1144 exam-type short-answer questions and answers.

Each question and answer was personally drafted by Steven Emanuel. The book covers the basic six first year subjects.

- *Civil Procedure* — 253 questions
- *Contracts* — 247 questions
- *Criminal Law* — 166 questions
- *Criminal Procedure* — 131 questions
- *Property* — 186 questions
- *Torts* — 161 questions

Note: About half of the Civil Procedure, Crim. Proc., Property and Torts questions in this book are reproduced in the current Emanuel Law Outlines for these subjects.

CONT'D PG. 21

Smith's Review, For Upper-Year Courses

Emanuel Law Outlines, Inc., also publishes the *Smith's Review* series of outlines. This series covers mainly upper-year courses. Each outline in the series is written by a law professor specializing in the subject. All *Smith's* follow the *Emanuel* style and format. They have big, easy-to-read type, extensive citations and notes, and clear, crisp writing. Most have capsule summaries and sample exam Q&A's. New *Smith's* titles this year are *Bankruptcy Law* and *International Law. Family Law* and *Federal Income Taxation* have been extensively revised.

Agency & Partnership
'89 Ed. $12.95

This volume is divided between the subject of Agency and the subject of Partnership. Agency is covered from a common-law perspective, with emphasis on the Second Restatement of Agency. Partnership, by contrast, is much more statutory, and our treatment focuses on the three principal Model Acts on which most state statutes are patterned: the Uniform Partnership Act, the Uniform Limited Partnership Act, and the Revised Uniform Limited Partnership Act.

Co-authors Myron G. Hill, Jr., Howard M. Rossen and Wilton S. Sogg are all practicing lawyers. Mr. Hill is adjunct professor at Antioch School of Law; Mr. Rossen is director of the Ohio Bar Review & BAR/BRI; Mr. Sogg is adjunct professor of law, Cleveland-Marshall College of Law.

List of Chapters

Rights and Duties of Principal and Agent

Knowledge of Agent Imputed to Principal

Power of Agent in Contract, Including Delegation of Authority

Relation Between Agent and Third Person

Ratification by Principal of Unauthorized Acts of Agent

Undisclosed Principal and Doctrine of Election

Principal and Third Person in Tort

Rights and Liabilities of Agent in Tort

Criminal Responsibility of Principal and Agent

Termination of the Agency Relationship

Analysis of Partnership

Nature of Partnership

Relations of Partners to Persons Dealing with Partnership

Relations of Partners to One Another

Property Rights of a Partner

Dissolution and Winding Up

Limited Partnership

Intellectual Property
'91 Ed. $15.95

Smith's Review on *Intellectual Property* covers three major areas:

Patents   Trademarks   Copyrights

It also covers six other areas: Trade Secrets; Undeveloped Ideas; Unfair Competition; Semiconductor Chip Protection; Right of Publicity; and Federal and State Conflicts.

The author, Margreth Barrett, is a professor of law at Hastings Law School. She has been widely published on the subject of Intellectual Property.

Summary of Contents

Law of Trade Secrets. . . • Status of Ideas • When Use or Disclosure is Actionable • Private Owners' Rights • Information Submitted to Government Agencies • Use by Employees and Former Employees • Misappropriation Remedies

Patents. . . • Utility • Design • Plants • Patent Treaties

Law of Undeveloped Ideas. . . • Nature • Novelty and Concreteness

Trademark Law. . . . • Nature • Types of Marks • Distinctiveness • Content of Marks • Acquiring Ownership • Registration • Cancellation of Registration • Infringement • Geographic

Family Law
Revised '94 Ed. $14.95

This book was extensively revised by Steve

Emanuel in 1994. It covers all topics typically treated in a Family Law or Domestic Relations course. Major topics include Divorce; Child Custody and Support; Separation Agreements; and Adoption.

The facts and holdings of hundreds of major cases are given in considerable detail. Uniform acts, such as the Uniform Reciprocal Enforcement of Support Act and the Uniform Child Custody Jurisdiction Act, are also covered.

Steve Emanuel's co-author was Myron Hill, adjunct professor at Antioch School of Law.

Special features:
• Exam question & answers (essay & True-False)

List of Chapters

Institution of Marriage

Types of Marriage

Rights of Women, Marriage, and Other Intimate Relationships

Annulment

Family Relationships

Divorce: Jurisdiction and Grounds

Divorce: Financial Aspects

Child Custody and Support

Separation Agreements

Adoption

Assisted Reproduction

Legitimacy and Illegitimacy

Special Features:

- Essay questions with sample answers
- Short-answer questions with sample answers
- Table of statutory references
- Table of cases
- Subject-matter index

Boundaries • Defenses to Infringement • Infringement Remedies • Gray Market Goods • Trademark Treaties

Unfair Competition. . . • Nature • Passing Off • Dilution • False Advertising • Misappropriation • Regulation • Disparagement • International Treaties

Copyright Law. . . • Purpose • Subject Matter • Rights Afforded • Derivative Works • Exclusive Right to Reproduce • to Publish • to Perform • to Display • Moral Rights • Infringement • Fair Use Defense • Ownership • Notice • Deposit and Registration • Duration of Protection • Renewals of Federal Copyrights • Termination of Transfers • Remedies for Infringement • Treaties Infringement

1984 Semiconductor Chip Protection Act

Right of Publicity

Commercial Paper '90 Ed.

$12.95

Smith's Review on *Commercial Paper* covers Articles 3 and 4 of the UCC. The coverage of Article 3 concentrates on negotiability, holder in due course, and the liabilities of various parties to instruments (including forged or altered ones.) Article 4 relates to bank deposits and collections, with special treatment of electronic fund transfers, credit cards, and letters of credit.

Author Clayton P. Gillette is the Pierce Bowen Professor of Law at the University of Virginia Law School. He has taught and written on the subject of Commercial Law since 1978.

Special features:

- **32-page 1992 supplement** covering the 1991 revisions to UCC Articles 3 & 4
- 80 True-False questions with explanatory answers
- Tables (cases, UCC references, subject-matter index)

List of Chapters

Concept of Negotiability

Forms and Requirements of Negotiable Instruments

Concept of Holding in Due Course

Liabilities of Parties

Liabilities on Forged and Altered Instruments

Checks and Check Collection

Bank's Relationship with its Customer

Electronic Funds Transfers and Credit Cards

Documentary Drafts and Letters of Credit

A lawyer shows up at the pearly gates, looks at St. Peter, and says, "There must be some mistake. I'm only 46." St. Peter checks his notes. "Sorry. According to the hours you billed, you're 107."

Bankruptcy Law
New '94 Title
$14.95

A new entry in the ever-expanding list of *Smith's Review* titles, this book covers every aspect of the Bankruptcy Code. Included are historical sources; an overview of the Code; the Debtor; the Trustee; the Creditor; the Estate; and extensive coverage of Chapters 7, 9, 11, 12, and 13 of the Code.

The author, Carl Felsenfeld, is a Professor of Law at Fordham Law School. Professor Felsenfeld teaches a course in Bankruptcy and is an authority in banking and commercial law.

Special features:

- Capsule Summary
- Subject-matter index

List of Chapters

Sources of Bankruptcy Law

Overview of the Bankruptcy Code

Beginnings of the Case

General Rules Dealing with the Debtor

The Trustee

General Rules Dealing with the Creditor

The Estate

The Trustee's Avoiding Powers

Chapter 7

Chapter 9

Chapter 11

Chapter 12

Chapter 13

Jurisdiction and Venue

More Titles from *Smith's Review*

Federal Income Taxation
Revised '94 Ed. $14.95

This outline covers all major aspects of Federal Income Taxation of Individuals. Cases, statutory sections, Revenue Rulings and Revenue Procedures are discussed and cited. Major topics include: definition of income (inclusions and exclusions); deductions; timing issues; capital gains and losses; and attribution.

Author Paul B. Stephan III is professor of law at the University of Virginia Law School. He has taught and written about tax law since 1979.

Special features:
- Capsule summary
- Glossary of Tax Terms
- Tables (cases, IRC references, references to Revenue Rulings and

Procedures, and Treas. Regs.)
- Subject-matter index

This outline was thoroughly revised in 1994 to reflect recent changes in Tax legislation and regulations.

Summary of Contents

Tax Policy and Tax Structure: Basic Concepts

Inclusions and Exclusions. . . • Compensation for Services • Imputed Income • Gratuitous Transfers • Windfalls and Involuntary Receipts • Loans • Illegal Income • Gain • Subsidies • Tax-Exempt Interest

Deductions. . . • Deductions and Exclusions • Business Expenses • Investment Expense • Personal Expenses • Capital Recovery • Losses and Bad Debts • Interest • Taxes • Charitable Contributions • Medical Expenses • Personal Adjustments

Timing. . . • General Consideration • Modifications of Taxable Year Concept • Cash Method Accounting • Accrual Method Accounting • Installment Sales • Nonrecognition of Gain • Commodity Straddles

Capital Gains and Losses. . . • Capital Assets • Sale or Exchange

Attribution. . . • Family Taxation • Assignment of Income

Labor Law
'88 Ed. $11.95

This volume covers both labor law and employment discrimination. Major topics include Unfair Labor Practices, Good-Faith Bargaining, Public Sector Bargaining, Picketing and Boycotts, and the entire range of laws prohibiting discrimination (Title VII, Equal Pay Act, Age Discrimination in Employment Act, etc.)

Co-authors Myron Hill, Jr., Howard Rossen and Wilton Sogg are all practicing lawyers (see *Agency & Partnership*).

List of Chapters

Glossary

Development of Labor Legislation

Procedure and Remedies

Employer Unfair Labor Practices

Good Faith Bargaining

Collective Bargaining Agreement

Public Sector Bargaining

Union Unfair Labor Practices

Picketing and Boycotts

Other Rights of Employees

Representation Proceedings

Other Laws Governing Labor Relations

Torts
'91 Ed. $13.95

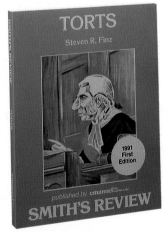

Smith's Review on *Torts* is a comprehensive overview of the field of Torts.

Smith's Review on *Torts* differs from the corresponding *Emanuel* on *Torts* in two major ways. First, it is a somewhat more abbreviated treatment. Second, it makes especially good use of hundreds of hypotheticals created by the author, as well as examples taken from reported cases.

The book is by Prof. Steven Finz (see *Products Liability,* next page).

Special features:
- Capsule summary
- Table of cases
- Subject-matter index

List of Chapters

Torts Involving Intent

Affirmative Defenses to Intentional Torts

Negligence

Affirmative Defenses

Strict Liability

Proximate Cause

Damage

Vicarious Liability

Nuisance

Misrepresentation

Interference with Business Advantage

Products Liability

Defamation and Related Torts

Invasion of Privacy

Misuse of Judicial Procedure

Immunities

Wills & Trusts
'93 Ed. $14.95

Smith's Review of *Wills & Trusts* also covers Probate, Administration and Fiduciaries. Approximately one-third of the book is devoted to intestacy and wills. The remaining two-thirds is devoted to trusts, including private express trusts, charitable trusts, constructive trusts, modification and termination of trusts, probate, and the trustee as fiduciary

This book is co-authored by Elizabeth A. Moody, Judith Permitt, Howard Rossen and William Sogg.

List of Chapters
Freedom of Testation and Intestate Succession

Protection of the Family

Execution, Validity and Components of Wills

Construction of Wills

Revocation and Republication of Wills

Nature of Trusts

Private Express Trusts

Charitable Trusts

Resulting Trusts

Constructive Trusts

Creation, Modification and Termination of Trusts

Limitations on Creation and Duration of Interests in Trusts

Jurisdiction Over Administration

Probate, Appointment of Personal Representative and Management of Estate

Trustee as Fiduciary

Products Liability
'93 Ed. $12.95

Smith's Review in *Products Liability* takes a detailed, sophisticated look at this increasingly important subject. In addition to discussing major reported cases, the author illustrates the subject with literally hundreds of examples that he himself has devised.

Author Steven Finz has served as adjunct professor of law at National University School of Law in San Diego, CA. Professor Finz has taught Torts and Products Liability since 1979. During that time, he has also been actively involved preparing students for the bar exam, as a writer and lecturer for Josephson/BRC, BAR/BRI, and PMBR.

List of Chapters
Intent

Negligence

Breach of Warranty

Misrepresentation

Strict Products Liability

Proximate Cause

Damage

Affirmative Defenses

Vicarious Liability

International law
New '94 Title $14.95

This new title in the *Smith's Review* Series illustrates our commitment to expand our publication base to reflect new areas of student interest. The book covers all aspects of international law, including issues affecting the environment.

The author is Linda Malone, Marshall Wythe Foundation Professor of Law, The College of William & Mary, Marshall Wythe School of Law.

The book includes a capsule summary which permits a thorough review of the subject before exam.

List of Chapters
The Concept of Public International Law

Sources of International Law

International Law & Municipal Law

States

Jurisdictional Principles in United States Law

International Organizations

International Dispute Settlement

The Rights of Individuals: International Law of Human Rights

The Law of Armed Conflict

The Law of the Sea

The Territorial Sea and Contiguous Zone

Air and Space Law

International Environmental Law

THE LAW IN A FLASH STUDY SERIES

America's Best-Selling Legal Flash Card

We're thrilled to announce that Emanuel is now the exclusive distributor of Law In A Flash products.

Imagine entering your exams, looking at your test paper, and seeing the issues jump off the page at you. Imagine feeling legal rules pop into your mind, and knowing that you can apply those rules to facts and analyze those issues quickly and flawlessly.

That's what you can achieve when you use Law In A Flash flashcards.

Each Law In A Flash title gives you from 350 - 650 cards. In each topic, you start with basic, blackletter principles, so you have all the theoretical tools you need at your finger-tips. You'll get lots of checklists and mnemonics to make them easy to remember.

Then you progress to short, interesting hypo-theticals that perfect your ability to apply theory to facts - the single skill that distin-guishes top law students. As you move through each topic, you'll answer questions that are progressively more difficult . . . but you'll be building on your knowledge one simple step at a time, so they won't seem tough to you! You'll soon find yourself answering complex questions quickly and easily. You'll reinforce what you know, and learn what you don't. And you won't be able to fool yourself into thinking you're prepared when you're not.

Try Law In A Flash and see for yourself how easy it can be to get better grades!

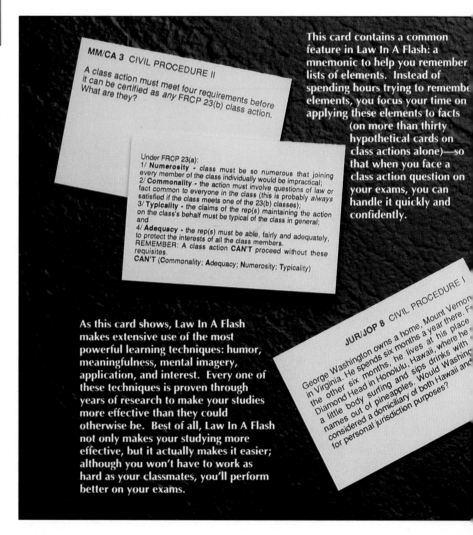

This card contains a common feature in Law In A Flash: a mnemonic to help you remember lists of elements. Instead of spending hours trying to remember elements, you focus your time on applying these elements to facts (on more than thirty hypothetical cards on class actions alone)—so that when you face a class action question on your exams, you can handle it quickly and confidently.

As this card shows, Law In A Flash makes extensive use of the most powerful learning techniques: humor, meaningfulness, mental imagery, application, and interest. Every one of these techniques is proven through years of research to make your studies more effective than they could otherwise be. Best of all, Law In A Flash not only makes your studying more effective, but it actually makes it easier; although you won't have to work as hard as your classmates, you'll perform better on your exams.

INDIVIDUAL FLASH CARD TITLES

Civil Proc. 1 (382 cards)*
Civil Proc. 2 (504 cards)*
Con. Law (616 cards)
Contracts (482 cards)
Corporations (644 cards)
Criminal Law (392 cards)
Crim. Pro. (420 cards)
*New 1994-95 Edition

Evidence (504 cards)
Future Inter. (353 cards)
Prof. Respons./MPRE
    (2-part set, 840 cards)
Real Property (644 cards)
Sales (Art. 2) (295 cds)*
Torts (616 cards)

All Titles $16.95, except Prof. Respon, $29.95

SETS

First Year Law Program (see oppos. pg.) $95.00
Multistate Bar Review Set (9 card titles + book, "Strategies & Tactics for the MBE") $165.00

Use Your Computer to Drill Yourself

Now there's Law In A Flash software. You get the full 350-650 questions for each title, in computer form. You can drill yourself, taking advantage of the computer's power. Here are some of the features you get:

■ **Scoring -** You can "check off" the questions you answer correctly, so you don't waste time reviewing them once you're comfortable answering them correctly.

■ **Two study modes -** review and testing.

■ **Printing -** You can print any question, answer, hint, and even your own answers.

■ **Color options -** A brilliant array of color choices for both the screen and text.

■ **Specialized sets available -** First Year Program (6 subjects + "Strategies & Tactics" Book); Multistate Bar Review Set

Indiv. Titles (Civ. Pr. 1 & 2, Con. L., Contr., Corp., Crim. L., Crim. Pro., Evid., Fut. Int., Real Prop., Sales, Torts): **$24.95**
First Yr. Progr. $145.00; Prof. Resp. Set, $39.95. Multistate Bar Review Set, $225.00

"I used to think Law In a Flash was a joke. Was I ever wrong. Law In A Flash enabled me to move from the top 50% of my class to the top 20% in one semester. . ."

"When I first heard about Law In A Flash during my first semester of law school, I had to laugh. Flash cards are for kids, not law students! Was I ever wrong. After my first round of exams I knew reading the case books and outlining wasn't enough; I needed a competitive edge. So during my second semester I decided to give Law In A Flash a try. What a difference! I'm not laughing any more. Law In A Flash made learning legal concepts more interesting and memorizing the blackletter law much easier. It gave me a system of learning the law and taking law school exams that enabled me to move up from the top 50% of my class to the top 20% at UNC in one semester."

Robert E. DiPaolo, University of North Carolina at Chapel Hill, School of Law

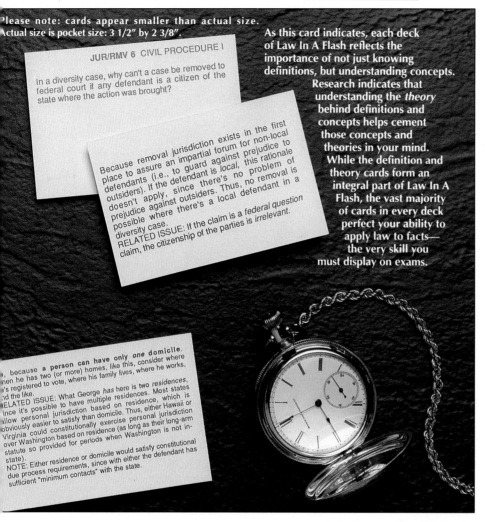

Please note: cards appear smaller than actual size. Actual size is pocket size: 3 1/2" by 2 3/8".

JUR/RMV 6 CIVIL PROCEDURE I

In a diversity case, why can't a case be removed to federal court if any defendant is a citizen of the state where the action was brought?

Because removal jurisdiction exists in the first place to assure an impartial forum for non-local defendants (i.e., to guard against prejudice to outsiders). If the defendant is *local*, this rationale doesn't apply, since there's no problem of prejudice against outsiders. Thus, no removal is possible where there's a local defendant in a diversity case.
RELATED ISSUE: If the claim is a federal question claim, the citizenship of the parties is irrelevant.

As this card indicates, each deck of Law In A Flash reflects the importance of not just knowing definitions, but understanding concepts. Research indicates that understanding the *theory* behind definitions and concepts helps cement those concepts and theories in your mind. While the definition and theory cards form an integral part of Law In A Flash, the vast majority of cards in every deck perfect your ability to apply law to facts— the very skill you must display on exams.

... because **a person can have only one domicile.**
when he has two (or more) homes, like this, consider where he's registered to vote, where his family lives, where he works, and the like.
RELATED ISSUE: What George *has* here is two *residences*, since it's possible to have multiple residences. Most states allow personal jurisdiction based on residence, which is obviously easier to satisfy than domicile. Thus, either Hawaii or Virginia could constitutionally exercise personal jurisdiction over Washington based on residence (as long as their long-arm statute so provided for periods when Washington is not in state).
NOTE: Either residence or domicile would satisfy constitutional due process requirements, since with either the defendant has sufficient "minimum contacts" with the state.

Learn the Secret of Top Exam Performance

Strategies & Tactics for First Year Law

With this book, you'll find valuable advice you can put to work immediately, including:

- The single study technique that can add a whole letter grade to your final score;
- The secret of taking notes that tell you what will be on the final exam;
- Nine steps to writing exceptional exam answers;
- How to guarantee you'll never miss a material issue on an exam;
- Why highlighting your text can hurt you more than help you;
- How to determine your professor's personality profile . . . *and much more!*

Strategies & Tactics for First Year Law $12.95 (also included in First Year Law Program)

All the Benefits of Law In A Flash In the Year When Your Grades Count the Most

The First Year Law Program

With the Law In A Flash First Year Program, you'll master the skills that characterize top law students— in the year when your grades count the most.

The program has two components: The Law In A Flash cards, for substantive review of every core first year course, and the book "Strategies and Tactics for First Year Law" (see description above right).

Every law student knows that doing what everyone else does results in average grades. The Law In A Flash First Year Program is the easiest, most effective way to gain the competitive edge.

First Year Law Program . . . $95.00 ($20 savings over components if bought separately.)

Siegel's Essay and Multiple-Choice Q&A's

Here's a whole series of books to show you how to handle law school examination questions. In 1992 we became the publisher and distributor of this series, which has been used by thousands of law students during the past decade. We have revised the text of the titles and put them into a more readable format.

Each title contains 20 to 25 essay questions, most taken from questions asked on the California bar exam, long known as the most difficult bar exam in America. Each essay comes with an extensive, well organized model answer written by Brian Siegel, a Columbia Law School graduate.

By writing your own answer, then comparing it with the model, you'll learn:

- How to **organize** your answer;
- How to **spot** and **articulate the issues**;
- How to **"elementize,"** by reducing the relevant legal principle to its individual elements; and
- How to **argue both sides** of a "gray" issue.

Plus, each scholarly answer prepared by Professor Siegel is like a mini-outline in its own right. And all are checked and rechecked to keep them current with changes in the law.

Each book also contains 90 to 100 Multistate-format questions, together with extensive explanatory answers. Most of these Multistate-format questions are taken from actual past Multistate Bar Examinations.

Each title . . . $15.95

Here are the titles available in this series:

- *Civil Procedure*
- *Constitutional Law*
- *Contracts*
- *Corporations*
- *Criminal Law*
- *Criminal Procedure*
- *Evidence*
- *Real Property*
- *Torts*
- *Wills & Trusts*

Practice Your Exam-Taking Skills

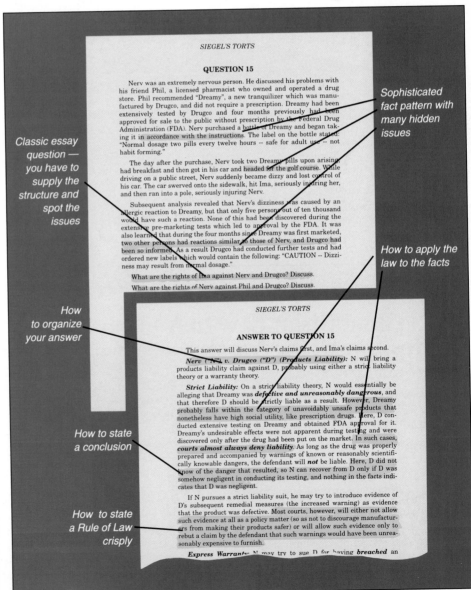

Classic essay question — you have to supply the structure and spot the issues

Sophisticated fact pattern with many hidden issues

How to apply the law to the facts

How to organize your answer

How to state a conclusion

How to state a Rule of Law crisply

The Bluebook $10.50

America's leading guide to the principles of legal citation. Compiled by the editors of the law reviews of Harvard, Columbia, Pennsylvania and Yale. Now in its Fifteenth Edition.

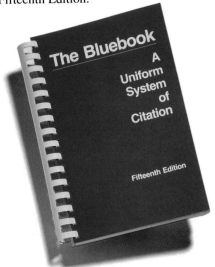

ELO T-shirt $9.95

Impress your friends and classmates with this memento of the old English judge who inspired the Emanuel covers. Specially designed for us by one of America's leading T-shirt manufacturers. 2 colors.

Available in X-large and large

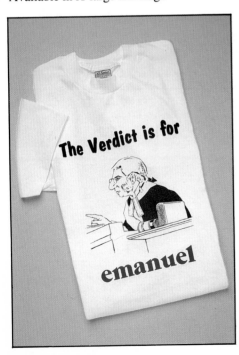

BUY any 3 of the Emanuel outlines in Contracts, Torts, Crim. Law, Crim. Pro. or Property and get **FREE** One Copy of Steve Emanuel's 1st Year Q&A's

NAME

ADDRESS

CITY

ST   ZIP

SCHOOL

GRAD YEAR   TEL:

Redeem to Emanuel Law Outlines, Inc., 1865 Palmer Avenue, Larchmont, NY 10538, with proof of purchase. For each outline, proof is retail receipt and copyright notice cut from title page. No Xerox or other mechanical reproduction accepted for any proof. Purchases must be dated after August 15. 1994

Purchase of all items required. All coupons must be postmarked not later than December 15. 1994. We are not responsible for late, lost or mutilated mail. Only original coupon is accepted. Offer void where prohibited, taxed or restricted by law. No substitution of items allowed.

BUY two or more Emanuel or Smith's outlines and get one **ELO T-shirt** FOR ONLY $5.95

NAME

ADDRESS

CITY

ST   ZIP

SCHOOL

GRAD YEAR   TEL:

Redeem to Emanuel Law Outlines, Inc., 1865 Palmer Avenue, Larchmont, NY 10538, with proof of purchase. For each outline, proof is retail receipt and copyright notice cut from title page. No Xerox or other mechanical reproduction accepted for any proof. Purchases must be dated after August 15. 1994

Purchase of all items required. All coupons must be postmarked not later than December 15. 1994. We are not responsible for late, lost or mutilated mail. Only original coupon is accepted. Offer void where prohibited, taxed or restricted by law. No substitution of items allowed.

ACLU Handbook Series

For law students who wish to learn about the rights of specific segments of American society. The paperbacks are published by the American Civil Liberties Union and cover virtually every group which has a special need to articulate its rights.

Titles: *The Rights of . . .*
• *Aliens and Refugees* **$8.95** • *Authors, Artists and other Creative People* **8.95** • *Crime Victims* **7.95** • *Employees and Union Members* **14.95** • *Indians and Tribes* **8.95** • *Lesbians and Gay Men* **8.95** • *Older Persons* **8.95** • *Patients* **9.95** • *Prisoners* **8.95** • *Public Employees* **8.95** • *Racial Minorities* **8.95** • *Single People* **5.95** • *Students* **8.95** • *Teachers* **7.95** • *Women* **8.95**

Also: *Your Right to. . .*
• *Government Information* **7.95** • *Privacy* **8.95** • *Protest* **8.95**

Briefing Pads

A briefing pad designed by Steve Emanuel for everyday use. 50 pages per pad . . . white-bond stock. . . 3 hole punched.

Each pad **$1.35**

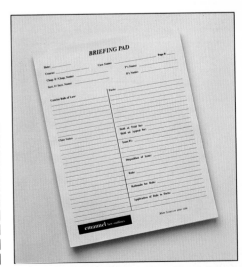

You can correspond with Steve Emanuel via E-mail at: 74224.3600@compuserve.com.

Socratutor Software —
It's an "Emanuel® on a diskette"!

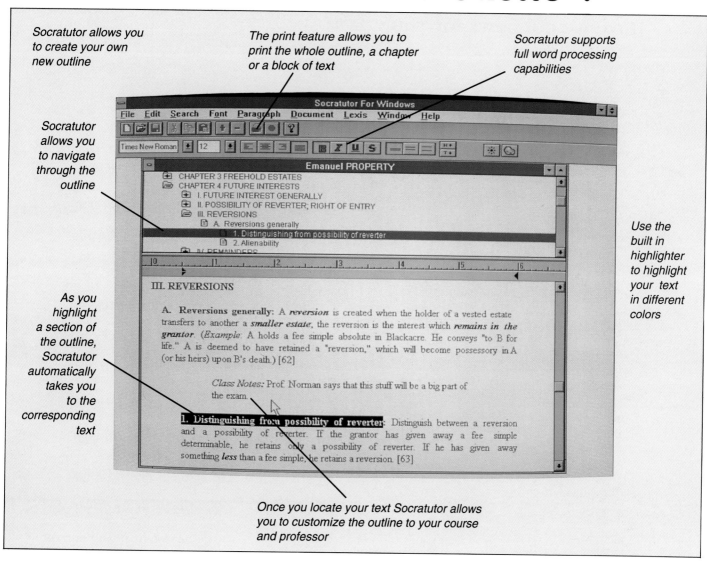

Socratutor allows you to create your own new outline

The print feature allows you to print the whole outline, a chapter or a block of text

Socratutor supports full word processing capabilities

Socratutor allows you to navigate through the outline

As you highlight a section of the outline, Socratutor automatically takes you to the corresponding text

Use the built in highlighter to highlight your text in different colors

Once you locate your text Socratutor allows you to customize the outline to your course and professor

---

Have you ever wished you could get an *Emanuel* or a *Smiths's* on a computer diskette? Then you could customize the outline into **your own personal course outline.**

Well, Socratutor is the answer to your prayer. Each Socratutor software package features an abridged *Emanuel* or a complete *Smith's* specially adapted for computer use. The text you get is similar to the capsule summary at the front of the *Emanuel* hard-copy outline, or the full *Smith's* text.

But Socratutor is much more than just an *Emanuel* or *Smith's* on disk. It's a self-contained **outlining software** package. It's got a **built-in word processor,** so you can add your own notes, delete materials, rearrange them, and otherwise produce your dream outline without

having to start from scratch. Plus, you get lots of other features:

- You can view a **Table of Contents,** then **zoom** into narrower topics and finally **zoom** into just the paragraph you want.

- Our **word search** feature lets you jump instantly to any word anywhere in the text.

- You can **print** just a portion of the outline, for use in class. **Or, print the whole outline.**

- For modified **open-book exams,** a customized Socratutor may qualify as an outline of your own preparation.

Socratutor is distributed under license from The Numina Group of Chicago, IL.

Socratutor is now available in DOS, Macintosh, and Windows.

Here are the courses now available:

Available in DOS, Macintosh and Windows

Emanuel Law Outlines. . . • Civil Procedure • Constitutional Law • Contracts • Corporations • Criminal Law • Evidence • Property • Torts

Smith's Review . . . • Agency & Partnership • Family Law • Labor Law • Wills

Additional titles in Macintosh and Windows only:

Emanuel Law Outlines. . . • Criminal Procedure • Secured Transactions

Smith's Review. . . • Bankruptcy • Commercial Paper • Federal Income Taxation • Intellectual Property • International Law • Products Liability • Torts

---

Each title...$19.95

Have we got news for you.

It's all about competitive advantage. And while access to legal information is vital, it's not all that's needed to win.

You could be missing some very critical information. News. Current news that could significantly affect your research. LEXIS®/NEXIS® is the only online service that provides access to current legal and news sources. And public records. And international materials.

LEXIS/NEXIS even lets you automatically validate your cites using a special feature called CheckCite™ software.

Quite simply, if your current search system limits you to just legal sources...you're only getting half the picture. Call LEXIS/NEXIS today, at 1-800-543-6862 because we've got news for you.

LEXIS·NEXIS
1-800-543-6862

LEXIS® and NEXIS® are registered trademarks of Mead Data Central. The WORLD IN YOUR HAND logo is a trademark of Mead Data Central, a division of The Mead Corporation. ©1994, Mead Data Central. All rights reserved. CheckCite is a trademark of Jurisoft Licensing Corporation.